Population Studies

2nd Edition

Population Studies:
Selected Essays and Research

KENNETH C.W. KAMMEYER
University of Maryland

RAND McNALLY COLLEGE PUBLISHING COMPANY/Chicago

Rand McNally Sociology Series
Edgar F. Borgatta, *Advisory Editor*

PREFACE TO THE SECOND EDITION

The major purpose of a second edition preface is to say what has changed and what remains the same. First, I shall say what remains the same. My perception of the audience for this book is largely unchanged from what it was at the time of the first edition. I have aimed again for a set of papers that will be interesting and enlightening for students taking the introductory population course. I make no presuppositions about the preparation of these students, sociological or otherwise. They still usually come to the population course because they are interested in or concerned about population or the "population problem." We do seem to have passed beyond that flurry of excitement that grew out of "ecology" concerns and which brought many students to the population class who wanted to learn more about population as the cause of the problem. The popular concern that might bring students to the study of population today is a concern about natural resources. The issue today is not so much one of despoiling the environment, but the frightening possibility that we may be using up the resources of our environment. This popular concern may be more lasting than the ecological concerns, since shortages are now promising to be a normal part of life, perhaps on an ever-more-severe scale. While this concern does reflect a long-standing population problem (see the discussion of Malthus in Section II), we must emphasize that there is more to the study of population than "the population-ecology-depletion of resources" problems. This collection again tries to present the many sides of the study of population, but it especially tries to show how demography is a theoretically guided science.

I have tried to bring together papers that will develop or explain some theoretical issue, or illustrate some principle of population, or show how a societal or social fact relates to some aspect of population. I have also been more inclined to select for inclusion those population studies that have some bearing on a dispute or debate; these may be theoretical, scientific, or in some cases political.

I believe that almost every paper in this book will give the reader at least one somewhat general principle, in addition to a major fact or set of facts. In other words, I have avoided the purely descriptive paper, even though much demographic and population research is descriptive. Every issue in the major American journal of population *Demography* contains many papers that describe some population fact about some specific population at a particular time. In some cases the time is historical, in others, contemporary. These papers are important, but they exemplify a highly sophisticated line of research and often lack the over-arching quality that is important for the introductory population course.

Now for what is different. Perhaps it will not be too strongly evidenced in this collection, but my personal orientation toward the study of population has undergone some changes since the first edition. Basically, I have accepted for myself a strongly social-demographic point of view. The first essay in Section I, by Philip Hauser, identifies population studies as research that interrelates "dependent demographic variables with independent sets of social, economic, genetic, psychological, historical, or other systems of variables." Among the systems of variables that may be used to explain demographic events, I am personally most interested in the social, or often even more narrowly, the social psychological. Through the years since the preparation of the first edition of this reader I have accepted more and more the basic ideas that Kurt Back expresses in the second paper of Section I. In this paper, Back makes the case for why a social psychological approach to the study of demographic events makes sense in the context of contemporary social life. I am sure that at least some of my selections have been influenced by the conviction that Kurt Back is right in the argument he makes.

While I openly proclaim my own affinity to a social psychological approach I have tried not to let that perspective dominate the papers selected, or to preclude some important aspects of formal demography. I have consciously attempted to retain some papers that illustrate a more formal demographic approach and explore some of the issues of formal demography. The collection does not, however, cover all systems of variables that have the potential for explaining variations in population. It was not possible, within the space limits we had set for ourselves, to give much attention to the influence of economics, genetics, and geography, just to mention a few. By and large the papers in this book relate most directly to formal demography and social demography (including the social psychological).

I did make one substantial addition in this revision: A section called

"Population Politics and Policies." If one considers any aspect of population a problem (such as growing too fast, growing too slowly, improper distribution) it seems to me that a resolution of the problem often rests on what happens politically. In short, the politics of population problems cannot be ignored. What happens to a population is *as* likely to be determined by political events as, for example, economic events.

When I first considered the revised edition of this reader I wondered which papers, if any, from the first edition should be retained in the second. While I had my personal choices, it occurred to me that the professors who have used the first edition would be my best advisors. So, I prevailed upon about twenty-five people who had adopted the book or were very familiar with its contents (such as my former students) to tell me what they thought I should retain. The results of the little survey were interesting, but not conclusive. There was no paper that was without at least one supporter. But, there were also no unanimous selections. Even more disconcerting were those instances where many of my respondents wanted to retain papers that I had already decided to drop. Altogether I ended up retaining five papers (or parts of papers) from the first edition. Basically, these are "timeless" papers—ones that have not been outdated and still retain their original importance. Some of these papers appear in a different section than they did in the first edition. In each case, the logic of their new placement seems just as right as did their first. This rearrangement is not something I am overly concerned with, for as I said in the preface to the first edition, I expect any instructor using this book of readings to select and assign the materials as they meet her or his needs. My only aim is to provide some things that will be useful to a reasonably large number of professors and students.

At this point I shall take the opportunity to thank my colleagues and friends who helped me by responding to my questions regarding the second edition. I appreciate the time and effort that many gave to my questions. I read each questionnaire and the often accompanying letters and papers carefully, and while I obviously couldn't follow each suggestion, I did consider carefully what each had to say.

I also wish to thank Leslie Anne Kammeyer, Carol Pennington, Priscilla Reckling, Nann Weaver, Gladys Graham, Dorothy Bowers, Donna Lichvar, and especially Bob Rucker for their assistance in preparing the manuscript.

CONTENTS

Preface to the Second Edition

SECTION I: THE STUDY OF POPULATION

Introduction: A. Frames of Reference   1
1. Demography in Relation to Sociology, *Philip M. Hauser*   6
2. New Frontiers in Demography and Social Psychology, *Kurt W. Back*   10

Introduction: B. Examples of Formal Demography and Population Studies   15
3. How Many People Have Ever Lived on Earth? *Annabelle Desmond*   18
4. How a Population Ages or Grows Younger, *Ansley J. Coale*   33
5. The Effect of the Great Blackout of 1965 on Births in New York City, *J. Richard Udry*   42
6. A Social Psychological Approach to Family Formation, *H. Theodore Groat and Arthur G. Neal*   46
7. Is Delinquency Increasing? Age Structure and the Crime Rate, *Roland Chilton and Adele Spielberger*   60

SECTION II: THE DATA AND THEORY OF DEMOGRAPHY

Introduction: A. The Data of Demography   69
8. John Graunt: A Tercentenary Tribute, *Ian Sutherland*   74
9. Historical Demography and Classical Demography, *Louis Henry*   94
10. Who Are the Uncounted People? *edited by Carole W. Parsons*   98

Introduction: B. The Theory of Demography   111
11.   Professor Malthus and His Essay, *Judy K. Morris*   114
12.   Developments in the Study of Population, *Kurt Mayer*   135
13.   A Re-Examination of Some Recent Criticisms of Transition
      Theory, *Kenneth C. W. Kammeyer*   156

SECTION III: MIGRATION

Introduction: A. Migration Theory   169
14.   Some Theoretical Guidelines Toward a Sociology of Migra-
      tion, *J. J. Mangalam and Harry K. Schwarzweller*   173
15.   A Theory of Migration, *Everett S. Lee*   188
16.   Migration in Relation to Education, Intellect, and Social
      Structure, *Everett S. Lee*   203

Introduction: B. Migration Research   212
17.   Some Tests of, and Comments on, Lee's Theory of Migra-
      tion, *Kenneth C. W. Kammeyer and McKee McClendon*   214
18.   Poverty Status and Receipt of Welfare Among Migrants
      and Nonmigrants in Large Cities, *Larry H. Long*   221

SECTION IV: MORTALITY

Introduction: A. Selected Research on the Social Causes of
               Death   239
19.   Mortality and the Relative Social Status of the Sexes in
      Ireland, *Robert E. Kennedy, Jr.*   244
20.   Sex, Marital Status, and Mortality, *Walter R. Gove*   257
21.   Deathday and Birthday: An Unexpected Connection,
      David P. Phillips   281

SECTION V: FERTILITY

Introduction: A. The Social Determinants of Fertility and
               Family Planning   295
22.   Social Pressure on Family Size Intentions, *Janet Griffith* 300
23.   The Revolution in Birth Control Practices of U.S. Roman
      Catholics, *Charles F. Westoff and Larry Bumpass*   313
24.   Voluntarily Childless Wives: An Exploratory Study, *J. E.
      Veevers*   323
25.   Continuities in the Explanation of Fertility Control, *John
      Scanzoni and Martha McMurry*   333

26. Coercive Pronatalism and American Population Policy, *Judith Blake*   346

27. A Small Failure in Birth Control, *Mahmood Mamdani*   370

SECTION VI: POPULATION POLITICS AND POLICIES

Introduction: A. Population Policy: National and Worldwide   375

28. Zero Population Growth, *Frank Notestein*   380

29. Discussion of Notestein's "Zero Population Growth," *Philip M. Hauser, Judith Blake, and Paul Demeny*   390

Introduction: B. President's Commission on Population Growth and the American Future   407

30. Population and the American Future: The Commission's Final Report, *Richard Lincoln*   409

Introduction: C. Birth Control and Black Americans   431

31. Race Consciousness and Fears of Black Genocide as Barriers to Family Planning, *William A. Darity, Castellano B. Turner, and H. Jean Thiebaux*   433

32. Birth Control and the Black American: A Matter of Genocide? *Robert G. Weisbord*   448

33. Family Planning Services and the Distribution of Black Americans, *Kenneth C. W. Kammeyer, Norman R. Yetman, and McKee J. McClendon*   474

Index   501

The Study of Population

Introduction: A. Frames of Reference

The scientific study of any phenomenon cannot usually be done without some *frame of reference*. By this term I simply mean some set of words or concepts that aids a person in making sense of what would otherwise be chaotic and confusing. There are different frames of reference in the scientific study of population (demography), but there is also a reasonable amount of agreement among demographers about a basic frame of reference that describes their field.

Almost every demographer would agree that the central aim of their science is to explain variations in demographic events. Specifically the job of the demographer is to explain why there are variations or changes in birth rates, death rates, migration rates (or patterns), population size, density or composition. Individual demographers who have their own special interests would add a number of things to that list, but most would agree this is the core of the science of demography. In short, the field of demography has as its primary purpose the explanation of population phenomena.

But that simple statement only leads to the next question: How do demographers explain these population events? What kinds of causal or explanatory factors may be used to account for demographic phenomena?

In the first paper of this section, Philip Hauser's "Demography in Relation to Sociology," the author develops the distinction between demographic analysis and population study. He describes demographic analysis as "concerned with the statistical analysis of population size, distribution, and composition and with components of variation and change." According to Hauser, demographic analysis is characterized in part by the techniques of statistical analysis that are used, and, more importantly, by the notion that population characteristics are used as independent variables to explain variations in other population characteristics (viewed as dependent variables). In contrast, population study is "the interrelating of a set of dependent demographic variables with independent sets of social, economic, genetic, psychological, historical and other systems of variables." To put this distinction as clearly as possible, if one is examining the influence that one demographic characteristic may have on another demographic characteristic, this is demographic analysis. For example, in the fourth paper, "How a Population Ages or Grows Younger," Ansley Coale analyzes the relationship between the mortality rate and the age structure of a population. The mortality rate is, of course, one of the basic dynamic characteristics of population (along with migration and fertility), while the age of a population is one of its structural or compositional characteristics. So we have in this paper a clear illustration of demographic analysis (some writers, including myself, prefer to call this formal demography).

By contrast, population studies are those studies that examine the influence of some nondemographic characteristic on a demographic variable (such as migration, mortality, fertility, age structure). As Hauser indicates, the nondemographic characteristics may come from a variety of other "systems of variables," so two quite different independent variables might be employed to explain variations in the same demographic variable. As a simple illustration, differences in fertility or changes in fertility may be explained by differences in family structure or marriage customs (sociological variables), fears and stereotypes about birth-control techniques (psychological variables) or differences in fecundity (a biological variable—fecundity is defined as the biological capacity to reproduce and is probably influenced by such things as diet, health, and heredity).

Hauser, in this introductory paper, notes that nondemographers may also use demographic factors in their studies. The nondemographer may use a population factor as an independent variable to show the influence that it may have on a nondemographic variable. For example, a political scientist could examine the age structure of a population to determine what effect it might have on the voting behavior of the group. Strictly speaking, this is not demography, but for convenience we may consider it one kind of population study. We might then have population studies type I, where other systems of variables are used to explain variations in demographic variables, and population studies type II, where demographic variables are used to explain variations in other systems of variables.

Following these distinctions, it will be clear that in this book I have tended toward the selection of those articles that would be labeled population study type I, and have chosen papers where the independent variables most often come from the social and cultural realms, or sometimes from the psychological.

In his paper on the relationship between sociology and demography, Hauser goes on to emphasize "that there is no logical reason why demography should be more closely related to sociology than to any one of a number of other disciplines." He suggests that "the fact that demography has become largely a subfield of sociology . . . in the United States is more a matter of historical accident than of special affinity. The relationships between demographic and sociological sets of variables are not necessarily closer, more compelling, and more fruitful than similar relationships with economic, psychological, geographic, genetic, or other sets of variables."

This assertion raises two questions. First, is Hauser correct when he claims that there is no special affinity between the study of population and sociology? Second, what are the historical conditions that led to the present situation, where the study of population is largely within the domain of sociology? The first of these two questions is worth considering, not because it contains the promise of a definitive answer, but because it will help to sensitize us to the nature of population study. Since the position that I might take on this issue is already indicated in the selections that have been made for this volume, and since taking an explicit position at this point might preclude further considerations by the reader, it might be most useful if I would only suggest some of the directions the discussion might take. It is to be hoped that this may help to ensure an ongoing consideration of the question as the reader continues through this book. While it could be argued that the question should not be considered at all until a person has developed an intensive and extensive familiarity with the study of population, I believe that the sensitizing benefits of the question are most important.

A discussion of the special nature of the relationship between population study and sociology might include a consideration of the following kinds of questions: Can one advance a logical argument for the position that there *is* a special affinity between sociology and the study of population? Might it be possible to rank the various academic disciplines and sciences in order of their importance in the explanation of population phenomena? If so, where would sociology fall in the ordered ranking? Does sociology have a special or strategic position relative to the study of specific population phenomena? Consider, for example, that sociological variables might be of great importance in understanding migration, but of much less importance in explaining variations in mortality. These are only a few of the lines that consideration of this issue can take, and although this volume will by its orientation and content imply that there is a special affinity between sociology and the study of population the issue is not one that is definitively answered.

One partial answer to the question is offered in the second article, Kurt Back's "New Frontiers in Demography and Social Psychology." Back draws the outlines of the two fields of study, demography and social psychology. When he discusses demography he is primarily describing what Hauser called demographic analysis or what I prefer to call formal demography. Back describes demography as the science of fate. It starts from the premise that the demographic events of man are largely outside of his control. Under these conditions whether people have babies or die is largely a matter of chance or probability. Back implies that under earlier historical circumstances the (formal) demographic approach might have been more appropriate for the study of population than it is today when many demographic events are within the control (or greater control) of the people who experience them.

Since, Back argues, control over individual demographic events is greater now than ever before, there is a much stronger case for an approach that examines the orientations of people and their decision making behavior. This is essentially the realm of social psychology, which is one of the subfields of sociology (or in the view of some, a field that falls between sociology and psychology). Back's point is that contemporary circumstances, such as modern science and medicine, birth-control methods, and high speed communication give people more control than ever before over their demographic fate. Back's argument, even if it is accepted only partially, does give greater credence to the idea that a social psychological approach is more appropriate for the study of demographic events than ever before. There are a number of papers in this volume that are built in some way on that idea, although not to the exclusion of other approaches or other scientific disciplines.

1

Demography in Relation to Sociology*

Philip M. Hauser

Demography may be conceived as consisting of two facets, demographic analysis and population studies. The former is concerned only with the study of population size and composition and components of variation and change; the latter, with the interrelationships of population and other systems of variables of which the sociological constitute but one set.

With the encouragement of the National Science Foundation, a review was recently undertaken of the status of demography as a science. This paper is drawn largely from the volume which reports the results of this undertaking.[1] The investigation necessarily entailed consideration of demography in relation to a number of other disciplines, including sociology.[2]

Courses in demography in the United States, although offered in a number of disciplines, are primarily concentrated in departments of sociology. In fact, about three-fifths of the members of the Population Association of America, and about half of those in the International Union for the Scientific Study of Population, had their basic training in sociology. The modal demographer in the United States is a Ph.D. in sociology serving as a faculty member in a university or college; 26 per cent of the members of the Population Association of America are so described.

The extent to which sociology has "captured" demography in the United States is an interesting phenomenon. Especially is this so when it is recalled that the study of population as a specialty probably antedated

Reprinted from *American Journal of Sociology*, 65, no. 2 (September, 1959), pp. 169–71, by permission of the author and the University of Chicago Press. Copyright © 1959 by the University of Chicago. Footnotes have been renumbered.

* Prepared for annual meeting of American Sociological Society, Seattle, 1958.

the emergence of sociology as a separate social science and that the close affinity between sociology and demography is largely a product of the last two or three decades.

It must be noted, however, that, although a large proportion of demographers are sociologists, only a small proportion of sociologists are demographers. Moreover, there would, in general, be agreement that most sociologists tend to ignore or to give scant attention to demographic considerations in their research and that some demographers have, on the whole, conducted their investigations without too much concern with, or attention to, problems of major sociological interest. In consequence, although demography in this country is primarily a subfield of sociology, the arrangement has been assumed to be more one of housekeeping convenience than of a fundamental theoretical, substantive, or methodological unity. By reason of these considerations it is appropriate to review the interrelationships of these fields and to explore the potentialities and prospects for their closer and more fruitful collaboration.

In the volume from which this paper is largely drawn, demography is conceived of as comprising two distinct facets, namely, demographic analysis and population studies.[3] The former is concerned with the statistical analysis of population size, distribution, and composition and with components of variation and change; the latter involves the interrelationships of demographic with other systems of variables. This distinction provides a logical framework for viewing the relationship of demography as a multiscience discipline to various disciplines, including sociology.

Scholars identified as "demographers," whether in sociology or other fields, have been primarily, although not necessarily exclusively, concerned with demographic analysis. Non-demographic scholars, however, also deal with demographic variables. For example, geographers, geneticists, ecologists, anthropologists, public health experts, psychologists, historians, economists, manpower specialists, and students of other disciplines, as well as sociologists, frequently consider population variables in the conduct of their research.

The demographer, whatever his training may be, is characterized by a major interest in demographic phenomena as dependent variables. He is concerned with accounting for the variability in demographic behavior, with the object of achieving predictability and control or explanation. In research designed to achieve this objective the demographer may use as independent variables either population or other phenomena. When the research of the demographer is confined to the interrelating of a set of dependent demographic variables with independent demographic factors, it is "demographic analysis"; when the research involves the interrelating of dependent demographic variables with independent sets of social, economic, genetic, psychological, historical, or other systems of variables, it is an example of "population studies." In the pursuit of such an interest the individual demographer is apt to work with the subject matter of the discipline in which he has been trained, as, for example, sociology, economics, psychology, genetics, or geography. Whatever may be their disciplinary origin, demographers have in common an interest in demographic analysis and are equipped, therefore, with a common body of theory, knowledge, and method for achieving it. In addition, they usually have general training in a social or natural science with departmental standing in academic organization.

The non-demographer, whether sociologist, geneticist, economist, or whoever else, who utilizes demographic variables to account for variability in sets of dependent variables in which he is interested, is also engaged in population studies. His interest may differ from that of the demographer, however, in that he is more likely to treat population phenomena as independent, rather than as dependent, variables in his effort to achieve predictability and explanation of his non-demographic phenomena.

Within this framework it is clear that there is no logical reason why demography should be more closely related to sociology than to any one of a number of other disciplines.[4] The fact that demography has become largely a subfield of sociology for instructional and academic housekeeping purposes in the United States is more a matter of historical accident than of special affinity. The relationships between demographic and sociological sets of variables are not necessarily closer, more compelling, and more fruitful than similar relationships with economic, psychological, geographic, genetic, or other sets of variables. Each of these configurations of interrelationships could conceivably make some contribution to achieving predictability and explanation of population phenomena considered as dependent variables. Conversely, population variables, considered as independent variables, could help to explain the behavior of the other sets of variables. But they have no closer relationship to the explanation of sociological than of other phenomena of social or natural science. There exists then as much justification for relating demography to any one of a number of natural as well as social sciences as there is for the relationship between demography and sociology.

These considerations are presented as a basis for neither the secession nor the expulsion of demography from sociology. On the contrary, a better understanding of the interrelations of these disciplines could conceivably lead to more fruitful research in both. . . .

NOTES

1. Philip M. Hauser and Otis Dudley Duncan (eds.), *The Study of Population: An Inventory and Appraisal* (Chicago: University of Chicago Press, 1959).

2. Explicitly treated were: "Ecology and Demography," chap. xxvii, by Peter W. Frank; "Human Ecology and Population Studies," chap. xxviii, O. D. Duncan; "Geography and Demography," chap. xxix, Edward A. Ackerman; "Physical Anthropology and Demography," chap. xxx, J. N. Spuhler; "Genetics and Demography," chap. xxxi, Franz J. Kallman and John D. Rainer; "Economics and Demography," chap. xxxii, Joseph J. Spengler; and "Sociology and Demography," chap. xxxiii, Wilbert E. Moore.

3. Hauser and Duncan, *op. cit.*, chap. i.

4. See also George A. Hillery, Jr., "Toward a Conceptualization of Demography," *Social Forces*, XXXVII, No. 1 (October, 1958), 45–51.

2

New Frontiers in Demography and Social Psychology*

Kurt W. Back

The topics of demography are those of human fate: birth, illness, marriage, occupation, and death. The methods of demography therefore relate global rates to major events, submerging the individual decision. The social psychologist observes the regularities of people's behavior in different social conditions and builds models from individual decisions. Since he looks at patterns independent of the event, the kind of event does not matter, and he tends to concentrate on trivial events which are amenable to research.

To the degree that man has obtained control over his environment, he is able to look at demographic events as less than fate. Social conditions have also given more control to the individual over many events over which he had no control previously, such as choice of a marriage partner or an occupational career. Thus, the classical methods of demography are frequently insufficient to deal with demographic data, and abrupt changes may occur because of vagaries of individual decisions. The more the demographic trends can be affected by individual decisions, the more the methods of social psychology become useful in understanding changes in population composition.

INTRODUCTION

The study of human life in its totality forms the background of the effort of a whole set of social sciences. However, each of these sciences specializes in some slice of human life, proposing a different partial model. Many of these models are more meaningful if placed in the context of a whole science

Reprinted from *Demography*, 4, no. 1 (1967), pp. 90–93, by permission of the author and the publisher.

* Revision of a paper presented at the annual meeting of the American Sociological Association, Chicago, August, 1965.

of human lives. We can liken the relation of the whole human life to particular sciences to the figure-ground relation of perception, where outlook of a particular science is highlighted. Backgrounds which give meaning to a figure are often taken for granted or forgotten. Thus, many social scientists tend to forget the place of their particular work within the total context of human life. It is the function of the background to locate the relative position of figures and to provide a contrast for them; to show what they can do and what they are lacking. By considering the several sciences in relation to human life, we may also discover their relations to each other and to the whole of human life and in this way make possible new methods for social studies of human lives. In many respects demography and social psychology represent two extremes, and so the two contrasting sciences (perhaps idealized) offer the most general framework for study. The difference can be polarized by two concepts—fate and control.

DEMOGRAPHY AND SOCIAL PSYCHOLOGY

Demography can be viewed as the science of fate. The demographer deals with such questions of fate as birth, death, illness, home, marriage, and occupation. As a matter of fact, in looking at the individual's concern with fate, we find exactly the topics with which demography deals. Further, the traditional demographer has dealt with this condition of human life in a fatalistic way. He prefers to look at trends, at rates, at the influence of long-time changes on these rates, and to make his results predictable without much regard for the individual. In dealing with rate and the events over which men traditionally have had little control, the classical model of man as a passive recipient is like that of a particle in the grip of physical, biological, and social forces.

The social psychologist proceeds in the opposite way. His unit of study is usually the individual, even if theory goes beyond strictly individual reactions. He is trying to construct the actions within a social system from the actions of the individual by observing the regularities of how people behave and feel in different social conditions. Characteristically, he also considers people interchangeable. The demographic characteristics of the people whom he studies matter little. The experimental social psychologist, for instance, picks his subjects from student populations, assuming that the kind of facts which he studies can be exhibited in any population which he selects. Even where demographic characteristics are stated, such as sex or age, they usually are used just as an item of information without any necessary connection to the results. The social psychologist's model of man is that of a modifiable organism loosely connected to society. It is this connection which he intends to study. As a result, he finds it easy to rely on a few psychological traits, and he is often fascinated by a theory emphasizing psychological reductionism.

In general, the social psychologist's approach is different from that of the demographer. Although some of the events that the demographer studies could be built up from some individual decisions, this is not the way the demographer proceeds. He works with aggregates; these global measures show greater regularities and permit simpler models than will be built up from individual actions.

Thus, demography deals with the important events in human life— birth, marriage, place of living, ways of making a living, illness, and death —but disregards the individual, who lives through these events, as an important factor in his theories and research. The social psychologist looks for a general pattern of the action of individuals, especially vis-à-vis other people, during the course of his life. Since he looks for a pattern independent of the particular event, the kind of event does not matter. Thus, he tends to concentrate on trivial events which are easily manageable for research. If we set each model within the framework of the whole individual life, we can see how a combination of the two approaches can help us better to understand the human life course. Several recent trends especially help in doing so; man's expanding control of his environment also tends to give him control of his "demographic fate." Correspondingly, theory and research in both fields have made an integration possible. We shall discuss some examples of the conditions which tend to balance demographic factors between fate and individual responsibility, control, and action.

FATE AND CONTROL IN LIFE EVENTS

Mortality: Epidemics v. way of life. It is still true today, of course, that man cannot control the length of his life and decide what it will be. The changing pattern of causes of mortality, however, has given this question a decidedly new meaning. Traditionally, death for infants has been caused through the conditions surrounding natality; for adults, through infectious diseases; for women, in childbirth; and, for the aged in general, by reaction to a strenuous life. Infantile mortality, epidemics, and general infections which spread through lack of knowledge of hygienic precaution were uncontrollable by the individual, everybody in the population being at risk. Incidence appears a random event. As seen from the individual viewpoint, it seems like blind chance or fate.

The importance of these causes of death has been receding in recent years. Infant mortality has been reduced, and the proportion of the contribution of infectious diseases to mortality has been diminished, both by the control of epidemics and by the use of new drugs. Of the invasions by micro-organisms, only cancer remains an important factor. As a result, major contemporary causes of death have a different character. For the young and middle-aged groups, accidents and suicide rank as the most important causes, to be superseded by cardiac and other chronic conditions among older age groups. Prevention of these conditions is no longer a problem of protection from contagion but is rather a question of the way of life of the individual. Exposure to these conditions depends more on the way a person organizes his life, what stresses he undergoes, how safely he drives, the risks he takes, and so forth. Even cure and prevention are no longer the province of an outside agent, such as a physician or sanitary engineer, alone. The agent has to talk to the person, and this interaction is important in convincing the individual that he is able to control the disease and, in many cases, that a change in values is necessary to reduce these factors which cause mortality. The confusing spread of plague or the curse of fate has given way to regimes controlling heart disease, arteriosclerosis, and accidents.

Fertility: Fecundity v. *planned parenthood.* Birth is another classical instance of the action of fate. Like death, in a biological sense, it corresponds clearly to the working of chance and necessity. In animals, the season for procreation is well defined and assumes at the point the function of a strong biological drive, combining both the sex act and procreation itself. We find that one of the distinguishing features of the human is that he can separate enjoyment of the sex act from its procreative function. Still, in most human societies, fertility is a rather uncontrolled, fateful concomitant of the expression of sexual desires. Thus, the question of whether to have children and, if so, when and how many is not considered to be a matter of individual plan or decision but at best is a matter of hope and fear. The widespread use of contraception, however, has changed this point of view, even where contraception is not practiced. Study after study has revealed that men and women have a definite idea of the number of children that they want and that they are increasingly able to have these children when they want them. With the decrease in infant mortality, each birth becomes a definite commitment to raising a child to maturity. We find that fertility has become dependent on a conscious decision to have children, although, as in mortality, biological factors which cannot be controlled at the present time still play a large role.

Migration: Necessity v. *selectivity.* The third main factor in vital rates is the migration pattern. In contrast to the first two, it is not primarily biologically but always socially defined. Traditionally, it has been a factor associated with the social group and not the individual. Membership in a social group, tribe, nation, polis, or other territorial unit has been socially determined as an ascribed characteristic, and the migrant was not free to enter it. Migration thus became a fact of interaction between nations, either as aggressors and conquerors or as being aggressed against and moved and dispersed. The individual migrant, the trader, or other person who sought out a new city for economic gain was rarer. The shifts in this balance are hard to assess quantitatively over the years, but it seems that individual mobility is relatively on the increase. This is certainly true of migration within the borders of national states. Relative freedom of movement and ease of transportation make individual trial decisions and final decisions much easier; and economic opportunity and livability in a particular section of a country can be taken into account in making individual decisions of a place to live.

Marital selection: Duty v. affiliation. Traditionally, marital selection has been controlled by kinship groups; the range of possible choice was very small. Further, many marital selection rules have been prescriptive as well as prohibitive; that is, people in certain relationships had to be married. Finally, the age of marriage frequently has been rigidly circumscribed; because of economic as well as social conditions, there was no choice of whether or not to get married. All these conditions have been changed. Even what is called the circle of eligibles defines only the preferred group from which to choose a mate and is not an exclusive rule. The circle itself is becoming larger and is no longer defined, except negatively, through kinship relations. Finally, it is at least economically possible for both men and women to have a position in society and to support themselves without being married. Thus, a person increasingly can make an active decision about whether to get married as well as whom to marry. This fact has been shown in the lessening importance of social and residential propinquity and in the rise of several kinds of intermarriage.

Occupational choice: Tradition v. interest. Social position has been long a determining factor in selection of occupation. Caste, family tradition, guild system, position within the family, and restriction on occupation and advancement have all made vocation a matter of fate. As in migration, membership in a social group no longer determines the action to be taken. Society presses for a higher standard of general education which ideally qualifies everybody for a variety of jobs and also equalizes their access to further specialized skills. There is still a relationship between social position and the level of occupational aspiration and achievement, but it is becoming less normative and more a deficiency to be overcome. In addition, the number of jobs at the same level leads to a multiplicity of possible choices which cannot be socially determined. Thus, increase in uniformity of upbringing, in contact, and in spatial mobility makes more vocational, as well as marital, choices possible and thus puts many of these into the realm of individual decisions. ·..

Introduction: B. Examples of Formal Demography and Population Studies

One way to get acquainted with a new field of study is to consider some illustrative examples. Analytic schemes are useful, but there is often a need to add some substance to the bare bones of the analytic categories. It is fine to talk about formal demography in which demographic variables are employed to explain changes in other demographic variables, but a paper such as that of Ansley Coale, referred to earlier, clearly demonstrates what a formal demographer can do and what surprising conclusions can be reached by formal demographic analysis. With that in mind I have selected a few papers that illustrate some of the methods, the theoretical approaches and the kinds of problems that demographers try to solve. The five papers that I have selected cannot suggest the full range of demography. But they are a sampling, and more importantly I have found the content of each to be interesting for the students in my classes.

The first paper of the set was published by the Population Reference Bureau. In it Annabelle Desmond summarizes what we know about the long history of the earth's population. She draws heavily on what is labeled historical demography. Historical demography as a field of populaton study has been growing steadily in recent years, though it has not yet flourished in the United States in the same way it has in Great Britain and France. In Section II there is a brief selection by Louis Henry, a French historical demographer, in which he looks at the field from the perspective of the data that are needed for historical studies of population.

In addition to illustrating historical demography, Desmond attempts to answer her title question: how many people have ever lived on earth? The conclusion and how it is arrived at merit special attention.

The paper by Richard Udry, "The Effects of the Great Blackout of 1965 on Births in New York City," is not so much an illustration of a particular kind of demography as it is a model of the scientific spirit that guides all good research. While almost everyone has heard about the Great Blackout of 1965 in New York and knows what effect it had on the birth rate nine months later, Udry's paper shows how a demographer establishes the facts.

As I have already mentioned, the social psychological approach to the study of fertility is becoming increasingly accepted by students of population, although one must admit that many studies of this genre have had disappointing results. Two researchers who have produced some interesting findings with a social psychological approach are Theodore Groat and Arthur Neal. They have used measures of the well-known concept alienation to see if the degree and type of alienation has any effect on the number of children people have. A summary of some of their major findings and their theoretical interpretations are reported in article 6.

The number of social psychological concepts that might be used to explain variations in fertility are unlimited, and one of the challenges of this approach is to select from all the possible orientations and psychological states those that will predict fertility most fully. This work has hardly begun although some trends and patterns are beginning to appear. The alienation concept used by Neal and Groat has within it a dimension that focuses on the degree to which people feel they have control over the future and their personal fate. This dimension, which might be called fatalism versus instrumentalism, is emerging as a possible important element in the fertility decision making of couples.

Most social psychologically oriented researchers are inclined to believe that the sex role orientations of males and females are also strong determinants of fertility behavior. The traditional feminine role strongly emphasizes the motherhood role, which has as its keynote the bearing and nurturance of children. If women believe that they are fulfilled only by becoming mothers it can hardly fail to have an impact on the number of children they have. These issues are discussed in several papers later in the book, but especially in articles 24, 25 and 26 in the section on fertility.

The final paper in this section illustrates how a demographic factor may influence a nondemographic factor. In this particular case Roland Chilton and Adele Spielberger examine the effects of the changing age structure of the State of Florida on the juvenile delinquency rates. In the 1960's juvenile delinquency and crime rates increased throughout the United States. There was much hand-wringing and head-shaking among the politicians and amateur social analysts who were inclined to see it as a breakdown of our moral fiber, or the result of a too affluent, coddled, Dr. Spock-raised generation. But, perhaps it was something much simpler that explained the increasing crime rates in American society during the 1960's. Perhaps it was a simple demographic factor: a changing age structure. Chilton and Spielberger argue effectively that fully three-fourths of the increase in Florida's juvenile delinquency rates might be attributed to the fact that there were more youngsters in the ages when juvenile crimes are most frequently committed.

The lesson of Chilton and Spielberger's paper is one that cannot be made too strongly. Anyone who has a rudimentary knowledge of demography should be highly sensitive to the effects of different population compositions. Whenever some social rate is compared from one time to another or one place to another the student of population should ask immediately: is this rate related to age or sex and does a changing age or sex composition of the population account for the difference or change? For example, if the divorce rate of a society goes up (as ours has in the United States in recent years), is it because divorce is more frequent at some ages than others (the answer is yes) and are those ages increasing proportionately in the society? If so, the changing age composition of the married population *may be* the cause of the increasing divorce rate. At least the demographic explanation should be considered before more fanciful explanations are advanced.

3

How Many People Have Ever Lived on Earth?*

Annabelle Desmond

How many people have ever been born since the beginning of the human race?

What percentage does the present world population of three billion represent of the total number of people who have ever lived?

These questions are frequently asked the Population Reference Bureau's Information Service. Because of the perennial interest and because of the credence sometimes given to what would seem to be unrealistic appraisals, this issue presents an estimate prepared by Fletcher Wellemeyer, Manpower, Education and Personnel Consultant, Washington, D.C., with Frank Lorimer of American University, Washington, D.C., acting as advisor. This estimate, based on certain statistical, historic and demographic assumptions set forth in an appendix, should be regarded as no more than a reasonable guess. It assumes that man first appeared about 600,000 years ago, a date which has been proposed for the dawn of the prehistoric era. However, this date obviously is a compromise, anthropologically speaking, between varying extremes.

Since then, it is estimated that about 77 billion babies have been born. Thus, today's population of approximately three billion is about 4.0 percent of that number.

Absolutely no information exists as to the size and distribution of prehistoric populations. Presumably they were not large, nor very widely distributed. If the 600,000 B.C. date is accepted as a sound compromise, then

Reprinted from *Population Bulletin,* 18, no. 1 (February, 1962), pp. 1–19, by permission of the publisher, Population Reference Bureau, Inc., Washington, D.C.

* The research report for this *Bulletin* was prepared by Fletcher Wellemeyer, with the technical assistance of Frank Lorimer. Georgine Ogden contributed supplemental research.

only about 12 billion people—less than one sixth of the total number ever born—are estimated to have lived before 6,000 B.C.

Anthropologists and paleontologists differ by hundreds of thousands of years as to when man first walked this earth. Recent discoveries strongly suggest that the life-span of the human species might date back as much as two million years. However, this time scale has not yet been accepted by all anthropologists.

If the "beginning" actually extended a million years prior to 600,000 B.C., the estimated number of births prior to 6,000 B.C. would be 32 billion, and the estimated total number, about 96 billion.

Prior to 1650, historical population data are very scanty for every part of the world. Despite this lack of knowledge, ancillary evidence exists which reveals the general pattern of human growth. Throughout the thousands of centuries which preceded the present technological age, human survival was such a touch-and-go affair that high fertility was essential to balance brutally high mortality. The human female—a relatively slow breeder, even among mammals—had to reproduce somewhere near her physiological limit in order for the family, the clan, the tribe, and the nation to survive.

As human culture developed over the ages, the chances of survival tended to improve. When the invention of agriculture provided a more stable food supply, the base was laid for the maintenance of large populations and for their spread into new areas. However, high death rates continued to check population growth.

Until recently, at least a half of all babies born died before reaching maturity. Man's quest for some formula to avert death included magic, incantations, and prayers, but none of these had shown any efficacy against the major killers. Then, with the advance of modern science, the mortality pattern of a million years was broken.

Jenner's dramatic discovery of vaccination for smallpox was the first of a multitude of discoveries destined to defer death, especially in infancy and childhood. This brilliant application of the scientific method to biology and medicine, together with improved agricultural technology, better transportation, and the vast and complex nexus of an emerging industrial culture, set in motion forces which drastically lowered death rates and thereby greatly increased the efficiency of reproduction. In some countries, the birth rate declined also, although more slowly than the death rate. During the 19th century, the industrial countries of the West were the first to experience the transition from high to low birth and death rates. This transition took about 150 years.

These epochal changes profoundly altered the patterns of survival and population growth. In those countries of northern Europe and North America which were the first to exploit effectively the new medical discoveries, life expectancy at birth rose rapidly from 30 years to 40, then to 50, and, by 1960, to 70 years and more. Infant mortality declined drastically: now, 95 out of every 100 babies born in Western industrial countries live to reach adulthood.

Although the power to defer death is one of the greatest advances in man's long history, it has been the principal factor in the acceleration in the rate of population growth during the past century. Now, public health programs reach even the world's most remote villages, and death rates in the less developed areas are falling rapidly. But the traditionally high birth rates—so essential to offset the high death rates of even the very recent past —remain high. Thus, population growth soars.

Therefore, over the long span of history, the rate of population growth has tended to accelerate—almost imperceptibly at first; then slowly; and recently, at a rapid clip. By the beginning of the Christian era, 200–300 million people are believed to have lived on earth. That number had grown to some 500 million by 1650. Then the growth curve took a sharp upward trend. By 1850, world population was more than one billion. Today, it is over three billion.

The quickening tempo of growth is even more dramatically expressed in doubling time. It took hundreds of thousands of years for world population to reach the quarter-billion mark, at about the beginning of the Christian era. Over 16 centuries more passed before that number reached an estimated half-billion. It took only 200 additional years to reach one billion, and only 80 more years—to about 1930—to reach two billion. Population growth rates are still going up. During all of the eons of time—perhaps as long as two million years—the human race grew to its present total of three billion. But it will take only 40 years to add the next three billion, according to United Nations estimates. In certain nations and larger areas, populations will double in 25 years or even less, if growth rates remain unchanged.

This historical review traces the proliferation of the human species through three very broad time spans: Period I extends from 600,000 B.C. to 6,000 B.C.; Period II extends to 1650 A.D.; and Period III, to 1962. These time periods are chosen because the dates mark important epochs in man's cultural development.

It should be emphasized, however, that not all portions of the globe experienced simultaneously the cultural and technological advances which mark these different stages of man's history. When the first European settlement was established in Australia in 1788, the aborigines there were in the Stone Age. Even today, some tribes living in New Guinea and elsewhere still remain at that level.

PERIOD I—THE OLD STONE AGE

Period I extends from 600,000 to 6,000 B.C. It begins early in the Paleolithic or Old Stone Age and continues to the beginning of the Neolithic or New Stone Age. It is estimated that during this period numbers grew to about five million, that man's birth rate was close to 50 per thousand, and that there was an approximate total of 12 billion births.

Little, if anything, is known about population size during this hunting and gathering stage of man's existence. The total land area of the earth is approximately 58 million square miles. It seems reasonable to assume that not more than 20 million square miles could have been used successfully by the relatively few who inhabited the earth at that time. The consensus of competent opinion indicates that, on moderately fertile soil in a temperate climate, about two square miles per person would be needed for a hunting and gathering economy.

It must be assumed that there were severe limitations on man's numbers during this period, and that his life cycle and average generation were much shorter than they are today. Man existed for the most part in wandering bands in order to survive. Our ancient ancestors were completely subject to all the vagaries of the weather and the ecological cycle of the game animals on which their existence depended. Food shortages were usually endemic, and the ravages of epidemics were routine—although the wide dispersal of the population tended to localize these hazards. Nevertheless, the picture that emerges is one in which births and deaths were roughly balanced, with births perhaps holding a narrow margin.

THE LONG TIME SPAN OF PREHISTORY

Anthropologists and paleontologists are gradually putting together, piece by piece, the great jigsaw puzzle that is the history of early man. Dr. T. D. Stewart, head curator of the Department of Anthropology, National Museum, in Washington, D.C., points out that only a few fossils of humans who lived in this period have been found. Nevertheless, man's long time scale is known today with far greater accuracy than ever before, mainly because of the new radioactive dating techniques. According to Dr. Stewart, new discoveries demand new theories or that existing theories be adjusted.

The remains of *Zinjanthropus*, recently found in the Olduvai Gorge of Tanganyika by L. S. B. Leakey, curator of the Coryndon Museum, Nairobi, Kenya, which Leakey believes date back almost two million years, probably do not represent the beginning of the line. *Zinjanthropus* has been called man because he was a toolmaker, in the crudest sense. Since his physical form represents a very early stage of human evolution, it is not advisable to assume so early a beginning for purposes of estimating human population growth.

However, it is generally believed that "man" had reached the point of being able to make simple tools and to talk by a half million or even a million years ago. Though he presumably emerged much earlier, *Homo sapiens* first appeared with great force in Europe sometime between 25,000 and 30,000 years ago. Very little is known about where he came from or about his connection with the Neanderthal people, who were one of many types of man to precede him. By 20,000 B.C., he had created the first great art in human history: the magnificent paintings and other artifacts found in certain caves in southern France and northern Spain. He engraved and carved bone and ivory with faithful representations of his women and of the animals he knew so well: the mammoth, the bison, and others. These were believed to have had magic significance—to bring fertility to the clan and success to the hunter.

No birth rates or death rates have ever been found on the walls of the prehistoric caves. Thus, what is the puzzle of man to the anthropologist and the paleontologist becomes the enigma of man to the demographer. A United Nations Report, *The Determinants and Consequences of Population Trends,* published in 1953, presents a comprehensive survey of world population through the whole of man's history. Readers are referred to it for a more complete historical survey than this limited space permits. The Report states:

> That men, using tools, have been living on this planet for at least one hundred thousand years, and possibly for over a million years, is proved by various types of evidence. For example, the definitely human skeletal remains found at Choukoutien, China, in association with artificial stone and bone implements and possible indications of the use of fire, were deposited during the second interglacial period, or earlier. There is evidence, also, that several divergent types of men emerged, some of whom had specialized characteristics which place them outside the ancestral line of all living races today. The Neanderthal people, who were dominant in Europe during the last (Würm) glaciation, were apparently such a divergent race.

PERIOD II—6000 B.C. TO 1650 A.D.

Starting with the beginning of the New Stone Age, this period extends through the Bronze and Iron periods, through classical antiquity and the Dark Ages, the Renaissance and the Reformation. It is estimated that world population increased one hundredfold during the period, growing from five million to half a billion, and that about 42 billion births occurred.

It is believed that at the beginning of the era the earth was still very sparsely settled and population was widely dispersed. Vast areas of the globe were not inhabited, partly because the last glaciations had just receded.

It was during this period that man began to *produce* food instead of simply consuming what nature had laid before him. In the Near East, he had already passed the stage of the most primitive village-farming communities which grew out of the earliest agriculture with its domestication of animals. Some of these ancient communities developed into the earliest known urban settlements. The development of agriculture with its settled farming community spread to other areas of the earth during this period. Eventually, it was to change drastically man's pattern of survival and his way of life.

The earliest scene of settled village-farming communities appears to have been in the Near East. Robert J. Braidwood, professor of the Oriental Institute of Chicago and field director of the Jarmo Project, a recently studied archeological site in Iraq, says: "It is probably very difficult for us now to conceptualize fully (or to exaggerate) the consequences of the first appearance of effective food production. The whole range of human existence, from the biological (including diet, demography, disease, and so on) through the cultural (social organization, politics, religion, esthetics, and so forth) bands of the spectrum took on completely new dimensions."

Braidwood describes the hilly piedmont and intermontane regions surrounding the great "Fertile Crescent," which starts in the valleys of the Tigris and Euphrates Rivers, sweeps around to the north to touch southern Turkey and Syria, then curves south to the shores of the Mediterranean and into Egypt. One radioactive-carbon date suggests that this development was well advanced by 4000 B.C.

Sheep, goats, pigs, cattle, and some kind of horselike animal were used by those living in the area. Their plants were wheat and barley. Braidwood notes that some sort of hybridization or mutation, particularly in domesticated plants, must have taken place before certain species could have been moved to other areas. However, they seem to have moved into the Danube Valley by 4000 B.C., and into western Europe by 2500 B.C.

In other words, man was learning to utilize his environment more efficiently; thus it could support more people than ever before. But numbers were still regulated by the food-producing quality of the land. Population grew in times of plenty and declined when food became scarce and when disease decimated large populations, as it did in Europe during the Dark Ages.

During the Bronze Age, man began to use copper and bronze and to build towns, cities, and states. Kings, advanced religions, social classes, writing, and enduring monuments, such as the Nile pyramids, appeared during this period. The Iron Age brought iron metallurgy, the invention of the alphabet, the use of coined money, and the spread of commerce and navigation.

The early and great empires and cultures developed: those of Egypt, Rome, and Greece; of King Asoka in India; of the Han dynasty in China; and, later, the empires of the Mayas and the Incas in the New World. The Hindu, Confucian, Buddhist, Jewish, Christian, Moslem, and other great religions emerged.

The City—Period II

The great cities of ancient times rose in rich valleys adjacent to the Mediterranean, the Red Sea, and the Persian Gulf, along the Indus and the Nile, and along the Yangtze in China. The first great urban civilization arose about 3500 B.C. in Mesopotamia, along the Tigris and Euphrates. Another grew up in Egypt before 3000 B.C. and still another in Crete. A fourth arose along the banks of the Indus in western India, but whether this grew directly out of Neolithic beginnings or was a transplant of the Sumerian culture of Mesopotamia is a matter of dispute. Urban civilizations developed in China at a later date, and still later in some areas of tropical Central America and in Peru.

The urban societies of Mesopotamia, China, and Egypt maintained complex centralized control of soil and water resources in order to provide irrigation and to control floods. These "hydraulic" civilizations supported very dense populations with highly integrated social systems. The individual peasant was allowed a small land area which produced more food than his family needed. Such civilizations have persisted in Egypt, India, China, and elsewhere to the present day, with little change in the economic basis of life but with periodic rises and declines.

The ancient Mediterranean, Asian and American urban civilizations appear to have been isolated flowerings of human culture which culminated in "golden ages" and then declined. The archeological record abundantly reveals their wavelike nature.

The A.D. Era of Period II

The United Nations study previously mentioned states that, at the beginning of the Christian era, the world's population was likely to have been between 200 and 300 million people. Discussing the lack of historic demographic information, the Report states:

Various kinds of evidence indicate that man's numbers became adjusted to the food-producing capacity of the land in ancient times—increasing as it rose and declining as it fell. Unfortunately little of this evidence is of a census type, and most of the remainder does not provide a basis for estimating the number of inhabitants of an area. Large parts of the world's population were subject to some sort of census enumeration near the beginning of the Christian era, but the information available from these censuses has limited value. Roman censuses were taken for administrative purposes and were restricted to "citizens," an expanding category as citizenship rights were extended to outlying regions. Moreover, only adult males were included in some of these censuses, while all household members except "children" were included in others. Chinese censuses at about this time provided reports on total population but interpretation of the results involves many difficulties. Elaborate records were kept by the ancient Incas, but their meaning is obscure.

J. C. Russell, professor of history at the University of New Mexico, who has contributed much to the demographic history of the West, has traced the population changes within the Roman Empire from the second century A.D. to the year A.D. 543, a period he characterizes generally as one of imperial decline:

> ... However, within the general picture there are great differences in the trends. Actually most of the decrease occurred in western Mediterranean lands: Italy, Gaul, Iberia, and North Africa, together with Greece and Egypt. In Syria the population seems to have held even while in Gaul and Britain something like recovery must have occurred at the end of the period. Eastern Asia Minor and the Slavic area probably increased markedly. The German and Scandinavian spheres apparently held even in spite of emigration. The information about the central, eastern, and northern parts of Europe is so vague and uncertain that there may have been a considerable increase in population. The general rise in temperature should certainly have reduced the semiglacial conditions of the northern countries and made them attractive for grain-growing groups.

In the second and third centuries A.D., Rome suffered two devastating epidemics which have not been identified, but their virulence suggests bubonic plague. According to Dr. Russell:

> The period from A.D. 543 to 950 probably marks the lowest ebb of population in Europe since the early Roman Empire. It covers the first great attack of the plague, the worst epidemic to strike the area with which we are concerned. Following it came the Mohammedan invasions from the seminomadic areas of the lands surrounding the Medi-

terranean. From the east in the tenth century the Hungarians scourged most of Europe and what they missed was visited by the terrible raids of the Vikings from the north. Some measure of the weakness of the European population is indicated by the feeble defense put up against these invaders by the governments of Europe. . . .

Endemic diseases such as malaria and tuberculosis were prevalent, and the latter was particularly fatal among young people. In fact, the combination of both diseases occurred quite frequently and was highly fatal. Dr. Russell speculates that during the periods of population decline in early medieval Europe, much carefully tilled and drained acreage lapsed into breeding grounds for mosquitoes; and that a period of wet, warm weather about 800–900 A.D. greatly increased the incidence of malaria.

The span of life (extreme length of life) seems to have been around 100 years, as it is now. Those who could avoid infection were likely to live to considerable ages. According to John Durand, assistant director in charge of population, the United Nations Bureau of Social Affairs, the best basis for making mortality estimates of the Roman period is a study of tombstone inscriptions for males dying between the ages of 15 and 42. This method corrects the exaggeration of years that humans are apt to indulge in, even on tombstones, and allows for the underrepresentation of children's deaths. On this basis, Durand concludes that life expectancy at birth for the whole population of the Roman Empire was probably only about 25 or 30 years.

After the year 1000, it appears that population began to increase; and, between 1000 and 1348, that growth was phenomenal, particularly in northern Europe. The empire of Charlemagne had already capitalized on the upward population movement, and stronger governments began to develop in Germany, Scandinavia, and even in Russia. The Crusades spread Christianity throughout the Middle East and brought contact between the Moslem and Christian worlds.

Then in 1348 the bubonic plague, which seems to have first appeared in the sixth century in Egypt, suddenly erupted in Europe in a more virulent form, taking a frightful toll of lives. Russell states that "the years 1348–1350 saw a very heavy loss of life, 20 to 25 per cent in most European countries. The decline continued with later epidemics until the population of about 1400 was near 60 per cent of the pre-plague figures. . . ."

Between 1500 and 1700, far-ranging social, economic, and intellectual revolutions began which formed the basis for the modern world. The era of medieval authority was first challenged in northern Italy, at the time of the Renaissance. This was followed by the age of discovery, with voyages around Africa and to the New World. At the same time, the Reformation set the stage for the revival of intellectual development in northern Europe. For the first time since the Golden Age of Greece, the human intellect began to look at the world objectively. This led to the birth of the scientific method: new concepts of the nature of matter, energy, and, ultimately, of life began to capture the minds of men. Out of this intellectual revolution came powerful new insights which were eventually to greatly change man's pattern of living and dying.

In Europe about the middle of the 17th century—after the end of the Thiry Years' War and the period of peace and stability which followed —agricultural methods improved, slowly at first and then rapidly. New crops were introduced and crops were rotated; manure and fertilizers were used more generally; and the soil was cultivated more extensively. Even though these more advanced methods increased food production, the margin of plenty continued to be precarious, especially for those who lived in cities. A comparable agricultural expansion seems to have occurred in China at about the same time.

Unfortunately, little is known about population growth and decline during this period for the vast continent of Asia, particularly for India and China. M. K. Bennett, director of the Food Research Institute, Stanford University, has recognized the need for a continent-by-continent or region-by-region survey. He estimates that world population in 1000 A.D. was somewhere around 275 million, or "probably less than half of the population of Europe in 1949; . . . that there has been one century, the fourteenth [the century of the Black Death in Europe], in which world population did not increase at all, but declined. . . ."

The earlier "hydraulic" civilizations became subject to disorders which checked and, in some cases, reversed their population growth.

The Americas had an estimated population of 16 million at the time of their discovery by Columbus. Julian Steward, research professor of anthropology, University of Illinois, has estimated the population of the different regions of the American hemisphere in 1492 as follows:

North America:	
North of Mexico	1,000,000
Mexico	4,500,000
West Indies	225,000
Central America	736,000
South America:	
Andean area	6,131,000
Remainder	2,898,000
Total	15,490,000

PERIOD III—1650–1962 A.D.

If man's existence on earth is viewed as a day, this period is less than a minute. But a fourth or more of all human beings ever born have lived during this brief span.

The period brought a sixfold increase in human numbers: from an estimated half-billion in 1650 to over three billion in 1962. There were approximately 23 billion births during this period—over half as many as in the preceding 76 centuries!

World population doubled between 1650 and 1850, growing beyond the one-billion mark. It doubled again, to reach two billion by 1930, in only 80 years. Since that time, the rate of growth has accelerated steadily. Now over 50 million more people are added each year. If the current rate remains unchanged, today's population will double again in less than 40 years.

A steadily falling death rate, especially during the last century, is mainly responsible for the very rapid acceleration in population growth. It is estimated that during 1650–1750, population was growing at about 0.3 percent a year; during 1750–1850, at about 0.5 percent; 1850–1950, at 0.8 percent. Currently, the rate is somewhere between 1.6 and 1.9 percent.

This period brings man through to the modern agricultural-industrial age with its tremendous scientific and technological discoveries which have greatly speeded up the rate of social change in the Western world and which have revolutionized agriculture, industry, communication, transportation, etc. These developments have made possible the support of the mammoth populations in numerous areas of the world. However, many of those technological advances are only beginning to touch the less developed areas where living levels for over half of the world's people are only a little, if any, above what they were during much of the earlier history of the race.

For the world as a whole, the mid-17th century is a benchmark in the pattern of population growth. Then, the upward surge in the numbers of people began. Just why the response to the early stirrings of the modern age was so rapid is not entirely clear, though many of the major factors which stimulated the increase in human numbers can be recognized. In Europe, the frightful famines and epidemics that marked the Dark Ages seem to have decreased, although hunger and disease were still endemic. The discovery of the New World opened the way for great transatlantic migrations to the rich, sparsely settled lands of the Americas. To some extent, this relieved the growing population pressure in Europe and provided a new source of food for the Old World. It also gave impetus to the tremendous growth of populations of European origin—at home and in European colonies—which amounted to a ninefold increase during the period.

The development of the scientific method and the application of this new knowledge to technology stimulated the Industrial and Vital Revolutions which so greatly changed man's way of life throughout the Western world. The Industrial Revolution brought the transition from agrarian to industrial societies—a transition which is beginning only now for large areas of Africa, Asia, and Latin America. The Vital Revolution brought the Western industrial nations through the demographic transition: from high birth and death rates to low birth and death rates. . . .

WHAT IS PAST IS PROLOGUE

Since man first appeared on earth, human arithmetic has moved from a relatively simple exercise in addition to a complicated one of geometric progression. It took all of the vast reaches of time to build today's population of slightly over three billion. But it will take only 40 more years for population to reach six billion, if the present growth rates remain unchanged.

Life on this earth was a precarious gamble for *Homo sapiens* for hundreds of thousands of years. Driven by his natural reluctance to endure an early death, man ultimately discovered and then perfected the power to defer death. That he has succeeded is a notable tribute to his genius and to his humanitarian and philanthropic instincts.

It is noteworthy that the desire to control fertility has never had the emotional imperatives which brought the power over death. Only modest efforts have been made thus far to discover effective methods of fertility control which would be acceptable to the people of all cultures and religions. Less than modest efforts have been made to disseminate what knowledge is now available to all of the world's people who would benefit from that knowledge. Consequently, during the past decade of rapid death-rate decline in the less developed countries, there has been no measurable reduction in high birth rates; so population growth has increased.

Rapid population growth cannot be maintained indefinitely in any part of the world. If birth rates do not decline in overcrowded lands, death rates eventually will rise to check growth.

The gulf which exists today between the peoples of the world has widened: life is better than ever before for those who live in the Western industrial countries. But the majority of the world's people still live close to the subsistence level, in poverty and squalor reminiscent of the Middle Ages. If the demographic transition to a balance between low birth and death rates could be hastened in the less developed countries, this gulf might yet be bridged in time to avert a Malthusian disaster.

APPENDIX

The statistical and general demographic assumptions used to determine the number of people who have ever been born were provided the Population

Reference Bureau by J. Fletcher Wellemeyer, an independent manpower consultant, Washington, D.C., in consultation with Frank Lorimer, American University, Washington, D.C.

The estimate was made on the basis of three time periods:

Period	Number of Years in Period	Number of Births per Year at Beginning of Period	Number of Births per Year at End of Period	Number of Births in Period
I. 600,000– 6000 B.C.	594,000	"1"	250,000	12 billion
II. 6000 B.C.– 1650 A.D.	7,650	250,000	25,000,000	42 billion
III. 1650–1962 A.D.	312	25,000,000	110,000,000	23 billion
Total				77 billion

To obtain the number of births at the beginning and end of these periods, certain assumptions were made regarding birth rates and the size of populations. It was assumed that at the beginning of the Neolithic era the population was five million and that the annual birth rate was 50 per thousand. The procedure assumes a smooth increase. The growth was undoubtedly irregular, but the estimates may fairly represent the net effect of the ups and downs.

By 1650, the annual number of births was estimated at 25 million, corresponding to a population of about 500 million. The 1962 world population of 3.05 billion, the number of births, and birth rate of 36 per thousand are based on United Nations estimates.

The 600,000 years' duration of the Paleolithic era is based on the assumption that manlike types were then in existence but in very small numbers. Earlier dates have been given a few species by certain authorities, but some of these dates are questionable, and the earlier species may have been considerably less than manlike. The 600,000-year period seems a reasonable compromise between extreme possibilities.

Once the number of births at the dates indicated was determined, the total number of births for each period was calculated at a constant rate of increase for the period.

The estimated rates of increase differ sharply. For the long Paleolithic period, the average annual rate of increase was only 0.02 per thousand; during 6000 B.C. to 1650 A.D., it rose to 0.6; and during 1650–1962, it reached 4.35.

For the figures derived here, the following equation was used:

$$\Sigma B_t = \frac{B_0 e^{rt}}{r}$$

B_0 is the number of births per year at the beginning of the period; t is the number of years in the period; e is the base of natural logarithms; and r is the annual rate of increase during the period.

The value of r is obtained by solving for r the equation

$$\frac{B_t}{B_0} = e^{rt}$$

where B_0 is the number of births the first year of the period and B_t is the number of births the final year of the period.

SOURCES

In the preparation of this *Bulletin*, the following sources were consulted. The reader is referred to them for additional information.

1. Bennett, M. K. *The World's Food.* New York: Harper and Brothers, 1954.

2. Braidwood, Robert J. "Near Eastern Prehistory." *Science.* 127 (3312). June 20, 1958.

3. Brown, Harrison. *The Challenge of Man's Future.* New York: The Viking Press, 1954.

4. Carr-Saunders, A. M. *World Population, Past Growth and Present Trends.* Oxford: Clarendon Press, 1936.

5. Collier, John. *Indians of the Americas.* New York: New American Library of World Literature, 1947.

6. Cook, Robert C. "World Population Growth." *Law and Contemporary Problems,* a quarterly published by the Duke University School of Law. 25 (3). Summer 1960.

7. Durand, John. "Mortality Estimates from Roman Tombstone Inscriptions." *American Journal of Sociology.* 45 (4). January 1960.

8. Huxley, Julian. *New Bottles for New Wine.* New York: Harper and Brothers, 1957.

9. Kroeber, A. L. *Anthropology.* New York: Harcourt, Brace and Company, 1948.

10. Russell, J. C. "Late Ancient and Medieval Population." *Transactions of the American Philosophical Society.* New Series 48 (part 3). June 1958.

11. *Scientific American.* Issue entitled "The Human Species." 203 (3). September 1960.

12. Steward, Julian. "The Native Population of South America." *Bureau of American Ethnology Bulletin.* No. 143.

13. Turner, Ralph. *The Great Cultural Traditions: Volume I, The Ancient Cities.* New York: McGraw-Hill Book Company, 1941.

14. United Nations, Department of Social Affairs, Population Division. *The Determinants and Consequences of Population Trends.* New York, 1953.

15. United Nations, Department of Economic and Social Affairs, Statistical Office.

    A. *Demographic Yearbook, 1960.* New York, 1960.

    B. *The Future Growth of World Population.* New York, 1958.

    C. *Population and Vital Statistics Reports* (Statistical Papers, Series A, Vol. XIII, No. 1). New York, 1961.

16. Willcox, Walter F. (editor). "Population of the Earth," by Willcox in *International Migrations,* Vol. II, Part I. New York: National Bureau of Economic Research, Inc., 1931.

4

How a Population Ages
or Grows Younger

Ansley J. Coale

The age of the whole human population could, I suppose, be measured
from the moment the species originated, and the age of a national population could be measured from the country's "birthday." The age (in this
sense) of the human population has been estimated as at least 100,000 and
no more than a million years, and the age of national populations ranges
from several thousand years for Egypt or China to a year or so for some of
the emerging nations of Africa.

In this chapter, however, when we speak of the age of a population we
refer to the age of its members, and to be precise we should use the term
age distribution of a population—how many persons there are at each age—
rather than the age of a population. The only way a single age can be given
for a group of persons is by using some sort of average. A *young* population,
then, is one that contains a large proportion of young persons, and has a
low average age, while an *old* population has a high average age and a large
proportion of old people.

The ages of various national populations in the world today are very
different, and in many countries the present age distribution differs markedly from the past.

The oldest populations in the world are found in Northwestern Europe.
In France, England and Sweden, for example, 12 percent of the population
is over sixty-five, and half of the population in these countries is over thirty-
three, thirty-six, and thirty-seven respectively. The youngest populations
are found in the underdeveloped countries—those that have not incorporated modern industrial technology in their economies—the populations of

Reprinted from *Population: The Vital Revolution,* ed. Ronald Freedman (Garden
City, N.Y.: Anchor Books, Doubleday & Co., 1964), pp. 47–58, by permission of the
author and the publisher.

Asia, Africa and Latin America. Half of the population of Pakistan is under eighteen years, of the Congo under twenty years, and of Brazil under nineteen years. The proportion over sixty-five in Brazil is less than one fourth what it is in France. The proportion of children under fifteen is twice as great in Pakistan as in England. Paradoxically enough, the oldest nations—China, India and Egypt—have very young populations.

The highly industrialized countries all have older populations than the underdeveloped countries, and also older populations than they did fifty to a hundred years ago. Since 1900 the median age has risen in England from twenty-four to thirty-six, in the United States from twenty-three to thirty, in Japan from twenty-three to twenty-six, and in Russia from twenty-one to twenty-seven. In the underdeveloped countries, however, the age distributions have changed only slightly, and they have, if anything, become slightly younger. In Taiwan, for example, the median age has declined from twenty-one to eighteen since 1915.

What accounts for these differences and these trends in the age distribution of populations? One obvious factor to consider is migration. A famous spa has an old population because old people come there for the cure, and university towns like Princeton have young populations because young people come there to study. But the age distribution of most national populations is not much affected by migration, especially today when almost everywhere international migration is restricted.

Whether a national population is young or old is mainly determined by the number of children women bear. When women bear many children, the population is young; when they bear few, the population is old.

The effect of fertility (as the rate of childbearing can be called) on the age distribution is clearest when a population continuously subject to high fertility is compared to one continuously subject to low fertility. The high-fertility population has a larger proportion of children relative to adults of parental age as a direct consequence of the greater frequency of births. Moreover, by virtue of high fertility a generation ago, today's parents are numerous relative to *their* parents, and hence the proportion of old people is small. Conversely, the population experiencing a prolonged period of low fertility has few children relative to its current parents, who in turn are not numerous relative to *their* parents. Prolonged high fertility produces a large proportion of children, and a small proportion of the aged—a population with a low average age. On the other hand, prolonged low fertility produces a small proportion of children and a large proportion of the aged—a high average age.

It is the small number of children born per woman that explains the high average age now found in industrialized western Europe, and the high birth rate of the underdeveloped countries that accounts for their young populations. The increase in average age and the swollen proportion of old people in the industrialized countries are the product of the history of falling birth rates that all such countries have experienced.

Most of us would probably guess that populations have become older because the death rate has been reduced, and hence people live longer on the average. Just what is the role of mortality in determining the age distribution of a population? The answer is surprising—mortality affects the age distribution much less than does fertility, and in the opposite direction from what most of us would think. Prolongation of life by reducing death rates has the perverse effect of making the population somewhat younger. Consider the effect of the reduction in death rates in the United States, where the average duration of life has risen from about forty-five years under the mortality conditions of 1900 to about seventy years today. Had the risks of death prevailing in 1900 continued unchanged, and the other variables—rates of immigration and rates of childbearing per mother—followed the course they actually did, the average age of the population today would be greater than it is: the proportion of children would be less and the proportion of persons over sixty-five would be greater than they are. The reduction of the death rate has produced, in other words, a younger American population.

These statements seem scarcely credible.

Does not a reduction in the death rate increase the average age at death? Are there not more old people as a result of reduced mortality than there would be with the former high death rates? How then can it be said that a reduction in the death rate makes a population younger?

It is true that as death rates fall, the average age at which people die is increased. But the average age of a population is the average age of living persons, not their average age at death. It is also true, as we all immediately realize, that as death rates fall, the number of old persons in a population increases. What we do not so readily realize is that reduced mortality increases the number of *young* persons as well. More survive from birth to ages one, ten, twenty, and forty, as well as more living to old age. Because more persons survive to be parents, more births occur.

The reason that the reduced death rates, which prolong man's life, make the population younger is that typical improvements in health and medicine produce the greatest increases in survivorship among the young rather than the old.

There is one kind of reduction in death rates that would not affect the age distribution of the population at all, that would lead to the same proportion of population at every age as if mortality had not changed. This particular form of reduced mortality is one that increases the chance of surviving one year by a certain amount—say one tenth of 1 percent—at every age. The result would be one tenth of a percent more persons at age one, five, ten, sixty, and eighty—at every age—than there would have been had death rates been unaltered. Because there would be one tenth percent more parents, there would also be one tenth percent more births. Therefore the next year's population would be one tenth percent larger than it would otherwise have been, but the proportion of children, of young adults, of the middle-aged, and of the aged would not be altered—there would be one tenth percent more of each.

Reductions in mortality of this singular sort that would not affect the age of the population at all are not found in actual human experience. However, there has been a tendency for persons at all ages to share some of the increased chances of survival, and the effect of reduced death rates on the age distribution has consequently been small—much smaller than the effect of reduced birth rates—in countries where both fertility and mortality have changed markedly.

As the average duration of life has risen from lower levels to sixty-five or seventy years, the most conspicuous advances in survivorship seem always to have occurred in infancy and early childhood. It is for this reason that reduced mortality has had the effect of producing a younger population, although the effect has usually been obscured by the much more powerful force of a falling birth rate that has occurred at the same time. Thus the population of the United States has actually become *older* since 1900, because of falling fertility; but falling mortality (with its tendency to produce a younger population) has prevented it from becoming older still.

The younger-population effect of reduced mortality is not an inevitable feature of all increases in length of life. The countries with the greatest average duration of life have by now about exhausted the possibility of increasing survivorship in a way that makes for a younger population. In Sweden today 95 percent survive from birth to age thirty, compared to 67 percent in 1870. At best, survivorship to age thirty in Sweden could approach 100 percent. No important increase in population at younger ages would result. If there are further major gains in the chances of prolonged life in Sweden, they must occur at older ages, and if they occur, will make the population older.

Every individual inexorably gets older as time passes. How old he gets depends on how long he avoids death. President Eisenhower remarked after his retirement that he was glad to be old, because at his age, if he were not old, he would be dead.

Populations, on the other hand, can get older or younger. They get older primarily as the result of declining fertility, and younger primarily as the result of rising fertility.

The most highly industrialized countries have all experienced a decline of fertility of about 50 percent since their preindustrial phase, and they all have older populations than they used to have. In France and the United States, for example, the number of children each woman bore declined for more than a century, reaching a minimum just before World War II. In each country during this period the population became progressively older. In fact, the "aging" of the population continued for a time after fertility had passed its minimum. Between 1800 and 1950 the median age of the French population rose from twenty-five to thirty-five years, and in the United States in the same interval the median age increased from sixteen to thirty. In both countries there has been a substantial recovery in fertility during the past twenty-five years from the low point reached in the 1930s. This rise in fertility has produced the first decrease in median age recorded in the statistics of either nation. Between 1950 and 1960 the median age in France fell from 35 to 33, and in the United States from 30.2 to 29.6.

This reversal in the trend toward an older population in the United States has been accompanied by a more pronounced reversal in the way proportions of children were changing. The long-term decline in fertility in the United States meant that the proportion of children to adults steadily shrank from about 0.85 children (under fifteen) per adult (over fifteen) in 1800 to 0.33 per adult in 1940. By 1960 the proportion had rebounded to 0.45 children per adult. In fact, the increase in the *number* of children in the population between 1950 and 1960—more than 15 million—was greater than the increase between 1900 and 1950.

The abrupt reversal of the long-term trend toward an older population has meant the first increase in the relative burden of child dependency in the history of the United States. The very productive American economy can certainly afford to support this burden, but it has not been painless. The extremely rapid increase in the number of children in the past decade has required the construction of many new schools and the training of many teachers. In some communities where foresight, willingness to pay increased taxes, or resources were inadequate, schools have been overcrowded and the quality of instruction has suffered.

The countries that have not undergone intensive industrialization have experienced no major changes in fertility, no trends of sustained decline and recovery such as occurred in France and the United States. Rather they have experienced a largely unbroken sequence of high birth rates. There has been in consequence little change in the age composition of underdeveloped areas. All have 40 percent of more under age fifteen, only 2 to 4 percent over sixty-five, and a median age of twenty years or less.

The age distributions of the industrialized countries on the one hand and of the preindustrial countries on the other are ironically mismatched with what each sort of country seems best equipped to accommodate. As we have noted before, the contrast in age of population is striking. In Pakistan or Mexico nearly one person of every two a visitor might encounter would be a child, and only two or three of every hundred would be old (over sixty-five); while in England only one in four would be a child and about one in eight would be old. In the industrialized countries where the proportion of the aged is so large, the importance of the family in the predominantly urban environment has diminished, and consequently the role of respected old patriarch or matriarch has nearly vanished. The wealthy industrial countries can readily afford to support a sizable component of old people but have not in fact always done so adequately. The aging of their populations has been accompanied by a weakening or a disappearance of the traditional claims of the aged on their descendants for material support and, perhaps more tragically, by a weakening or disappearance of a recognized and accepted position for old people in the family.

In the underdeveloped countries, on the other hand, the relatively few old people are accorded traditional respect and whatever economic support their families have to offer, and hence the aged are less subject to special economic and social deprivation.

Because of extremely young age distributions, adults in the impoverished underdeveloped countries must support a disproportionately large dependent-child population—twice as great a burden of dependency per adult in the working ages of fifteen to sixty-five as in typical industrialized countries—a burden these poor countries can scarcely afford. The enormous proportion of children makes it extraordinarily difficult, where incomes are extremely low, to provide adequate shelter, nourishment, and education for the young.

Moreover, the preindustrial countries can expect no relief from dependency as a result of the spectacular drop in death rates now occurring. Unless fertility declines, this drop in mortality will only make the populations younger, adding to the already extreme burden of dependent children.

In sum, it is the industrialized countries that, better able to afford a high burden of child dependency, have only half the proportion of children found in underdeveloped areas, and that, having abandoned the institutions giving a meaningful role to the aged, have four times the proportion of the elderly found in preindustrial countries.

The last question considered in this brief survey of the age of populations is the past trend in age distribution from man's origin to the present, and what alternative trends may possibly develop in the future.

The human population as a whole has always been and is now a young population, consisting of at least 40 percent children, and having a median age of no more than about twenty years, because the over-all human birth rate has always been about 40 per 1,000 or higher. It is almost certain that until perhaps two hundred years ago all sizable national or regional populations likewise were young, with about the same age characteristics as the population of the world.

These statements can be made with confidence, even though no reliable records of the age distribution of the world, or of world birth rates, or even records of many national populations exist for most of man's history. We can be confident that the world's population has always been young because until the last two centuries it was not possible for any population to achieve low mortality for any sustained period, and any population with a low birth rate would therefore have become extinct.

It is simply not possible for a population to have a birth rate much below its death rate for a prolonged period, as can be shown by the following example. The population of the world has grown from about one-quarter billion to about three billion since the time of Julius Caesar—it has been multiplied by about twelve. But the average annual rate of increase has been very little—about 1 per 1,000 per year. If the world birth rate has averaged 40 per 1,000 (a reasonable guess), the world death rate by logical necessity has averaged 39 per 1,000. A world birth rate only two points lower (38 instead of 40 per 1,000) would have led to an annual *decrease* of 1 per 1,000, and the current population would be only one twelfth instead of twelve times the population of Caesar's day. A birth rate of 35—that of England or the United States in 1880—would have reduced the 250 million of two thousand years ago to less than one hundred thousand today.

The industrialized countries have been able to reduce their birth rates without having their populations shrink drastically because they first reduced their death rates. Beginning in the late eighteenth century some countries made preliminary steps in the improvement in living conditions and sanitation that has continued until today, and in the latter half of the nineteenth century there began the remarkable development of modern medicine and public health that so greatly extended the average duration of life in the industrially more advanced countries.

In the past few decades modern medical techniques and public health methods have been introduced into the underdeveloped countries, causing an extraordinary drop in death rates, and since birth rates have not changed, the growth of world population has sharply accelerated so that it is now 2 percent per year.

Just as it is not possible for a population to maintain for long a birth rate much below its death rate, because such a population would shrink to extinction, it is not possible to maintain for long a birth rate much *above* a death rate, because then the population would grow to a physically impossible size. For example, had the current 2 percent rate of growth existed since the time of Caesar, the population of the world would have been multiplied by about 135 quadrillion instead of twelve, and there would be more than 30,000 times the entire world's current population on each square mile of land area on the earth. Starting with today's three billion persons, it would take only about 650 years for a 2 percent rate of increase to produce one person per square foot, and about twice that long to produce a total that would outweigh the earth.

In short, the present combination of a high world birth rate and a moderate and rapidly falling death rate can only be temporary. The only combinations that can long continue are birth and death rates with the same average levels.

If man chooses to continue the high birth rate that he has always had, the human population will remain a young one—but in the long run it can remain young only by returning to the high death rate and short average life it has always had. Sustained geometric increase is impossible.

If, on the other hand, mankind can avoid nuclear war, and bring the fruits of modern technology, including prolonged life, to all parts of the world, the human population must become an old one, because only a low birth rate is compatible in the long run with a low death rate, and a low birth rate produces an old population. In fact, if the expectation of life at birth of seventy years—now achieved or exceeded in many industrialized countries—becomes universal, the average number of children born per woman must decline to about two from five or more in the underdeveloped areas, slightly more than three in the United States, and some two and a half in Europe. Such a decline in fertility would give the whole world as old a population as any country has had to date—only about 21 percent under fifteen, at least 15 percent over sixty-five, and as many persons over thirty-six as under.

A world population with the age composition of a health resort is a mildly depressing prospect. Such a population would presumably be cautious, conservative, and full of regard for the past. A young, vigorous, forward-looking population perhaps appears more attractive, but in the long run the world can keep its youth only by tolerating premature death.

We find at the end, then, that although the birth rate determines how old a population is, the death rate determines what the average birth rate in the long run must be. If prolonged life produces by its direct effects a younger population, it is nevertheless compatible only with an older population.

SUGGESTIONS FOR FURTHER READING

L. Dublin and A. Lotka. "On the True Rate of Natural Increase." *Journal of the American Statistical Association.* Vol. 20, 151, September 1925, pp. 305–39.

A classic article in which the interrelations of fertility, mortality, growth, and age distributions were presented with the ingenious invention of a new concept, "the stable age distribution."

United Nations. "The Cause of the Aging of Populations: Declining Mortality, or Declining Fertility?" *Population Bulletin* No. 4, December 1954, pp. 30–38.

Ansley J. Coale. "How the Age Distribution of a Human Population Is Determined." *Cold Springs Harbor Symposium on Quantitative Biology.* Vol. 22, 1957, pp. 83–88.

Two short articles, the second somewhat technical, explaining the respective roles of fertility and mortality in shaping age distributions.

Ansley J. Coale. "Population and Economic Development," in *The Population Dilemma,* edited by Philip M. Hauser. Englewood Cliffs: Prentice-Hall, 1963, pp. 46–69.

Includes a discussion of the significance of age distributions for economic development.

5

The Effect of the Great Blackout of 1965 on Births in New York City

J. Richard Udry

Electric power went out in New York City and much of the Northeast in the late afternoon November 9, 1965, and stayed out for up to ten hours. On Wednesday, November 10, 1965, the *New York Times* carried a banner headline on page one, "POWER FAILURE SNARLS NORTHEAST; 800,000 ARE CAUGHT IN SUBWAYS HERE; AUTOS TIED UP, CITY GROPES IN DARK." Light and power first went out at 5:27 P.M. in New York City, and power in all areas was back on at 4:00 A.M.

On Wednesday, August 10, 1966, also in the *Times*, a page one midsection headline announced, "BIRTHS UP 9 MONTHS AFTER THE BLACKOUT." Under the signature of Martin Tolchin, the following story appeared.

A sharp increase in births has been reported by several large hospitals here, 9 months after the 1965 blackout.

Mount Sinai Hospital, which averages 11 births daily, had 28 births on Monday. This was a record for the hospital; its previous one-day high was 18. At Bellevue there were 29 new babies in the nursery yesterday, compared with 11 a week ago and an average of 20.

Columbia Presbyterian averages 11 births daily and had 15 Monday; St. Vincent's averages 7 and had 10; Brookdale averages 10 and had 13; and Coney Island averages 5 and had 8. However, New York and Brooklyn Jewish hospitals reported that their number of births was normal. . . .

There were 16 babies at Mount Sinai yesterday, 13 at Columbia Presbyterian, and 10 at St. Vincent's, all above average. The number of births was reported normal in Nassau and Suffolk counties, many of whose commuters were stranded in the city November 9, in Newark and Jersey City which were not affected, and in hospitals in Albany,

Reprinted from *Demography*, 7, no. 3 (August, 1970), pp. 325–27, by permission of the author and the publisher.

Rochester, New Haven and Providence, where the lights went on in mid-evening.

Sociologists and obstetricians were requested to comment on the reported event. One sociologist was quoted as saying, "The lights went out and people were left to interact with one another." Others said that the disruption in routine caused by the blackout and the absence of television might have contributed to the phenomenon. Christopher Tietze was more cautious in his opinion: "I am skeptical until I see the data from the entire city. There can be daily fluctuations in individual hospitals that can be misleading. If it should be true, I would think it is because people may have had trouble finding their accustomed contraceptives, or just because it was dark." (Tolchin, 1966).

The effect of the blackout on birth rates is a relatively easy matter to determine. Through the cooperation of Carl Erhardt and the New City Health Department, I obtained the number of births for each calendar day for the years 1961 through 1966. I took November 10, 1965, as the date of conception for the blackout babies, and assumed that the average gestational length was 280 days, counting from the last menstrual period, and therefore about 267 or 266 days from conception. Using a distribution of gestational ages at birth derived from vital statistics (Vital Statistics of the U.S., 1965), it was estimated that more than 90 percent of the births conceived on November 10th would have been born between June 27 and August 14. I reasoned that if there were an unusual number of conceptions on November 10th, then the period between June 27 and August 14, 1966, would contain a greater percentage of the year's births than that contained by the same period in other years. Table 1 presents the percentage of the year's birth occurring per week from June 27 through August 14 for the years 1961 through 1966. It can be seen that 1966 is not an unusual year in this comparison. For those who still imagine that all babies conceived on a given date are also born on an exact date 267 days later, Table 1 presents the number of births and proportion of the year's births born on the date corresponding to 267 days after the blackout, also for the years 1961 through 1966. This number of births is not at all remarkable for 1966 when compared to the previous five years. Figure 1 presents the critical data graphically. The unshaded area in Figure 1 is the limits of variation for the years 1961–1965 in percent of the year's births occurring in each of the critical weeks. The dotted line gives the average percent of the year's births occurring in each of these weeks for 1961–1965. The solid line is the percent of the year's births for each of these weeks for 1966.

For no week is the 1966 value significantly above average for the previous five years. We therefore cannot conclude from the data presented

TABLE 1.   Births Occurring in New York City from June 29 to August 16 Except 1964 When It Was June 28–August 15 During the Years 1961 through 1966

Yr.	Mean births per		Pct. of year's total births	Number of births on 267th day
	Day	Week		
61	478.7	3350.6	13.9	475
€2	467.2	3270.1	13.9	497
63	476.2	3333.7	13.9	431
64	470.2	3291.3	13.9	406
65	457.7	3203.7	14.1	468
66	434.5	3041.6	13.9 <	431 <

Source: Unpublished tabulations furnished by the New York City Department of Health.

here that the great blackout of 1965 produced any significant increase (or decrease) in the number of conceptions.

Let us not imagine that a simple statistical analysis such as this will lay to rest the myth of blackout babies. Nine months after the Great Snow of 1967 in Chicago, hospitals reported that they were preparing their facil-

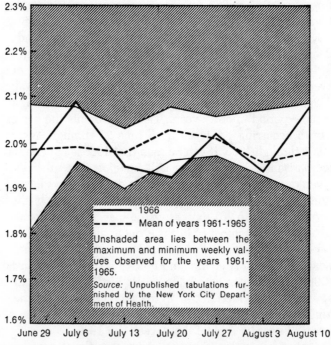

FIGURE 1.   Percent of Year's Births Occurring by Week from June 29 to August 16, for the Years 1961–1966

ities for an avalanche of "snow babies." It is evidently pleasing to many people to fantasy that when people are trapped by some immobilizing event which deprives them of their usual activities, most will turn to copulation.

ACKNOWLEDGMENTS

This research was completed under a grant from the Faculty Research Council of the University of North Carolina at Chapel Hill. Thanks to Marie Cloney, Thomas Graham, and Charles Chase for tabulation. Gratitude is expressed to Carl Erhardt and the New York City Department of Health for making the data available to me.

REFERENCES

New York Times, November 10, 1965.

Tolchin, Martin. "Births Up Nine Months After Blackout," *New York Times*, August 10, 1966, p. 1.

Vital Statistics of the U.S. 1965 Vol. I—Natality. U.S. Dept. of H.E.W. Public Health Service, National Center for Health Statistics, Table 1–42 and Table 1–46.

6

A Social Psychological Approach
to Family Formation*

H. Theodore Groat and Arthur G. Neal

The census approach to population growth is valuable as a way of describing fertility occurrences or happenings within given societies. Certainly the "world population problem," with the well-known dilemma of high birth rates outpacing low or declining death rates, has demonstrated the importance of aggregate behavior as supraindividual facts. Population studies relating demographic data to large-scale economic and social trends will of course continue to command our attention in the years ahead. Through survey research, to supplement census and vital statistics data, we are now on the threshold of knowing a great deal more about the diffusion of contraceptive knowledge and use, changing patterns of differential fertility, and some of the broader sociological and economic factors affecting fertility in many parts of the world.

But childbearing, as both an individual and a collective act, is more than an occurrence or a statistic. Fertility trends may also be viewed as an aggregate outcome of the intentions, motives, and decisions of vast numbers of individual couples. If we are interested in understanding fertility behavior we must go beyond the descriptive social facts and take into account the values and aspirations surrounding the production and rearing of children, as well as the problems related to unsuccessful fertility control. As governments throughout the world move increasingly toward policy decisions on populations, it is important that they be informed by research that taps behavior on this more proximate level. While nations and regions of the world do indeed have overall fertility problems, the individual and

This paper was prepared especially for the second edition of this reader.

* Part of the research upon which this publication is based was supported by Contract No. NIH-71-2028 with the Center for Population Research, National Institutes of Health, Department of Health, Education, and Welfare.

family units comprising these populations also have their own problems: contraceptive availability and use, unwanted pregnancies, and short intervals between children, to name a few.

Davis and Blake (1956) have pointed out that fertility behavior must relate to factors affecting intercourse, conception, and gestation. This framework describes an exhaustive causal chain, each step of which may be affected by broad sociocultural variables such as urbanization and industrialization, and mediated by such social-psychological influences as motives and attitudes. As members of family units move through the life cycle, from marriage to first pregnancy, from first child to completed family size, we may profitably seek determinants of family-forming behavior in the mediating context of world views, decision-making and contraceptive efficacy.

SOCIAL-PSYCHOLOGICAL PERSPECTIVES

Analytically, we might ask why individuals and couples *decide* to have a first child, another child, or no children at all. The mere asking of this question implies some kind of rational decision-making, an assessment of the available means and alternative goals as well as the potential consequences. Presumably, within this decisional framework, couples are seen as weighing the "costs" against the "rewards" of childbearing. Here costs and rewards are defined broadly to include not only such objective factors as time and money, but the subjective values of convenience, freedom from responsibility, and many other positive and negative reinforcements.

From this perspective, the reasons people have children, or large versus small families, are the result of choices between alternative combinations of costs and rewards. A pregnancy might mean that a young working wife, for example, must give up her job. So the costs of potential income loss are weighed against the potential rewards of having a baby. If we wish, this line of reasoning can be carried even to decisions regarding contraceptive behavior. For a couple not planning a pregnancy the decision *not* to use contraception would then be based on the inconvenience, psychic, and other costs of using a contraceptive vis-a-vis the rewards of sexual intercourse unencumbered by contraceptive concerns. The possibility of an unwanted pregnancy would, of course, also be weighed as a possible cost consequence of noncontracepted intercourse (Easterlin, 1969).

An alternative approach questions the assumption that fertility behavior results from rational decision-making. Instead, decision-making varies in kind and degree, and deliberate planning may be placed along a continuum ranging from very little or none to a great deal. After all, contraceptive and fertility behavior, indeed all heterosexual behavior, involves at least two people. Ultimate decision-making, then, is contingent upon nearly perfect communication between the man and the woman. How can a joint decision be made, in other words, without a mutual sharing of the relevant concerns of both partners? Yet we know that communication between sexual partners is highly variable. Nuances and subleties involving the socio-sexual identities of both partners must surely be implicated in the communication patterns. Further, different cultural groups and social strata are characterized by different definitions of sex roles and different cultural and organizational patterns which may either enhance or inhibit the probabilities of full and open communication and joint decision-making (Rainwater, 1965). Despite the liberalizing trends apparent in our present society, sexuality is still a sensitive and emotion-laden area of human behavior.

In sum, instead of asking *how* fertility-related decisions are made, the social psychologist and social demographer might address the questions of *whether* they are made and, if so, *to what extent* they are made, and *under what conditions* they are made. We really know very little about the *units* of fertility decision-making. Do married couples actually decide on a next pregnancy? If so, within what time frame? Are alternatives to childbearing considered? Do young, unmarried sexual partners jointly make contraceptive decisions? Are the decisions made primarily by the male, or by the female? Under what conditions do the sexually active fail to contracept? The thrust of these questions is meant to suggest that the involvement of any given couple in fertility decision-making is primarily a matter of degree.

If this is indeed the case, we should then be able to research kinds and degrees of decision-making related to intercourse, conception, and gestation, at various stages in the family-forming process. Social psychologically oriented fertility research is needed to inform us more clearly about what attitudes, values, and world views interact with and influence contraceptive and family planning behavior. The special need is for conceptual models of social psychological variables to provide refinements of correlations between as well as within the broader demographic and socioeconomic categories.

In recent years, a social psychological approach to fertility behavior has slowly been gaining momentum as a promising direction for research. The basic premise, common to social psychology in general, is that personalities are organized differentially within the broader societal contexts of social class, religion, and other cultural and organizational auspices. Attitudes and beliefs about oneself and the relationships between oneself and the larger society of which one is a part are organized in different ways among different people. We know that some people seem better able to carry out planned courses of action than others, and a greater understanding of this phenomenon has an obvious relevance to fertility and family planning. Since voluntary family planning programs so crucially depend on the planfulness of their clients, attitudinal variables that interfere with the effective practice of contraception are clearly in need of scientific examination.

THE ALIENATION FRAMEWORK

Drawing upon the alienation framework, a series of empirical studies has been conducted by the authors to clarify relationships between generalized measures of estrangement from the larger society and specific attributes of fertility behavior (Groat and Neal, 1967, 1973; Neal and Groat, 1970, 1973). The alienation studies have emphasized the variables of powerlessness, meaninglessness, normlessness, and social isolation. These variables were not initially regarded as determinants of fertility in their own right, but as intervening between the structural conditions of social class and religion and intimate aspects of family life. Prior research had clarified conditions of alienation as obstacles to rational decision-making, especially as related to low receptiveness to control-relevant cues and information readily available in one's environment (Seeman and Evans, 1962; Seeman, 1963; Bickford and Neal, 1969).

The *powerlessness* dimension of alienation was designed to elicit expectancies (subjectively held probabilities) that the outcome of political and economic events cannot be adequately controlled by oneself or collectively by persons like oneself. The issues of concern relate to war and peace, the concentration of power, influence on government decisions, world opinion of the United States, and inflation. In its more intense form, powerlessness implies fatalism, a belief in unregulated occurrences, an emphasis upon "historical drift." In contrast, low powerlessness reflects a sense of mastery and confidence that the outcomes of national and international events are related to human efforts and intentions.

Feelings of powerlessness, we reasoned, are likely to be generalized from expectancies about events in general to specific forms of everyday behavior. Rather than seeing family-formation as stemming from one's own efforts and desires, such outcomes as pregnancies and child-care responsibilities are likely to be regarded as occurrences, "the will of God," or as "something which just happens." Our major hypothesis about powerlessness holds that those with more intense feelings of helplessness are likely to be characterized by a lower level of contraceptive knowledge, a lower likelihood of using contraception effectively, and a higher probability of experiencing an unwanted pregnancy.

In view of the relevance of the powerlessness dimension to planning and information-seeking, it seems reasonable to expect additional measures of alienation to be related in a consistent fashion to the same kinds of behavior. Conditions of *meaninglessness*, for example, may divert attention from the kinds of information that are necessary for making events intelligible and coherent. This measure of alienation indexes the degree to which national and international events are regarded as overwhelmingly complex, as chaotic, and as unpredictable. For those high in meaninglessness, events in society at large are lacking in coherence and the minimal standards for clarity in prediction and understanding are not being met. By way of contrast, for those low in meaninglessness, events involving the larger society appear orderly, predictable, and coherent.

Similarly, the suspicion and distrust involved in feelings of *normlessness* may create a preoccupation with "hidden motives," and thus interfere with the personal acceptance of information for planning and decision-making that is readily available. The measure of normlessness taps the expectancy that socially unapproved behavior is necessary for goal attainment. From this standpoint, normlessness involves a moral judgment on one's own society in terms of the extent to which its ethical standards must be violated in the attainment of socially approved goals. High scores on normlessness imply that society's moral standards have lost their hold over conduct, and that social norms carry weak sanction.

Finally, the detachment and anonymity in feelings of *social isolation* may create barriers to forming the very kind of social relations supportive of information transmission and retention so necessary for effective planning. This measure of alienation reflects the extent to which the individual experiences a cleavage between himself and his fellow man. Those high in social isolation feel that social relations are no longer predictive and supportive, and that the individual is thrown back on his own resources. Other people are regarded as unfriendly and disinterested, and one's own position is that of anonymity and aloneness.

Drawing upon these alienation concepts, we hypothesized that the measures of meaninglessness, powerlessness, normlessness and social isolation would be predictive of differential fertility and family planning behavior. Successful family planning, we reasoned, should be associated with rational decision-making, a sense of mastery over the outcome of events, a positive judgment on the normative order, and the perception of social relations as integrative and supportive.

In contrast, unwanted pregnancies and maximized fertility should, in theory, be associated with aimlessness and drift, fatalistic resignation, low regard for the normative order, and a sense of personal loneliness. For those high in powerlessness, fertility seems more likely to constitute an occurrence, a chance happening, an unmanaged event. Similarly, we expected those high in meaninglessness and normlessness to be unlikely to link immediate experiences with future consequences. A sense of uprootedness, aloneness, and isolation, we predicted, would be associated with the attempt to gain social integration through having and rearing children.

Thus, for those high in alienation in its various forms, a large number of births may result from the operation of "drift," chance occurrence, good or bad "luck," and failure to engage in long-range rational planning of the more important aspects of life. One such implicit use of the alienation framework may be found in Rainwater's (1960: 167–68) study of working class fertility, where he maintained "The lack of effective contraception . . . *is embodied in particular personalities, world views, and ways of life which have consistency and stability and which do not admit such foreign elements as conscious planning and emotion-laden contraceptive practices"* (Rainwater's italics).

Following Rainwater's insights, there are reasons for believing that a significant number of women are in a sense "victimized" by a high fertility which stems from a cognitive life-style with a heavy loading of alienation components. From this perspective, the major control-relevant implication is that ineffective family planning derives not so much from lack of knowledge or of access to methods as from the social psychological inaccessibility of "knowledge," generating dominance of emotional over rational elements in the decision-making process.

EMPIRICAL FINDINGS

In exploring relationships between alienation and fertility, our initial study was concentrated on a random sample of 750 mothers who delivered a baby during the calendar year of 1962 in the Toledo, Ohio, metropolitan area. The results generally indicated a substantial relationship between levels of alienation and fertility and family-planning behavior (Groat and Neal, 1967). In most of the comparisons with religion and socioeconomic status controlled, the higher the levels of alienation the larger the number of children. Further, the results suggested that the more highly alienated were more likely to continue their childbearing after the age and marital duration levels of completed family size for most women.

The data collected, however, did not permit an empirical assessment of two critical questions. First, data collected at a single point in time could not adequately answer the primary causal question. Do high levels of alienation tend to generate high levels of fertility, as we argued, or do high levels of alienation result from the presence in the home of a large number of children, especially unplanned ones? Panel data, in other words, were required for a rigorous test of the direction of causality between the alienation and fertility variables. Secondly, a clarification of the related question as to *why* alienation variables are predictive of fertility behavior could be obtained by analyzing data drawn from an identical sample at two different points in time.

It was possible to shed additional light on the explanatory problems by collecting identical data on the same subjects in 1971, allowing for a time lag of about eight years. If the longitudinal data indicated significantly higher levels of fertility for those women who scored high, in contrast to those who scored low, on the alienation measures in 1963, we would then have supportive evidence for including alienation variables among the causal factors underlying differential patterns of fertility. On the other hand, if differential fertility in 1971, within religious and socioeconomic categories, could not be predicted from alienation scores in 1963, the results would suggest that a large number of children may generate high levels of alienation, rather than the other way around.

A variety of procedures were utilitized in 1971 for relocating our initial respondents, including the use of telephone and city directories, and phone calls to the 1963 places of residence. In all, we were able to verify current addresses for 408 of our 1963 subjects. Utilizing a mailed questionnaire, a return rate of 82 percent was obtained from our relocated subjects, providing us with a parallel set of alienation data from 334 respondents. To determine the possibility of sample bias, a comparison was made of respondents with nonrespondents and unlocated subjects. The results indicated no statistically significant differences in either kinds and degrees of alienation or in 1963 parity levels.

Our particular sampling procedure was designed to assure the inclusion of women with proven fecundity, as well as to test for possible alienation to fertility relationships operative *during* the childbearing years. As such, the sample incorporated varying ages and marital durations, and included parity levels from one to sixteen. Additionally, only women with marriages uninterrupted by death or divorce between 1963 and 1971 were included in our longitudinal analysis.

Between 1963 and 1971, 43 percent of our subjects had no additional children, 33 percent had one additional child, and 24 percent gave birth to two or more additional children. Thus, the explanatory efficacy of the alienation variables was evaluated within the context of these variations in subsequent fertility over an eight-year period.

Table 1 shows that the overall pattern was the expected one of high alienation in 1963 generally associated with high subsequent fertility. We have listed the unadjusted, or observed, means for the total sample along with means by a series of controls adjusted for religion. Fertility differentials by the unadjusted means are invariably in the hypothesized direction, and applying standardization procedures to the control variables did not alter the direction or appreciably diminish the overall magnitude of these mean fertility differences by high and low alienation.

TABLE 1. Subsequent Fertility (1963 to 1971) by Kinds and Degrees of Alienation in 1963, Standardized on Religion, Age, Marital Duration, 1963 Parity, Education, and Husband's Occupation.

| | Kinds and Degrees of Alienation in 1963 | | | | | | | |
| | Meaning-lessness | | Social Isolation | | Norm-lessness | | Power-lessness | |
	Low	High	Low	High	Low	High	Low	High
	Mean Number of Children Between 1963 and 1971							
Unadjusted Total	(161)	(147)	(173)	(135)	(185)	(123)	(198)	(110)
	.79	1.08	.84	1.04	.86	1.02	.87	1.03
Controls Adjusted by Religion:[a]								
Age	.78	1.07	.87	1.02	.95	.96	.86	1.02
Marital Duration	.76	1.11	.86	1.08	.89	1.04	.89	1.14
1963 Parity	.78	1.09	.85	1.04	.87	.99	.87	1.05
Education	.77	1.08	.83	1.04	.87	1.02	.86	1.07
Husband's Occupation	.78	1.09	.84	1.03	.86	1.04	.87	1.02
Adjusted Total Means[b]	.77	1.09	.85	1.04	.89	1.01	.87	1.06
P (t test)[c]	.001		.05		ns		.05	

a Mean scores were adjusted for each of the control variables by drawing upon the techniques of test factor standardization suggested by Meuller, Schuessler, and Costner (1970), and Rosenberg (1962).
b Standardized in religion, age, marital duration, 1963 parity, education, and husband's occupation.
c Significance levels were based on the one-tailed test.

In each instance with the means adjusted for religion, sizeable fertility differentials were sustained within age, marital duration, previous parity, education, and occupation categories. Meaninglessness, social isolation, and powerlessness were most highly related to having subsequent children, while normlessness was in the expected direction, though less impressively. When these separate controls were combined into an adjusted total mean, the greatest fertility differentiation was obtained for meaninglessness, followed by social isolation and powerlessness. Regardless of religious differences, then, three of the four measures of alienation were significantly predictive of fertility differentials within a series of demographic and socioeconomic controls. The directionality was one of high alienation in 1963 associated with higher levels of subsequent fertility by 1971.

In assessing what appear to be small differences in the mean number of children, we need to bear in mind that the variance in subsequent fertility was also relatively small. Through initially selecting subjects by the fecundity criterion of having delivered a baby during the preceding calendar year, our cross-sectional sample was necessarily skewed in the direction of high-fertility mothers. Women with small families, in other words, had a lower probability of being selected in our sampling of recent mothers. Additional reproduction over the subsequent eight years, then, was occurring among subjects already characterized in 1963 by generally high levels of fertility (Mean Family Size = 3.05). Relating 1963 alienation levels to subsequent fertility, however, is reflective of women who had exhibited a high degree of fertility control over the next eight years, successfully terminating their childbearing, as well as women who had experienced continued fertility beyond the age and marital duration of completed family size for most women.

In any event, our longitudinal results corresponded with those obtained from our initial cross-sectional study. Using multiple indicators of alienation, the general pattern supported the view that conditions of alienation are associated with subsequent fertility. But to clarify the feasibility of the general explanatory framework under review, it is important to know if the obtained subsequent fertility derived primarily from the desire for additional children or from a lack of success in fertility control.

The data presented in Table 2 permit us to address this issue. The

TABLE 2. Percent of Subjects With One or More Unplanned Children by Kinds and Degrees of Alienation in 1963, Standardized on Religion and Socioeconomic Status.

	Meaning-lessness		Social Isolation		Norm-lessness		Power-lessness	
	Low	High	Low	High	Low	High	Low	High
	Percent with one or more unplanned children between 1963 and 1971							
Protestants	31%	50	33	51	36	48	46	37
	(59)	(60)	(72)	(47)	(73)	(46)	(57)	(62)
Catholics	34	50	32	51	39	48	33	56
	(35)	(40)	(34)	(41)	(46)	(29)	(43)	(32)
Total	32	50	33	51	37	48	41	44
(Standardized)	(94)	(100)	(106)	(88)	(119)	(75)	(100)	(94)
P (Phi Coefficient)	.01		.01		.05		ns	
Working Class	29	53	34	54	40	50	41	47
(Manual)	(54)	(83)	(68)	(69)	(81)	(56)	(66)	(71)
Middle Class	34	35	31	42	32	41	37	30
(Non-Manual)	(40)	(17)	(38)	(19)	(40)	(17)	(34)	(23)
Total	30	48	33	51	37	47	40	42
(Standardized)	(94)	(100)	(106)	(88)	(119)	(75)	(100)	(94)
P (Phi Coefficient)	.01		.01		ns		ns	

Note: Subjects were excluded from this analysis who indicated in 1963 that they expected to have an additional child.

information obtained in 1963 on preferences for additional children provided a basis for partially assessing the motivational argument that the higher fertility of the more highly alienated may derive from a desire for larger families. Our subjects were asked in 1963 whether or not they wanted to have additional children. By concentrating on those who indicated that no more children were wanted, we could derive a measure of "unplanned" or "unwanted" fertility over the next eight years. The data in Table 2 are listed by religion and socioeconomic status separately and standardized within these religion and social class categories.

By religion, the data show consistently higher incidences of unplanned subsequent fertility among wives scoring high than among those scoring low on each of the four alienation measures. For example, while 50 percent of Protestants and Catholics scoring high in meaninglessness in 1963 had at least one unplanned child by 1971, their counterparts scoring low in meaninglessness had significantly lower proportions with unplanned births (31 and 34 percent, respectively). The results are similar for social isolation and normlessness, and in all three instances the differentials between total means, standardized on religion, reach statistical significance at either the .01 or .05 level. The data for powerlessness, while providing a striking differential among Catholics, indicate a slight reversal for Protestant mothers which, of course, suppresses the differential for the total means standardized on religion.

Turning to the social class categories, based on husbands' occupations, the results are quite similar to those by religion. Meaninglessness and social isolation generate the greatest differentials in unplanned births, with the data for normlessness, as well as for powerlessness among working-class subjects, also in the expected direction. The total, standardized means for the latter two alienation dimensions, however, failed to reach levels of statistical significance.

These data in Table 2 demonstrate, of course, that sizeable proportions of women in all the control categories had unplanned fertility over the eight-year period. While it is possible that some of our subjects simply changed their minds about desired fertility levels, this is not a likely explanation of the "excess" fertility, for during this same time-interval the mean *ideal* family size for our subjects was reduced from 3.86 to 3.34 children. Thus by drawing upon the criterion of 1963 birth expectations, our index of unplanned fertility appears to be a conservative one. The variations in unplanned fertility generally follow the same pattern as for the mean number of additional children presented in Table 1, and suggest that increased childbearing for our high-fertility subjects tends correspondingly to be associated with a greater degree of unwanted fertility. The explanation for the higher fertility of our more highly alienated subjects would then appear to be more reasonably attributed to a lack of success in fertility control than to an actual desire for a large number of children.

Since our data show that high alienation tends to be associated with unplanned fertility, we might expect a lack of effective family planning to be generative of higher levels of alienation. This question is central to our explanation of causality in the obtained alienation-fertility relationships. If increasing fertility does in fact lead to increasing alienation, our data should show that rates of increasing alienation are greater for mothers who had additional children than for those who demonstrated effective fertility control by having no additional children over the eight-year period in question.

In a separate analysis (data not shown here), we tested for this possibility under controls for religion, socioeconomic status, and 1963 levels of parity. Virtually no support was found for the contention that increasing fertility is accompanied by increasing alienation. Instead, alienation levels *generally* increased for our subjects during the 1960s and early 1970s, but these increases were not associated with either the number of children in 1963 or in 1971. Increases were as great among women with small families and no subsequent fertility as among women with large families and additional children. Our data thus provide strong support for the view that conditions of alienation come prior to and generate high levels of fertility, rather than the other way around.

DISCUSSION

As we have operationalized the dimensions of alienation, the relationships reported above between high alienation and high fertility should, by the theory under review, be understood as a differential capacity for control-relevant behavior in the area of family planning. Our intent has been to identify social psychological variables empirically correlated with information seeking and retention, planning and decision-making, and the recognition of future consequences of conduct. Thus the theoretical orientation of our research has somewhat paralleled that of other researchers who have studied the predictive values of differences in "capacities for self-determination," or "subjective efficacy" (De Charms, 1968; Rotter, 1966; Lefcourt, 1966). These convergent lines of theory and research have been interpreted (Smith, 1973) as involving clusters of self-attitudes that operate as a kind of self-fulfilling prophesy. In other words, persons who feel they are mere "pawns" of individual and social causation tend to behave in ways that ultimately confirm their beliefs. Several studies have provided some direct evidence in this regard relative to fertility. Contraceptive use (MacDonald, 1970; Keller, *et al.*, 1970) and attitudes (Williamson, 1969), for example, have been empirically implicated in research along these lines.

Our own research with the alienation variables, and that by several of our graduate student colleagues, has also been directed at contraceptive use and knowledge (Cornelius, 1973; Knisely, 1973), and age at marriage, child spacing, and premarital pregnancy (Mathews, 1973). In each instance, corroborative support was provided for the usefulness of alienation variables in differentiating fertility-control kinds of behavior. For example, the more highly alienated tend not only to have higher levels of unplanned fertility throughout different ages and parities, but also to experience greater incidences of premarital pregnancy and to marry at younger ages.

Considerable research, therefore, has now pointed to alienation as a key factor in understanding variations among populations in their capacities for decision-making and long-range planning in the area of family formation. Nonetheless, this is only a beginning. We need to know much more about the possible associations between kinds and degrees of alienation as they relate to the sexual intercourse, conception, and gestation variables of fertility behavior, as well as to each stage in the family-forming process, from courtship and marriage through the birth of the last child.

The early years of family formation, especially, seem crucial from both an individual and societal point of view. Planning (or lack of planning) for the first birth, for example, may be the single most important stage in the family-forming process. This is because so many individual and demographic consequences seem to be associated with the timing of the first birth (Coombs, et al., 1970; Pohlman, 1968; Freedman and Coombs, 1966; Christensen, 1963; Lowrie, 1965; Campbell, 1970). Premarital pregnancy and illegitimacy rates, in particular, have shown a striking persistence in the face of widespread contraceptive knowledge and availability (Davis, 1972; Sklar and Berkov, 1974). The empirical and theoretical utility of alienation research may well help fill in some of the gaps in our present understanding of these phenomena.

Finally, what are the practical implications of what we have learned so far? Since inadequate decision-making, poor planning, and fatalistic outlooks seem clearly related to fertility problems, we might ask how a society could go about increasing the individual's sense of personal efficacy and attenuating feelings of alienation. Needless to say, this is a large order. But it is not difficult to imagine educational and mass media attempts at generating greater personal efficacy in at least the realm of family planning. Family *planning* needs to become a salient value among the highly alienated, especially the young, if all pregnancies are to be wanted pregnancies and the deliberate outcome of a decisional process between sexual partners. Clearly, making sex and contraceptive information and materials available in a physical sense is not enough. The next step in public policy might well be directed toward making effective contraceptive information and supplies available to those for whom they are as yet unavailable in a social psychological sense.

REFERENCES

Bickford, H. L., and A. G. Neal. 1969. "Alienation and Social Learning: A Study of Students in a Vocational Training Center." Sociology of Education 42 (Spring):141–53.

Campbell, F. L. 1970. "Family Growth and Variation in Family Role Structure." Journal of Marriage and the Family 32:45–53.

Christensen, H. T. 1963. "Childspacing Analysis via Record Linkage: New Data Plus a Summing Up From Earlier Reports." Marriage and Family Living 25:272–80.

Coombs, L., R. Freedman, J. Friedman, and W. H. Pratt. 1970. "Pre-marital Pregnancy and Status Before and After Marriage." American Journal of Sociology 75 (March):800–820.

Cornelius, R. M. 1973. "Correlates of Contraceptive Knowledge Among Married Women." Unpublished M.A. Thesis, Bowling Green State University.

Davis, K., and J. Blake. 1956. "Social Structure and Fertility: An Analytic Framework." Economic Development and Cultural Change 4:3 (April):211–35.

Davis, K. 1972. "The American Family in Relation to Demographic Change," in C. F. Westoff and R. Parke, Jr. (Eds.), Demographic and Social Aspects of Population Growth, Vol. 1 of Commission Research Reports, pp. 439–66. Washington, D.C.: Government Printing Office.

De Charms, R. 1968. Personal Causation: The Internal Affective Determinants of Behavior. New York: Academic Press.

Easterlin, R. A. 1969. "Towards a Socioeconomic Theory of Fertility: A Survey of Recent Research on Economic Factors in American Fertility," in S. J. Behrman, L. Corsa, Jr., and R. Freedman (Eds.), Fertility and Family Planning, pp. 127–56. Ann Arbor: University of Michigan.

Freedman, R., and L. Coombs. 1966. "Childspacing and Family Economic Position." American Sociological Review 31 (October):631–48.

Groat, H. T., and A. G. Neal. 1967. "Social Psychological Correlates of Urban Fertility." American Sociological Review 32 (December):945–49.

Groat, H. T., and A. G. Neal. 1973. "Social Class and Alienation Correlates of Protestant Fertility." Journal of Marriage and the Family 35 (February): 83–88.

Keller, A. B., J. H. Sims, W. E. Henry, and T. J. Crawford. 1970. "Psychological Sources of 'Resistance' to Family Planning." Merrill-Palmer Quarterly 16:286–302.

Knisely, E. C. 1973. "Correlates of Catholic Contraceptive Behavior." Unpublished M.A. Thesis, Bowling Green State University.

Lefcourt, H. M. 1966. "Internal versus External Control of Reinforcement." Psychological Bulletin 65:206–20.

Lowrie, S. H. 1965. "Early Marriage, Premarital Pregnancy and Associated Factors." Journal of Marriage and the Family 27:48–56.

MacDonald, A. P., Jr. 1970. "Internal-external Locus of Control and the Practice of Birth Control." Psychological Reports 21:206.

Mathews, L. I. 1973. "Age at First Marriage and the Timing of the First Birth." Unpublished M.A. Thesis, Bowling Green State University.

Neal, A. G., and H. T. Groat. 1970. "Alienation Correlates of Catholic Fertility." American Journal of Sociology 76 (November):460–73.

Neal, A. G., and H. T. Groat. 1973. "Alienation Predictors of Differential Fertility: A Longitudinal Study." Paper presented at the annual meetings of the American Sociological Association, New York, New York.

Pohlman, E. 1968. "The Timing of the First Birth: A Review of Effects." Eugenics Quarterly 15:252–63.

Rainwater, L. 1960. And the Poor Get Children. Chicago: Quadrangle Books.

Rainwater, L. 1965. Family Design: Marital Sexuality, Family Size, and Contraception. Chicago: Aldine.

Rotter, J. B. 1966. "Generalized Expectancies for Internal versus External Control of Reinforcement." Psychological Monographs 80:1–28.

Seeman, M., and J. W. Evans. 1962. "Alienation and Learning in a Hospital Setting." American Sociological Review 27 (December):772–82.

Seeman, M. 1963. "Alienation and Social Learning in a Reformatory." American Journal of Sociology 59:270–84.

Sklar, J., and B. Berkov. 1974. "Teenage Family Formation in Postwar America." Family Planning Perspectives 6 (Spring):80–90.

Smith, M. B. 1973. "A Social-Psychological View of Fertility," in J. T. Fawcett (Ed.), Psychological Perspectives on Population, pp. 3–18. New York: Basic Books.

Williamson, J. B. 1969. "Subjective Efficacy As an Aspect of Modernization in Six Developing Nations." Unpublished Ph.D. Dissertation, Harvard University.

7

Is Delinquency Increasing?
Age Structure and the Crime Rate*

Roland Chilton and Adele Spielberger

An age-specific analysis of juvenile court referrals in Florida illustrates
the crucial role of changing age structure in the interpretation of crime
and delinquency statistics. Although the number of acts which resulted
in referrals to Florida's juvenile courts rose sharply from 1958 to 1967,
an examination of data submitted by the courts and the public school
districts of the state for the period suggests that most of this increase
could be predicted by changes in the number of children eligible for
delinquency referral. The study also suggests (1) that the variation in
delinquency rates observed both within and among counties is probably
the result of differences in reporting practices, and (2) that increases
in FBI crime rates for the state and its six SMSAs for the same period
are probably inflated by the inability of the crime index to take into
account Florida's changing age structure.

Crime statistics for Florida, like those for other populous and growing
states, suggest that there has been a rapid increase in crime and delinquency. Specifically, the FBI's *Uniform Crime Reports* indicate that the
number of offenses known to the police in Florida rose by *154* percent
from 1958 to 1967, while the total population of the state increased by
approximately *35* percent for this same period of time (FBI, 1958:52; 1967:
69). In addition, the number of children brought to the attention of Florida's juvenile courts in delinquency charges rose from almost *18,700* in 1958
to over *38,200* in 1967 (Florida Department of Public Welfare, 1958:3;
1967:xxv). When used in conjunction with the number of children in

Reprinted from *Social Forces*, 49, no. 3 (March, 1971), pp. 487–93, by permission
of the authors and the publisher.

* Revised version of a paper presented at the annual meeting of the Southern
Sociological Society, 1969.

grades two through twelve of Florida's public schools to compute juvenile delinquency rates for the state, these figures suggest a less rapid but still impressive increase in the juvenile crime rate for the state from 236 per 10,000 eligible children in 1958 to 312 in 1967, an increase of 32 *percent*.[1]

Increases in the number of children committed to the state's training schools for this period provide a third indication of a rising volume of delinquency throughout the state, although the rates of increase are less striking. The number of children committed to the training schools in 1958 was 1,167, as compared to 2,035 for 1967, an increase of 74 percent. Figure 1 presents the commitment rates for this period, using the number

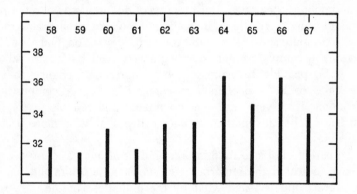

FIGURE 1. Commitment rate (number of children committed to the state training schools per 10,000 children enrolled in grades seven through twelve) for Florida, 1958 through 1967.

of children in grades seven through twelve as a base, and illustrates the 23 percent increase in this rate.[2]

The less rapid rise in this commitment rate might be interpreted as an indication that serious and persistent crime by juveniles was not increasing as fast as less serious offenses. However, the periodic fluctuations in the commitment rate suggest that the number of children committed might have been influenced by the number of beds and staff members available at the training schools rather than by the number of crimes committed. There appears to have been a two-year cycle, for the years from 1958 to 1967, with increases occurring in the even-numbered years and decreases or minimal increases occurring in odd-numbered years. This pattern corresponds closely with the biennial meetings of the state legislature, which were regularly held in odd-numbered years during this period. And it is conceivable that budgetary fluctuations caused by biennial sessions had some bearing in this pattern. In any case, it is clear that factors other than the number of crimes reported or children referred to the juvenile courts influenced commitment rates in the state during the period from 1958 to 1967.

IMPORTANCE OF AGE STRUCTURE

Although commitment figures are not a useful index of delinquent activity, the use of other juvenile court data, specifically the number of children referred, appears to be meaningful and important. Such juvenile court referral counts may even be superior to offenses known to the police as an indicator of changing patterns of crime, because they permit an examination of the impact of changes in the age composition of a population on crime and delinquency rates. Since reports of offenses known to the police do not, and cannot, provide an indication of the ages of offenders, there is no way to compute age-specific rates for such information. Only if uniform and reasonably complete annual arrest data were available for several years, would it be possible to estimate the proportion of change in arrest figures which could be explained by changes in the age composition of a population. However, until more complete and reliable arrest information is available, juvenile court data will probably be more useful in such analyses.

Two earlier efforts to examine the impact of age structure on crime rates have indicated the importance of such analysis, although both attempts were hampered somewhat by the limitations of the data which were available. The Space General Corporation's (1965) 1964 study, for example, pointed to the increase in the number of young people in California to explain increases in crime observed there. And the National Crime Commission, despite limitations of nationwide arrest data, was able to illustrate the probable importance of changes in age structure and in urban–rural residence for reported increases in crime in the United States. The commission's analysis indicated that from 40 to 50 percent of the increase in arrests reported for 1960 and 1965 could be accounted for by changes in the nation's age composition (The President's Commission, 1967:25).

The juvenile court data used in this analysis have a number of limitations, which are discussed below, but still present some distinct advantages over current arrest data. Their primary advantage is the extent to which they approximate complete coverage of juvenile delinquency referrals in a rapidly growing state for a period of approximately ten years. Continuity and completeness, combined with a rather consistent uniformity, make it possible to examine and compare juvenile court data for each county in the state for the years since 1958.[3]

RESULTS

In general, our age-specific analysis of data provided by the juvenile courts of Florida for the years 1958 through 1967 illustrates the inappropriateness of comparisons which emphasize percentage increases in the absolute numbers of offenses reported for two periods of time and indicates that even comparisons of some general crime rates may be quite misleading. Taking the data presented above as an example, in 1958 approximately *18,700* children came to the attention of the juvenile courts of Florida on delinquency charges, while for 1967 this figure had grown to over *38,200*, an increase of *103* percent. For this same period of time, the number of children enrolled in grades two through twelve of the public schools grew from *789,000* to *1,224,000*, an increase of *55* percent. A superficial interpretation of these figures might suggest that delinquent acts increased twice as fast as the relevant population. Actually, as a result of changes in the number of children in high-risk age categories, it would not have been surprising if this 55 percent increase in the number of children between seven and seventeen years of age had been accompanied by a larger percentage increase in the number of delinquency referrals. Table 1 illustrates this assertion. It suggests that *70* percent of the increase in the referrals for delinquency in the state from 1958 to 1967 could quite reasonably be expected as a result of changes in the number of children in specific age groups.[4]

When a similar analysis is performed for the counties constituting Florida's Standard Metropolitan Statistical Areas and nine other large counties in the state, the results suggest that *79* percent of the increase in delinquency referrals is the result of a changing age structure. These twenty counties contain 85 percent of the state's population and 83 percent of its school-age children. Therefore, it is not surprising that, in 1967, officials in these counties reported 87 percent of the delinquency referrals for the state. Table 2 presents the observed age-specific rates for this set of twenty counties in 1958, the school enrollment figures for relevant grades in 1967, the expected number of delinquency referrals for each age group in 1967, and the number of delinquency referrals actually reported for 1967. The estimated figures for 1967 are those which would be predicted if the 1958 rates had remained relatively constant and only the number of children in each age group had changed.[5]

Finally, a similar analysis of delinquency referrals and school enrollment figures, limited only to those counties which constitute Florida's SMSA's, indicates that 85 percent of the rise in delinquency referrals in these eleven counties was probably the result of increases in the number of children in high-risk age categories. The greater impact of age group

TABLE 1.   Number of expected and observed delinquency referrals for sixty-six Florida counties for 1967, nine specific age groups, expected counts based on 1958 age-specific rate and 1967 school enrollment data*

Age Group	1958 Delinquency Rates (Referrals per 10,000 Children)	1967 School Enroll- ment (Grades Two through Twelve)	1967 Expected Delinquency Referrals	1967 Observed Delinquency Referrals
Under 10	33.83	386,473	1,307	1,422
10	73.01	123,028	898	1,078
11	110.01	117,731	1,295	1,560
12	170.23	121,074	2,061	2,670
13	312.81	113,284	3,544	4,668
14	547.24	107,197	5,866	7,334
15	845.92	100,189	8,475	8,988
16	1,018.20	83,833	8,536	10,059
17 and over	61.49	71,331	439	445
Total		1,224,140	32,422	38,224
Increase over 1958 referrals			13,724	19,526
Percent of the increase that would have occurred if the age-specific rates had not changed		70		

* Delinquency data for one county (1967 population estimate, 5,000) were not available.

changes in these most populous counties of the state appears despite the fact that two of the eleven SMSA counties reported increases in delinquency referrals far in excess of the growth in their school-age populations.[6] Table 3 presents the data for this set of counties which contain 66 percent of the state's population, 64 percent of its school children and two-thirds of its delinquency referrals.

LIMITATIONS OF THE DATA

These age-specific analyses of delinquency referrals for a rapidly growing state like Florida suffer from a number of specific hazards. One of these is the impact on statewide totals of a few very rapidly growing counties. For example, primarily as a result of the federal space program, the population of Brevard County, and a few counties contiguous to it, expanded more rapidly than the populations of larger counties and much more rapidly than the population of the state. Consequently, the procedure for handling children accused of delinquent conduct underwent extensive change during the period examined. With the construction of a new juvenile court building and increases in staff, the possibilities for more formal and complete reporting procedures probably produced the meteoric rise in delinquency

TABLE 2. Number of expected and observed delinquency referrals for twenty Florida counties for 1967, nine specific age groups, expected counts based on 1958 age-specific rates and 1967 school enrollment data*

Age Group	1958 Delinquency Rates (Referrals per 10,000 Children)	1967 School Enroll-ment (Grades Two through Twelve)	1967 Expected Delinquency Referrals	1967 Observed Delinquency Referrals
Under 10	37.86	319,932	1,211	1,261
10	79.11	101,883	806	952
11	122.25	97,733	1,195	1,403
12	190.05	100,306	1,906	2,342
13	349.39	94,412	3,299	4,059
14	595.97	87,312	5,323	6,237
15	906.51	84,425	7,653	7,683
16	1,068.68	70,800	7,566	8,422
17 and over	61.77	60,164	372	350
Total		1,018,967	29,331	32,709
Increase over 1958 referrals			12,972	16.350
Percent of the increase that would have occurred if the age-specific rates had not changed		79		

* This set of counties includes the eleven counties in the state's SMSAs and nine other counties with populations over 65,000.

referral rates observed in Brevard County from 1958 to 1967. It is likely that something similar may also have occurred in Volusia County where delinquency referral rates rose from 78 per 10,000 school-age children in 1958 to 806 per 10,000 children in 1967. When Brevard and Volusia are removed from the large county analysis, the proportion of the increase in delinquency referrals attributable to changes in age structure rises to 92 percent.

Another limitation in the use of statewide juvenile court data is the variability of reporting procedures. Variation in rates from county to county appear to be the result of such differences rather than reflections of changes in juvenile misconduct. The evidence for this assertion cannot be presented in detail in this paper. But, in general, it is the result of comparisons of changes in general delinquency rates for the ten-year period from 1958 through 1967 for specific counties with changes in school enrollment figures and with rates of offenses known to the police for the same counties. These comparisons suggest that the increases in the reported numbers of children referred to the juvenile courts of these counties do not always accurately reflect the conduct of school-age children. Officials of some counties appear to have been underreporting delinquency referrals in recent years while the officials of other counties appear to have been overreporting for some of the years in the same period.

TABLE 3.   Number of expected and observed delinquency referrals for eleven Florida counties for 1967, nine specific age groups, expected counts based on 1958 age-specific rates and 1967 school enrollment data*

Age Group	1958 Delinquency Rates (Referrals per 10,000 Children)	1967 School Enrollment (Grades Two through Twelve)	1967 Expected Delinquency Referrals	1967 Observed Delinquency Referrals
Under 10	39.60	243,624	965	954
10	80.79	77,887	629	701
11	124.77	74,818	933	1,093
12	194.82	76,691	1,494	1,796
13	356.27	72,465	2,582	3,091
14	605.50	68,992	4,177	4,754
15	909.83	65,599	5,968	5,775
16	1,077.73	54,788	5,905	6,175
17 and over	53.52	45,900	246	282
Total		780,764	22,900	24,621
Increase over 1958 referrals			9,819	11,540
Percent of the increase that would have occurred if the age-specific rates had not changed		85		

* These counties constitute the eight SMSAs of the state.

CONCLUSIONS

In spite of the limitations of the data available for this study, the importance of a changing population for the interpretation of crime and delinquency statistics is again illustrated. The analysis presented above clearly indicates that at least 70 to 80 percent of the increase in delinquency referrals in Florida was the result of a rise in the number of children eligible for delinquency referral or, more specifically, that it was the result of increases in the number of children in high-risk categories. This does not minimize the seriousness of increased referrals but provides a basis for a rational interpretation of such increases.

The results suggest that variations in the rates observed in some counties and variations among counties are probably the result of differences in reporting practices and that variations in commitment rates appear to have been influenced by the availability of commitment facilities. But perhaps the most important implication of this analysis is that it calls attention to an inherent limitation of offenses known to the police as a crime index.

Increases in the FBI's crime index cannot be examined in the light of a changing age structure because no information about the ages of the offenders is available. All that is known is that a specific number of crimes have come to the attention of the police. If the same situation prevailed in regard to Florida's juvenile court data, we could only observe that in 1967 there was an increase of 103 percent in the number of persons suspected of committing delinquent acts in comparison to the number suspected in 1958. If no age information at all were available—not even that the individuals involved were juveniles—we could only relate increases in the number of persons suspected to increases in the total population. Since the number of referrals doubled between 1958 and 1967, and the total population of the state increased by only 35 percent, journalistic interpretations of these figures might suggest that delinquent acts were increasing 2.8 times as fast as the population. Whereas, we have seen that at least 70 to 80 percent of the increase in delinquency referrals in the state can quite plausibly be related to changes in population and that an examination of increases in crime without regard to age structure—a situation which of necessity occurs when offenses known to the police are examined—will necessarily produce misleading results.

It should be clear that this type of analysis does not "explain away" increases in crime. It suggests that the increases, for the most part, are real and understandable in light of specific population changes. With few exceptions, the urban counties of Florida have experienced a rapid increase in the number of children in age categories most likely to be involved in crime and delinquency. And these increases have exceeded by far the growth of the general population.

Although school-age children have probably not become more delinquency prone, there are more of them in high-risk age categories. This means more crime, more work for police agencies, and more work for juvenile court personnel and others working with children in trouble. But it does not suggest any widespread failure of socialization processes. It does not call for more laws or more repressive measures to deal with crime. Nor does it require the abandonment of traditional American safeguards against the abuse of official power. It does suggest that there are serious limitations of currently acceptable measures of crime and that many currently popular interpretations of crime are probably inaccurate because of the failure to take into account the changing age structure.

NOTES

1. Although the number of children in grades two through twelve is a more relevant base than the total population, the number of children in grades seven through twelve might also constitute a relevant and justifiable population base. When such a base is used to compute delinquency rates, the results suggest an increase in the rate of *16* percent from 1958 to 1967. However, grades two through twelve are used in this analysis because they provide a more complete set of age-specific delinquency rates. For training school rates, the number of children in grades seven through twelve is used because few children under twelve, and almost no children under ten, are admitted to the training schools. School enrollment data were provided by the Florida Department of Education.

2. Training school data were provided by the Florida Division of Youth Services, Department of Health and Rehabilitative Services.

3. Juvenile court data were provided by the Florida Division of Youth Services and the Florida Division of Family Services (formerly the Department of Public Welfare).

4. Computer work for this paper was performed at the Florida State University Computing Center using machines financed in part by National Science Foundation Grants (NSF-GP-671 and NSF 1981).

5. Children in grades two through four are assumed to be under ten years old, those in grade five are assumed to be ten years old and those in grade six, eleven years old. Similar assumptions are made about the children in each higher grade, with those in grade twelve assumed to be seventeen years óld or older.

6. It is not clear why this occurs but Duval and Escambia counties report increases in delinquency referrals greatly in excess of increases in their school-age populations and the FBI's crime index.

REFERENCES

Federal Bureau of Investigation. 1958–1967. *Uniform Crime Reports.* Washington, D.C.: Government Printing Office.

Florida Department of Public Welfare. 1958–1967. *Florida Juvenile Court Statistics.* Jacksonville: Department of Public Welfare.

The President's Commission on Law Enforcement and the Administration of Justice. 1967. *Task Force Report: Assessment of Crime.* Washington, D.C.: Government Printing Office.

Space General Corporation. 1965. *A Study of Prevention and Control of Crime and Delinquency.* Elmonte, California: Space General Corporation.

The Data and Theory of Demography

Introduction: A. The Data of Demography

Demography, or the study of population, is an empirical science. It is the goal of every science to describe, explain, and predict the occurrences connected with some particular phenomena; Demography must fulfill these tasks with regard to people and populations. In order to achieve these general goals of science it is necessary to have data or facts, and in the case of demography the facts that are needed are about the activities of human populations.

Demography has been labeled an "observational science," in contrast to the "experimental sciences."[1] The observational sciences are those whose data are produced primarily by records that are made of naturally occurring events. By contrast, the experimental sciences are those in which the data are generally produced by experiments

---

[1] Philip M. Hauser and Otis Dudley Duncan, eds., *The Study of Population* (Chicago: University of Chicago Press, 1959), pp. 4–5.

conducted in the laboratory under conditions that are greatly controlled by the experimenter. While demography is an observational science, this does not mean that experimental procedures cannot be and have not been used to acquire knowledge that is useful for an understanding of population phenomena. It simply means that on balance the demographer is more likely to get his data from some process other than the laboratory experiment.

Hauser and Duncan have pointed out that demography is an observational science because the data are "spread out."[2] The data are spread out in two senses: in time and in space. The events that interest the demographer—births, deaths, migration—are spread out over vast geographical areas, and go back in time to the beginning of man's existence. The primary implication of the spread-out nature of population data is that a single demographer can gather only a very small proportion of the data that are necessary when he wants to describe population phenomena, to test population hypotheses, or to build generalizations about population.

The work of the demographer can be only as good as the quality of the data he uses, and yet the demographer often uses data that are gathered by others, and under circumstances over which he has little or no control. Furthermore, the very facts that are to be gathered are often decided upon by individuals other than the demographer.

Whenever a scientist does not have personal control over the data-gathering process, he must be on guard against the errors and inadequacies in the data he is using. It is for this reason that this part of Section II is devoted to several articles that focus on the data used by demographers. Each of the papers in this part relates to some of the events, issues, or problems connected with population data.

The paper by Ian Sutherland on John Graunt describes the work of one of the first and probably the most prominent of a group of seventeenth- and eighteenth-century scholars who have been labeled the "political arithmeticians." The political arithmeticians of England and the European continent were often men who had been trained in the natural sciences, or else, as in the case of Graunt, men who recognized the possibilities of applying the observational techniques of the natural sciences to political and social phenomena. It can be argued that the political arithmeticians were the first real demogra-

---

2 Ibid, p. 5.

phers, and thus it would follow that they should be given credit for stimulating and initiating the study of population as an empirical science. However, this latter assumption is not strongly supported by the facts, because it is difficult to establish a continuous scholarly lineage from the political arithmeticians to the demographers of the nineteenth century. The only apparent exception is in the analysis of mortality, especially the construction of life-expectancy tables, which started with the political arithmeticians and proceeded in a fairly unbroken line since their time. The reason for the continuing interest in and development of life tables appears to have been the growing need of insurance societies for ever better actuarial data.

There were two major factors that seemed to motivate the political arithmeticians of the seventeenth century. First, for many of them the basic reason for gathering data on population (and other resources as well) was to assess the resources of the nation, particularly as these were vested in the royal family. Second, the political arithmeticians accepted the intellectual challenge that was inherent in any attempt to describe the size and characteristics of the population in an era when the data had to be extracted from whatever records were at hand.[3]

With the advent of the modern census, beginning at the end of the seventeenth century, the data on population became more available, and one would guess that the intellectual challenge that motivated the early political arithmeticians no longer existed. Thus, as suggested above, the intellectual line of the political arithmeticians appears to have waned, except in the area of mortality.

It is beneficial to read an account of the life and work of one of the political arithmeticians, such as we are able to do in Sutherland's tribute to John Graunt, because it reminds us that only 300 years ago in one of the most advanced countries of the world there was scarcely any knowledge of some of the most elementary population facts. In our age, when statistical data seem to exist on all aspects of life, it is difficult to imagine an England in which such data were not available. It also brings into focus again the spread-out character of population data. In this case we see more clearly that historical population data, even for European countries, is likely to be very limited for

---

[3] Some additional details on the political arithmeticians are presented in Kurt Mayer's "Developments in the Study of Population" in part B of this section.

any present-day researcher who might want to reconstruct the demographic past.

In the short essay that follows the paper on Graunt, Louis Henry reviews some of the issues related to demographic data and historical demography. Henry emphasizes that demography need not, indeed should not, be limited only to the data produced by the governmental statistical services—the census and vital registration. He urges broadening the data base of demography in two ways. First, for contemporary data he notes the increasing importance of the sample survey, which can be designed to get precisely the information one needs to answer a scientifically relevant question. Henry's second point is that historical demography, which utilizes data coming from precensus times, is a necessary part of any complete science of population.

Henry's view that census and vital registration data may have shortcomings or limitations for population research raises an important demographic issue. Censuses of national populations conducted by governments are relatively recent in origin. While there were earlier censuses, the United States census of 1790 was one of the first national population counts and probably deserves to be recognized as the first regularly scheduled national census. The voluminous amounts of data gathered in all the subsequent decennial censuses of the United States have provided a great amount of population data and surely stimulated the science of demography. Many useful demographic techniques and measurements have been developed and used by Census Bureau personnel, but the census is not without its critics and the charges that are made are not insignificant. One of these is the criticism already implied by Henry. The census simply may not provide the information that would be most useful for our increased theoretical understanding of population processes. There is a danger that demographers, attracted by all the available free data collected by the census, may spend their time studying irrelevant or inconsequential problems. Or, alternatively, they may attack important questions, but limit themselves to the use of census data that may be only partially adequate for the task. In short, census data, collected by governments for their own purposes, may attract demographers away from the most important demographic questions, or it may keep them from collecting the best possible data to answer the important questions.

Another criticism of census data focuses on the quality of the data. The employees of census-taking organizations, both in the United States and in other countries, have often been their own severest critics. The people who work with the census have often reported just how much error is contained in census data. The errors are basically those of misclassification, or else overenumeration or underenumeration. There is much evidence that when large numbers of people are questioned (even a 5 percent sample of the United States will be as many as ten million people) there are many known and unknown errors that pervade the data. Furthermore there has been ample demonstration that when a census is taken of any large population a substantial number of people will be missed, while others will be enumerated twice. This issue of missing people has become increasingly recognized and important, because it is obvious that the people who are missed are not simply randomly distributed throughout the population. There are some things about them, some characteristics, that give certain people a higher probability of being missed by the census-taking machinery. "Who Are the Uncounted People?" (article 10) analyzes the data from the 1960 census to see who the Americans were who were most frequently missed by the census. Analysis of the coverage of the 1970 census has already been reported, but the reports are quite technical and not appropriate for inclusion in this reader. For the student who wishes to explore this issue further, I recommend a paper by Jacob Siegel titled "Estimates of Coverage of the Population by Sex, Race, and Age in the 1970 Census."[4] Siegel reports that in 1960, 2.7 percent of the population of the United States was missed, while in 1970 the percentage was 2.5. It is clear that no substantial improvement has been made in our coverage of the population. Again in 1970, as it was in 1960, the percentage of blacks missed by the census far exceeded that of whites. Young black males were once again the most frequently missed segment of the population in 1970. Article 10 gives a full review and analysis of why and how people are missed by the census.

---

[4] Jacob Seigel, "Estimates of Coverage of the Population by Sex, Race, and Age in the 1970 Census," *Demography*, 11 (February, 1974), pp. 1–23.

8

John Graunt: A Tercentenary Tribute

Ian Sutherland

John Graunt was a London draper who, three hundred years ago, published some "Natural and Political Observations on the Bills of Mortality." These observations represent the first, and an extremely competent, attempt to draw scientific conclusions from statistical data. The present study illustrates Graunt's careful scientific approach, his ability to extract the essence from what by modern standards are distinctly untrustworthy demographic data, and his intuitive appreciation of the amount of interpretation his findings would stand. Graunt's analysis was largely based upon ratios and proportions of vital events and consideration of the way in which these altered in different circumstances, and is remarkably free of major statistical errors. His statistical understanding was considerable; for example, we owe to him the first scientific estimates of population size, the concept of the life table, the idea of statistical association, the first studies of time series, and a pioneer attempt to draw a representative sample. Graunt's book is well worth reading today, not only for entertainment and instruction, but because it laid the foundations of the science of statistics.

1. INTRODUCTION

Just 300 years ago, in 1662, a small book was published under the title *"Natural and Political* OBSERVATIONS Mentioned in a following INDEX, and made upon the Bills of Mortality." The author was *"JOHN GRAUNT,* Citizen of LONDON." A celebration of the tercentenary of publication of a small seventeenth-century book by a little-known author requires some initial justification, and this is perhaps best provided by a nineteenth-century inscription in a copy in the library of our Society. "Captain John Graunt of London merits the high honour of being the founder of Statistics.

Reprinted from the *Royal Statistical Society Journal,* Series A, 126 (1963), pp. 537–56, by permission of the author and the publisher.

His natural & political Observations on the Bills of Mortality . . . first directed public attention to the important inferences that might be deduced from correct registers of Births, deaths, & marriages." This is indeed a high claim; we may be prepared to concede that he was the first to study *medical* statistics, but to attribute the beginnings of the whole scientific discipline to him may sound a little extravagant. I hope to show, however, in the course of what follows, that the claim is justified, and that we are really celebrating the tercentenary of statistics as well as that of Graunt's book. . . .

2. A BIOGRAPHICAL SKETCH

John Graunt was born in London on April 24th, 1620, to Henry and Mary Graunt, and was christened a week later at St. Michael, Cornhill. His father was a draper who had moved to London from Hampshire, and carried on his business in Birchin Lane. John was the eldest of a large family and, after serving an apprenticeship, took up and eventually succeeded to his father's business, as a "Haberdasher of small-wares," which he carried on in the family house for the greater part of his life. He became a Freeman of the Drapers' Company ("by Patrimony") at the age of 21, was granted the Livery of the Company when he was 38, and rose to the distinguished position of Renter Warden three years before his death at the age of 53. In this and other ways Graunt became a respected London citizen. He passed through the various ward offices of the city and was eventually elected to the common council for two years. He was a captain in the (military) trained band for several years and a major for two or three more. Even before he was 30 his influence was sufficient to procure the professorship of music at Gresham College for his friend Dr. William Petty.

From the comments of those who knew him we can tell that he must have been an unusually likeable person. Aubrey describes him as "A man generally beloved; a faythfull friend. Often chosen for his prudence and justnes to be an Arbitrator." He was "very facetious and fluent in his conversation" and "very hospitable." In addition he was a man of some accomplishment and taste. He was, to his friend Richard Smyth, "an understanding man of quick witt and a pretty schollar," to Aubrey a "very ingeniose and studious person" who "rose early in the morning to his Study before shop-time. He understood Latin and French." He "wrote Shorthand dextrously," and "had an excellent working head." He was acquainted with Samuel Cooper, the miniaturist, and John Hales, also a portrait painter, and had both professional and social dealings with Samuel Pepys, who, on a visit to Graunt's house, much admired his collection of prints—"indeed . . . the best collection of anything almost that ever I saw, there being the prints of most of the greatest houses, churches and antiquitys in Italy and

France, and brave cutts." Despite these links with the arts, however, there is unfortunately no known portrait of Graunt.

Graunt's house, and presumably much of the contents, was burnt down in the Fire of London in 1666, and was rebuilt with financial assistance from Petty. Graunt's business probably suffered too, but it seems that his financial position did not become acute until shortly before his death. He had been brought up a Puritan and was throughout his life deeply religious, using his shorthand to make notes on the many sermons he went to hear. For several years he adhered to Socinian, that is unitarian, beliefs, but eventually turned Catholic, giving up his civil and military offices on this account. This doubtless played a major role in his change of fortune, but the full reasons are obscure; the family house passed to Petty, and Graunt moved into Bolt Court, in the parish of St. Dunstan-in-the-West, Fleet Street. He died in poverty on April 18th, 1674, of jaundice, and was buried in St. Dunstan's church on the 20th; later in the year his widow was granted an annual pension of £4 by the Drapers' Company "in regard of her low condition." Aubrey gives us details just where in the church John Graunt was buried, and comments "what pitty 'tis so great an Ornament of the Citty should be buryed so obscurely!" If it was obscure then, it is more so now, as the church was rebuilt in about 1830 on a rather different site, and neither the old church nor the new had any monument to Graunt. Graunt's best monument, however, is undoubtedly his *Observations*, and no apology is needed for celebrating the tercentenary of its publication rather than any other event in Graunt's life. Although he also wrote some "Observations on the Advance of Excise," these were not published and the manuscript has not come down to us.

3. THE "OBSERVATIONS"

This distinctly unusual tradesman, at the age of 41, published a distinctly unusual book. One of the dedicatory epistles is dated the 25th of January, 1662; on February 5th, 50 copies of the book were presented by Graunt to the Royal Society of Philosophers, and he was proposed as a candidate for membership. A Committee was appointed to examine the book and reported favourably; on February 26th, only a month after publication, Graunt was elected to the Royal Society. He continued as a Fellow for some years, and was a member of the Council of the Society from November 1664 until April 1666.

The admission of Graunt to so distinguished a gathering may have surprised some people, but it was approved by King Charles II. Sprat (1667, p. 67) describes "the recommendation which *King* himself was pleased to make, of the judicious Author of *the Observations on the Bills of Mortality*:

In whose Election, it was so farr from being a prejudice, that he was a Shop-keeper of *London;* that His Majesty gave this particular charge to His Society, that if they found any more such Tradesmen, they should be sure to admit them all, without any more ado." Indeed, the Society was able to follow this precept in Charles's lifetime, and elect not merely another distinguished shopkeeper, but another draper; Anthony Leeuwenhoek, of Delft, was elected a Fellow in 1679, in recognition of his pioneer microscopial discoveries.

The *Observations* evidently made an impact elsewhere too. Samuel Pepys (who did not become a Fellow until later) bought a copy in March 1662, commenting that the observations "appear to me on first sight to be very pretty," and later in the year a new edition was printed. In 1665, in the early months of the Great Plague, a third and fourth edition appeared. These are described as "much enlarged," but the only important additions are a fairly short appendix and some related tables. The fifth edition was published in 1676, two years after Graunt's death, probably having been seen through the press by Sir William Petty; it contains a very few "further observations."

4. GRAUNT'S SCIENTIFIC APPROACH

The first point that strikes one on reading the book is the modesty of the author. This appears not merely in the dedications at the beginning—where it might be only false modesty—but underlies much of the text. The preface affords a particularly good example:

> Having been born, and bred in the City of *London,* and having always observed, that most of them who constantly took in the weekly Bills of *Mortality,* made little other use of them, then to look at the foot, how the *Burials* increased, or decreased; And, among the *Casualties,* what had happened rare, and extraordinary in the week currant: so as they might take the same as a *Text* to talk upon, in the next Company; and withall, in the *Plague-time,* how the *Sickness* increased, or decreased, that so the *Rich* might judge of the necessity of their removall, and *Trades-men* might conjecture what doings they were like to have in their respective dealings:
>
> 2. Now, I thought that the Wisdom of our City had certainly designed the laudable practice of takeing, and distributing these Accompts, for other, and greater uses then those above-mentioned, or at least, that some other uses might be made of them: And thereupon I casting mine Eye upon so many of the General *Bills,* as next came to hand, I found encouragement from them, to look out all the *Bills* I could, and (to be short) to furnish my self with as much matter of that kind, even as the Hall of the *Parish-Clerks* could afford me; the which,

when I had reduced into Tables (the Copies whereof are here inserted) so as to have a view of the whole together, in order to the more ready comparing of one *Year, Season, Parish,* or other *Division* of the City, with another, in respect of all the *Burials,* and *Christnings,* and of all the *Diseases,* and *Casualties* happening in each of them respectively; I did then begin, not only to examine the Conceits, Opinions, and Conjectures, which upon view of a few scattered *Bills* I had taken up; but did also admit new ones, as I found reason, and occasion from my *Tables.*

3. Moreover, finding some *Truths,* and not commonly-believed Opinions, to arise from my Meditations upon these neglected *Papers,* I proceeded further, to consider what benefit the knowledge of the same would bring to the World; that I might not engage my self in idle, and useless Speculations, but like those Noble *Virtuosi* of *Gresham-Colledge* (who reduce their subtile Disquisitions upon Nature into downright Mechanical uses) present the World with some real fruit from those ayrie Blossoms.

4. How far I have succeeded in the Premisses, I now offer to the World's censure. Who, I hope, will not expect from me, not professing Letters, things demonstrated with the same certainty, wherewith Learned men determine in their *Scholes;* but will take it well, that I should offer a new thing, and could forbear presuming to meddle where any of the Learned Pens have ever touched before, and that I have taken the pains, and been at the charge, of setting out those *Tables,* whereby all men may both correct my *Positions,* and raise others of their own: For herein I have, like a silly Schole-boy, coming to say my Lesson to the World (that Peevish, and Tetchie Master) brought a bundle of Rods wherewith to be whipt, for every mistake I have committed.

It is clear from this that Graunt was, quite understandably, conscious of his lay status; he was no doctor, no mathematician, no politician, but an enquiring citizen who rated his efforts no higher than to "offer at a new thing," and took pains to tabulate his basic material so that his readers could check his deductions and add others he had overlooked (I do not believe that any of them have been able to). It seems to me that Graunt's lay status may have been an advantage in his enquiries rather than the reverse, by encouraging a degree of detachment from, and modesty towards, the handling of his data. These qualities are just as essential for an effective statistician today as they were in Graunt's time, but a statistician must now learn to combine them with an extensive knowledge of his particular field of application.

Secondly, Graunt shows a methodical tidiness throughout the book. *"THE Observations, which I happened to make (for I designed them not) upon the* Bills of Mortality, *have fallen out to be both* Political, *and* Natural, *some concerning* Trade, *and* Government, *others concerning the* Air, Countries, Seasons, Fruitfulness, Health, Diseases, Longevity, *and the proportions between the* Sex, *and* Ages of *Mankinde."* Since his observations fall into these two distinct classes, there are two dedications in the book, one of the political observations to the Lord Privy Seal, and one of the natural observations to the President of the Royal Society. This is perhaps a trivial example. The preface, quoted above, gives a better illustration of Graunt's methodical approach; it is as good a statement as one could hope to find, in any age, of the reasons for undertaking a scientific enquiry, of the thorough collection of relevant data, of the need to check first impressions against more extensive facts, and of the drawing of practical conclusions from the findings. This careful logical approach pervades the book, as you will see from my later examples.

Thirdly, Graunt devotes much space to a description of the bills of mortality, explaining how they were compiled and in what way they had developed. A lesser man would have thought this unimportant, or would not have bothered on the grounds that most of his readers would know it all already. As it is, his modern readers are in as good a position as Graunt's contemporaries were to understand the basis for his deductions. Moreover, and this is crucial, having described his sources, Graunt does not accept the information they contain without further question; he is critical both of their completeness and of their accuracy. Indeed, such appraisal of the data is often an integral part of his argument, affecting his deductions and conclusions, and giving them a validity they could not otherwise possess. Again, I shall be illustrating this below.

These three points I have touched upon, namely a humility of approach, a tidiness born of logic, and a critical appraisal of the basic data, are fundamental to any scientific enquiry. To find them adopted and pursued, at the very beginnings of serious scientific research, by a London draper, is a further justification for this celebration. Even though his scientific approach may have been intuitive rather than conscious, we can recognize in Graunt a pioneer of scientific method, quite apart from his contribution to statistics. . . .

5. THE BILLS OF MORTALITY

At some time early in the sixteenth century, a system arose whereby the totals of burials in each London parish, distinguishing deaths from the plague, were collected each week. It is likely that these weekly "bills of mortality" were at first prepared only during times of plague, but from about 1563 onwards they appear to have become a regular manuscript series. The earliest printed bills date from the first years of the seventeenth century, and in this form eventually became available to the public.

The weekly totals of christenings in each parish were included with those of burials from an early date, and causes of death other than plague were first recorded in about 1604, although not included in the printed bills until 1629.

Graunt gives us an excellent description of the way in which the bills of mortality for London were compiled during the seventeenth century.

> When any one dies, then, either by tolling, or ringing of a Bell, or by bespeaking of a Grave of the *Sexton*, the same is known to the *Searchers*, corresponding with the said *Sexton*.
>
> 11. The *Searchers* hereupon (who are antient Matrons, sworn to their Office) repair to the place, where the dead Corps lies, and by view of the same, and by other enquiries, they examine by what *Disease*, or *Casualty* the Corps died. Hereupon they make their Report to the *Parish-Clerk*, and he, every *Tuesday* night, carries in an Accompt of all the *Burials*, and *Christnings*, hapning that Week, to the *Clerk* of the *Hall*. On *Wednesday* the general Accompt is made up, and Printed, and on *Thursdays* published, and dispersed to the several Families, who will pay four shillings *per Annum* for them.

From about 1604 onwards, these weekly bills were consolidated at the end of December, and a general bill for the year was published. . . .

Graunt's statistical data for London were drawn almost exclusively from the series of annual bills from 1604 to 1660—although he turns to the weekly bills in connection with some of his observations on plague, and includes annual and some weekly figures for years up to 1665 in later editions of the book. Essentially his data consisted of the annual numbers of christenings and burials for the above period, subdivided by parish, and, from 1629 onwards, by sex. He also had statements of the causes of death under a large number of headings (not subdivided by sex or age) from 1629 until 1660; deaths from "that extraordinary and grand *Casualty* the *Plague*," however, had been shown separately since the beginning of the period.

Graunt's table of the annual deaths by cause, taken from the annual bills, is qualified by the following note: "Memorandum, *That the 10 years between 1636 and 1647 are omitted as containing nothing Extraordinary, and as not consistent with the Incapacity of a Sheet.*" It is sad that Graunt did not use a less incapacious sheet for his table, as no annual bills for the omitted years appear to have survived the Fire of London, and Graunt's table is the sole authority for nearly all the other years included on it. One might think that after such an interval this does not matter much, but the bills are still studied today; a recent historical study of attitudes to suicide in England contains the annual series of proportionate mortality rates from suicide in London from 1629 to 1800—complete apart from these 10 years Sprott, 1961, p. 159).

In addition to these data from the London bills, Graunt had some statistics for the country parish of Romsey in Hampshire, namely the annual number of weddings, and the christenings and burials by sex, from 1569 to 1658. For later editions this was supplemented with corresponding information for Tiverton in Devon and Cranbrook in Kent.

6. GRAUNT'S ARGUMENTS AND METHODS

From this very limited material, for he had no information, when he first wrote, on the size of London's population, and never had any on its age-distribution, Graunt discovered a surprising amount about the vital statistics and demography of seventeenth-century England. Amongst other things, he was the first to direct attention to the extremely high rates of mortality in infancy, and to the higher rate of mortality in London than in the country. He made the first realistic estimates of the size of the population of London, and of the country as a whole, showed that the populations of both were increasing, and that there was a steady migration into London from the country. He even made something of the extremely rudimentary data on causes of death, for example, distinguishing between endemic and epidemic diseases, noting for the first time the stability from year to year of accident and suicide rates, arguing cogently that rickets was an increasing disease and syphilis an under-recorded one, and demonstrating that the causes of death in infancy were often confused. He showed, too, that plague was under-recorded by about a quarter as a cause of death, examined which of the plague years had the greatest mortality, discovered the extent to which London depopulated itself in plague years, and then found how rapidly it repopulated itself.

But interesting though these conclusions are (and I have given only a selection), the arguments by which Graunt reached them are even more interesting. He had a remarkable and enviable facility for handling numerical data of mixed reliability and drawing valid conclusions from them, and in the process he founded a methodology of descriptive statistical analysis. One of the best examples of his approach is his discussion on rickets.

> 19. My next Observation is, that of the *Rickets* we finde no mention among the *Casualties,* untill the year 1634, and then but of 14 for that whole year.
>
> 20. Now the Question is, whether that Disease did first appear

about that time; or whether a Disease, which had been long before, did then first receive its Name?

21. To clear this Difficulty out of the Bills (for I dare venture on no deeper Arguments:) I enquired what other Casualties before the year 1634, named in the Bills, was most like the *Rickets;* and found, not onely by Pretenders to know it, but also from other Bills, that *Liver-grown* was the nearest. For in some years I finde *Liver-grown, Spleen* and *Rickets,* put all together, by reson (as I conceive) of their likeness to each other. Hereupon I added the *Liver-growns* of the year 1634, *viz.* 77, to the *Rickets* of the same year, *viz.* 14, making in all 91, which Total, as also the Number 77 it self, I compared with the *Liver-grown* of the precedent year, 1633, *viz.* 82. All which shewed me, that the *Rickets* was a new Disease over and above.

This, the reader may think, is not very convincing, being based on a rise from 82 to 91. Graunt did not think so either.

22. Now, this being but a faint Argument, I looked both forwards and backwards, and found, that in the year 1629, when no *Rickets* appeared, there was but 94 *Liver-growns;* and in the year 1636, there was 99 *Liver-grown,* although there were also 50 of the *Rickets:* onely this is not to be denyed, that when the *Rickets* grew very numerous (as in the year 1600, *viz.* to be 521) then there appeared not above 15 of *Liver-grown.*

23. In the year 1659 were 441 *Rickets,* and 8 *Liver-grown.* In the year 1658, were 476 *Rickets,* and 51 *Liver-grown.* Now, though it be granted that these Diseases were confounded in the judgment of the *Nurses,* yet it is most certain, that the *Liver-grown* did never but once, *viz. Anno* 1630, exceed 100, whereas *Anno* 1660, *Liver-grown,* and *Rickets* were 536.

24. It is also to be observed, That the *Rickets* were never more numerous then now, and that they are still increasing; for *Anno* 1649, there was but 190, next year 260, next after that 329, and so forwards, with some little starting backwards in some years, untill the year 1660, which produced the greatest of all.

Here is another, less frequently quoted, example of Graunt's understanding of his material, which has a number of points of interest.

11. The *Lunaticks* are also but few, *viz.* 158 in 229250, though I fear many more then are set down in our *Bills,* few being entred for such, but those who die at *Bedlam;* and there all seem to die of their *Lunacie,* who died *Lunaticks;* for there is much difference in computing the number of *Lunaticks,* that die (though of *Fevers,* and all other Diseases, unto which *Lunacie* is no *Supersedeas*) and those, that die by reason of their *Madness.*

The wording is perhaps a little strange to our ears, but there is no doubt that Graunt had a clear grasp of the distinction between mortality and morbidity from a specific disease; the difficulty of making this distinction in practice has bedevilled official mortality statistics in all countries ever since. I find the ensuing paragraph very entertaining.

> 12. So that, this *Casualty* being so uncertain, I shall not force my self to make any inference from the numbers, and proportions we finde in our Bills concerning it: onely I dare ensure any man at this present, well in his Wits, for one in the thousand, that he shall not die a *Lunatick* in *Bedlam*, within these seven years, because I finde not above one in about one thousand five hundred have done so.

Graunt evidently knew just how one might run an insurance business. He allows himself some leeway from the risk of 1 in 1,500 to a premium of 1 in 1,000 and then slips in a couple of extra clauses about "well in his Wits" and "within these seven years," to "make assurance double sure." He was writing just 100 years before the first commercial life office (the Equitable) was opened in London.

7. POPULATION MOVEMENTS

Graunt, having no direct information on the size of the population of London, uses the information on christenings and burials most ingeniously, to study the movements and other characteristics of the population. I shall now outline some of these arguments in the sequence in which they occur, because they illustrate not only the variety of conclusions he is able to draw from his data, but the careful logical structure of the book. Graunt proceeds deliberately from one topic to another, and has frequent occasion to build his earlier findings into his later arguments.

His first mention of the numbers of christenings is when he relates the numbers of abortions and stillbirths to the christenings, this incidentally being just the form of stillbirth rate adopted by the World Health Organization for international use nowadays. He immediately comments that between 1629 and 1659 either the stillbirth rate must have increased or the christenings must have decreased; he prefers the latter explanation, because the numbers of christenings, having been almost equal to the burials from 1603 to 1642, had by 1659 become less than half the burials; and this he attributes principally to increasing religious dissension during the Commonwealth period. He notes that, if the stillbirth rate had been the same at the end of this period as at the beginning, the number of births in 1659 (as distinct from the number actually christened) would have been about three-quarters of the number of burials. He then points out that a better account is kept of women dying in child-bed than of abortions and still-births and so prefers instead to base his calculations on a constant maternal mortality rate. This gives him an estimate of the number of births in 1659 which is much closer to the number of burials, a most satisfying conclusion.

Graunt then uses the christenings explicitly as an indicator of changes in size of the population in London in times of plague, in preference to burials, "because few bear children in *London* but *Inhabitants*, though others die there." He concludes that two out of five expectant mothers died, fled or miscarried during years when plague was epidemic (notably 1603 and 1625), but found that christenings, and by implication the population, returned on each occasion to their former level within two years.

Graunt next compares the numbers of burials and christenings, deliberately restricting his comparison to the period 1604–43, for which he trusted the figures of christenings. He finds more burials than christenings in London, but rejected one obvious conclusion, that this implied a decline in the population, because he had other evidence that the population of London was increasing (as we have today), namely the "daily increase of Buildings upon new Foundations, and . . . the turning of great Palacious Houses into small Tenements. It is therefore certain, that *London* is supplied with People from out of the Countrey, whereby not onely to repair the overplus difference of *Burials* above-mentioned, but likewise to increase its *Inhabitants* according to the said increase of housing."

Next, he has figures to show that in the country the reverse applies, namely, that there were more christenings than burials. He estimates, in three ways, that the population of England and Wales was about 6,440,000, namely about fourteen times that of London, which he estimates elsewhere (also in three ways) to have been about 460,000. This enables him to show, in a rather intricate but quite valid argument, assuming his country area to be typical, that the excess of christenings over burials in the whole country was about three times as many as would provide London with an influx of population large enough to account for the observed excess of burials, the remainder either making the country more populous, or emigrating. He concludes "That the People of the whole Nation do increase, and consequently the decrease of *Winchester, Lincoln,* and other like places, must be attributed to other Reasons, then that of refurnishing *London* onely."

Once Graunt comes to deal with the numbers of the two sexes in the population he immediately extends his data to include figures after 1643, noting in justification that the general decrease in christenings has not affected the relative proportions of the sexes. He finds more male christenings than female, and more male burials than female, each in the proportion fourteen to thirteen; from this he concludes that there were more males alive than females. This would be a fair conclusion if age-specific death

rates for males and females were equal, but is not necessarily correct otherwise. (Similar excesses of male over female births and male over female
deaths are found in England and Wales today, but because age-specific
death rates are uniformly higher among males than females, there are fewer
males than females living.) Unfortunately Graunt, who had no data which
would permit a statistical examination of the point, leaves us in some
uncertainty whether he regarded male and female death rates as equal or
not. On the one hand, he suggests "that men, being more intemperate then
women, die as much by reason of the Vices, as the women do by the In
firmitie of their *Sex*, and consequently, more *Males* being born, then *Females*, more also die." On the other hand, he implies a differential death
rate, at least among young adults, in a famous statement which eventually
influenced Malthus: "that although more men die violent deaths then
women, that is, more are *slain* in Wars, *killed* by mischance, *drowned* at
Sea, and die by the *Hand of Justice*. Moreover, more men go to *Colonies*,
and travel into foreign parts, then women. And lastly, more remain unmarried, then of women, as *Fellows* of *Colleges*, and *Apprentises*, above eighteen, &c. yet the said thirteenth part difference bringeth the business but
to such a pass, that every woman may have an Husband, without the allow-
ance of *Polygamy*." Apparently Graunt realized that a differential mortality
rate would affect the relative numbers of adult males and females, but
missed the corollary, that his conclusion (of more males alive than females) was unlikely to be valid unless the age-specific death rates of males
and females were closely similar. This is one of the very few places in the
book where one can legitimately criticize the logic of one of Graunt's
deductions.

The final item in this sequence consists of Graunt's assessment of the
increase in London's population. Here he wishes to deal with the whole
period from 1593 to 1659, and so has to rely upon the burials as his indicator
of the population rather than christenings. But he uses these data with his
customary instinct for a correct statistical approach. He subtracts plague
deaths from the total deaths throughout, he leaves out the years when
plague was epidemic and those immediately following, because of the
exodus of the population, and to make the comparisons more reliable he
bases them on averages of two years rather than on single years. He concludes that the total population of London had increased from "two to five"
in 54 years (1605–59), the greatest increases being in the parishes outside
the walls of the city, and "That the City of *London* gradually removes
Westward." This last observation is not original, having been made by
Evelyn the previous year in "Fumifugium," the famous first treatise on
atmospheric pollution in London, but Graunt was the first to demonstrate it
statistically.

8. ESTIMATES OF THE SIZE OF THE POPULATION

I referred above to Graunt's estimates of population size, and in this field too his approaches are most instructive. He tells us that his interest in estimating the population of London was aroused by hearing an assertion that there were 2 million more people in London in 1661 than before the plague in 1625. He begins, characteristically, by pointing out that this would imply a total population of about 6 or 7 million in London in 1661, which, from the deaths recorded in the bills, would mean that the annual mortality would have been less than 1 in 400. He next shows that another popular belief, "That it is esteemed an even Lay, whether any man lives ten years longer," when applied to an estimate of the adult deaths, led to a figure for the total population which he clearly regards as much too small.

Graunt then describes three ways in which he "endeavoured to get a little nearer" the truth; each involved estimating the number of families in London, and multiplying this by the average size of family, which Graunt took to be eight, made up of a man and his wife, three children, and three servants or lodgers. Graunt's estimates of the number of families were made respectively via births, deaths and houses.

> 4. I considered, that the number of *Child-bearing women* might be about double to the *Births:* forasmuch as such women, one with another, have scarce more then one Childe in two years. The number of *Births* I found, by those years, wherein the *Registries* were well kept, to have been somewhat less then the *Burials.* The *Burials* in these late years at a *Medium* are about 13000, and consequently the *Christnings* not above 12000. I therefore esteemed the number of *Teeming women* to be 24000: then I imagined, that there might be twice as many Families, as of such women; for that there might be twice as many women *Aged* between 16 and 76, as between 16 and 40, or between 20 and 44. . . .

This gives him 48,000 families, and a population of 384,000.

> 5. Secondly, I finde by telling the number of Families in some Parishes within the walls, that 3 out of 11 families *per an.* have died: wherefore, 13000 having died in the whole, it should follow, there were 48000 Families. . . .
>
> 7. And lastly I took the Map of *London* set out in the year 1658 by *Richard Newcourt,* drawn by a scale of Yards. Now I guessed that in 100 yards square there might be about 54 Families, supposing every house to be 20 foot in the front: for on two sides of the said square there will be 100 yards of housing in each, and in the two other sides 80 each; in all 360 yards: that is 54 Families in each square, of which there are 220 within the Walls, making in all 11880 Families within

the Walls. But forasmuch as there dy within the Walls about 3200 *per Annum,* and in the whole about 13000; it follows, that the housing within the Walls is ¼. part of the whole, and consequently, that there are 47520 Families in, and about *London,* which agrees well enough with all my former computations: the worst whereof doth sufficiently demonstrate, that there are no Millions of People in *London,* which nevertheless most men do believe.

Graunt's estimate of 460,000 for the population of London, which I mentioned earlier, arises by the addition of one-fifth to the figure of 384,000 to encompass "*Westminster, Stepney, Lambeth,* and the other distant Parishes."

Graunt's first argument "that *England* hath fourteen times more People" than London is that "*London* is observed to bear about the fifteenth proportion of the whole Tax." His second is based upon a computed density of population of 220 to the square mile in his country parish (Romsey), "of which I abate ¼ for the overplus of People more in that Parish, then in other wilde Countries"; this leads him to the figure quoted earlier of 6,440,000 persons in the whole country (including London), which has an area of 39,000 square miles. The third estimate, of 6 million, is based upon a suggested average population of 600 in each of the 10,000 parishes in the country.

It is, of course, easy to criticize individual items in the edifice of assumptions and approximations behind each of these estimates, but to do this is to miss the point. The importance of these paragraphs is that they represent the earliest attempts to estimate population size scientifically, and the results show very clearly how much a scientific guess is to be preferred to an unscientific guess. By using a variety of approaches to each population figure Graunt shows that he is well aware of the shortcomings of the data, and at the same time the consistency of the various estimates (even though it may be in part artificial) is at least confirmation that Graunt's orders of magnitude are likely to be correct.

It is of especial interest that, after making these estimates, Graunt was able to apply a check to his figure for London. An enumeration of the population of the city and liberties of London had been made in 1631 for taxation purposes, but the findings were not generally available, and Graunt was clearly unaware of their existence when he first published the *Observations.* He later obtained the figures and included them with the appendix in the third and later editions of the book. When scaled up in accordance with his own estimate of the population increase in the city and liberties in the interval of 30 years, and again in accordance with his estimate of the relative populations of all London, and the city and liberties, in 1661, the total figure Graunt obtains is 403,000; from which "it will appear, that I computed too many rather than too few, although the most part of men have thought otherwise."

9. THE FIRST LIFE TABLE

I turn to what is commonly regarded as Graunt's masterpiece, the first life table.

> 9. Whereas we have found, that of 100 quick Conceptions about 36 of them die before they be six years old, and that perhaps but one surviveth 76, we, having seven *Decads* between six and 76, we sought six mean proportional numbers between 64, the remainder, living at six years, and the one, which survives 76, and finde, that the numbers following are practically near enough to the truth; for men do not die in exact Proportions, nor in Fractions: from whence arises this Table following.

Viz. of 100 there dies within the first six years	36
The next ten years, or *Decad*	24
The second *Decad*	15
The third *Decad*	09
The fourth	6
The next	4
The next	3
The next	2
The next	1

> 10. From whence it follows, that of the said 100 conceived there remains alive at six years end 64.

At Sixteen years end	40
At Twenty six	25
At Thirty six	16
At Fourty six	10
At Fifty six	6
At Sixty six	3
At Seventy six	1
At Eighty	0

There has been much speculation how Graunt derived his column of survivors—indeed the production of rival explanations seems to have become almost a statistical parlour-game in the nineteen-twenties and thirties. More recently, Glass (1950) suggested that Graunt used a method of diminishing differences for distributing the deaths, and this appeals to me more than the earlier efforts because it involves an arithmetical approach more likely to have occurred to Graunt.

The life table is derived from a distribution of deaths by age, and not, as a modern one would be, from mortality rates based on the population.

Greenwood (1948) pointed out that as a consequence this table would be valid as a description of the dying-out of the population only if the population were stationary (which, Graunt had shown, was not so) and discusses whether Graunt realized this. I find it hard to convince myself that Graunt would have appreciated so abstruse a point. Greenwood appears to assume tacitly that Graunt approached the problem of compiling his table from the standpoint of a modern actuary or statistician, and this I am sure he did not. Thus, Greenwood refers to Graunt's "great achievement, the estimation of rates of mortality at ages when the numbers and ages of the living were not recorded." But this is not what Graunt set out to achieve; he had, as I suggest below, a much more practical aim. Nor, in this context, was the lack of information on the living his problem; it was the lack of information about the dead. He had estimated—and estimated is here the right word—that of 100 children born alive 36 would die before they were six years old, and it would naturally occur to him to wonder when the remaining 64 would die. He had no information on ages at death from which to estimate this and so he fell back on a piece of arithmetical guesswork; he distributed the 64 deaths into a diminishing series which would link smoothly with the initial figure of 36 and leave the last of his deaths to occur at a suitably advanced age. If his procedure was that suggested by Glass this would lead him to a final death at an age exceeding 76, and this may be the origin of Graunt's otherwise unsupported suggestion "that perhaps but one surviveth 76." Graunt then built up the column of survivors.

Now Graunt introduces his table just after estimating London's population to consist of 199,000 males and 185,000 females. His reason for introducing it is to compute how many of the 199,000 are "fighting Men," and he does this by deriving from the column of survivors the proportion of the population aged between 16 and 56, applying this to the total of 199,000. But at this point he commits an important statistical error. What he derives from the column of survivors and uses in his calculation is not the proportion living at ages 16 to 56, but the proportion *dying* between those ages. No one appears to have noticed this error for more than 250 years (Westergaard, 1932, p. 23), so Graunt may perhaps be excused for having made it. Nevertheless, as Greenwood said, "Graunt was not at all clear in his mind as to how to use a life table."

Graunt, having introduced the table for a specific purpose, and having as he thought, achieved this, makes no further reference to it; he gives no sign of having perceived its actuarial uses. Nor does Petty, who made a similar table (Hull, 1899, 1, 144), and committed the same error, at a later date (although Petty did indicate in a different context that, if certain information were available for the population, one could calculate mortality rates at ages and put these to actuarial use—see Greenwood, 1948, 15). It was left to Halley (1693a, b) to derive a realistic age-distribution of a stationary population from records of ages at death, and to describe its actuarial uses. It seems to me that unless Graunt had first realized the actuarial potentialities of *his* table, the point discussed by Greenwood would certainly not have occurred to him.

If this account of the origins of Graunt's table is correct, he retains the honour of making the first attempt to describe the dying out of a population cohort, but cannot be regarded, actuarially speaking, as having compiled the first life table. The distinction may seem a fine one, but I believe that it is historically correct.

10. FURTHER STATISTICAL APPROACHES

Most of Graunt's arguments, as we have seen, are based upon the study of ratios, differences between ratios and time-trends in ratios. But what Graunt describes as *"the* Mathematiques *of my Shop-Arithmetique"* extended further than that. He knew how to study associations, to "counterpoise the Opinion of those who think great *Plagues* come in with *Kings* reigns, because it hapned so twice, *viz, Anno* 1603, and 1625, whereas as well the year 1648, wherein the present *King* commenced his right to reign, as also the year 1660, wherein he commenced the exercise of the same, were both eminently healthful, which clears both *Monarchie,* and our present *King's Familie* from what seditious men have surmised against them." Two against two may not wholly convince a modern statistician, but there is nothing wrong with the approach. Again, Graunt noted an inverse association between christenings and burials, both in London and in the country, years with the more burials having the fewer christenings, and vice versa.

He made a rational attempt to study time-series, defining a sickly year as one in which there were not more than 200 deaths from plague and in which the burials exceeded those of the preceding and succeeding year. He even touched upon the classic problem of epidemiology, the course of an epidemic, noting, among other characteristics, that plague took longer to rise to its peak than to decline from it, in the proportion of three to two.

He was also interested in geographical variations, particularly in the relative numbers of male and female births, and this led him to attempt what can only be described as the first sample survey. "I have here inserted two other Countrey Bills, the one of *Cranbrook* in *Kent,* the other of *Tiverton* in *Devonshire,* which with that of *Hantshire,* lying about the midway between them, give us a view of the most Easterly, Southerly, and Westerly parts of *England:* I have endeavoured to procure the like account from *Northumberland, Cheshire, Norfolk* and *Nottinghamshire;* Thereby to have a view of seven Countries most differently situated, from whence I am sorry to observe that my Southern friends have been hitherto more curious and diligent than those of the North."

11. THE LIMITS OF GRAUNT'S STATISTICAL PERCEPTION

Perhaps the main single impression which Graunt leaves with a modern statistical reader is one of his sure-footed progress through a mass of untidy numerical data, apparently instinctively keeping clear of that which was unanalysable and extracting the maximum of information from the rest; he seems, too, to have had an intuitive appreciation of just how much interpretation his findings would stand, and takes care not to exceed this.

I have referred to Graunt's two major statistical errors, in connection with the relative numbers of the two sexes and in using his life table. I do not consider that these detract from Graunt's achievement. A pioneer must be judged by the amount of new ground he explores, not by the fact that he is eventually brought to a halt. Graunt's errors both arise at the extreme limits of what he might have been expected to appreciate. In a situation in which no ages at death were recorded, and there was no prospect of information about the numbers and ages of the living, it is not surprising that Graunt should have failed to appreciate the subtle interplay between birth-rates, age-specific death-rates and the size of the living population. Even today a student of demography may pause at the apparent paradox of more male than female births and more male deaths, and yet fewer males than females alive; and may make the mistake of regarding a column of survivors at various anniversaries as if it represented an age-distribution of a living population.

In one section of the book, Graunt emphasizes the much greater proportionate variation from year to year in the numbers of births and deaths in his small country parish than was found in London. He has consequently been criticized (Hull, 1899, 1, p. lxxvi) for failing to appreciate that the smaller numbers would be inherently more variable. But surely he did appreciate this—otherwise why should he have combined the burials for consecutive years when studying the trends in size of London's population over a period of years? Moreover, as Greenwood (1948) showed, the variations in the country districts were substantially greater than would be expected from chance alone, and he suggested that Graunt might have recognized this intuitively.

12. THE AUTHORSHIP OF THE "OBSERVATIONS"

I have deliberately left until now a matter on which some comment might have been expected earlier. It concerns the allegation that Graunt never wrote the *Observations* at all, these being the work of his friend Sir William Petty. This allegation was not made, as far as we know, until after Graunt's death, but it has persisted in some quarters until the present day. It would, unfortunately, take too long even to outline the arguments on the two sides (see Hull, 1899, 1, p. xxxix; Willcox, 1937 or 1939; Greenwood, 1948, p. 36), but it is sufficient, in the present context, to say that statisticians have never been in any serious doubt that Graunt wrote his own book. Assessing them as statisticians, there is no comparison between the two men. There is sufficient evidence above the validity of Willcox's (1937 or 1939) comment that "To the trained reader Graunt writes statistical music," and there is little difficulty in verifying the antithesis, that "Petty is like a child playing with a new musical toy which occasionally yields a bit of harmony."

There can, however, be little doubt that the two men, who were then close friends, discussed the book while it was in preparation, and Petty may well have suggested additions and perhaps even supplied some draft. But by far the greater part of the text, and certainly all the statistically important parts, could never have come from Petty. This is not to deny Petty's many other merits. He was an inventive man, and full of good ideas, even though they did not all come to fruition as fast or as successfully as he wished. In particular, he advocated, in detail, the setting up of a General Register Office in this country more than 150 years before it was achieved, and it was he who was responsible for carrying forward Graunt's isolated statistical effort into the beginnings of political arithmetic, or, as we now call it, demography....

ACKNOWLEDGMENTS

It is a pleasure to thank Professor E. S. Pearson for allowing me to consult the manuscripts of Karl Pearson's lectures on the history of statistics, and Professor D. V. Glass for keeping me informed of his own recent discoveries about Graunt. I am indebted to Mr. E. C. Chamberlain, Fitzwilliam Museum, Cambridge, and to Mr. R. Williams, British Museum, for their efforts to locate a portrait of Graunt, and to Dr. H. Campbell for pointing out the parallel between Graunt and Leeuwenhoek.

REFERENCES

Glass, D. V. (1950), "Graunt's life table," *J. Inst. Actu.*, **76**, 60–64.

Greenwood, M. (1948), *Medical Statistics from Graunt to Farr*. Cambridge University Press.

Halley, E. (1693a), "An estimate of the degrees of the mortality of mankind, drawn from curious tables of the births and funerals at the city of Breslaw;

with an attempt to ascertain the price of annuities upon lives," *Phil. Trans.,* **17,** 596–610.

——— (1693b), "Some further considerations on the Breslaw bills of mortality," *Phil. Trans.,* **17,** 654–656.

Hull, C. H. (Ed.) (1899), *The Economic Writings of Sir William Petty together with the Observations on the Bills of Mortality more probably by Captain John Graunt.* (Including a reprint of the fifth edition, 1676.) Cambridge University Press.

Royal Statistical Society (1934), *Annals of the Royal Statistical Society, 1834–1934.* London.

Sprat, T. (1667), *The History of the Royal Society of London, for the Improving of Natural Knowledge.* London.

Sprott, S. E. (1961), *The English Debate on Suicide from Donne to Hume.* La Salle, Illinois: Open Court.

Todhunter, I. (1865), *A History of the Mathematical Theory of Probability from the Time of Pascal to That of Laplace.* London: Macmillan.

Tukey, J. W. (1962), "The future of data analysis," *Ann. math. Statist.,* **33,** 1–67.

Westergaard, H. (1932), *Contributions to the History of Statistics.* London: King.

Willcox, W. F. (1937), "The founder of statistics," *Rev. Inst. int. Statist.,* **5,** 321–328.

——— (Ed.) (1939), *Natural and Political Observations made upon the Bills of Mortality by John Graunt.* (A reprint of the first edition, 1662.) Baltimore: Johns Hopkins Press.

9

Historical Demography and Classical Demography

Louis Henry

The history of demography, since the start of the science in 1662, has been marked by two preoccupations. The first demographers concentrated on the study of mortality to such an extent that the first century of demography—from John Graunt to Per Wargentin—consists of the progressive discovery of correct procedures for the measurement of current mortality. In the nineteenth century, official statistical services were created to record the size and movement of population. The information and knowledge thereby acquired had both an administrative and scientific utility.

These two facts are not independent of each other. A study of mortality is hardly possible without a census which records the number of people and their classification by age. When, at a very late date, demographers turned their attention to the study of other demographic phenomena—birth and marriage—they modeled this study on the earlier analyses of mortality, without questioning too deeply whether it was necessary to proceed in this way. As a result, in demography everything was studied by a judicious combination of the data extracted from two sources: the census and vital statistics. When vital statistics failed to provide certain information, they were supplemented by the census, so that the latter became the keystone in the arch of the demographic edifice.

Because a census could be taken only by a statistical service, this service had a monopoly on statistical observation—that is to say, a monopoly on demography itself. Until the last war, all that was not classical demography was marginal and without real importance. The lines of thought that classical demography followed often led to impasses because

Reprinted by permission of *Daedalus,* Journal of the American Academy of Arts and Sciences, Boston, Massachusetts, vol. 97, no. 2.

its methods were too rigorously focused on the present—on events of the moment. At the time, however, no one was concerned that it should be otherwise.

After 1945, the situation was modified by several changes whose repercussions will be felt for a long time. In the United States and Britain, the analysis of demographic phenomena by periods (transversal analysis) was thought to be ill-suited to phenomena other than mortality. Demographers in Britain and the United States, thus, substituted an analysis based on the experience of each generation or cohort throughout its lifetime (longitudinal analysis) for transversal analysis. Today longitudinal analysis has largely conquered demographic studies; even mortality, which has so far escaped, begins to be menaced.

Reflection on the procedures of statistical observation has made the need of the double source of data—the census and vital statistics—somewhat less imperative. It was seen that, for the past, almost everything required could be found from vital statistics alone, provided they were accurate. It became apparent, even for studies of the present, that it was not possible to answer all the needs of demography by combining the data of the census and the vital statistics.

A new means of statistical observation—sample surveys—came into wide use. Although often conceived simply as a complementary procedure, the sample survey offers new possibilities and puts demographic observation within the reach of more organizations (for example, universities and research institutes). The *de facto* monopoly of the statistical services can no longer be justified.

Requirements for information and opinions in the field of economics and demography have increased so sharply within government that the statistical services have become more and more occupied by current events. Providing data has clearly become, at the expense of scientific analysis, the predominant focus of statistical services. The disequilibrium between collection and analysis has led to an almost total disinterest in the past, even when it belongs to the statistical era.

Since the war, permanent or temporary organizations for research have been created or launched. These organizations do not pose demographic problems in the same terms as the statistical services. Scientific concerns predominate; the preoccupation with events of the moment is diminished.

Such changes have great importance for historical demography. Longitudinal analysis is naturally inclined toward a historical perspective. The importance it has acquired tends to make all demography a history of successive generations. Historical demography, which quite naturally uses longitudinal analysis, therefore became an integral part of demography as a whole, just as the history of the eighteenth century is an integral part of history as a whole.

To fail to observe demographic phenomena in the manner of the statistical services is no longer considered erroneous; moreover, historical demography is now completely independent of the statistical service and is free to pursue its observations in terms of its needs, taking into account all relevant documents. No other branch of demography now benefits from an equal autonomy.

The diminished participation of the statistical service in the development of demography as a science minimizes the importance of purely contemporary events. As a result of this evolution, the frontier between historical demography and current demography has been reduced, if not eradicated.

Demographic phenomena are inscribed in time. Such phenomena cannot be explained nor understood unless they have been traced through the concatenations of many decades or centuries, as far back as available observations and documents permit us to go. To study demography only from current events is equivalent to the study of astronomy without benefit of earlier observation or to the construction of a theory of evolution with attention to none but presently living species. Can one imagine a meterology which did away with the information of the last century under the pretext that it was no longer current?

We do not know whether laws analogous to those which regulate natural phenomena exist for demography, but what we do know shows that any future cannot proceed from a given present. If there are no permanent and rigid statistics in demography, there are certainly relations among phenomena. By studying these, we can hope to improve our knowledge and our ability to forecast. Only the observation of as long a chronological series as is possible will furnish all the relations observable up to the present. In demography, therefore, the important factor is not to possess the most recent information about the population of a certain country or city, but to be able to dispose of homogeneous retrospective statistics extending as far into the past as possible. If this is accepted, it is hardly a paradox to say that historical demography is all demography—or, to put it another way, that from the scientific point of view demography has as its object the study of all observable populations, past and present. Given the actual state of affairs, however, I prefer the first formula, for it focuses more clearly on the primary importance of time.

The paradox to which I subscribe is not inspired by a particular love of the past. I am not a historian, and I came to historical demography because I needed information on natural fertility (fertility unlimited by birth control). Because historical demography furnished this information, it was possible to advance the study of biological factors in fertility and to construct a model that could serve as a guide to biologists in certain studies of the physiology of reproduction. As a demographer, I also know that modern statistics do not furnish so much diverse information as can be collected from the study of rural families of the eighteenth century. This lack could easily be corrected by a few sample surveys—that is, if one gives, finally, more weight to studies in depth than to peripheral current happenings.

10

Who Are the Uncounted People?

edited by Carole W. Parsons

Net underenumeration in the Censuses of 1950, 1960, and 1970 is estimated on the basis of findings produced by three independent methods; postcensal re-enumeration in a sample of geographic areas, record-matching samples, and demographic analysis. In the case of the third, which is now the preferred method of evaluating census coverage, estimates are developed by comparing census totals with expected population figures derived from analysis of the results of previous censuses and from separate records of births, deaths, immigration, and emigration.

Demographic methods are inexpensive to use. Their limitations arise primarily from the lack of adequate migration data. The other methods, though usually more informative, are costly and have specific technical weaknesses. For example, experience has shown that the carefully controlled, intensive interviewing procedures of a special postcensal survey, while useful for identifying *completely unenumerated households,* are not much more likely than standard census procedures to find *persons missed within enumerated living quarters.* Similarly, although record matching is immensely useful for assessing the reliability and validity of information provided by enumerated households, there is reason to suspect that record linkage techniques may never provide acceptable estimates, at reasonable cost, of the error in census counts of persons.

Matching technologies, still relatively poorly developed, will be improved and made less expensive. However, there is the added difficulty that, for some persons, not being counted in a census may be symptomatic of not being listed in any other comparable record system. Whether it is ethically desirable to use matching techniques extensively is also open to question. Reinterviews and record matching were both used to evaluate

Reprinted by permission from *America's Uncounted People,* Publication ISBN 0–309–02026–3, Advisory Committee on Problems of Census Enumeration, Division of Behavioral Sciences, National Academy of Sciences-National Research Council, Washington, D.C., 1972.

coverage in the 1950 and 1960 Censuses. In 1970, in contrast, reinterviews were used only for measuring the quality of responses actually elicited by the 1970 Census questions, and record matching for coverage estimation purposes was limited to those few selected instances where opportunities existed for comparison with record systems, such as Medicare, that are believed to offer relatively thorough coverage of specific population categories.

DEMOGRAPHIC CHARACTERISTICS OF THE UNDERENUMERATED

Undercount estimates derived from demographic analyses are, of course, affected by errors in previous censuses, by imperfect vital statistics, and particularly by flawed immigration and emigration statistics. Nevertheless, demographic methods provide relatively inexpensive evidence of deficiencies in the national counts for many groups.[1]

Table 1 presents such an estimate of the number of uncounted persons in the 1960 Census by sex, color, and age. The percentages are most reliable for persons under 25, since birth and death registration areas covered the entire United States only after 1933. For other ages, the soundness of the figures depends on the choice of demographic techniques used, the adequacy of assumptions made in applying those techniques, and the quality of the basic demographic data employed. Typically, Table 1 indicates that although, in absolute numbers, more whites than nonwhites[2] were missed by the 1960 Census, the estimated number of uncounted nonwhites, as a percentage of the total estimated nonwhite population, was disproportionately large (about 10 percent). Moreover, approximately 15 percent of all nonwhite males between the ages of 20 and 40 are estimated not to have been counted, with the highest proportion (20 percent) in the 25–29 age group. Similar patterns can be observed among females. While women in both color groups were generally more completely enumerated than men in corresponding age categories, nonwhite females were noticeably less well enumerated than white females, not only at ages over 45 (at which nonwhite females appear to have been even less well counted than nonwhite males) but also in the age groups in which nonwhite men were markedly undercounted.

SOCIAL CHARACTERISTICS OF THE UNDERENUMERATED—THREE HYPOTHESES

The reasons for the persistence of undercounting from one census to the next, and for the greater underenumeration of nonwhites, especially young nonwhite males, are not known. Three hypotheses, derived largely from

TABLE 1.   Estimated Amount and Percentage of Net Underenumeration of the Population by Age, Sex, and Color, in the 1960 Census[a]

Sex and Age	White, 1960 (April 1)		Nonwhite, 1960 (April 1)	
	Amount (thousands)	Percentage[b]	Amount (thousands)	Percentage[b]
Male, all ages	2,256	2.8	1,218	10.9
0–4	177	2.0	124	7.7
5–9	205	2.4	78	5.7
10–14	194	2.5	59	5.2
15–19	233	3.8	114	12.5
20–24	209	4.3	133	17.5
25–29	208	4.2	150	19.7
30–34	167	3.1	138	18.0
35–39	142	2.5	107	14.5
40–44	97	1.9	82	12.8
45–49	77	1.6	69	11.5
50–54	159	3.6	97	17.8
55–59	15	0.4	25	5.9
60–64	97	3.0	31	9.7
65 and over	276	3.8	11	1.8
Female, all ages	1,297	1.6	924	8.1
0–4	102	1.2	101	6.4
5–9	126	1.6	66	4.8
10–14	108	1.5	47	4.2
15–19	144	2.4	91	10.1
20–24	121	2.4	75	9.6
25–29	68	1.4	67	8.7
30–34	32	0.6	46	5.9
35–39	−11	−0.2	47	6.2
40–44	−11	−0.2	42	6.4
45–49	35	0.7	52	8.4
50–54	194	4.2	103	18.2
55–59	62	1.6	45	10.0
60–64	151	4.2	50	14.1
65 and over	176	2.1	92	12.2

[a] Reprinted with permission from Jacob S. Siegel, "Completeness of Coverage of the Nonwhite Population in the 1960 Census and Current Estimates, and Some Implications," in David M. Heer (Ed.), *Social Statistics and the City* (Cambridge, Massachusetts: Harvard University Press for the Joint Center for Urban Studies of the Massachusetts Institute of Technology and Harvard University), 1968, Table 2, pp. 42–43.

[b] These percentages were computed in the following manner: For a particular sex–color–age category, let C represent the Census-reported count and let E represent the "corrected" population count. Then, the percentage is $\left(\dfrac{E-C}{E}\right)$ 100. The numbers in the "Amount" columns are the values of $E-C$. Footnote 2 on page 16 of Siegel gives the sources for the E values.

census field experience and research, have strongly influenced recent thinking about the problem. One directs attention to incomplete reporting of the number of persons attached to enumerated living quarters; another centers on the possibility that uncounted persons may not reside in any place enumerated by standard census procedures; and a third concerns the urban-rural distribution of uncounted persons.

The 1950 and 1960 Census Post-Enumeration Surveys (PES), and the results of demographic analyses of those two censuses, provide evidence that in 1950 and 1960 incomplete coverage of whites, both male and female, stemmed in large measure from failure to enumerate entire households. The most important inference to be drawn from the Post-Enumeration Surveys and related work, however, is that white and nonwhite undercount patterns seem to have differed markedly. While 70 percent of the *whites* known to have been missed in the 1960 Census were subsequently found in completely missed households, only 30 percent of the uncounted *nonwhites* appear to have been missed because their entire households were missed.[3] This evidence, plus the additional observation that persons loosely attached to households, such lodgers and members of extended families, are more likely to be missed by the census than household heads, wives, and children,[4] has led to speculation that a large majority of missed nonwhites are "either present but unreported in enumerated living quarters or ... not staying in any kind of place covered by the census."[5]

The second hypothesis—that some individuals are not counted because they are not staying in conventionally enumerated places—receives support not only from the 1960 PES but also from a small body of evidence developed during tests of 1970 Census field operations. In the spring of 1967, the Bureau of Labor Statistics and the Bureau of the Census jointly initiated a pilot research program aimed at improving the quality of statistical information about residents of urban poverty areas. Part of the effort was designed to develop data on the labor force characteristics of persons thought to be inadequately represented in sample surveys, mainly black men between the ages of 20 and 50, by means of a procedure called the "casual setting interview." Experimental interviews were conducted during the New Haven, Connecticut, pretest of the 1970 Census and later in conjunction with a full-scale census "dress rehearsal"[6] in Trenton, New Jersey.[7]

"Casual setting interviews," in the census context, are conducted in such places as bars and poolrooms and on street corners. Lists of the names and addresses of interviewed persons are compiled for later matching with census records to determine the enumeration status of each person contacted. In New Haven, the procedure consisted of an initial encounter between interviewer and respondent in a casual setting, followed by an attempt to find and reinterview persons who, by checking census lists, could be definitely identified as uncounted in the census pretest. In Trenton, time and budget limitations precluded a second interview, but the lack of follow-up was partially offset by the larger scope of the Trenton project and by the fact that less than one in six of the men whose names could not be matched in New Haven were subsequently locatable for follow-up interviews at addresses they had given to casual setting interviewers.[8]

The findings of the two studies cannot be interpreted as descriptive of all uncounted men in the areas in which the research was conducted (or, in the case of New Haven, as representative of the universe of potentially relocatable persons). Many uncounted individuals may not have frequented the particular casual settings in which interviews took place or may have deliberately avoided contact with the interviewers. Nevertheless, the evidence gathered by the two studies does suggest that men who could be identified as uncounted tended, in comparison with enumerated men, to be more poorly educated, to have fewer family ties, and to exhibit a marked proclivity for frequent changes of residence. In New Haven, only 33 percent of the uncounted group were married, compared with 57 percent of those who had been enumerated. In Trenton, the respective percentages were 35 and 58. In New Haven, 46 percent of the uncounted individuals interviewed a second time had lived at their present addresses only a year or less, compared with 12 percent of the enumerated. In Trenton, where length of time at present address was ascertained during the casual setting interview, the observed tendency was in the same direction, though less noticeable. The respective percentages were 14 and 9.[9]

It is not clear whether the more stable living arrangements indicated by the Trenton data simply reflect bias in the selection of persons to be interviewed or point to some underlying aspect of culture or social structure.[10] But the New Haven experience alone would seem to encourage further exploration of the "not staying in any place" hypothesis. Even though such individuals may, from time to time, stay in enumerated living quarters, their lack of regular attachments to such places makes it conceivable that neither they nor anyone else regard them as "usual residents" or, for that matter, as having "a usual residence elsewhere." It may well be that, for practical purposes, such persons should be considered "to live" on street corners and in bars, poolrooms, and other "casual settings" in which censuses are not customarily taken.

A third hypothesis about the social characteristics and circumstances associated with underenumeration posits a relationship between census field office difficulties and undercounting in urban areas. Results of the 1950 and 1960 Post-Enumeration Surveys suggested that failure to enumerate entire households occurred most often in the inner zones of large cities, where there is an abundance of multiunit housing structures, and in remote, sparsely populated rural areas. Moreover, the 1960 Census Time and Cost Study revealed that "when urban block cities [i.e., cities of 50,000 or more inhabitants for which data were to be published by city block], urban non-block cities, and rural areas were compared, urban block cities appeared to be the most difficult in which to take the Census. They had the lowest proportion of enumerations completed on the first visit, . . . the highest closeout rate, . . . and took the longest time to complete. . . ."[11] These observations, along with more recent reports of similar difficulties encountered by other survey organizations,[12] led the Census Bureau to hypothesize a possible connection between 1960 field office difficulties and 1960 undercounts by age, sex, and race. That such difficulties would grow in 1970 also seemed reasonable to expect in the light of Current Population Survey data indicating increasing Negro population densities in major urban centers,[13] and given what is known or suspected about the demographic and social consequences of Negro migration out of the rural South.[14]

Accordingly, in 1970, the Census Bureau invested several million dollars in special efforts to assure an accurate count of people living in economically depressed areas of large cities, principally in the North and Midwest.[15] There was no opportunity to conduct an independent test of the presumed relationship between field office difficulties and differential census undercounting, but the hypothetical connection seemed reasonable.[16] In census field operations, the crucial linkages are the incomplete household enumeration and the "close-out," wherein follow-up interviewers are instructed to collect information from neighbors about persons residing in households to which enumerators have failed to gain access after several attempts. Close-out cases in 1960 were relatively more numerous in cities with populations of 50,000 or more. The 1960 PES also indicated that one third of the persons identified by the PES as missed by the census within enumerated living quarters were indeed attached to households that had originally been enumerated by close-out.[17] However, the inability of the PES to add a large proportion of uncounted black persons to the 1960 Census totals did caution against associating field office difficulties with suspected urban undercounts, and the presumed relationship has, therefore, remained an open issue.

Indeed, as preparations for the 1970 Census proceeded, the Bureau continued to consider the possibility that a large portion of the 1960 undercount occurred in parts of the South.[18] To date, evidence on this point is inconclusive, and may be supported only by assumptions about the accuracy of census data on interstate and interregional migration. If sufficiently refined, however, undercount estimates for states could provide an independent basis on which the hypothesis that guided the choice of places for intensive enumeration in 1970 could be re-examined.

Finally, it is conceivable that very little of what is known or suspected about undercounting in 1960 is relevant to what occurred in the 1970 Census or will occur in the future. Population mobility can reasonably be thought to have impeded census operations in the North and Midwest 10 years ago, but, in 1970, the principal problems may have stemmed from the hostility and resistance of groups that find themselves trapped in decaying urban ghettos. Or it may be that the rapid growth of a number of southern cities during the last decade had important, though unanticipated, effects on the pattern of undercounting there. One of the most important lessons to be learned from the many attempts to achieve complete or nearly complete census coverage is that the census is inextricably embedded in a network of social relationships that are undergoing change sufficiently significant in scale to strain even the most carefully designed efforts to understand and reduce counting deficiencies.

OTHER HYPOTHESES ABOUT CENSUS UNDERCOUNTING

Much speculation about the causes of census underenumeration centers on the high incidence of undercounting among young black men. This focus, as noted earlier, is the result of a fairly recent confluence between exigent social policy concerns and census coverage priorities.[19] Following the 1950 Census, when the first comprehensive studies of census undercounting were completed and published,[20] speculation about the causes of underenumeration ranged more widely and led to an initial array of experiments and procedural changes that crisscrossed a wide spectrum of possibilities.

For example, a study of the completeness of census counts of infants was undertaken in 1950. Unexpectedly, the test revealed that in 80 percent of the cases where infants had been missed, their parents, often young adults living in the homes of relatives, had also been missed.[21]

Similarly, it has long been suspected that age-reporting errors account for a large proportion of what otherwise appear to be undercounts of persons over 50 years of age. The contention is that undercount estimates contain a net overstatement of the number of persons aged 65 and older, with a corresponding net understatement in the immediately preceding age categories. Modest research efforts have thus far produced no significant conclusions one way or the other, but the age-reporting hypothesis has never been completely discarded.[22]

Another line of inquiry that has been intensively pursued might be termed the "frictional undercount" hypothesis—that is, the contribution to errors in a census made by persons who are hired to collect and process census data under unusually heavy workload conditions. The experience of all survey research organizations attests to the advantages of having a corps of highly trained individuals to carry out the detailed operations that large household surveys characteristically involve. Moreover, a study of learning curves for Current Population Survey interviewers (who are permanent, part-time Census Bureau employees) "has shown that two and one-half years are required for an interviewer to achieve peak performance ... as measured by noninterview rates and the frequency of edit [misclassification] problems...."[23]

Such extensive on-the-job training is not possible for the thousands of enumerators who are hired to take the census once every 10 years. Numerous opportunities for error are also created by the rapid, short-term organizational expansion that each census requires. Consequently, the Census Bureau early concluded that underenumeration might well be due in part to deficiencies in its own field operations.

Two decades of procedural innovation, testing, and evaluation have, however, yielded fewer encouraging results than originally anticipated. Two post-enumeration surveys and several enumerator and coding variance studies have identified and measured census staff contributions to reporting and tabulation errors, but the principal light they shed on the causes of undercoverage was the finding that enumerators missed more than half the estimated number of uncounted persons identified by the 1960 PES because they failed to canvass entire households. Such a finding was significant. It is one factor that accounts for the introduction of the census-by-mail in 1970, but it also has suggested to the Census Bureau that there are limits to the explanatory potential of what once appeared to be a most promising line of investigation.

There are aspects of frictional undercounting that still merit exploration. The 1970 Census evaluation program includes, for example, studies of the adequacy of the mail address register, of errors occasioned by misapplication of the census housing definition, and of reporting and tabulation inaccuracies. There has also been measurement of the errors associated with certain standard features of the census, such as the length of census questionnaires, and continuing discussion of the possible effects of the mandatory response requirement and of respondents' doubts about official assurances that census data on individuals will be held in strictest confidence.

The Census Bureau regards the two-stage enumeration procedure used in the 1960 Census as, in effect, a nationwide experiment with a shorter questionnaire that produced no substantial change in net undercoverage.[24] However, whether a different kind of short questionnaire would have produced different results remains a topic for further inquiry.

The mandatory response and confidentiality provisions have been examined only tentatively. It has been felt that the former is likely to encourage enumeration among the groups that are least well counted and that the second cannot be adequately studied until more is known about the social characteristics and distinguishing ways of life of uncounted persons. The government has rarely prosecuted anyone for failing to respond to census queries, and long experience with household surveys has convinced the Bureau that most people do not have to be persuaded to cooperate, *once they have been personally contacted by an enumerator*. The difficulty is that missed persons are, by definition, not contacted by anyone, anywhere, so that it is impossible to know with certainty what may cause them to remain uncounted. Disclosure surely has different implications for illegal occupants of public housing than for middle-class citizens concerned about alleged government "snooping." So also, misreporting on income and other census items may be motivated by a variety of considerations corresponding to specific circumstances in which respondents find themselves or to their different perceptions of the uses of census data. But it remains a matter of conjecture whether what is known or might be learned about such circumstances and perceptions will prove in any way useful for understanding why the very existence of certain persons is overlooked or concealed.

THE IMPORTANCE OF MULTIPLE LINES OF INQUIRY

In retrospect, the limited explanatory capacity of so many common-sense hypotheses about the causes of underenumeration can be seen to have slowly turned attention away from alleged defects in census field operations toward closer examination of the social characteristics and hypothesized life ways of undercounted groups. The BLS-Census studies of uncounted men in New Haven and Trenton are symptomatic of the changed perspective. So, in fact, is the establishment of the Advisory Committee on Problems of Census Enumeration. Both reflect a tentative reformulation of the undercount problem in terms of adaptive human behavior associated with being poor, a victim of racial or social discrimination, and an inhabitant of blighted places seldom visited by the society's more affluent and more secure members.

It would, however, be unfortunate if the new cast of thinking were to lead to a narrowing of the range of hypotheses advanced or of the categories of undercounted persons to be considered. There is still insufficient evidence to warrant concluding that the majority of uncounted persons is to be found at one extreme of the economic spectrum, or to assert that being black makes a person less likely to be counted than, say, being poor or functionally illiterate, or even moderately wealthy and very mobile.

The attention recently focused on black undercounts is long overdue and should be maintained, but race should not be viewed as an explanatory variable of such overwhelming importance as to discourage investigation of other characteristics that more directly account for the exclusion of people from the census. While undercount estimates by age, sex, and race serve clear purposes in the collection and publication of official social statistics, they are not adequate guides for the design of research intended to improve census coverage. There is a danger, in other words, that the practice of presenting census undercount estimates by age, sex, and race will turn out to be an unfortunate example of the way in which data-classification frameworks affect thinking about social problems.

Several different factors are surely responsible for underenumeration. Hence, although the evidence of black undercoverage is dramatic, there is a need for research along other lines of investigation tied to different causal hypotheses. For example, an unexplained result of demographic analysis of census counts is that coverage of nonwhite females appears to decline as the cohorts age, while the pattern for nonwhite males is, also inexplicably, the reverse. The data hint, moreover, that not being counted, for both whites and Negroes, has something to do with being young and, therefore, perhaps relatively unencumbered by conventional social linkages that make the vast majority of the population readily locatable. Inquiry into the distinguishing characteristics and life styles associated with under-coverage of middle-aged black women and young adults would be worth-while in itself and might also illuminate the enumeration problems of other categories of undercounted persons.

The need for multiple research approaches and complementary lines of inquiry should be strongly stressed. In later chapters of this report, several additional research approaches are recommended. However, both the Census Bureau and other sponsors and performers of census-related research should also rethink and rework the findings of previous studies of undercounting in the light of recent hypotheses. Census research and field reports suggest that data from the 1960 PES, for example, could be retabulated to provide greater information on the relationship between the social characteristics of "subsequently found" households and the social and behavioral characteristics of enumerators and other census field personnel who failed to count such households in the census but located them in the PES.

In addition, it is important to be aware of how the objectives and intellectual style of the research staffs of the Census Bureau and other agencies with an interest in enumeration problems appear to have affected past research on the census. Much of the evaluative research on the census during the last two decades has concentrated on developing statistical procedures and household interviewing methods that would improve the quality of the census generally. Hence, strong emphasis has been placed both on measuring the extent of systematic error and dispersion in the responses made to standard census queries by various groups in the population and on devising new enumeration techniques, such as the census-by-mail.

That work has been highly successful. Moreover, the basic mode of analysis is a powerful tool for many purposes, as the greatly improved quality of census statistics indicates. It seems reasonable to expect, however, that research on the census and on similar social data-gathering activities could be further improved by expanding the amount of attention given to the behavioral and social aspects of the enumeration process. The Census

Bureau has already made a start in that direction, as indicated by its role in the casual setting interview studies and by its demonstrated interest in ethnographic research as a means of developing new hypotheses about the causes of census errors.[25] Nevertheless, development of behavioral and social science research perspectives could be more fully encouraged and should be made a more central feature of the overall census research effort.

NOTES

1. For detailed expositions of the estimation methods used, see Ansley J. Coale, "The Population of the United States in 1950 Classified by Age, Sex, and Color—A Revision of Census Figures," *Journal of the American Statistical Association*, 50, 1955, pp. 16–54; Morris H. Hansen, Leon Pritzker, and Joseph Steinberg, "The Evaluation and Research Program of the 1960 Censuses," *Proceedings of the Social Statistics Section of the American Statistical Association*, 1959, pp. 172–180; Conrad Taeuber and Morris Hansen, "A Preliminary Evaluation of the 1960 Censuses of Population and Housing," *Proceedings of the Social Statistics Section of the American Statistical Association*, 1963, pp. 56–73; U.S. Bureau of the Census, *Evaluation and Research Program of the U.S. Censuses of Population and Housing, 1960: Record Check Studies of Population Coverage*, Series ER60, No. 2 (Washington, D.C.: U.S. Government Printing Office), 1964; Melvin Zelnik, "Errors in the 1960 Census Enumeration of Native Whites," *Journal of the American Statistical Association*, 59, 1964, pp. 437–459; Jacob S. Siegel and Melvin Zelnik, "An Evaluation of Coverage in the 1960 Census of Population by Techniques of Demographic Analysis and by Composite Methods," *Proceedings of the Social Statistics Section of the American Statistical Association*, 1966, pp. 71–85; Melvin Zelnik, "An Examination of Alternative Estimates of Net Census Undercount by Age, Sex, and Color," Paper contributed to the Annual Meeting of the Population Association of America, New York, N.Y., April 1966; Jacob S. Siegel, "Completeness of Coverage of the Nonwhite Population in the 1960 Census and Current Estimates, and Some Implications," in David M. Heer (Ed.), *Social Statistics and the City* (Cambridge, Massachusetts: Harvard University Press for the Joint Center for Urban Studies of the Massachusetts Institute of Technology and Harvard University), 1968, pp. 13–54; and Jacob S. Siegel, "Coverage of Population in the 1970 Census: Preliminary Findings and Research Plans," Paper presented at the Annual Meeting of the American Statistical Association, Detroit, Michigan, December, 1970.

2. In 1960, the color category "nonwhite" included Negroes, Indians, Japanese, Chinese, Filipinos, Aleuts, Eskimos, Hawaiians, part-Hawaiians, Asian Indians, Koreans, Malayans, and other racial or ethnic groups of non-European or non-Near Eastern origin. An explanation of the concept of race, as used by the Census Bureau in 1960, will be found in U.S. Bureau of the Census, *Characteristics of Population, 1960 Census of Population*, Part I, "U.S. Summary" (Washington, D.C.: U.S. Government Printing Office), November 1963, p. xli. Since Negroes comprise over 90 percent of all nonwhites in the United States, the 1960 count of nonwhites is often used to represent the Negro population. In 1970, however, separate tabulations will normally be made for whites, Negroes, and "other races."

3. Leon Pritzker and N. D. Rothwell, "Procedural Difficulties in Taking Past Censuses in Predominantly Negro, Puerto Rican, and Mexican Areas," in David M. Heer (Ed.), *Social Statistics and the City* (Cambridge, Massachusetts: Harvard University Press for the Joint Center for

Urban Studies of the Massachusetts Institute of Technology and Harvard University), 1968, p. 66.

4. *Ibid.*, p. 64.

5. *Ibid.*, p. 66.

6. The distinction between a "pretest" and a "dress rehearsal" is that no previously untried procedures are used in the latter.

7. The Trenton study was actually funded by the Trenton Model Cities Agency.

8. In a third related project, the Bureau of Labor Statistics (B L S) attempted to obtain household interviews with individuals identified from lists of workers in low-paying jobs in New York City. Results of all three studies have been summarized by Deborah P. Klein in "Determining the Labor Force Status of Men Missed in the Census," U.S. Bureau of Labor Statistics, *Special Labor Force Report 117* (Washington, D.C.: U.S. Government Printing Office), March 1970. An earlier report on the New Haven and New York experience will be found, alog with a description of the B L S pilot research program, in U.S. Bureau of Labor Statistics, *Pilot and Experimental Program on Urban Employment Surveys, Report No. 354* (Washington, D.C.: U.S. Government Printing Office), March 1969.

9. Interestingly, however, a principal finding of the New Haven and Trenton studies was that "the labor force status of the undercount group was very much like the labor force status of their neighbors who were counted." Klein, *op. cit.*, p. 28.

10. For example, one fifth of the Trenton respondents were recent immigrants from Puerto Rico. Differences in industrial and residential location patterns could also be a factor. A wise recommendation emanating from the casual setting interview research is that similar studies be carried out "in cities and towns of different sizes and with different racial compositions." *Pilot and Experimental Program on Urban Employment Surveys, op. cit.*, p. 27.

11. U.S. Bureau of the Census, "A Proposed Coverage-Improvement Program for the 1970 Census," Response Research Branch Report No. 67–14 (Unpublished), May 5, 1967, p. 2. In addition, field canvass records for the 1960 Census show that, while 98 percent of the enumeration had been completed by April 30, "the remaining two percent was not completed until mid-July. Lags were concentrated in New York, Chicago, Los Angeles, and several other large cities." Pritzker and Rothwell, *op. cit.*, p. 70.

12. See, for example, George Gallup's remarks in the *New York Times* of November 1, 1968: ". . . the difficulties of doing a scientific poll in Harlem are extreme. . . . The normal living patterns are completely disarranged. . . . They just don't want to talk to a stranger." Quoted in Earle J. Gerson, "Methodological and Interviewing Problems in Household Surveys of Employment Problems in Urban Poverty Neighborhoods," *Proceedings of the Social Statistics Section of the American Statistical Association*, 1969, p. 23.

13. See U.S. Bureau of Labor Statistics and U.S. Bureau of the Census, "The Social and Economic Status of Negroes in the United States, 1969," *BLS Report No. 375*, and *Current Population Reports*, Series P–23, No. 29 (Washington, D.C.: U.S. Government Printing Office), 1970.

14. See, for example Pritzker and Rothwell *op. cit.*, p. 68:

. . . a low sex ratio has been historically an urban phenomenon both for native whites and for Negroes. Although the observed consistently low urban sex ratios for whites as well as for Negroes may result from differential migration of women to cities, our conjecture is that relatively high underenumeration of males in urban areas also contributes to it. At any rate, it is clear that the observed decline in combined urban and rural Negro sex ratios, as measured, can be entirely accounted for by the rapid urbanization of the Negro population. Standardization based on the 1900 Census proportions of rural and urban population produces nearly identical sex ratios in every decade from 1900 to 1960.

15. The special efforts included (a) establishment of a corps of "community educators" six months in advance of the census; (b) use of publicity media and local organizations to heighten awareness that a census was being taken; (c) more intensive training and supervision of

enumerators; (d) more extensive use of hourly-rate enumerators; (e) a special check of the completeness of the mail-out/ mail-back address register; and (f) a "missed persons" campaign to identify persons who thought they were not counted, or whom others regarded as not likely to have been counted.

16. The hypothesis was explored further, albeit with inconclusive results, by a Subcommittee of the Advisory Committee. For details, see Appendix B, pp. 130–138 in *America's Uncounted People*.

17. Pritzker and Rothwell, *op. cit.*, p. 64.

18. U.S. Bureau of the Census, "The Coverage-Improvement Program for the 1970 Census," Response Research Branch Report No. 69–9 (R) (Unpublished), July 22, 1969, p. 3.

19. For an illuminating overview of the historical linkages between coverage priorities and public policy issues, see Hyman Alterman, *Counting People: The Census in History* (New York: Harcourt, Brace & World), 1969, especially Chapters 7 and 8.

20. Coale, *op. cit.*, and U.S. Bureau of the Census, "The Post Enumeration Survey: 1950," Bureau of the Census Technical Paper No. 4 (Washington, D.C.: U.S. Government Printing Office), 1960. A number of earlier studies using demographic analysis had shown problems in the coverage of infants in the population census, not only in the United States but also in other parts of the world.

21. U.S. Bureau of the Census, *Infant Enumeration Study: 1950*, Procedural Studies of the 1950 Censuses, No. 1 (Washington, D.C.: U.S. Government Printing Office), 1953.

22. Hansen and Taeuber have seriously questioned it, however. See Hansen and Taeuber, *op. cit.*, pp. 59–60.

23. Gerson, *op. cit.*

24. In the 1960 Census, households were enumerated in two stages. In the initial round, respondents were asked to answer only the eleven basic demographic and housing questions. Longer sample questionnaires were not delivered until enumerators canvassed each household to retrieve the information on the short forms.

Introduction: B. The Theory
of Demography

Throughout this book there are a number of theories relating to different aspects of population (especially migration and fertility). I have tried to select papers for this section that show something about those population theories that purport to explain the totality of population growth or decline.

As the article by Judy K. Morris shows, the famous *Essay on the Principle of Population* by Thomas Robert Malthus was such a total theory of population, even though it was also a political-philosophical-moralistic document. Malthus argued from some simple premises about the potential of humans to reproduce and the potential of the earth to provide the resources necessary to support a growing population. Basically, his theory advanced the principle that the capacity for human reproduction was much greater than the earth's production of resources. Therefore, he concluded, the earth and its resources would always set severe limits on population growth. While Malthus's theory is still widely accepted today as an explanation of human poverty and hardship, it cannot be said that it is a highly sophisticated theory of population. The importance of Malthus's work lies more in the area of what it has meant for the growth and development of demography and its influence on the population policies of many countries. Malthus did two things with regard to the study of population: (1) he brought the study of population into the realm of empirical science, i.e., the testing of theory with data, while at the same time (2) he emphasized the poverty and misery associated with excessive numbers of people, and thus made population a *social prob-lem*. Since the main thrust of early sociology in the United States was a concern about social or societal problems, it was probably natural that some American sociologists should be attracted to the study of population.

In addition to a theory of population there was clearly an ideo-logical side to the work of Malthus. He was a political economist, and he was convinced that any governmental efforts to improve the condi-tions of the poor (through welfare plans) would only serve to let them have more children, which would lower their living conditions even more. The most noteworthy negative reaction to this ideological posi-tion, and thus the theory, was that of Karl Marx. Marx argued that the poverty and misery of many people was not caused by overpop-ulation, but by the unequal distribution of resources under the capital-ist economic system. This opposition of Marx to Malthus has carried through in socialist doctrine until this very day. Many socialist politi-cal leaders have refused to accept the idea of overpopulation and a "population explosion" and have therefore opposed population poli-cies that would limit or curtail birth rates.

While the socialist position opposing population control has been an impediment to efforts to control population growth, there are now signs that in the communist countries there is a recognition of the dangers of a rapidly growing world population. In particular, the Soviet Union has changed from its long-standing anti-Malthusian po-sition to a policy of limited support for population control. The Chi-nese, while vacillating between energetic birth-control programs and no program at all, now seem to be taking many steps that will keep their population from growing too fast.

Other theories of population are well defined and characterized in the article by Kurt Mayer. In this paper Mayer summarizes and evaluates most of the major historically important population the-ories. He closes with a discussion of "transition theory" in which he notes that while it has been acclaimed for some time "the validity of transition theory has been severely questioned in recent years." My paper (article 13) takes a close look at one of those criticisms and finds that much of the criticism has not been as carefully scrutinized as it might have been. The theory of modern demographic transition remains "as one of the best documented generalizations in the social sciences."[1] Students who want to get a grasp of what has happened to world population in the last three hundred years, and what has "caused" the population explosion in the twentieth century will find it a convenient and parsimonious explanatory framework.

---

[1] William Petersen, *Population* (2nd ed.; New York: Macmillan & Co., 1969), p. 11.

11

Professor Malthus and His Essay

Judy K. Morris

I think I may fairly make two postulata.

First, that food is necessary to the existence of man.

Secondly, That the passion between the sexes is necessary, and will remain nearly in its present state.

Assuming, . . . my postulata as granted, I say, that the power of population is indefinitely greater than the power in the earth to produce subsistence for man.—Robert Malthus, 1798

The Reverend Robert Malthus (Malthus preferred to drop the "Thomas"), Professor of History and Political Economy at East India College, Hailey-bury, England, was not a man one would expect to stir up controversy. He took religious orders, according to the head of his college, because "the utmost of his wishes was a retired living in the country."

In an age when prolonged public debate was a major British pastime, Malthus avoided the game. Eager for discussion with the economist David Ricardo, he "took the liberty of introducing himself," hoping that, "as we are *mainly* on the same side of the question, we might supersede the necessity of a long controversy in print respecting the points in which we differ, by an amicable discussion in private."

The first edition of Malthus's famous work, *An Essay on the Principle of Population,* was published anonymously.

But this reticent man, when quite young, stumbled upon a subject which dominated his life and caused his name to be very much on the public tongue: his controversial "principle of population." The essential concept of the principle lay in what Malthus saw as a tendency toward imbalance between the rates of growth of a population and its food supply. To

Reprinted from *Population Bulletin,* 22, no. 1 (February, 1966), pp. 7–27, by permission of the publisher, Population Reference Bureau, Inc., Washington, D.C.

balance the two, Malthus said, nature used both "preventive" and "positive" (war, plague, famine, and the ubiquitous "vice") checks to population.

Interest generated by his pronouncements, as well as a flow of new information, led Malthus to revise and republish his *Essay* five times. Malthus's principle of population appears to be as relevant today—200 years after his birth—as it was in 1798, when the *Essay* first appeared. That Malthus's views remain controversial is perhaps symbolic of the confusion in which the population problem is cast, even in this assumedly enlightened age.

Even today Malthus is still coolly dismissed or roundly denounced in some quarters. But, while population is growing as never before, in most of the world it does not thrive. The number of people now on the verge of falling victim to what Malthus saw as the ultimate check to population—famine—*is twice the total population of the world when he wrote his* Essay.

Malthus's fundamental concept remains unchallenged: *Unchecked population growth accelerates faster than the greatest increases of food that man is able to wrest from the earth on a sustained basis.*

The controversy which this idea engendered has had such wide-ranging consequences that Malthus stands as one of the select few who have made unique and enduring contributions to man's understanding of himself and of his place on this planet.

THE MISUNDERSTOOD MAN

Any controversial figure is subject to rumor, innuendo, and misunderstanding, and Malthus was no exception. For example, he has come to be known as the "gloomy parson."

Actually, he was rather a cheerful person. It is true that he was not one to gloss over the grim realities of life, as in this statement: "It has appeared, that from the inevitable laws of our nature, some human beings must suffer from want. These are the unhappy persons who, in the great lottery of life, have drawn a blank." But he also called life "a blessing." In his introduction to the *Essay*, he attempted to forestall a "gloomy" view of his personality by denying he had "a jaundiced eye, or an inherent spleen of disposition."

Technically, Malthus was a "parson." In 1803, he was appointed to a rectory in Haileybury, a position he held the rest of his life. Actually, he left his parish in the charge of a succession of curates. His real vocation was as a professor of political economy. No less an authority than John Maynard Keynes has given him the highest marks in economics: "If only Malthus, instead of Ricardo, had been the parent stem from which nineteenth-century economics proceeded, what a much wiser and richer place the world would be today!"

A more serious misconception links Malthus with the movement promoting the use of birth-control devices. In fact, he abhorred even the idea of contraception, which he referred to delicately as "improper arts." As will be noted later in this discussion, he paradoxically advocated large families at the same time forecasting the imminence of mass famine.

Perhaps most surprising, Malthus thus by no means frowned on large and growing populations. On the contrary, he said: "That an increase of population, when it follows in its natural order, is both a great positive good in itself, and absolutely necessary to a further increase in the annual produce of the land and labour of any country, I should be the last to deny. The only question is, what is the order of its progress?"

Malthus wanted men to "unite the two grand *desiderata*, a great actual population and a state of society in which abject poverty and dependence are comparatively but little known." In the appendix to the third edition of his *Essay*, he complained of criticism which proceeded ". . . upon the very strange supposition that the *ultimate* object of my work is to check population, as if anything could be more desirable than the most rapid increase of population, unaccompanied by vice and misery. But of course my ultimate object is to diminish vice and misery, and any checks to population which may have been suggested are solely as means to accomplish this end."

Malthus was concerned with nature's often cruel ways of eliminating "redundant" populations. He never referred to a "population problem," only to the problems of misery and vice, of poverty and labor surpluses, resulting from too-rapid growth.

He frequently discussed the application of his "principle of population" as it related to social conditions in England. His conviction—shocking to many then and now, but based for Malthus on the feudal antecedents of his society—was that the poor, through overbreeding, were largely responsible for their condition. He said, in effect, those who have ceased to have the power to eat or to live, ceased to have the right: that there is no inherent right to sustenance. By pretending otherwise, society misleads and cruelly disappoints the poor. He advised the poor to forgo marriage until they could support their offspring, thus limiting their numbers, tightening the labor market, and raising wages.

Malthus was not a prudish person who disapproved of sex. The *Essay* contains occasional hymns to "virtuous love":

> Virtuous love, exalted by friendship, seems to be that sort of mixture of sensual and intellectual enjoyment, particularly suited to the nature of man, and most powerfully calculated to awaken the sympathies of the soul, and produce the most exquisite gratifications. Perhaps there is scarcely a man, who has once experienced the genuine delight of vir-

tuous love, however great his intellectual pleasures may have been, who does not look back to that period as the sunny spot in his whole life. . . .

He regarded "the passion between the sexes" as mankind's unique characteristic and a great force for potential good: ". . . we appear to have under our guidance a great power, capable of peopling a desert region in a small number of years; and yet, under other circumstances, capable of being confined by human energy and virtue to any limits however narrow, at the expense of a small comparative quantity of evil."

Malthus was indebted to the work of many other men for ideas which contributed to the development of his theories. Conversely, others were indebted to him. For instance, Charles Darwin found the inspiration for his law of evolution by natural selection in the *Essay:*

> I happened to read for amusement Malthus on Population, and being well prepared to appreciate the struggle for existence which everywhere goes on, from long-continued observation in the habits of animals and plants, it at once struck me that under these circumstances favourable variations tend to be preserved, and unfavorable ones to be destroyed. The result of this would be the formation of new species. Here then I had at least got a theory by which to work.

Alfred Russel Wallace, who simultaneously and independently arrived at an identical theory, also found his inspiration in the *Essay.* As the crucial spark for this epochal idea alone, Malthus's place in history is secure.

CURRICULUM VITAE

Depending upon the source one chooses, Thomas Robert Malthus was born either on St. Valentine's Day, February 14, 1766, or on the 13th. In any case, according to a brief biography of the essayist by Lord Keynes, Jean Jacques Rousseau and David Hume visited Malthus's father three weeks after his son's birth. Keynes suggests these "two fairy godmothers . . . may be presumed to have assigned to the infant with a kiss diverse intellectual gifts." The baby was not so lucky in another respect: Malthus had a harelip which rendered his speech defective throughout his life.

Malthus was born into a middle-class family at a small but elegant mansion in farming country near Dorking, just south of London. Among his forebears were the Vicar of Northolt, the apothecary to King William, and a director of the South Sea Company. Malthus's father, Daniel, was an Oxford-educated country gentleman, who led an earnestly intellectual life. Daniel corresponded with Rousseau and, according to family legend, with Voltaire. Young Robert was brought up in a world of very advanced ideas.

James Bonar, a late 19th-Century biographer, described the England of Malthus's youth:

> The early life of Malthus . . . coincides of necessity with the accomplishment of England's greatest industrial revolution. Malthus was born in 1776, three years after the Peace of Paris. There was an end, for the time, to foreign wars; and trade was making a brave start. The discoveries of coal and iron in northern England, going hand in hand with the inventions of cotton-spinning and weaving, were beginning to convert the poorest counties into the richest, upsetting the political balance. The new science of chemistry had begun to prove its usefulness. Wedgwood was perfecting his earthenware, Brindley cutting his canals, Telford laying out his roads, Watt building his steam-engines. England in Roman days had been a granary; in later ages she had been a pasture-ground; she was now becoming the land of machinery and manufacture, as well as the centre of foreign trade.

Malthus was tutored at home during his early years, then went to Jesus College, Cambridge, which was then becoming a center of intellectual ferment. He took his Holy Orders about 1788, but spent little time at his ecclesiastical post.

He married in 1804, the year after the second edition of the *Essay* was published. Of his three children, two were daughters, one of whom died young. According to Lord Keynes, Malthus has no descendants today.

In 1805, Malthus was appointed to the college established by the East India Company for the training of young men entering its service. He apparently enjoyed teaching, for he remained in his Chair at Haileybury for the rest of his life. And his students apparently enjoyed him, for they called him "Pop." A Whig, he was by no means isolated from current political and economic ideas and Mrs. Malthus's evening parties drew the elite of the London scientific world.

His duties as a professor included occasional preaching, frequently on the benevolence of God. His continuing religious dedication is obvious, particularly in the conclusion of the first edition of his *Essay*, where he defends God against those who complained that He brought misery, the "checks" to population, into man's life. Even in the more worldly second edition, he saw the Creator's plan thus:

> . . . we can have no reason to impeach the justice of the Deity because his general laws make this virtue [restraint from marriage] necessary and punish our offences against it by the evils attendant upon vice, and the pains that accompany the various forms of premature death. A really virtuous society, such as I have supposed, would avoid these evils. It is the apparent object of the Creator to deter us from vice by

the pains which accompany it, and to lead us to virtue by the happiness that it produces.

Malthus produced so many books, articles, and papers in his field of political economy as to suggest that early 19th-Century academe had its own version of the "publish or perish" dictum. Perhaps his greatest legacy in the field is the long series of letters exchanged during his friendly debate with David Ricardo. Their friendship, begun with Malthus's hesitant self-introduction in 1811, lasted until Ricardo's death in 1823. Malthus said of Ricardo: "I never loved anybody out of my own family so much. Our interchange of opinions was so unreserved, and the object after which we were both enquiring was so entirely the truth . . . that I cannot but think we sooner or later must have agreed."

In his biography, Lord Keynes described the varying approaches of Malthus and Ricardo, and then cast his own vote:

> Here indeed, are to be found the seeds of economic theory, and also the divergent lines—so divergent at the outset that the destination can scarcely be recognised as the same until it is reached—along which the subject can be developed. Ricardo is investigating the theory of the *distribution* of the product in conditions of equilibrium, and Malthus is concerned with what determines the *volume* of output day by day in the real world. Malthus is dealing with the monetary economy in which we all happen to live; Ricardo with the abstraction of a neutral money economy. . . .
>
> One cannot rise from a perusal of this correspondence without a feeling that the almost total obliteration of Malthus's line of approach and the complete domination of Ricardo's for a period of a hundred years has been a disaster to the progress of economics. Time after time in these letters Malthus is talking plain sense, the force of which Ricardo with his head in the clouds wholly fails to comprehend.

Applying his "plain sense" to another field, Malthus believed that authors who were proclaiming the perfectibility of man and society could not ignore the tendency of population to outgrow food supplies. The down-to-earth scholar took on the idealists in 1798, with the publication of the first edition of his *Essay*. He was 32.

His concern for getting to the truth of the human condition led him into extensive research and travel to find evidence to corroborate his theories. His findings and expanded thought led to the second edition in 1803. He continued to expound his themes in additional revised editions, the last in 1826, and in an article for the 1824 supplement to the *Encyclopaedia Britannica*. Malthus died at age 68 in 1834.

THE BEST OF TIMES, THE WORST OF TIMES

Like the rumblings of the scientific revolutions, those of the American and the French revolutions promising universal equality were heard in all Western nations at the turn of the 19th Century. Charles Dickens was to call this "the best of times . . . the worst of times." Liberals dreamed of drastic changes in the social order which would enable man to achieve his potential best. Those in power had nightmares of mass uprisings which would sweep away their established rule. The English Poor Laws—in effect since the time of Queen Elizabeth—quite obviously were not alleviating the lot of the poverty-stricken; rather, the poor grew in number. The English aristocracy feared any worsening of conditions might well trigger a revolution.

It was a time when theories abounded—aired in multitudinous pamphlets and shouted in the public houses. An idea was advanced and immediately answered, often with a volley of tracts. Everyone, it seemed, had his own intellectual foxhole. In Malthus's opinion:

> The late rage for wide and unrestrained speculation seems to have been a kind of mental intoxication, arising perhaps from the great and unexpected discoveries which had been made in various branches of science. To men elate and giddy with such successes, everything appeared to be within the grasp of human powers; and under this illusion they confounded subjects where no real progress could be proved with those where the progress had been marked, certain, and acknowledged.

It was a time of war and uneasy peace. Perhaps the radical concepts in Malthus's *Essay* were as widely accepted as they were, despite much dissent, because England was in and out of war, and the island nation could well imagine the horrors of food shortages. Five years of poor harvests preceded the publication of the first edition; severe food shortages continued through the first quarter of the 19th Century.

England's population was growing rapidly, although the surprising dimensions of the growth were not then known. The first British census (1801) was not taken until three years after the *Essay* first appeared. Compulsory registration of births and deaths did not begin until 1837, three years after Malthus died. Until then, church records of baptisms and burials served as the vital statistics of the realm. Nevertheless, with his acute interest in the economic situation, Malthus recognized that the poor were increasing with a consequent growth in unemployment.

Demographers have established that England's death rate began a long and steady decline in 1740, whereas the birth rate remained fairly high until the last quarter of the 19th Century. Offhand references in Malthus's *Essay* bring home sharply what a high death rate meant: "One out of five children is a very unusually small proportion to lose in the course of ten years," he said. And later, "The average age of marriage will almost always be much nearer to the average age of death than marriage is to birth. . . ."

In 1740 both birth and death rates were about 36 in England and Wales; in 1840, the birth rate was 37, the death rate was down to 23. In the half century before Malthus wrote his *Essay*, England's population grew sizeably. And, during the years he was revising it, the population took on a new pattern of very rapid growth. England and Wales had an estimated population of about 6 million in 1700; the 1801 Census counted 8.6 million; the 1901 Census counted a fourfold increase to 32.5 million. This rapid growth occurred despite massive emigration. Farming techniques improved, industry demanded more people to man its factories, industrial England traded with the world and was able to support her additional millions partly by increased agricultural production but mainly by food imports. Although poverty was not banished, the population of England boomed.

Amid the turmoil of ideas, Malthus's were not new. Forty years earlier, Dr. Robert Wallace mentioned excessive population growth as an obstacle to a more perfect human society. In his first preface, Malthus described his debt to, and differences from, earlier writers:

> It is an obvious truth, which has been taken notice of by many writers, that population must always be kept down to the level of the means of subsistence; but no writer, that the Author recollects, has inquired particularly into the means by which this level is effected; and it is a view of these means, which forms, to his mind, the strongest obstacle in the way to any very great improvement of society.

THE SIX EDITIONS, AND HOW THEY GREW

Malthus wrote his *Essay on the Principle of Population* to put in order thoughts roused in continuing discussion with his father, Daniel, over the "future improvement of society." The seed of the argument lay in some proposals by William Godwin, a utopian anarchist, political philosopher, and sometime novelist.

Godwin's treatises criticizing established society and proposing a system based on reason and innate human justice rather than on law had attracted a substantial and vociferous following, including the poet Percy Bysshe Shelley. . . .

Daniel Malthus supported Godwin's convictions. His son Robert thought Godwin, and others who postulated ideal societies, made a fatal error in ignoring population growth and the forces which checked it. If ideal societies were established, he reasoned, hunger, jealousy, and antagonism would soon mar these perfect states and restore the familiar competitive world.

His *Essay* held that the various proposals for the perfectibility of society had not been subjected to careful and dispassionate scrutiny. This first edition presented an untypically abstract formulation of Malthus's understanding of population growth and checks, with brief references to existing and former societies. It was marked by a philosophic, even theological, acceptance of the demographic situation as Malthus saw it.

The full title of the first edition was: *An Essay on the Principle of Population as it affects the Future Improvement of Society, with remarks on the Speculations of Mr. Godwin, M. Condorcet, and other writers.* The concluding chapter heading suggested a somber outlook indeed: "Moral evil probably necessary to the production of moral excellence."

The second edition took a more hopeful view. It was entitled: *An Essay on the Principle of Population or, A view of its past and present effects on Human Happiness; with an enquiry into our prospects respecting the future removal or mitigation of the evils which it occasions.* The final chapter heading carried a definite banner of hope: "Of our rational expectations respecting the future improvement of society."

Fully half the second edition was devoted to a detailed examination of how the principle of population worked and identification of the checks which operated in past and contemporary societies. In this extensive revision, Malthus adjusted and fleshed out his basic theory. His approach, this time, was altogether worldly. The second edition was cast in the terms of politics, economics, and history.

He refuted the systems of equality suggested by Godwin *et al.*, and applied his own analysis to the economic and political problems of contemporary England: the Poor Laws, the Corn Laws, the optimum proportions of agriculture and commerce for a national economy. For instance, Malthus warned England that the new nation, America, would soon be setting up mills and factories and processing its own raw materials. England, he said, must be prepared to cease counting on America both as a supplier of raw goods and as a buyer of finished goods.

The last quarter of the book introduced his most important new principle: the possibility of encouraging moral restraint as a means of checking population growth with a minimum of human unhappiness.

Between the first (1798) and second (1803) editions, Malthus developed—from a reading of history, from current records, and from firsthand observations—the factual basis and substantive analysis he preferred to his first rather abstract approach. Among the sources cited are Robertson's *History of America* (1780), *Voyage dans l'Intérieur de l'Afrique,*

Cook's accounts of his three voyages, Hume's *Essays*, the Bible, Tacitus's *De Moribus Germanorum*, Gibbon's *Decline and Fall of the Roman Empire*, Tooke's *View of the Russian Empire*, and Plato's *The Republic*.

More current sources included parish registries, scientific papers, transactions of meetings, population abstracts, and bills of mortality. While, as Malthus noted, the first edition was written "on the impulse of the occasion, and from the few materials which were then within my reach in a country situation," he completely overcame this deficiency. The second edition—almost 600 pages of small type in the *Everyman* edition—is about four times the length of the first.

In his research on population growth, he found "much more had been done than I had been aware of . . . and the most violent remedies proposed, so long ago as the times of Plato and Aristotle." Many of his contemporaries, he reported, had treated the subject "in such a manner . . . as to create a natural surprise that it had not excited more of the public attention."

Some of the information he gathered during two European tours was too subjective to be of scientific value. About Norway—the country to which he gave highest marks for a robust economy and an awareness of the dangers of rapidly growing population—he said, "I particularly remarked that the sons of housemen and the farmers' boys were fatter, larger, and had better calves to their legs than boys of the same age and in similar situations in England."

Why the great variation in tone and content between the first two editions? Bonar suggested the "happy coincidence" that England was at war when the first was written and at peace five years later. Whatever the reason, one critic said that Malthus's changes, particularly the advocacy of moral restraint, indicated the essayist had abandoned his original argument. Another suggested it was Godwin himself, in a letter to Malthus (now lost), who recommended prudence to circumvent the dreadful checks.

As new information accumulated, and in order to respond to criticism and questions stirred by his work, Malthus revised and added to his *Essay* through a total of six editions. However, the later editions (1806, 1807, 1817, 1826) differed little from the second.

Joseph J. Spengler, Professor of Economics at Duke University, found increasingly in later editions the assertion that population growth depends on the availability of employment. In Malthus's *Principle of Political Economy* (1820), Spengler found this idea most fully developed: that the availability of sustenance determines the upper bound of population size, but within this limit the amount of available and prospective employment conditions the rise and fall of population.

THE PRINCIPLE OF POPULATION

Malthus's principle is succinct. After stating that "the power of population is indefinitely greater than the power in the earth to produce subsistence for man," he continued:

> Population, when unchecked, increases in a geometrical ratio. Subsistence only increases in an arithmetical ratio. A slight acquaintance with numbers will show the immensity of the first power in comparison of the second.
>
> By that law of our nature which makes food necessary to the life of man, the effects of these two unequal powers must be kept equal.
>
> This implies a strong and constantly operating check on population from the difficulty of subsistence. This difficulty must fall somewhere; and must necessarily be severely felt by a large portion of mankind. . . .
>
> Among plants and animals [the effects of this great restrictive law] are waste of seed, sickness, and premature death. Among mankind, misery and vice. . . . This natural inequality of the two powers of population, and of production in the earth, and that great law of our nature which must constantly keep their effects equal, form the great difficulty that to me appears insurmountable in the way to perfectibility of society. . . . I see no way by which man can escape from the weight of this law which pervades all animated nature. No fancied equality, no agrarian regulations in their utmost extent, could remove the pressure of it even for a single century.

In addition to the "positive" population checks (the "misery and vice" of famine, war, pestilence; "vicious customs with respect to women, great cities, unwholesome manufactures, luxury"), Malthus also noted the "preventive" check of restraint from early marriage during hard times, which tended to lower the number of births.

He cited the known doubling of the population in 25 years in the United States of America as proof that such a rate of increase was possible, though perhaps near a maximum.

Malthus said that, with great effort, a country might double its agricultural production in 25 years, but that it was impossible to double production again, to four times the original output, in the succeeding 25 years. The utmost one could hope for, he surmised, was an increase again equal to the original production: an arithmetical increase.

If, to begin with, the food supply met the needs of the population, it would again be sufficient after both had doubled in the first 25-year interval. If, during the succeeding 25 years, population again doubled but food only increased by the original amount, the food available per capita would be reduced by a fourth. With numbers pressing on marginal subsistence

Malthus saw the positive and preventive checks rigidly limiting further population growth.

Malthus was positive that in the end the checks would come into action:

> The different modes which nature takes to prevent, or repress a redundant population, do not appear, indeed, to us so certain and regular; but though we cannot always predict the mode, we may with certainty predict the fact. If the proportion of births to deaths for a few years indicate an increase of numbers much beyond the proportional increased or acquired produce of the country, we may be perfectly certain, that unless an emigration takes place, the deaths will shortly exceed the births. . . .

Actually, this tendency to geometric increase is a property of all living things. The *potential* for rapid increase is much greater in agricultural crops and herds than in human populations. Crop plants have a potential doubling time of less than one year, a fact which is utilized by plant breeders to multiply new strains with fantastic speed.

In agricultural practice, however, making two blades of grass or two bushels of wheat or rice grow where one grew before is no easy matter. Most of the good agricultural land in the world is already under cultivation. The land available for crops remains effectively constant from year to year. It is being farmed by methods—and with resources—which change very slowly. There is no question that improved techniques, better varieties, and increased use of fertilizer could provide an adequate diet for all the world's people. Agricultural production, world-wide, is currently increasing by about 1 percent a year, which will double production in 75 years. By that time, at the present rate of increase, the number of people would have grown to over 13 billion, four times the present population.

In the second edition, Malthus conceded that "the comparison between the increase of population and food . . . had not perhaps been stated with sufficient force and precision." He made less of the ratios and relied more heavily on his many examples of populations which grew when food was plentiful, only to suffer cruel ravages when supplies were scarce.

Malthus held that food scarcity was the ultimate barrier against which population growth faltered. The action of both the preventive and positive checks he related to the food supply.

For instance, as people weakened from hunger, they were more vulnerable to plagues. Thus sickness actually caused death, although scarcity of food had paved the way. (WHO has recently stated that in Latin America "among the children aged 1 to 4 about half the deaths are attributable to malnutrition.") The quantity of employment, he said, while related to food production, did not vary as much from year to year as did food supplies. Therefore, it was a much steadier check, and, since it encouraged or discouraged marriage, acted as a preventive, rather than a harsher, positive check.

Malthus dramatically described the awesome power of famine in proscribing man's increase in one of the few highly colored passages in his generally restrained prose:

> Famine seems to be the last, most dreadful resource of nature. The power of population is so superior to the power in the earth to produce subsistance for man, that premature death must in some shape or other visit the human race. The vices of mankind are active and able ministers of depopulation. They are the precursors in the great army of destruction; and often finish the dreadful work themselves. But should they fail in this war of extermination, sickly seasons, epidemics, pestilence, and plague, advance in terrific array, and sweep off their thousands and ten thousands. Should success be still incomplete, gigantic inevitable famine stalks in the rear, and with one mighty blow, levels the population with the food of the world.

MALTHUS'S HOPE: MORAL RESTRAINT

In the first edition, Malthus's proposals for limiting the misery resulting from overpopulation were little more than recommendations of various new measures for dealing with the poor. Not until the second edition did he declare that moral restraint from imprudent marriage should be encouraged in order to stave off, not population growth, but the vices and miseries which are the natural checks to population growth.

He did note, in the first *Essay*, that a preventive check existed in England and in "all old states," when some individuals chose to put off marriage because of financial hardship or the exigencies of social ambition.

Malthus was distressed to note that restraint from marriage, "almost necessarily, though not absolutely," resulted in vice. Although he frowned on imprudent early marriage, he had compassion for those who, "guided either by a stronger passion or a weaker judgment, break through these restraints; and it would be hard indeed if the gratifications of so delightful a passion as virtuous love, did not sometimes more than counterbalance all its attendant evils." He was certain, however, that the consequences of imprudent marriages usually justified his forebodings.

Moral restraint, as introduced in the second *Essay*, was no haphazard natural check but a carefully defined series of stages which Malthus hoped would comprise a program to be generally encouraged, especially among the poor. He called it "a restraint from marriage from prudential motives, with a conduct strictly moral during the period of this restraint."

First, then, moral restraint demanded the postponement of marriage until the individuals were sure of sufficient income to support a family without relying on the state for aid. Malthus here meant a purposeful, knowledgeable decision by the parties involved, rather than the preventive check of the first edition, where restraint from marriage was "unconnected with its consequences."

Second, moral restraint imposed complete sexual continence before the postponed marriage. The probability that this requirement would not be met Malthus allowed to be the only plausible objection to his plan. Curiously, he countered this objection by saying that sexual vices were not

> . . . the only vices which are to be considered in a moral question; [nor are they] . . . even the greatest and the most degrading to the human character. They can rarely or never be committed without producing unhappiness somewhere or other, and therefore ought always to be strongly reprobated: but there are other vices the effects of which are still more pernicious. . . . Powerful as may be the temptations to a breach of chastity, I am inclined to think that they are impotent in comparison of the temptations arising from continued distress.

Malthus did not believe the greatest threat to chastity came from a code of celibacy before marriage: ". . . marriage has been found to be by no means a complete remedy. . . . Add to this, that abject poverty, particularly when joined with idleness, is a state the most unfavourable to chastity that can well be conceived. The passion is as strong, or nearly so, as in other situations: and every restraint on it from personal respect, or a sense of morality, is generally removed."

The third aspect of moral restraint is most surprising: that within marriage there should be no restriction on family size. While this was not part of the definition first given in the *Essay*, scholars accept it as part of Malthus's thought. In the *Essay* he referred to contraceptives as "improper arts," and in the appendix to the 1817 edition made his position completely clear:

> . . . I should always particularly reprobate any artificial and unnatural modes of checking population, both on account of their immorality and their tendency to remove a necessary stimulus to industry. If it were possible for each married couple to limit by a wish the number of their children, there is certainly reason to fear that the indolence of the human race would be very greatly increased, and that neither the population of individual countries nor of the whole earth would ever reach its natural and proper extent.

Malthus's enthusiasm for the efficacy of moral restraint was un-bounded: "the only line of conduct approved by nature, reason, and religion."

He built what looks suspiciously like an entire war on poverty on the single pillar of moral restraint: "The operation of the preventive check in this way, by constantly keeping the population within the limits of the food, though constantly following its increase, would give a real value to the rise of wages and the sums saved by laborers before marriage . . . all abject poverty would be removed from society; or would at least be confined to a very few."

The chances for establishing a general practice of moral restraint, he felt, were fair. He acknowledged that moral restraint "does not at present prevail much among the male part of the society . . . [but] it can scarcely be doubted that in modern Europe a much larger proportion of women pass a considerable part of their lives in the exercise of this virtue than in past times and among uncivilised nations."

SOCIAL IMPLICATIONS: HARDHEARTED OR HARDHEADED?

Although Malthus believed the government had a "very considerable" obligation "in giving the best direction to those checks which in some form or other must necessarily take place," his conclusion was that the poor themselves must accept responsibility for their condition.

With typical bluntness, he said it was necessary to "impress as strongly as possible on the public mind that it is not the duty of man simply to propa-gate his species, but to propagate virtue and happiness; and that, if he has not a tolerably fair prospect of doing this, he is by no means called upon to leave descendants.

He condemned the Poor Laws for removing any need for prudent doubts among those poor who might otherwise hesitate to marry. By pro-viding precious food for the poorest, least industrious citizens, the laws deprived those who were more industrious of their just share and thus were likely to push more people into dependence on the state.

"Fortunately for England," said Malthus, "a spirit of independence still remains among the peasantry. The poor-laws are strongly calculated to eradicate this spirit." The laws, he said, diminished "both the power and the will to save, among the common people, and thus to weaken one of the strongest incentives to sobriety and industry, and consequently to happiness."

But it was not only as a weapon against poverty and hunger, or as an incentive to sobriety and industry, that Malthus recommended the practice of moral restraint. He thought it could be a strong buffer to the tide of revolution which many feared would shortly sweep across the Channel. He believed that: "A mob which is generally the growth of a redundant population goaded by resentment for real sufferings, but totally ignorant of the quarter from which they originate, is of all monsters the most fatal to freedom."

The poor, who quite rightly disliked their position, tended to blame the government in power, and this was the seed of revolution. The prevention, Malthus said, was to teach the poor the true cause of their condition—imprudent marriage—and explain to them that "the withholding of the supplies of labour is the only possible way of really raising its price, and that they themselves, being the possessors of this commodity, have alone the power to do this."

He stated further:

If these truths were by degrees more generally known . . . the lower classes of people, as a body, would become more peaceable and orderly, would be less inclined to tumultuous proceedings in seasons of scarcity, and would at all times be less influenced by inflammatory and seditious publications, from knowing how little the price of labour and the means of supporting a family depend on a revolution.

Malthus's theories, and the political and social views he derived from them, fully supported the *status quo*. He had no doubt that he was revealing a "natural law" of society. He was very skeptical about inherent "natural rights":

Nothing would so effectually counteract the mischiefs occasioned by Mr. Paine's Rights of Man as a general knowledge of the real rights of man. What these rights are it is not my business at present to explain; but there is one right which man has generally been thought to possess, which I am confident he neither does nor can possess—a right to subsistence when his labour will not fairly purchase it. Our laws indeed say that he has this right, and bind the society to furnish employment and food to those who cannot get them in the regular market; but in so doing they attempt to reverse the laws of nature; and it is in consequence to be expected, not only that they should fail in their object, but that the poor, who were intended to be benefited, should suffer most cruelly from the inhuman deceit thus practised upon them.

In another statement he recognized that "social laws" did enhance the "right to subsist," but that this right appears not to be divinely ordained:

The Abbe Raynal has said that "Avant toutes les loix sociales l'homme avoit le droit de subsister" ["Before all social laws, man has the right to survival"]. He might with just as much propriety have said that, before the institution of social laws, every man had a right to live a hundred years. Undoubtedly he had then, and has still, a good right to live a hundred years, nay a thousand *if he can,* without interfering with the right of others to live; but the affair in both cases is principally an affair of powers not of right. Social laws very greatly increase this power, by enabling a much greater number to subsist than could subsist without them, and so far very greatly enlarge *le droit de subsister;* but neither before nor after the institution of social laws could an unlimited number subsist, and before as well as since, he who ceased to have the power ceased to have the right.

Obviously, Malthus would stand aghast at the modern welfare state—whose existence has been made possible by the remarkable increases in productivity since his time.

Perhaps in answer to the charges of social injustice, Malthus occasionally stressed his liberal persuasion. For all his claim that imprudent marriage is an "immoral act," for instance, he stated firmly that the nation could not take away a man's right to marry whenever he chooses.

And Malthus wanted to improve the social status of single women, not only so that women would feel less compelled to marry, but also in deference to "the plainest principles of equity." Malthus was for a general system of public education, as a means of teaching the poor his own ideas of "the real nature of their condition," and also to render them less vulnerable to the spell of "interested and ambitious demagogues."

Even his suggestion for reducing population growth was basically democratic—if somewhat naïve: give the poor the facts and they will surely act wisely in their own best interests.

REACTIONS: RUMPUS AND RESPECTABILITY

Reaction to the *Essay* was instinctively violent. Lord Keynes describes the magnitude of Malthus's suggestion that man restrain his procreative powers: "The voice of objective reason had been raised against a deep instinct which the evolutionary struggle has been implanting from the commencement of life; and man's mind, in the conscious pursuit of happiness, was daring to demand the reins of government from out of the hands of the unconscious urge for mere predominant survival.

The public returned a volley of outraged protest. Typical of the sniping was this comment by William Hazlitt, a combative critic and essayist in London's literary and political world, who said Malthus had produced:

> . . . a complete theory of population, in which it is clearly proved that the poor have no right to live any longer than the rich will let them. . . .

Is it an argument that because the pressure of a scarcity does not fall directly upon those who can bear it best, viz. the very rich, that it should therefore fall upon those, (sic) who can bear it least, viz., on the very poor? Unless Mr. Malthus can contrive to starve someone, he thinks he does nothing.

Malthus had brought a new subject to the tireless pamphleteers of London and the universities, a subject relatively unexplored, with overtones of philosophy and politics, and—though who was to say it then—an undertone of psychology. Comments and protests appeared in letters, humor magazines, parliamentary speeches, and scholarly and popular journals. Many responses showed careless reading of Malthus, or no reading at all; some were fanciful exaggeration. Others constituted thoughtful, well-founded criticism.

Opponents attacked Malthus's rather loose and arbitrary exposition of the geometrical and arithmetical growth ratios of food and population. The seeming precision and authority, critics felt, helped popularize his theory. In Hazlitt's opinion: "Mathematical terms carry with them an imposing air of accuracy and profundity, and ought, therefore, to be applied strictly, and with greatest caution, or not at all."

Some dismissed Malthus's argument as a truism. Obviously there can be no more people than the food to feed them; obviously population stays within bounds. Samuel Taylor Coleridge, who attended Cambridge when Malthus was in a position of some authority there and apparently had reason to resent the essayist, made this marginal note on his copy of the Essay: "Are we now to have a quarto to teach us that great misery and great vice arise from poverty, and that there must be poverty in its worst shape wherever there are more mouths than loaves and more Heads than Brains?"

For all the barrage, the Essay gathered more and more adherents. By 1820, the nay-sayers had been so ineffectual that William Godwin himself felt called upon to publish a lengthy refutation. The good standing of Malthus's theory can be surmised from the fact that the self-aggrandizing Godwin took pains to remind his readers that it was his own work which stimulated Malthus's original effort.

Malthus lived to see the revision of the English Poor Laws in the direction he had suggested. The stern new laws would not encourage anyone to marry out of a certainty that his children would be raised by the state. According to D. V. Glass, Professor of Sociology at the London School of Economics, Malthus's views colored British attitudes towards social services for a century or more.

The reaction in America was preponderantly negative, although far less attention was paid the *Essay*—a scattering of brief comments, mostly in journals. The first American edition, reprinted from the third London edition, was published in 1809. Commentators in the young and optimistic nation simply felt there was no shortage of land. If there ever should be? Well, a man's ingenuity and a little sweat could make the earth yield twice as much and twice as much again.

The *Essay* was translated into German and French during Malthus's lifetime. In Germany, hard times brought on a short-lived and inconclusive government-ordained Malthusian regime of restrictions on marriage.

In England, arguments about the principle of population raged long after Malthus's death in 1834. By the last half of the 19th Century, the brunt of public attack had moved to the neo-Malthusian proposal that births should be controlled within marriage by what Malthus had once decried as "improper arts."

The manifold developments of the 19th Century had the greatest bearing on the long-term reaction to Malthus's theory. Cities sprang up and spread. Power, production, and transportation facilities were invented and put to use everywhere. By the end of that century, the major checks to population—famine, plague, and war—had been greatly mitigated for that part of mankind living in Europe.

The new inventions and machines led to an outpouring of industrial production which not only revolutionized life at home, but also prodded the major European nations to seek foreign colonies as consumers and to supply raw materials. These colonies shipped a continuing stream of foodstuffs. New methods applied to domestic agriculture greatly increased yields. It seemed that Europe need never again fear empty larders.

Developments in medicine and public health paralleled gains in industry and agriculture. Together with the sustained adequate food supplies, these innovations led to rapid declines in mortality. However, birth rates remained high, and population grew rapidly. Although there was some unemployment and working conditions were horrendous, most of the additional people either were absorbed into the new industrial plants or migrated to the colonies.

While war was not eliminated on the continent in the 19th Century, the almost continuous clashes of the 18th Century were over.

In the second half of the century individuals began to limit the size of their families and national birth rates slowly dropped. The gloomy spectre of masses of starving people receded. Malthus was "proved" a false prophet.

Nevertheless, Malthus remained an important figure in economic history. In 1921, The Macmillan Company of New York and London published parallel chapters from the first and second editions in its *Economics*

Classics series. In 1926, the Royal Economic Society reproduced the first edition: "with the least possible change, preserving its features not only in the lines, pages, and spellings but, it is hoped with fair success, in colour of paper and style of binding."

A unique example of the spontaneous application of moral restraint was Ireland. Contrary to the popular view, it was well before the terrible potato famine of 1848–1852 that the Irish people evolved a custom of late marriages which has continued for over a century. Prophetically, Malthus had warned of the dangers of adopting the potato as a one-crop basic staple:

> In Ireland, or in any other country, where the common food is potatoes, and every man who wishes to marry may obtain a piece of ground sufficient, when planted with this root, to support a family, prizes may be given till the treasury is exhausted for essays on the best means of employing the poor. . . . When the commons were all divided, and difficulties began to occur in procuring potato-grounds, the habit of early marriages, which had been introduced, would occasion the most complicated distress; and when, from the increasing population, and diminishing sources of subsistence, the average growth of potatoes was not more than the average consumption, a scarcity of potatoes would be, in every respect, as probable as a scarcity of wheat at present; and, when it did arrive, it would be beyond all comparison more dreadful.

This is almost an exact description of what was to happen in Ireland. The people of Ireland drastically modified their traditional pattern of early marriage. They adopted, whether or not purely by coincidence, the "preventive checks" which Malthus advocated. Ireland's population has declined from 8 million in 1846 to less than 3 million today. As far as many individuals are concerned, this has definitely been a painful and frustrating solution of the population problem. That it is infinitely better than famine can hardly be gainsaid.

The controversy centering around Malthus's views continues. A recent critique of Malthus by a British economist, Kenneth Smith, notes that the world has been unfair to those critics of Malthus who "forecast that population would both grow, and grow richer. . . ." This did indeed happen for a time, and in certain fortunate areas.

Smith's disdain of Malthus leads him to posit a principle of indefinite growth which is as naïve in its way as some of Malthus:

> Man and his food supplies are governed by similar principles of growth, and which can outstrip the other will depend on the relative rates of growth of each. With regard to minerals, which have been laid down once and for all, the annual produce is great or small according to the effort put forth and the skill with which it is applied. The limit in regard to plants and animals is space; in regard to minerals the exhaustion of

the deposits. But these are long-run positions. In the short run no principle emerges which makes it impossible for man to cater for his growing numbers.

Smith did see another check beginning to operate: "In the days when Malthus wrote, space was not a limiting consideration. It is possible that it now is; that the long-run position is being reached; that the world is full."

Writing only 15 years ago, Smith cited populations, such as some in Asia and Latin America, which grew enormously (after medical science reduced the incidence of disease), without having increasing backlogs of food to encourage such growth.

Today the food crisis is engulfing these very populations which obviously did not grow beyond the point of minimal subsistence, but which are now confronting—*in the short run*—the action of the primary checks envisioned by Malthus.

Malthus's ideas of the dynamics of population change were elementary, and his suggestions for checking multiplication of people were naïve. Yet the continuing controversy which has centered around his name has highlighted a problem which is central in world affairs today, and for which a solution has not yet been found.

SOURCES

Bonar, James. *Parson Malthus*. Glasgow: James Maclehouse, 1881.

———. *Malthus and His Work*. New York: Harper and Brothers, 1885.

Brown, Lester R. *Increasing World Food Output: Problems and Prospects*, U.S. Department of Agriculture Foreign Agricultural Economic Report No. 25. Washington, April 1965.

Carr-Saunders, A. M. *World Population*. Oxford: Clarendon Press, 1936.

Glass, D. V. *Introduction to Malthus*. London: Watts and Company, 1953.

Keynes, John Maynard. "Robert Malthus" in *Essays in Biography*. New York: W. W. Norton & Company, Inc., 1963. (Note: First published in Great Britain in 1933.)

Malthus, T. R. *An Essay on the Principle of Population*. (Parallel chapters from the First and Second Editions.) New York: The Macmillan Company, 1921.

———. *An Essay on Population*. Volume One. London: J. M. Dent and Sons, Ltd., and New York: E. P. Dutton and Company, no date.

———. *An Essay on Population*. Volume Two. London: J. M. Dent and Sons, Ltd., and New York: E. P. Dutton and Company, no date.

Smith, Kenneth. *The Malthusian Controversy*. London: Routledge and Kegan Paul, 1951.

12

Developments in the Study of Population[1]

Kurt Mayer

In recent years there has been widespread concern with population questions. Stagnation and impending population decline, the popular clichés of
the thirties, have been replaced by population explosion and urban sprawl
as slogans of the fifties and sixties. Unfortunately, the bewildered layman
finds little relief by turning to the demographers, because the professional
students of population problems have been notoriously unsuccessful not
only in predicting future population growth, but even in explaining past
population changes. These shortcomings of a discipline that ostensibly
deals with hard, quantifiable data may seem surprising at first glance, but
an examination of the development of population studies may reveal some
of the reasons for their predicaments and permit some assessment of their
future progress. For this purpose it is useful first to distinguish between two
aspects of population studies, demography and population theory, which,
though equally indispensable, have often traveled along different roads.[2]

Demography is concerned with three main tasks: ascertaining the
numbers, the characteristics, and the distribution of people in a given
area; determining changes in numbers, characteristics, and distribution
over time; and explaining the major factors accounting for these changes.
The explanation of population changes relies on three basic variables—
fertility, mortality, and migration (the latter will not be discussed in this
article)—for any factors affecting the numbers and distribution of people
must operate through one or more of these variables; a population cannot
change in any other way. The statistical measurement of fertility, mortality,
and migration forms the core of formal demographic analysis. Formal
demography stands out among the social sciences in its strong emphasis

Reprinted from *Social Research: An International Quarterly of the Social Sciences*,
29, no. 3 (Autumn, 1962), pp. 293–320, by permission of the author and the publisher. Footnotes have been renumbered.

on quantification and its persistent use of precise mathematical models and various statistical techniques.

However, the study of population is not confined to measuring, counting, collecting, and analyzing statistical data. For it is evident that fertility, mortality, and migration are not independent variables; they are to a large extent socially and biologically determined. The numbers of births, deaths, and migrants are affected by a whole host of physical, biological, social, and psychological factors. In turn, population changes have far-reaching effects on the social organization and the economic system of the societies in which they occur. Any meaningful interpretation of the causes and effects of population changes must therefore extend beyond formal statistical measurement of the components of change, and draw on the theoretical framework of several other disciplines for assistance. This analysis of the causal determinants and consequences of population changes forms the subject matter of population theory. Demography thus deals with the inner or formal variables in the population system, while population theory is concerned with the outer or ultimate variables, which are biological, economic, and sociological.

Despite their logical interdependence, formal demography and population theory have not developed at an even pace historically. The progress of demographic measurement has depended partly on the evolution of mathematical statistics, and to a large extent on the supply of basic demographic statistics, which are collected at great public expense, often primarily for administrative rather than for scientific purposes. The development of population theory, on the other hand, has been conditioned not only by the availability of demographic data, but also by the growth of other sciences, some of which are of fairly recent origin, like sociology and psychology. Moreover, determining which of the sciences could provide the most suitable frame of reference for the causal analysis of demographic events posed a thorny question, which has found varying answers in the course of time. As a result of their uneven rates of progress, the relations between demography and population theory have often been tenuous. At times the formal analysis of demographic variables developed along strictly empirical lines, with little reference to causal interpretations. The development of population theory, however, was influenced by shifting interests and by preoccupations with the changing economic, social, and political problems of the day. Its progress has been marked by constant controversy, often taking a purely speculative and deductive turn, with only slight and casual references to empirical demographic phenomena. The study of population phenomena has thus been retarded by the disjointed way in which population theory and demography have often developed. Fortunately, there is some evidence of the emergence at long last of a modern population science in which formal demographic analysis and causal interpretation appear better integrated and more closely interrelated. However, we cannot properly understand recent developments in this complex field—the main concern of this paper—without a brief survey of historical origins.

EARLY DEVELOPMENTS

The origins of formal demography antedate the development of a systematic population theory by a full century. The latter did not develop until late in the eighteenth century, when lively controversies about national population trends broke out both in England and in France. The first empircial investigations of demographic data, on the other hand, date back to the seventeenth-century mercantilist and cameralist writers, who called their studies "political arithmetic." In 1662 John Graunt published his *Natural and Political Observations . . . Made upon the Bills of Mortality*. These "bills of mortality" were weekly reports of buryings and christenings occurring in the London area. Analyzing these materials, Graunt observed the numerical regularity of deaths and births; calculated mortality rates, fertility ratios, sex ratios; classified deaths and death rates by cause; and constructed a London life-table in skeleton form. His work greatly influenced Sir William Petty, who published similar *Observations* on the Dublin mortality bills in 1676 and 1683; the astronomer Halley, who in 1693 calculated a much more detailed life-table; and Johann Peter Suessmilch, who in 1742 wrote the first complete treatise on population, *Die Göttliche Ordnung in den Veränderungen des menschlichen Geschlechts aus der Geburt, dem Tode und der Fortpflanzung desselben erwiesen* [*The Divine Order in the Changes of the Human Race Shown by Its Birth, Death and Reproduction*]. Yet, as the title of Suessmilch's volume so clearly indicates, while the demographic measurements of these writers were scientific, their causal interpretations were not. They interpreted the uniformity and the predictability of demographic phenomena as manifestations of the divine ordering of human events. This naïve theological approach inhibited the further development of the new discipline. The discovery of previously unknown quantitative relations in the processes of life and death was considered an end in itself; since they represented the will of God, it was superfluous to search for causal interpretations.

Lacking an adequate theory, political arithmetic could not burgeon into a full-fledged science. Its methods of empirical inquiry were further developed only along one fairly narrow line: the analysis of mortality and the formulation of life expectancies, both propelled by the demand of insurance companies for more accurate actuarial values and by the increasingly scientific approach of public-health authorities in the control of diseases.

Systematic causal interpretations of population change began to develop when the Enlightenment replaced Christian metaphysics, and when theological explanations of demographic phenomena no longer appeared satisfactory in an age of rationality. Instead, population processes were now interpreted as determined by natural laws that rest on biological factors. Population dynamics were explained as the result of fixed universal relationships between man's biological nature and the physical environment. Although he was not the first proponent of this doctrine, Malthus, in his *Essay on the Principle of Population,* first published in 1798, became the most famous and the most influential expositor of the biological thesis. Postulating that man's powers of procreation are always and everywhere greater than nature's ability to produce food, Malthus asserted that man can increase means of subsistence only in arithmetic progression, whereas population tends to grow in a geometric ratio. Therefore population always tends to outgrow the limit of subsistence, but is contained within the limit by the operation of positive checks like famine, war, and disease, which raise the death rate, and by preventive checks operating through deferment of marriage and abstinence within marriage, which lower the birth rate.

Malthus' *Essay* aroused a storm of controversy that dominated the literature throughout the nineteenth century and has not yet completely diminished. Actually many, though by no means all, of Malthus' opponents shared the biological point of view. Although they violently attacked his pessimistic conclusions, they substituted other biological explanations, claiming that advancing civilization leads to a reduction of natural fecundity. The argument varied, but the different writers—like Spencer, Doubleday, and Sadler—shared the underlying causal assumption that population changes are determined by the relation of the human species to its physical environment.

Although the biological approach predominated in nineteenth-century population writings, the Malthusian debate also brought forth other theories, which drew on sociological and economic frames of reference rather than biological ones. One of the first to categorically reject the existence of any universal laws of population was Marx, who stated that every historic mode of production has its own laws of population, historically valid only within that period. Marx and his followers acknowledged the existence of population pressure on resources, but attributed its causes to the characteristics of the capitalistic mode of production, not to man's biological proclivities.

It is remarkable that the Malthusian controversy, which produced an abundance of theoretical writings, had comparatively little direct influence on the development of formal demography. The bulk of the many books, pamphlets, and articles on "the population question" which were published during the middle decades of the nineteenth century contained only slight and casual references to any empirical demographic data. Only a few of the scholars who engaged in the theoretical discussions undertook any serious empirical studies.

This does not mean, of course, that formal demography made no headway at all during this period. Indeed, a large measure of progress was made during the nineteenth century in developing population censuses and vital statistics. But the development of these basic sources of demographic data was stimulated only very indirectly by the debate on th. population question. It was caused primarily by the administrative requirements of national governments that needed increasingly detailed information for the fulfillment of their rapidly expanding functions. The first reliable, periodic census count continuing into present days was instituted in Sweden in 1749, in the United States in 1790, and in both England and France in 1801. Thereafter the practice of taking regular national census counts was adopted by a steadily increasing number of nations. At the same time, the scope of the enumerations expanded and their accuracy increased. But even today there are large underdeveloped areas where reliable counts have never been made and where we must still rely on very rough estimates.

Systematic records of births, deaths, and marriages date back to the fifteenth and sixteenth centuries, when clergymen in most European countries were required to keep registers of all weddings, baptisms, and burials at which they officiated. In England and Ireland the ecclesiastical records were supplemented by the independently collected and published "bills of mortality." As pointed out before, these bills provided the basic sources for the "political arithmetic" of the seventeenth and early eighteenth centuries. The church registers laid the foundation for the subsequent development of national civil registration systems, although this transformation took considerable time. It was achieved first in Sweden, where a continuous series of national vital statistics has been available since 1748. In England and Wales a national system of civil registration was established in 1837; other European countries followed suit somewhat later in the nineteenth century. In general, the development of vital statistics had advanced in step with the development of census enumerations, with the notable exception of the United States, where more than a century elapsed between the inauguration of a periodic census program and the establishment of a nationwide vital-statistics system.

DEVELOPMENTS SINCE 1870

Beginning with the 1870s, a combination of factual events and scientific developments opened up a new era of progress for both population theory and formal demography. First, a rapid expansion of economic production in manufacturing and extractive industries greatly improved conditions in Western countries. In the West, therefore, Malthus' positive checks lost their significance and the previous preoccupation of theorists with the relation of population to the means of support no longer seemed relevant. Second, in some of the economically most advanced countries the birth rate began to decline in the 1870s; in other countries a precipitate drop began around the turn of the century. This was brought about through the spreading use of birth control after marriage, a factor that neither Malthus nor Marx had taken into consideration. Third, the great improvement and extension of census and registration statistics had made available a vast body of appropriate and relatively accurate data, which now permitted new refinements in the methods of analyzing demographic statistics.

Social and Cultural Theories of Declining Fertility

The events and discoveries that rendered the Malthusian fears obsolete, at any rate for the West, led many contemporary students of population to concentrate their attention on the decline of the birth rate. The causes of this decline became the subject of considerable conjecture and controversy, while its effects were viewed with a good deal of alarm. Interest centered particularly on the phenomenon of differential fertility. Differences in the fertility of social classes had long existed in the Western world, but these differences had been relatively small and quite stable. The general decline in the birth rate, however, greatly increased the existing group differentials. While all occupational and economic groups were eventually affected by the general fertility decline, it was evident that the groups of the highest socio-economic status were the leaders. Numerous statistical investigations undertaken from the 1890s onward came to essentially similar conclusions, an almost universal inverse relationship between social status and fertility: the more fortunate and favorable the social and economic circumstances of a group or class, the lower was its fertility.

Most of the various theories that attempted to provide a causal explanation of the general decline of the birth rate and the widening fertility differentials advanced some sort of sociological interpretation, although their proponents were often economists by profession rather than sociologists or demographers. Among the most prominent explanations for a time was the theory of increasing prosperity, which attracted much attention, first in France, the classical country of declining fertility, and later on also in Germany. In the late nineteenth century French scholars like Leroy-Beaulieu, Bertillon, Levasseur, and others advanced the thesis that the desire for a high standard of living or wealth motivates couples to limit the number of their offspring: the greater the family's prosperity, the smaller its size. A more sophisticated attempt to explain fertility differentials also originated in France. In 1890 Dumont pointed out that there is no direct causal relationship between declining fertility and increasing prosperity; instead, both must be viewed as products of an underlying common cause, the striving of individuals to move up in the prestige hierarchy of their society. Dumont compared the individual's drive for social recognition to the capillarity of fluids: wherever there is a social hierarchy, the individual aspires to move up. Social capillarity is most effective in the open-class societies, where obstacles to movement from class to class are comparatively few. Here the acquisition of wealth tends to be the most important avenue of social mobility. At the same time children are encumbrances that retard or prevent the individual's struggle for advance. Therefore, Dumont concludes, prosperity varies directly, whereas fertility varies inversely, with social capillarity.

Along with social mobility and increasing wealth, urbanization has often been considered a major factor influencing the attitude of individuals toward parenthood. The decline in fertility was preceded and accompanied in all Western countries by a massive shift of the population from the country to the cities. Leroy-Beaulieu, Dumont, and many others suggested, therefore, that the rapid increase in the proportion of the population living in the cities is causally connected with the decline in fertility. It had long been known that urban populations are generally less fertile than rural populations. Urban-rural fertility differentials existed in many countries long before the onset of the decline in the birth rate. But as in the case of class differentials, the general decline of the birth rate increased the existing fertility differences between town and country, because fertility declined more rapidly at first in the urban areas. This evidence was cited by many observers who analyzed various aspects of urban life which they believed to be particularly favorable to family limitation. First, the upbringing of children is more expensive in the city. Second, family life is less cohesive and plays a smaller role in the city. The urban adult tends to be involved in a broad range of outside interests and activities that draw him away from home; a large family would interfere with these varied urban pursuits. Third, as Dumont pointed out in his discussion of social capillarity, opportunities to gratify status aspirations are more plentiful in the cities, but those who wish to take advantage of them find children a liability in their upward struggles.

As time went on, it became increasingly evident that the decline in fertility was not confined to the upper classes and the urban population. By the second and third decades of the twentieth century, family limitation had spread widely among the working classes and the farm population in many Western countries. It appeared obvious, therefore, that theories that had sought to attribute the decline exclusively or primarily to such factors as urban residence, increasing wealth, or competition from social advancement could not adequately explain a phenomenon that was affecting very different population groups. A workable theory needed to explain not only the low fertility of the upper classes, but also the recent fertility decline among the proletariat and the farmers. Hence some authors developed theories attributing the cause of the overall fertility decrease to the spread of a rationalistic mentality, a specific product of capitalism, inherent in the spirit of striving which started with the urban bourgeoisie but eventually permeated all classes of society: the proletariat now imitates the behavior of the upper classes, adopting their rationalistic attitude toward life and a correspondingly rationalistic reproductive-behavior pattern. Others, however, have warned against exaggerating the connection between capitalism and the motives in the minds of modern couples which guide their reproductive behavior, and some writers have rejected altogether the invocation of any unquantifiable "spirit" to explain historical changes in fertility patterns.

Despite considerable differences in emphasis, the various theories reviewed above generally agree that the explanation of the fertility decline must be sought in an interplay of various social and economic factors and their effects on the attitudes of individual couples. As to the causal connection between social factors and individual attitudes, most theories could offer no more than plausible inferences. There was no lack of empirical investigations that discovered and confirmed statistical relationships between fertility and socio-economic factors. Usually, however, the data of these studies were primary population statistics of the census type. That is, the data had been collected for other purposes, and the theories advanced to explain the statistical relationships discovered were developed ex post facto.

In the early 1930s a series of studies was undertaken in which data were specially collected to investigate the role of contraception in bringing about class differences in fertility. These studies furnished strong evidence that class fertility differentials can be accounted for almost entirely by differences in the prevalence and effectiveness of contraceptive practices; but they did not inquire into the causes underlying these differences. Obviously, contraception is the immediate means of family limitation; the causes are the factors that encourage or discourage its practice. In 1938, however, a committee of demographers, sociologists, and psychologists was organized in the United States for the specific purpose of undertaking a field study of the social and psychological factors underlying reproductive behavior. This research, popularly known as the Indianapolis Study, was the first major empirical investigation designed to test causal hypotheses, by inquiring directly into the motivations and attitudes of married couples regarding the planning and having of children, and the factors responsible for differences in fertility. For various reasons the committee decided to restrict the study to native-born white, urban, Protestant couples, married from twelve to fifteen years, living in the city of Indianapolis.

The Indianapolis Study clearly confirmed both the importance of contraception in the general reduction of fertility and the key role of socio-economic status in the effectiveness of contraceptive practices. Some form of contraception was practiced by virtually every couple in the sample; nevertheless, slightly over half of all the pregnancies occurred while birth control was being practiced. As expected, the effectiveness of contraceptive practices varied inversely with socio-economic status: the higher the income, occupational status, education, and the like, the greater was the proportion of couples practicing contraception effectively. Of special significance, however, was the finding that among those couples who had exercised complete and effective fertility control and therefore had no unplanned pregnancies, there obtained a *direct* relationship between fertility and socio-economic status: the higher the income, occupation, and education, the larger the size of the planned families.

Although the Indianapolis Study was a pioneer attempt to go beyond the collection of primary population statistics in order to investigate some of the complex causal factors underlying reproductive behavior, its success was limited. Because of a variety of weaknesses in conceptualization, limitations in the sample, and deficiencies in the data, most of the hypotheses that attempted to unravel the social and psychological variables underlying fertility differences were neither adequately confirmed nor decisively refuted. The Indianapolis Study thus adds comparatively little to the various theories that have attempted to explain the general decline in fertility. The same is true of another major study of family limitation undertaken in Great Britain in 1946, on behalf of the Royal Commission on Population. This investigation was based on interviews with 10,297 female patients in general hospitals, widely distributed throughout the country. The findings clearly demonstrate the continuously increasing usage of birth control in Britain since the early years of this century. They also show the familiar inverse relationship of birth-control practice and social class, but give some indication that these differences are narrowing as knowledge and practice of contraception are increasing in all social classes. Although particularly valuable for international comparative purposes, the research was sheerly empirical and adds nothing new to the existing theories of declining fertility.

Most of these theories suffer from the same major limitation: they are all ad hoc theories, dealing only with one specific historical phenomenon, the decline of the birth rate and of family size in the Western world during the nineteenth and twentieth centuries. Limited in time and space, these theories do not meet the exacting qualifications of a comprehensive theory of population change, which must provide causal explanations also of the population dynamics of other societies and of different historical epochs. But though only small progress has been made to date toward the elaboration of a truly comprehensive sociological theory of population change, there has been no dearth of attempts to find universally valid laws of population growth outside the sociological frame of reference. While sociologically oriented theorists have focused their attention mainly on the phenomenon of overall decreasing fertility and fertility differentials, biologists and economic theorists have developed some ambitious theories of considerably wider scope. At the same time considerable progress has been made in the development and further refinement of formal demographic models.

Biological Theories of Population Change

The search for biological laws of population growth, which had dominated the early Malthusian controversy, had a vigorous though fairly brief revival during the present century. In the 1920s the biometrician Raymond Pearl stirred up considerable excitement by reasserting the hypothesis of biological determinism and advancing a mathematical formula of population growth. Like other biological theorists, Pearl contended that the law of human population growth is fundamentally the same as that which regulates the growth of plants and animals: all living organisms increase in size in cyclical fashion, growing rapidly at first, slowly thereafter, until the organism finally dies. Arguing by analogy, Pearl assumed that the growth of collectivities like entire populations resembles that of individual organisms. Population growth, too, occurs in cycles consistent with the observed rhythm of growth characteristic of all living matter. Since populations always grow in a finite area, they must have an upper limit, but in the case of human populations several successive growth cycles can occur in the same area, which reflect changes in the economic organization of society. Thus the transition from an agricultural to an industrial society, for example, creates the possibility of additional population growth in a new cycle. In the early stages of each growth cycle, population increases at an accelerating rate, until the midpoint is reached; thereafter the growth rate decreases. Represented graphically, population growth cycles form an elongated S-shaped curve, which in mathematical terminology is known as the logistic curve, discovered in 1838 by Verhulst.

Comparison of the calculated values of the curve with the actual census data of several countries resulted in a remarkably good fit. Pearl therefore assumed that future population growth could be predicted with some confidence. He was not satisfied, however, with the purely empirical nature of the logistic formula, and attempted to explain the causal mechanism underlying it: the reason why population increases logistically in a spatially limited area is that fertility correlates inversely with population density, that is, as density increases, fertility declines. Pearl proclaimed this to be a biological principle that universally regulates the growth of all living matter throughout nature, adducing experimental evidence from the behavior of yeast cells and fruit flies in a bottle. However, this altogether too simple analogy was clearly refuted by Pearl's own later empirical investigations of contraceptive practices, which he had undertaken with the expectation of proving that variations in social conditions other than density have only a negligible influence on human fertility. As a result, the excitement about the logistic formula has subsided; it is now generally recognized that with respect to human populations the logistic curve is a purely empirical formula, which sometimes accurately describes the past course of population growth of a given area but does not necessarily predict its future development.

The evidence provided by Pearl's study, as well as by other investigations of the prevalence and nature of contraceptive practices, also contradicts the theories of those contemporary writers who have argued on various grounds that increasing prosperity tends to decrease the reproductive capacity of human beings. First advanced during the Malthusian controversy, such ideas were revived by some twentieth-century authors, especially Gini, who attributed the fertility decline and the widening of group fertility differentials to decreases in reproductive capacity, allegedly induced by the strains and stresses of social mobility, which lead to the physical exhaustion of the upper classes. However, the accumulating evidence about the extent of contraception has documented rather decisively the lack of class differences in physiological capacity to reproduce. The Indianapolis Study, for example, found approximately the same proportion of sterile couples in each socio-economic status group, and among the fecund couples the fertility rates during periods of noncontraceptive exposure were strikingly similar, regardless of social class. In view of such evidence, Gini partly shifted his ground. Accepting the fact that the major part of the fertility decline is the result of contraception, he held that the spread of contraceptive practices is itself the result of biological decadence, an assertion that neither he nor anyone else has ever been able to prove.

The Concept of the Optimum Population

In contrast to the exponents of the biological approach, many of the professional economists who have contributed to population theory have been less concerned with finding and expounding the *causes* of population change than with assessing its *results*. They have been interested in the economic and social effects of population growth or decline on natural resources, labor supply, levels of consumption and production, and so forth, rather than in the mode or rate at which population changes. In attempting to analyze the complex and intricate interrelationships between population and the economy, certain economists have raised the intriguing question: "What size of population is economically most advantageous in given circumstances?"

The theory of an optimum population size is the outgrowth of the synthesis of two different bodies of generally accepted economic theory. On the one hand there is the notion that a growing population results in an enlarged market and a greater division of labor, and consequently brings about an increase in productivity per capita. On the other hand there is the doctrine of diminishing returns, which holds that if other factors are held constant, productivity per capita will diminish if the number of people working given resources increases beyond a certain point. From a combination of these two doctrines, it logically follows that there must be a point at which the two opposing tendencies are in equilibrium: an optimum point at which a given (optimum) size of population results in maximum productivity per capita. Two further concepts follow from this premise: if the size of the population exceeds the (optimum) point that provides the highest possible level of per capita output, the area is overpopulated; and conversely, if population size is below the optimum, the area is underpopulated.

It has also been pointed out that the optimum point is never static but continually shifts, because the quantity and quality of resources and technology are constantly changing. It is clear, therefore, that empirical measurement of the optimum population presents enormous difficulties, and it is not surprising that to date no satisfactory statistical indicators of overpopulation or underpopulation have been devised, in spite of frequent attempts to do so. The theory of the optimum population is an ideal-typical construct that enables us to understand hypothetically the influence of population size on economic productivity. At the present state of knowledge, however, the optimum concept cannot be translated into empirical terms of any precision, and therefore it does not lend itself as an instrument of practical population policy, despite the tempting policy implications inherent in its very terminology.

Formal Demography

During the last thirty years considerable progress has been made in the development of a different body of abstract and logically interrelated principles which appears to be more fruitful as a guide in the examination and interpretation of empirical population data. The theory concerns the universal relationships that always obtain between the basic components of population change—fertility, mortality, and migration. It has variously been called analytical theory, pure demography, or formal demography. The fact that a population consists of organisms that are subject to the inescapable biological processes of birth, maturation, and death makes it possible to view any human population as a sex and age structure that is determined by the vital processes and migration. Leaving migration out of account, the age and sex structure of a "closed" population at any given time is the result of the operation of specific mortality and fertility frequencies in the past. In turn, this structure influences and sets limits for future variations in fertility and mortality. It is therefore possible to establish deductively a series of mathematical theorems, much like geometrical axioms, which define the relationships between sex and age composition and the vital rates.

Pure demographic theory involves as a central core the concept of the "stable population," a hypothetical model of a particular age and sex structure that would ultimately develop in any population subject to age-specific fertility and mortality rates continuing unvaried for an extended period of time, if there were meanwhile no migration or other disturbing influences. The population that would eventually result from the long-time operation of constant vital rates is called "stable" because the proportion of the population in each age group will not vary in time, even though the size of the population as a whole might increase or decrease. In a stable population, the birth rate, death rate, and rate of natural increase remain constant and can be computed mathematically.

Although the basic principle of a stable population dates back to the development of Halley's life-table in 1693, the theory was not fully developed until 1925, when Lotka and Dublin introduced the idea of the reproduction of generations into the analysis of the stable population. They proved that the stable age distribution and the net reproduction rate are both the result of the same conditions, that is, of a long-time regime of constant age-specific fertility and mortality rates. A net reproduction rate is a measure of the number of daughters that one cohort of newborn girls would bear *if* the age-specific fertility rates and mortality rates of the current life-table were to continue unchanged to the end of their child-bearing period. A net reproduction rate is thus an estimate of the extent to which a cohort of women of an actual population will replace itself, *provided* current fertility and mortality conditions continue unchanged. Therefore the net reproduction rate represents not only a replacement index of an actual population, but also the ultimate rate of increase of the stable population. If now this rate of increase is expressed per annum instead of per generation, it corresponds to the intrinsic or "true" rate of natural increase of an actual population. The corresponding intrinsic or "true" birth and death rates of the actual population (which are also at the same time the crude death and birth rates of the stable population) can be calculated easily. Since in all three of the intrinsic rates the effect of age is controlled, these rates can be used for comparing the reproductive activities of actual populations regardless of differences in their age and sex composition. Intrinsic rates, like the net reproduction rate, measure correctly the current reproductive activity of an actual population, but since current conditions rarely remain unchanged, they have no predictive power and should not be used to forecast future population change, as has frequently been done with disastrous results.

The stable-population model, the net reproduction index, and the intrinsic vital rates are used in demographic research to discover relationships underlying actual vital processes but not visible in the observed crude rates of birth, death, and natural increase—just as geometrical models are used in engineering to measure concrete relations. Major interest attached to the indexes of reproductivity, especially during the 1920s and 1930s. It appeared at that time that the decline in the birth rate had temporarily inflated the proportion of persons in the childbearing ages. Consequently the crude rate of natural increase seemed to be spuriously high in Western nations, presenting a picture of continued population growth. At the same time, however, calculations of the intrinsic rates showed the "true" death rate exceeding the "true" birth rate, and the net reproduction rate well below unity in many countries, thus indicating that the current cohorts of women were not then giving birth to enough daughters to replace their numbers. Demographers therefore concluded that the observed vital rates were actually concealing a trend toward incipient decline, and did not hesitate to forecast the end of population growth and even population decline in the foreseeable future.

However, the unanticipated postwar upsurge of the birth rate brought massive population growth to most of the countries that had been labeled as those of "incipient decline," especially the United States and Canada. This made it painfully clear that net reproduction and intrinsic rates cannot serve as predictive instruments, because fertility and mortality are assumed constant in their computation. A further difficulty lies in the fact that the net reproduction rate is computed by the summation of age-specific fertility rates of all women in the childbearing ages during a *single year*. The net reproduction rate thus gives a cross-sectional view of the reproductive activity of a hypothetical generation, an artificial cohort. It cannot, therefore, measure the basic changes in the fertility behavior of real cohorts over time. This limitation very clearly indicates the need for longitudinal analysis of reproduction in terms of real cohorts of women; for example, all women in the population born in the same year or married in the same year. The reproductive behavior of any given cohort is determined not only by conditions of the moment, but also by past circumstances and by anticipation of future conditions. The fertility history of every real cohort is thus shaped by many factors, which do not necessarily operate the same way on different cohorts. It is imperative, therefore, to study fertility behavior over time if one wants to detect genuine trends.

Intensive efforts to study fertility and reproduction from the real cohort or longitudinal point of view were first begun in the 1940s, and this type of work continues prominently in the forefront of formal demographic endeavors at the present time. The substantive findings of these studies indicate, first, that most of the sharp fluctuations of the crude birth rate in the 1930s and 1940s reflect changes in the timing of family-building behavior of different cohorts; depression, war, and postwar prosperity caused a great deal of postponing, making up, and moving ahead of births. The findings show, second, that over and above such changes in the timing of births, a definite change in the long-time downward trend of fertility is evident. For example, in the United States the total number of children per 1,000 women born to each cohort of native white women declined continuously from the 1875 to the 1909 cohort, the total drop amounting to one-third. However, the cohorts of women born in 1910 and later give definite indications of having reversed the trend. It is too early as yet to gauge the extent of the change in fertility trends with any precision, but it does appear that the long-term trend toward smaller family sizes has been halted in practically all countries of "incipient decline." In the countries of northwestern Europe, fertility seems to be stabilized for the time being at slightly above prewar levels, while in the United States and in the British Dominions a trend toward larger families is unmistakable.

Current Fertility Research

In the United States the unanticipated upturn in fertility, which clearly demonstrated the urgent need for improved measures of replacement and forecasting, has stimulated two major new field researchers of fertility behavior and the social and psychological factors that affect it. The first of these studies, undertaken jointly, in 1955, by the Scripps Foundation for Research in Population and the Survey Research Center of the University of Michigan, involved interviews with 2,713 married white women, aged 18–39 years, selected through a national area probability sample, including all religious groups.[3] The women were questioned about the following topics: socio-economic status, marital history, pregnancy history, physical impairment of fertility, birth-control practices and attitudes toward birth control, expectations about the number and birth dates of additional children and the reasons for these expectations, attitudes toward children, and beliefs about what constitutes the "ideal" family size.

The results indicate three main conclusions. First, family limitation is now almost universally approved in the United States, and is practiced widely and effectively by white couples. Second, women of all social classes are largely agreed on the number of children wanted and expected. The average number of expected children is approximately three and, with the exception of religion, the traditional fertility differentials appear sharply reduced if not eliminated. Catholics desire and expect more children than Protestants and Jews, but the difference lies within the range of two to four children generally accepted as the norm. Third, if the present family growth plans are continued and actually realized, the American population will continue to grow rapidly. Although fecundity impairments are widespread, they will not materially reduce the rate of population growth. Since all conclusions were based on expectations only, the study was repeated in 1960, albeit with a different sample, in order to ascertain how expectations reported in 1955 compared with actual performance during the ensuing five-year period. Preliminary indications are that although there were numerous differences between expectations and performance, these differences canceled out, so that the aggregated number of children born by 1960 approximated closely the number expected in 1955.[4]

The other project, a successor to the Indianapolis Study, was undertaken by the Office of Population Research of Princeton University, and is designed in longitudinal form. It is based on interviews and questionnaires obtained in 1957 from a sample of 1,165 native-born couples, selected at random in seven large metropolitan areas and including all religions. All of these couples had a second child in September 1956. The data gathered initially relate to the pregnancy and contraceptive histories, socioeconomic status and related attitudes, personality characteristics and marital adjustment, aspirations with respect to having a third child, and the total size of family desired. The couples were reinterviewed after about thirty months to ascertain how the actual fertility situation had developed. This study is therefore a prediction study of a metropolitan sample of couples with two children, which attempts to isolate factors associated with future childbearing, especially with respect to the timing of a third child. Inherent in the research design are provisions for testing the correctness of the prediction.

To date only the findings of the first round of interviews have been published.[5] They strongly corroborate the conclusions of the Michigan-Scripps study. Only 11 percent of the couples were not using contraception after a second birth. Family sizes of two, three, and four children were equally popular, and accounted for 90 percent of the reported preferences. While class differentials were negligible, religion exerted a strong influence on fertility, with Catholics desiring larger families than Protestants, and Jews wanting the smallest number of children. Preliminary reports from the second phase of the survey show that the religious differences were clearly manifested in actual fertility behavior. Three-fifths of the Catholic, one-half of the Protestant, but barely more than one-fourth of the Jewish couples actually had additional pregnancies in the two-and-one-half-year interval between the first and second interviews.[6]

Perhaps the most interesting aspect of current American fertility research is the virtual disappearance of the traditional class differences in the number of children American couples desire and expect. Moreover, the remarkable convergence on an average of three children means that fertility will be high enough to maintain a rapid rate of population increase in the foreseeable future. This represents a definite change from the prewar situation. However, the basic causes that have brought about this change cannot possibly be ascertained by interviewing methods. Field research in fertility behavior has definite limitations. It may reveal the shifts in attitudes and motivations which directly result in fertility "fashion changes." Yet shifts in motivation and corresponding changes in fertility behavior are themselves but reflections and symbols of underlying long-term changes in social structure and economic systems of human societies. Such basic factors cannot be studied by means of attitude and opinion surveys; they require comprehensive analysis of social structure and cultural norms in historical depth.

Comprehensive Structural Population Theories

The lack of an adequate frame of reference that would permit us to understand the fundamental social changes behind major shifts in reproductive behavior, not only in Western but also in many other societies, has recently prompted renewed attempts to formulate comprehensive sociological theories of population change. One such theory, which has been developed during the last thirty years, especially by American and British demographers, is known in the literature as the theory of the demographic transition. Briefly described, this theory explains the rapid growth of the world's population during the last three hundred years as the result of a transition from high to low birth and death rates which societies undergo in the process of industrialization and modernization. This growth began with reductions in mortality in Europe, caused by increases in food supply brought about by agricultural innovations and improved transportation, followed later by spectacular sanitary and medical advances. Fertility, less responsive to the processes of modernization, declined less rapidly at first. The widening gap between the two rates provided the tremendous growth of the European population and caused its swarming overseas. Eventually, however, the new urban-industrial conditions of life provided strong incentives to couples to limit their fertility through birth control, until finally a new demographic balance of low mortality plus low fertility was achieved, resulting in approaching population stability and possible decline.

Different countries reach different stages of the demographic cycle at different times. It is therefore possible to divide the world's population into three categories, according to the stages reached in the transition cycle. First, there are the countries of "incipient population decline," which have nearly completed the transition. This category includes the populations of northwestern and central Europe, North America, Australia, and New Zealand. Second are the countries in the stage of "transitional growth," where mortality is declining sharply and fertility has begun to decline but is still lagging behind, with the result that these populations are now experiencing very rapid growth. The nations in this stage include Eastern Europe, the Soviet Union, Japan, and parts of Latin America. Finally, we have the countries of "high growth potential," which have not yet begun the transition or are only on the verge of it. Here births and deaths are still high and growth is slow, but it could become explosive if and when the characteristic gap between mortality and fertility decline develops. Most of Africa, Asia, the Middle East, and much of Latin America belong in this category.

Although widely acclaimed for a time, the validity of the transition theory has been severely questioned in recent years. Examination of the demographic experience of several Western countries shows considerable variations in their history of population growth which do not fit the postulated three stages. Thus in France and in North America the decline in the death rate began early, preceding modernization, while in England and the Netherlands fertility increases preceded the decline in mortality and accounted for the population growth in the eighteenth and through most of the nineteenth century. The accuracy of the theory as a description of past demographic history in the Western world is therefore in doubt. Moreover, major questions have been raised about its predictions of future population growth and the assumed sequences on which they are based. Analysis of recent population trends in underdeveloped countries leads to serious question whether the countries now assumed to be in the "transitional growth" stage will actually recapitulate either the demographic or the industrial experiences of the West. Furthermore, the strong postwar fertility upsurge in some of the countries in "incipient decline" casts doubt about the predictive aspects of the theory even if it is limited to the West. Some critics have therefore suggested that further stages should be added to the transition theory or that the United States and the British Dominions represent a special case where low mortality and moderately high fertility have resulted in a substantial rate of population increase.

Such modification and revisions reduce the status of the demographic transition concept to that of yet another ad hoc theory, limited in time and space, valid only for specific historical situations. Thus it would appear reasonable for population theorists and demographers to be finally willing to learn the lesson taught by two centuries of continued failures: there simply is no universal law of population change; therefore attempts to develop general theories designed to explain population changes occurring under widely differing social and cultural conditions by the same set of causal factors must necessarily be futile. This does not mean, however, that population theory must be confined to purely empirical generalizations or ad hoc hypotheses. On the contrary, there is urgent need for comprehensive sociological analyses of population dynamics, but such theories must clearly recognize the cultural relativity of demographic phenomena. Sociologically adequate theories must show how variations in the social structure and the cultural context produce differences in population structure. They will not imply a single or uniform factor as the cause for varying rates of population change. Instead, they will identify distinctive types of causal factors which operate differently in different social contexts.

Although an adequate conceptual framework for an acceptable structural population theory is still lacking, it is encouraging to note that real progress is now being made. Some preliminary steps in this direction have recently been taken in the United States by Lorimer and by Kingsley Davis, who have employed a structural-functional approach in analyzing specific aspects of social organization and cultural norms that are functionally related to fertility and mortality controls in different societies.[7] Their work illustrates what may be called a cross-cultural approach leading to a comparative sociology of population dynamics. It lacks, however, the historical depth that some recent European theories attempt to supply.

A sociologically and historically sophisticated theory has been advanced in Germany by Mackenroth, and his work has inspired a brief but excellent analysis by the Swiss economist and demographer Bickel.[8] Departing from the insight originally provided by Marx, that every historical epoch has its own laws of population, Mackenroth proceeds to trace the historical development of different European populations from mediaeval days to the present, relating in each instance the specific features of the changing social structure to the reproductive-behavior pattern typical of the particular historical context. Extending this analysis also to European settlements overseas and to non-Western societies, Mackenroth distinguishes typical demographic patterns, or population dynamics, as Bickel calls them, each of which is historically unique, depending on the reciprocal relationship between social structure, culture, and reproductive behavior.

As Mackenroth points out, however, the analysis of this relationship is complicated by two factors. Since every society is socially differentiated and stratified, its demographic pattern is not uniform; rather, every major social group has its own patterns of reproductive behavior, which must be identified separately. Moreover, since neither social structures nor population patterns are static, there is rarely a perfect synchronization between them. On the contrary, the reproductive behavior of a given group or of a society as a whole frequently overlaps different historical epochs, causing time lags and survivals to arise. For example, time lags tend to develop between changes in the social structure and the fertility behavior of different social groups whose population dynamics can often be understood only by reference to past rather than present conditions. At the same time the presence of group differences facilitates both statistical analysis and causal interpretation. Mackenroth interprets as lag phenomena not only class fertility differences but also the rapid population growth of Western nations during the nineteenth century. He attributes the latter to the overlapping of fertility mores and ethics typical of pre-industrial conditions into the epoch of urbanization and industrialization, where they were no longer appropriate. The subsequent decline in fertility can then be understood as an adaptation of reproductive behavior to changed social conditions.

Although neither Mackenroth nor Bickel offers an analysis of the postwar changes in fertility trends, this mode of analysis can be extended to include the most recent developments. For example, analyzing the American experience, this writer has recently argued that basic changes in the social structure cause large swings in reproductive-behavior patterns.[9] The decline of American fertility below the replacement level in the 1930s represents the extreme point in a long swing that occurred as a reaction to the fundamental transformation from an agricultural to an urban-industrial society. Once the structural transformation was completed, the pendulum swung back, and the current convergence of fertility differentials marks the adaptation of the reproductive behavior of different population groups to an increasingly homogeneous social structure. To be sure, such hypotheses require rigorous testing, but it would seem that only systematic historic-structural analyses can ultimately lead to adequate interpretations.

NOTES

1. This is a revised and abbreviated version of an article contributed to a German symposium, edited by René König, *Handbuch der empirischen Sozialforschung*, vol. 1 (Stuttgart 1962), pp. 453–79, under the title "Bevölkerungslehre und Demographie."

2. Two recent works present extensive accounts of the historical development of population theories and of the current status of demography: *The Determinants and Consequences of Population Trends*, published by the Population Division of the United Nations (New York 1953); and Philip M. Hauser and Otis Dudley Duncan, eds., *The Study of Population: An Inventory and Appraisal* (Chicago 1959). Instead of presenting a copious apparatus of footnotes, I refer the reader to the extensive bibliographies contained in these works. Only a few recent publications will be cited here.

3. Ronald Freedman, Pascal K. Whelpton, Arthur A. Campbell, *Family Planning, Sterility and Population Growth* (New York 1959).

4. P. K. Whelpton, Arthur Campbell, Richard Tomasson, "Preliminary Results from the 1960 Study of Growth of American Families," unpublished paper presented at the annual meeting of the Population Association of America, New York, May 5, 1961.

5. Charles F. Westoff, Robert G. Potter, Jr., Philip C. Sagi, and Elliot G. Mishler, *Family Growth in Metropolitan America* (Princeton 1961).

6. Charles F. Westoff, Robert G. Potter, Jr., and Philip C. Sagi, "Preliminary Results from the Study of Family Growth in Metropolitan America," unpublished paper presented at the annual meeting of the Population Association of America, New York, May 5, 1961.

7. Frank Lorimer *et al.*, *Culture and Human Fertility*. Unesco (Paris 1954); Kingsley Davis and Judith Blake, "Social Structure and Fertility: An Analytical Framework," in *Economic Development and Cultural Change*, vol. 4 (April 1956), pp. 211–35; see also Kingsley Davis, *Human Society* (New York 1949), Chapters 20–21.

8. Gerhard Mackenroth, *Bevölkerungslehre: Theorie, Soziologie und Statistik der Bevölkerung* (Berlin 1953); Wilhelm Bickel, "Bevölkerungsdynamik und Gesellschaftsstruktur," in *Schweizerische Zeitschrift für Volkswirtschaft und Statistik*, vol. 92 (September 1956), pp. 317–28. The interesting recent publication by Andreas Miller, *Kultur und menschliche Fruchtbarkeit* (Stuttgart 1962), which presents a sophisticated equilibrium theory of population developments, was received too late to be considered in this article.

9. Kurt Mayer, "Fertility Changes and Population Forecasts in the United States," in *Social Research*, vol. 26 (Autumn 1959), pp. 347–66.

13

A Re-Examination of Some Recent Criticisms of Transition Theory*

Kenneth C. W. Kammeyer

The theory of the modern demographic transition was presented in its inchoate form by Thompson (1929). This early paper was not an attempt to set forth a completely formulated theory, but was written to summarize and categorize the then available worldwide data on vital rates. Since other demographers of that era were similarly engaged, it is not surprising that there should be differing opinions about the origins of transition theory. For example, Glass (1965) has seen the beginnings of transition theory in the work of European scholars. He has cited the work of the French demographer Landry (1934), who described three "regimes" of population that are parallel to the customary three stages of population in transition theory. Glass also credited Carr-Saunders (1936:60–66) with introducing the idea of the "staggered phasing of mortality and fertility decline" (Glass, 1965:14).

Although there are differences of opinion regarding the beginnings of transition theory, there is a consensus about its subsequent development. Notestein's (1945) presentation of the "long view" of population along with Blackner's (1947) elaboration of the population stages—in which he increased the number from three to five—are important early landmarks in the development of the theory. Davis (1949:598–600) adopted transition theory in his introductory sociology text, and in the process contributed a partial rationale for the differential effects of modernization on birth and death rates. Cowgill (1949, 1963) produced two excellent papers relating

Reprinted from *Sociological Quarterly*, 11, no. 4 (Fall, 1970), pp. 500–510, by permission of the author and the publisher.

* This paper was written while I was a Research Associate with the Institute for Social and Environmental Studies at the University of Kansas. I want to thank my colleagues, D. Stanley Eitzen, Gary M. Maranell and L. Keith Miller for improving both the tone and structure of the paper.

the modern demographic transition (or cycle), first to other cyclical theories and later to Malthusian theory. Hertzler (1956) also contributed to transition theory in his analysis of the "crisis in world population." An indication of the acceptance of transition theory in the 1950's may be seen in the fact that Vance (1952:12), in his famous call for more theory in demography, saw transition theory emerging as an "integrated theory of a high order...."

In its essential features, transition theory emphasized a sequence of three stages. The following description of these stages is taken from Cowgill's (1963) summary:

> Stage 1 is the primitive condition of high birth rates and high death rates, and equilibrium having been previously achieved, these vital rates tend to balance each other and the population tends to remain relatively stable.
>
> The second stage is that of transition or change; it marks the transition from a condition of high birth rates and high death rates to that of low birth rates and low death rates. Thus far the expected pattern is one in which death rates fall first and most rapidly for a time, resulting in rapid population growth or what in recent times has been dubbed 'the population explosion.'
>
> Stage 3, as yet largely hypothetical, is that condition of low birth rates and low death rates which presumably follows the transition stage.

A key element of the theory, and one that is under special consideration in this paper, is the assertion that in Stage Two, as modernization begins, the mortality rate drops earlier and faster than the fertility rate. Again, in Cowgill's words (1963:272): "Under conditions of industrialization and urbanization, given the technology of birth control and death control, there is a marked tendency for the technology of death control to be applied earlier and more extensively resulting in rapid population growth...."

Davis (1963:352) has given further emphasis to the point by arguing that declines in fertility have typically been in response to the new conditions of lowered mortality: "Under prolonged drop in mortality with industrialization, people in Northwest Europe and Japan found that their accustomed demographic behavior [high fertility] was handicapping them in their effort to take advantage of the opportunities being provided by the emerging economy. They accordingly began changing their behavior."

As the theory of the demographic transition became established and accepted, it also developed its critics. The very fact that transition theory was fairly explicit made it vulnerable to attack. A more imprecise theory would have been less clear about hypothesized causal sequences, and thus not as open to criticism. The criticisms have come from various quarters; have focused on different characteristics and capabilities of transition theory; and have employed varying criteria for judging its utility. It is not the objective of this paper to deal with all criticisms of transition theory. The primary objective is to counter, or perhaps neutralize, the effects of some criticisms that have been quite influential and relatively unchallenged. Since Petersen's work (1960:1; 1961:11–14, 376–402; 1969:11–14, 401–429) stands out as the most detailed and oft-cited criticism, this discussion will center around his case against transition theory.

Petersen's critical attention has been especially directed toward the reasons for population growth in the *early stages of modernization*. He has argued against the tenet of transition theory which holds that the initial growth of the population is caused by a decline in mortality. A number of other demographers have taken similar or supportive positions, and their work will be cited as it is relevant to the following discussion.

It is noteworthy, however, that Petersen's view of the *utility* of modern demographic transition theory seems to be more favorable in the recent edition of his text than it had been in his earlier writing. He now says, "although some of its details have proved to be false and some of its implications misleading, in its simplest form the theory of the demographic transition is nevertheless one of the best documented generalizations in the social sciences. Duly amended and supplemented, it is one useful framework within which to organize an analysis of population" (Petersen, 1969: 11). The view that transition theory is most useful as a framework within which large scale population changes can be more readily comprehended is one that most supporters of the theory would stress. However, the effect of much of the criticism of transition theory has been to cast doubt on its usefulness. This paper addresses itself to some of these criticisms with a view to modifying such effects.

THE DUTCH AND ENGLISH CASES AS NEGATIVE EVIDENCE

Petersen (1960) considered several features of demographic transition theory in the light of certain known or estimated demographic events in the Netherlands from the sixteenth to the twentieth century. The major question under consideration was the cause of the population increase that had occurred in the Netherlands after 1650, and especially during the nineteenth century. Petersen asked whether the increase in the Netherlands was the result of declining mortality, as transition theory would have it, or the result of increasing fertility? According to the theory, the fertility rate at the beginning of the period would have been at an already high level, and thus could *not* have accounted for much of the natural increase by going still higher. However, it should be noted that the idea of some increase in fertility occurring as a result of more favorable and healthful living conditions would not be inconsistent with the theory. Hertzler (1956: 46) suggested that the first tendency of the birth rate at the beginning of modernization is often slightly upward. In the Dutch case the actual demographic data were not available to determine if it was reduced mortality or increased fertility that accounted for the population increase of the nineteenth century. But Petersen argued from known medical and social institutional facts (the latter were primarily changes in the structure of the family), that the cause was probably increased fertility rather than decreased mortality.

In his 1961 text, and again in 1969, Petersen produced much the same kind of analysis for England, and arrived at the same conclusion as he had for the Netherlands (Petersen, 1961:376–402; 1969:401–423). Again in this case, and in Petersen's words, "it is impossible to build from national data a sound statistical argument concerning population growth up to 1840" (1961:381; 1969:406). But he continued, "What we propose to do here is to examine the theory of the demographic transition in the context of English social history, reinforced with statistical data only when these are reasonably precise" (1961:381–382; 1969:406). Thus, in the two European cases at hand, Petersen set for himself the task of proving, or at least amassing arguments that: a) declining mortality did not account for the natural increase of the population during the early stages of modernization, and b) that increasing fertility did account for it.

DECLINING MORTALITY AND EARLY STAGES OF MODERNIZATION

Taking up the mortality issue first, Petersen asked, "Was the considerable population growth before the introduction of modern medicine and public health (about 1880) also the consequence, whether wholly or mainly, of a prior decline in mortality?" (Petersen, 1960:339). "While it is not possible to answer these questions directly from mortality statistics, at least plausible hypotheses can be suggested from known institutional changes and their probable effect on the death rate" (1960:339). Petersen built the beginning of his case by following McKeown and Brown (1955) who analyzed the factors affecting mortality in eighteenth century England. The McKeown and Brown paper had been originally written with a dual thrust. It was first of all a counter to Habakkuk's (1953) argument (which is substantially the same as Petersen's) that increased fertility was the likely cause of eighteenth century population increases in England rather than mortality decreases. The second task of the McKeown and Brown paper was to analyze critically the thesis of Griffith (1926) that improvements in medical practices and hospital care caused the decline in mortality.

Petersen, in both the Dutch and English cases, followed the McKeown and Brown argument *up to the point* where they concluded that declining mortality in the eighteenth century could not be accounted for by changes in medical practices and hospital care, or by reductions in the virulence of infective organisms, or increasing human resistance. However, he was skeptical of McKeown and Brown's final conclusion that the probable cause of declining mortality was to be found in the improvements in environmental and living conditions that would have reduced the risk of infection or increased the survival rate among those infected. In the case of the Netherlands, Petersen said that "it is hardly possible to speak of 'improvements' in Dutch living conditions during the century from 1750 to 1850" (Petersen, 1960:339). Regarding the Dutch case, he concluded, "If there was any decline in general mortality, then, it was probably quite small" (1960:341). In the case of England he did allow that there "probably was a more or less continuous decline in mortality from roughly 1760 to 1840.... The most important factor seems to have been better food supply, and possibly the improved living conditions, in other respects, enjoyed by the lower class" (1969:417).

Both cases were summarized by arguing that there is insufficient evidence that declining mortality was responsible for population increases in the eighteenth century and, "a *prima facie* case here for the probability that fertility rose" (Petersen, 1960:341; 1969:417). This runs counter to several historical demographers who have also considered the issue. McKeown and Brown (1955:138) carefully assembled and presented their reasons "for preferring a decrease in the death rate to an increase in the birth rate as an explanation of the rise in population in the eighteenth century." Helleiner (1957:7) has commented that

> ... most students of the history of population seem to agree that a significant reduction in mortality was the primary cause of the demographic upswing; and though the statistical evidence is inconclusive, we see no reason why this proposition shall be challenged. Indeed it can be shown that when mortality is high (as it was in the eighteenth century), a decline in death rate is inherently a more powerful causative factor of population growth than a rise in the birth rate.

On the other side of the argument, Habakkuk (1953) has argued that an increased need for labor produced the population increase of the eighteenth century. But, as he put it: "This still leaves open the mode of operation of this increased demand. Was its principal effect to lower the age at marriage, and in this way to increase births? Or to increase the ability of labourers to feed their children?" (1953:133). He concluded his argument by saying that one "purpose of this essay is to reinstate, as a hypothesis, the view that the first effect was more important, i.e., that the increased demand operated more via the birth rate than the death rate" (1953:133). Essentially Habakkuk made no stronger claim for his position than that it was a hypothesis that should be reopened for consideration.

Krause (1958, 1959a, 1959b) has argued that more frequent marriage and a decline in the age at marriage acted to increase fertility during the nineteenth century, but even Wrong (1967), one of the critics of transition theory, has noted that Krause's conclusions go far beyond the evidence. Petersen, while mentioning Krause's position, does not utilize his arguments to support his own (1969:428). Finally, Glass has also recently opened to question the "old orthodoxy" that mortality declines came first in the demographic transition, but he offered no evidence in support of his suggestion (Glass, 1965:17). And so the argument goes on, as it can so easily in the absence of reliable population data. One cannot escape the feeling when reading these discussions that making inferences about vital rates on the basis of social-historical information is an exercise of dubious worth. The researcher seems usually to have enough freedom in the selection of his evidence to reach the conclusion he prefers.

But what is the case when population data can be found? The Scandinavian countries, which have notably good demographic data for the eighteenth century, provide evidence for the prior decline of mortality. For example, Myrdal (1968: 17–28) has presented the vital rates for the Swedish population beginning with the year 1751. The Swedish death rate dropped from approximately 21 to 15 in the century between 1750 and 1850, while the birth rates moved generally downward from about 35 to 31 during that century. A recent excellent study of Norway's demographic history by Drake (1969) also showed that it was the prior decline of mortality that was the crucial factor producing a steady natural increase of the population after 1815. Drake provided several visual and tabular presentations showing the influence of a declining death rate (1969:42, 48, 49), and stated firmly that, "Whatever the ultimate cause [i.e., the actual cause of the falling death rate] of the rapid expansion of population in Norway after 1815, there can be little doubt that the immediate one was the fall of the death rate" (1969:73). Both the Swedish and Norwegian cases provide sound *demographic* evidence in support of that part of transition theory which claims that mortality declines in the early stages of modernization account for population increases.

FERTILITY IN THE EARLY STAGES OF MODERNIZATION

The second part of Petersen's critical argument is that an increase in the birth rate could have accounted for population increases in the early period of modernization. The case rests almost entirely on a series of deductions about the possible effects of the breakdown of traditionalism during the early period of modernization. The elements of the argument for the Netherlands case are that the breakdown of the traditional joint family households allowed some people to marry who would otherwise have remained as unmarried siblings in the household. The same conditions might have reduced the age at marriage (Petersen, 1960). In England, the long apprenticeship of the Medieval guilds imposed restraints against early marriage, and with the breakdown of the guilds in the early modern period these restraints were eased. Again, the effect of such institutional change could have been to increase rates of marriage and decrease the age at marriage. Petersen also argued that illegitimacy might have increased, and that the birth control practices previously used (within marriage) might have been reduced as the restraints of the older order were removed. Finally Petersen noted that in England the Poor Laws might have lowered the age at which people married, and might further have increased the number of children they had, because the existence of the welfare system would reduce the need for self constraint (Petersen, 1961:396; 1969:419). The entire argument, as Petersen forthrightly admits, is an inferential one derived from "sparse, often dubious, sometimes contradictory data concerning the interrelation of economic and demographic trends in Britain" (1969:401). Despite the admitted shakiness of those arguments about changes in fertility and mortality rates during the early stages of modernization, they are often cited as evidence of important weaknesses in transition theory (e.g., Wrong, 1967:21).

THE JAPANESE CASE

In the recent edition of his population book Petersen has introduced a new body of evidence—this time demographic evidence—that would, if accepted at face value, buttress the previously well received deductive arguments. The new evidence is the case of Japanese modernization that started during the latter part of the nineteenth century.

The Japanese case is particularly crucial because the unique history of that country fixes the date of the beginning of modernization almost exactly. The Tokugawa regime, which lasted from the beginning of the seventeenth century until 1867, kept Japan isolated from the Western world (Taeuber, 1958:17–18). With the Meiji Restoration, between 1867 and 1871, the way was cleared for modernization to begin. The new government played an active role in the process, and during the decades of 1870 and 1880 modernization was getting underway in Japan (Taeuber, 1958: 38). The vital rates that prevailed in these years after the Meiji Restoration provide an important test of the part of transition theory under consideration.

Petersen's presentation of the demographic facts are quoted here *verbatim*.

> From 1873, shortly after the Meiji regime was installed, to 1918, when the initial phase of rapid industrialization was over, the population of Japan went up from 35.2 to 55.0 million. The rate of annual growth increased from 0.75 per cent in the 1870's and 1880's to not quite 1 per cent in the 1890's, and to almost 1.5 per cent in the first two decades of the twentieth century. This accelerating growth was not the consequence of a substantial decline in mortality, as one would anticipate from the transition theory. On the contrary, the death rate apparently remained almost constant at around 20 per thousand throughout these decades. The birth rate rose from about 20 to over 30 (Taeuber, 1958, p. 41), for the incidence of infanticide was much reduced: children who had no place in the village economy could now migrate to industrial jobs in the cities or to overseas posts in the colonies. This rise in fertility during the first period of industrialization, puzzling to one anticipating the contrary, was not a spurious artifact of improved records but a social reality (*ibid.*, p. 232; but cf. Morita, 1963). In short, the higher fertility that by our surmise accompanied early British industrialization (or, for that matter, the modernization of almost any Western society; for the Dutch case, cf. Petersen, 1964) can be established with somewhat greater certainty in the Japanese case (Petersen, 1969:426).

This presentation of the evidence on Japan's period of transition does support the proposition that early population growth was more the result of increasing fertility than decreasing mortality. However, the best available evidence on the Japanese vital rates during the period after 1870 is not in agreement with several points made in the quotation above.

To begin, there are two factual errors in the references to Taeuber's data above. First, the birth rate in the 1870's as reported by Taeuber (using official statistics) was not 20 per thousand, but was about 25 per thousand (Taeuber, 1958:41, 50). If a ten point or more increase in the fertility rate had occurred between 1870 and 1918 it would have been a dramatic increase, and a very likely contributor to population growth. But no such increase occurred, for even the unadjusted official figures show the rate to be about 25 per thousand in 1875. What happened to the mortality rate during this same period? Petersen indicates that the "death rate remained almost constant at about 20 per thousand." Actually if the official statistics are taken at face value—as they are reported by Taeuber—the death rate *went up* from about 18 to 22.5 between 1875 and 1919 (Taeuber, 1958:50).

This is a demographic statistic which, if true, would be consistent with Petersen's thesis. Yet when the official statistics of Japan show mortality actually going up during the first fifty years of modernization one must immediately be skeptical of their validity; as indeed many scholars have been, including Taeuber (1958, 1960).

There is a second crucial inaccuracy in Petersen's discussion in the statement that "this rise in fertility during the first period of industrialization, 'puzzling' to one anticipating the contrary, was not a spurious artifact of improved records but a social reality" (*Ibid.*, p. 232; but cf. Morita, 1963) (Petersen, 1969:426). Taeuber's discussion on page 232 of her study of Japan's population was not, however, a defense of the validity of official fertility data between 1870 and 1918, but was in fact a consideration of the increase in fertility that occurred in Japan in the 1920's. Taeuber was explaining that the birth rate increase between the 1915–1919 era· and the 1920's was not an artifact of faulty data (Taeuber, 1958:232).

Regarding the validity of the mortality statistics for the period in question (1870–1918), Taeuber was quite clear. She recognized that the registration system of Japan—which started in 1871 and was the source of population data until 1918—achieved accuracy and completeness only gradually (1958:50). She discussed the official mortality rate which showed an increase after 1870, and considered a number of factors that *might have increased* the death rate during the early period of modernization. However, she ultimately concluded (contrary to the official tabular data accompanying her text and contrary to Petersen's reading of her) that "increasing activities designed to prevent deaths resulted in substantial and continuing declines in mortality from the 1860's or 1870's onward. Declining mortality was a factor leading to population increase in an industrializing Japan as it had been earlier in the West" (1958:55).

On the question of fertility changes during the same period, Taeuber was more equivocal, and it is difficult to draw a firm conclusion. She first presented a variety of hypothetical reasons for believing that the birth rate might actually have been as high as 38 or 40 per thousand in the early Meiji period (as contrasted with the official rate of 25). She did not, however, conclude that the birth rate was actually that high. She concluded her discussion by saying, "Moreover, in Japan the initial impact of economic modernization tended toward an increase in fertility" (1958:55). It is not completely clear how she arrived at that conclusion.

Returning to Petersen's treatment of the issue at hand, it will be noted in the quotation from his text that after the reference to Taeuber's statement that the trend in birth rates is no artifactual, he refers to a paper by Morita published in 1963. Preceded as it is by the suggestion "but, cf.," there is at least a hint that Morita may disagree with Petersen (and the position he attributed Taeuber) about the quality of the official data coming out of the early Meiji period. Indeed this is certainly the case. Morita (1963) has estimated the vital rates of Japan during the early Meiji period, and they vary considerably from the official registration figures. His analysis started from an assumption of under-registration of both births and deaths during the first decades after the Meiji Restoration, and his method involved an examination of the internal consistency of the data over time. By working backward from a time when the registration of births and deaths was more complete, he estimated the amount of under-registration during the early years of the registration system. This mode of analysis led Morita to state the following conclusions:

1. The crude birth rate in the early 1870's could never have been as low as was indicated in official statistics. The estimated birth rate for this period is 32 per 1000 as against the official rate for this period of 24. This estimated rate stands approximately at the same official birth rate in the 1900's (Morita, 1963:48).
2. The crude birth rate was very probably about 30 per 1000 or higher from the very beginning of the Meiji period, and the low rate in the official vital statistics should obviously be attributed to the incomplete registration of births in those years (Morita, 1963:49).
3. As for the death rate, we observe again, a significant difference between the estimated and official rates. According to our estimation, the crude death rate in the early 1870's was between a maximum of 24 and a minimum of 22 per 1000 as against the official rate of 18. The trend of the estimated death rates was slightly declining. . . . It may be noted that the estimated death rate declines from the very beginning of the Meiji period as against the official statistics which showed an upward trend until the 1890's (Morita, 1963:49).

Morita's analysis indicated that both the birth rate and the death rate, as reported in the official statistics of Japan for the 1870's, were too low. The lower rates would be the likely outcome of a registration system that was newly established and only partially understood or accepted by the people. The people of Japan probably did not register all births or deaths until some years after the introduction of the registration system (Morita, 1963:35–36). If the total count of the base population was reasonably accurate, the obvious effect of such underreporting would be a lowering of the vital rates. Then, over time, as the registration procedure became more universally accepted there would be an apparent increase in these rates.

While it might be possible to argue that Morita's conclusions are not valid, it is not possible to dismiss them casually while using the Japanese case as a refutation of transition theory. The Japanese case, as Petersen suggests, is nearly like a controlled experiment (1969:423). It provides an unequalled opportunity for examining what happens to vital rates during the early stages of modernization.

The ultimate question is, "What are the demographic facts?" It may never be possible to know precisely what did happen to the birth and death rates of Japan between 1870 and 1900, but the opposing views of the demographers considered in this paper are clear. Petersen has argued that birth rates went up and death rates remained almost constant. He based his argument on the official registration statistics, even though the demographers of Japan have routinely questioned their validity. Morita, on the other hand, has used the registration figures for the later part of the period to estimate the probable fertility and mortality rates after 1870. He has concluded that the fertility rate fluctuated around 32 per 1000 beween 1870 and 1900. He estimated that the death rate declined slightly during the same period. Given the contradictory nature of these conclusions, it is nearly impossible to accept the Japanese case as a clear refutation of transition theory. Only by accepting the official registration figures uncritically can the Japanese case be offered as evidence contrary to transition theory. We would argue on the basis of Morita's conclusions that the Japanese vital rates during the last decades of the nineteenth century are supportive of the theory. The more cautious might want to withhold judgment, but it must be considered inappropriate to argue that the Japanese case is contrary evidence.

SUMMARY AND CONCLUSION

Transition theory emerged about forty years ago. In the decades after 1930, the theory was elaborated and used by a wide variety of demographers and students of population. Some of the criticisms of transition theory have been widely quoted and apparently influential.

One criticism of the theory questions the nature of the changes in birth and death rates during the early stages of modernization. Some critics have argued that population growth during the early years of modernization was caused more by an increase in fertility than a decrease in mortality. While particular historical demographers argue on both sides of the issue, their evidence is largely deduced from various social, economic, or medical facts. The demographic evidence for European countries is difficult to find, although in both Norway and Sweden—with good quality demographic data covering the early stages of modernization—the evidence points toward the prior decline of mortality as the more important factor in population growth. Japan is a non-European case that appears to support the same conclusion although critics of transition theory have used it as contrary evidence. They have done so by using official Japanese statistics and ignoring a more sophisticated analysis which has highlighted the biasing effects of under-registration during the early Meiji period. When these biases are corrected the Japanese case is quite consistent with the theory of the modern demographic transition.

REFERENCES

Blacker, C. P. 1947. "Stages in population growth." The Eugenics Review 39 (October):88–102.

Carr-Saunders, Alexander M. 1936. World Population—Past Growth and Present Trends. Oxford: Clarendon Press.

Cowgill, D. O. 1963. "Transition theory as general population theory." Social Forces 41 (March):270–74.

———. 1949. "The theory of population growth cycles." The American Journal of Sociology 55 (September):163–70.

Davis, Kingsley. 1963. "The theory of change and response in modern demographic history." Population Index 29 (October):345–65.

———. 1949. Human Society. New York: The Macmillan Co.

Drake, Michael. 1969. Population and Society in Norway 1735–1865. Cambridge University Press.

Glass, Davis V. 1965. "Population growth and population policy." Pp. 3–24 in Mindel C. Sheps and Jeanne C. Ridley (eds.), Public Health and Population Change. Pittsburgh: University of Pittsburgh Press.

Griffith, G. Talbot. 1926. Population Problems of the Age of Malthus. Cambridge: Cambridge University Press.

Habakkuk, Hrothgar J. 1953. "English population in the eighteenth century." Economic History Review, 2nd series, 6:117–33. Reprinted in D. V. Glass and D. E. C. Eversley (eds.), Population in History. Chicago: Aldine Publishing Company, 1965:269–84.

Helleiner, K. F. 1957. "The vital revolution reconsidered." Canadian Journal of Economics and Political Science 23 (No. 1):1–9. Reprinted in D. V. Glass and D. E. C. Eversley (eds.), Population in History. Chicago: Aldine Publishing Company, 1965:79–86.

Hertzler, Joyce O. 1956. The Crisis in World Population. Lincoln: University of Nebraska Press.

Krause, J. T. 1959a. "Some implications of recent work in historical demography." Comparative Studies in Society and History 1 (January):164–88.

———. 1959b. "Some neglected factors in the English industrial revolution." Journal of Economic History 19 (December):528–40.

———. 1958. "Changes in English fertility and mortality, 1781–1850." Economic History Review, 2nd series, 11 (August):52–70.

Landry, Adolphe. 1934. La Revolution Demographique. Paris: Librairie du Recueil Sirey.

McKeown, Thomas and R. G. Brown. 1955. "Medical evidence related to English population changes in the eighteenth century." Population Studies 9 (November):119–41. Reprinted in D. V. Glass and D. E. C. Eversley (eds.), Population in History. Chicago: Aldine Publishing Company, 1965:285–307.

Morita, Y. 1963. "Estimated birth and death rates in the early Meiji period of Japan." Population Studies 17 (July): 33–56.

Myrdal, Alva. 1968. Nation and Family. Cambridge: The M.I.T. Press. Original edition: 1941, New York: Harper & Brothers.

Notestein, Frank W. 1945. "Population—the long view." Pp. 31–51 in Theodore W. Schultz (ed.), Food for the World. Chicago: University of Chicago Press.

Petersen, William. 1969. Population. 2nd ed. New York: The Macmillan Company.

———. 1964. "The demographic transition in the Netherlands." Pp. 166–92 in The Politics of Population. Garden City, N.Y.: Doubleday and Co.

———. 1961. Population. New York: The Macmillan Co.

———. 1960. "The demographic transition in the Netherlands." American Sociological Review 25 (June):334–47.

Taeuber, Irene B. 1960. "Japan's demographic transition re-examined." Population Studies 14 (July):28–39.

———. 1958. The population of Japan. Princeton, New Jersey: The Princeton University Press.

Thompson, W. S. 1929. "Population." American Journal of Sociology 34 (March): 959–75.

Vance, R. B. 1952. "Is theory for demographers?" Social Forces 31 (October): 9–13.

Wrong, Dennis H. 1967. Population and society. 3rd ed. New York: Random House.

Migration

Introduction: A. Migration Theory

There are three basic questions connected with the study of migration: 1. What is migration? 2. What are the causes of migration? 3. What are the effects of migration? Some partial answers to all of these questions will be provided in the pages that follow, but, of course, the answers will be selective and reflect only some points of view. With regard to theory, I have selected papers that reflect the most recent sociological thinking, not the earlier migration theories.

For years many writers complained that there was too little theoretical work being done in the area of migration. There was a substantial amount of empirical work, but little theory to guide that work. In the last decade that situation has changed, for a number of writers have advanced theories of migration that may now be used to guide research. The three papers of this part of Section III reflect a good deal of the sociological thinking that has been done on the subject.

In general migration theories concentrate on the causes of migration, but most theorists begin theoretical discussions by identifying and defining what it is. This raises one of the interesting problems of migration theory: there is little consensus among demographers about the best definition of migration.

Mangalam and Schwarzweller (article 14) define migration as the "relatively permanent moving away of a collectivity, called migrants, from one geographical location to another, preceded by decision-making on the part of the migrants . . . resulting in changes in the interactional system of the migrants." By contrast, Everett Lee in "A Theory of Migration" defines migration very simply as ". . . a permanent or semipermanent change of residence." Lee's brief definition leaves many questions unanswered. Even the more elaborate definition of Mangalam and Schwarzweller raises a number of questions.

Both definitions agree that the move must be a semipermanent change of residence. A trip from one place to another is not migration if there is no intention of changing residence. Mangalam and Schwarzweller have strongly emphasized the group or collectivity aspects of migration. If by collectivity they mean a married couple or a family, it is of course quite true that most migration is done in groups. But individuals also migrate and most researchers would not want to exclude them from consideration. But Mangalam and Schwarzweller are implying that migrants should always be viewed as part of a collectivity. In an earlier writing Mangalam has said that even though only one individual with a specific set of characteristics is moving from one place to another, he or she is still likely to be a member of some collectivity of individuals sharing these same characteristics.[1] This position might be called the "strong sociological" view of migration. Many theorists and writers would not insist that migration *always* be viewed as the action of a collectivity. Almost all would agree, though, that when a natural social unit is involved—a family, a tribe, a village—it is quite reasonable to take the norms of the group and statuses of the individuals into account if one is to understand the decision-making process that leads to migration. James Beshers has made this point very strongly, emphasizing that migration is most often going to be the outcome of a joint decision by a husband and wife, in marriages where the spouses accept the traditional sex roles.[2] Traditional sex roles call for the husband to have the greatest

---

[1] J. J. Mangalam, *Human Migration: A Guide to Migration Literature in English 1955–1962* (Lexington, Ky.: University of Kentucky Press, 1968), p. 9.

[2] James M. Beshers, *Population Processes in Social Systems* (New York: The Free Press, 1967), pp. 135–39.

voice in the economic and occupational aspects of migration, while the wife's opinion is traditionally given more weight in the realm of social and familial matters.

One final issue about which many writers hold differing opinions is found again in the contrasting definitions of Mangalam-Schwarz-weller and Lee. The former writers feel that migration only occurs when there is a change in the interactional system of the migrants. While they admit that it may be difficult to prove that a move from one place to another can occur without some change in the interactional system of the individuals, they nevertheless cling to the possibility that it could occur. I am much more inclined to believe that any change of residence will produce *some* change in the interactional system of the individual, and thus it might be taken as an assumption. The difficulty with this position is illustrated by Lee's definition of migration in which he does not require that migration involve a significant change in the interactional systems of the individuals. Following this notion, he concludes that "a move across the hall from one apartment to another is counted as just as much an act of migration as a move from Bombay, India, to Cedar Rapids, Iowa. . . ."

There is no final answer to this question of exactly what constitutes migration, except as one arbitrarily asserts one thing or the other. In research the scientist simply has to make his definition known and be specific about his measurement. If other scientists think the definition or measurement is unreasonable, they may disregard the findings.

The two theories of migration presented in articles 14 and 15 are distinguishable generally because the first is more sociological while the second is more individualistically oriented. They both represent needed efforts to clarify and identify what we are talking about when we use the word migration. More importantly, they present testable hypotheses that can guide research. More will be said about the characteristics of migration theory and the hypotheses derived therefrom in the paper by Kammeyer and McClendon below (article 18).

The final paper in this part of Section III is another statement by Everett Lee in which he speculates on the role of migration in American society. He is especially concerned with the way in which migration is a necessary and integral part of the American educational and social structure. In a specific way Lee is arguing, as he has before, that the migrating habits of the American population are unusual, if not unique, and they are instrumental in shaping the kind of society we have.[3]

---

[3] See also: Everett S. Lee, "The Turner Thesis Re-examined," *American Quarterly*, XIII (1961), pp. 77–83; See also: George W. Pierson, "The Migration Factor in American History," *American Quarterly*, XIV (1962), Supplement, pp. 275–89.

14

Some Theoretical Guidelines
Toward a Sociology of Migration[1]

J. J. Mangalam and Harry K. Schwarzweller

The question is beginning to be debated in the field of migration studies as to whether it is possible to formulate an explanatory theory general enough to cover the whole process of emigration and immigration. Charles Price thinks it is doubtful that we are ready for a general account couched in terms of formal theory (*Australian Immigration: A Bibliography and Digest,* 1966, p. A52). On the other hand, Everett S. Lee has attempted to present a general theory ("A Theory of Migration," *Demography,* 3, 1966, pp. 47–57). The following article by Mangalam and Schwarzweller takes a middle of the road position by formulating a middle-range theory of migration. This is a preliminary effort which other researchers will hopefully modify, clarify, and expand.

Students of human migration are becoming increasingly aware that a general theoretical orientation, preferably with a multidisciplinary emphasis, is lacking in most studies of migration.[2] There have been attempts to construct typologies[3] and many efforts at model-building to explain various aspects of migration on the part of many scholars.[4] At least one scholar, more recently, has formulated even a theory of migration.[5] However, for reasons stated in our recent review of contemporary studies of migration, a sociological theory of migration which meets the stringent demands of formal theory is not likely to materialize in the near future. For, despite a long history of empirical inquiry, researchers are only beginning to do the hard work of conceptualization of the phenomenon, systematically positing causal sequences, and testing relevant hypotheses, all of which must necessarily precede a formal statement of theory. And no one should entertain any

Reprinted from *International Migration Review,* 4, no. 2 (Spring, 1970), pp. 5–20, by permission of the authors and the Center for Migration Studies.

false illusion that such a theory of migration is in the offing here. Our far more modest aim is to suggest some guidelines and sociologically relevant foci which may serve to stimulate further effort by other social scientists in building *toward* the goal of a general, sociological theory of migration.

For purposes of the discussion at hand, we conceive of migration as a phenomenon, having some aspects located within the culture system, some within the social system and some within the personality system sectors of human social organization. Our main concern is with the collectivity dimensions of the phenomenon, modified as appropriate and meaningful by its culture and personality systems dimensions.[6]

In developing a sociological framework for the study of any social phenomenon one must, of course, attend to a number of important tasks. To begin with, that part of the phenomenon which is sociologically relevant must be abstracted from the totality of its dimensions; that is, it must be drawn from the reality of specifics and considered as a general object for study apart from special circumstances.[7] This abstraction must be embodied in the form of a definition which, in effect, charts out the proper sociological concerns in dealing with the phenomenon. A sociological frame of reference for the study of society must then be outlined (or selected) and the phenomenon of interest located within that framework. Finally, in order to demonstrate or "to test" the utility of this approach, crucial questions derived from the proposed theoretical treatment should be indicated and examined as to their researchability and their potential contribution to our knowledge of the phenomenon and hence about society. We have endeavored to follow the above procedure.[8]

SOCIOLOGICAL DIMENSIONS OF MIGRATION

As noted earlier,[9] our systematic review of the current literature on migration, paying particular heed to the manner by which researchers define and approach this phenomenon, reveals a number of misconceptions about the nature of migration as well as serious inadequacies and errors of omission in directing sociologically relevant research. Typically, researchers view migration as an individual event (although migration of a collectivity is not necessarily excluded from consideration), and they describe this event as a physical movement of people from one spatial location to another entailing a more or less permanent change of residence. Often other aspects are specified, but not in consistent fashion, and other dimensions emphasized, but these usually depend upon the unique characteristics of the case being studied.[10]

We contend that the prevailing view of migration and the modes of defining it as commonly employed by researchers reflect basic inadequacies in the abstracting of its sociological content from the concrete and specific realities under observation. We cannot pursue in detail here the evidence and reasoning which give rise to these assertions. Rather, we shall begin with the end-product of our mental deliberations, namely, a definition of migration which, though by no means exhaustive of its sociological content inherent in the phenomenon, takes us a bit further in calling attention to some major sociological concerns in the study of migration. *Migration is a relatively permanent moving away of a collectivity, called migrants, from one geographical location to another, preceded by decision-making on the part of the migrants on the basis of a hierarchically ordered set of values or valued ends and resulting in changes in the interactional system of the migrants.*

It is our thesis that the identification of instances of migration in these terms is a necessary precondition for the proper sociological study of migration. Let us not confuse the purpose of a conceptual definition of this kind with that of an operational definition; the latter, an essential step in designing research, is guided by the former. The terms included in the above definition set the theoretical boundaries and specify the sociological foci in studying the phenomenon; hence, the implications of these terms need to be made clear.

Permanent moving away. Change in the geographical location of residence is the most frequently stressed aspect of migration and a necessary, though not sufficient condition for determining what is or is not an instance of migration. By emphasizing the permanency of spatial movement we rule out such cases as commuters, salesmen, tourists, and the like. The period of time implied by the term *permanent,* however, cannot be generalized for all instances but must be operationalized for each specific case. Likewise, the determination of locational change must be tailored to situational circumstances and research questions. In setting these spatial and temporal limits, of course, one will be guided by additional requirements imposed in meeting the demands of the remaining dimensions of migration as specified in the definition.

A collectivity, called migrants. The formulation of generalizations about groups or categories of people is a central concern in the discipline of sociology, and indeed, the *raison d'etre* of sociology as a science. In the past, for various reasons, the collectivity aspects of migration have tended to be ignored; to build toward a sociology of migration, this fundamental dimension should be emphasized.

Though the collectivity criterion in essence negates interest in the individual cases, these cannot be rejected outright; deviant case analysis may yield fruitful insights about those patterns of behavior the sociologist is researching. An individual migrant, for example, abstracted from his immediate environment and conceptualized as an actor with certain attributes can be considered as a representative of a particular category of actors within a normative system different from that of the collectivity in question. In that sense, at least, many of the sociodemographic studies of migration have taken into account the collectivity dimension of migration phenomenon, though often not for explicitly theoretical reasons.

Preceded by decision-making on the basis of a hierarchically ordered set of values. Whether specified in these terms or in terms denoting similar concerns of a sociopsychological nature,[11] this criterion is an important directive toward studying the dynamics of the migration process and the adjustment phase that follows in the wake of physical relocation. As an object of scientific inquiry, migration cannot be treated as random behavior. To be sure, there are individuals who appear "to simply pick up and go"; in these cases, however, we must assume that our data are insufficient rather than that human behavior is erratic.

It is when the existing social situation fails to satisfy individual needs, at least minimally, that certain members of the collectivity entertain the notion of moving away to other places, where as they see it, they will have a better chance of satisfying their unmet needs and of overcoming their felt deprivation. Yet all people experience deprivations of one kind or another; the mere existence of some deprivations does not necessarily induce migration. In order to explore the dynamics of migration, therefore, one must undertake to discover the criteria by which, and the process through which, existing deprivation effect the decision to migrate.

We contend that it is useful to posit values, which are overtly expressed in terms of valued ends, as the criteria used by a collectivity in determining the relative importance of existing deprivations.[12] Assuming that values and valued ends tend to be ordered hierarchically within a given social organization, the deprivation of ends more highly valued will have greater positive effect upon the decision to migrate than the deprivation of ends less highly valued, all other things being equal. Furthermore, if those deprivations that led to migration persist after relocation, and if high value continues to be attached to those desired ends, then adjustment difficulties (manifested, perhaps, by a second migration or a "return migration") can be anticipated.

Of course, a high degree of deprivation of highly valued ends is not a sufficient condition for migrating. We must take into account, for example, that a given social organization does provide various means for the pursuit of valued ends. Only when a collectivity is blocked from contesting, for example in the economic or political arena, and only when such barriers are perceived as factors intrinsic to the local system (i.e., the residential situation seen as a determining condition) will relative deprivation become a force affecting migration. But by the same token we should not assume that migration is a "final answer" or "last resort" in response to relative deprivations; indeed, migration may be a normatively sanctioned means toward the attainment of valued ends and, in that sense, a structurally prescribed behavior integral to the fabric of the local social organization.

Furthermore, the decision to migrate is a subjective act. What matters is how members of the collectivity feel about the situation irrespective of the objective facts of the structure of opportunity. Readiness to migrate is more a function of perceived reality than a response to structural conditions *per se*.

Unless other conditions are also satisfied, however, readiness to migrate alone will not induce migration. The availability and characteristics of potential places of destination, for example, must be taken into account. In societies where they are reasonably free to move about, individuals will tend to migrate to places where they perceive ways to overcome their felt deprivations without having to give up those aspects of life they had been enjoying at the place of origin. Values, of course, enter into the process of establishing priorities and of making such choices.

To be sure, the factors inducing migration are not always recognized overtly nor logically articulated by migrants or potential migrants. But we must assume that these elements are present in varying degrees in any given case of migration and, subsequently, affect all phases of the migration process. Their detection and delineation are important tasks for the researcher; their study is a proper area of inquiry for the sociologist.

Changes in the interactional system. Emphasizing the social system aspects of migration, this criterion directs the sociologist's attention toward structural changes concomitant with residential relocation. We are suggesting, in effect, that to study migration from the sociological point of view one must regard it as a phenomenon that produces changes in the interactional system. Insofar as this social change producing character of migration is not delineated, its introduction into a general theory of social organization is not only difficult to rationalize but also, from a strictly sociological standpoint, perhaps not proper.

A change in residence *per se*, however, does not *necessarily* mean a change in the interactional system of the actors involved. It is conceivable, for instance, that members of a collectivity may travel some distance, establish residence in a new area, yet still not experience, nor contribute to, any basic changes in the interactional system of which it is a part. Despite residential relocation, in other words, the essential structural features of the shared interactional system may not have been altered. But the burden of proof then is on the researcher to demonstrate that he has indeed explored all conceivable, sociologically relevant ways in which change might have occurred, and this, of course, is a task that offers very little chance of closure.[13] In the study of migration, then, the sociologist is called upon to seek out, through empirical research guided by a general conceptual scheme, *the sense* in which the phenomenon of relocation has disturbed the interactional system of the migrating collectivity.

It is an error, for example, to assume that peasants basically retain their original social organization when they move from village to cities.[14] Change in occupation alone, which is almost always the overriding reason for such rural to urban movements, is sufficient to bring about significant changes in the interactional system of those migrants. Then too, there are other important behavioral changes—in visiting patterns, recreational activities, shopping practices, and the like—which are situationally induced through relocation[15] and which, if not seriously disturbing in an immediate sense, at least erode over time the framework of social organization the peasants carry with them into the city, even if it is to a migrant enclave. The mistaken notion that migration occurs without significant change in the interactional system of the migrants can be traced, more often than not, to a conceptualization of this phenomenon within the context of social organization theory somewhat different from that suggested here; we shall clarify our position in a subsequent section. At this point, let us explore a bit further how one might approach the study of changes in the interactional system of a migrating collectivity, and the importance of such study in understanding significant problems associated with migration.

We conceive of migration as a social process linking two systems of social organization. Pursuant to this conceptualization, knowledge about both systems, whether empirically delineated or historically reconstructed, is essential for an adequate understanding of the intricate social dimensions bound up in the phenomenon. To take into account only the *recipient system,* at the place of destination, or only the *donor system,* at the place of origin, represents an inadequate sociological approach and yields incomplete knowledge about the dynamics of this social process.[16]

Furthermore, social problems arising out of the process of migration can be fully understood only by careful delineation of those sectors of social organization where interactional changes have taken place. Consider, for example, the problems of social control associated with migration. Why should migration result in an increase or decrease of crime, alcoholism, and other forms of deviant behavior? There is no inherent reason why the physical movement of people from one geographic locale to another should affect deviant behavior, unless the interactional pattern that had stabilized the migrants' social organization prior to their migration is somehow upset in the process of residential relocation of the collectivity.

In short, for defining a sociologically relevant instance of migration, this criterion of changes in the interactional system of the migrants, couched in these or similar terms, suggests one of the essential sociological properties of human migration.[17] In building toward a sociology of migration this property must be given a central position in the conceptualization of that phenomenon.

The foregoing discussion, which specifies the sociological content of migration, calls for a consideration of this phenomenon's location within the context of a general and theoretical orientation for the study of society. In our own research we have employed a functional approach, and we have found that an action-theory framework, with emphasis upon the interactional system, is most suitable and consistent with our perspective of migration as an integral part of social organization. A brief review of the central notions in this approach are in order.[18]

Four basic *conditions* may be postulated which together determine the patterns of behavior in an on-going society at any given point in time. These are: the size and quality of its population; the natural and man-made environment; the historical time context; and the available technological base. Under the given parameters of these *contingent conditions*, the members of a society interact to produce a particular type of social organization.[19]

For analytical purpose, a social organization can be understood to have three interrelated components: the culture, social, and personality systems. The culture system represents the *symbolic-meaningful* aspects (e.g., values expressed in such elements as language, art, style of life, etc.) which serve to guide behavior.[20] The personality system has relevance to immediate action, essentially, but largely on an individual rather than collectivity level; reference points for action tend to be within the realm of the individual psyche. The social system is inter-individual and, in that sense, *relational-normative;* reference points for action are relevant to functional problems faced by a collectivity and action is governed by the demands of the normative structure of the society. An essential difference between the social and personality systems is one of relative emphasis on group or collective pressure versus individually perceived needs. Whereas both the social and personality systems have direct bearing on action, the influence of the culture system is indirect and usually less pressing.

In the *relational-normative* sense, the functional problems of a social system are many. They include the problems of patterning of the normative structure, its maintenance, and continued patterning; of adapting or allocating of scarce means to desired ends; of attaining collective goals; of coping with the structural strains produced by the on-going social process; and of integrating the totality of the social processes and actions into a meaningful whole.[21] These functions are interrelated in the social system, which in turn is interrelated with both the culture and personality systems to form the overall social organization of a given society at a particular point in time.

The functioning of this social organization over a period of time inevitably results in a new set of relationships, giving rise to a different or changed social organization. Because of the interrelated nature of the elements, sociocultural changes, of course, can be initiated in any part of the social organization and its contingent conditions.[22]

Now let us consider the location of the phenomenon of migration within some definite sector of social organization. Given the nature of migration, we find it most useful to conceptualize it within the social system component of social organization and, reasoning that migration is a response to relative deprivations perceived by a collectivity, as integral to the functional area of adaptation. In other words, we conceive of migration as an adaptive process for maintaining the dynamic equilibrium of the social organization at the place of origin (i.e., of the *donor sub-system*).

Whereas migration is thus the result of certain inadequacies in the functioning of a given social organization (i.e., a legitimized means for providing members of the collectivity ways to overcome their perceived deprivations), it sets in motion a series of changes in the entire social organization. Furthermore, the social organization at the place of destination (i.e., the recipient sub-system) by accommodating the social organization of the migrating collectivity, must itself change. A complete understanding of migration, therefore, demands that it be considered as a phenomenon effecting two social organizations, one at the place of origin and the other at the place of destination.

The migrant collectivity itself should be regarded as a third social organization which, either through direct interactional ties or through symbolic interchanges such as gifts and letters, links the other two. Structural strains within the migrant social organization are of a crucial nature and can result from changes in practically all functional areas. New ways of patterning, adapting, goal gratification, and integration are called forth almost at once. Moreover, new deprivations are usually generated as a result of migration and these provide important clues to the identification and solution of adjustmental problems with which the migrants must now cope.[23]

Placing a middle-range "theory" of migration, or an *ad hoc* hypothesis, or even a specific research design within the framework of a general theoretical scheme such as that suggested here would, we believe, enable students of migration to see the dynamics of the phenomenon in its proper perspective and far beyond that of the narrower framework of isolated studies. It would aid in the cumulative growth of a general theory of migration and it would help to assure that migration studies ultimately contribute to an integrated body of sociological knowledge and to a broader and deeper understanding of change processes.

SOCIOLOGICALLY RELEVANT TOPICS IN THE STUDY OF MIGRATION

We shall now briefly attempt to demonstrate the usefulness of our approach by pointing out how sociologically relevant questions concerning migration can be viewed within the context of this approach.

Who Are Migrants?

From a sociological point of view, our interest focuses on the delineation of migrant characteristics in terms of relevant elements of social organization. Relevance is determined by differentials between the social organizations (and their respective contingent conditions) of the migrant collectivity and that of the donor subsystem. In a particular case of migration *some* of these differentials take on greater importance than others, although it cannot be established *a priori* in which characteristics such differentials exist.

From general considerations of the nature of social organization, however, the following kinds of information would seem to be pertinent: 1. aspects of contingent conditions affecting the migrants' social organization, such as population characteristics, ecological factors, historical antecedents, technological skills; 2. kinds of interaction, such as the extent of cooperation, competition, conflict, and the available communication facilities; 3. the overall nature of the migrant collectivity's social organization as differentiated from the social organization at the place of origin (say, for example, in terms of the rural-urban continuum); 4. cultural system components, such as style of life, ideological commitments, values, language; 5. personality system components, such as health, needs, aspirations, role performance in significant statuses. And, in particular, one should consider 6. the social system components including a) socialization practices, b) type of economy, c) clarity of goal definitions, d) kinds of stress within the system, and e) level of integration. These topics are illustrative of the kinds of information needed for a sociological understanding of the migrating collectivity which, in turn, will suggest some answers to the question: Why did they migrate?

Some of the above factors come under sociodemographic variables and these are well represented in the studies of migration. Some attention also has been paid to such personality variables as attitudes, aspirations, and health. Occasionally, studies have focused on neighborhood relations and community satisfactions. But the existing literature is very weak in describing migrant collectivities in terms of differentials in culture and social system components and, until such differentials are delineated, answers to the above question will continue to be couched in more or less nonsociological terms.

Why Did They Migrate?

At noted earlier, the mere existence of differentials between the migrating collectivity and the collectivity at the place of origin is not a sufficient condition for migration to occur. All societies, for example, have some kind of stratification system and this implies the existence of sectors of society which differ in some elements of their social organizations. Yet in many such societies no extensive migration occurs. The more important factor, of course, is how the migrating collectivity views these differentials.

When differentials exist in the form of deprivations for the migrant in highly valued goals, and if the collectivity cannot perceive the means to attain those goals within the existing social organization, and if they perceive resources to overcome their deprivations outside the social organization of their place of origin, then migration is likely to occur. Thus we have members of a collectivity, called migrants, who become part of two social organizations: the one in which they were reared but in which they feel deprived of opportunities for the realization of highly valued goals, and the other known perhaps only vaguely to them but in which they sense the accessibility of necessary resources to overcome their deprivations.

A migrating collectivity, however, is seldom if ever able to take full cognizance of new deprivations that might arise as a consequence of migration. Furthermore, migrants almost never totally reject all elements of the social organization of the migrant collectivity and these differ only in *some* aspects from the social organization of the place of origin; they have a good many things in common and these continue to influence the life of the migrants and their subsequent adjustment in the host community.

Where Did They Migrate?

Migrants seek a destination where: 1. their unmet wants can be satisfied and where; 2. the social organization is as similar as possible to that at the place of origin. In other words, we are saying that the migrants prefer to relocate in a situation that disturbs to a minimum their own social organization, i.e., their internalized patterns of behavior. And in the selection process, of course, values play an important part (e.g., in determining what elements of the social organization at the place of origin can be "sacrificed" through a move).

One can conceive of situations where the first, but not the second aim is fulfilled.[24] Compromises must be made and, in such circumstances where various highly valued elements of social organization have been jeopardized through migration, a number of alternative behaviors can be predicted: 1. the migrants may live in literally two worlds, maintaining semi-permanent attachment to both the place of origin and place of destination;[25] 2. they may introduce their own kind of social organization into the new situation; 3. they may plan a second migration elsewhere; 4. they may return to the area of origin; or 5. they may abruptly break away from their own cultural heritage and social organization and accept the new.

What Are the Consequences of Migration?

The consequences of migration affect all three social organizations: of the migrants, of the area of origin, and of the area of destination. A population interchange between the donor and recipient subsystems has, of course, occurred. The migrating collectivity also experiences changes in some of its contingent conditions (ecological, historical time dimension) which bring about changes in its social organization, theoretically, in all three components: culture, personality, and social systems.

All resulting changes, however, are not necessarily consequential; this is a matter for empirical delineation, guided by appropriate and limited theoretical guidelines of the middle range type. It is important to recognize, nevertheless, the possibility that changes in the social organizations at the place of origin and destination also affect changes in the social organization of the migrating collectivity. It is in this sense, namely, of the interrelatedness of the three social organizations, that we speak when we refer to these as one *migration system*. Interchanges of elements of social organization take place among these social organizations through the medium of the migrants (who, on the one hand, are unit carriers of a particular kind of social organization, and on the other hand effective advocates of change, implicitly if not explicitly).

Mapping out all possible consequences for any particular instance of migration would be a colossal, if not an impossible, task. We believe, however, that the notion of a migration system comprised of three social organizations with interlinkages operating through the migrating collectivity is a useful theoretical device for organizing sociologically relevant research on the consequences of migration.

CONCLUSION

In conclusion, let it be understood that the foregoing discussion should not be interpreted as a delineation of an all-encompassing theory of migration. Rather, as explicitly stated in the title, it outlines certain theoretical guidelines which can lead to fruitful results in building *toward* a comprehensive theory of migration. We have tried to conceptualize migration within a setting of human interaction, the generic stuff that gives rise to the phenomenon of social organization. And we have located migration as an adaptive process within the social system component of social organization; this indicates our own preference for the study of social organization as a theoretical framework rooted in motivated, goal-oriented social action. We have argued for the notion of migration system, consisting of a donor subsystem and a recipient subsystem, linked by the subsystem of the migrating collectivity. We have spelled out briefly what seem to us the advantages of these theoretical guidelines while considering the four important questions about human migration: Who are the migrants? Why do they migrate? Where do they migrate? And what are the consequences of migration? We should perhaps finally add that the above theoretical considerations emerged as useful in our struggle with the empirical problems encountered in our own research on one small sector of the universe of human migration.[26]

NOTES

1. This is one of a series of papers from the Beech Creek Study sponsored by the National Institute of Mental Health in cooperation with the Kentucky Agricultural Experiment Station. The authors gratefully acknowledge the suggestions of our colleague, James S. Brown, and Sylvia Mangalam, and the patient work of our able assistant, Mrs. Cornelia Morgan. This paper continues the discussion that we began in our earlier paper, J. J. Mangalam and Harry K. Schwarzweller, "General Theory in the Study of Migration: Current Needs and Difficulties," *International Migration Review*, 3 (1968).

2. For example, see Gunther Beijer, *Rural Migrants in Urban Setting*, The Hague: Martinus Nijhoff, 1963, p. 316; Everett S. Lee, "A Theory of Migration," *Demography*, 3 (1966): 47–57; Philip M. Hauser, "Present Status and Prospects of Research in Population," pp. 70–85 in Joseph J. Spengler and Otis Dudley Duncan (editors), *Population Theory and Policy*, Glencoe, Illinois: The Free Press, 1956; Rupert B. Vance, "Is Theory for Demographers?" pp. 88–90, in Joseph J. Spengler and Otis Dudley Duncan, *op.*

cit.; and George L. Wilber, "Determinants of Migration Research and Their Consequences," *Population Research and Administrative Planning*, Mississippi State University, Division of Sociology and Rural Life, Conference Series no. 10, pp. 52–61.

3. For example, see Otis D. Duncan, "The Theory and Consequences of Mobility of Farm Population," in Joseph J. Spengler and Otis Dudley Duncan, *op. cit.*, pp. 417–34; Ajit Das Gupta, "Types and Measures of Internal Migration," *International Population Conference Proceedings*, Vienna: International Union for the Scientific Study of Population, 1959, pp. 619–24; R. Heberle, "Types of Migration," *Southwestern Social Science Quarterly*, 36 (1955): 65–70; William Petersen, "A General Typology of Migration," *American Sociological Review* 23 (1958): 256–66.

4. For example, see Albert F. Anderson, *Theoretical Considerations in the Analysis of Migration*, unpublished doctoral dissertation, Iowa State University of Science and Technology, 1962, 141 pp.; John K. Folger, "Models in Migra-

tion," in *Selected Studies of Migration Since World War II*, New York: Proceedings of the 34th Annual Conference of the Milbank Memorial Fund, 1957, Part III, pp. 155–64; Harold Frank Goldsmith, *The Meaning of Migration: A Study of the Migration Expectations of High School Students*, unpublished doctoral dissertation, Michigan State University, 1962, 322 pp.; Eleanore Noble Nishtura, *Internal Migration in Indiana*, unpublished doctoral dissertation, Purdue University, 1959, 293 pp.; and Ronald Taft, "A Psychological Model for the Study of Social Assimilation," *Human Relations*, 10 (1957): 141–56; Allen Richardson, "A Theory and a Method for the Psychological Study of Assimilation," *International Migration Review*, 2 (1967): 3–29.

5. Everett S. Lee, *op. cit.*

6. "A collectivity," according to Parsons, "is a system of concretely interactive roles." See Talcott Parsons, *The Social System*, Glencoe, Illinois: The Free Press, 1951, p. 41. There are at least three types of collectivities that can be distinguished: group, category, and aggregate. See Joseph H. Fichter, *Sociology*, Chicago: University of Chicago Press, 1957. When we use the term, we shall be referring to group *and* category.

7. The distinction drawn here between abstraction of a phenomenon and its conceptualization is a simple but necessary one. Abstraction implies what Lazarsfeld has called "originating observation." By conceptualization we mean translating this original imagery to communicable words in the form of a workable definition, not necessarily operationalized. This is step 1 in Lazarsfeld's "translating this imagery into empirical research instruments." See Paul F. Lazarsfeld, "Problems in Methodology," in Robert K. Merton, Leonard Broom, and Leonard S. Cottrell, Jr. (editors), *Sociology Today*, New York: Basic Books, 1959, pp. 39–78.

8. As noted earlier, our endeavors to deal with migration as a sociological phenomenon began with the study of migrants from Beech Creek, a three-neighborhood locality in eastern Kentucky, to urban-industrial Ohio and adjoining states. See James S. Brown, Harry K. Schwarzweller, and Joseph J. Mangalam, "Kentucky Mountain Migration and the Stem Family:

An American Variation on a Theme by Le Play," *Rural Sociology*, 28 (1963): 48–69.

9. J. J. Mangalam and Harry K. Schwarzweller, *op. cit.*

10. Illustrations of such definitions are many. Some typical ones can be found in S. N. Eisenstadt, *The Absorption of Immigrants: A Comparative Study Based on the Jewish Community in Palestine and the State of Israel*, Glencoe, Illinois: The Free Press, 1955, p. 1; David Hannerberg, Torsten Hägerstrand, and Bruno Odering (editors), *Migration in Sweden: A Symposium*, Lund: The Royal University of Lund, 1957, p. 28; William Petersen, *Population*, New York: Macmillan, 1961, p. 592; Brinley Thomas, "Internal Migration," in Philip M. Hauser and Otis D. Duncan (editors), *The Study of Population*, Chicago: University of Chicago Press, 1959, p. 510; and Abraham A. Weinberg, *Migration and Belonging: A Study of Mental Health and Personal Adjustment in Israel*, The Hague: Martinus Nijhoff, 1961, pp. 265–66. All of them conceive of migration as something more than mere movement of people through physical space; but none of them taken alone has grasped the core of the phenomenon.

11. As for example, in Thomas' definition of migration as "the movements (involving change of permanent residence) from one country to another which take place through the volition of the individuals or families concerned." See Brinley Thomas, *op. cit.*

12. We are using the term "values" in the sense of selection principles from "available means, modes and ends of action." See Clyde Kluckhohn, "Values and Value-Orientations in the Theory of Action: An Exploration in Definition and Classification," in Talcott Parsons and Edward A. Shils (editors), *Toward a Theory of Action*, Cambridge: Harvard University Press, 1952.

13. The problem we are pointing out is somewhat analogous to that of a scientist arguing a null hypothesis.

14. An example of this sort of position is found in the statement made by Oscar Lewis during a conference on rural-urban migration. See National Institute of Mental Health, *Proceedings of the Rural-*

Urban Migration Conference, Bethesda, Maryland, 89 pp.

15. Appalachian mountain people, for example, who move to urban, industrialized areas of the Ohio Valley find that many things they were accustomed to in the social organization of mountain communities are lacking or changed in the social organization of the urban, host communities. Housing, food, primary group relations, kin-oriented activities, legal demands, etc., appear to have taken new dimensions. The migrants must learn to cope with these new deprivations as well as overcome the old deprivations that gave rise to the decision to migrate in the first instance.

16. For a further explanation of the *donor subsystem* and the *recipient subSystem,* which together make up the migration system, see James S. Brown, Harry K. Schwarzweller, and Joseph J. Mangalam, *op. cit.* What we want to emphasize here is that there is an important difference between the manner in which migration system (stream) is used in demographic literature and the manner in which we are using it here. Our usage is in the sociological context, emphasizing the interactional context of human migration.

17. We should also add that it represents the core concern in the study of migration as a social problem.

18. Attack and defense of functionalism, particularly of the variant known as structural-functional analysis, has been going on for some time. We have no intention to enter this battle on either side. However, any objective observer is likely to find a considerable amount of common elements in the approaches of such modern theorists as Kingsley Davis (*Human Society,* 1949), M. J. Levy (*The Structure of Society,* 1952), Robert K. Merton (*Social Theory and Social Structure,* 1957), Talcott Parsons (*The Structure of Social Action,* 1937; *The Social System,* 1951; *Essays in Sociological Theory,* 1954), Pitirim Sorokin (*Society, Culture, and Personality,* 1947), and Robin M. Williams, Jr. (*American Society,* 1951). It is this general tradition that we have called functional approach.

19. The social organization so produced has been characterized in an overall sense by such dichotomies as rural-urban

(Sorokin), sacred-secular (Becker), mechanical-organic (Durkheim), gemeinschaft-gesellschaft (Tönnies), Folk-urban (Redfield), and community-association (McIver). Each contrasting dichotomy is actually a continuum in the sense that types as defined by each side of the dichotomy are really ideal states or conditions and never come into real life as a pure type. A given social organization at a given time has, for example, some of the secular and some of the sacred elements, although one of them might be present only in a very small measure.

20. The distinction drawn here between culture system and social system follows the recommendations made jointly by Alfred L. Kroeber and Talcott Parsons. See their "The Concept of Culture and of Social System," *American Sociological Review,* 23 (1958): 582–83.

21. Although the functional problems listed here follow more closely Parson's view, other similar lists are available. See Kingsley Davis, *op. cit.,* and M. J. Levy, *op. cit.*

22. This bare outline of a general perspective is a very highly condensed version, suggesting only the major building blocks of what is known as a functional theory for the study of society. We shall not attempt to elucidate it further except to note that we have found the concepts *norm, status-role, institution* and values useful for the tasks at hand.

23. For a critical review of the notion of social adjustment, see J. J. Mangalam, Harry K. Schwarzweller and James Brown, "A Reconsideration of the Notion of Adjustment: An Explanation," *Proceedings,* Association of Southern Agricultural Workers Annual Meeting, 1962, Agricultural Economics and Rural Sociology Section, Vol. II.

24. As for example, in a case of migration from a folk village or tribal situation to a modern, metropolitan center.

25. See for example, Josef Gugler, "Life in a Dual System," East African Institute of Social Research Conference Papers, January 1965.

26. The general theoretical approach we suggest here has been illustrated in the Beech Creek Study of eastern Kentucky migrants to urban-industrial Ohio and neighboring states. See James S.

Brown, Harry K. Schwarzweller and J. J. Mangalam, *op. cit.;* Harry K. Schwarzweller and James S. Brown, "Social Class Origin, Rural-Urban Migration, and Economic Life Chances: A Case Study," *Rural Sociology,* 32 (1967): 5–19; Harry K. Schwarzweller and John F. Seggar, "Kinship Involvement: A Factor in the Adjustment of Rural Migrants," *Journal of Marriage and Family,* 29 (1967): 662–71; J. J. Mangalam, *Human Migration,* University of Kentucky Press, 1968, 194 pp.; and J. J. Mangalam and Harry K. Schwarzweller, *op. cit.*

15

A Theory of Migration*

Everett S. Lee

It was a remark of Farr's to the effect that migration appeared to go on without any definite law that led Ravenstein to present his celebrated paper on the laws of migration before the Royal Statistical Society on March 17, 1885.[1] This paper was based upon the British Census of 1881, but in 1889 Ravenstein returned to the subject with data from more than twenty countries.[2] Finding corroboration for his earlier views in this broader investigation, he also entitled his second paper, "The Laws of Migration," though he noted that it was ambitiously headed and warned that "laws of population, and economic laws generally, have not the rigidity of physical laws." An irreverent critic, Mr. N. A. Humphreys, immediately retorted that "After carefully reading Mr. Ravenstein's former paper, and listening to the present one, [I arrived] at the conclusion that migration was rather distinguished for its lawlessness than for having any definite law."[3] Mr. Stephen Bourne's criticism was less devastating but logically more serious: "that although Mr. Ravenstein had spoken of 'Laws of Migration,' he had not formulated them in such a categorical order that they could be criticized."[4] Nevertheless, Ravenstein's papers have stood the test of time and remain the starting point for work in migration theory

As found in the first paper and extended or amended in the second, Ravenstein's laws are summarized in his own words below. The first five of these items include the laws as they are usually quoted, while items 6 and 7, though taken from the general conclusions of his second paper, are not ordinarily included. This, however, is due more to Ravenstein's way of

Reprinted from *Demography*, 3, no. 1 (1966), pp. 47–57, by permission of the author and the publisher.

* Presented at the Annual Meeting of the Mississippi Valley Historical Association, Kansas City, April 23, 1965 ("Population Studies Center Series in Studies of Human Resources," No. 1). This paper has benefited greatly from discussions with Professor Surinder K. Mehta.

188

numbering the laws and to his somewhat tentative statement of the dominance of the economic motive than to his own estimate of the importance of his conclusions.

1. *Migration and distance.* *(a)* "[T]he great body of our migrants only proceed a short distance" and "migrants enumerated in a certain center of absorption will . . . grow less [as distance from the center increases]" (I, pp. 198–99).[5] *(b)* "Migrants proceeding long distances generally go by preference to one of the great centers of commerce and industry" (I, p. 199).

2. *Migration by stages.* *(a)* "[T]here takes place consequently a universal shifting or displacement of the population, which produces 'currents of migration,' setting in the direction of the great centers of commerce and industry which absorb the migrants" (I, p. 198). *(b)* "The inhabitants of the country immediately surrounding a town of rapid growth flock into it; the gaps thus left in the rural population are filled up by migrants from more remote districts, until the attractive force of one of our rapidly growing cities makes its influence felt, step by step, to the most remote corner of the kingdom" (I, p. 199). *(c)* "The process of dispersion is the inverse of that of absorption, and exhibits similar features" (I, p. 199).

3. *Stream and counterstream.* "Each main current of migration produces a compensating counter-current" (I, p. 199). In modern terminology, stream and counterstream have been substituted for Ravenstein's current and counter-current.

4. *Urban-rural differences in propensity to migrate.* "The natives of towns are less migratory than those of the rural parts of the country" (I, p. 199).

5. *Predominance of females among short distance migrants.* "Females appear to predominate among short-journey migrants" (II, p. 288).

6. *Technology and migration.* "Does migration increase? I believe so! . . . Wherever I was able to make a comparison I found that an increase in the means of locomotion and a development of manufactures and commerce have led to an increase of migration" (II, p. 288).

7. *Dominance of the economic motive.* "Bad or oppressive laws, heavy taxation, an unattractive climate, uncongenial social surroundings, and even compulsion (slave trade, transportation), all have produced and are still producing currents of migration, but none of these currents can compare in volume with that which arises from the desire inherent in most men to 'better' themselves in material respects" (II, p. 286).

This century has brought no comparable excursion into migration theory. With the development of equilibrium analysis, economists abandoned the study of population, and most sociologists and historians are reluctant to deal with masses of statistical data. A crew of demographers has sprung up, but they have been largely content with empirical findings and unwilling to generalize. Indeed, Vance, in his presidential address to the Population Association of America, entitled "Is Theory for Demographers?" contends that demography, for lack of theory, remains unstructured and raises the question, "Is there room [in demography] for the bold and audacious?"[6]

In the three-quarters of a century which have passed, Ravenstein has been much quoted and occasionally challenged. But, while there have been literally thousands of migration studies in the meantime, few additional generalizations have been advanced. True, there have been studies of age and migration, sex and migration, race and migration, distance and migration, education and migration, the labor force and migration, and so forth; but most studies which focused upon the characteristics of migrants have been conducted with little reference to the volume of migration, and few studies have considered the reasons for migration or the assimilation of the migrant at destination. So little developed was the field in the 1930's that Dorothy Thomas and her associates concluded that the only generalization that could be made in regard to differentials in internal migration was that migrants tended to be young adults or persons in their late teens.[7] Later Bogue and Hagood trenchantly summed up the current state of knowledge under the heading "An Approach to a Theory of Differential Migration,"[8] and Otis Durant Duncan contributed a valuable essay on "The Theory and Consequences of Mobility of Farm Population,"[9] but both were restricted to the United States and both were hampered by a lack of data which has since been partially repaired. Most essays in migration theory have dealt with migration and distance and advanced mathematical formulations of the relationship. Perhaps the best known of recent theories of migration is Stouffer's theory of intervening opportunities.[10]

Except for Dudley Kirk,[11] Ravenstein seems to have been the last person to make a detailed comparison of the volume of internal migration or the characteristics of migrants within a goodly number of nations. Generally speaking, considerations of internal migration have been divorced from considerations of immigration and emigration, and very short moves, such as those within counties in the United States or within *Kriese* in Germany, have not been considered along with the longer distance movement that is labeled migration. Also, such forced migration as the refugee movements of World War II and its aftermath have not been grouped with the so-called free migration.

It is the purpose of this paper to attempt the development of a general schema into which a variety of spatial movements can be placed and, from a small number of what would seem to be self-evident propositions, to deduce a number of conclusions with regard to the volume of migration, the development of streams and counterstreams, and the characteristics of migrants. As a starting point for this analysis, a definition of migration is introduced which is considerably more general than that usually applied.

DEFINITION OF MIGRATION

Migration is defined broadly as a permanent or semipermanent change of residence. No restriction is placed upon the distance of the move or upon the voluntary or involuntary nature of the act, and no distinction is made between external and internal migration. Thus, a move across the hall from one apartment to another is counted as just as much an act of migration as a move from Bombay, India, to Cedar Rapids, Iowa, though, of course, the initiation and consequences of such moves are vastly different. However, not all kinds of spatial mobility are included in this definition. Excluded, for example, are the continual movements of nomads and migratory workers, for whom there is no long-term residence, and temporary moves like those to the mountains for the summer.

No matter how short or how long, how easy or how difficult, every act of migration involves an origin, a destination, and an intervening set of obstacles. Among the set of intervening obstacles, we include the distance of the move as one that is always present.

FACTORS IN THE ACT OF MIGRATION

The factors which enter into the decision to migrate and the process of migration may be summarized under four headings, as follows:

1. Factors associated with the area of origin.
2. Factors associated with the area of destination.
3. Intervening obstacles.
4. Personal factors.

The first three of these are indicated schematically in Chart 1. In every area there are countless factors which act to hold people within the area or attract people to it, and there are others which tend to repel them. These are shown in the diagram as + and − signs. There are others, shown as 0's, to which people are essentially indifferent. Some of these factors affect most people in much the same way, while others affect different people in different ways. Thus a good climate is attractive and a bad climate is repulsive to nearly everyone; but a good school system may be counted as a + by a parent with young children and a − by a houseowner with no children because of the high real estate taxes engendered, while an unmarried male without taxable property is indifferent to the situation.

Clearly the set of +'s and −'s at both origin and destination is differently defined for every migrant or prospective migrant. Nevertheless, we may distinguish classes of people who react in similar fashion to the same general sets of factors at origin and destination. Indeed, since we can never specify the exact set of factors which impels or prohibits migration for a given person, we can, in general, only set forth a few which seem of special importance and note the general or average reaction of a considerable group. Needless to say, the factors that hold and attract or repel people are precisely understood neither by the social scientist nor the persons directly affected. Like Bentham's calculus of pleasure and pain, the calculus of +'s and −'s at origin and destination is always inexact.

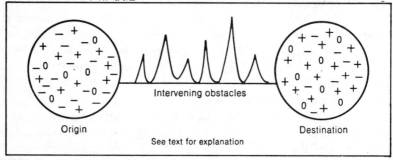

CHART 1.   Origin and Destination Factors and Intervening Obstacles in Migration.

There are, however, important differences between the factors associated with the area of origin and those associated with the area of destination. Persons living in an area have an immediate and often long-term acquaintance with the area and are usually able to make considered and unhurried judgments regarding them. This is not necessarily true of the factors associated with the area of destination. Knowledge of the area of destination is seldom exact, and indeed some of the advantages and disadvantages of an area can only be perceived by living there. Thus there is always an element of ignorance or even mystery about the area of destination, and there must always be some uncertainty with regard to the reception of a migrant in a new area.

Another important difference between the factors associated with area of origin and area of destination is related to stages of the life cycle. For many migrants the area of origin is that in which the formative years have been spent and for which the general good health of youth and the absence of annoying responsibilities create in retrospect an overevaluation of the positive elements in the environment and an underevaluation of the negative elements. On the other hand, the difficulties associated with assimilation in a new environment may create in the newly arrived a contrary but equally erroneous evaluation of the positive and negative factors at destination.

While migration may result from a comparison of factors at origin and destination, a simple calculus of +'s and −'s does not decide the act of migration. The balance in favor of the move must be enough to overcome the natural inertia which always exists. Furthermore, between every two points there stands a set of intervening obstacles which may be slight in some instances and insurmountable in others. The most studied of these obstacles is distance, which, while omnipresent, is by no means the most important. Actual physical barriers like the Berlin Wall may be interposed, or immigration laws may restrict the movement. Different people are, of course, affected in different ways by the same set of obstacles. What may be trivial to some people—the cost of transporting household goods, for example—may be prohibitive to others.

The effect of a given set of obstacles depends also upon the impedimenta with which the migrant is encumbered. For some migrants these are relatively unimportant and the difficulty of surmounting the intervening obstacles is consequently minimal; but for others, making the same move, the impedimenta, among which we must reckon children and other dependents, greatly increase the difficulties posed by intervening obstacles.

Finally, there are many personal factors which affect individual thresholds and facilitate or retard migration. Some of these are more or less constant throughout the life of the individual, while others are associated with stages in the life cycle and in particular with the sharp breaks that denote passage from one stage to another.

In this connection, we must note that it is not so much the actual factors at origin and destination as the perception of these factors which results in migration. Personal sensitivities, intelligence, and awareness of conditions elsewhere enter into the evaluation of the situation at origin, and knowledge of the situation at destination depends upon personal contacts or upon sources of information which are not universally available. In addition, there are personalities which are resistant to change—change of residence as well as other changes—and there are personalities which welcome change for the sake of change. For some individuals, there must be compelling reasons for migration, while for others little provocation or promise suffices.

The decision to migrate, therefore, is never completely rational, and for some persons the rational component is much less than the irrational. We must expect, therefore, to find many exceptions to our generalizations since transient emotions, mental disorder, and accidental occurrences account for a considerable proportion of the total migrations.

Indeed, not all persons who migrate reach that decision themselves.

Children are carried along by their parents, willy-nilly, and wives accompany their husbands though it tears them away from environments they love. There are clearly stages in the life cycle in which the positive elements at origin are overwhelmingly important in limiting migration, and there are times in which such bonds are slackened with catastrophic suddenness. Children are bound to the familial residence by the need for care and subsistence, but, as one grows older, ages are reached at which it is customary to cease one stage of development and begin another. Such times are the cessation of education, entrance into the labor force, or retirement from work. Marriage, too, constitutes such a change in the life cycle, as does the dissolution of marriage, either through divorce or the death of a spouse.

Many more or less random occurrences can also greatly reduce the hold of an area upon a person and increase the attractiveness of other areas. Victims of injustice as well as the perpetrators of crime may be forced to leave the area in which they are living. These and other events which affect but a few persons in the total community may nevertheless bulk large in the motivation of the migrant group.

This conceptualization of migration as involving a set of factors at origin and destination, a set of intervening obstacles, and a series of personal factors is a simple one which may perhaps be accepted as self-evident. It is now argued that, simple though this is, it provides a framework for much of what we know about migration and indicates a number of fields for investigation. It is used below to formulate a series of hypotheses about the volume of migration under varying conditions, the development of stream and counterstream, and the characteristics of migrants.

VOLUME OF MIGRATION

1. *The volume of migration within a given territory varies with the degree of diversity of areas included in that territory.* If migration, as we have assumed, results in part from a consideration of positive and negative factors at origin and destination, then a high degree of diversity among areas should result in high levels of migration. These we find in countries which are being opened up for settlement, as was the United States in the nineteenth century, eastern Europe during the twelfth and thirteenth centuries, and Siberia in the twentieth century. Under such conditions, opportunities arise which are sufficient to attract to them persons whose dissatisfaction with their places of origin is little more than minimal. Very great attractions spring up suddenly, as, for example, the discovery of gold in California, of silver in Colorado, and the opening up of Indian Territory for white settlement. The servicing of such a movement, in terms of provid-

ing transportation, protection, supplies, and the niceties as well as the necessities of life, creates highly specialized but often very lucrative opportunities. Thus, pioneers and settlers are accompanied by soldiers and merchants and ladies of fortune, who indeed may push ahead of the wave of settlement to establish outposts and nodal points.

The end of the period of settlement does not necessarily imply a decrease in areal diversity. On the contrary, the industrialization, which has traditionally followed settlement, is a great creator of areal diversity. In a dynamic economy, new opportunities are continually created in places to which workers must be drawn, and old enterprises are ruthlessly abandoned when they are no longer profitable.

2. *The volume of migration varies with the diversity of people.* The diversity of people also affects the volume of migration. Where there is a great sameness among people—whether in terms of race or ethnic origin, of education, of income, or tradition—we may expect a lesser rate of migration than where there is great diversity. A diversity of people implies the existence of groups that are specially fitted for given pursuits. Thus, we find throughout northern Europe, where land has been reclaimed from the sea or marshes drained, villages which still bear the stamps of their Dutch origin. The settlement of the American West would have been more difficult had it not been for the Jewish merchant who came with or even preceded the rush of migrants, and the conditions which attended Irish and Chinese immigration made them especially responsive to the demands for railroad laborers. Indeed, it is a common finding that immigrant groups specialize in particular occupations and become scattered throughout the country wherever the need for such work is found. Thus, Chinese laundry operators and Greek restaurant owners in the United States had their counterparts in the widely spread German and Jewish craftsmen of eastern Europe.

A diversity of people inevitably implies that the social statuses of some groups will become elevated above those of others. Discrimination among racial or ethnic groups is the rule rather than the exception, and the degree of discrimination varies from place to place, often in as extreme a manner as in the United States. Though discrimination leads to the establishment of ghettos, it also operates to bring about vast movements of people from one area to another—witness the recent migration of the American Negro.

Ethnic diversity may disappear as minorities become assimilated, but a major aim of modern civilization is to inaugurate other kinds of diversity among people. The aim of prolonged education is to create specialists, for many of whom the demand is small in any one place but widespread. For them migration is a concomitant of their vocations. Thus, engineers and professors have become peripatetic, but so have business executives and actors.

3. *The volume of migration is related to the difficulty of surmounting the intervening obstacles.* This hypothesis hardly needs elaboration. One of the most important considerations in the decision to migrate is the difficulty of the intervening obstacles. To tunnel under the Berlin Wall is a hazardous task not to be undertaken lightly; nor was sea passage to the Americas in the seventeenth and eighteenth centuries. The removal of immigration restrictions within the Common Market countries has been accompanied by large migrations of workers from one of these countries to another. There are many other instances in history where the removal of obstacles has set in motion large flows of migrants, and others in which the imposition of new obstacles or the heightening of old ones has brought about the sharp diminution of a long continued flow.

4. *The volume of migration varies with fluctuations in the economy.* Business cycles affect the volume of migration in many ways, but a crucial consideration is the manner in which they affect the comparison of positive and negative factors at origin and destination. During periods of economic expansion, new businesses and industries are created at a rapid rate, and old industries begin to recruit workmen from afar. Such opportunities, however, are by no means evenly spread, and parts of the country remain in a state of relative stagnation. The contrast between the positive factors at origin and destination is therefore heightened, and the negative factors at origin seem more distressing. During depressions, however, some of the newly created businesses fail and others cease to expand. A leveling of opportunities occurs, and sheer familiarity with the place of residence (which in itself constitutes an element of safety) militates against moving to places where positive factors no longer so heavily outweigh those at home. Many tests of this hypothesis have been made, but among them the most revealing and confirming are the studies of Jerome in relation to immigration to the United States[12] and of Thomas in relation to migration within the United States.[13]

5. *Unless severe checks are imposed, both volume and rate of migration tend to increase with time.* The volume of migration tends to increase with time for a number of reasons, among them increasing diversity of areas, increasing diversity of people, and the diminution of intervening obstacles. As indicated above, industrialization and Westernization, the explicit or implicit goals of most countries, increase the diversity of areas. It is also true that in both developed and developing countries the differences between areas, both in terms of economics and of amenities, become heightened. On an international scale, the economic differences between advanced and backward countries are increasing rather than diminishing,

and within all countries the differences between agricultural and urban areas are becoming more pronounced.

Other factors which tend to bring about an increase in the volume of migration are both the increasing differences among people and the view taken of these differences. In a primitive or agricultural society, specialization is limited and the development of differences among people tends to be discouraged. In an advancing society, however, specializations multiply, and there is an increased realization of both the existence and the need for special aptitudes or training. Thus, even in an agricultural area children are trained for urban pursuits, and an increased variety of developed aptitudes renders the population more susceptible to the appeal of highly special positive factors in scattered places.

Increasing technology plays an important role in diminishing intervening obstacles. Communication becomes easier, and transportation relative to average income becomes cheaper. Even if there were no change in the balance of factors at origin and destination, improving technology alone should result in an increase in the volume of migration.

Also operating to increase migration is migration itself. A person who has once migrated and who has once broken the bonds which tie him to the place in which he has spent his childhood is more likely to migrate again than is the person who has never previously migrated. Furthermore, succeeding migration lowers inertia even more. Once a set of intervening obstacles has been overcome, other sets do not seem so formidable, and there is an increasing ability to evaluate the positive and negative factors at origin and destination.

6. *The volume and rate of migration vary with the state of progress in a country or area.* As Ravenstein remarked, "Migration means life and progress; a sedentary population stagnation."[14] The reasons why this is true are similar to those advanced above under item 5. In an economically progressive country, the differences among areas are accentuated by industrial development and the differences among people by education. At the same time, intervening obstacles to migration within the country are lessened by improving technology and by political design.

We should, therefore, expect to find heavy immigration to developed countries where this is permitted and within such countries a high rate of internal migration. On the other hand, in the least developed countries we should find a largely immobile population which usually changes residence only under duress and then en masse rather than through individual action. In the United States, economically the most advanced of nations, rates of migration are unbelievably high, one in five persons changing his residence each year. In other economically advanced countries, like Sweden, Canada, or West Germany, we find this repeated at a somewhat lower level. We may

argue that a high rate of progress entails a population which is continually in a state of flux, responding quickly to new opportunities and react-
ing swiftly to diminishing opportunities.

STREAM AND COUNTERSTREAM

1. *Migration tends to take place largely within well defined streams.*
It is a common observation that migrants proceed along well defined routes
toward highly specific destinations. This is true in part because opportunities tend to be highly localized and in part because migrants must usually
follow established routes of transportation. Perhaps just as important is
the flow of knowledge back from destination to origin and, indeed, the actual recruitment of migrants at the place of origin. The overcoming of a
set of intervening obstacles by early migrants lessens the difficulty of the
passage for later migrants, and in effect pathways are created which pass
over intervening opportunities as elevated highways pass over the
countryside.

Thus the process of settlement tends to be a leapfrogging operation
in which military outposts or trading centers become the focus of migration
streams and the filling-up of the passed over territory is left to a later stage
of development. From this point of view, the real frontiersmen are not the
farmers but the merchants, the missionaries, and the military. It was in
this fashion that German colonization east of the Elbe was accomplished,
and it was in this fashion that the American West was won.

In many cases, large movements take on the form of streams which
are highly specific both in origin and destination. For example, Italians
from Sicily and southern Italy migrated chiefly to the United States and
within the United States to a few northern cities, while high proportions
of their countrymen from Lombardy and Tuscany went to South America
and, in particular, to Buenos Aires. There are many examples of even more
specific streams. Goldstein has noted that high proportions of Negroes
resident in Norristown, Pennsylvania, in 1950 had come from Saluda,
South Carolina, where a small contingent of Negroes had been recruited
by the Pennsylvania Railroad as laborers and sent to Norristown during
World War I.[15] At the present time, a small stream of miners is proceeding
from Appalachia to copper-mining centers in the West, and this movement
has been paralleled in the past by the movement of British mechanics to
New England and British potters to Ohio.

2. *For every major migration stream, a counterstream develops.* A
counterstream is established for several reasons. One is that positive factors
at origin may disappear, or be muted, as during a depression, or there may
be a re-evaluation of the balance of positive and negative factors at origin

and destination. The very existence of a migration stream creates contacts between origin and destination, and the acquisition of new attributes at destination, be they skills or wealth, often makes it possible to return to the origin on advantageous terms. Migrants become aware of opportunities at origin which were not previously exploited, or they may use their contacts in the new area to set up businesses in the old. Accompanying the returning migrants will be their children born at destination, and along with them will be people indigenous to the area of destination who have become aware of opportunities or amenities at the place of origin through stream migrants. Furthermore, not all persons who migrate intend to remain indefinitely at the place of destination. For example, many Italian immigrants to the United States intended to stay only long enough to make enough money to be comfortable in Italy.

3. *The efficiency of the stream (ratio of stream to counterstream or the net redistribution of population effected by the opposite flows) is high if the major factors in the development of a migration stream were minus factors at origin.* Again, this point is so obvious that it hardly needs elaboration. Few of the Irish who fled famine conditions returned to Ireland, and few American Negroes return to the South.

4. *The efficiency of stream and counterstream tends to be low if origin and destination are similar.* In this case, persons moving in opposing flows move largely for the same reasons and in effect cancel each other out.

5. *The efficiency of migration streams will be high if the intervening obstacles are great.* Migrants who overcome a considerable set of intervening obstacles do so for compelling reasons, and such migrations are not undertaken lightly. To some degree, the set of obstacles in stream and counterstream is the same, and return migrants are faced with the necessity of twice negotiating a nearly overwhelming set of obstacles. For example, migrants from Pennsylvania to California are deterred from returning by the very expense of the journey.

6. *The efficiency of a migration stream varies with economic conditions, being high in prosperous times and low in times of depression.* During boom times the usual areas of destination, that is, the great centers of commerce and industry, expand rapidly, and relatively few persons, either return migrants or others, make the countermove. In times of depression, however, many migrants return to the area of origin, and others move toward the comparatively "safer" nonindustrialized areas. In extreme instances stream and counterstream may be reversed, as was the case with movement to and from rural areas during the worst years of the Great Depression. More recently, the mild recession in 1949 seems to have reversed the usual net flow from Oklahoma to California.

CHARACTERISTICS OF MIGRANTS

1. *Migration is selective.* This simply states that migrants are not a random sample of the population at origin. The reason why migration is selective is that persons respond differently to the sets of plus and minus factors at origin and at destination, have different abilities to overcome the intervening sets of obstacles, and differ from each other in terms of the personal factors discussed above. It would seem impossible, therefore, for migration not to be selective. The kind of selection, however, varies, being positive in some streams and negative in others. By positive selection is meant selection for migrants of high quality and by negative selection the reverse.

2. *Migrants responding primarily to plus factors at destination tend to be positively selected.* These persons are under no necessity to migrate but do so because they perceive opportunities from afar and they can weigh the advantages and disadvantages at origin and destination. For example, highly educated persons who are already comfortably situated frequently migrate because they receive better offers elsewhere. Professional and managerial people are also highly mobile, and often because migration means advancement.

3. *Migrants responding primarily to minus factors at origin tend to be negatively selected; or, where the minus factors are overwhelming to entire population groups, they may not be selected at all.* Examples of the latter are political expulsions like that of the Germans from Poland and East Prussia or the Irish flight which followed the failure of the potato crop. On the whole, however, factors at origin operate most stringently against persons who in some way have failed economically or socially. Though there are conditions in many places which push out the unorthodox and the highly creative, it is more likely to be the uneducated or the disturbed who are forced to migrate.

4. *Taking all migrants together, selection tends to be bimodal.* For any given origin, some of the migrants who leave are responding primarily to plus factors at destination and therefore tend to be positively selected, while others are responding to minus factors and therefore tend to be negatively selected. Therefore, if we plot characteristics of total migrants along a continuum ranging from poor to excellent, we often get a J-shaped or U-shaped curve. Such curves are found, for example, where the characteristic is either occupational class or education.

5. *The degree of positive selection increases with the difficulty of the intervening obstacles.* Even though selection is negative or random at origin, intervening obstacles serve to weed out some of the weak or the incapable. Thus, the rigors of the voyage to America in the seventeenth and

eighteenth centuries eliminated many of the weak, and the same kind of selection is apparent among the German refugees from eastern Europe during and after World War II. It is also commonly noted that as distance of migration increases, the migrants become an increasingly superior group. At the other extreme, we have the milling-around in restricted areas of persons who, by any definition, are less capable; for example, uneducated slum dwellers often move round and round within a few-block radius. Such short distance movements were also characteristic of sharecroppers in the pre–World War II days in the United States.

6. *The heightened propensity to migrate at certain stages of the life cycle is important in the selection of migrants.* To some degree, migration is a part of the *rites de passage.* Thus, persons who enter the labor force or get married tend to migrate from their parental home, while persons who are divorced or widowed also tend to move away. Since some of these events happen at quite well defined ages, they are important in shaping the curve of age selection. They are also important in establishing other types of selection—marital status or size of family, for example.

7. *The characteristics of migrants tend to be intermediate between the characteristics of the population at origin and the population at destination.* Persons with different characteristics react differently to the balance of plus and minus factors at origin and destination. Even before they leave, migrants tend to have taken on some of the characteristics of the population at destination, but they can never completely lose some which they share with the population at origin. It is because they are already to some degree like the population at destination that they find certain positive factors there, and it is because they are unlike the population at origin that certain minus factors there warrant migration. Many studies have shown this intermediate relationship. The fertility of migrants, for example, tends to fall between that of the population at origin and the population at destination, and the education of migrants from rural areas, while greater than that of nonmigrants at origin, is less than that of the population at destination. Thus, we have one of the paradoxes of migration in that the movement of people may tend to lower the quality of population, as expressed in terms of some particular characteristic, at both origin and destination.

SUMMARY

In summary, a simple schema for migration has been elaborated, and from it certain hypotheses in regard to volume of migration, the establishment of stream and counterstream, and the characteristics of migrants have been formulated. The aim has been the construction of a related set of hypotheses within a general framework, and work is proceeding toward further development in regard to the assimilation of migrants and in regard to the effect upon gaining and losing areas.

Where possible, the hypotheses have been put in such form that they are immediately testable with current data. For others the necessary data are not now available, and others require restatement in terms of available data. It is to be expected that many exceptions will be found, since migration is a complex phenomenon and the often necessary simplifying condition—all other things being equal—is impossible to realize. Nevertheless, from what is now known about migration, encouraging agreement is found with the theory outlined in this paper. Full testing depends, of course, upon the amassing of materials from different cultures. Fortunately, recognition of the importance of internal migration in social and economic development has spurred research, and more and more countries publish detailed migration data from their censuses or population registers.

NOTES

1. E. G. Ravenstein, "The Laws of Migration," *Journal of the Royal Statistical Society*, XLVIII, Part 2 (June, 1885), 167–227. Also Reprint No. S-482 in the "Bobbs-Merrill Series in the Social Sciences."

2. Ravenstein, "The Laws of Migration," *Journal of the Royal Statistical Society*, LII (June, 1889), 241–301. Also Reprint No. S-483 in the "Bobbs-Merrill Series in the Social Sciences."

3. "Discussion on Mr. Ravenstein's Paper," *Journal of the Royal Statistical Society*, LII (June, 1889), 302.

4. *Ibid.*, p. 303.

5. In the quotations from Ravenstein, "I" refers to the 1885 paper and "II" to the 1889 paper.

6. Rupert B. Vance, "Is Theory for Demographers?" *Social Forces*, XXXI (October, 1952), 9–13.

7. Dorothy Swaine Thomas, *Research Memorandum on Migration Differentials* (New York: Social Science Research Council, Bulletin 43, 1938).

8. Donald J. Bogue and Margaret Marman Hagood, *Subregional Migration in the United States, 1935–1940*, Vol. II: *Differential Migration in the Corn and Cotton Belts* (Miami, Ohio: Scripps Foundation Studies in Population Distribution, No. 6, 1953), pp. 124–27.

9. Otis Durant Duncan, "The Theory and Consequences of Mobility of Farm

Population," *Oklahoma Agriculture Experiment Station Circular No. 88* (Stillwater, Okla., May, 1940). Reprinted in Joseph J. Spengler and Otis Dudley Duncan, *Population Theory and Policy* (Glencoe, Ill.: Free Press, 1956), pp. 417–34.

10. Samuel A. Stouffer, "Intervening Opportunities: A Theory Relating Mobility and Distance," *American Sociological Review*, V (December, 1940), 845–67, and "Intervening Opportunities and Competing Migrants, *Journal of Regional Science*, II (1960), 1–26.

11. Dudley Kirk, *Europe's Population in the Interwar Years* (Princeton, N.J.: Princeton University Press, 1946).

12. Harry Jerome, *Migration and Business Cycles* (New York: National Bureau of Economic Research Inc., 1926).

13. Hope T. Eldridge and Dorothy Swaine Thomas, *Population Redistribution and Economic Growth, United States, 1870–1950*, Vol. III: *Demographic Analyses and Interrelations* (Philadelphia: American Philosophical Society, 1964), 321 ff.

14. Ravenstein, "The Laws of Migration," *Journal of the Royal Statistical Society*, LII (June, 1889), 288.

15. Sidney Goldstein, *Patterns of Mobility, 1910–1950: The Norristown Study* (Philadelphia: University of Pennsylvania Press, 1958), p. 38.

16

Migration in Relation to Education, Intellect, and Social Structure*

Everett S. Lee

To the foreign observer, two of the most striking aspects of American life are the incessant, crisscrossing migration of the population and the attempt to educate outrageously high proportions to advanced levels. I shall argue that there is a necessary relationship between the two and that without high rates of migration mass education would lose much of its value. I shall further maintain that our attitudes toward migration and education reflect an implicit view of the structure of intellect that leads to a high degree of educational and occupational specialization. And as the division of labor becomes more intricate, competition becomes fiercer, but rewarding to a larger number, to so many, in fact, that the traditional view of a broadly based but abruptly narrowing social structure can no longer be maintained.

From the earliest times to the present, there have been those who deplored the American readiness to leave the homes of their ancestors and to begin life anew in distant places. Among them were Joseph Kennedy, the Superintendent of the Census for 1850, who opined, "The roving tendency of our people is incident to the peculiar condition of their country, and each succeeding Census will prove that it is diminishing. When the fertile plains of the West shall have been filled up, and men of scanty means cannot by a mere change of location acquire a homestead, the inhabitants of each State will become comparatively stationary, and our countrymen will exhibit that attachment to the homes of their childhood, the want of

Reprinted from *Population Index*, 36, no. 4 (October–December, 1970), pp. 437–44, by permission of the author and the publisher. Footnotes have been renumbered.

* This is the revised text of the address delivered by Everett S. Lee, University of Massachusetts, President of the Population Association of America, at the banquet on the evening of April 17, 1970, at Atlanta, Georgia, as part of the annual meeting of the Association.

which is sometimes cited as an unfavorable trait in our national character."[1]

Kennedy's prediction was not fulfilled, and from his point of view our national character remains as bad as ever. From historical data we can find no evidence that there has been a long-term downward movement in rates of migration. And from the Current Population Survey, which gives us annual estimates of migration over the last twenty years, we find that with surprisingly little variation, one American in five has changed his place of registration each year, one in fourteen has migrated from one county to another, and one in thirty has made the longer move from one state to another.

Kennedy was right, however, in his judgment that marked differences in regions, especially in regard to the degree of settlement, furnish powerful inducements to migration. But the end of settlement does not imply the end of spatial differentiation. The desirable or undesirable features of an area change with technology, with the shifting importance of a given resource, with the spread of transportation and communication, and with the location of industry. And it should not be forgotten that areas are differentiated in social and psychological aspects. Discrimination can be a powerful determinant of migration. Important spatial differences, therefore, remain, but it could be argued that they have diminished. A goodly proportion of the population now lives in metropolitan fringes, and much of our migration is from one suburb directly to another. Among these there is such deadly similarity that areal differentiation may well have decreased in importance as an impelling force in migration.

This brings us to one of the anomalies of American migration. As the country was settled and the distribution of population came to depend chiefly upon the location and spread of urban conglomerates, migration might have been expected to decrease. The farm population has been reduced to a point where it no longer furnishes a major reservoir of surplus population. The migration of people, and the same is true of the migration of industry, has become largely a movement within urban agglomerations or between essentially similar metropolises.

The decrease in migration that could have been expected to occur as empty areas filled and as the different regions grew in similarity, I shall now argue, has not occurred because there has been an offsetting increase in the diversity of people. A major factor in this regard is an educational system devoted to increasing certain important differences among people.

No other country has attempted to educate so high a proportion of its population beyond the elementary level, and no other country has given such enthusiastic support to education at the college and university level. At present about three-quarters of American youths complete high school, and more than half of the graduates attempt some sort of additional education. High as these proportions are, we may expect them to increase, since the education of parents is an important determinant of the educational attainment of the child. Where both parents are college graduates, all but a tiny fraction of the children complete high school and about seven out of eight go on to college.[2] Projections of recent trends into the not too distant future indicate that we shall have a young adult population, more than a third of whom will be college graduates, while one in five will have training beyond that level. To many, these projections are horrifying and indeed have been cited by Europeans as indicating still another of the many American follies. An influential business group in West Germany, for example, has opposed their participation in such a ludicrous design by maintaining that no more than ten percent of any age class is intellectually qualified for higher education.

Even here Cassandras have arisen to bemoan the supposed glut of Ph.D.'s, and a number of graduate schools have restricted enrollments. One is reminded of Seymour Harris' postwar predictions of an oversupply of college graduates. The American public, however, perhaps wiser in the ways of the world than university deans, still answers the question, "How many educated intelligences does a modern community need?" in much the same way as did the Scottish psychologist, Godfrey Thompson, "In short, as many as they can get."[3]

In contrast to traditional European educational systems that were designed for elites, the American system has featured the education of the masses. On the whole, the European conception has been that intelligence is largely determined by some overall global factor, and higher education came to depend upon the ability to master either foreign languages, particularly the dead ones, or mathematics. By contrast, the implicit assumption underlying the American system is that inability in a particular branch of knowledge is not a necessary deterrent to all learning or to future productivity. By varying the curriculum and shaping the courses for the students, rather than the reverse, the American system proclaims the eminent usefulness of persons who, judged by narrower criteria, would have been shunted at an early age into the lower and middle ranks of the labor force.

In the American system there is a recognition, more implicit than explicit, of a structure of intellect something like that expressed by such psychologists as J. P. Guilford. Without necessarily denying the existence of some global factor that may raise or lower whole batteries of abilities, it is presumed that the interaction of several basic intellectual processes gives rise to a rather large number of abilities possessed by each person in varying degrees. For nearly all of us the majority of our abilities are about average, but there are some that we possess to a better than usual degree and some that are better not mentioned. We are all mosaics of abilities, and for each of us there should be some things that we can do well and some that we can do but poorly.

We need not be concerned here with whether manifest abilities are determined more by heredity or by environment. The fact is that the expression of basic abilities can be heightened through the arousal of interest and through training and practice. This is evident in the seemingly miraculous performances of star athletes, but is no less remarkable in the ingenious solution of mathematical problems. The arousal of interest and the sharpening of abilities can begin very early and have considerable effect. It is not simply the inheritance of certain basic abilities that causes the sons of doctors and the sons of lawyers to follow in their father's footsteps. It is also the arousal of interest and the creation of a milieu that emphasize the desirability of a particular vocation.

Very early the American educational system expanded to take in a wide segment of the population and persons with varying abilities. It seems that the purpose of primary education has been to make people alike in that certain basic knowledge has been imparted to all students, but beginning in high school pupils have been differentiated according to perceived abilities. Rather than demanding that all students adapt themselves to a single rigidly prescribed series of courses, there has been an attempt to adapt different types of instruction to the abilities of the students. From high school onward, the purpose of education has been to make people different by heightening selected series of abilities.

The flexibility of the schools is reinforced by the insistence of the economy upon workers with highly specialized skills. The increase in the size of enterprises, both public and private, encourages the division of labor, and the farther one proceeds up the educational or socio-economic ladder, the greater the degree of specialization. Thus we have no more "chemists" but "organic chemists" or "biochemists," and within the tiny fraternity of demographers the generalist is yielding to experts in fertility, mortality, or migration.

A particular specialization requires the possession of a particular set of abilities. This does not mean that a person with a specific set of abilities should ideally pursue only one occupation, but rather it indicates a number of possibilities from which one can be chosen. Individuals can and do change occupations while continuing to exploit the same series of abilities. Nevertheless, an increasing number of specializations have arisen that require specific training and that are engaged in by relatively few people. There is little feeling in this country for the gifted amateur, the "liberal arts" graduate, who traditionally has risen to top management in Britain to become the bane of their faltering industrial system. Nor is there the British pattern of social and economic discrimination against the technician, or the relegation of applied science and technology to institutions of lesser repute.

While specialization is most apparent among the best educated, it extends into areas that are less demanding in terms of years of school completed. Thus air traffic controllers may be counted as highly specialized as are urologists, and we have all become aware of our dependence upon the whims of such a small group. Similar considerations hold for diamond cutters and for pipefitters, for oil drillers and for ballistics experts. While it is true that the practitioners of certain specialties, say diamond cutting, may be concentrated in a few places like New York, Amsterdam, and Israel, the demand for many kinds of specialists, while small at a given place, is widespread in space. Air traffic controllers and demographers are needed in Atlanta and Seattle as well as in New York. Even psychiatrists are found outside the confines of Manhattan, a situation that may attest as much to the spread of wealth as to the incidence of need.

Whatever the genetic factors in intellect, they are not likely to operate in such fashion that persons with a given set of abilities are likely to be born in the places where they eventually pursue careers. They will be born and raised in many places, but they are likely to be brought together in a very few places for advanced training. From the educational institutions they must be dispersed throughout the country, and rarely will they return to the place of birth except in those instances where the locality, like New York City, Chicago, Los Angeles, London, or Tokyo, is practically a nation in itself.

Before proceeding further, let us establish some of the connections that were promised at the beginning of this discourse. It is well known that there is a close and positive relationship between the rate of migration and the number of years of school completed. This relationship is nearly as invariable as that between age and migration, and it holds for every country for which I have been able to find data. This is particularly true of long-distance migration. In 1955–1960, for example, more than half of the whites and a third of the nonwhites in the age group 25–29 moved from one county to another within the United States. In general the rate of migration was twice as high for college graduates as it was for persons at the bottom of the educational scale. While there was a great deal of intracounty movement by the poorly educated, their rate of migration, relative to that for the college trained, fell sharply as the distance of migration increased.

That the postulated relationship between migration and education exists needs no further demonstration. But is it a necessary one? I argue that it is. And proceeding immediately to *reductio ad absurdum,* I note that the University of Illinois would soon inundate Champaign-Urbana with chemists were it not that they move away. The hopes of farmers for their children are doubtless considerable, but when they have been processed through the universities there is little need for their new skills in the open country. For the uneducated, perception is limited to the immediate vicinity or to places included in the information network of friends and relatives. For the most educated, however, the labor market is national or international. The aircraft engineer in Baltimore is well aware of happenings in Seattle, and the Boeing designer knows about the troubles at Lockheed.

While I do not deny that laborers, or others at the bottom of the economic heap, develop some measure of specialization, they usually depend upon a wide range of abilities in performing the shifting and generalized tasks to which they are usually assigned. They find a variety of demands for the manual or poorly intellectualized skills that they have to offer, and are perhaps more often driven to migration by generally poor economic conditions at origin than they are attracted by lucrative offers or climatic amenities in distant places. For the highly educated specialist, however, the demand can be urgent and locally unfillable. For this man, there are many inducements to migration, not all of them pecuniary. For the best educated, society has created an impressive series of rewards for migration. Presidencies of firms and professorships in universities come fastest to those who are willing to migrate, and many organizations have adopted a deliberate policy of moving their top employees from place to place. Key specialists can seldom be stockpiled, nor can they be replaced by persons moving upward from lesser positions. Thus the interests of the economy and of the individual are best served by the fluid movement of those who are hardest to replace. The relationship between migration and education is indeed a necessary one.

Let me summarize up to this point by noting that our immigrant experience has served us well. A nation of migrants, we have achieved a freedom from binding ties to home and locality—the counterbalance to the rootlessness deplored by Superintendent Kennedy a century ago—that permitted the rapid settlement of a continental expanse and that still facilitates the quick exploitation of economic opportunity, no matter where it arises. While we probably have the highest rates of migration in the world, particularly when we restrict consideration to long-distance movement, we find high rates of migration in other advanced countries such as Canada and Sweden. At best the data are sketchy, but it is probably safe to assert that the highest rates of migration are found in those countries having the highest per capita income or in those that are in states of rapid transition from traditional to modern economies. Sustained economic growth and development depend upon maximizing the usefulness of human resources through the development, primarily in formal educational settings, of specific abilities, and the fluid movement of highly trained persons to any place where they may be needed. Neither will occur without the implicit assumption that intellect is multifaceted and that high proportions of the population possess natural abilities that can be brought to near perfection through the arousal of interest and the proper training.

Let us now consider some of the consequences in terms of competition for status and social structure. In a primitive or agrarian society, cooperation rather than competition may be stressed. Here the differences between people are minimized because everyone uses a wide range of abilities in the performance of daily tasks. Since most of the abilities possessed by an individual are average in character, achievements tend to be similar. Most people, in fact, perform the same tasks. There is some specialization, of course, but even that may be based primarily upon inheritance, as is suggested by the many names, like Smithson, which include the designation for a male child coupled with the name of an occupation. Leadership itself is inherited. Chiefs are the sons of chiefs, and the possession of land is a common attribute of status. People ordinarily die in the same status in which they were born, and social mobility occurs only under extreme conditions. A brave man may rise from peasantry to leadership in the course of battle, while epilepsy may elevate the swineherd to shaman. Everybody knows everybody else, and there is no escaping one's inheritance or the follies of one's youth. A man lives and dies in the place where he was born, rules of endogamy permitting, or if migration occurs the whole village may move together. A geographically static society is a socially static society.

Quite a different set of social relations appears in modern societies. Leadership is no longer hereditary, and no male is judged on the basis of overall abilities. Instead, opportunities are provided for developing a specific set of abilities that lead in turn to the adoption of specializations. Competition within the specialization is keen, since, except for the unfortunate and the ill advised, the requisite abilities are possessed by almost all the practitioners of the art. Nevertheless, a relatively large number of people can have the aura of high achievement. How many have the comfortable feeling of being one of a handful of leading experts on mathematical demography, or on cohort analysis in fertility, or of similar esoteric specialties? How many have been directors of respected associations? How many are fellows of learned societies, and to how many have senators and governors, even the White House, turned for advice?

The greater the degree of specialization, the greater the number of intellectual compartments into which we fit ourselves, and the greater the number who can achieve some semblance of eminence. A feeling of rare achievement comes to many, but even for those who never make the pages of leading journals and who never sit at head tables, there are compensations. Recall that specialists tend to be scattered geographically and that their services are frequently crucial. An air traffic controller may not be the best of his ilk, but when he fails to show up for work in Kansas City, we miss him sorely. The only cardiologist in a corn-shaded county of Iowa may be no great shakes as far as his colleagues in the metropolitan hospitals are concerned, but to the general public in time of emergency and to the local medical men with whom he consults, he is a man of nearly boundless authority. The state of the entire economy can depend upon a few key specialists, as can our lives, and we tend to reward them not only in accordance with their capacities but also in accordance with our needs.

There is, of course, no precise way of evaluating one specialty against another. From time to time one rises to special attention, as did nuclear physics in the 'forties and 'fifties and molecular biology in the 'sixties. The 'seventies will doubtless see considerable expansion of demography and ecology, and there will emerge many industrial specializations not yet dreamed of but that will be just as tiny and just as crucial to the national economy as the group of air traffic controllers. Within our own specializations we may reap encomiums, but we must nevertheless pay homage to each of the others.

There are therefore many ways of achieving status, and this multiplicity of avenues to the top has created a social structure that is no longer one with a tiny group of leaders and fashion setters, lording it over a large, undifferentiated mass of lesser beings. The top of the social structure is much wider, and it continues to broaden. It consists, however, of an elite that is geographically mobile, with loose ties to place and neighbors, with broad and national rather than narrow and local concerns.

The top of the social structure is broader, but it is no longer one, like that of Malthus's England, where the intellectual and the ruling elites all know each other. Instead, relationships tend to be concentrated within a discipline or within a vocation, a tendency encouraged by the telephone and the airplane. Like professional soldiers, other specialists form relationships despite separation in space, and events occurring across the continent may be deemed more immediate in effect than local happenings. These elite may never meet their neighbors, yet maintain the liveliest of contacts with colleagues across hundreds of miles.

A disturbing view of our developing society? In many ways, yes. What sense of community can these wanderers have, and if they have little regard for local surroundings since they may soon leave, who will lead the fight on local blight? Do wives and children adjust as easily to new surroundings as do family heads, whose relationships with the place of destination were well developed even before migration? Is a large part of the upper stratum of the social order to live in a constant state of anomie?

Surely the costs of this kind of social change are great, but so are the benefits. Mass education and migration have greatly increased the possibilities of social advancement, and they have brought profound changes to the social structure. Both depend, however, upon a concept of intellect that assigns many but uneven abilities to the individual. The end result may perhaps be viewed as a broadening of democracy through the multiplication of elites.

NOTES

1. Joseph Kennedy. *Report of the Superintendent of the Census for December 1, 1852*. Washington, 1853. P. 15.

2. U.S. Bureau of the Census. *Current Population Reports*. Series P-20, No. 190. School enrollment: October 1968 and 1967. Washington, 1969. [i], II, 57 pp.

3. Godfrey Thompson. Intelligence and civilization. In: Stephen Wiseman, Editor. *Intelligence and ability*. Baltimore, Penguin Books, 1967. P. 123.

Introduction: B. Migration Research

The research on migration is literally voluminous, though much of it is purely descriptive and does not bear on theoretical or problematic issues. I have selected only two papers for this section to illustrate the kind of research that does try to test theoretical hypotheses or answer relevant practical questions.

The first paper (Kammeyer and McClendon) illustrates the traditional kind of migration research in which migration *rates* between regions of the United States serve as the dependent variables. The importance of this paper is not so much the research findings, but the conclusions that are made about the relationship between migration theory and migration research. This paper again illustrates the points made in Section I where, in discussing Kurt Back's essay (article 2), I argued that the social psychological approach may be most relevant for studying many kinds of demographic phenomena today.

The second paper is one of several good recent articles by Larry Long in which he answers some politically and socially relevant questions about migration-related phenomena. In a paper not reprinted here, Long has investigated the effects of women's participation in the labor force on the migration of couples and has found that the migration of families that occurs because of the husband interferes substantially with the career development of wives.[1] Long has also investigated the effect that migration has on the grade level achieve-

---

[1] Larry H. Long, "Women's Labor Force Participation and the Residential Mobility of Families," *Social Forces*, 52 (March 1974), pp. 342–48.

ment of the children of parents who migrate. On the basis of his data, Long concluded that "even though long-distance migration may interfere with children's progress in school, areas with high rates of inmigration tend to have children of above-average scholastic ability, presumably because of the overrepresentation of highly-educated parents among migrants."[2] In the paper reprinted in this section, Long considers the validity of the often heard claim that people move to cities in order to take advantage of the welfare benefits that cities offer. He does not find support for that reasoning, even though politicians often base their arguments against welfare programs on this charge.

---

[2] Larry H. Long, "Does Migration Interfere with Children's Progress in School?" Paper presented at the annual meeting of the American Sociological Association, August, 1973, New York City, p. 10.

17

Some Tests of, and Comments on, Lee's Theory of Migration

Kenneth C.W. Kammeyer and McKee McClendon

The plea for more theory in the field of population has been made so often in the last two decades that it has become a cliche. But now it also is fast becoming an anachronism. It can no longer be said that demographers are *only* concerned with descriptive data and empirical research. Increasingly they have turned their attention to the production of theoretical models that promise to guide and illuminate their empirical work.

This has certainly occurred with regard to theories of migration. A decade ago it could have been said with validity that in the field of migration there had been almost no theorizing since the late nineteenth century work of Ravenstein (1885, 1889). The only obvious exception to this assertion would have been the "intervening opportunities" model of Stouffer (1940, 1960), and the work of a few other "gravitational" model theorists (e.g., Stewart, 1948; Dodd, 1950).

In the late 1960's, three well-formulated theories of migration emerged. All three had a distinctly sociological orientation. They were published in successive years by Everett Lee (1966), James Beshers (1967), and J. J. Mangalam (1968).

These three theoretical contributions to the study of migration are now in need of critical analysis and empirical testing to establish their utility and validity. This paper offers some empirical evidence and critical comment, with special attention to the migration theory of Lee.

LEE'S THEORY OF MIGRATION

Lee posited four very general factors that enter into the decision to migrate and the process of migration:

This paper was prepared especially for the second edition of this reader.

1. Factors associated with the area of origin,
2. Factors associated with the area of destination,
3. Intervening obstacles, between the place of origin and the place of destination,
4. Personal factors.

The inclusion of personal factors in Lee's conceptual model is of critical significance because it is this element that gave the theory a distinct social psychological character. Lee used the concept of personal factors in two different senses. First, personal factors appeared to be the objective personal characteristics of an individual, such as his or her sex, age, family status, or life cycle stage. The second meaning that Lee attached to personal factors related more to the personality and the perception of the individual. "In this connection," he said, "we must note that it is not so much the actual factors which result in migration. Personal sensitivities, intelligence, and awareness of conditions elsewhere enter into the evaluation of the situation at origin, and knowledge of the situation at destination. . . ." (Lee, p. 51).

There is no particular disadvantage in developing a social psychological theory of migration, for, as Kurt Back (1967) has forcefully argued, at this particular historical time, the social psychological approach to demographic events is most likely to be fruitful. However, a social psychological theory of migration will be most useful for producing hypotheses at the level of the individual or family. Yet many of the hypotheses that Lee developed, and both the hypotheses being tested in this study, are at the aggregate level. The unit of analysis implied by most of Lee's hypotheses is the socioecological system, and not the individual or family. We would expect a reduction in the explanatory-predictive power of a theory when the level of analysis changes from the theory to the hypotheses derived therefrom.

THE HYPOTHESES TO BE TESTED AND THE RESEARCH PROCEDURES

In this paper we will report the tests of two of the hypotheses that Lee derived from his theoretical model. They are as follows: 1. "the volume of migration within a given territory varies with the degree of diversity of areas included in that territory," and 2. "the volume of migration varies with the diversity of people." The key concepts in these two hypotheses are: 1. diversity (area and people), and 2. volume of migration.

The units of analysis that we used to test the hypotheses were the 119 economic subregions of the continental United States. The economic, educational, and residential characteristics of these subregions were used to measure the diversity of *pairs* of subregions; and the combined stream and counterstream migration between any two subregions was used as a measure of migration volume. The data on migration and subregion characteristics came from the 1960 census reports.

The procedure used to test the validity of the hypotheses can be illustrated by describing the test of hypothesis 1: "The volume of migration within a given territory varies with the degree of diversity of areas included in that territory."

The hypothesis stated in this way says that if a number of territories are examined the territories with the greatest diversity (say in income, or labor force composition) will have the greatest amount of migration. Conversely, if a territory is completely homogeneous, a total sameness throughout, then there should be little migration because there should be very little reason to move from one place to another that is just the same. Therefore, in order to use the migration data for economic subregions of the United States and still test Lee's hypotheses, the following derivative hypothesis was tested: the rate of migration between pairs of areas, within a given territory, will vary positively with the degree of diversity between pairs of areas. For this hypothesis to be valid, the volume of migration between pairs of economic subregions of the United States would have to be positively correlated with measures of dissimilarity between the pairs. The most dissimilar pairs, according to the hypothesis, would have the greatest amount of migration between them; the least dissimilar, the least migration. To test hypothesis 1 the percentage distributions of the industrial composition of the labor force were compared for all pairs of subregions. The diversity between every pair of subregions was calculated by applying the Index of Dissimilarity (Duncan and Duncan, 1965) to pairs of percentage distributions. Table 1 shows the details of each of the four diversity variables used in the study: area diversity included Industry and Rural-urban; people diversity included Education and Income. Table 1 also presents an example of how the Index of Dissimilarity was calculated for one pair of subregions.

The migration between every pair of subregions was based on the movement of people from one subregion to another between 1955 and 1960, as reported by the 1960 census. For each pair of subregions a total rate of migration was calculated from the number of migrants moving in each direction. Rates of migration were used instead of volume to eliminate the effects of different sized base populations.

In the test of the hypothesis that migration would be greatest when the diversity between areas was greatest, the distance between areas was a confounding factor. Distance has often been employed as an index of intervening obstacles to migration, and it is well established that as the distance between two places increases the volume of migration decreases. Since

TABLE 1.   Diversity Variables and the Index of Dissimilarity

Industry
Agriculture, forestry, fisheries
Mining
Construction
Durable Goods Manufacturing
Nondurable Goods Manufacturing
Transport, Communication,
   & Other Public Util.
Wholesale & Retail Trade
Finance, Insurance, and Real Estate
Business & Repair Services
Personal Services
Entertainment and
   Recreational Services
Professional and Related Services
Public Administration
Industry not Reported

Urban-Rural Residence
Urban (2,500 and above)
Rural Nonfarm
Rural Farm

Education (25 years and above)
No school years completed
Elementary: 1 to 4 years
            5 to 6 years
            7 years
            8 years
High School: 1 to 3 years
            4 years
College: 1 to 3 years
            4 years

Income (total family income)

Under $1,000	$6,000–$6,999
$1,000–$1,999	$7,000–$7,999
$2,000–$2,999	$8,000–$8,999
$3,000–$3,999	$9,000–$9,999
$4,000–$4,999	$10,000 and over
$5,000–$5,999	

Sample Index of Dissimilarity for Residence

Residence Categories	Economic Subregion 1 Number	%	Economic Subregion 2 Number	%	Absolute Difference Between Percentages
Urban	330,546	37.12	729,796	64.84	27.72
Rural Nonfarm	489,983	55.02	366,451	32.56	22.46
Rural Farm	69,969	7.86	29,276	2.60	5.26
Sum	890,489	100.00	1,125,523	100.00	55.44

Index of Dissimilarity $= 55.44/2 = 27.72$

there is also a greater probability that proximate places will have more characteristics in common than distant places, it follows that the distance between two areas will have to be introduced as a control when the relationship between dissimilarity and the volume of migration is being considered. The diversity hypotheses will receive their most severe test by examining the partial correlation coefficients between measures of diversity and migration, while controlling for distance.

THE FINDINGS

Table 2 shows that the diversity of the industrial composition of the labor force is *negatively* correlated with the rate of migration ($-.232$), and not positively, as hypothesized. When the distance between subregions is controlled, the partial correlation remains negative ($-.189$).

In other words, the hypothesis derived from the theory led us to expect a positive correlation between the diversity of subregions and the amount of migration between them. Presumably, people would not move to a new place if it did not differ in some way from the place they were leaving (though this assumption will be reconsidered below).

TABLE 2. Correlation Coefficients Between Selected Measures of Diversity and the Rate of Migration Between Pairs of Economic Subregions, Partialled by Distance

Migration Rate Between Pairs of Economic Subregions N = 7021		
Diversity	Zero-order	Partialled by distance
Industry	−.232	−.189
Rural-Urban	−.092	−.086
Education	−.261	−.221
Income	−.141	−.119

In a similar manner all of the other measures of diversity also correlated negatively with the rate of migration. Controlling for distance did not change the direction of the correlation. (Rural-urban $r = -.086$, Education $r = -.221$, Income $r = -.119$.) Hypotheses 1 and 2, as derived from Lee's theory, received no support from these tests.

CONCLUSION AND DISCUSSION

The correlation coefficients produced in our tests of Lee's hypotheses were nonsupportive. There are a number of possible answers to the question "Why?" We would like to emphasize one that was alluded to earlier. As Lee moved from his theoretical discussion to the derived hypotheses, there was clearly a shift in the conceptual level and the unit of analysis. In the theory, the unit of analysis was the individual migrant (or a family) and the behavioral act was the decision to migrate or the fact of migration. In the hypotheses the unit of analysis (at least in the particular hypotheses we tested) changed to territories and their objective economic and population characteristics. The act or action shifted to the volume of migration within the territories or, in the case of our test, the rates of migration between areas within a territory. The theory was developed at the individual or family level and the hypotheses were formulated at the aggregate and socio-ecological level.

Furthermore, Lee developed a conceptual model of migration that gave the perception and the decision-making of the individual a position of preeminence. Yet in the formulation of the hypotheses, presumably derived from the theory, the individual's perception of the situation was of no relevance. This is best illustrated by recalling Petersen's (1958) important, but too seldom used, distinction between "innovative" and "conservative" migration. Essentially, innovative migrants are moving to change their way of life, while conservative migrants are moving to retain their way of life. Lee's hypotheses would be best supported if most of the migration occurring were innovative. But, in the United States today that may not be the case. Many migrants may move to places that are very much like the places they have left. They do so because their occupation or profession calls for them to be mobile. They are likely to see their migration as one that allows them to retain their way of life. In any event, it would be important to know something about the values, objectives, and perceptions of the migrants. *The emphasis should be on the perceptions and the decision-making processes of the individual migrants, or the family as a decision-making unit.* This is clearly the emphasis of Lee's theoretical model, but his derived hypotheses shift ground dramatically, and end up being formulated in the more traditional formal-demographic mold.

It might be noted that there is a parallel shift in Beshers' (1967) discussion of a theory of migration. He developed his theoretical model around a modified Weberian typology of modes of orientation, augmented by the notion of family decision-making. From this social psychological, decision-making model Beshers somehow derived what he called the "classical points of migration literature." Paraphrased, they are: 1. net migration can be interpreted as an effort to increase economic opportunity; 2. volume of migration between pairs of cities stands in some direct relation to the populations of the two cities, and in some relation to the distance between them; 3. there is a marked difference in age and sex characteristics of migration streams between different types of areas (p. 142). It is very difficult to see the connection between Beshers' theoretical discussion and at least the last two familiar propositions of formal demography.

We believe that what we are seeing in these theoretical efforts of present-day demographers is a well-ingrained pattern of ultimately considering the subject of population only from a formal demographic, aggregate level. Even after having formulated what are essentially social psychological or decision-making theories, they are inclined to revert back to the perspectives of formal demography.

Kurt Back has suggested, and we agree, that as people gain increasing control over the demographic events of their lives, the approach of formal demography will have to give way to sociological, and especially social psychological data and research. Movement in this direction has been made in these recent theories of migration, but the research hypotheses and the suggested methodological approaches will have to move toward a more social psychological character. In large measure, this can be done by having the research reflect the existing theories with greater fidelity.

REFERENCES

Back, Kurt W. 1967. "New Frontiers in Demography and Social Psychology." Demography 4:90–97.

Beshers, James M. 1967. Population Processes in Social Systems. New York: The Free Press, Chapter 5.

Dodd, Stuart D. 1950. "The Interactance Hypothesis: A Gravity Model Fitting Physical Masses and Human Groups." American Sociological Review 15: 245–56.

Duncan, Otis Dudley, and Beverly Duncan, 1965. "Residential Distribution and Occupational Stratification." American Journal of Sociology 60:493–503.

Lee, Everett S. 1966. "A Theory of Migration." Demography 3:47–57.

Mangalam, J. J. 1968. Human Migration. Lexington, Kentucky: University of Kentucky Press, pp. 1–20.

Ravenstein, E. G. 1885. "The Laws of Migration." Journal of the Royal Statistical Society 48 (Part 2):167–227.

————. 1889. "The Laws of Migration." Journal of the Royal Statistical Society 52:241–301.

Stewart, John W. 1948. "Demographic Gravitation: Evidence and Applications." Sociometry 11: 31–57.

Stouffer, Samuel A. 1940. "Intervening Opportunities: A Theory Relating Mobility and Distance." American Sociological Review 5:845–67.

————. 1960. "Intervening Opportunities and Competing Migrants." Journal of Regional Science 2:1–26.

18

Poverty Status and Receipt of Welfare Among Migrants and Nonmigrants in Large Cities*

Larry H. Long

Data from the 1970 census show that black migrants to six of the nation's largest cities were less likely to be poor or on welfare in 1970 than blacks born and raised in these cities. The cross-sectional pattern suggests that black migrants from the South may initially experience fairly high rates of poverty and welfare dependence, but after a few years the Southern migrants are more successful in escaping from poverty and welfare dependence than blacks native to large cities in the North.

Among whites in the six cities there is no consistent relationship between migration status and being poor and on welfare, except for slightly higher than average rates of poverty and receipt of welfare among the Southern born.

These findings are placed in the context of previous research on differences between first-generation black Northerners and second- (and later) generation black Northerners. Some explanatory hypotheses are offered.

There is widespread belief in the United States that differing levels of welfare payments greatly influence migration patterns. Since large cities generally have much higher welfare payments than rural areas and small towns, policy makers and administrators have often suggested that this differential attracts poor people to cities and is a major reason for increases in welfare rolls of large cities. Empirical research has neither supported nor refuted this explanation of the rapid rise in recent years in the number and proportion of persons on welfare.

Reprinted from *American Sociological Review*, 39, no. 1 (February, 1974), pp. 46–56, by permission of the author and the publisher.

* Revised version of a paper presented at the annual meeting of the Population Association of America, New Orleans, La., April 26–28, 1973.

This paper has three purposes. First, it will establish the widespread nature of beliefs concerning the relationship between migration patterns and differing levels of welfare payments. Second, the validity of these beliefs will be tested by examining what is already known about the motivation and characteristics of migrants and by examining data from the 1970 census on the inter-relationships among race, region of birth, recency of arrival, and the likelihood of being poor and on welfare in selected large cities in 1970. Finally, a set of explanatory hypotheses will be advanced to explain the findings and suggest future research strategies.

Because the hypothesized link between migration and size of welfare payment is usually offered with respect to blacks, this paper focuses primarily on migration patterns of blacks.

POPULAR BELIEFS ABOUT WELFARE AND MIGRATION

The rapid increase in the number of persons on welfare (mostly Aid to Families with Dependent Children) beginning around 1966 has been described as "startling" (Banfield, 1969:89) and referred to as an "explosion" (Gordon, 1969:65; Piven and Cloward, 1971:187). This dramatic change is often explained by contrasting what Southern states pay welfare recipients and what New York City pays and concluding that the large difference motivates poor people to move from areas with low average welfare payments to areas with high average welfare payments.

Writing about welfare in 1968, Daniel Moynihan commented (1968: 28) that "the differential in payments between jurisdictions . . . *has* to encourage *some* migration toward urban centers in the North" [emphasis in original]. He noted that at the end of 1966 New York state paid AFDC families an average of $226.85 per month, while South Carolina paid $62.10; and in the years 1961–65 New York's caseload went up 104 percent, while South Carolina's went down 26 percent. "There is no solid evidence," wrote Moynihan (1968:28), "that migration had anything to do with these changes, but the possibility is surely strong, and it is absurd to suppose that a one-year residence restriction would discourage such obviously rational moves."

In spite of Moynihan's acknowledgment of the absence of "solid evidence," the idea has become widespread that differing levels of welfare payments attract to high-benefit areas large numbers of poor people who disproportionately increase the welfare rolls. In a cover story on the economy, *Time* magazine (1972:74) referred to:

. . . the scandalous situation under which the citizens of states such as New York and Illinois in effect subsidize low tax and welfare levels in other areas, predominantly the South, whose poor still flock to the high-welfare states in order to collect more money.

The Wall Street Journal asserted with almost equal force (Garnett, 1972:1) that Southern blacks "will continue to be attracted to the North. if only because the welfare payments are better."

Such statements apparently reflect the views of many Americans. In a 1969 nationwide survey of 1,017 adults, 41 percent agreed with the statement that "A lot of people are moving to this state from other states just to get welfare money here" (Feagin, 1972:107). Only 31 percent disagreed with the statement, and 28 percent were uncertain of their views on this subject. Since the survey was nationwide and since persons in states with very low welfare payments appear unlikely to agree with the statement, one could reasonably conclude that a majority of the population in states with above-average welfare benefits believe that "a lot of people" are moving in to avail themselves of welfare.

THE EXISTING EVIDENCE

In view of these widely-held beliefs, it is a little surprising that so few tests of the responsiveness of migration patterns to differences in welfare benefits have been made. Correlation studies of areal characteristics using size of welfare payment as one variable have been attempted (DeJong and Donnelly, 1972) but their results are not conclusive.

A methodological difficulty in such studies is the high correlation between median family income and average AFDC payment per family. For example, for the fifty states and the District of Columbia the zero-order correlation between these two variables in 1970 was .67, meaning that about 45 percent of the variation among the states in size of AFDC payment can be accounted for simply by differences in median family income (income data from 1970 census; AFDC data from National Center for Social Statistics for February 1970). Rank-order correlation (Spearman's rho) is even higher—.72. Thus one can conclude that there is a rather strong tendency for states with high incomes to offer relatively generous welfare payments.[1]

Traditional economic theory postulates that people in economically depressed areas tend to move to areas where income-earning possibilities are greater. But with correlations of areal characteristics, one cannot tell how many people who moved to high income/high welfare states moved for the high income and how many for the high welfare.

Another approach is to interview welfare recipients about their residential backgrounds. Such evidence, however, is hard to evaluate without similar information on a control group of persons not on welfare. Nevertheless, based on correlation studies and data from interviews of welfare recipients, Steiner (1971:87) cautiously concluded that:

> ... there seems reason to doubt that benefit differences between low paying southern states and high paying northern states are themselves pulling millions of southern blacks into the slums of New York, Newark, Chicago, Philadelphia, or Detroit.

With interviews of welfare recipients in New York City, Sternlieb and Indik (1973:29) came to a similarly guarded conclusion.

Piven and Cloward (1971) were less cautious in dismissing the hypothesis. They deny that changes in the number of persons on welfare reflect changes in the number eligible. But even if such were the case, they note (1971:189–91) that migration could not have changed the number of persons eligible enough to account for the rise in the number of welfare recipients that occurred around 1966. The volume of black migration out of the South was fairly steady from year to year during the 1960's and showed no increase that could account for the 1966 rise. During the 1960's the South actually experienced net immigration of whites for the first time in many decades (U.S. Bureau of the Census, 1971).

Still, none of the above studies had direct information on residential background of both receivers and nonreceivers of welfare. The Survey of Economic Opportunity, taken in 1967, "contains the first national information on receipt of money income from welfare programs, by migration status" (Beale, 1971:305). This survey contained several questions on residential background, including one on type of residence (urban vs. rural) when the respondent was sixteen years old. Beale tabulated current (i.e., 1967) type of residence with type of residence at age sixteen and concluded (1971:305):

> Among blacks the rural-urban migrant family or individual was nominally slightly more likely than urban natives to have received welfare income assistance [during the preceding year] . . . However, these differences are not statistically significant from a sampling standpoint and, if real, would be rather minor in any meaningful effect on welfare programs.

From the same data file other researchers prepared slightly different tabulations and limited consideration to the New York City metropolitan region. Their study concluded that "Negroes born in the area have a higher rate of welfare dependency than any but quite recent Negro migrants" (Lowry, et al., 1971:41). The small number of cases, however, prevented any firm conclusions, and there is legitimate doubt whether the example of the New York City metropolitan area can be generalized to other metropolitan areas.

In short, no study has presented empirical evidence for the hypothesis that welfare payments themselves have attracted large numbers of persons to states or cities with high benefit levels. Most factual analyses of welfare have considered the hypothesis and refuted it, but the evidence presented has not been entirely convincing. To provide a more definitive test, several tabulations were designed to take advantage of data collected in the 1970 census.

DATA FROM THE 1970 CENSUS

The 1970 census contained questions on state of birth, county or city of residence in 1965, and total money income in 1969 from various sources (including public assistance). Thus for individual cities we can identify persons born in and out of the state, separating the latter into those who moved to the city in question before 1965 and those who moved after 1965. In addition, Southern-born persons can be separated from the total population born in other states. The percent poor and the percent receiving public assistance income during the preceding year were tabulated for each of six major cities according to these migration categories. These data are shown in Table 1 for black family heads and in Table 2 for white family heads not of Spanish heritage.

These six cities—New York City, Philadelphia, Chicago, Detroit, Los Angeles, and Washington, D.C.—were chosen because each had at least 500,000 Negro population. The definition of poverty level is that currently used by the federal government for statistical purposes and is based on total family income, size of family, and whether residence is farm or nonfarm (see U.S. Bureau of the Census, 1972:29–31, Appendix B). White persons of Spanish heritage—excluded from Table 2—consist of persons of Puerto Rican birth or parentage in New York City and Philadelphia, Spanish speaking people in Chicago, Detroit and Washington, D.C., and Spanish speaking people or people with a Spanish surname in Los Angeles. A family was considered to be receiving public assistance if any member reported any income in 1969 from this source.

Table 1 shows that for each of the six cities black family heads born in other states were *less* likely to be on welfare than those born in the respective states. The differences are not great, but they are consistent; and it is clear that blacks born out-of-state are less dependent on city welfare systems than those born in the state.

In five of the six cases, black family heads who were recent migrants (since 1965) were slightly more likely to be on welfare than the early migrants. But even the recent migrants were less likely to be on welfare than the native blacks in each city.

TABLE 1.   Migration, Receipt of Public Assistance, and Poverty Status, for Black Families in Six Cities: 1970

	New York City	Phila-delphia	Chicago	Detroit	Los Angeles	Wash., D.C.
	Percentage of Families Receiving Public Assistance					
Total*	20.8	19.6	17.7	15.2	23.8	8.2
Family head:						
Born in state of 1970 residence	23.7	21.4	19.4	18.3	24.8	9.6
Born in other states	22.0	17.9	17.1	14.0	23.9	7.2
Moved to city before 1965	22.0	17.8	17.1	13.9	23.8	7.6
Moved to city after 1965	22.7	18.9	17.6	14.2	24.6	4.5
Born in South	22.7	18.0	17.4	14.1	24.7	7.6
Moved to city before 1965	22.6	17.9	17.4	14.0	24.4	8.0
Living in South in 1965	25.6	19.2	19.6	13.6	29.2	5.1
Living elsewhere in 1965	21.2	18.8	15.6	16.0	23.8	4.3
Incomplete migration data	20.7	20.6	16.8	15.5	23.9	8.6
	Percentage of Families Below Poverty Level					
Total*	20.7	21.5	20.6	18.8	21.5	15.6
Family head:						
Born in state of 1970 residence	23.3	24.4	23.7	22.9	27.4	17.9
Born in other states	19.9	17.9	19.0	16.8	20.7	13.1
Moved to city before 1965	19.8	17.5	18.6	16.3	20.0	13.5
Moved to city after 1965	21.6	23.1	23.1	20.0	24.1	10.1
Born in South	20.4	18.0	19.4	17.1	21.4	13.6
Moved to city before 1965	20.3	17.6	18.9	16.6	20.6	13.9
Living in South in 1965	24.0	26.6	27.5	22.7	31.4	12.6
Living elsewhere in 1965	19.0	19.5	20.2	17.9	21.6	6.6
Incomplete migration data	22.8	24.2	21.1	20.9	20.8	17.9

* Includes family heads born abroad and family heads with incomplete migration data (i.e., with no report on either place of birth or residence in 1965).
Source: 1970 Census of Population, *Mobility for Metropolitan Areas,* Tables 17–22.

When we look at poverty status, the same kind of picture emerges—namely, blacks born in other states appear to be doing better economically than those born in the state where the city is located. For each city the percent below the poverty level is lower among blacks born in other states. In each city recent black inmigrants are more likely to be poor than early migrants, but even the recent inmigrants are less likely to be poor than blacks native to the cities in question.

The same pattern emerges when we look at blacks of Southern origin. In each city, blacks born in the South were less likely to be poor and less likely to be on welfare than blacks born in the states where each city is located. Recent arrivals from the South (since 1965) were usually more likely to be poor and dependent on welfare than early migrants from the South, and the recent arrivals from the South were even more likely to be poor than the urban natives. But in every case Southern-born blacks who had lived in the cities for five years or more were less likely to be on welfare and less likely to be poor than the urban natives.

In short, the information in Table 1 indicates that being born in one of the six cities can in some ways be a greater handicap for blacks than Southern birth. The urban-born blacks rely more on urban welfare institutions than all but the most recent migrants from the South.

Do the same conclusions apply to whites? As Table 2 shows, the answer is generally no. Among whites there are no consistent differences between those born in their state of 1970 residence and those born in other states with respect to being on welfare. But for each city whites born in the South were more likely to be on welfare than those born in other regions.

Looking at poverty status among whites in the six cities, one finds that the total out-of-state-born persons are less likely to be poor than those born in their 1970 state of residence. But the Southern-born whites are more likely to be poor than either the whites born in other regions or the whites born in their 1970 state of residence.

In Table 2 note the relatively high incidence of poverty among white family heads of Southern birth living in Chicago or Detroit in 1970. This may reflect the fact that these two cities are known to be major destinations of whites moving from economically depressed Appalachian areas.

Analyses of this kind are hampered by troublesome non-response rates. In Tables 1 and 2 the lines for "Incomplete migration data" include persons who failed to report either of the two migration items—state of birth or county or city of residence in 1965. These non-responses are caused not only by respondents leaving the questions blank but also by machine malfunctions and other errors in data processing. For whatever reason, blacks were about twice as likely to be missing information on either of these two items as were whites. For the total U.S. population, 4.4 percent had no information on state of birth (8.3 percent among blacks), and 5.2 percent had no information on county or city of residence in 1965 (8.3 percent among blacks).

It seems doubtful that having information on the non-responders would alter the preceding findings. At least for blacks, the non-responders did not differ much from all blacks with respect to percent receiving public assistance or being poor. And the findings for blacks are consistent with the results of other recent empirical research on how inmigrant blacks differ from blacks born and raised in large cities. These other studies will be considered in the next section.

The same kinds of tabulations as shown in Tables 1 and 2 were pre-

TABLE 2. Migration, Receipt of Public Assistance, and Poverty Status, for White Families not of Spanish Heritage in Six Cities: 1970

	New York City	Philadelphia	Chicago	Detroit	Los Angeles	Wash., D.C.
	Percentage of Families Receiving Public Assistance					
Total*	4.2	3.2	2.6	3.6	5.4	1.3
Family head:						
Born in state of 1970 residence	3.7	3.1	2.4	3.4	5.0	1.6
Born in other states	3.7	3.1	3.4	3.9	5.4	1.3
Moved to city before 1965	4.0	3.3	3.4	3.9	5.1	1.5
Moved to city after 1965	2.0	2.3	3.4	4.1	6.2	0.8
Born in South	5.9	3.6	4.7	5.8	6.4	1.9
Moved to city before 1965	6.7	3.9	4.9	6.0	6.1	2.0
Living in South in 1965	3.4	3.0	5.1	5.6	4.3	2.2
Living elsewhere in 1965	2.7	1.4	3.3	5.1	8.1	0.9
Incomplete migration data	6.1	4.7	3.6	4.9	6.5	1.5
	Percentage of Families Below Poverty Level					
Total*	6.7	6.3	5.5	6.2	5.5	4.2
Family head:						
Born in state of 1970 residence	5.3	5.5	4.5	5.4	5.9	5.1
Born in other states	4.7	4.9	5.7	5.9	4.8	3.3
Moved to city before 1965	4.7	4.4	5.5	5.7	4.2	3.2
Moved to city after 1965	4.8	6.6	6.5	7.2	6.6	3.6
Born in South	6.6	6.7	8.4	8.7	6.3	4.9
Moved to city before 1965	7.0	6.1	8.1	8.1	5.6	5.0
Living in South in 1965	6.2	15.5	13.4	12.7	6.7	6.4
Living elsewhere in 1965	4.8	4.9	6.6	10.1	8.5	0.9
Incomplete migration data	8.9	9.6	7.6	9.5	7.1	5.6

* Includes family heads born abroad and family heads with incomplete migration data (i.e., with no report on either place of birth or residence in 1965).

Source: 1970 Census of Population, *Mobility for Metropolitan Areas,* Tables 17–22.

pared for female family heads, as shown in Tables 3 and 4. The data for female family heads support the above conclusions.

In five of the six cities, black women who head families and who were born in other states were less likely to be on welfare than black women born in their 1970 state of residence. And in all cities, black women heading families were less likely to be poor if born in other states. Even Southern-born black women heading families were less likely to be poor or on welfare than black women born in their state of 1970 residence. Only among recent (since 1965) arrivals from the South were black female heads more likely to be poor or on welfare than the urban native female family heads.

An interesting comparison in Tables 3 and 4 is that black women who failed to respond to one of the two migration questions did not differ greatly with respect to being poor or on welfare from other black women who responded to both questions. In contrast, white women who failed to respond to either migration question were much more likely to be poor or on welfare than other white women who answered both questions. Why these differences exist is not clear.

TABLE 3. Migration, Receipt of Public Assistance, and Poverty Status, for Families Headed by Black Women in Six Cities: 1970

	New York City	Philadelphia	Chicago	Detroit	Los Angeles	Wash., D.C.
	Percentage of Families Receiving Public Assistance					
Total*	43.0	40.0	42.8	40.3	47.0	19.9
Family head:						
Born in state of 1970 residence	46.9	43.4	44.8	44.4	45.7	21.9
Born in other states	45.2	35.8	42.4	38.4	47.6	18.7
Moved to city before 1965	44.9	35.4	42.1	37.7	47.2	19.1
Moved to city after 1965	48.4	42.1	46.6	43.0	49.1	15.1
Born in South	46.0	36.2	43.4	39.3	49.2	19.3
Moved to city before 1965	45.8	35.8	43.0	38.5	48.3	19.6
Living in South in 1965	48.3	43.4	52.8	44.7	56.1	16.8
Living elsewhere in 1965	52.4	38.9	42.2	45.3	49.4	15.1
Incomplete migration data	41.2	41.9	38.7	40.3	47.7	19.5
	Percentage of Families Below Poverty Level					
Total*	40.4	43.6	46.3	45.9	44.3	32.8
Family head:						
Born in state of 1970 residence	44.9	48.4	50.4	51.2	50.4	35.5
Born in other states	39.6	36.6	43.8	43.0	43.6	28.9
Moved to city before 1965	39.4	36.0	42.8	40.9	42.5	28.9
Moved to city after 1965	43.0	45.3	54.9	56.6	47.8	28.8
Born in South	40.0	36.9	44.9	43.7	44.9	29.3
Moved to city before 1965	39.8	36.4	43.8	41.8	43.5	29.1
Living in South in 1965	42.8	49.8	64.7	64.4	58.3	32.1
Living elsewhere in 1965	43.9	37.1	48.1	49.5	44.0	28.0
Incomplete migration data	44.4	48.8	46.0	47.8	42.0	37.0

* Includes family heads born abroad and family heads with incomplete migration data (i.e., with no report on either place of birth or residence in 1965).
Source: 1970 Census of Population, *Mobility for Metropolitan Areas*, Tables 17–22.

TABLE 4. Migration, Receipt of Public Assistance, and Poverty Status for Families Headed by White Women not of Spanish Heritage in Six Cities: 1970

	New York City	Phila-delphia	Chicago	Detroit	Los Angeles	Wash., D.C.
	Percentage of Families Receiving Public Assistance					
Total*	14.1	9.8	8.7	13.6	16.1	3.1
Family head:						
Born in state of 1970 residence	13.8	9.6	8.2	13.9	17.4	4.1
Born in other states	11.8	10.8	13.0	16.0	15.8	3.1
Moved to city before 1965	12.2	10.9	12.5	15.6	14.5	2.7
Moved to city after 1965	7.4	9.8	16.6	19.1	19.9	5.6
Born in South	19.0	13.7	17.1	25.9	17.5	4.4
Moved to city before 1965	19.9	12.9	17.5	25.4	15.1	3.3
Living in South in 1965	11.8	**	15.3	**	11.1	12.1
Living elsewhere in 1965	9.0	**	13.7	23.8	26.0	**
Incomplete migration data	21.5	15.7	10.0	20.2	17.6	2.1
	Percentage of Families Below Poverty Level					
Total*	17.0	17.0	15.3	18.8	18.6	7.4
Family head:						
Born in state of 1970 residence	16.6	17.2	14.6	20.1	23.9	10.8
Born in other states	14.7	14.1	16.4	20.1	17.1	5.6
Moved to city before 1965	13.8	12.6	14.8	19.0	14.3	4.5
Moved to city after 1965	22.9	26.0	28.0	28.6	26.0	11.9
Born in South	20.9	21.4	25.1	30.9	20.0	6.2
Moved to city before 1965	20.0	16.8	23.5	28.2	17.2	6.1
Living in South in 1965	25.0	**	35.2	**	19.2	5.4
Living elsewhere in 1965	34.7	**	36.3	44.5	28.7	**
Incomplete migration data	27.3	24.8	22.3	29.3	21.4	10.1

* Includes family heads born abroad and family heads with incomplete migration data (i.e., with no report on either place of birth or residence in 1965).

** Too few cases to compute rate.

Source: 1970 Census of Population, *Mobility for Metropolitan Areas,* Tables 17–22.

DISCUSSION OF FINDINGS

For the six cities with the largest black populations, this paper has shown that blacks most likely to be poor and on welfare are those born and raised in the city and living there at the time of the 1970 census. Only recent (since 1965) arrivals from the South were found to have rates of poverty and welfare dependence as high as blacks born and raised in their city of 1970 residence.

That blacks having recently arrived from the South have higher rates of poverty and welfare dependence than earlier migrants may suggest either of two interpretations: (1) after an initial period of adjustment the recent migrants from the South will be more successful in finding and holding jobs than blacks born in the cities where they were living in 1970, that is, after a few years the recent inmigrants from the South may come to resemble the earlier migrants; or (2) the recent black inmigrants from the South represent a change in migration patterns and will continue to have rates of poverty and welfare dependence as high as the urban born, that is, the recent Southern migrants may not come to resemble earlier migrants.

Only time will decide which of these hypotheses is true. Several studies dating back to around 1960 seem to support the former. These studies have found that on several indices black migrants to Northern cities have lower rates of social disorganization than blacks native to the cities.

One of these studies is by Savitz on juvenile delinquency in Philadelphia. In a high delinquency section of the city, he studied about nine hundred Negro boys and found that those born and raised in the city had higher delinquency rates than the inmigrants. Savitz concluded that (1960:16):

> There was no confirmation of internal migration as a disorganizing process in modern life. The migrants not only tended to be lower than the natives in the frequency and seriousness of delinquencies, but were also less likely to come from broken homes, have illegitimate siblings or engage in considerable intracity mobility.

Unfortunately, subsequent studies of juvenile delinquency have not controlled for residential background to confirm Savitz's findings.

Kinman and Lee (1966) studied rates of imprisonment in Pennsylvania and found that among blacks the rates were higher for those born in Pennsylvania than those born in other states. Tilly (1970) in his study of "Race and Migration to the American City" emphasized the studies by Savitz and Kinman and Lee.

Crain and Weisman (1972) did a study based on interviews made in 1966 of a sample of adult blacks living in the North. Comparing blacks born in the North with migrants from the South who moved North before and after age ten, Crain and Weisman concluded (1972:13) that "whichever category of migrants is used for comparison, the data indicate that native Northerners are slightly more likely to have been arrested than are migrants." Interestingly, Crain and Weisman were apparently unaware of the previous work on this subject by Savitz and Kinman and Lee, who had come to similar conclusions. Nor, it appears, were Crain and Weisman aware of Green's study (1970), which seems to be the only recent study to argue that black migrants to Northern states are more prone to criminal behavior than blacks born in the North.

Finally, we may consider the studies of participation in the riots in black ghetto areas in 1967–68. A Presidential commission was set up to investigate the causes of the riots and the characteristics of participants (Kerner Commission, 1968). One of the studies carried out for the commission was by Caplan and Paige, who concluded (1968:18):

> In both Detroit and Newark 74 percent of the rioters reported that they had been raised in the North. Among the nonrioters 64 percent in Detroit and 48 percent in Newark said they were raised in the North. It is, then, the long-term residents—those who know Northern living patterns and the city best—and not the unassimilated migrants who are most likely to riot.

Studies of riots and rioters in other areas have come to similar conclusions (see Tilly, 1970:164–5).

These studies do not show that black migrants to large cities in the North have no problems of adjustment. They do, however, show that black migrants seem to be less socially disorganized and less prone to deviant behavior than blacks born in their city of residence. The present study's finding that black migrants in the six cities were generally less likely to be poor or on welfare than black urban natives is in accord with these previous studies.

If assimilation means that migrants come to be like urban natives, then the assimilation of Southern blacks in Northern cities may not be a desirable goal. This conclusion has actually been suggested by Elliot Liebow. At a conference on "Demographic Aspects of the Black Community," Daniel Price observed that his own interviews of blacks in Chicago indicated that the inmigrants were better able to obtain and hold jobs than blacks born and raised in the city (reported in Kiser, 1970:62). Liebow spoke of a study he had carried out on peer group formation and peer group associations among teenagers in an all-black area of Washington, D.C. According to Liebow (Kiser, 1970:67):

> [Black teenagers] who were not well integrated into one or another peer group invariably did much better in school and elsewhere than those who were. For whatever reason they were not accepted and did not participate fully in peer group life, but they fared better in school than those who were well integrated into their local peer groups. . . .
> It may well be that the inmigrants, unable to break into the on-

going social life very easily, and unable to establish an integrated life with their peers who were already there, are, for the same reasons as the kids, also faring better in education and jobs.

Liebow did not specify clearly what he meant by "the same reasons," but he is suggesting that black inmigrants may do relatively well because they are not "assimilated."

Price's conclusions about black inmigrants being more successful at finding and holding jobs (see also Price, 1971) have been re-confirmed by recent research of Masters (1972). In addition, Crain and Weisman (1972:11) found in their sample that black migrants to the North actually had slightly higher incomes than blacks born in the North. Weiss and Williamson (1972), in an analysis of the 1967 Survey of Economic Opportunity, found that blacks who had moved from the South to the North had higher earnings than blacks native to the North. In another analysis of the Survey of Economic Opportunity, Bacon (1971) found slightly lower rates of poverty among the South-to-North black migrants than among native Northern blacks.

In conclusion, the evidence from recent empirical research indicates that black migrants to the North become more economically successful and less likely to engage in criminal behavior than blacks born in the North. The present study has added to this body of findings by showing that in the six cities with largest black populations, black migrants were less likely to be below the poverty level or on welfare than blacks native to their city of 1970 residence.

It is true that black migration has added to the welfare rolls of Northern cities simply because black migration has added to the total population of Northern cities. But the important conclusion of this study is that black migrants have accounted for a less-than proportionate increase in the welfare rolls. Evidence presented here and elsewhere (see Masters, 1972) shows that recent black arrivals from the South often have difficulty adjusting initially to big-city living, and in such cases welfare may help "weather the crisis."

TOWARD AN EXPLANATION

An explanation is obviously needed to account for why blacks born in big cities in the North appear somewhat more likely to (1) engage in criminal behavior, (2) be unsuccessful in obtaining steady employment, and (3) be dependent on welfare than black inmigrants. An encompassing theory to account for these findings is not available, for the existence of these differences between Southern-born and Northern-born blacks is not generally recognized. Nevertheless, some speculations may be advanced as a guide to future research.

One consideration is that Southern black migrants are selected along social-psychological dimensions not commonly measured in censuses or surveys. Often noted is the fact that black South-to-North migrants traditionally have had higher levels of education than blacks who remained in the South (Beale, 1971). In recent decades black migrants to large Northern cities have had levels of education about as high as nonmigrant Northern blacks (Taeuber and Taeuber, 1965a and 1965b), although a year of education in the South has generally been of slightly lower quality than education elsewhere (estimates of how much lower are given in Coleman et al., 1966:274). But why do the Southern-born blacks seem to get more from their education in terms of employment and income than the Northern-born?

Perhaps the Southern black migrants are highly selected on the basis of intelligence, motivation and ambition. Merely the act of moving may demonstrate a positive action taken to improve one's condition. Perhaps motivational factors more than compensate for shortcomings in education and make the Southern migrants more goal-oriented and, in the end, more economically successful.

On the other hand, perhaps Southern migrants are distinguished by their attitudes toward life and work. The traditional absence of welfare in the South, the absence of an ideology to justify the "right" of welfare (cf. the National Welfare Rights Organization), and the open hostility toward welfare recipients may have made Southern blacks especially self-reliant and hesitant in applying to official agencies for welfare. Perhaps their environment engenders in Southern blacks the feeling that life is hard and hard work is all one can expect. This attitude may lead transplanted Southern blacks to persist in low-paying jobs which have no future but which provide just enough income to keep their families off welfare and above the poverty line.

It is possible that in Northern ghetto areas daily exposure to drugs, crime, violence, and overcrowded living conditions makes growing up and leading stable adult lives especially difficult. In the words of Crain and Weisman (1972:7): ". . . the data from our survey suggest that life in the North is so disruptive that [black] migrants from the South are actually better off than those who were born in the North." If this is in fact the case, then birthplace in the urban North has become for blacks the economic and social handicap that birth in the rural South was often alleged to be.

Furthermore, blacks born and raised in the North may develop a heightened sensitivity about the extent of discrimination and at the same time may develop a pessimistic attitude about the rate of economic progress which blacks have made. Wattenberg and Scammon (1973) have asserted that black economic gains are often understated or even denied in public discussions. If so, such a focus may have a more pronounced effect in the North and may engender in Northern blacks a heightened sense of relative deprivation and feelings of anger and frustration which lead to withdrawal. According to Crain and Weisman (1972:140): "Thus, while white prejudice is not more severe in the North, the northern respondent may be more aware of it and depressed by his awareness."

Northern blacks may also develop high expectations regarding suitable employment. Blacks raised in the North may be led to aspire for jobs beyond their education and may become angry, frustrated and withdrawn when their hopes are not fulfilled. Southern-born blacks may have more modest expectations and may take low-status, low-paying jobs which the Northern-born would view as not paying a "decent" wage. The Northern-born may then be more likely to choose street-corner life or welfare over such "dead-end" jobs.

These possibilities are merely speculation and represent ex post facto theorizing, in that they were developed to account for empirical regularities. Research is needed on the extent to which these and other processes may operate. The evidence in this paper shows that more surveys should include questions on residential background (where respondents were born, where educated, and when they moved to their present area of residence). This recommendation applies especially to studies of urban problems which are often assumed (without much evidence) to have a substantial rural origin.

NOTE

1. Interestingly, for the fifty states and the District of Columbia there is zero correlation between AFDC payment level and the percent of population receiving AFDC. The zero-order correlation is –.03 and rank-order correlation is –.04. In other words, states that put a high proportion of their population on welfare are not necessarily generous toward the recipients.

REFERENCES

Bacon, Lloyd. 1971. "Poverty among interregional rural-to-urban migrants." Rural Sociology 36 (June):125–40.

Banfield, Edward. 1969. "Welfare: a crisis without 'solutions'." The Public Interest 16 (Summer): 89–101.

Beale, Calvin L. 1971. "Rural-urban migration of blacks: past and future." American Journal of Agricultural Economics 53 (May):302–7.

Caplan, Nathan S. and Jeffrey M. Paige. 1968. "A Study of ghetto rioters." Scientific American 219 (August):15–21.

Coleman James S., Ernest Q. Campbell, Carol Hobson, James McPartland, Alexander M. Mood, Frederic D. Weinfield, and Robert L. York. 1966. Equality of Educational Opportunity. Washington, D.C.: U.S. Government Printing Office.

Crain, Robert L. and Carol Sachs Weisman. 1972. Discrimination, Personality, and Achievement. New York: Seminar Press.

DeJong, Gordon F. and William L. Donnelly, 1972. "AFDC payment levels and nonwhite migration to cities." Pp. 187–91 in American Statistical Association, Proceedings of the Social Statistics Section, 1971. Washington, D.C.: American Statistical Association.

Feagin, Joe R. 1972. "Poverty: we still believe that God helps those who help themselves." Psychology Today 6 (November):101–11.

Garnett, Bernard E. 1972. "More black Americans return to south from 'exile' in north." The Wall Street Journal, November 10, page 1.

Gordon, David M. 1969. "Income and welfare in New York City." The Public Interest 16 (Summer):64–88.

Green, Edward. 1970. "Race, social status, and criminal arrest." American Sociological Review 35 (June):476–90.

Kerner Commission. 1968. Report of the National Advisory Commission on Civil Disorders. New York: Bantam Books.

Kinman, Judith and Everett S. Lee. 1966. "Migration and crime." International Migration Digest 3:7–14.

Kiser, Clyde V. (ed.). 1970. Demographic Aspects of the Black Community. New York: Milbank Memorial Fund.

Lowry, Ira S., Joseph S. DeSalvo, and Barbara M. Woodfill. 1971. Rental Housing in New York City. Volume II. The Demand for Shelter. New York: The New York City Rand Institute.

Masters, Stanley H. 1972. "Are black migrants from the south to northern cities worse off than blacks already there?" Journal of Human Resources VII (Fall):411–23.

Moynihan, Daniel P. 1968. "The crises in welfare." The Public Interest 10 (Winter):3–29.

National Center for Social Statistics. Public Assistance Statistics, December 1970. NCSS Report A-2 (12/70). U.S. Department of Health, Education, and Welfare. Social and Rehabilitation Service.

———. Public Assistance Statistics, February 1971. NCSS Report A-2 (2/71). U.S. Department of Health, Education, and Welfare. Social and Rehabilitation Service.

Piven, Frances Fox and Richard A. Cloward. 1971. Regulating the Poor. New York: Pantheon Books.

Price, Daniel O. 1971. "Discussion: migration of blacks." Social Biology 18 (December):367–8.

Savitz, Leonard. 1960. Delinquency and Migration. Philadelphia: Commission on Human Relations.

Steiner, Gilbert. 1971. The State of Welfare. Washington, D.C.: The Brookings Institution.

Sternleib, George S. and Bernard P. Indik. 1973. The Ecology of Welfare: Housing and the Welfare Crisis in New York City. New Brunswick, New Jersey: Transaction Books.

Taeuber, Karl E. and Alma F. Taeuber. 1965a. "The changing character of Negro migration." American Journal of Sociology 60 (January):429–41.

———. 1965b. Negroes in Cities. Chicago: Aldine Publishing Company.

Tilly, Charles. 1970. "Race and migration to the American city." Pp. 144–69 in James Q. Wilson (ed.), The Metropolitan Enigma. Garden City, New York: Doubleday and Company, Inc.

Time Magazine. 1972. "Empty pockets on a trillion dollars a year." March 13: 66–74.

U.S. Bureau of the Census. 1971. "Whites account for reversal of south's historic population loss through migration." United States Department of Commerce News (press release), No. CB71–84.

———. 1972. Census of Population: 1970. General Social and Economic Characteristics, Final Report PC(1)-C1, United States Summary, Washington, D.C.: U.S. Government Printing Office.

———. 1973. Census of Population: 1970. Subject Reports. Final Report PC(2)-2C, Mobility for Metropolitan Areas. Washington, D.C.: U.S. Government Printing Office.

Wattenberg, Ben J. and Richard M. Scammon. 1973. "Black progress and liberal rhetoric." Commentary 55 (April): 35–44.

Weiss, Leonard and Jeffrey G. Williamson. 1972. "Black education, earnings and interregional migration." American Economic Review LXII (June): 372–83.

Mortality

Introduction: A. Selected Research on the Social Causes of Death

Sociologists and other social scientists have given much less of their attention to death than they have to fertility and migration. This relative lack of attention to mortality is understandable if we recognize that death is in the last analysis always associated with some biological, physical or medical factor. Of course, so is the birth of a child, and yet the social causes that produce fertility are so much more obvious. The social causes of death are less clear because they are farther removed from the event itself. The proximate cause of death is the thing we tend to focus on, not the style of life, or the social or psychological factors that lead to that proximate cause. It takes a little closer examination to reveal the social and psychological causes. One purpose of this section is to present some evidence that will sensitize us to the social and psychological factors that influence mortality.

One fundamental sociological principle relative to death is that a person's position in the social structure of a society will influence his or her chances of living. Any ongoing social system will develop some kind of structure, which simply means that there will be some kind of organized set of statuses or positions, into which most people will fall. The status into which a person is placed is often determined by some characteristic of birth or a biological characteristic. For example, gender still determines a person's major status placement; race is also often the basis for status placement. A person's age determines various statuses as one progresses through the age structure. These bases for status placement are often labeled *ascribed* characteristics since the individual has little chance or likelihood of changing them. There are also *achieved* characteristics that influence status placement. These are things like educational and occupational achievement. Regardless of the basis for placement, the result of large numbers of people being placed in similar categories is a societal structure. One interesting thing about these resultant structural features of society is that once they are established the individuals who compose them have certain prescribed relationships toward each other. Sometimes they must avoid each other; often a member of one social- structural category must give deference to persons in another category, and so on. The kinds of relationships between social structural categories are many and quite varied, but one feature seems to be ubiquitous: there is always some kind of hierarchical arrangement. One status has advantages, privileges, rights, powers, and material things that are not given to those of lesser status. These advantages will lead to greater life chances, including a greater chance to live. To reformulate the principle we started with: people in the lower statuses of the social structure of a society are likely to die younger than those in the higher statuses.

Sociologists have shown repeatedly that a person's position in the social class system (or the socioeconomic structure of the society) will have an effect on his or her length of life. At the University of Chicago, research has been carried on for decades that shows just how crucial one's position in the class structure may be in determining the number of years one is likely to live.[1] In 1930 the white males and

---

[1] Evelyn M. Kitagawa and Philip Hauser, "Trends in Differential Fertility and Mortality in a Metropolis—Chicago," in *Contributions to Urban Sociology*, edited by Ernest W. Burgess and Donald J. Bogue (Chicago: University of Chicago Press, 1964), pp. 59–85.

females of Chicago who came from the highest socioeconomic group had a life expectancy of eleven to twelve years longer than the lowest status white group and twenty-three to twenty-four years longer than the lowest status nonwhite group. In 1950, the life expectancy of the white males and females in the highest status group exceeded that of the white males and females in the lowest status group by eight and six years respectively, and exceeded that of the lowest status non-whites by thirteen and fourteen years. The Chicago researchers often analyzed differential mortality by asking "How many of the deaths in Chicago would not have occurred if all people in the city had had the same life chances as the highest status white group?" For the year 1950, they concluded that one-third of all deaths in Chicago would not have occurred if all people had had the same death rate as the highest status white group. They also noted that fifty percent of the nonwhite deaths would not have occurred in that year if they had had the death rate of the highest status white group.

But these findings came from only one city. In 1960 the Chicago researchers initiated a national study of differential mortality.[2] By using census information gathered in 1960, they were able to identify the status characteristics of the adults who died in the first several months after the 1960 census. In this study the researchers used educational level as the measure of social status. (Other common indicators of socioeconomic status such as income and occupation are not appropriate for mortality research since many people who die have retired or have unusually low incomes. Also many women do not have formal occupations.) Kitagawa and Hauser continued to find differences in the length of life according to one's status. (Their initial report dealt only with the white population, since there were problems in dealing with the nonwhite data caused by the under-enumeration of nonwhites.) For white women between the ages of 25 and 64 years the death rate for the least educated group (less than 8 years of school) was 61 percent higher than for the women who had at least some college. For the white males between 25 and 64, the death rate of the least educated group was 48 percent higher than that of the college educated. Over the age of 65, there was not much difference in mortality for the males who had different levels of edu-

---

[2] Evelyn M. Kitagawa and Philip M. Hauser, "Educational Differentials in Mortality by Cause of Death: United States, 1960," *Demography* 5(1968):318–53.

cation, but for females the death rate was still 59 percent higher for the least educated group. These researchers estimated that for the white population of the United States in 1960, 9.4 percent of white-male deaths and 29.3 percent of white-female deaths would not have occurred if people at all status (educational) levels had experienced the same life chances as the whites who had at least some college.

Exactly what the differentials in death rate are today we cannot say, but there is every reason to believe that people who fall into the lower strata of American society still have a distinct disadvantage when it comes to length of life. One indication of this is a comparison between the death rates of whites and nonwhites in American society. At all ages, within each sex group, the death rate for nonwhites is invariably greater than the death rate for whites.[3]

The first paper in this section is an interesting illustration of the way in which status in a social system influences mortality. Robert Kennedy has done extensive research on various demographic characteristics of the Irish people. In this excerpt from his book *The Irish*,[4] Kennedy presents evidence to show that the subordinate status of women in Ireland probably lowered their length of life compared to what it might have been if they had enjoyed a higher status. In this instance it is the sex-role structure of the society that reveals the disadvantage of being in a lower position in the social structure.

Walter Gove (article 20) adds a new dimension to an established relationship between marital status and death. Very simply, married persons have lower death rates than single persons, who in turn have lower rates than widowed or divorced persons. This general pattern holds up, even when age is held constant. However, while Gove demonstrates this relationship again as he looks at many causes of death separately, he also shows that the differences are much less between the death rates of the married women and unmarried women than they are between married and unmarried men. Gove argues on the basis of his evidence that while the married status gives a mortality advantage to both sexes, it gives much more of an advantage to men. Gove believes that the relative disadvantage of married women

---

[3] U.S. Bureau of the Census, *Statistical Abstract of the United States: 1972*, 3rd edition. (Washington, D.C.: U.S. Government Printing Office, 1972), p. 56.

[4] Robert E. Kennedy, Jr., *The Irish: Emigration, Marriage and Fertility* (Berkeley: University of California Press, 1973).

compared to married men is attributable to the traditional marital sex role our society provides for women. Gove and others are finding increasing empirical support for the idea that marriage has more advantages, both psychological and physical, for men than it has for women. Sociologist Jessie Bernard has identified these differences qualitatively by describing what she calls the "husband's marriage" and the "wife's marriage."[5] Basically she argues against the popular cultural idea that it is the man who pays a high price for marrying.

In the final paper in this section, David Philips illustrates the general proposition that individual deaths are related to the way that a person is a part of, or integrated into, his society. In his previous research Philips has demonstrated in a number of ways how the deaths of individuals go down immediately before certain ceremonial occasions. In the present paper he illustrates how deaths go down in the month before a person's birthday. He has conducted a similar analysis in which he examined what he calls the death-dip before a religious holiday (the Jewish Day of Atonement) and before presidential elections.[6] Philips concludes from his analysis that at least some persons postpone death until after the occasion of important personal, religious or national events.

Even though death is usually considered a physiological phenomenon, there is evidence in all of the papers reprinted here, and others cited, to show that both social and psychological factors may play a part in producing differences in mortality.

---

[5] Jessie Bernard, *The Future of Marriage* (New York: World Publishing Co., 1972).

[6] David P. Philips and Kenneth A. Feldman, "A Dip in Deaths Before Ceremonial Occasions: Some New Relationships between Social Integration and Mortality," *American Sociological Review* 38(1973):678–96.

19

Mortality and the Relative Social Status of the Sexes in Ireland

Robert E. Kennedy, Jr.

Even though mortality rates cannot be taken as indicators of economic or social opportunity, they may reflect the relative social status of persons within the same community. If food, shelter, clothing, and medical care are unequally divided, then this practice should show up in unequal mortality rates. The mortality rates of the religious and occupational groups in Ireland would be relevant to this question; unfortunately, such data do not exist. As we have said, the available data deal only with sex, age, region, cause of death, and marital status. Were there social practices which favored one sex in the allocation of vital resources to the extent that they affected mortality rates? My assumption is that if such practices were important enough to have influenced mortality rates, they also should have been readily apparent both to the Irish themselves and to foreign observers of Irish culture. Before presenting the patterns of mortality by sex for Ireland, I shall briefly give a few illustrations of the way some writers have seen the relative social status of the sexes in Ireland.

It has been said that Ireland is divided by a boundary even more pernicious than that between the North and the South—the boundary between the sexes.[1] Arensberg and Kimball described the situation as it existed in County Clare in 1932: "Men and women are much more often to be seen in the company of members of their own sex than otherwise, except in the house itself. . . . They go to mass, to town, or to sportive gatherings with companions of their own sex. Till recently and even now in remote districts, a conventional peasant woman always kept several paces behind her man, even if they were walking somewhere together."[2]

Reprinted from *The Irish: Emigration, Marriage and Fertility* (Berkeley, Calif.: University of California Press, 1973), pp. 51–65, by permission of the author and the publisher. Footnotes have been renumbered, table numbers (9–15) retained.

244

The act of a female walking behind the male was symbolic of the inferior position of females generally in Irish rural society. Women and children did not eat their meals until after the men and older boys had had their fill,[3] a practice which systematically made the more nutritious food and larger helpings available to the favored sex. The practice of males getting the better food, and more of it, apparently also prevailed among the urban working classes. Sean O'Casey mentioned the custom in his play *The Shadow of a Gunman.* A married couple were described: "He is a man of forty-five, but looks, relatively, much younger than Mrs. Grigson. . . . He has all the appearance of being well fed; and, in fact, he gets most of the nourishment, Mrs. Grigson getting just enough to give her strength to do the necessary work of the household."[4] The exploitation of females by males was one of the major motifs of O'Casey's *Juno and the Paycock.* At one point Juno says to her husband: "Shovel! Ah, then, me boyo, you'd do far more work with a knife an' fork than ever you'll do with a shovel! If there was e'er a genuine job goin' you'd be dh'other way about—not able to lift your arms with the pains in your legs! Your poor wife slavin' to keep the bit in your mouth, and you gallivantin' about all the day like a paycock!"[5]

The subordination of daughters in many Irish families was severe. Although things had changed considerably by the late 1950s, an observer was still able to describe the status of teenage girls in the rural areas of Limerick in the following way: "When a daughter reaches sixteen, if she remains on the farm, she must do a full day's work, and too often her life is one of unrelieved drudgery. . . . [Girls] are favoured neither by father nor mother and accepted only on sufferance. This is, perhaps, too strong a conclusion, and it would be better to say that they are loved but not thought of any great importance. In general, the girl is subservient to all other members of the family and shares no confidences with either her parents or her brothers. Her only right is to a dowry if she marries with her parents' consent."[6]

In contrast to the daughter, the son in the Irish family system was given preferential treatment. Although sons were in a subordinate position to their father, they were above everyone else in the household in the way they were treated by their mother. The preference of the mother for her sons over her daughters is shown by an attitude, found both in rural and urban areas and among all social classes, that daughters were expected "to provide the sons with special service and comforts."[7] As a 26-year-old Dublin woman told an observer in the early 1950s, in front of her mother and brothers (who agreed with her comments): "If I am sitting in the easy chair there and Matt or Charley come home, I am expected to get up and give them the chair. They just say 'Pardon me' and up I get. . . . There is no use fighting against it. I used to, but I soon found out which way the wind blew—we have to wait on the boys from sole to crown. I do not mean that the boys do not do anything for us. Matt, for example, will always fix my bike. But Mammy is just a slave to them, a willing slave, and we are expected to be, too. And that is general. That's the common attitude."[8]

Although females were subservient to males both in rural and urban Ireland, there were two practices prevalent in rural areas which especially favored males in the allocation of vital resources. On almost all Irish farms the income from the sale of animals and cash crops was kept by the husband, who was under no obligation even to tell his wife how much he had. He was bound by custom to provide for his wife and family, but only after looking after his own personal needs and those of the farm and livestock.[9] Under this system the wife and children were liable to suffer if the husband overindulged himself in drinking and gambling, was otherwise irresponsible, or if he was willing to have his family lead a spartan existence so that he could buy more land or livestock. As in the matter of eating priorities, there was the chance that the wife and children would be supported by leftovers, with the sons getting the largest share.

The second rural practice which favored males was the matter of division of labor. Generally men took care of the fields and the animals when they were in the fields, while women were responsible for feeding the animals when they were in the barn, milking the cows and processing the milk, and taking care of the vegetable garden, in addition to the usual duties of cooking, housework, and child care. Whether the initial division of labor was equal or not (since the latter half of the nineteenth century only a small proportion of Irish agricultural land was tilled, most of it being in pasture),[10] the more important point is that women were expected to help do the men's work, but men would be ridiculed for helping with the women's work.[11] Women were usually called out into the fields during turf cutting, during the planting, cultivation, and lifting of potatoes, and during haymaking time when the pitching, raking, and some building of haycocks was left to the women.[12]

The situation of females in urban areas was much better, at least in so far as the family income and expected workload was concerned. According to Humphreys, the Dublin family of the early 1950s was a partnership arrangement with both spouses agreeing how to spend their income, and with many wives actually being responsible for the money.[13] Very few married women were employed outside their homes; at each census between 1926 and 1966 about 5 to 6 percent of married women were working.[14] Even though few rural or urban wives were employed, the workload of the two groups differed considerably. The urban housewife was expected only to keep house, cook, and care for her husband and children.

The great amount of farm work which the rural wife did was in addition to her normal duties as a mother and wife, but it was not considered to be work done outside the home.

On the basis of these comments and impressions, one could reasonably conclude that males were dominant in Irish society, and that they controlled many of the resources needed for good health in the rural areas. When we turn to the mortality statistics, the relatively worse position of Irish compared with American or English females becomes apparent. The relevant comparison here is the difference between the sexes in Ireland contrasted with the difference between the sexes in other countries. For example, the excess of female over male life expectation between 1871 and 1946 was less in Ireland than in England; females lived from three to five years longer than males in England but only 0.1 to 1.9 years longer in Ireland (Table 9). The greater longevity of females in all three countries

TABLE 9. Excess of Female over Male Expectation at Birth in Years in Ireland, the United States, England and Wales, 1850 to 1960–62.*

Approximate Period	Ireland	United States[a]	England and Wales
1850	na	3.1	1.9
1870–72	1.3	na	3.2
1880–82	0.5	na	3.5
1890–92	0.1	na	3.7
1900–02	0.3	2.9	3.9
1910–12	0.5	3.4	3.9
1925–27	0.5	2.8	4.0
1935–37	1.4	4.0	4.2
1945–47	1.9	5.2	4.7
1960–62	3.8	6.9	5.9

Source: Calculated from Table 6.
(*) For specific dates and periods see note a, Table 6.
(a) White population in reporting area.

was in large part a biological phenomenon. Females generally could be expected to have lower mortality rates, since males have higher mortality rates during foetal life,[15] and also in a number of species other than the human.[16] The greater physical soundness of females has been attributed to genetic causes, specifically the fact that the male possesses only one x-chromosome while the female possesses two.[17] The possible impact of environmental factors on the adult mortality of the sexes was virtually controlled for in a careful study of the mortality of teaching Catholic monks and nuns: in these establishments the females continued to have a better mortality record than males.[18] The effect of social factors is to widen or narrow the biological advantage enjoyed by females.

Just how unusual was the relatively low excess of female over male life expectancy in Ireland? Before 1900 on a world-wide basis it probably was not unusual for males to have even greater longevity than females, and the present pattern of lower female mortality at every age became typical in the West only after the 1920s.[19] In addition to the decline in maternal mortality, another environmental factor explains the widening advantage enjoyed by adult females in Western nations, especially in recent decades: this is the greater increase in cigarette consumption among males.[20] A case has been made that environmental factors also account for the greater longevity of males and females in Ceylon, India, and Pakistan—specifically maternal mortality and the preferential treatment given to males at almost all ages.[21] The remainder of this chapter will attempt to show that the Irish case is an excellent Western illustration of the linkage of male dominance with relatively high female mortality. Irish mortality patterns by sex were not unique; where Ireland was unusual for a European nation was in the persistence into the mid-twentieth century of the social customs sustaining male dominance.

A consideration of some other countries in which the excess of female over male life expectancy at birth was less than one year at some time eliminates many possible explanations of the phenomenon which might be peculiar to Ireland alone (Table 10). The sexual puritanism of Irish Catholicism, for example, might be thought to contribute to the subordinate status of single females (although the strong veneration of the Virgin Mary in Ireland could be argued to enhance the status of married women). Yet an even worse pattern of female mortality existed in Northern Ireland during the first decade of the twentieth century, and this region is predominantly non-Catholic.

One trait which all nine of these countries may have shared was the extreme degree of the male dominance which is often found in rural societies: male dominance carried to such an extent that it considerably reduced the advantage in longevity which females normally would have expected for biological reasons. For example, the greater loss of expected female longevity in the rural areas of both Ireland and the United States is shown in Table 7, but the Irish pattern was much more extreme. The excess of female over male life expectancy was 3.4 years more in the urban areas of Ireland, compared with 1.3 years more in the urban areas of the United States. The advantage in mortality enjoyed by females over males in urban areas existed in Ireland as early as 1841. Even though the life expectancy of both sexes was lower in the less healthful cities, the excess of female over male life expectation was five years greater in Dublin than in Irish rural areas (where females actually had a lower life expectancy than males, Table 3). The advantage of the Irish urban over rural areas in

TABLE 10. Countries with an Excess of Female Over Male Life Expectation at Birth of Less than One Year at Various Times.*

Country and Period or Year	Expectation of Life in Years		Excess
	Female	Male	
	(A)	(B)	(A–B)
Northern Ireland			
1890–92	45.7	46.3	−0.6
1900–02	46.7	50.7	−4.0
1910–12	51.0	54.2	−3.2
1925–27	56.1	55.4	0.7
Bulgaria			
1900–05	42.2	42.1	0.1
1905–06	42.9	43.7	−0.8
1925–28	46.6	45.9	0.7
India			
1891	25.5	24.6	0.9
1901	24.0	23.6	0.4
1911	23.3	22.6	0.7
1931	26.6	26.9	−0.3
China (Rural)			
1929–31	34.6	34.8	−0.2
Ireland			
1881–83	49.9	49.4	0.5
1890–92	49.2	49.1	0.1
1900–02	49.6	49.3	0.3
1910–12	54.1	53.6	0.5
1925–27	57.9	57.4	0.5
Italy			
1876–87	35.5	35.1	0.4
1891–1900	43.2	42.8	0.4
1901–10	44.8	44.2	0.6
1910–12	47.3	46.6	0.7
Union of South Africa Colored Population			
1935–37	40.9	40.2	0.7
Japan			
1899–1903	44.8	44.0	0.8
1908–13	44.7	44.2	0.5
Ukraine			
1895–98	36.2	35.3	0.9

Sources: *Censuses of Population of Ireland, 1946 and 1951,* "General Report," Table 51, p. 68; L. I. Dublin, A. J. Lotka, and M. Spiegelman, *Length of Life: A Study of the Life Table,* rev. ed.; New York: Ronald Press, 1949, Tables 85–90, pp. 344–53.

* Out of 39 countries listed in the second source.

female compared with male mortality has continued to at least 1960–62, when females at birth had an expectation of life 5.3 years longer than males in urban areas, but only 3.8 years longer than males in the nation as a whole (Table 5).

Even though the loss of expected female longevity was a predominantly rural phenomenon, it also occurred among young urban persons in Ireland during both the nineteenth and twentieth centuries. Although no detailed analysis of the 1841 Census data on mortality would be warranted because of probable differences in the amount of under-reporting of deaths in various sub-categories, the general pattern of mortality by age, sex, and rural-urban residence was striking and was similar to that existing a century later (Table 11). The mortality rate of females was greater than that

TABLE 11. Estimated Average Annual Death Rates for 1831–41 (32 Counties), and Death Rates for 1931 (26 Counties), by Age, Sex, and Rural-Urban Residence.

Period and Age-group in Years	Deaths per 10,000 of the Same Age and Sex				Female Death Rates as a Percentage of the Male	
	Rural Areas		Urban Areas		Rural	Urban
	Males	Females	Males	Females		
1831–41						
5 and under	371	364	417	414	98	99
6–10	73	80	96	105	110	109
11–15	46	56	49	61	122	124
16–25	156	153	169	171	98	101
26–35	141	165	204	205	117	100
36–45	160	181	274	254	113	93
46–55	225	218	342	295	97	89
56–65	384	408	475	450	106	95
66–75	509	512	578	540	100	93
1931						
Under 5	162	142	341	279	88	82
5–9	20	18	36	26	90	72
10–14	14	18	20	23	128	115
15–19	26	29	34	37	112	109
20–24	39	42	48	48	108	100
25–34	43	54	52	57	126	110
35–44	53	67	88	78	126	89
45–54	93	104	178	132	112	74
55–64	238	238	373	317	100	85
65 and over	746	693	878	773	93	88
All ages	139	143	160	149	103	93

Sources: *Census of Ireland, 1841,* "Report," p. lxxxiv; Saorstat Eireann, *Annual Report of the Registrar General, 1931,* Table 19, p. 29.

of males generally after early childhood in the rural areas, and between the ages of about 10 and 34 years in urban areas both in the 1830s and in 1931. This finding is consistent with the impression given of the subordinate status of daughters in Irish families both in rural and urban areas, and of the additional disadvantages experienced by females at almost all age groups in rural areas.

The long term trends in relative Irish mortality by age and sex between 1864 and 1967 are given in Table 12. With the possible exception of the first several years after the compulsory registration of vital statistics began in Ireland in 1864, there is little reason to believe that the under-registration of deaths was greater for one sex than the other. In some male-dominated societies there is a greater under-registration of female deaths, and if this had happened in Ireland during the 1860s and early 1870s the effect would have been to understate the actual degree of excess female mortality. The

TABLE 12. Female Age-Specific Death Rates as a Percentage of the Male in Selected Age Groups in Ireland, 1864–1967.

Period	Age Group in Years							
	Under 5	5–9	10–14	15–19	20–24	25–34	35–44	55–64
1864–70	90	102	112	96	79	92	95	95
1871–80	91	106	120	102	83	91	90	95
1881–90	90	109	129	115	89	96	96	98
1891–1900	89	109	134	122	92	93	96	101
1901–10	88	113	140	123	95	92	99	101
1911–20	88	114	129	112	94	94	98	98
1921–30	86	104	120	115	98	105	105	98
1931–40	84	101	113	111	108	113	105	94
1941–50	81	89	109	109	111	113	100	86
1951–60	77	87	85	77	83	87	91	73
1961–67	79	79	73	50	54	72	77	62

Source: Calculated from, Ireland, *Report on Vital Statistics, 1967,* Table 9, p. 11.
Note: Original death rates were expressed as average annual deaths per 1,000 of the corresponding population classified by age and sex, and were carried to two decimals.

most dramatic aspect of the data is the sudden improvement in relative female mortality between the 1940s and the 1950s. This may have been due to a great change in the social status of females, but it also may have been due to improvements in medical care and public health measures which benefited females more than males (Table 6), and to the increased urbanization of Ireland (Appendix Table 3). For the period before 1950 the greater female than male mortality is obvious, especially among older children and young adults—age-groups which include very few persons who are not living as sons and daughters in their parents' home. The relatively lower ratio of female to male mortality for children under five is probably due to two things. The greater male mortality expected for biological reasons is higher among infants and young children than among older children; and sex differentials may have been less important in the way infants were treated since the adult males of the Irish family had little to do with the everyday care of children of either sex until after early childhood.[22]

The reasons for this rise in the ratios among teenagers after the 1870s, and among older women between 1921 and 1950, are a matter of speculation. There may have been some selective migration of the healthier rural women, but I am not aware of any data which could serve to negate or verify this hypothesis. It is as logical to argue that the healthy rural women would have had less reason to emigrate than their less fit sisters since they would have been better able to cope with the physical demands made upon them. If there had been some under-registration of female deaths during the first few years of compulsory registration of vital statistics in the 1860s and early 1870s, part of the increase in female mortality recorded would have been due to more accurate statistics. An interesting conjecture is the impact of the changing land laws on female mortality.[23] Although the laws were eventually designed so that no more money was needed to purchase a holding than one had been paying for rent, and that the legal cost of transfer was met out of public funds,[24] the fact remains that the decade of greatest transfer of land ownership was also the decade of highest excess female mortality among young women: at this time among persons aged 10 to 14 years the female death rate was 140 percent of the male. Could there have been other expenses associated with land ownership which resulted in some of the more land-hungry farmers buying fields with money taken away from the support of their families? The subsequent rise in relative female mortality among older persons a decade or so later may have been due, at least in part, to the aging of this cohort. The males of this generation perhaps felt less of an obligation to share their incomes with their wives; the females may have demanded less, having been raised to expect very little (that is, the females who did not choose to migrate to urban areas).

When the age-specific mortality rates of females are higher than those of males, there is no doubt that the females have lost some of their biological advantage over males in longevity. Females also may have lost some advantage in those age-groups where the ratio of female to male deaths, while less than 100, is nevertheless relatively high compared with other countries. In the mid-1930s, for example, the Irish pattern was quite different from that of the United States and England (Table 13). Although the source used for the table compared ages from 25 to 69, there is no reason to assume that the American and English proportions in the younger age-groups were higher than the very high Irish proportions recorded in Ireland at this time (Table 12). The United States and England were roughly similar in their proportions of female to male death rates; the greatest discrepancy was 11 percentage points in the 25 to 29 years age-group. But both countries contrasted with Ireland. While the Irish proportions at no time fell below 91 percent, the American proportions at no

TABLE 13.   Deaths per 10,000 in Certain Age Groups by Sex in Ireland, 1935–37, England and Wales, 1939, and the United States, 1939.

Age Group	Ireland		England and Wales		United States [a]	
	Male	Female	Male	Female	Male	Female
25–29	41	49	26	24	26	21
35–39	53	57	37	30	42	33
45–49	91	85	80	58	93	64
55–59	188	175	195	123	205	140
65–69	407	370	445	316	441	331
Female death rates as a percentage of the male						
25–29	120		92		81	
35–39	108		81		79	
45–49	93		72		69	
55–59	93		63		68	
65–69	91		71		75	

Source: W. A. Honohan, "Irish Actuarial Data," *Journal of the Statistical and Social Inquiry Society of Ireland,* Vol. XVII (1944–45), Table VI, p. 387.

(a) White population in reporting area.

time rose above 81 percent. In each of the five age-groups the discrepancy between the Irish and English proportions was at least 20 percentage points.

The loss of female advantage in mortality in several age-groups in Ireland is also shown by an international comparison of cause of death by sex and age. Although there may have been some differences in determining cause of death owing to dissimilarities in diagnostic procedures between England, Wales, and Ireland on the one hand and the United States on the other, the pattern is clear. For example, among persons aged 5–14 years in the early 1950s, mortality from infectious and parasitic diseases was much greater for Irish females than for Irish males or for both sexes in the United States and in England (Table 14). When the female rates were higher than the male for certain causes in England (two) or in the United States (one), the differences were small and of an entirely different order than the excess female mortality in Ireland.

The more rapid aging of Irish females as compared to males, commented upon in descriptions of the relative social status of the sexes, also shows up in international comparisons of cause of death by age and sex. Comparing Ireland with the United States, among older persons the mortality rates from anemias and from certain types of nervous and circulatory system disorders were higher among Irish females than males, while the reverse was true in the United States (Table 15). Although English females did have higher death rates than English males for some causes of death, the differences generally were smaller than those of the Irish.

Mortality statistics have confirmed the impression given by descrip-

TABLE 14. Deaths per 100,000 Persons of the Same Sex and Aged 5–14 Years, Due to Certain Causes in Ireland, 1951, the United States, 1955, and England and Wales, 1955.*

Cause of Death	Ireland Females	Ireland Males	United States Females	United States Males	England and Wales Females	England and Wales Males
Tuberculosis of the respiratory system	4.5	0.7	0.1	0.1	0.3	0.1
Rheumatic fever	4.1	1.4	1.0	1.0	0.9	0.4
Ill-defined and unknown	3.8	2.2	0.4	0.7	0.0	0.0
Miscellaneous infectious and parasitic diseases	2.6	1.1	1.0	1.1	0.7	0.8
Chronic rheumatic heart disease	1.9	0.7	0.2	0.1	0.4	0.5
Scarlet fever and strep-tococcal sore throat	1.9	0.7	0.1	0.1	0.1	0.1
All causes	70.0	76.8	38.0	58.4	34.2	47.1
Female death rates as a percentage of the male:						
Tuberculosis	640		100		300	
Rheumatic fever	290		100		220	
Ill-defined	170		60		100	
Miscellaneous infectious	240		90		90	
Rheumatic heart disease	270		200		80	
Scarlet fever	270		100		100	
All causes	91		65		72	

Source: United Nations, *Demographic Yearbook, 1957,* Table 17, pp. 494, 508, 516.

* Causes in Ireland in 1951 resulting in at least 1.0 more female than male deaths per 100,000 persons of the same age and sex. There was no cause of death in either England and Wales or in the United States where the female mortality rate was 1.0 higher than the male for this age group.

tions of Irish life that sons received preferential treatment both in rural and urban regions, and that males generally were favored in the allocation of vital resources in Irish rural areas. The less adequate diet given to females in many Irish families probably contributed to the lower resistance of females to infectious and parasitic diseases. Malnutrition and fatigue resulting from continued heavy workloads also probably explained at least part of the more rapid aging of Irish females.[25] Rural housewives in other countries also experienced some loss of longevity for these reasons,[26] but compared with the United States and several northwest European countries in the twentieth century, the Irish pattern was extreme.

While mortality rates cannot be used as indicators of either the direction or the magnitude of the migration stream, nor as indicators of economic or social opportunities in different regions, they can be used as indicators of the relative social status of persons within the same community. The high female compared with male mortality was due, at least in part, to the subordinate status of females in rural areas, and of daughters in the Irish family system. Because the opportunities for improving one's social

TABLE 15. Deaths per 100,000 Persons of the Same Sex and Aged 45–64 Years, Due to Certain Causes in Ireland, 1951, the United States, 1955, and England and Wales, 1955.*

Cause of Death	Ireland		United States		England and Wales	
	Females	Males	Females	Males	Females	Males
Vascular lesions affecting central nervous system	142.0	98.1	95.5	110.3	109.6	111.2
Hypertension without mention of heart	31.0	23.7	6.4	8.5	11.8	17.5
Chronic rheumatic heart disease	22.2	17.5	24.1	25.5	37.4	23.8
Anemias	19.4	12.3	1.4	1.7	3.1	2.1
Diabetes mellitus	13.4	9.9	26.1	18.5	8.2	4.5
Rheumatic fever	3.5	2.1	0.6	1.0	0.5	0.5
All causes	1,206.1	1,527.1	837.5	1,534.1	768.2	1,353.5
Female death rates as a percentage of the male						
Vascular lesions	145		87		99	
Hypertension	131		75		67	
Rheumatic heart disease	127		95		157	
Anemias	158		82		148	
Diabetes mellitus	135		141		182	
Rheumatic fever	167		60		100	
All causes	79		55		57	

Source: United Nations, *Demographic Year Book, 1957*, Table 17, pp. 494, 508, 516.

* Causes in Ireland in 1951 resulting in at least 1.0 more female than male deaths per 100,000 persons of the same age and sex. There were no other causes of death in either England and Wales or in the United States where the female mortality rate was 1.0 higher than the male for this age-group.

status were relatively much greater for females than for males away from their families, and in urban rather than in rural areas, we would expect migration to urban areas to appeal more strongly to Irish females than males. The subordinate status of females in rural Ireland was also probably a factor contributing to the reluctance of many Irish women to marry rural men.

NOTES

1. Ussher, "The Boundary Between the Sexes," in O'Brein (ed.), *The Vanishing Irish*, pp. 154–155.

2. Arensberg and Kimball, *Family and Community in Ireland*, pp. 202–203.

3. *Ibid.*, pp. 35–57.

4. O'Casey, *Three Plays*, p. 115.

5. *Ibid.*, pp. 13, 14.

6. McNabb, "Social Structure," *The Limerick Rural Survey, 1958–1964*, Newman (ed.), pp. 230–231.

7. Humphreys, *New Dubliners*, p. 162.

8. *Ibid.*, p. 163.

9. Arensberg and Kimball, *Family and Community in Ireland*, pp. 47–48.

10. It is generally agreed that pasture requires less labor than plowed land. The highest proportion of agricultural land ever recorded as plowed was in 1851 when it was 29 per cent; this dropped to 18 per cent in 1881, and to 13 per cent in

1926. Ireland, *Agricultural Statistics, 1847–1926,* "Report and Tables," Dublin, 1928, p. lx.

11. *Ibid.,* p. 49.

12. *Ibid.,* pp. 33–50.

13. Humphreys, *New Dubliners,* pp. 34, 236.

14. *Censuses of Population of Ireland, 1926,* Vol. V, Part II, Table 1B, p. 5; *1936,* Vol. V, Part II, Table 1B, p. 5; *1946,* Vol. V, Part II, Table 1B, p. 5; *1961,* Vol. V, Table 1B, p. 5; *1966,* Vol. V, Table 1B, p. 9.

15. Shapiro, Schlesinger, and Nesbitt, *Infant, Perinatal, Maternal, and Childhood Mortality,* p. 43.

16. Dublin, Lotka, and Spiegelman, *Length of Life,* p. 129.

17. The female thus has two parallel sets of genes while the male does not since the segments of his x-chromosome do not exactly match those of his y-chromosome. The chances for a deleterious or lethal gene finding expression in the phenotype of an individual are therefore greater among males than females. G. Herdan, "Causes of Excess Male Mortality in Man," Acta Genetica et Statistica Medica, Vol. 3 (1952), pp. 351–375.

18. Madigan, "Are Sex Mortality Differentials Biologically Caused?" *The Millbank Memorial Fund Quarterly,* Vol. XXXV, No. 2 (April 1957), pp. 202–223.

19. Stolnitz, "A Century of International Mortality Trends: II," *Population Studies,* Vol. X (July 1956), pp. 22–25.

20. Preston, "An International Comparison of Excess in the Death Rates of Older Males," *Population Studies,* Vol. XXIV (March 1970), pp. 5–20.

21. El-Badry, "Higher Female than Male Mortality in Some Countries of South Asia: A Digest," *Journal of the American Statistical Association,* Vol. 64 (December), pp. 1234–44.

22. Arensberg and Kimball, *Family and Community in Ireland,* p. 59.

23. See Chapter Two (of Kennedy, *The Irish: Emigration, Marriage, and Fertility*).

24. Beckett, *The Making of Modern Ireland,* p. 407.

25. There is evidence that fatigue resulting from continued hard physical labor, especially after 40 years of age, contributes to premature death. L. I. Dublin, A. J. Lotka, and M. Spiegelman, *Length of Life: A Study of the Life Table,* rev. ed. (1949), p. 233.

26. The higher death rates from tuberculosis, pneumonia, and influenza among rural than urban females in the United States has been attributed to the harder working life of rural housewives and the resulting greater fatigue and lower resistance. *Ibid.,* p. 78.

20

Sex, Marital Status, and Mortality[1]

Walter R. Gove

This paper explores the relationship between marital status and mortality for both men and women. It is shown that, controlling for age, the married have lower mortality rates than the single, the widowed, or the divorced and that the differences between the married and unmarried statuses are much greater for men than for women. It is argued that these relationships can, at least in part, be attributed to the characteristics of the marital statuses in our society, for: (1) precisely the same pattern is found in studies of psychological wellbeing and mental illness; (2) the evidence from specific types of mortality indicates that this pattern is characteristic primarily of types of mortality in which one's psychological state may greatly affect one's life chances; (3) a role explanation can account for the way the pattern varies with changes in age; and (4) it appears that the alternative explanation, namely, that the relationships are due to selective processes, does not account for most of the variation in rates.

In the final analysis, mortality is due to a physical phenomenon. However, social processes play a role in the etiology of many disorders that lead to death and frequently determine how promptly and persistently one seeks treatment. And, of course, with some types of mortality, such as suicide, the role of social factors is obvious. This paper will explore the possibility that the psychological states and life-styles associated with the different marital roles in our society affect life chances with regard to selected types of mortality.

The data on psychological well-being (Gurin, Veroff, and Feld 1960;

Reprinted from *American Journal of Sociology*, 79, no. 1 (July, 1973), pp. 45–67, by permission of the author and the University of Chicago Press. Copyright © 1959 by the University of Chicago.

Bradburn and Caplovitz 1965; Bradburn 1969) uniformly indicate that the married, at least with regard to psychological variables, are better situated than the unmarried. As Gurin et al. (1960, p. 232) state, "The most striking finding is that married respondents report feeling happier than those that are unmarried, and the difference is a sharp one for both men and women." The studies of mental illness likewise almost invariably show that the unmarried, whether single, widowed, or divorced, have higher rates of mental illness than the married (e.g., Gove 1972a). Probably, as Gurin et al. (1960, pp. 230–31) indicate, the key difference between the roles of the married and the unmarried (whether single, widowed, or divorced), is that the unmarried live a relatively isolated existence which lacks the close interpersonal ties that the data suggest are a key factor in maintaining a sense of well-being.

Another very consistent finding, at least in recent years, is that married women are more likely to be emotionally disturbed than are married men. In a recent paper (Gove 1972a) I show that every study in Western industrial countries conducted after World War II has found that married women have higher rates of mental illness than married men. These results are supported by the studies on psychological well-being (Gurin et al. 1960; Bradburn and Caplovitz 1965; Bradburn 1969) which indicate that married women, compared with married men, find their roles constricted and frustrating. For example, Gurin et al. (1960) found that women are less happy in their marriages and report more marital problems than men. Furthermore, they found that women are more negative about parenthood than men, reporting less satisfaction with being a parent and more problems of adjustment.

The situation is quite different when we compare single men and women, for in this category it is the women who appear to be better situated. The pioneering study by Gurin et al. (1960, p. 233) found that "single women apparently experience less discomfort than do single men; they report greater happiness, are more active in their working through of the problems they face, and appear in most ways stronger in meeting the challenges of their positions than men." This finding is supported by the subsequent work on psychological well-being (Bradburn and Caplovitz 1965; Bradburn 1969), and a large majority of the studies of mental illness indicate that single men have higher rates of mental illness than single women (Gove 1972a). Probably a major difference between single men and women is that single women are apt to have stronger ties to family and friends (e.g., Gurin et al. 1960, pp. 232–35).

There is much less data on the other unmarried statuses. However, Gurin et al. (1960, pp. 236–38) did find that widowers are more poorly situated than widows, a finding substantiated by the fact that most of the studies on mental illness which provide a sex breakdown of widowed persons find that widowed men have higher rates than widowed women (Gove 1972a). Comparing the divorced on mental illness produces similar results, that is, the substantial majority of the studies indicate that divorced men have higher rates of mental illness than divorced women. However, the pattern for the divorced is not as clear as for the widowed, since the limited data on the psychological well-being of the divorced (Gurin et al. 1960, pp. 235–36) are not consistent with the data on mental illness.

To summarize, the data on psychological well-being and mental illness suggest that the married are in a more advantageous position than the never married, the widowed, and the divorced. There are, however, important sex differences. Being married appears to be more advantageous to males than females, while being single, widowed, and probably divorced is more disadvantageous to males. These results allow us to construct some testable hypotheses regarding the relationship between marital status and mortality—if we assume that one's emotional state affects one's life chances with regard to at least certain types of mortality. First, if being married is more advantageous than not being married, the coefficient formed by the ratios (single mortality rate)/(married mortality rate), (widowed mortality rate)/(married mortality rate), and (divorced mortality rate)/(married mortality rate) should be larger than one. Second, if the analysis of the sex differences is correct, then the coefficients for men should be consistently larger than the coefficients for women.[2]

This paper focuses on the size of these coefficients across selected types of mortality, paying particular attention to variations between the sexes.[3] It should be noted at this point that Durkheim (1951) used this same coefficient in his classic work on suicide, referring to it as the coefficient of preservation. Implicit in this term, and explicit in his analysis, is the assumption that marriage, through its strong social ties, provides a person with a sense of meaning and importance, thereby serving to inhibit the destructive impulses associated with suicide. Durkheim is able to support this assertion with empirical evidence. First, he demonstrates that the large value of the coefficient of preservation is not primarily due to the selective processes associated with marriage, that is, it is not primarily due to stable persons being more likely to marry than unstable persons (Durkheim 1951, pp. 182–93). Durkheim (1951, pp. 185–202) then demonstrates that the size of the coefficient of preservation varies directly with the presence of children.[4] Finally, he finds that as one moves from country to country, the sex that has the higher coefficient of preservation appears to be a response to the nature of marital roles in a society and the sex that is favored will vary from society to society. In a recent paper (Gove 1972b) I looked at three forms of suicidal behavior (threats, attempts, and completions) and showed that for such behaviors men tend to have larger coefficients of preservation in both the United States and Western Europe.

For the analysis of the relationship between sex, marital status, and mortality, I will rely primarily on a recent publication of the National Center for Health Statistics (1970) that provides age-specific mortality rates for selected causes by race, sex, and marital status for the years of 1959–61. Because the death rates of whites and nonwhites are quite different and because much less is known about the nature of the marital roles of nonwhites, I will deal only with the mortality of whites. Furthermore, for a number of reasons, I will be primarily concerned with the ages 25 through 64. First, this is the age span with which the role explanation is most concerned, for it is during this time of the life cycle that people are involved in their full range of adult roles. Second, before the age of 25, mortality rates from many causes tend to be unreliable simply because there are very few cases of mortality. The lack of reliability is particularly a problem in the widowed and divorced categories. Third, before this age the patterns of mortality are more complex and less easily interpreted,[5] perhaps because many persons are not yet established in their adult roles. Therefore, for reasons of accuracy, space, and coherence I will not, in this paper, deal with mortality for persons under the age of 25. By the age of 65 the role configuration of most people has shrunk, and we might expect the differences in mortality between the married and the unmarried to have also diminished. Furthermore, the older age groups have high rates of mortality, which, to some extent may override and thus mask the influence of social factors. For these reasons the differences between the marital groups in the older categories are perhaps less relevant to my role analysis. However, given their high mortality, their rates should be reliable, so the relevant coefficient will be presented.

One last note before turning to the data. With the exception of work on suicide (e.g., Durkheim 1951; Gove 1972b), I have been unable to locate any studies in the sociological literature dealing with how the mortality of men and women differs between the various marital states. There are, however, a few studies in the medical literature (e.g., Shurtleff 1956; Kraus and Lilienfeld 1959) and the public health literature (e.g., Berkson 1962; Sheps 1961; Carter and Glick 1970) that do make such a comparison. With the exception of Carter and Glick (1970), who use 1959–61 data, all of these studies use 1949–51 data. Although some of the studies are very concerned with establishing the validity of the statistics, they present little in the way of either a medical or sociological framework for interpreting their data. I would note that data for the two time periods 1949–51 and 1959–61 are in general similar.

MORTALITY DUE TO OVERT SOCIAL ACTS

In this section I will look at the relationship between sex and marital status, and mortality due to suicide, homicide, and various types of accidents. In all instances I assume that there will be an inverse relationship between close, meaningful social ties and mortality. Following the research on psychological well-being and mental illness, I presume that such ties are more characteristic of the married than the unmarried and that the differences between the married and unmarried statuses are greater for men than for women.

The assumption that suicide is inversely related to close interpersonal ties is, of course, a standard one in the sociological literature. Regarding accidental death, I postulate that a lack of close interpersonal ties frequently results in carelessness and even recklessness which may lead to death.[6] In the case of homicide I assume that in many instances persons who are murdered have to some degree precipitated the act by their behavior and that this behavior frequently reflects frustration and dissatisfaction with life. Just as with accidental death, it is probably also the case that recklessness increases the likelihood of being murdered. It should be noted that, with regard to some accidental deaths, and probably with some homicides, this person killed may be in no way responsible. This is particularly clear in some motor accidents, where the person killed may be simply a passenger, a situation that is probably very common among married women. There is, in some cases, also the issue of differential exposure to risk; thus, it is possible, for example, that at younger ages single persons drive more than married persons and thus experience a greater risk.

The data on suicide, homicide, and accidental death are presented in tables 1 through 5. Each table presents the ratios produced by dividing the mortality rate of the unmarried (single, widowed, or divorced) by the mortality rate of the married, with each sex taken separately. In the first section of the table the age-specific ratios are presented, while in the second section the averages of these ratios are presented. The first average in this latter section deals with all ages 25 and over, and the second average deals with ages 25 through 64. This last figure deals with the age span with which we are primarily concerned, for it is during this time in the life cycle that persons are involved in the full range of their adult roles. I would call the reader's attention to the fact that the time span is not constant in the age-specific categories and that in calculating the average of these ratios each age-specific ratio was weighed according to the time span covered. If the reader wishes, he may view the average ratios as being based on age-standardized rates which are calculated using a theoretical population in which each year is equally weighed.[7]

The suicide data are presented in table 1. As can be seen from the last column, for ages 25 through 64 single men are, controlling for age, exactly twice as likely to commit suicide as married men. In contrast, comparable single women are 51% more likely than married women to commit suicide. Turning to the widowed, we see that between these ages, widowed men commit suicide five times more frequently than married men, while widowed women commit suicide 2.2 times more frequently than married women. The divorced show a similar pattern.

The data on homicide are generally similar to the data on suicide, except that single women have a lower mortality than married women (see

TABLE 1. Suicide: Ratios Produced by Dividing the Suicide Rate of the Unmarried by the Rate of the Married, Whites, United States, 1959–61*

Unmarried Category (Ratio)	Age								Average Ratio	
	25–34	35–44	45–54	55–59	60–64	65–69	70–74	75+	25+	25–64
Single:										
Male	2.47	2.07	1.74	1.68	1.75	1.92	2.22	2.11	2.02	2.00
Female	2.13	1.63	1.16	1.09	1.12	1.10	1.61	0.90	1.42	1.51
Widowed:										
Male	8.15	5.79	3.52	2.65	2.51	2.28	2.35	2.05	4.25	5.01
Female	3.32	0.94	1.87	1.82	1.64	1.39	1.79	1.49	2.04	2.21
Divorced:										
Male	6.08	5.38	3.95	3.54	3.61	2.88	3.24	3.03	4.28	4.75
Female	5.36	3.74	2.33	2.05	2.52	2.68	2.36	4.25	3.34	3.43

* Ratios calculated by the author from the mortality rates presented by the National Center for Health Statistics (1970).

Editor's note: Since the empirical evidence in Gove's paper is presented in a series of tables, the reader is advised to make sure of the meaning of the figures. Gove explains what the figures in the tables mean, but I would add the following clarification: any number found in the table signifies how much larger the mortality rate is for the unmarried than it is for the married (with the same age and sex characteristics). If the number is 2.00 it means that the unmarried people in that category have a mortality rate that is twice as large as the married people of the same age and sex. A number of 1.00 means the rate is the same for the married and unmarried. A number of less than 1.00 (say .87) means that the unmarried in that category actually enjoy an advantage over the married. For example, in Table 2, because there are numbers smaller than 1.00, one can see that single females often have a lower mortality rate due to homicide than married females. Table 3 shows a similar pattern for motor accident deaths. These instances are, of course, unusual, and exceptions to the general rule that married persons have a mortality advantage over the unmarried. Throughout Gove's paper the tables show that being married gives one a greater chance of living (since most figures are larger than 1.00), but since the male figure is almost always larger than the female figure it also shows that being married helps males live longer than it helps females.—K. K.

table 2). Thus, for women the shift from being single to being married increases the likelihood of being murdered, while for men the shift decreases their chances. For both men and women, the shift from being married to being widowed markedly increases their likelihood of being murdered, with the difference noticeably greater for men than women. The data indicate that the divorced, particularly divorced men, are especially likely to be murdered.

TABLE 2. Homicide: Ratios Produced by Dividing the Homicide Rate of the Unmarried by the Rate of the Married, Whites, United States, 1959–61*

Unmarried Category (Ratio)	Age								Average Ratio	
	25–34	35–44	45–54	55–59	60–64	65–69	70–74	75+	25+	25–64
Single:										
Male	2.02	2.31	1.95	1.70	2.69	2.00	3.05	2.79	2.25	2.12
Female	0.90	0.68	0.35	0.42	0.55	1.13	0.73	0.94	0.69	0.60
Widowed:										
Male	5.09	3.17	2.69	3.49	3.69	2.42	2.81	1.90	3.29	3.64
Female	4.21	3.42	1.59	1.42	1.18	1.25	0.87	0.82	2.18	2.63
Divorced:										
Male	8.48	8.10	7.21	6.27	6.73	3.85	10.05	5.79	7.30	7.57
Female	6.26	4.95	3.94	3.42	2.64	0.50	0.93	3.71	3.77	4.54

* Ratios calculated by the author from the mortality rates presented by the National Center for Health Statistics (1970).

Accidental deaths show a pattern similar to deaths due to suicide and homicide. Looking at mortality due to motor accidents (excluding pedestrian mortality), we find again that the single statuses appear to be worse for men than for women. As with homicide, single women are less likely to be killed than married females, while with all other comparisons the married have lower mortality rates than the unmarried (see table 3). Pedestrian deaths are much more likely to occur among the unmarried than the married, and again the differences between the marital statuses are significantly greater for men than for women (see table 4). Accidental deaths due to all other causes have exactly the same pattern as pedestrian deaths, although the differences between the marital statuses, and to some extent the differences between the sexes, are not as great (see table 5).

Taken together, these data show a pattern that very closely parallels the data on psychological well-being and mental illness. In all cases, the shift from being single to being married appears, from the mortality rates, to have a more favorable effect on men than on women, while the shift from the married to an unmarried state appears to have a more unfavorable effect on men than on women. For men, being unmarried is uniformly associated with mortality rates that are higher than those of the married, with the

TABLE 3. Motor Accident Deaths (Excluding Pedestrian Deaths): Ratios Produced by Dividing the Mortality Rate of the Unmarried by the Rate of the Married, Whites, United States, 1959–61*

Unmarried Category (Ratio)	Age								Average Ratio	
	25–34	35–44	45–54	55–59	60–64	65–69	70–74	75+	25+	25–64
Single:										
Male	1.79	1.49	1.20	1.00	1.02	0.97	0.89	0.84	1.24	1.36
Female	1.28	0.82	0.54	0.63	0.63	0.60	0.57	0.49	0.74	0.82
Widowed:										
Male	5.37	3.68	2.73	2.36	2.06	1.94	1.72	1.21	2.99	3.50
Female	5.80	3.15	1.66	1.15	0.91	0.85	0.69	0.65	2.32	2.91
Divorced:										
Male	4.58	4.26	3.28	2.34	2.43	2.23	2.15	1.59	3.18	3.63
Female	4.38	3.04	1.60	1.08	0.99	0.59	0.81	0.73	2.02	2.51

* Ratios calculated by the author from the mortality rates presented by the National Center for Health Statistics (1970).

widowed and divorced having especially high rates. The data for women are generally similar, although the relationships are neither as strong nor as consistent.

Another pattern worth noting is that in most instances the disparity between being married and unmarried diminishes with age. The drop in the size of the ratio usually starts by the age of 44 and frequently by the age of 34. The younger ages are, of course, the time young children are in the home, and it is possible, as Durkheim noted, that having young children provides a form of protection. It is perhaps worth emphasizing that at the relatively early ages, the differences between the married and unmarried rates are often very large. For example, between the ages of 25 and 34, ·

TABLE 4. Pedestrian Deaths: Ratios Produced by Dividing the Mortality Rate of the Unmarried by the Rate of the Married, Whites, United States, 1959–61*

Unmarried Category (Ratio)	Age								Average Ratio	
	25–34	35–44	45–54	55–59	60–64	65–69	70–74	75+	25+	25–64
Single:										
Male	2.86	4.94	4.89	4.30	4.07	3.89	3.78	2.87	4.03	4.22
Female	2.50	1.83	1.50	1.77	2.10	2.41	2.46	2.43	2.08	1.94
Widowed:										
Male	3.71	6.77	4.65	4.81	2.82	3.01	2.73	2.16	4.16	4.74
Female	3.25	2.50	2.50	2.06	2.50	2.31	2.17	1.67	2.47	2.63
Divorced:										
Male	5.79	8.29	9.62	8.19	5.77	4.41	4.65	3.51	6.72	7.67
Female	6.50	3.67	3.17	4.59	2.50	1.69	2.51	2.38	3.67	4.22

* Ratios calculated by the author from the mortality rates presented by the National Center for Health Statistics (1970).

TABLE 5. All Other Accidental Deaths: Ratios Produced by Dividing the Mortality Rate of the Unmarried by the Rate of the Married, Whites, United States, 1959–61*

Unmarried Category (Ratio)	Age								Average Ratio	
	25–34	35–44	45–54	55–59	60–64	65–69	70–74	75+	25+	25–64
Single:										
Male	1.68	2.56	2.53	2.41	2.41	3.00	2.97	2.27	2.42	2.30
Female	2.44	2.06	1.56	1.53	2.06	1.60	1.67	2.17	1.92	1.96
Widowed:										
Male	3.43	3.19	2.99	2.51	2.42	2.37	2.14	2.22	2.81	3.02
Female	3.54	2.78	2.31	1.69	1.69	1.44	1.42	1.94	2.31	2.58
Divorced:										
Male	3.18	5.08	5.40	4.70	4.44	4.25	3.79	2.49	4.27	4.56
Female	3.51	3.37	2.73	2.66	2.21	1.86	2.08	1.74	2.71	3.02

* Ratios calculated by the author from the mortality rates presented by the National Center for Health Statistics (1970).

widowed men are 8.2 times more likely to commit suicide than married men, and in the same age bracket divorced men are 8.5 times more likely than married men to be murdered.

MORTALITY ASSOCIATED WITH THE USE OF SOCIALLY APPROVED "NARCOTICS"

In this section I will look at two types of mortality associated with the use of socially approved 'narcotics," namely, cirrhosis of the liver and lung cancer.

In a recent article Terris (1967) presents convincing evidence that a very major determinant of death due to cirrhosis of the liver is the consumption of alcohol. Alcohol use is, of course, in part regulated by social norms. However, heavy users of alcohol frequently appear to be trying to "drown" their troubles. If this is the case, then it would seem to follow that the mortality rates for cirrhosis of the liver should conform to the pattern associated with deaths due to overt social acts.

The data on mortality due to cirrhosis of the liver are presented in table 6. As can be seen in the last column, for the ages 25 through 64 single men are, controlling for age, 3.3 times more likely to die of cirrhosis of the liver than married men. In contrast, single women are only slightly more likely than married women to die of cirrhosis of the liver, and in fact, in the older ages, single women have noticeably lower mortality rates than married women. Widowed men and women are both more likely to die from cirrhosis of the liver than their married counterparts, with the difference being greater among men. The divorced have the same pattern as the widowed, but their mortality rates are markedly higher, especially for males. In fact,

TABLE 6. Cirrhosis of the Liver: Ratios Produced by Dividing the Mortality Rate of the Unmarried by the Mortality Rate of the Married, Whites, United States, 1959–61*

Unmarried Category (Ratio)	Age								Average Ratio	
	25–34	35–44	45–54	55–59	60–64	65–69	70–74	75+	25+	25–64
Single:										
Male	4.07	3.85	2.76	2.37	2.58	2.39	2.00	1.50	2.93	3.29
Female	2.15	1.06	0.78	0.74	0.76	0.76	0.76	0.74	1.07	1.19
Widowed:										
Male	2.50	7.23	5.08	3.85	3.39	3.09	2.15	1.40	3.95	4.61
Female	6.54	3.81	2.05	1.54	1.30	1.28	1.15	1.04	2.83	3.45
Divorced:										
Male	11.29	10.61	7.84	6.16	5.10	4.16	2.99	2.06	7.27	8.84
Female	8.54	4.71	2.55	2.01	1.82	1.56	1.38	1.30	3.61	4.43

* Ratios calculated by the author from the mortality rates presented by the National Center for Health Statistics (1970).

in the 25 to 34 age bracket, divorced men are 11.3 times more likely to die than married men from cirrhosis of the liver.

There is quite strong evidence that smoking is causally related to lung cancer (Public Health Service 1964a). People smoke, of course, for a wide variety of reasons. One of these reasons, although perhaps not a major one, is to relax. If we assume that relaxation as a reason for smoking is important enough to affect overall patterns of use, is seems plausible that mortality due to lung cancer would show, in a moderate form, the pattern found with cirrhosis of the liver. The data on mortality due to lung cancer are presented in table 7, and they do in fact show the same pattern, although the differences between the marital statuses are not nearly as great.

I might note that these mortality data do not completely correspond to

TABLE 7. Lung Cancer: Ratios Produced by Dividing the Mortality Rate of the Unmarried by the Mortality Rate of the Married, Whites, United States, 1959–61*

Unmarried Category (Ratio)	Age								Average Ratio	
	25–34	35–44	45–54	55–59	60–64	65–69	70–74	75+	25+	25–64
Single:										
Male	1.07	1.24	1.14	1.84	2.88	1.17	1.11	1.06	1.36	1.45
Female	1.33	1.09	0.97	1.06	1.02	1.16	1.06	1.01	1.01	1.11
Widowed:										
Male	2.33	1.92	1.74	2.49	3.46	1.39	1.26	1.15	1.98	2.24
Female	0.67	1.53	1.40	1.35	1.09	1.22	1.14	1.17	1.20	1.20
Divorced:										
Male	2.73	2.78	2.63	3.34	4.96	1.88	1.80	1.68	2.72	3.07
Female	1.67	2.00	1.59	1.71	1.43	1.25	1.75	1.24	1.63	1.71

* Ratios calculated by the author from the mortality rates presented by the National Center for Health Statistics (1970).

the available information on smoking patterns in the United States. The surveys by Hammond and Garfinkel (1961) and Haenszel, Skinkin, and Miller (1956) indicate, as do the mortality data, that the widowed and especially the divorced, of both sexes, are more likely to smoke than married individuals. However, both of these studies suggest that single men and women are somewhat less likely to smoke than their married counterparts, while the mortality data would suggest a lower rate among the married. It is possible that the lower rates of mortality caused by lung cancer among the married are not due to higher rates of lung cancer but instead to how promptly and diligently people seek treatment.

MORTALITY ASSOCIATED WITH DISEASES REQUIRING PROLONGED AND METHODICAL CARE

It seems logical that one's willingness to undertake the very prolonged and methodical care required in the treatment of certain diseases would be related to one's emotional state, willingness to take risks, etc. If the unmarried find their roles less satisfying than the married, and this is more true for men than for women, then we might expect this fact to be reflected in the mortality statistics of diseases requiring prolonged, attentive care. In this section I will look at the mortality statistics of two such diseases, tuberculosis and diabetes.

Tuberculosis is an infectious disease whose effective treatment requires the careful scheduling of one's life. Effectively treated tuberculosis will usually move into a latent phase; however, it is apt to become activated again if one becomes physically dissipated due to poor diet, lack of rest, etc. Furthermore, it appears to be the case that psychological stress and physical dissipation are related to initial infection (Derner 1953; Wolff 1953, pp. 27–32).

The data on tuberculosis are presented in table 8. As can be seen in the last column, between the ages 25 and 64 single men are, controlling for age, 5.4 times more likely than married men to die from tuberculosis, while the comparable figure for women is 3.3. Widowed and divorced men are even more likely than single men to die of tuberculosis. For the widowed, the differences reach 11.5 times the married rate between the ages 25 and 34, and reach a similar value among the divorced during the ages 35 through 44. For widowed and divorced women we find a different pattern, namely, that they are somewhat less likely than single women to die from tuberculosis. This, of course, means that when we compare the coefficients of preservation for men and women across the widowed and divorced categories, the differences are especially large.

In contrast to tuberculosis, the likelihood that one will become diabetic

TABLE 8. Tuberculosis: Ratios Produced by Dividing the Mortality Rate of the Unmarried by the Mortality Rate of the Married, Whites, United States, 1959–61*

Unmarried Category (Ratio)	Age								Average Ratio	
	25–34	35–44	45–54	55–59	60–64	65–69	70–74	75+	25+	25–64
Single:										
Male	5.67	6.64	5.20	4.30	3.87	3.47	3.12	2.57	4.74	5.37
Female	4.50	3.29	3.04	2.23	2.58	2.09	1.70	1.75	2.91	3.31
Widowed:										
Male	11.50	8.82	6.69	4.22	3.33	2.71	2.08	1.62	6.18	7.70
Female	3.88	2.62	2.11	1.47	1.94	1.51	1.39	1.29	2.26	2.58
Divorced:										
Male	7.67	11.45	10.63	7.79	6.87	4.77	4.57	2.77	7.84	9.27
Female	4.00	3.38	2.78	2.30	2.21	1.35	1.76	1.16	2.65	3.10

* Ratios calculated by the author from the mortality rates presented by the National Center for Health Statistics (1970).

is determined largely by one's genetic inheritance (Duncan 1964; Knowles 1965). However, at least among those who have a propensity for diabetes, social factors such as diet, and possibly such factors as stress, affect one's chances of becoming diabetic. It is necessary for most diabetics to carefully schedule major aspects of their life. They must be especially careful about what they eat and when they eat, as well as remember to take medications, etc.

TABLE 9. Diabetes: Ratios Produced by Dividing the Mortality Rate of the Unmarried by the Mortality Rate of the Married, Whites, United States, 1959–61*

Unmarried Category (Ratio)	Age								Average Ratio	
	25–34	35–44	45–54	55–59	60–64	65–69	70–74	75+	25+	25–64
Single:										
Male	3.56	3.37	2.21	1.70	1.52	1.29	1.07	0.93	2.25	2.69
Female	3.19	3.13	1.10	0.76	0.63	0.53	0.54	0.54	1.62	2.03
Widowed:										
Male	3.83	2.26	1.88	1.86	1.85	1.49	1.47	1.32	2.18	2.46
Female	1.69	2.29	1.59	1.37	1.13	1.14	1.09	1.08	1.54	1.71
Divorced:										
Male	6.78	5.66	2.98	2.05	1.71	1.66	1.31	1.19	3.52	4.32
Female	2.50	2.21	1.11	0.87	0.83	0.85	0.77	0.71	1.42	1.67

* Ratios calculated by the author from the mortality rates presented by the National Center for Health Statistics (1970).

The mortality data on diabetes are presented in table 9. Again, the unmarried have higher rates of mortality than the married, and the differences are noticeably greater for males than for females. As with tuberculosis, widowed and divorced women have a somewhat lower mortality rate than single women. Among the males, the mortality rate of the widowed is relatively similar to the rate of those who are single, while the divorced have a noticeably higher mortality rate.

MORTALITY LARGELY UNAFFECTED BY SOCIAL FACTORS

Assuming that one's marital status is related to how promptly and diligently he seeks treatment, one would expect some relationship between almost any cause of mortality and marital status. However, in cases where one's emotional state is unrelated to the etiology of a disorder and interacts minimally with the potential effectiveness of treatment, we would, following a role analysis, expect the relationship between mortality and marital status to be slight. Two such disorders are leukemia and aleukemia.

The relationship between deaths due to leukemia and aleukemia and marital status, by sex, are presented in table 10. These data indicate that

TABLE 10. Leukemia and Aleukemia: Ratios Produced by Dividing the Mortality Rate of the Unmarried by the Mortality Rate of the Married, Whites, United States, 1959–61*

Unmarried Category (Ratio)	Age								Average Ratio	
	25–34	35–44	45–54	55–59	60–64	65–69	70–74	75+	25+	25–64
Single:										
Males	1.25	1.08	1.07	0.84	0.94	0.91	1.01	0.84	1.03	1.07
Females	1.26	1.27	1.08	1.01	1.16	0.78	0.92	0.93	1.09	1.17
Widowed:										
Males	0.71	0.81	1.01	1.10	1.12	1.10	1.06	1.08	0.96	0.91
Females	0.95	1.27	1.10	1.05	1.10	0.99	1.04	1.10	1.08	1.10
Divorced:										
Males	1.38	1.08	1.29	1.38	1.36	1.08	1.21	1.10	1.24	1.28
Females	1.47	0.89	0.90	1.24	1.01	1.19	0.83	1.34	1.10	1.10

* Ratios calculated by the author from the mortality rates presented by the National Center for Health Statistics (1970).

there is in fact very little relationship between marital status and mortality caused by leukemia and aleukemia. Note also that in the case of the single and the widowed, it is the women and not the men who tend to have the larger coefficient of preservation—a finding that runs counter to the other types of mortality presented. I would also note that an analysis of the relationship between marital status and mortality caused by cancer of the digestive organs shows only slightly larger relationships than those found for leukemia and aleukemia (data not shown; see National Center for Health Statistics 1970).

The data on leukemia and aleukemia bear on a possibility raised by

Sheps (1961), who suggested that a major reason the unmarried groups appear to have higher rates of mortality than the married is that unmarried, particularly the widowed and divorced, are underenumerated in the census. Furthermore, he suggests that this underenumeration is greater for males than for females, which would account for the generally larger coefficients of preservation among males. However, if this were true, then the effects of underenumeration should be constant for all causes of mortality. If Shep's proposal were valid, then with regard to leukemia and aleukemia, the data would show the unmarried to have markedly higher rates of mortality than the married, and these differences would be greater for men than for women. However, for the widowed, particularly widowed males, the data clearly indicate that underenumeration is not an important issue. Among the divorced the data are consistent with the possibility that divorced males may be slightly underenumerated; however, the differences between the statuses are quite small. In short, it is clear that the relationships presented above could, at most, have been only marginally affected by underenumeration (also see Kraus and Lilienfeld 1959).

MORTALITY—ALL CAUSES

The relationships between marital status and mortality due to all causes are presented in table 11. The unmarried have, controlling for age, notice-

TABLE 11.   Mortality, All Causes: Ratios Produced by Dividing the Mortality Rate of the Unmarried by the Mortality Rate of the Married, Whites, United States, 1960*

Unmarried Category (Ratio)	Age								Average Ratio	
	25–34	35–44	45–54	55–59	60–64	65–69	70–74	75+	25+	25–64
Single:										
Male	2.23	2.25	1.83	1.49	1.50	1.46	1.43	1.38	1.81	1.95
Female	2.29	1.88	1.42	1.16	1.11	1.04	1.05	1.49	1.55	1.68
Widowed:										
Male	3.85	2.86	2.16	1.83	1.56	1.49	1.42	1.56	2.33	2.64
Female	2.43	1.82	1.54	1.29	1.26	1.22	1.18	1.45	1.64	1.77
Divorced:										
Male	3.92	4.07	3.14	2.58	2.27	1.99	1.83	1.59	2.96	3.39
Female	2.86	2.00	1.56	1.41	1.31	1.28	1.26	1.38	1.77	1.95

* Ratios calculated by the author from mortality rates presented by Grove and Hetzel (1968, p. 335).

ably higher mortality rates than the married, with the differences being significantly greater for men than for women. As one would expect, these differences, although substantial, are generally not as great as the differences associated with those types of mortality where social factors would appear to be especially important. In general, the more detailed differences shown by these data closely parallel the patterns associated with the specific causes of mortality previously presented, and this is a good place to summarize these patterns.

From the last column in table 11 it is obvious that for men there are marked differences in mortality associated with the three unmarried statuses. Divorced men have, controlling for age, a much higher mortality rate than widowed men, who in turn have a much higher mortality rate than single men. In contrast, mortality rates for women across these three marital statuses are quite similar. From these data it appears that when women shift from a married to an unmarried state, their life chances simply revert to those associated with the single status. However, this is not the case for men, for here the formerly married have higher mortality rates than the never married. It may be that, as men (apparently) benefit more from marriage than do women, they also experience more of a "shock" on reverting to an unmarried state, a shock which has the effect of decreasing their life chances.

Previously I noted, when discussing mortality associated with overt social acts, that the coefficient of preservation is largest during the early ages and drops off rapidly thereafter. This pattern also occurs with most of the other types of mortality where the social element appears to be particularly important, and can be seen in table 11, where all types of mortality are grouped together. As is shown in this table, for women the disparity between the three unmarried statuses and the married status is in each case greatest between the ages 25 through 34. For men the disparity between being married and being single or divorced is greatest between the ages 35 and 44 (although it is almost as large between 25 and 34), while the disparity between being married and widowed is greatest between the ages 25 to 34. These ages correspond closely to the time most families have young children in the home (see table 12), and it may be, as Durkheim indicated, that children provide a form of "protection" (through their effect on the concerns and behavior of parents).

TABLE 12. Presence of Children in Husband-and-Wife Families, 1959, by Percent*

Presence and Age of Own Children	Age of Husband			
	25–34	35–44	45–64	65+
With own children under 18 and at least some under 6	74.6	42.9	8.1	0.1
With own children under 18 but none under 6	11.2	42.9	34.9	3.2
Without own children under 18	14.2	14.2	57.0	96.7

* Data taken from Bureau of the Census (1960, table a).

I would note also that between the ages 25 and 34 the disparity between being married and being single is actually slightly larger for women than for men. Furthermore, as one moves to the older ages, where children tend not to be present in the home, the relative drop in the size of the coefficient of preservation tends to be larger for women than for men. It may be that young children provide more "protection" for women than for men. This is what Durkheim (1951, p. 189, n.27) concluded from his analysis of suicide. Furthermore, the data of psychological well-being suggest that this is a plausible possibility. For example, Gurin et al. (1960, p. 130) found that women "view children as more essential to their growth as a person, to their stability and maturity, and to the focusing of their life, giving such responses as: 'children provide a goal in life,' 'they are a fulfillment.' "

DISCUSSION

This paper analyzes the relationship between sex, marital status, and mortality. Previous research on psychological well-being and mental illness indicates that the married of both sexes find life more satisfying than the unmarried. This research, however, suggests that there are important differences between the sexes, namely, that males find being married more advantageous than do females and being single, widowed, or divorced more disadvantageous. This paper is based on the premise that if the research on psychological well-being and mental illness is valid, then similar relationships should appear in the data on mortality, particularly among those types of mortality which are clearly affected by such things as one's emotional stability and willingness to take risks.

As we have seen, the mortality rates of the unmarried statuses are, controlling for age, higher than those of the married, and the differences between the married and unmarried statuses are much greater for men than for women. The evidence from specific types of mortality suggests that these differences can be largely attributed to characteristics associated with one's psychological state. More precisely, the variations in the mortality rates are particularly large where one's psychological state (1) appears to play a direct role in death, as with suicide, homicide, and accidents, (2) is directly related to acts such as alcoholism that frequently lead to death, and (3) would appear to affect one's willingness and ability to undergo the drawn-out and careful treatment required for diseases such as tuberculosis. In contrast, there is little difference between the marital statuses in the mortality rates for diseases such as leukemia and aleukemia, where one's psychological state has little effect on either the etiology of the disease or treatment.

Further support for attributing the variation in mortality rates to variations in psychological factors related to the marital roles is provided by patterns in the way the rates vary. For both men and women the coefficients of preservation are large during the time children tend to be at home and then drop markedly thereafter. Furthermore, children appear to "protect" women more than men, a result previously noted by Durkheim and one that is suggested by the data on psychological well-being.

The pattern of mortality that is found between the marital statuses of the sexes is one that would be predicted by a role framework. However, other authors have suggested an alternative explanation, namely, that most of the observed differences are due to selective processes associated with marriage (e.g., Zalokar 1960; Sheps 1961; and to some extent Carter and Glick 1970, pp. 324–57, although see pp. 341–42). The selective argument is essentially as follows. Marriage is a selective process, and persons who are emotionally unstable and/or physically handicapped are much less likely to get married than those who are emotionally and physically healthy. Furthermore, the selective processes are such that the man (because he plays the dominant role in courtship) finds it more difficult to get married if he is handicapped than does a woman.[8] The first part of the argument seems quite reasonable, and I would assume that handicapped persons do find it difficult to marry. The question in my view is how much of the variation in the mortality rates between the marital states can be attributed to selective processes. The second part of the argument I find less convincing, although plausible. I would think that neither a man nor a woman would want a spouse who was emotionally unstable or about to die, and that there would be little difference between the sexes in this desire. Unfortunately, with the available evidence it is impossible to evaluate either of these selective arguments in a definitive fashion. However, it is possible to begin such an evaluation.

If, as the selective argument holds, more unstable women than men marry, this means that among persons who become either widowed or divorced, a higher proportion of women, as compared with men, would be emotionally unstable. A similar analysis can, of course, be made with regard to physical disability. This being the case, we would not expect, at least on the first analysis, the coefficients of preservation to be smaller for divorced and widowed women than for comparable men. In fact, at least with those coefficients relating to instability, we might expect them to be larger for women. It seems reasonable to assume that instability contributes to the likelihood of divorce, and this, in concordance with the selective hypothesis, suggests that a particularly large number of divorced women would be unstable (while a large number of divorced men would not be unstable but would simply have been formerly married to unstable women).

Proponents of the selective hypothesis would reply to this argument that, although the unstable and physically disabled would be more frequent among divorced and widowed women than among divorced and widowed men, the divorced and widowed frequently remarry and this screening process may result in the residual divorced and widowed population having proportionately more disabled and unstable men than women. It is, of course, true that many widowed and divorced persons remarry. I would note, however, that both the widowed and divorced have successfully passed through one selective process, and one would not expect a second, fairly comparable screening to produce greater differences than the initial screening. (In fact, I would expect it to produce a smaller difference.) This seems particularly obvious with regard to the widowed. However, the divorced and widowed, particularly males, have, controlling for age, higher mortality rates than the never married. Furthermore, as can be seen from table 11, the differences between the sexes tend to be greater among the widowed and divorced than among the never married.

In his classic work on suicide, Durkheim (1951, pp. 182–83) attempted to evaluate the relative validity of the selective and role explanations of the high rates of suicide among the never married. He argued that if the reason single persons have higher rates of suicide than the married is because stable persons tend to marry and unstable persons tend not to, then we would expect the differences between the single and married to be greater in the later years after virtually everyone who is going to marry has married, and smaller in the earlier years when the single category still contains a sizable number of stable persons who will eventually marry. As we have seen, not only with suicide but also with most forms of mortality, the difference between the never married and the married is greater during the early years and undergoes a marked decline over time. However, although these data are consistent with the role explanation, at our present state of knowledge they could also plausibly be explained by a selective explanation. For example, from a selective perspective it could be argued that (1) as it is "misfits" who die early there would be fewer misfits at risk in later years regardless of marital status and (2) the relative importance of selective processes may diminish with increasing age as mortality rates from most causes increase. It is going to take considerable work, with better data, before the relative importance of these explanations can be adequately assessed.[9]

Further evidence that the differences in mortality between the various marital statuses is not due primarily to selective processes associated with marriage is provided by Kraus and Lilienfeld (1959). Noting that the 1949–51 U.S. data on mortality indicated that the young widowed group had very high rates of mortality from certain causes, they attempted to see whether these differences could be attributed to the remarriage of healthy widows, which had left a residual "ill" widowed population. To do this they made very generous estimates of the characteristics of the widowed population that had remarried (i.e., they overestimated the number of widows who had remarried and assumed that none of the remarried widows had died), added the "remarried" widows to the residual widow population, and calculated the mortality rate of all widows (whether remarried or not). Although this reduced the difference between the widowed and married somewhat, most of the difference remained, and they were forced to conclude that at least for the young widowed group, the selective hypothesis could, at best, explain only a slight part of the differences in the mortality rates of the unmarried and married.

Another piece of evidence that strongly suggests that, at least for our purposes, the selective processes are not of major importance are the mortality patterns associated with diseases where the role explanation suggests little variation in mortality across the marital statuses but where the selective explanation suggests there should be marked variations. The mortality rates associated with leukemia and aleukemia provide an excellent example. These diseases are almost inevitably fatal, but persons who have been stricken with them may live for a long time, time for the selective processes, if they are important, to produce marked variations in the mortality rates associated with the different marital statuses. However, as is shown in table 10, for these diseases there is very little variation in the mortality rate between the marital statuses. Furthermore, the mortality rates associated with these diseases may be interpreted as indicating that it is disabled women and not disabled men who are the least likely to get married.

In this paper I have suggested that the different mortality patterns for men and women across the married and unmarried statuses can be largely explained by the nature of the marital roles. Although we have looked at selective processes as an alternative explanation of the data, we have, to this point, ignored the traditional independent variable of sociology—social class. As one's socioeconomic position in society has a strong inverse relationship to both mortality (e.g., Antonovsky 1972) and mental illness (e.g., Hollingshead and Redlich 1958; Rushing 1969; Kohn 1968), a few words are in order. Unfortunately, the national data used in this study do not allow for economic controls. Nevertheless, on the basis of national data for 1960 it is possible to show that it is very unlikely that the particular pattern of mortality dealt with in this paper is a product of economic factors. First, the average economic position of married men and women can, almost by definition, be taken as comparable. Second, the economic position of never-married white men and women is quite comparable, with women slightly better off (e.g., Carter and Glick 1970, p. 318). Third, white widowed women and white divorced women have much less income than their male counterparts (e.g., Carter and Glick 1970, pp. 266, 295). Thus, if it were the economic situation of men and women that determined the mortality pattern across the marital statuses, we would expect very little differences between men and women in the size of the never married/married ratio (the women's ratio might be slightly smaller), while we would expect the ratios of divorced/married and widowed/married to be much larger for women than for men. However, as we have seen for two out of the three marital categories, the ratios are the reverse of what the economic perspective would suggest

In conclusion, with regard to the relationship between marital status and mortality for men and women, the married have lower mortality rates than the unmarried and the differences between being married and being single, widowed, or divorced are greater for men than for women. These differences are particularly marked among those types of mortality where one's psychological state would appear to affect one's life chances. It would seem that these results can be tentatively attributed to the nature of marital roles in our society—in part, because the data on psychological well-being and mental illness indicate the same pattern of relationships; in part, because the "protective" aspects of marriage appear to be greatest at the time the role explanation would predict; and, in part, because the alternative explanation, namely, that the differences are due primarily to selective processes associated with marriage, tends not to be supported by the available data. I would note, however, that we know very little about how such variables as emotional instability and physical disability affect the likelihood of marriage. This is particularly true with regard to possible sex differences. Until such information is available, the precise weighing of the relative importance of the role explanation and the selective explanation of the mortality data must, in my view, remain tentative.

NOTES

1. I would like to note that in writing this paper I have benefited from conversations with Omer Galle, and I would like to thank Antonina Gove and William Parish for their comments on an earlier draft. The research for this paper was supported by the Vanderbilt University Research Council.

2. In some cases, death among the widowed is probably related to the death of the widowed's spouse. For example, if the spouse of a widowed person had died of an infectious disease, the widowed person is probably more likely than the average person to have been infected and is thus also more likely to die. This means that to some extent the size of the widowed/married ratio is affected by processes we are not considering. However, unless one assumes that such effects are sex specific (e.g., that a husband of a sick wife is more likely to get infected than the wife of a sick husband), such effects should have only minimal impact on the sex differences in the size of the ratios. I would note that if there is a sex differ-

ence in the likelihood of infection from one's spouse, I suspect it would be wives who would be more likely to become infected because of their presumed greater tendency to care for others. This, of course, would tend to increase the size of the women's ratio, producing an effect counter to the predicted one.

3. Since men and women have different mortality rates, the use of these coefficients allows us to avoid many of the problems involved in comparing the mortality of men and women. Some of the factors creating different life chances for men and women are noted below. First, there is considerable evidence that women have a longer life-span than men (e.g., Madigan 1957). Second, the life chances of men and women are differentially affected by social norms; it has, for example, been socially more appropriate for men to smoke and drink, which increases the likelihood that men will die because of lung cancer and cirrhosis of the liver. Third, men and women characteristically have quite different life styles, which may affect their life chances due to different rates of exposure to disease and to the possibility of accidents. Fourth, men and women appear to have different ways of behaving, which would affect their life chances. For example, men in general appear to be more aggressive and willing to take risks. Such ways of behaving would not only increase the death rate of men due to accidents but might also mean that men would be less apt to enter treatment early and be less likely to persist in the prolonged and careful treatment that is necessary for many disorders such as tuberculosis and diabetes. I would note that the different behavioral patterns of the sexes have long been recognized in the study of suicide, where investigators do not simply compare the rates of men and women but instead look for patterned variations (e.g., Durkheim 1951; Gove 1972b).

4. Parish and Schwartz (1972), like Durkheim, show that the size of the household was inversely correlated in France during the latter part of the 19th century. Their analysis, however, suggests that it is the number of adults in the household and not the number of children that is responsible for variations in the

suicide rate. Their conclusions are, in my view, open to question, in part because they are based on ecological data. However, even if they are valid they do not challenge Durkheim's contention that the presence of children has a "protective" effect on the married. For example, Durkheim (1951, p. 186) demonstrated (in a section not discussed by Parish and Schwartz) that in France in 1889–91 the "protective" effect of marriage among married men with children was almost four times as great as it was for married men without children. Similarly, he showed that married women without children had a significantly higher rate of suicide than unmarried women, while married women with children experienced considerable protection (Durkheim 1955, pp. 188–89). Furthermore, the protective effect of children persisted into widowhood. It may be that beyond the first child the number of additional children made little difference (which might explain the Parish and Schwartz results), but there can be little question that the presence or absence of children was of major importance.

5. For example, as had been noted by Durkheim (1951) and others (e.g., Maris 1969), in the very young age groups married persons frequently have higher suicide rates than single persons. A similar pattern occurs with some but not most other forms of mortality. I hope in a later paper to deal with the issue of marital status and mortality in the younger age groups.

6. For a recent discussion of the relationship between social control, deviance, and accidents see Suchman (1970).

7. The typical way of calculating age-standardized rates would be to standardize on the U.S. population. However, for our purposes such a procedure is likely to produce misleading results. In the United States we have more young people than old people, which means the young age groups will contribute more heavily to the age-standardized rate. However, in the present instance the younger ages are not, a priori, more important, and I see no theoretical reason why they should be weighed more heavily. Perhaps even more important is the fact we have subpopulations with very different age struc-

tures. The typical form of standardization would mean, for example, that in developing the age-standardized rates for the widowed, one would find that the rates of young widows play a much greater role than the rates of older widows. This would obviously be a questionable procedure, in part because widowed persons in the younger age groups are very rare and their rates thus unreliable, but also because they are a very atypical segment of the widowed population.

8. Carter and Glick (1970, pp. 258, 337) posit a third explanation with regard to the divorced. They suggest that divorced women, because of their status (presence of children, etc.), find it more difficult to remarry than divorced men. On the basis of this assumption they suggest that because more divorced men than divorced women remarry, and as it is the healthy who remarry, the residual divorced population will contain few healthy males (and thus the mortality rate of divorced males will be high) and many healthy females (and thus the mortality rate of divorced females will be low). However, their basic assumption is incorrect, for slightly more divorced women than divorced men remarry (Public Health Service 1964b, table 2–22.). I would note that the remarriage rate among the living divorced population is higher for males than for females. This is true because even after controlling for age and sex differences, divorced men have a higher mortality rate than divorced women. From a selective perspective, this means that among the persons who get divorced, approximately an equal number of (healthy) males and females remarry, but that more *unhealthy* divorced males than females are selected out (i.e., die early), which hypothetically would mean that at any given time the remaining population of divorced males should be healthier than the remaining population of divorced females.

9. I would note that Bradburn (1969, pp. 152–56) performed an analysis similar to that of Durkheim's on single males to see whether his results could be explained by selective processes and concluded that the "unhappy" state of single males was largely due to their reaction to their roles. Because of the nature of his data, it is very unlikely that his results could be attributed to the selective mortality of "misfits."

REFERENCES

Antonovsky, Aaron. 1972. "Social Class, Life Expectancy and Overall Mortality." In *Patients, Physicians and Illness,* edited by E. Gertly Jaco. New York: Free Press.

Berkson, Joseph. 1962. "Mortality and Marital Status." *American Journal of Public Health* 52 (August):1318–29.

Bradburn, Norman. 1969. *The Structure of Psychological Well-Being.* Chicago: Aldine.

Bradburn, Norman, and David Caplovitz. 1965. *Reports on Happiness.* Chicago: Aldine.

Bureau of the Census. 1960. "Household and Family Characteristics." *Current Population Reports,* ser. P-20, no. 100 (March 1959). Washington, D.C.: Government Printing Office.

Carter, Hugh, and Paul Glick. 1970. *Marriage and Divorce: A Social and Economic Study.* Cambridge, Mass.: Harvard University Press.

Derner, Gordon. 1953. *Aspects of the Psychology of the Tuberculous.* New York: Hoeber.

Duncan, G. C. 1964. *Diseases of Metabolism.* Philadelphia: Saunders.

Durkheim, Émile. 1951. *Suicide: A Study in Sociology.* New York: Free Press.

Gove, Walter R. 1972a. "The Relationship between Sex Roles, Marital Roles and Mental Illness." *Social Forces* 51 (September):34–44.

———. 1972b. "Sex, Marital Status and Suicide." *Journal of Health and Social Behavior* (in press).

Grove, Robert, and Alice Hetzel. 1968. *Vital Statistics Rates in the United States 1940–1960* (National Center for Health Statistics). Washington, D.C.: Government Printing Office.

Gurin, Gerald, Joseph Veroff, and Sheila Feld. 1960. *Americans View Their Mental Health.* New York: Basic Books.

Haenszel, W., M. Skinkin, and H. Miller. 1956. *Tobacco Smoking Patterns in the United States.* Public Health, Monograph no. 45 (Public Health Service Publication no. 463). Washington, D.C.: Government Printing Office.

Hammond, E. Cuyler, and Lawrence Garfinkel. 1961. "Smoking Habits of Men and Women." *Journal of the National Cancer Institute* 27 (August):419–42.

Hollingshead, August, and Fredrick Redlich. 1958. *Social Class and Mental Illness.* New York: Wiley.

Knowles, H. C. 1965. "The Incidence and Development of Diabetes Mellitus." In *Diabetes,* edited by R. H. Williams. New York: Harper & Row.

Kohn, Melvin. 1968. "Social Class and Schizophrenia: A Critical Review." In *The Transmission of Schizophrenia,* edited by David Rosenthal and Seymour Kety. New York: Pergamon.

Kraus, Arthur, and Abraham Lilienfeld. 1959. "Some Epidemiologic Aspects of the High Mortality Rate in the Young Widowed Group." *Journal of Chronic Diseases* 10 (September):207–17.

Madigan, Francis. 1957. "Are Sex Mortality Differences Biologically Caused?" *Milbank Memorial Fund Quarterly* 21 (January):145–55.

Maris, Ronald. 1969. *Social Forces in Urban Suicide.* Homewood, Ill.: Dorsey.

National Center for Health Statistics. 1970. *Mortality from Selected Causes by Marital Status,* ser. 20, no. 8. Washington, D.C.: Government Printing Office.

Parish, William, and Moshe Schwartz. 1972. "Household Complexity in Nineteenth-Century France." *American Sociological Review* 37 (April):154–73.

Public Health Service. 1964a. *Smoking and Health: Report of the Advisory Committee to the Surgeon General of the Public Health Service.* Public Health Service Publication no. 1103. Washington, D.C.: Government Printing Office.

———. 1964b. *Vital Statistics of the United States 1960.* Vol. 3. *Marriage and Divorce.* Washington, D.C.: Government Printing Office.

Rushing, William. 1969. "Two Patterns in the Relationship between Social Class and Mental Illness Hospitalization." *American Sociological Review* 34 (August):533–41.

Sheps, Mindel. 1961. "Marriage and Mortality." *American Journal of Public Health* 51 (April):547–55.

Shurtleff, David. 1956. "Mortality among the Married." *Journal of the American Geriatrics Society* 4 (July):654–66.

Suchman, Edward. 1970. "Accidents and Social Deviance." *Journal of Health and Social Behavior* 11 (March):4–15.

Terris, Milton. 1967. "Epidemiology of Cirrhosis of the Liver." *American Journal of Public Health* 57 (December):2076–88.

Wolff, Harold. 1953. *Stress and Disease*. Springfield, Ill.: Thomas.

Zalokar, Julia. 1960. "Marital Status and Major Causes of Death in Women." *Journal of Chronic Diseases* 11 (January):50–60.

21

Deathday and Birthday:
An Unexpected Connection

David P. Phillips

In the movies and in certain kinds of romantic literature, we sometimes come across a deathbed scene in which a dying person holds onto life until some special event has occurred. For example, a mother might stave off death until her long-absent son returns from the wars. Do such feats of will occur in real life as well as in fiction? If some people really do postpone death, how much can the timing of death be influenced by psychological, social, or other identifiable factors? Can deaths from certain diseases be postponed longer than deaths from other diseases?

In this essay we shall see how dying people react to one special event: their birthdays. We want to learn whether some people postpone their deaths until after their birthdays. If we compare the date of death with the date of birth for a large number of people, will we find fewer deaths than expected just before the birthday? If we do find a dip in deaths, we may conclude that some of these people are postponing death until after their birthdays.

We shall use elementary statistical methods in approaching the problem. For example, the comparison of an actual number of events with the number that might be expected is one of these methods; others will be noted later.

NATURE OF THE DATA TO BE INVESTIGATED

We shall examine only the deaths of famous people. There are two reasons for this. First, it seems likely that ordinary people look forward to their

Reprinted from *Statistics: A Guide to the Unknown*, ed. J. M. Tanur, E. Mosteller, et al. (San Francisco: Holden-Day, Inc., 1972), by permission of the author and the publisher.

birthdays less eagerly than do famous people because a very famous person's birthday, generally, is celebrated publicly, and he may receive a substantial amount of attention, gifts, and so on. In contrast, much less attention is paid to the birthday of an ordinary person, and he may have relatively little reason to look forward to it. Hence famous people may be more likely to postpone deaths than less famous ones. Second, it is easier to examine the deaths of the famous than of other people. To discover whether there is a dip in deaths before the birthday, we need information on the birth and death dates of individuals. This type of information is not available from conventional tables of vital statistics; therefore, we cannot easily determine the birth and death dates of large numbers of ordinary people. On the other hand, we can easily determine the birth and death dates of famous people because there is much biographical information available about them.

In all, we shall examine the birth and death dates of more than 1200 people. It is tedious to classify these dates by *day*, so we shall examine the *month* of birth and *month* of death. Thus, for the purpose of this analysis, we shall be concerned, not with the relationship between the birthday and the day of death, but rather with the relationship between the birth month and the death month. For our purposes, a person is said to have died in his birth month if the month of his death has the same name as the month of his birth. For example, if a person was born on March 1, 1897, and died on March 31, 1950, he died in his birth month. On the other hand, if he was born on March 1 and died on February 28, he did not die in his birth month; rather, he died in the month just before his birth month. Although we gain convenience by examining events by month rather than by day, we lose precision; if we find a dip in deaths in the month before the birth month, we cannot tell whether a dying person is hanging on for a few days or for a few weeks.

IS THERE A DIP IN DEATHS BEFORE THE BIRTH MONTH?

Table 1 shows the month of birth and month of death of people listed in *Four Hundred Notable Americans*. For example, we can see from the first column that one person who was born in January died in January, two people who were born in January died in February, and so on. The column labeled "Row Total" gives the total number of people who died in each month and the row labeled "Column Total" gives the total number of people born in each month.

Table 1 enables us to compare two hypotheses. The first hypothesis states that the death month is related to (is dependent on) the birth month in that some people postpone death in order to witness their birthdays. This

TABLE 1. Number of Deaths by Month of Birth and Month of Death (Sample 1)

Month of Death	Month of Birth												Row Total
	Jan.	Feb.	Mar.	Apr.	May	June	July	Aug.	Sept.	Oct.	Nov.	Dec.	
Jan.	1	1*	2	1	2	2	4	3	1	4	2	4	27
Feb.	2	3	1*	3	1	0	2	1	2	2	6	4	27
Mar.	5	6	5	3*	1*	0	5	1	2	5	3	1	37
Apr.	7	6	3	2	1	3	3	1	3	2	4	4	39
May	4	4	2	2	1	2*	4	1	3	2	1	5	31
June	4	0	4	5	1	1	1*	2*	1	2	4	0	25
July	4	0	3	4	3	3	4	1*	6	4	2	5	39
Aug.	4	4	4	4	2	2	3	3	1*	1	2	0	30
Sept.	2	2	1	0	2	0	2	4	2	0*	5	2	22
Oct.	4	2	2	3	1	2	2	3	3	1	4*	5	33
Nov.	0*	2	0	2	1	1	0	3	3	3	1	0*	16
Dec.	1*	2	2	1	2	1	4	1	4	0	2	2	22
Column Total	38	32	29	30	19	17	34	24	31	26	36	32	
Total													348†

Source: R. B. Morris, ed., Four Hundred Notable Americans (New York: Harper & Row, 1965).

* Deaths corresponding to month preceding birth month.

† The total number of deaths is less than 400 because (1) some of those in the source volume have not yet died; (2) for some of those in the volume, the month of birth and/or death is not known.

will be called the *death-dip hypothesis*. The second hypothesis states that no deaths are being postponed and that the month of death is not related to (is independent of) the month of birth. This will be called the *independence hypothesis*. (When we formulate our problem in terms of two hypotheses, one that we wish to disprove in order to lend credence to the other, and try to decide which hypothesis seems more consistent with the data, we are using a standard statistical testing procedure. The concept of "independence" is also an important part of many statistical hypotheses.)

Our general plan is to see whether the month immediately preceding the birth month has fewer deaths than the independence hypothesis suggests. As we explain below, it turns out that if the independence hypothesis were true, about ½ of the deaths would occur in each of the six months preceding the birth month, ½ in the birth month, and ½ in each of the five following months. Although this may seem obvious, it actually depends upon detailed calculations because we must take into account that some calendar months produce more deaths than others and some produce more births than others. It is intuitively satisfying, nevertheless, that for the independence hypothesis, the calculations give nearly equal expected numbers of deaths for each of the twelve months preceding, during, and following the birth month.

We now compare the actual number of deaths before the birth month with the number of deaths that are expected, on the average, if the independence hypothesis is true. If the observed number of deaths is noticeably less than the expected number, there is a dip in deaths before the birth month.

First, we count the actual number of deaths in the month just before the birth month. If we sum the numbers in the starred cells in Table 1, we will have the total observed number of deaths in this period. This number is 16.

Now we calculate the total expected number of deaths in the month just before the birth month. If the independence hypothesis is true, then the death month is independent of the birth month. This means that the deaths of those born in any given month should be distributed throughout the year in the same way as the deaths of those born in any other month. Thus, because 6.32% this is $[(22/348) \times 100]$ of all the deaths in Table 1 fall in December, 6.32% of those born in January should die in December, 6.32% of those born in February should die in December, and so on. In Table 1, we see that 11.2% $[(39/348) \times 100]$ of all deaths fall in April. Then, if independence holds, we would expect 11.2% of those born in any month to die in April. For example, there are 19 people born in May; we expect 11.2% of these people, that is $(11.2/100) \times 19 = 2.1$, to die in April. In a similar fashion, we can work out the expected number of deaths in each of the 12 starred cells in Table 1. If we sum these 12 numbers, we will have the total number of deaths that we expect to occur in the month before the birth month *if* the independence hypothesis is true. This expected number is 28.3.

The more intuitive method mentioned earlier estimates the total expected number of deaths in the starred cells to be simply 348/12 = 29.0. In other words, we expect about ¹⁄₁₂ of all deaths to occur one month before the birth month. In fact, we expect about ¹⁄₁₂ of all deaths to occur in the birth month or in any month before or after it. In general, this rough-and-ready method of estimating the total expected number for any month gives results very close to those provided by more precise methods.

We can now compare the observed number of deaths before the birth month with the expected number in this period. No matter which "expected number" we use, it is considerably higher than the number of deaths observed just before the birth month: we expect about 28 or 29 deaths, but we observe only 16—about 12 fewer than expected. In other words, we observe a dip in deaths in the month before the birth month as predicted by the death-dip hypothesis. As we shall soon see, the discrepancy is much more than might reasonably be explained by chance.

IS THERE A DEATH RISE AFTER THE BIRTH MONTH?

If the death-dip hypothesis is true, what will become of the 12 or so people who presumably have postponed death until their birthdays? When are they expected to die? There is no way of answering this question a priori because, even if the death-dip hypothesis is true, the death dip might have come about in a number of different ways; some of these different ways imply differing periods of survival for those who have postponed death. For example, the death dip could result entirely because some people who were hovering between life and death unexpectedly recovered; in this case, it might be years before these people die, and we could expect no rise in deaths immediately after the birth month. On the other hand, the death dip could appear solely because those who do not die just before their birthdays live a few days or weeks longer than expected; in this case, there should be a peak in deaths soon after the birth month. Depending on the way in which the death dip came about, we would or would not expect a rise in deaths after the birth month: we cannot tell what to expect on the basis of the death-dip hypothesis.

Although the death-dip hypothesis is not helpful here, practical experience with another sample (of famous Englishmen) suggests that we look for a rise in deaths in the four-month period consisting of the birth month and the three months thereafter. Thus, although we searched for a *death dip* in a *one-month* period, we shall search for a *death rise* in a *four-month* period, because past experience, not theory, makes this approach seem promising.

Table 2 gives the observed number of deaths six months before the birth month, five months before, and so on, down to zero months before, one month after, and so on up to five months after the birth month. Because $n = 348$ is the total number of people in sample 1, $n/12 = 29.0$ is the number expected to die six months before the birth month, five months before, and so on. From this table it is evident that not only is there a dip in deaths before the birth month, but there is also a rise in deaths during the birth month and during the three months thereafter. We expect about $\frac{4}{12}$ of all deaths in the first sample [$348 \times (\frac{4}{12}) = 116$] to fall in this four-month period, but we observe 140 deaths during this time.

COULD THE DEATH DIP AND DEATH RISE BE DUE TO CHANCE?

We know that surprising phenomena sometimes occur just by chance and for no other reason. For example, a person might deal himself a straight in poker; ordinarily, we attribute this happy event to the vagaries of providence, not to the dishonesty of the dealer. In much the same way, we might wonder whether the death dip and death rise have arisen by chance and for no other reason.

Now suppose our poker player were to deal himself not just one straight, but four straights in a row in the four times he deals while playing with us. This *could* have happened by chance, but it is so unlikely that we would prefer some other explanation. The less likely an event is to occur by chance, the more we prefer some other explanation. Similarly, if we find a death dip and death rise in, say, four samples and not just one, there is a small possibility that these phenomena could have occurred by chance, but another explanation might be more plausible.

In sample 1 we observed that there are fewer deaths than expected in the month before the birth month, and more deaths than expected in the four-month period consisting of the birth month and the three months thereafter. Can we find a similar death dip and death rise in other samples of people?

MORTALITY IN THREE MORE SAMPLES

Three new samples were taken, consisting of people who are famous for two reasons. First, they achieved high status in their lifetimes: they were listed in *Who Was Who in America*. Second, they came from well-known

TABLE 2. Number of Deaths, Before, During, and After the Birth Month (Sample 1)

	6 Months Before	5 Months Before	4 Months Before	3 Months Before	2 Months Before	1 Month Before	The Birth Month	1 Month After	2 Months After	3 Months After	4 Months After	5 Months After
Number of Deaths	24	31	20	23	34	16	26	36	37	41	26	34

$n = 348$
$n/12 = 29.0$

Source: Table 1.

families (e.g., Adams, Vanderbilt, Rockefeller) which are listed in "The Foremost Families of the U.S.A.," an appendix to *Royalty, Peerage and Aristocracy of the World* (vol. 90, 1967). We have ensured that the new samples do not overlap each other or sample 1.

Three volumes of *Who Was Who* were examined, those for the years 1951–60, 1943–50, and 1897–1942. Sample 2 contains all who are listed in the first of these volumes and have their surnames in "Foremost Families." Sample 3 contains all who are listed in the second *Who Was Who* volume and have their surnames in "Foremost Families." Sample 4 contains *every other* person who is in the third volume of *Who Was Who* and has his surname in "Foremost Families." We chose every other person rather than every person because the third volume is so much larger than the other volumes that it would be tedious to examine every person who meets our selection criteria.

Table 3 gives the observed number of deaths before, during, and after the birth month for samples 2, 3, and 4. The last number in each row of this table is the expected number of deaths six months before the birth month, five months before, and so on. We can see that the death dip and death rise evident in sample 1 also appear in samples 2, 3, and 4. In each of these samples there are fewer deaths than expected in the month before the birth month and more deaths than expected in the four-month period consisting of the birth month and the three months thereafter.

If we now combine the data in all four samples, we get the results seen in Table 4. A graph of these results appear in Figure 1, where we can see a death dip just before the birth month and a death rise during and after it.

In summary, just before the birth month, in each of the four samples presented, we found fewer deaths than would be expected under the hypothesis that the month of death is independent of the month of birth. In each of the four samples presented, more deaths occur during and immediately after the birth month than would be expected if independence held. The similarity of results in each of the four samples helps to convince us that the death dip and death rise are real phenomena and are not merely chance fluctuations in the data.

THE SIZE OF THE DEATH DIP AND DEATH RISE

Let us estimate the size of the death dip before the birth month and the size of the death rise thereafter for the aggregate sample of 1251 people. Out of 1251 people, 86 died in the month before the birth month. Given independence between the birth month and the death month, we would expect about 1/12 of all 1251 deaths, or approximately 104 deaths, to fall in

TABLE 3.   Number of Deaths Before, During, and After the Birth Month Samples 2, 3, and 4

Number of Deaths	6 Months Before	5 Months Before	4 Months Before	3 Months Before	2 Months Before	1 Month Before	The Birth Month	1 Month After	2 Months After	3 Months After	4 Months After	5 Months After	Total	Total 12
Sample 2*	17	23	26	27	28	28	42	32	31	34	36	30	354	29.5
Sample 3†	10	14	12	11	8	12	15	15	15	13	20	13	158	13.2
Sample 4‡	39	32	29	35	31	30	36	35	38	26	31	29	391	32.6

* Sample 2 excludes those listed in *Who Was Who in America 1951–1960* who died outside of that period and those listed in *Four Hundred Notable Americans.*
† Sample 3 excludes those listed in *Who Was Who in America 1943–1950* who died outside of that period or during World War II and those listed in *Four Hundred Notable Americans.*
‡ Sample 4 excludes those listed in *Who Was Who in America 1897–1942* who died outside of that period or during both World Wars and those listed in *Four Hundred Notable Americans.*

TABLE 4.   Number of Deaths Before, During, and After the Birth Month (All Samples Combined)

	6 Months Before	5 Months Before	4 Months Before	3 Months Before	2 Months Before	1 Month Before	The Birth Month	1 Month After	2 Months After	3 Months After	4 Months After	5 Months After
Number of Deaths	90	100	87	96	101	86	119	118	121	114	113	106

$n = 1251$
$n/12 = 104.3$

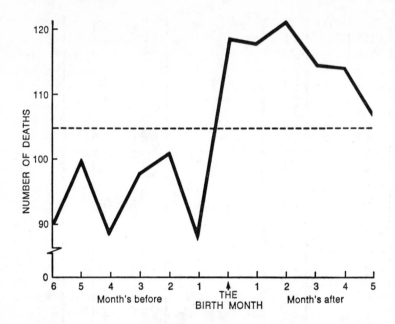

**FIGURE 1.   Number of deaths before, during, and after birth month
(all samples combined)**

this period. Thus, just before the birth month only about 83% (86/104) of
the deaths expected actually occurred. To put this another way, in the
month before the birth month there were about 17% fewer deaths than we
would expect under independence.

Similarly, we can estimate the size of the death rise during the birth
month and the three months thereafter. There were 472 deaths in the
period including the birth month and one, two, and three months thereafter. Given independence between birth and death months, the expected
number of deaths in this four-month period is estimated to be $\frac{4}{12}$ of all
deaths, or 417 deaths [($\frac{4}{12}$) $\times$ 1251 = 417]. Thus the actual number of
deaths in and just after the birth month is $\frac{472}{417}$ = 11% more than the number expected.

We can see that the death dip and death rise for sample 1 are larger
than the death dips and death rises for the other three samples examined.
In the month before the birth month, sample 1 has 45% fewer deaths than
independence leads us to expect. In the remaining three samples combined, we observe 70 deaths in the month before the birth month; given
independence, we expect about 75.25 [($\frac{1}{12}$) $\times$ 903] in this period. Thus,
just before the birth month, the observed number of deaths in samples 2,
3, and 4 combined is approximately 7% less than the number expected
under independence.

Similarly, it is evident that the death rise in sample 1 is larger than the death rises in the remaining samples. We estimate that in sample 1, in the birth month and in the three months thereafter, there are 20% more deaths than expected. The equivalent figure for samples 2, 3, and 4 is 10%.

The death dip and death rise in the sample 1 may be larger than in the other samples because the members of sample 1 are considerably more famous than the members of the other samples. The 348 people in sample 1 are supposed to be the most famous people in American history. The larger number of people in the remaining samples were less stringently selected.

RELATION BETWEEN FAME AND THE SIZE
OF THE DEATH DIP AND DEATH RISE

We have referred several times to the notion that a group of famous people is expected to produce a larger death dip before the birth month than a group of ordinary people. Now we shall assess this idea more carefully. We classify the members of sample 1 into three groups according to how famous they are and examine the sizes of the death dip and death rise produced by each of these groups. If we are right, we should find that the more famous a group is, the larger its death dip and death rise.

There are obviously many ways to classify groups by fame. The method used here is convenient and seems plausible. The best-known members of "the four hundred" are those whose names have become household words in the "common culture." The "common culture" may be said to consist of the knowledge shared by almost all the members of a society—in other words, some sort of lowest common denominator of knowledge. To find which of the four hundred is "in" the common culture, we must find a set of people who know only what is in that culture. The members of the four hundred who are known to this group of people have names that are part of the common culture.

Of all the people in a society, children come closest to having no more knowledge than is in the common culture. If a child has heard of someone in the four hundred, he is very famous indeed. Thus the members of the four hundred who appear in children's biographies may be judged to be better known than members who do not appear in such biographies.

Two series of children's biographies were examined: Dodd, Mead's (1966) and Bobbs-Merrill's (1966). The criterion of coverage or noncoverage in these series can be used to classify members of the four hundred into groups of differing fame. Three different subgroups were formed from the original four hundred.

Group 1 consists of those of the four hundred whose names are found in both of the children's biography series. For example, George Washington, Thomas Jefferson, Benjamin Franklin, Mark Twain, and Thomas Edison are in group 1.

Group 2 consists of those of the four hundred whose names are in only one of the series. For example, John Quincy Adams, John Hancock, Jefferson Davis, Edgar Allen Poe, and Alexander Graham Bell are in group 2.

Group 3 consists of those of the four hundred whose names are in neither series. For example, Samuel Adams, Millard Fillmore, Rutherford B. Hayes, H. L. Mencken, and Nikola Tesla are in group 3.

For our purposes, the members of group 1 are judged to be more famous, on the average, than the members of group 2, and the members of group 2 are judged to be more famous, on the average, than the members of group 3. We say "on the average" because single individuals could be moved readily from one group to another if we used a third or fourth biography series to judge fame. But we think that the groups as a whole are ordered with respect to fame in the way we want them to be.

We can now measure the death dip and death rise produced by each of these groups. Table 5 gives the relevant information.

TABLE 5.   The Size of the Death Dip and Death Rise for Groups of Differing Fame

Group	Size of Death Dip (%)	Size of Death Rise (%)	Total No. in Group	No. of Deaths in the Birth Month and 1, 2, 3 Months Thereafter	No. of Deaths in the Month Before the Birth Month
1	−78	58	55	29	1
2	−63	23	129	53	4
3	−20	−3	164	53	11

As predicted, the more famous a group is, the larger is its death dip. Group 1 produces a larger death dip than group 2, and group 2 produces a larger death dip than group 3. The death dip for the most famous group is quite large. About 78% of the deaths that are expected to fall in the month before the birth month do not do so. It should be stressed, however, that the number of people in group 1 is not large.

From Table 5 we can see also that the more famous the group is, the larger is the death rise that it produces. In group 1 (the most famous group) the observed number of deaths during and just after the birth month is about 58% greater than the number expected. Note that there is no death rise at all for group 3, the least famous group.

SUMMARY

We have noted two sets of findings that are consistent with the notion that some people postpone death to witness a birthday because it is important to

them. There is a death dip before the birth month and a death rise thereafter in four separate samples. We have noted also a consistent relation
between the fame of a group and the size of its death dip and death rise:
the more famous the group, the larger the death dip and death rise it produces. These results might be due to chance, but this possibility is sufficiently small that we would prefer some other explanation of these
phenomena.

There are indications that some people postpone dying in order to witness events other than their birthdays. There are fewer deaths than expected
before the Jewish Day of Atonement in New York, a city with a large Jewish population. In addition, there is a dip in U.S. deaths, in general, before
U.S. Presidential elections.

We have anecdotal evidence that the timing of death might be related
to other important social events. For example, many people have noted that
both Jefferson and Adams died on July 4th, 50 years after the Declaration
of Independence was signed. We may find it easier to believe that this is
not coincidental if we read Jefferson's last words, quoted by his physician.

> About seven o'clock of the evening of that day, he [Jefferson] awoke,
> and seeing my staying at his bedside exclaimed, "Oh Doctor, are you
> still there?" in a voice however, that was husky and indistinct. He then
> asked, "Is it the Fourth?" to which I replied, "It soon will be." These
> were the last words I heard him utter.[1]

---

[1] Merrill Peterson, *Thomas Jefferson and the New Nation* (New York: Oxford
University Press, 1970), p. 1008.

Fertility

Introduction: A. The Social Determinants of Fertility and Family Planning

Having babies is a socially motivated behavior. This basic principle for understanding fertility has been precisely stated by Kingsley Davis: ". . . if it were admitted that the creation and care of new human beings is socially motivated, like other forms of behavior, by being a part of the system of rewards and punishments that is built into human relationships, and this is bound up with the individual's economic and personal interests, it would be apparent that the social structure and economy must be changed before a deliberate reduction in the birth rate can be achieved."[1]

There have been many alternative explanations and theories of fertility, both popular and scientific, but I believe that not one holds up as well as the social explanation. Some writers still try to explain variations in fertility in physiological terms, but biological theories of fertility are much less popular today than they were in the nine-

[1] Kingsley Davis, "Population: Will Current Programs Succeed?" *Science* 158 (1967):7.

teenth century. The typical biological theory of fertility had as its basic argument the claim that the number of babies born depended on the biological capacity of the people to reproduce. Occasionally the effects of some biological cause can be observed, as when some disease or infection produces widespread sterility in a population, but that is really quite rare and does not usually have much impact on the levels of fertility.

Some of the popular explanations of fertility differences and fertility change are most interesting, but usually wrong. For example, since sexual intercourse is the prime cause of conception and thus fertility, many people seem to believe that the frequency of sexual relations or the "sexuality" of some people is the primary cause of differences in fertility between groups. People in underdeveloped societies where there is usually high fertility are often assumed to have high rates of sexual intercourse. J. Mayone Stycos in an excellent essay reprinted in the first edition of this book, identified this attitude as one of the "elite" theories of lower-class fertility[2] and identified it properly as a condescending and patronizing attitude of the upper classes toward the lower classes. This idea is generally used as an explanation for why some lower-class group is having such high fertility rates. The first objection to this facile theory is that we have no substantial evidence that the frequency of sexual intercourse varies that much from one group to another, and, if it does, that the groups with traditionally high fertility also have greater sexual frequency. As Davis and Blake pointed out in discussing the related issue of sexual abstinence, some groups who are poor and rural (peasants) have religious customs that prohibit sexual intercourse many days during the year.[3] Also, many lower-class people may not have sexual intercourse as often because of the very hard physical labor they have to do, and because sickness is more likely to make sexual intercourse unpleasant or impossible.

To jar my classes out of this kind of simplistic thinking I often assert that "'sex has very little to do with how many babies people have." A simple exercise will reveal how ludicrous it is to assume that

---

[2] J. Mayone Stycos, "Obstacles to Programs of Population Control—Facts and Fancies," *Marriage and Family Living* 25(1963):8–9.

[3] Kingsley Davis and Judith Blake "Social Structure and Fertility," *Economic Development and Cultural Change* 4(1956):232.

the frequency of sexual intercourse is a crucial determinant of the number of children a couple will have. First, the number of children that couples have almost always falls within the range between zero and ten. Babies born at a higher birth order are demographically inconsequential. So most couples have fewer than ten children, and in most societies the substantial majority of children born per couple is between two and five. Consider now the number of times that a married couple may have sexual intercourse during the twenty years that a woman is typically married and fecund. It is much, much greater. Even by making conservative estimates of the frequency of intercourse the number must run generally into the thousands. The great disparity between the two sets of numbers must surely show that frequency is not the crucial factor. What is obviously more important, especially in present-day societies, is the kind of precaution that people take to avoid conception. This leads us to the second popular, but also inadequate, explanation of fertility differences: the technical advances in contraception.

Fertility declines in American society in the last fifteen years or so are often attributed to the birth control pill (or occasionally the intrauterine contraceptive device). It is, of course, true that the more effective and efficient a contraceptive method is the more it should reduce fertility. But, it is equally true that people must be motivated to use a contraceptive method (any contraceptive method) or it will not be effective. Westoff and Bumpass (article 23) show the dramatic changes that have taken place among American Catholics in the last decade regarding their use of contraception. There has obviously been some change in the attitudes and orientations of many Catholics toward birth control that caused them to change their behavior, because the contraceptive techniques they are using are no less contrary to Catholic doctrine than earlier mechanical-chemical methods.

Explaining the decline in American fertility since 1957 by saying that the oral contraceptive is responsible simply overlooks the fact that the "pill" was not even developed beyond testing until the early 1960's and it was not that widely used even as late as the middle '60's, yet fertility was going down steadily. Furthermore, a careful examination of the aggregate use of oral contraceptives and declining fertility during those years led Ryder and Westoff to conclude that "what has been happening to fertility in the 1960's would have happened in direction if not in degree even if the oral contraceptive had not appeared on the scene. . . ."[4]

Finally, one must note that an explanation of changes in the rate of fertility in the United States that is based upon the influence of contraceptive technology would be hard-pressed to account for some dramatic ups and downs over the last forty years. Fertility in American society is very low in the 1970's, but it was equally low in the 1930's, when most of the presently used contraceptive methods were not in common use. Essentially one must conclude that birth control technology may be a facilitator in bringing down birth rates, but only when individual couples have reasons to limit the number of children they have will they use these methods. The articles in this section will reveal that the system of rewards and punishments that Davis spoke of are the real causes, the social causes, of fertility.

The first three articles (22, 23 and 24) approach the issue of fertility as a social behavior primarily from the point of view of the social pressure for having children. Janet Griffith's paper examines the pressures that people feel to have certain numbers of children. Griffith's research clearly identifies the pressures to have at least two children, but she also finds some pressure for couples today to limit childbearing after they have had five children.

Charles F. Westoff and Larry Bumpass, as mentioned earlier, illustrate the effect that religion can have on keeping people from using the available methods of birth control. Up until very recent years the prohibition on the use of birth control has been very effective among U.S. Catholics. But the research by Westoff and Bumpass shows how that has changed dramatically since 1965.

The paper by Jean Veevers comes from her study of childless couples who made the conscious decision to remain childless. Among other things, the voluntarily childless couples reveal how difficult it is to make the decision to remain childless in a social system that pressures for the bearing of children. Unless couples make the conscious decision before marriage to remain childless (and about one-third of Veevers' sample did) they usually go through a number of years during which they think and say that they are going to have children but are postponing the actual time for one reason or another. During many of these years the childless couple is often subject to

---

[4] Norman R. Ryder and Charles F. Westoff, "The United States: The Pill and the Birth Rate, 1960–1965," *Studies in Family Planning* 20(1967):3.

subtle (and not so subtle) pressures to have children. The voluntarily childless couples must learn to use mechanisms of defense justifying the fact that they have not yet had children. For example, they may say that they plan to have children after they have done one thing or another, or say that they may adopt children later. What research by Veevers suggests is that there may be many couples, who, not having thought about remaining childless very carefully or explicitly, may simply succumb to the pressures and have children.

The remaining papers in this section (25, 26 and 27) tend to show the positive rewards for having children. That is, they more often reflect the rewards that the social system offers for those who meet societal expectations. These three papers also give some consideration to the issues of fertility-control programs and policies.

The Scanzoni-McMurry paper (25) and Judith Blake's paper (26) emphasize the way in which the sex roles of the society are set up to encourage fertility. Blake has been especially strong in expressing the idea that most societies cannot reach a zero population growth level unless the population policy takes into account the strong pressures and rewards that are causing couples to *want* to have babies. Blake has emphasized in several of her writings how the role of parenthood is integrally linked with the masculine and feminine roles. There is a strong and widespread feeling that men and women are not truly fulfilled unless they have children. For most people there is no acceptable substitute for having children.

The final paper in this section (27) comes from a book by Mahmood Mamdani called the *Myth of Population Control*. In this brief excerpt Mamdani recounts the failure that was experienced when government officials tried to introduce birth control into a Punjab Indian village. He argues that the failure of the Indian villager to accept birth control is simply a function of his class and economic position in the society. The poor people in the village not only want children, they *need* children, because without them they would end their lives living on the charity of their neighbors. Mamdani argues that the family-planning program has a middle-class bias that simply does not recognize the problems of life among the poor. He obviously feels that a change in the economic structure of Indian society is necessary before there can be a change in the response to family planning among the great majority of the Indian people whose lives are embedded in poverty.

22

Social Pressure on Family Size Intentions

Janet Griffith

Although there is considerable information concerning the "ideal" and "expected" family size of American couples of childbearing age, there has been little exploration of the upper and lower family size limits which most couples deem socially "acceptable," and of the kinds of social pressures brought to bear on couples whose family size intentions or performance falls outside this "acceptable" range. The research reported in this paper shows that there is a sharp lower boundary, with two children widely regarded as the minimum acceptable family size. There is a less precise upper limit, with four-child families regarded as acceptable by a majority, and families of five or more increasingly less acceptable. There appears to be considerable social pressure on couples to have a first and second child, and, for women particularly, substantial pressure to limit family size after having a fifth child. The data also show that while men and women feel there are social pressures to have or not to have specific numbers of children, both direct and indirect pressures are anticipated by women more than men. These findings of expectations of social pressure to bring family size within "acceptable" limits are of particular interest in relation to data indicating a longstanding preference in the United States for family sizes in the two-to-four-child range. The results of surveys dating back to the 1930s show a consistent preference among Americans for the two-to-four-child family, with relatively few respondents regarding as "ideal" family sizes of fewer than two children or more than four, and relatively few "expecting" to have fewer than the lower limit or more than the upper.[1] Highlighting this trend was the finding of the 1965 National Fertility Study that 92 percent of a national sample of 5,617 ever-married women of reproductive age said that two, three or four children was an "ideal" size for an average American

Reprinted from *Family Planning Perspectives*, 5, no. 4 (Fall, 1973), pp. 237–42, by permission of the author and the publisher. Footnotes have been renumbered.

family, compared with seven percent who said five or more is "ideal," and fewer than one percent who said that the family with one child or none is "ideal."[2] Similarly, with regard to "expected" family size, a 1973 survey of the reproductive intentions of young wives reported a large increase since 1967 in the proportion of wives under 25 years of age who expect to have exactly two children, and a corresponding decrease in the proportion expecting three or more.[3] For example, 57 percent of wives aged 22–24 in 1973 said they expected to have precisely two children, compared with 38 percent of wives that age in 1967. In the same age group, the proportion expecting three or more almost halved in the same period, from 55 percent in 1967 to 30 percent in 1973. During this period, the survey showed, there was an increase in the proportion of young wives expecting to remain childless (4.0 percent from 1.7 percent) or to have only one child (from five percent to nine percent).

While there has been considerable variation in the preferences for family sizes within the two-to-four-child range, the persistence over time of the concentration within this range raises theoretical and practical questions about the kinds of social mechanisms that contribute to the maintenance of this pattern. In addition, important questions are raised by the data indicating a recent downward trend in preferred and expected family size. These include questions as to whether the trend toward a family size of exactly two children represents a long-term, possibly irreversible trend, and whether the apparent trend to family sizes smaller than two children may be weakened by social pressures to have families of at least two children.

METHODOLOGY

To obtain data on the limits to acceptable family size and on social pressures on family size intentions, a series of questions was concluded in the July 1972 Opinion Research Corporation Caravan survey, a national probability sample survey of Americans aged 18 and older living in the continental United States.[4] This article reports on the responses of 311 ever-married men and 412[5] ever-married women from 18 to 39 years of age to two sets of questions:

In the first set, the questions were, "In general, what number of children do you think makes a family too small?" and "what number makes a family too large?" The number or other response (e.g., "no number") given by the respondent was recorded and used in the analyses.

In the second series, the respondents were asked about their expectations of disapproval or pressure to change in three hypothetical family size situations, i.e., if they were going to remain childless, have only one child, or if they already had four and were expecting a fifth child.

The questions asking respondents what family sizes they regarded as "too large" and "too small" were designed to elicit information on the limits to acceptable family size by obtaining *disapproved* family sizes rather than simply ones that are preferred or idealized. This was done because much social pressure involves attempts to redirect behavior *away* from disapproved alternatives, rather than to bring it into conformity with the most preferred alternative.

ONE TOO FEW, FIVE TOO MANY

The data in the upper panel of Table 1 show a very clear boundary between two children and one child as constituting acceptable family sizes: Very few say a family of two or more children is too small, but almost two-thirds of the men and three-fourths of the women say a one-child family is too small.[6] (The remainder, just over one-third of the men and one-fourth of the women, say either that zero children makes a family too small or that no number does.)

At the upper end of the family size continuum, there is no single break as sharp as that between one and two children at the lower end, but a family with five children is regarded as too large by the majority, while a four-child family is more generally acceptable, especially among women

TABLE 1.   Cumulative percentages* of ever-married men and women aged 18–39 stating that successive numbers of children make a family "too small" or "too large"

Number of children	Percent respondents who think family too small	
	Men (N = 302)*	Women (N = 412)*
0/no number	100	100
1	64	75
≧2	2	5
	Percent respondents who think family too large (N = 299)	(N = 397)
2	3	0
3	15	5
4	39	25
5	59	54
6	71	70
≧7/no number	100	100

* Percentages are weighted. Number of respondents is the raw number for each category. The numbers vary because of different numbers of nonrespondents.

(just one-fourth of the women and two-fifths of the men say it is too large).

These patterns show a sharp lower boundary and a less precisely specified upper boundary range. The data demonstrate the nearly universal acceptability of the two-child family as neither too large nor too small, and the wide acceptance of three- and four-child families. Overall, women are more disapproving than men of a one-child family and are somewhat more accepting of three- and four-child families.

SOCIAL PRESSURES ON FAMILY SIZE

To explore the kinds of direct and indirect social pressures affecting the family size intentions of couples, respondents were asked a series of questions about how they thought others would respond to them and how they would feel if they were childless, had one child or were expecting a fifth child.[7] The childless and one-child situations were chosen because the lower limit of two children was predicted to be very sharp, and because somewhat different pressures were expected at each of these two parties. For instance, we would predict strong pressure from parents or other close relatives for the couple to have a first child so that the couple's parents could become grandparents, to 'carry on the family name', or for other reasons involving the family's perceived welfare and interests. Pressures to have a second child appear more likely to be put in terms of the first child's welfare and may involve relatively more internalized pressures and peer pressure than does the first birth.

The situation in which the couple is expecting their fifth child was chosen because of the data on family size preference and ideals that indicate a sharp break between four and five children as the accepted or preferred family sizes.

As Table 2 shows, half or more of both men and women expect overt family and peer pressure at each of the three parities studied: pressure to have a first and a second child, and to limit family size after having a fifth one. However, there are important differences between parities and between men and women in their expectation of these and other kinds of family size pressures.

More than three-fourths of both men and women (78 percent) expect family pressure to have a first child. But, while almost as many women expect family pressure to have a second and to stop childbearing after a fifth child, considerably fewer men expect such pressures. Sixty-two percent of men expect family pressure to have a second child, and 54 percent expect family pressure to limit family size after having five, compared with 76 percent and 72 percent of women expecting family pressure at these parities.

TABLE 2. Percentages of ever-married men and women aged 18–39 expecting social pressures from family, friends or others if they remained childless, had one child or were expecting a fifth

Question*	Percent Agreeing†	
	Men (N = 311)	Women (N = 407)
If childless:		
a. "Parents or other close relatives would urge you to have a child."	78	78
b. "You would feel out of place when you got together with relatives."	34	43
c. "Friends would urge you to have a child."	62	69
d. "You would feel out of place when you got together with other married (women/men)."	33	54
e. "People would say you were selfish."	40	51
If had one child:		
a. "Parents or other relatives would urge you to have another child."	62	76
b. "Friends would urge you to have another child."	52	66
c. "People would say your child would be spoiled."	81	83
d. "You would worry that it would be bad for the child."	57	72
Expecting a fifth child:		
a. "Parents or other close relatives would urge you to think about limiting your family."	54	72
b. "Friends would urge you to think about limiting your family."	51	62
c. "People would say you were wrong to have so many children."	58	72

* The wording of the question was: "I'd like to ask you now about some things that might happen if you had different numbers of children. Some of these may really have happened to you, some may not, but please try to imagine what each would be like." The wordings for the three parities were: Childless: "First, try to imagine what it would have been like if you had been married for quite a while and did not have any children." One child: "Now—can you try to imagine what it would be like if you had one child and people thought you might not have another one." Expecting fifth child: "Now, can you try to imagine what it would be like if you already had four children and found out you were going to have another." For each parity, the interviewer read a list of possible consequences. The response alternatives were "Definitely happen," "Probably happen," "Probably not happen," and "Definitely not happen."

† The percentage base includes respondents who said "Don't know," but not nonrespondents. Percentages are weighted. Number of cases is raw number.

Fewer men and women expect peer pressure than expect family pressure, at each parity, but overt peer pressures are expected by a substantial proportion: 69 percent of women and 62 percent of men expect pressure from their friends to have a first child, and half or more expect pressure from friends to have a second child or to limit family size after a fifth. As with pressure from family, more women than men expect pressure from friends after having a first or fifth child.

Thus, the burden of overt pressure to bring family size intentions into conformity with the expectation that couples should have a minimum of two children and should not exceed some upper limit of around five appears to fall more heavily on women than on men. And, as the data in Table 2 indicate, other kinds of social pressures are also greater for women than men at each of the hypothetical parity levels.

Several of these are of particular interest in terms of the kinds of indirect pressures that act on couples' family size intentions. Considerably more women than men expect that being childless would make them feel out of place with married friends of approximately the same age, and somewhat more expect that others would say they were selfish not to have children.

Expectations of one's own and others' concerns if the couple were to have only one child reflect the widespread belief that only children are socially and personally disadvantaged. Four-fifths of both men and women expect others would say the child would be spoiled. (This response and family pressure to have a first child are expected by more men and women than any other response at any of the three parities and, in addition, these are the only two items on which there is no sex difference. This gives an indication of the strength and pervasiveness of the belief in the "spoiled only child" and of the family's perceived interest in the birth of the first child.) But, despite this similarity in men's and women's expectation that others would feel an only child would be disadvantaged, more women than men express a corresponding personal concern that the child would be harmed if they stopped at one child (71 percent of women, compared with 57 percent of men).

The majority of both men and women expect others would say they were "wrong to have so many children" if they had a fifth child, but more women than men expect this evaluation, as more women than men expect family or peer pressure not to have additional children. The sex differences in response to these items show consistently higher expectations of family limitation pressures by women than men.

Overall, the data for both men and women indicate expectations of substantial direct and indirect pressures both to have a first and second child, and to limit family size after having a fifth.

The data on these and the family-size boundary questions, taken together, support the basic thesis of the study: that there is disapproval of family sizes outside the boundaries of the two-to-four or five-child range, and that this social response is reflected in direct and indirect pressures on couples to bring their family size intentions and performance into conformity with social expectations about "acceptable" family sizes.

ADDITIONAL ANALYSES

In addition to the basic analysis of men's and women's expectations of family size pressures at different parities, a series of further analyses was carried out. This included analyses by: age (comparing respondents 18–29 with those 30–39) to study possible changes in family size pressures associated with recent trends to smaller family size intentions; religion (Catholic and non-Catholic), in order to determine whether Catholics' relatively large family size experience is reflected in qualitatively different kinds of family size pressures at different parities; educational level (high school graduate or less and attended and/or completed college); and, for women, current employment status. The findings of these analyses can be briefly summarized:

Age. Age differences are small and do not support the idea of a major trend to weaker social pressures to have a first or second child. For instance, somewhat fewer of the younger men and women expect overt pressure to have a first child, but even among the younger respondents, three-fifths of the men and two-thirds of the women expect such pressures. And, while somewhat more of the younger respondents expect peer and family pressure to limit family size after having a fifth child, the age differences are not great (around eight percent). Greater differences might have been found for the intermediate parities (having a third or fourth child), but this cannot be studied with these data.

Women's Employment Status. When employed and nonemployed women are compared, they do not show large or consistent differences in the expectation of family size pressures. Employed women are not insulated from pressures to have a first or second child, nor do they expect greater peer pressure to limit family size after a fifth child than do women who are not employed. This supports the argument frequently made that adult roles for women are defined primarily in terms of being a wife and being a mother and that occupational roles do not provide an alternative basis for confirming adult status for women.[8]

Religion. When respondents' expectations of family size pressures are analyzed by religion and sex, the responses show a clear and somewhat unexpected pattern. On the one hand, Catholic and non-Catholic women differ little in their expectations of family size pressures. Somewhat more Catholic than non-Catholic women expect pressures to have a first child, but non-Catholic women are *not* more likely than Catholics to expect pressures to limit family size after having a fifth child. Catholic men, however, expect substantially less pressure to have a second child or to limit their family after a fifth child than do Catholic women or non-Catholics of either sex.

Because of the lack of comparable data from earlier research, it is not possible to determine whether the sex difference in Catholics' expectations of family size pressures represents a long-standing difference or a more recent change. It may be that Catholic women have been more directly exposed to and sensitive to the recent trend away from large families than have Catholic men, and thus are more aware of social pressures for family limitation. Catholic men, by contrast, appear to be quite insulated from these kinds of changes.

The unexpected finding that Catholic and non-Catholic women do not differ in their expectations of pressure to limit family size after having a fifth child was examined further in a tabulation controlling for educational status. This tabulation showed that, among the less-educated (high school graduate or less education), religious differences in the expectation of family limitation pressures were small, while among the better-educated (at least some college education), fewer of the Catholic than the non-Catholic women expect such pressures. And, among Catholic women, more of the less-educated than the better-educated expect pressure to limit family size after a fifth child. Analyses of other data in the survey showed that less-educated Catholic women express greater tolerance of relatively large family sizes and attitudes more favorable to large families than do better-educated Catholic women. It appears that much of the family limitation pressure on Catholic women reflects practical concerns about the problems of raising a large family, and does not necessarily indicate a major change away from values favorable to family sizes at least moderately larger than those of non-Catholics. Other recent data showing greater use of nonsanctioned means of contraception appear to reflect the same kind of practical accommodation to changing social and economic conditions.[9] Whether these changes and the convergence in the family size desires of Catholics and non-Catholics over recent years indicate a corresponding convergence in values relating to family size and family life generally is less clear.

Education. The effect of educational level on expectations of family size pressures was examined. The educational level categories used in the analysis were high school graduate or less, and attended and/or completed college.

The major finding of the analysis is that men and women with a high school education or less are generally similar to each other in their expectations of social pressures to have a first and second child, while among those with some college, the pressures appear substantially greater for women than for men. In particular, among the well-educated, more women than men expect: pressure from friends to have a first child (74 percent, compared with 55 percent); feeling out of place with married friends if they remained childless (62 percent, compared with 24 percent); pressure from friends to have a second child (71 percent, compared with 49 percent); and personally worrying that being an only child would be bad for the child (70 percent, compared with 48 percent). Among the less-educated, the differences are in the same direction, but are smaller in size.

Expectations of family and peer pressure to limit family size after a fifth child show sex differences (more women than men expect such pressures), but no educational level differences within each sex. These patterns persist when a control for religion is included.

These differences and, in particular, the well-educated men's low expectation of peer pressures to have a first and second child or internalized pressures to have a second, can be partially interpreted in terms of sex and occupational role differences. Well-educated men have access to highly valued occupational positions, performance in which provides confirmation of their standing as "successful" adults, whether or not they have children. Such positions may also provide a basis for friendships and activities in which children are less important than they are in the more neighborhood- and family-based friendships of lower status men and those of women of both status levels. In any event, whatever the basis of the difference, the greater discrepancies between high-status men and women in their expectations of pressures to have a first and, particularly, a second child have important implications for questions of family size decision-making and couples' family size intentions. These data on women's expectations of peer and personal pressure to have a first and second child, combined with other data indicating that, within status levels, more women than men oppose a family size as small as one child, suggest that among well-educated couples, the woman may be the internal lobby for having a second child, and perhaps for having a first child as well. From the data, it appears that, at higher status levels, the structure of external pressures and the kinds of concerns felt by the woman are quite different from those experienced by the man. For lower status men and women, the social context within which decisions about the first two births are made (or not made, as, for instance, through contraceptive 'accidents' or non-use of contraception) appears more congruent, or at least is perceived as more congruent by respondents at this level.

These findings indicate the practical and theoretical importance of examining qualitative differences in the kinds of considerations that influence family size decisions for well-educated men and women and the processes by which couples come to decisions about having a first and second child. In the terms of household decision-making analysis, it appears that remaining childless or having only one child has considerably higher personal and interpersonal costs for well-educated women than for comparable men.

SUMMARY AND COMMENT

The data on family size boundaries and expected social pressures at boundary parities demonstrate the existence of limits to acceptable family size and, particularly at the lower limit, the anticipated occurrence of social pressures to bring family size intentions into the acceptable family size range. The greater expectation of social pressure by women than by men is interpreted in terms of sex role differences in the importance of child-bearing and child-rearing and in the greater opportunities child-related activities provide for the communication and enforcement of expectations about the limits to acceptable family size.

The sex differences further suggest that the woman is the one through whom external social (as distinct from financial) pressures are brought into the couple's family size decisions.

The findings raise several questions about the recent trend toward intended family sizes of exactly two children, and the possible increase in the proportion expecting to have a one-child family.[10] While some young wives expect to have only one child, the findings of this study indicate that they are likely to be under considerable pressures, not only from family and friends but from their own concern for the child's welfare, to have a second child. Young women who have a child early in marriage and expect to have no more are exposed to the risk of accidental pregnancy for a long period. But, in addition, they are "exposed to the risk" of social pressure to have an additional child. The combination of these factors may well mean that relatively few women will complete child-bearing with only one child (subfecundity, divorce, or other external reasons excluded). Even for women who want to combine work and childbearing, social pressure to have a second child and personal concern for the child's welfare are likely to make a decision to have only one child a very difficult one to make and carry out.

Achievement and maintenance of average family sizes at or around the replacement level can be achieved either if there is a dispersion of family sizes around the level of two children (i.e., if the proportion having fewer than two children roughly balances the proportion having more than two), or if there is a great concentration of family sizes at exactly two children.

Data on "ideal" and preferred family sizes show a marked resistance to family sizes smaller than two children, as do data from the present study on family sizes regarded as "too small." And the findings about expected social pressure to have a first and second child indicate the existence of social pressures that help to maintain the two-child lower limit to acceptable family size and to discourage couples from having fewer than two children. Thus, unless major social or economic changes occur, there is reason to believe that, at least in the near future, the proportion of couples having one child or remaining childless will not be sufficiently large to counterbalance any substantial tendency for couples to have families larger than two children. This raises the question of whether the trend away from relatively large families to a family size of exactly two children is so firmly established that no trend to larger family sizes is likely to occur. The present study was primarily concerned with social pressures to influence family size intentions at the boundaries to the two-to-four-child family size range, so no data were obtained regarding family limitation (or expansion) pressures after having two, three, or four children. Because of this limitation, direct answers to the question cannot be offered on the basis of these data. Indirect evidence is available, however, from the data on family sizes reported as "too large" by respondents to the survey. These data (shown in Table 1) suggest that social pressures to limit family size after having a second, or even a third or fourth child may not be intense or widespread. The data show that somewhat more than half the men and women respondents think a family as large as five children is "too large," a figure consistent with the substantial proportion expecting social pressures to limit family size after having as many as five children. However, while two-fifths of the men say a four-child family is "too large," only one-fourth of the women say it is, and far fewer regard a three-child family as too large. These figures indicate widespread tolerance of families as large as three or four children by men and women in the main reproductive ages. Many couples may choose to have no more than two children, for social, personal or other reasons, and the data indicating that few people regard a two-child family as "too small" suggest that those who choose to have a family of exactly two children will not be under social pressure to have any more than two. However, the apparent tolerance for three- and four-child families suggests that couples who want to have three or four children will not be subject to strong social pressure *not* to have them.

These data suggest the absence or weakness of overt *social* pressures on couples to avoid having a third or fourth child. If such pressures are relatively weak, such personal factors as preference for one rather than another number of children (within the two-to-four-child range) or personal and financial circumstances are likely to serve as the major determinants of family size. Below two children and after five children, data from this study indicate that overt social pressures are brought to bear on couples to bring them into conformity with expectations about the limits to acceptable family size if they have "too few" children, or to prevent them from deviating further if they have "too many," but the expressed tolerance for three- and four-child families suggests that comparable social pressures will not be as strong at these intermediate parities within the acceptable family size range.

Insofar as such social pressures are weak, couples are relatively free to revise their family size intentions upward or downward within the acceptable family size range. Under these conditions, family size decisions are likely to be constrained primarily by personal or financial considerations rather than external social pressures. In this situation, the downward trend toward family sizes of exactly two children will not necessarily reverse, but it appears unsafe to assume that it necessarily will *not* reverse if economic or other conditions change. At least several possible economic and social changes that could contribute to a moderate upward revision of family size intentions can be suggested. For instance, a shift to a shorter work week and increased leisure time could contribute to greater involvement in family and family-related activities. If the relative costs of children did not increase at the same time, an expansion of family size to a third or fourth child could be attractive to many couples. The relatively low marginal costs of a third or fourth child—both the financial and the perceived personal or psychological costs—could facilitate such a moderate upward revision of family size intentions. A second kind of change that could affect family size intentions concerns employment opportunities for women. For married women, employment has been negatively associated with fertility, and employment can be regarded as a factor that exerts a downward pressure on fertility. A recent study projecting female labor supply and demand estimates concludes that in the next several decades job opportunities (particularly jobs attractive to better-educated women) may not expand sufficiently to absorb the supply of women wanting to work.[11] If this were to happen, one possible outcome could be a withdrawal of younger married women from the labor force into more home-centered activities and interests. Under these circumstances, it is possible to anticipate at least a moderate upward shift in fertility intentions, particularly in view of the apparent acceptance of three- and four-child families as not exceeding the socially prescribed upper limits to family size.

A shift to family sizes as large as five children seems unlikely. Such families have not been desired or achieved by any very large proportion of American families in recent decades.[12] And data from the present study indicating that a majority regard a five-child family as too large, and expect family and peer pressure to limit family size at that level, support the expectation that a shift to large family sizes (five or more) will not occur. However, even a "moderate" upward shift to three- and four-child families would have substantial demographic impact, in the absence of compensating increases in childless or one-child marriages.

The present research has focused largely on negative responses to family sizes outside the boundaries to acceptable family size. Data are needed on positive responses to both middle and extreme parities. If negative social responses are conceived of as a kind of "interpersonal cost" associated with a parity, positive responses can be regarded as a form of "interpersonal benefit." Data are also needed as to whether there are conditions under which couples who remain childless or have only one child are less subject to social pressure to have children, and the means by which couples effectively resist the pressures to which they are subject.

NOTES

1. J. Blake, "Ideal Family Size Among White Americans: A Quarter of a Century's Evidence," *Demography*, 3: 154, 1966; and "Coercive Pronatalism and American Population Policy," in R. Parke, Jr., and C. F. Westoff, eds., *Aspects of Population Growth Policy*, Vol. 6 of U.S. Commission on Population Growth and the American Future research reports, U.S. Government Printing Office, Washington, D.C. (GPO), 1972.

2. N. B. Ryder and C. F. Westoff, *Reproduction in the United States: 1965*, Princeton University Press, Princeton, N.J., 1971, p. 28.

3. U.S. Bureau of the Census, "Birth Expectations of American Wives: June 1973," *Current Population Reports*, Series P-20, No. 54, October 1973.

4. The Opinion Research Corporation of Princeton, New Jersey, fields survey questionnaires to a nationally projectable sample of 2,000 adults every two months on a variety of topics, and commercial or academic organizations may pay to have specific questions included.

5. This is the maximum of respondents to these questions. The numbers in the tables vary slightly because of varying numbers of nonrespondents.

6. The table entries are the cumulative percentage of respondents saying "n" or more children makes a family too small (top panel), and the cumulative percentage saying "n" or fewer children makes a family too large (bottom panel). The rationale for the cumulation procedure is that each individual's response is assumed to represent a limit, and to be transitive (e.g., if a respondent says five children makes a family too large, we are assuming that he also would say that six, seven or any larger number is too large, but that a family of four or fewer children is not too large). The cumulation procedure gives an aggregate limit by showing, for each number of children, the proportion of respondents for whom that number makes

a family too large or too small. The size of the 'step' between consecutive family sizes (the additional percentage saying one child more makes a family too large, or one child fewer makes it too small) is an indication of the sharpness of the boundary between these family sizes.

7. While it would have been desirable to include questions covering the whole range from three to six or more children, this was not done because of cost, and concern that the question sequence would have become repetitive and tedious. As a consequence, we do not have a full picture of the expectations of social sanctions through the whole moderate-to-large family size range. We may assume that those who expect pressure to limit family size after having a fifth child would also expect such pressure after having a sixth or higher order birth. But we cannot be sure that the respondents who expect social pressures to limit family size after a fifth birth would not also expect it after a fourth. The break in acceptability between four- and five-child families discussed in the preceding section suggests this may occur, but we cannot determine this with the data collected in this study.

8. A. S. Rossi, "Transition to Parenthood," *Journal of Marriage and the Family*, 30:26, 1968; and J. Blake, "Coercive Pronatalism . . . ," 1972, op. cit.

9. C. F. Westoff, "Changes in Contraceptive Practices Among Married Couples," in C. F. Westoff, et al., eds., *Toward the End of Growth*, Prentice-Hall, N.J., 1973, p. 19.

10. A. A. Campbell, "Three Generations of Parents," *Family Planning Perspectives*, 5:106, 1973; and L. L. Bumpass, "Is Low Fertility Here to Stay?" *Family Planning Perspectives*, 5:67, 1973.

11. V. K. Oppenheimer, "Demographic Influence on Female Employment and the Status of Women," *American Journal of Sociology*, 78:946, 1973.

12. A. A. Campbell, 1973, op. cit.

23

The Revolution in Birth Control Practices of U.S. Roman Catholics

Charles F. Westoff and Larry Bumpass

Ever since the 1968 papal encyclical ended the period of ambiguity and speculation about the Roman Catholic Church's position on birth control, there has been considerable interest in how American Catholics would respond to the reaffirmation of the traditional ban on methods of contraception other than the rhythm method. The trend toward conformity documented in the 1965 National Fertility Study (NFS) (*1*), the observed reduction in the rate of unwanted births among all groups, including Catholics, during the 1960's (*2*), and the sharp decline in U.S. fertility rates all combine to enhance the plausibility of the hypothesis that Catholic couples have increasingly adopted unapproved methods of contraception. An analysis based on reinterviews with Catholic women in the 1965 study supports this view (*3*).

This report presents data from the 1970 NFS, a probability sample survey in which 6752 ever-married women of reproductive age (under 45) were interviewed across the nation (*4*). Our analysis is based on currently married, white Catholic women living with their husbands. Data for our subsample of the 1970 NFS are analyzed in conjunction with data on comparable women in the 1965 NFS and two earlier U.S. fertility surveys conducted in 1955 (*5*) and 1960 (*6*).

CONCEPTS AND MEASURES

While "current use" is appropriate for describing the contraceptive practices of the population at any given time, "most recent use" is more appro-

Reprinted from *Science*, 179, no. 5 (January, 1973), pp. 41–44, by permission of the author and the publisher. Copyright 1973 by the American Association for the Advancement of Science.

priate for measuring the *usual* contraceptive practices. At any given time, many couples are not using any method simply because the wife is pregnant, trying to become pregnant, or in postpartum. Others may not be practicing birth control for a variety of reasons such as illness, involuntary sterility, or temporary separation. It is a couple's usual method of contraception that is most relevant to the issue of Catholic conformity. Of course, some couples who are not currently using any method will change methods when they begin practicing birth control again; and to the extent that such changes are away from conformity, as seems most likely, our measure understates the level of nonconformity.

The concept of "conformity" is defined here as following the traditional teaching of the Roman Catholic Church, reaffirmed by the encyclical, which prohibits the use of any method of fertility control other than periodic continence, the so-called rhythm method. There are two categories of Catholic women who are classified as conforming to Church doctrine: those who have never used any method of contraception and those whose most recent practice was the rhythm method (7).

TREND IN CATHOLIC CONFORMITY

By linking the 1955 and 1960 Growth of American Family studies with the 1965 and 1970 National Fertility studies, we can observe the trend in Catholic conformity over a 15-year period. Table 1 shows a dramatic

TABLE 1. Percentage of white, married Catholic women age 18 to 39 who have never used any method of contraception or who most recently used rhythm or some other method (1, 5, 6). Data for 1965 differ from earlier data because "sterilization for contraceptive reasons" was not previously included as a form of contraception.

Most recent method	Women per year (%)			
	1955 (N = 787)	1960 (N = 668)	1965 (N = 846)	1970 (N = 1035)
None	43	30	21	18
Rhythm	27	31	28	14
Other	30	38	51	68

change in the adherence of Catholic women to their Church's teaching on birth control. The proportion of Catholic women between the ages of 18 and 39 (8) who use methods of contraception other than rhythm has increased from 30 percent in 1955 to 68 percent in 1970, with the greatest changes occurring in the last 5 years. Between 1965 and 1970, the percentage of Catholic women deviating from official teaching on birth control has risen from 51 to 68 percent. It seems clear that the papal encyclical has not retarded the increasing defection of Catholic women from this teaching.

This trend is even more apparent when the data are examined by the women's age and year of birth across all four studies (vertical comparisons, Table 2). There has been a spectacular increase in nonconformity among

TABLE 2. Percentage of white, married Catholic women not conforming to Church teaching on birth control. In the 1955 and 1960 studies (on the top and second diagonals, respectively), a woman is classified as not conforming to Church teaching if she had ever used any method of contraception other than rhythm. In the 1965 and 1970 data (third and bottom diagonals, respectively) the classification relates to the method most recently used.

Year of birth	Age of women (years)				
	20 to 24 (%)	25 to 29 (%)	30 to 34 (%)	35 to 39 (%)	40 to 44 (%)
1916–1920				28	45
1921–1925			30	46	43
1926–1930		37	40	52	50
1931–1935	30	40	50	50	
1936–1940	43	54	68		
1941–1945	51	74			
1946–1950	78				

Catholic women in the youngest age groups. Among women aged 20 to 24 in the year of each study, the proportion not conforming was 30 percent in 1955, 43 percent 5 years later, 51 percent by 1965, and 78 percent by 1970. The increase from 1955 to 1970 was almost as great for the next two age groups: from 37 to 74 percent for ages 25 to 29 and from 30 to 68 percent for ages 30 to 34.

The increase in nonconformity that occurs as women grow older is revealed by the horizontal comparisons in Table 2. For example, of Catholic women born between 1936 and 1940, 43 percent were deviating from Church teaching by age 20 to 24 in 1960, 54 percent by age 25 to 29 in 1965, and 68 percent were not conforming by the time this cohort had reached 30 to 34 years of age in 1970. It is not surprising that women tend to adopt more effective methods as they grow older; as a cohort ages, increasing proportions have had all of the children they want and thus face the risk of unwanted pregnancies. In this light, it is interesting to speculate about the ultimate nonconformity of the youngest women in these studies. Women who were age 20 to 24 in 1970 were already at the 78 percent level, and it seems likely that their birth control practices will become indistinguishable from those of non-Catholics, reaching a maximum of around 90 percent. (The remaining 10 percent will be comprised of those who discover subfecundity before ever having practiced contraception and therefore never use any method as well as a small fraction who use the rhythm method successfully.)

EDUCATION

In 1965, nonconformity was greatest (57 percent) among Catholic women who had not completed high school and least (40 percent) among those who had attended or graduated from college (1, pp. 198–200) (Table 3).

TABLE 3. Percentage of white, married Catholic women, by age and education, who have never used any method of contraception or whose most recent method was rhythm or the pill ("College" refers to women who attended or graduated from college).

| | Age of women (years) | | | | | |
| | Under 45 (%) | | Under 30 (%) | | 30 to 44 (%) | |
Education	1965	1970	1965	1970	1965	1970
	Not conforming (%)					
College	40	65	42	78	38	53
Grade 12	47	67	51	76	45	58
Less than grade 12	57	63	57	73	57	55
Total	49	65	51	76	48	56
	Pill (%)					
College	13	29	24	42	6	16
Grade 12	13	29	24	38	6	20
Less than grade 12	11	25	23	35	5	17
Total	12	28	24	38	6	19
	Other (%)					
College	27	36	19	35	32	36
Grade 12	34	38	26	38	39	38
Less than grade 12	45	38	34	37	52	38
Total	37	37	28	37	42	37
	Rhythm (%)					
College	39	19	36	10	41	27
Grade 12	34	16	31	12	36	20
Less than grade 12	13	7	11	4	14	9
Total	28	14	25	10	29	19
	None (%)					
College	21	16	22	12	21	21
Grade 12	19	17	18	12	19	22
Less than grade 12	30	30	31	23	29	35
Total	23	19	23	14	23	24
	Size of sample (No.)					
College	166	262	59	127	107	135
Grade 12	548	701	211	351	337	350
Less than grade 12	369	287	131	121	238	166
Total	1083	1250	401	599	682	651

By 1970, this relationship had reversed among younger Catholics, with college women deviating from Church teaching slightly more than women who had not completed high school.

These changes are due to a dramatic increase in nonconformity among the more educated Catholic women, an increase that has taken the form of a marked reduction in reliance on rhythm and a corresponding increase in the use of the pill. The college-educated and the high school-educated are now virtually indistinguishable in terms of birth control practice. The rhythm method is at least popular among the least educated women, but the largest proportion of women who have never used contraception are still found in this group.

RELIGIOUSNESS

It is important to determine whether the increase in nonconformity between 1965 and 1970 is the result of attrition from the Church in general or simply of rejection of the prohibition against birth control in particular. Our analysis seems to indicate that both trends are occurring: that Catholic women (and presumably men as well) are moving away from traditional formal practice, but, much more important for the increase in nonconformity, that those women who continue such formal practice are increasingly just ignoring Church teaching on birth control.

It should be emphasized that we have not undertaken any extensive or intensive study of the religious practices or attitudes of Roman Catholics in this country. Our conclusions are based on only one index of religious behavior although a very significant one: the frequency with which a woman receives Holy Communion. We have divided the women into two categories: those who receive Communion at least once a month (the more committed) and those who receive it less frequently (the less committed). Since receiving Communion at least once a month exceeds the minimum obligation (which is once a year), this dichotomy differentiates Catholics who adhere more closely to their faith from those whose attachment is weaker or just nominal.

There has been a decrease in the proportion of Catholic women who receive Communion at least monthly, from 52 percent in 1965 to 44 percent in 1970. Most of this change has been concentrated among the younger women, for whom the proportion receiving Communion monthly or more frequently declined from 52 to 37 percent.

Overall, nonconformity to teachings on birth control increased 16 percent between 1965 and 1970 (from 49 to 65 percent). If there had been no change in the proportion of women receiving Communion at least monthly, the increase in nonconformity would have been 14 percent. Thus, the change caused by a decline in religious practice is fairly small, amounting to about an eighth of the overall increase in nonconformity. This is true as well among the younger women, whose deviation from Church teaching on birth control has been greatest; only 2 percent of the 24 percent increase in nonconformity is attributable to a decline in religious practice.

Consequently, the primary source of the increase in nonconformity is a willingness to deviate from Church teaching on this particular issue. In 1970, the majority (53 percent) of the more committed Catholic women were deviating from the official position on birth control, a remarkable increase from the 33 percent so classified in 1965 (Table 4). Even more remarkable, and perhaps an indication of changes yet to come, is the increase in nonconformity among the younger, more committed Catholic women: from 38 percent in 1965 to 67 percent by 1970. The increase among older, more committed Catholic women was from 30 to 44 percent.

Among less committed Catholic women there has been an increase in nonconformity only in the younger generation—from 66 percent in 1965 to 81 percent in 1970. Only the older, less committed Catholic women showed no change in conformity over the 5-year period: at both times, some two-thirds were not conforming to Church teaching on birth control.

The pill has played a major role in the decreasing conformity of the more committed Catholic women. Among women under 30, its use increased from 20 percent in 1965 to 37 percent in 1970. Almost exactly the reverse obtained for the rhythm method, which declined in use from 38 percent in 1965 to 18 percent in 1970. There was also a significant decrease in the proportion of more committed women in the younger generation who had never used any method (from 24 percent in 1965 to 15 percent in 1970) and an increase in the proportion of those using unapproved methods other than the pill (from 18 to 30 percent). Most of this latter increase was brought about by the adoption of newer methods—the intrauterine device (IUD) and foam.

Among older Catholic women, the more committed shifted from rhythm to the pill, but among the less committed women of this generation the increase in the popularity of the pill was at the expense of methods other than rhythm.

THE CONVERGENCE OF RELIGIOUS DIFFERENCES

One consequence of the increasing nonconformity of Catholics in the area of birth control has been to diminish the differences between Catholic and non-Catholic contraceptive practices. In the period between 1965 and 1970, a marked convergence has occurred (Table 5) in the proportion using every method except surgical sterilization. The blurring of the dif-

TABLE 4. Percentage of white, married Catholic women, by age and frequency of receiving Holy Communion, who have never used any method or who most recently used rhythm, the pill, or other methods.

Age of women (years)

	Receive Communion at least monthly						Receive Communion less than monthly					
	Under 45 (%)		Under 30 (%)		30 to 44 (%)		Under 45 (%)		Under 30 (%)		30 to 44 (%)	
Most recent method	1965 (N= 558)	1970 (N= 554)	1965 (N= 207)	1970 (N= 221)	1965 (N= 351)	1970 (N= 323)	1965 (N= 525)	1970 (N= 706)	1965 (N= 199)	1970 (N= 378)	1965 (N= 331)	1970 (N= 328)
None	25	23	24	15	25	29	21	17	22	14	20	21
Rhythm	42	23	38	18	45	27	12	8	12	5	12	11
Pill	11	26	20	37	5	18	14	30	28	39	6	19
Other	22	27	18	30	25	26	53	45	39	41	61	48
Total not conforming	33	53	38	67	30	44	67	75	67	80	67	67

TABLE 5. Method of contraception used most recently by married, white non-Catholic (NC) and Catholic (C) women, by age.

Most recent method	Under 45 (%)				Age of women (years) Under 30 (%)				30 to 44 (%)			
	1965		1970		1965		1970		1965		1970	
	NC (N= 2666)	C (N= 1090)	NC (N= 3708)	C (N= 1255)	NC (N= 1038)	C (N= 403)	NC (N= 1723)	C (N= 602)	NC (N= 1628)	C (N= 687)	NC (N= 1985)	C (N= 653)
Sterilized†	10	4	12	5	5	2	5	2	12	5	19	8
Pill‡	21	12	33	28	37	24	49	38	11	6	19	19
IUD§	1	*	5	6	1	*	6	7	1	*	4	4
Diaphragm¶	12	4	7	4	8	1	3	3	15	5	10	5
Condom‖	20	14	12	10	17	11	10	10	22	15	15	11
Withdrawal	4	6	2	2	3	2	1	1	5	9	2	3
Foam	3	1	6	5	5	2	8	8	2	1	3	3
Rhythm	4	28	3	14	3	25	2	10	5	29	4	19
Douche	5	3	4	3	4	3	2	3	6	3	5	3
Other#	6	5	4	3	6	5	3	4	6	4	4	2
None	13	23	12	19	12	23	9	14	15	23	15	24

* Less than 1 percent.   † Surgical procedures undertaken at least party for contraceptive reasons.   ‡ Includes combinations with any other method.
§ Includes combinations with any method other than the pill.   ¶ Includes combinations with any method other than the pill or the IUD.   ‖ Includes combinations with any method other than the pill, IUD, or diaphragm.   # Includes other multiple, as well as single, methods and a small percentage of unreported methods.

ference between Catholics and non-Catholics is most evident among younger women, which suggests that the differential for all women will diminish even further in the years ahead. It does not seem at all unlikely that by the end of the decade Catholics and non-Catholics will be virtually indistinguishable in their birth control practices. This will occur as the proportion of Catholics who have never used any method and those who use the rhythm method continues to decline and the proportion using the pill (and perhaps even the more radical procedure of sterilization) increases.

SUMMARY AND CONCLUSIONS

There has been a wide and increasing defection of Roman Catholic women from the traditional teaching of their Church on the subject of birth control over the past two decades and a resulting convergence of Catholic and non-Catholic contraceptive practices. By 1970, two-thirds of all Catholic women were using methods disapproved by their Church; this figure reached three-quarters for women under age 30. Considering the fact that most of the one-quarter of young Catholic women conforming to Church teaching had never used any method, the percentage of those deviating may well reach 90 as these women grow older and the problems of fertility control become more important.

Much of this increasing deviation has been among the more educated Catholics, who were formerly the most faithful adherents to Church teaching. The change between 1965 and 1970 was especially striking for Catholic women who had attended college.

Perhaps the most significant finding is that the defection has been most pronounced among the women who receive Communion at least once a month. Even among this group, the majority now deviates from Church teaching on birth control; among the younger women in this group, the proportion not conforming reaches two-thirds.

It seems abundantly clear that U.S. Catholics have rejected the 1968 papal encyclical's statement on birth control and that there exists a wide gulf between the behavior of most Catholic women, on the one hand, and the position of the more conservative clergy and the official stand of the Church itself, on the other. That many Catholics can continue in their other religious practices and simultaneously deviate on the issue of birth control is an interesting commentary on the process of social change.

Ultimately this crisis of authority will probably be resolved by a change in official teaching, since it seems doubtful that such a major discrepancy can continue indefinitely without other repercussions. At a minimum, the cost to the Roman Catholic Church will be a loss of authority in a major area of life: that of sex and reproduction.

REFERENCES AND NOTES

1. N. B. Ryder and C. F. Westoff, *Reproduction in the United States: 1965* (Princeton University Press, Princeton, N.J., 1971).

2. ———, in *Demographic and Social Aspects of Population Growth*, C. F. Westoff and R. Parke, Jr., Eds. (Government Printing Office, Washington, D.C., in press).

3. C. F. Westoff and N. B. Ryder, *Stud. Fam. Planning No. 50* (1970), p. 1.

4. The 1970 National Fertility Study is supported by the Center for Population Research of the National Institute for Child Health and Human Development under contract with the Office of Population Research, Princeton University. The fieldwork was conducted by the Institute for Survey Research, Temple University.

5. R. Freedman, P. K. Whelpton, A. A. Campbell, *Family Planning, Sterility and Population Growth* (McGraw-Hill, New York, 1959).

6. P. K. Whelpton, A. A. Campbell, J. E. Patterson, *Fertility and Family Planning in the United States* (Princeton University Press, Princeton, N.J., 1966).

7. This measure differs somewhat from that employed in the 1965 National Fertility Study, which included in the measure of conformity only those women who had never used any contraception or whose *only* practice, rather than whose most recent practice, was rhythm. This redefinition reduces only slightly the estimate of nonconformity; for example, in 1965 the estimates of nonconformity were 28 and 25 percent, respectively, under the two definitions.

8. The age range of 18 to 39 is used when comparisons are involved with the earlier studies because of their sample design. Subsequent tables are based on women under 45.

24

Voluntarily Childless Wives:
An Exploratory Study*

J. E. Veevers

In-depth unstructured interviews with a non-random sample of 52 voluntarily childless wives suggest that most remain childless through a series of postponements of child-bearing, involving at least four separate stages. Informal sanctioning of childless couples is most intense during the fourth and fifth years of marriage. Factors related to satisfaction with childlessness are discussed in terms of the symbolic importance of adoption and of supportive ideologies.

Students of the family have generally tended to accept the dominant cultural values that married couples should have children, and should want to have them. As a result of this value bias, although parenthood (especially voluntary parenthood) has been extensively studied, the phenomenon of childlessness has been virtually ignored.[1] This selective inattention is unfortunate, for to a large extent the social meanings of parenthood can be comprehensively described and analyzed only in terms of the parallel set of meanings which are assigned to nonparenthood.[2] Although sociologists have occasionally discussed the theoretical relevance of voluntary childlessness, and have speculated regarding some empirical aspects of it,[3] virtually no direct research has been conducted. As a preliminary step towards filling this gap in the sociological study of the family, an exploratory study of voluntarily childless wives was conducted. The present article will not attempt to describe this research in its entirety, but rather will be

Reprinted from *Sociology and Social Research*, 57 (April, 1973), University of Southern California, Los Angeles, California, 90007, pp. 356–66, by permission of the author and the publisher.

* A revised version of a paper presented at the Annual Meeting of the National Council of Family Relations held in Portland, Oregon, November 1–4, 1972. The author is indebted to Professor Norman Bell of the University of Toronto for his many suggestions and for his assistance at all stages of the research.

concerned with brief discussions of four aspects of it: first, the career paths whereby women come to be voluntarily childless; second, the social pressures associated with that decision; third, the symbolic importance attributed to the possibility of adoption; and fourth, the relevance of supportive ideologies relating to concern with feminism, and with population problems.

SELECTION AND NATURE OF THE SAMPLE

Conventional sampling techniques cannot readily be applied to obtain large and representative samples of voluntarily childless couples.[4] Only about five percent of all couples voluntarily forego parenthood,[5] and this small deviant minority is characterized by attitudes and behaviors which are both socially unacceptable and not readily visible. The present research, which is exploratory in nature, is based on depth interviews with a purposive sample of 52 voluntarily childless wives. Although the utilization of non-random samples without control groups is obviously not the ideal approach, and can yield only suggestive rather than definitive conclusions, in examining some kinds of social behaviors it is often the only alternative to abandoning the inquiry.

In the present study, respondents were solicited by three separate articles appearing in newspapers in Toronto and in London, followed up by advertisements explicitly asking for volunteers. Of the 86 individuals who replied, 52 wives were selected. Three criteria were evoked in these selections. First, the wife must have stated clearly that her childlessness was due to choice rather than to biological accident. Second, she must either have been married for a minimum of five years, or have been of post-menopausal age, or have reported that either she or her husband had been voluntarily sterilized for contraceptive purposes. Third, she must have affirmed that she had never borne a child, and had never assumed the social role of mother.

The interviews, which were unstructured, averaged about four hours in length, and included discussion of the woman's life history, considerable detail concerning her marriage and her husband, and attitudinal and evaluative aspects of her responses to the maternal role. Data are thus available on the characteristics of 104 voluntarily childless husbands and wives, whose demographic and social characteristics may be briefly summarized as follows. The average age of the sample is 29, with a range from 23 to 71 years. All are Caucasian and living in urban areas, most are middle class, and many are upwardly mobile. Although educational experience ranges from grade school to the post doctoral level, most have at least some university experience. With the exception of one housewife, all are either employed full-time or attending university. Most individuals are either atheists or agnostics from Protestant backgrounds, and of the minority who do express some religious preference, almost all are inactive. Most individuals come from stable homes where the mother has been a full-time housewife since her first child was born. The incidence of first born and only children is much higher than would ordinarily be expected.

With the exception of two widowers, all of the subjects in the present research are involved in their first marriage. The average marriage duration is seven years, with a range from three to twenty-five years. Most couples have relatively egalitarian relationships, but still maintain conventional marriages and follow the traditional division of labor. Configurations of marital adjustment cover the entire continuum described by Cuber and Haroff,[6] ranging from conflict-habituated to total relationships, with many wives reporting vital or total relationships with their husbands.

All of the couples agree on the desirability of preventing pregnancy, at least at the present time. Most of the wives had never been pregnant, but about a fifth had had at least one induced abortion, and most indicate they would seek an abortion if pregnant. More than half of the wives are presently on the pill. About a quarter of the husbands have obtained a vasectomy, and another quarter are seriously considering doing so. Many of the women express positive interest in tubal ligation, but only one, a girl of 23, has actually been sterilized.

THE NATURE OF CHILDLESS CAREERS

In reviewing the processes whereby couples come to define themselves as voluntarily childless, two characteristic career paths are apparent. One route to childlessness involves the formulation by the couple, before they are even married, of a definite and explicitly stated intention never to become involved in parental roles; a second and more common route is less obvious, and involves the prolonged postponement of childbearing until such time as it was no longer considered desirable at all. These two alternatives will be elaborated.

Nearly a third of the wives interviewed entered into their marriages with a childlessness clause clearly stated in their marriage "contract." Although none of these women had a formal written contract in the legal sense of the word, the husband and wife explicitly agreed upon childlessness as a firm condition of marriage. The woman deliberately sought a future mate who, regardless of his other desirable qualities, would agree on this one dimension. Generally the negative decisions regarding the value of children were made during early adolescence, before the possibility of marriage had ever been seriously considered. In contrast, a few of the wives had indifferent or even vaguely positive attitudes towards childbearing until they met their future husbands. During their courtship and engagement, they gradually allowed themselves to be converted to the world view of voluntary childlessness, and by the time of their marriage were quite content to agree to never have children.

More than two thirds of the wives studied remained childless as a result of a series of decisions to postpone having children until some future time, a future which never came. Rather than explicitly rejecting motherhood prior to marriage, they repeatedly deferred procreation until a more convenient time. These temporary postponements provided time during which the evaluations of parenthood were gradually reassessed relative to other goals and possibilities. At the time of their marriages, most wives involved in the postponement model had devoted little serious thought to the question of having children, and had no strong feelings either for or against motherhood. Like conventional couples, they simply assumed that they would have one or two children eventually; unlike conventional couples, they practiced birth control conscientiously and continuously during the early years of marriage.[7]

Most couples involved in the postponement pattern move through four separate stages in their progression from wanting to not wanting children. The first stage involves postponement for a definite period of time. In this stage, the voluntarily childless are indistinguishable from conventional and conforming couples who will eventually become parents. In most groups, it is not necessarily desirable for the bride to conceive during her honeymoon. It is considered understandable that before starting a family a couple might want to achieve certain goals, such as graduating from school, travelling, buying a house, saving a nest egg, or simply getting adjusted to one another. The degree of specificity varies, but there is a clear commitment to have children as soon as conditions are right.

The second stage of this career involves a shift from postponement for a definite period of time to indefinite postponement. The couple remains committed to the idea of parenthood, but becomes increasingly vague about when the blessed event is going to take place. It may be when they can "afford it," or when "things are going better" or when they "feel more ready."

The third stage in the cycle involves another qualitative change in thinking, in that for the first time there is an open acknowledgment of the possibility that in the end the couple may remain permanently childless. The third stage is a critical one, in that the very fact of openly considering the pros and cons of having children may increase the probability of deciding not to. During this time, they have an opportunity to experience directly the many social, personal, and economic advantages associated with being childless, and at the same time to compare their life styles with those of their peers who are raising children. It seems probable that the social-psychological factors involved in the initial decision to postpone having children may be quite disparate from the social-psychological factors involved in the inclination to remain childless, and to continue with the advantages of a life style to which one has become accustomed. At this stage in the career, the only definite decision is to postpone deciding until some vague and usually unspecified time in the future.

Finally, a fourth stage involves the definite conclusion that the couple are never going to have children, and that childlessness is a permanent rather than a transitory state. Occasionally this involves an explicit decision, usually precipitated by some crisis or change in the environment that focuses attention on the question of parenthood. However, for most couples, there is never a direct decision made to have or avoid children. Rather, after a number of years of postponing pregnancy until some future date, they gradually become aware that an implicit decision has been made to forego parenthood. The process involved is one of recognizing an event which has already occurred, rather than of posing a question and then searching or negotiating for an answer. At first, it was "obvious" that "of course" they would eventually have children; now, it is equally "obvious" that they will not. The couple are at a loss to explain exactly how or when this transition came about, but they both agree on their new implicit decision, and they are both contented with its implications.

CHILDLESSNESS AND INFORMAL SANCTIONS

All of the wives interviewed feel that they are to some extent stigmatized by their unpopular decision to avoid having children, and that there exists an ubiquitous negative stereotype concerning the characteristics of a voluntarily childless woman, including such unfavorable traits as being abnormal, selfish, immoral, irresponsible, immature, unhappy, unfulfilled, and non-feminine.[8] In addition, these devaluating opinions are perceived to have behavioral consequences for their interaction with others, and to result in considerable social pressure to become mothers. Some of the sanctions reported are direct and obvious, including explicit and unsolicited comments advocating child-birth and presenting arguments relating to the importance of motherhood. Other pressures are more subtle, and in many cases are perceived to be unintentional. For example, the childless frequently complain that, whereas parents are never required to explain why they chose to have children, they are frequently required to account for their failure to do so.

Childlessness is of course not always a disapproved state. Couples are rewarded, not punished, for remaining childless for the first several months of marriage, and thereby negating the possibility that they were "forced" to get married. After the minimum of nine months has passed, there is a short period of time when the young couple is excused from not assuming all of their responsibilities, or are perceived as having been having intercourse for too short a period of time to guarantee conception. The definition of how long a period of time child bearing may be postponed and still meet with conventional expectations is difficult to determine, and apparently varies considerably from one group to another. In most groups, the first twelve months constitutes an acceptable period of time. After the first year, the pressure gradually but continually increases, reaching a peak during the third and fourth years of marriage. However, once a couple have been married for five or six years there appears to be some diminution of negative responses to them. Several factors are involved in this change: part may be attributable to the increased ability of the childless to avoid those who consistently sanction them; part may be attributable to the increased ability of the childless to cope with negative and hostile responses, making the early years only seem more difficult in retrospect; and part may reflect an actual change in the behavior of others. After five or six years, one's family and friends may give up the possibility of persuading the reluctant couple to procreate or to adopt, and resign themselves to the fact that intervention, at least in this case, is ineffective.

It is noteworthy that although all wives report considerable direct and indirect social pressures to become mothers, most are remarkably well defended against such sanctions. Although on specific occasions they may be either indignant or amused, in most instances they are indifferent to negative responses, and remain inner-directed, drawing constant support and reaffirmation from the consensual validation offered by their husbands. Many strategies are employed which "discredit the discreditors"[9] and which enable the voluntarily childless to remain relatively impervious to the comments of critics and the wishes of reformers. One such strategy concerns the possibility of adoption.

A recurrent theme in discussions with childless wives is that of adoption. Most wives mention that they have in the past considered adopting a child, and many indicate that they are still considering the possibility at some future date. However, in spite of such positive verbalizations, it is apparent that adoption is not seriously contemplated as a viable alternative, and that their considerations are not likely to result in actually assuming maternal roles. The lack of serious thought about adoption as a real possibility is reflected in the fact that generally they have not considered even such elementary questions as whether they would prefer a boy or a girl, or whether they would prefer an infant or an older child. With few exceptions, none of the couples have made even preliminary inquiries regarding the legal processes involved in adoption. Those few that had made some effort to at least contact a child placement agency had failed to follow through on their initial contact. None had investigated the issue thoroughly enough to have considered the possibility that, should they decide to adopt, a suitable child might not be immediately available to them.

For the voluntarily childless, the importance of the recurrent theme of adoption appears to lie in its symbolic value, rather than in the real possibility of procuring a child by this means and thereby altering one's life style. This symbolic importance is twofold: the reaffirmation of normalcy: and the avoidance of irreversible decisions. A willingness to consider adoption as a possibility communicates to one's self and to others that in spite of being voluntarily childless, one is still a "normal" and "well-adjusted" person who does like children, and who is willing to assume the responsibilities of parenthood. It is an effective mechanism for denying the possibility of considerable psychological differences between parents and non-parents,[10] and legitimates the claim of the childless to be just like parents in a number of important respects.

The possibility of adoption at a later date is of symbolic value, in that it prevents the voluntarily childless from being committed to an irreversible state. One of the problems of opting for a postponement model is that eventually one must confront the fact that childbirth cannot be postponed indefinitely. The solution to this dilemma is to include possibility of adoption as a satisfactory "out" should one be needed. The same strategy is employed by many couples who chose sterilization as a means of birth control, but who are not entirely comfortable with the absolute and irreversible solution. The theoretical possibility of adoption is also comforting when faced with the important but unanswerable question of how one will feel about being childless in one's old age.

THE RELEVANCE OF SUPPORTIVE IDEOLOGIES

The voluntarily childless appear to be in a state of pluralistic ignorance, in that they are unaware of the numbers of other individuals who share their world view. Although the deliberate decision to avoid parenthood is a relatively rare phenomenon, it is not nearly as rare as the childless themselves perceive it to be, especially among urban and well-educated middle class couples. A large proportion of wives indicated that until they read the article and/or advertisement asking for subjects for the present study, they had never seen the topic of voluntarily childlessness discussed in the mass media. Many reported that they did not know any other couple who felt as they did about the prospect of parenthood, and many others reported having met only one or two like-minded people during the course of their marriage.

Feelings of uniqueness and of isolation are somewhat mitigated by the explicit agreement of husbands on the appropriateness of foregoing parental roles. However, regardless of how supportive the husband is in his reaffirmation of the legitimacy of childlessness, and how committed he is personally to avoiding fatherhood, because of cultural differences in sex roles he does not share an entirely comparable situation. He may be totally sympathetic, but he has a limited ability to empathize. The childless wife may be generally comfortable with her decision not to have children, and still express the wish that she could discuss her situation with other like-minded women who might have shared similar experiences within the female sub-culture, and who might provide a model for identification.

It is noteworthy that within the psychological world of the voluntarily childless, existing social movements concerned with population or with feminism have surprisingly little relevance, and provide relatively little intellectual or emotional support. The concern with population problems, especially as manifest in the Zero Population Growth movement, does provide a supportive rationale indicating that one is not necessarily being socially irresponsible and neglectful of one's civic obligations if one does not reproduce. However, although there is a clear statement that procreation is not necessary for all, most ZPG advocates are careful to indicate that it is not procreation *per se* they are opposed to, but rather excessive procreation. The slogan "Stop at Two" asserts that one should have no more than two children, but also implies that one perhaps should have at least one or two. Some of the childless wives are superficially involved in ZPG and sympathetic with its goals, but in all cases this identification is an *ex post facto* consideration, rather than a motivating force, and their satisfaction with being childless is related to concerns other than to their contribution to the population crisis.

It is sometimes suggested that an inclination to avoid motherhood is a logical extension of the new feminism. It is difficult to generalize about a social phenomenon as amorphous as the women's liberation movement, a rubric which incorporates many diverse and even contradictory attitudes. However, "A significant feature of the women's liberation movement is that, although its demands have been made on the basis of equity for women, it has not usually been anti-marriage or anti-children."[11]

In many instances, the ideological statements endorsed by the women's liberation movement are implicitly or explicitly pro-natalist. Motherhood is not perceived as an unfulfilling and unrewarding experience; rather, it is perceived as a positive experience which, although desirable, is not sufficient in and of itself for maximum self-actualization. Considerable concern is expressed with the problems involved in combining successful motherhood with comparable success in other careers. Rather than advising women to give up having children, the new feminist literature advises them to consider other careers in addition to motherhood, and advocates changes in society which would make the motherhood role easier. For example, there is considerable stress on the provision of maternity leaves, on increased involvement of fathers in childcare, on accessibility to adequate day care facilities. Although advocates of the new feminism may provide some support for the idea that motherhood is neither necessary nor sufficient for fulfillment, they do still advocate that normally it will be an important part of that fulfillment. Only a few of the voluntarily childless are at all concerned with women's liberation, and these few apparently came into the movement after their decision was made and their lifestyle was established.

Although none of the voluntarily childless are actively seeking group support for their life style, many would welcome the opportunity to become involved in a truly supportive social movement. The first example of such an association is the National Organization for Nonparenthood (NON), which was formed in California in 1971. Because of the state of pluralistic ignorance which surrounds voluntary childlessness, and because of the inadequacy of demographic and feminist movements in expressing the world view of the childless, such attempts to formulate a counter-culture might be expected to be very successful.

SUMMARY

The present research on a purposive sample of 52 voluntarily childless wives is exploratory in nature. Although it is not possible to make definitive statements regarding the nature of childless couples, several tentative conclusions are offered. It is suggested that couples come to be voluntarily childless by a number of diverse paths beginning both before and after marriage, and that considerable diversity might be expected between those who enter marriage only on the condition of a clear childlessness clause in the marriage contract, and those who remain childless after a series of postponements of parenthood. Although considerable social pressures are directed towards the childless, most of the individuals involved appear to be very well defended against such sanctions, and the mechanisms of redefining situations and of protecting themselves are worthy of further study. One such mechanism appears to be the use of the possibility of adoption to deny the status of voluntary childlessness while not seriously threatening the accompanying life style. Finally, it is suggested that existing social movements do not provide much relevant support for the voluntarily childless, and that an explicit counter-culture, such as the National Organization of Nonparenthood, might be expected to meet with considerable success.

NOTES

1. J. E. Veevers, "Voluntary Childlessness: A Neglected Area of Family Study," *The Family Coordinator,* 21 (April, 1972), forthcoming.

2. J. E. Veevers, "The Social Meanings of Parenthood," *Psychiatry: Journal for the Study of Interpersonal Processes,* forthcoming.

3. Edward Pohlman, "Childlessness: Intentional and Unintentional," *The Journal of Nervous and Mental Disease,* 151 (number one, 1970), 2–12.

4. Susan O. Gustavus and James R. Henly, Jr., "Correlates of Voluntary Childlessness in a Select Population," *Social Biology,* 18 (September, 1971), 277–84.

5. J. E. Veevers, "Factors in the Incidence of Childlessness in Canada: An Analysis of Census Data," *Social Biology,* 19 (December, 1972), forthcoming.

6. John F. Cuber and Peggy B. Haroff, *Sex and the Significant Americans: A Study of Sexual Behavior Among the Affluent* (Baltimore, Maryland: Penguin Books, 1966).

7. Pascal K. Whelpton, Arthur A. Campbell and J. E. Patterson report in one study that nearly two out of three newlyweds do not start using contraception before the first conception. See their *Fertility and Family Planning in the United States* (Princeton, New Jersey: Princeton University Press, 1966), 221.

8. J. E. Veevers, "The Violation of Fertility Mores: Voluntary Childlessness as Deviant Behavior," in Craig L. Boydell, Carl F. Grindstaff and Paul C. Whitehead (eds.), *Deviant Behavior and Societal Reaction* (Toronto: Holt, Rinehart and Winston, 1972), 571–92.

9. J. E. Veevers, "The Moral Career of Voluntarily Childless Wives: Notes on the Construction and Defense of a Deviant World View," in S. Parvez Wakil (ed.), *Marriage and the Family in Canada* (Toronto: Longmans Green, 1973) forthcoming.

10. J. E. Veevers, "The Social Meanings of Parenthood," *op. cit.*

11. Commission on Population Growth and the American Future, *Report* (Washington, D.C.: Commission on Population Growth and the American Future, 1972), 68.

25

Continuities in the Explanation of Fertility Control

John Scanzoni and Martha McMurry

The issue of fertility control is discussed in a context of reward-alternatives. Specifically, the suggestion is made that redefinitions by some younger women of the female sex role may be a critical factor influencing fertility differentials, particularly as long-standing fertility predictors appear to be losing some of their discriminatory power. Also discussed are implications for male sex role and family structure, and implications for the traditionally inverse association of social position and fertility.

Social scientists have traditionally relied heavily on demographic variables in their attempts to explain reproductive behavior. Taeuber and Taeuber (1966:154) maintain that these attempts have been relatively unsuccessful, and the same could be said of various efforts to incorporate certain social psychological variables. Furthermore, the demographic factors which previously had been the best predictors of fertility (income, education, occupation) have been gradually declining in predictive power as contraceptives became diffused throughout the population, and as fertility desires seem to range between two and four children for most Americans throughout the status structure (Kiser, 1968).

Declining fertility differentials have not, however, produced total homogeneity among all Americans with respect to: (1) family size desires; (2) contraceptive efficacy; or (3) completed family size. In this paper we shall attempt to contribute to the explanation of continued variation in these three classic dependent variables of fertility research. We shall take the position that at a general level, norms and behaviors surrounding fertility

Reprinted from *Journal of Marriage and the Family*, 34, no. 2 (May, 1972), pp. 315–22, by permission of the authors and the publisher. Copyright 1972 by National Council of Family Relations.

can be viewed in a context of "reward alternatives"; and that at a more specific level, varying definitions of the female sex role may have an impact on fertility desires and control.

SEX ROLE AND FERTILITY

It is possible to argue that having children is a socially motivated form of behavior that provides institutionalized rewards to parents. To the extent that other kinds of rewards are seen as alternatives to childbearing and are also perceived as accessible, the motivation to have children may be reduced and fertility may then be depressed. This point of view is argued cogently by Blake (1965) who states:

> Children are high on the list of adult utilities. Offspring are not simply outlets (and inlets) for affection, they are the instrumentalities for achieving virtually prescribed social statuses ("mother" and "father"), the almost exclusive avenues for feminine creativity and achievement. . . . Until nonfamilial roles begin to offer significant competition to familial ones as avenues for adult satisfaction, the family will probably continue to amaze us with its procreative powers.

Besides Blake, there are others who have iterated the sex role-fertility theme. Hoffman and Wyatt (1960) point out that,

> having a child is highly creative both in the sense of producing it and in the social sense of molding it . . . the care of the infant provides an area where the woman (in America) is not replaceable. . . . Bearing and mothering children are important as proofs of femininity . . . this is the traditional feminine role. . . .

Or, as Davis (1967) puts it:

> If it were admitted that the creation and care of new human beings is socially motivated, like other forms of behavior, by being a part of the system of rewards and punishments that is built into human relationships, and thus is bound up with the individual's economic and personal interests, it would be apparent that the social structure and economy must be changed before a deliberate reduction in the birth rate can be achieved.

For Davis, "changes in social structure" include, among other things,

> modification of the complementarity of the roles of men and women. Men are now able to participate in the wider world, yet enjoy the satisfaction of having several children because the housework and childcare fall mainly on their wives. Women are impelled to seek this role by their idealized view of marriage and motherhood and by either the

scarcity of alternative roles or the difficulty of combining them with family roles. [1967]

Concomitant with less differentiation of male-female roles within the family should come, Davis (1967) alleges, changes in the economic opportunity structure with respect to married female employment: "If . . . women were paid as well as men and given equal educational and occupational opportunities . . . many women would develop interests that would compete with family interests."

Furthermore, Goldberg has suggested that higher fertility observed among Catholics might be attributable to a more traditional definition of the female sex role held by Catholics when compared to Protestants (1960: 144). Catholic women may be more likely to see "motherhood" and related traditional behaviors in sacred terms, so that fulfillment of these kinds of behaviors may provide a sense of reward and satisfaction that they do not see as attainable in any other way. Evidence for the idea that Catholicism encourages higher fertility by strongly reinforcing traditional sex role ideals is found in the Westoff and Potvin (1967) study of college women.

At the same time, Westoff and Ryder (1969) concluded from comparing trends in the 1955, 1960, and 1965 national fertility studies, that religious differences in attitudes toward fertility control have declined considerably. Nonetheless, greater or lesser traditionalism in conceptions of the married female role remain and may become an even more significant variable in explaining fertility differentials, particularly as other factors, including religious affiliation, become less salient. Substantial literature from the advocates of "women's liberation," (or neo-feminism) as well as some scholarly speculation, exists to suggest that the role of women may be undergoing large-scale alteration in the United States, and that such changes may be likely to continue.

Historically, one of the most obvious indicators of long-term changes in the status of women has been wife employment outside the home (Goode, 1963; 54ff). The incidence of wife employment has been steadily increasing for some years, and is consistently found to be negatively related to fertility both in Western and non-Western societies (Collver and Langlois, 1962; Blake, 1965).

As far back as 1955, Freedman *et al.* found

> that among fecund wives 35–39 years old who had been in the labor force for a long time, Catholics are rather similar to Protestants with respect to the proportion trying to limit family size, the success of their efforts, and their ideals about the expected number of children. . . . We interpret this to mean that common experiences and contacts in the working situation outside the family minimized the effects of religious differences. [1959:141]

A similar conclusion was reached by Blake (1965) in a study based on a sample of white college and high school girls. Whether the girls intended to work outside the home for an extended period of time after marriage was about equally as important as religious affiliation in determining family size desires.

Both these studies suggest that wife employment can equal or perhaps exceed even the powerful variable of religion in the strength of its correlation with fertility control. Changes occurring in the social structure are likely to decrease the effects of organized religion owing to secularization and to changes in the official Catholic position on birth control. On the other hand the incidence of wife employment is not likely to decrease but instead can be expected to increase substantially.

As a complement to the reasoning of theorists such as Goode (1963) that ongoing changes in female status are the result of the pervasive spread of historic individualism and personal freedom, Oppenheimer (1970) has devised a demographic model to account for the substantial increases in wife employment—both past and projected for the future. Her conclusion is that the unprecedented rapid growth of our economy, particularly since 1940, created a great demand for female labor. But the supply of *preferred* females—those never married and the young prior to marriage—was at the same time declining. To meet the increased demand, married women, who had formerly experienced job discrimination, began to be accepted into the labor force at all stages of the life-cycle, and markedly so at the middle and later stages.

Her projection (based among other things on continued economic expansion and on current age distributions) is that demand for female labor will continue to outstrip available supply, and that increasing numbers of wives will work at all life-cycle stages, including the period before their children start school. Finally, she predicts that these kinds of demographic changes will contribute substantially to redefinitions of the female role.

> Women's family statuses may be becoming less important determinants of their labor force status than other factors such as economic aspirations, marketable skills, occupational commitments. . . . [They] will start to consider work a possible lifetime activity . . . one of their major adult roles. . . . To the extent this is happening it will become more and more difficult to dismiss many of the complaints emanating from women's liberation groups as simply the distorted thinking of a lunatic fringe. [1970:33]

Although studies in the United States and elsewhere consistently point to a strong inverse linkage between wife employment and fertility, the causal problem has been a thorny one. It is possible to argue: (1) that women who are subfecund are more likely to work merely because of fewer home responsibilities; or (2) that some women work because of a perceived necessity to provide a higher standard of living for their families; or (3) because they want to work and enjoy doing so, some women therefore seek and manage to limit the size of their families. Whelpton *et al.* found in both fecund and subfecund subsamples that women who worked because they wanted to had fewer children than those working out of necessity, who in turn had fewer children than those who did not work at all (1966:108). It is possible to conclude from these comparisons that some women who see working as desirable in its own right do indeed manipulate their contraceptive behavior so as to permit them to achieve this goal. It would appear that even women who work only because the number of children already present puts a strain on family life style, women who might prefer not to work, also exercise caution in contraceptive behavior in order to be able to continue to work. These same investigators also found that when comparing employed Protestant and Catholic wives who worked because they *wanted* to, and who also had worked 1.5 years or more, family size expectations were quite similar (p. 110).

It will be recalled that the conclusion reached by Freedman *et al.* (1959) that wife employment had as powerful an influence on fertility as religion, was based on a fecund subsample. Likewise, in a later study, using a sample of "proven fecundity," Freedman and Coombs provide additional evidence which they took to suggest that work behavior and work expectations exert some "causal influence" on family size expectations (1966:218).

ROLE DEFINITION AND CAUSALITY

The possibility of ongoing, fundamental changes in female sex role definitions may be able to shed some light on this particularly difficult instance of directionality. Assuming fecundity, if increasing numbers of younger women redefine their roles both in and out of the family, (1) they can be expected to *desire* fewer children; (2) more of these women will remain single; (3) those who marry will do so at a later age; and (4) the completed size of their families can be expected to be less than the family size of those with more traditional role orientations. What is the nature of this sex role redefinition that it would have these kinds of potentially far-reaching consequences?

One of the major goals of most neo-feminists is opportunity for occupational achievement equal to that of anyone else in the society (Harbeson, 1967). Most women who work now do not possess the same degree of commitment as do men, neither is individualistic occupational achievement central to their work behaviors. There is virtually unanimous agreement with Degler's observation (1965) that their concern has been with "jobs" rather than with "careers." Even as late as 1967, the Census Bureau (October, 1969) verified the longstanding inverse relationship between husband's income and proportion of wife employment, continuing to affirm the generalization that heretofore when women worked, it was chiefly at a "job" necessary to supplement the family income. These census data show that once the husband is able to earn $7,000, wives begin to drop out of the labor market, with the percentage of nonemployment rising sharply with husband's income. The lack of "career-orientation" is also evidenced by the low median earnings reported by working wives.[1] Median earnings for working wives whose husbands earn $7,000 to $7,999 is $2,900 for a ratio of 0.38. The highest median earnings ($3,600) of all working wives is found among those whose husbands earn $25,000 and over, for a ratio of 0.10 (Current Population Reports: October, 1969).

In the event of a clash of interests between the occupations of husband and wife, it is the latter who generally give way. (For instance, rarely if ever would the husband quit his job and follow a career-oriented wife to another city so that she could take a "more challenging" position.) Nevertheless, occupational achievement remains, in modern society, a prime vehicle for fulfillment, satisfactions, and rewards, both in terms of prestige and material goods. If more and more younger women came to define individualistic occupational achievement as desirable and as desired for them as it is for men (i.e., in terms of career interests), then we might expect, among many other things (such as tax-supported day care centers), the four kinds of consequences described above.

Tomasson (1966), in comparing America and Sweden, describes the relationships between role definitions and fertility in the two societies. First he observes that Sweden's birth rate in 1960 was 14 per thousand population compared with America's 24. "Swedish wives born in the 1930's will probably have an average of 2.2 or 2.3 children by the time they complete the childbearing years, compared with a minimum estimate of 3.3 children for their counterparts in America (and 3.0 children for those who are not Catholic)" (1966:335). He also takes note of the increasingly large proportion of Swedish females who are located in traditionally "male professions," compared to actually decreasing proportions of American females in such occupations.

What is significantly different in the two societies is the increase in acceptable role possibilities for women that has occurred in Sweden over the past generation. The neo-traditional role for women has few spokesmen in the Swedish press and mass media compared to the United States. The feminism that became abortive in the United States about the time of World War II continued unabated in Sweden and has had far reaching effects in the society. Typical views of Swedish university students on women's roles are less differentiated and more egalitarian than those of [American college students]. The minimizing of sexual differentiation and the maximizing of sexual equality in education are guiding principles in the radical school reform in Sweden in the postwar years. . . . I Think it is suggestive that more Swedish wives regard two children as "ideal" than any other number (48 percent compared with 19 percent of American wives), whereas more American wives so regard four children than any other number (41 percent). [Tomasson, 1966:337]

Along with influencing family size desires and actual fertility, sex role redefinitions may be expected to influence "contraceptive efficacy" as well. Ryder and Westoff (1969) report that in their 1965 National Fertility Study, only 25 percent of women who intended no more children were actually successful in their family-planning goals. And 67 percent of those who intended additional children experienced timing failure. They conclude that there is "substantial lack of success in fertility planning across the entire sample, regardless of race, religion, or education" (1949:443). Apparently some two-thirds to three-quarters of American women have considerable difficulties in planning their families the way they say they would like to. If this level of "failure" cannot be blamed on the highly efficient technologies which are currently available, to what then may it be attributed? One hypothesis is that up to this point in time many married women perceived no compelling reward alternative to (an) additional child(ren). Consequently they may tend to be sloppy, haphazard, and careless in their contraceptive behavior. If changes in role definitions and achievement aspirations among some younger women are actually beginning to occur, then we might expect some upgrading in the rigor of their contraceptive behavior.

Ryder contends that "contraception is a difficult task, even for a sophisticated population . . . more important than this is the consideration that contraceptive efficacy . . . is a function not only of competence . . . but also of the perceived gravity of the consequences of failure" (1968:8–9). His key phrase is "perceived gravity of the consequences of failure." The more traditional a female is in her role definitions the less perhaps is the "perceived gravity of failure." Consequently her contraceptive behavior may be less rigorous. Her completed family size is therefore likely to be larger than that of a woman who defines her role in the more modern, achievement-oriented terms described above and who may perceive the gravity of an additional child as immense in terms of her own individual educational and occupational interests. The latter may be less likely to take risks, to chance a(n) (additional) pregnancy.

STUDIES OF SEX ROLE AND FERTILITY

Significantly, there is some limited evidence (besides that pertaining to wife-employment per se) which indicates that sex role definitions may indeed be linked to fertility control in the ways suggested. Clarkson *et al.* (1970), using a subsample of 60 Catholic women between ages 45 to 59, husband present, with at least two children, administered a series of 122 self-evaluative items measuring sex role stereotypes. Their stated objective was to test the Davis-Blake thesis cited above. The range of items included those indicating "stereotypic male-valued" characteristics, *i.e.*, items describing a "rational, competent, mature individual." The range also included "female-stereotypic" items indicating "warmth, expressiveness, sensitivity," etc. The investigators found that "mothers with high competency [high on the masculine stereotype] self-concept scores were found to have [statistically] significantly fewer children (mean = 3.12) than mothers who perceive themselves to be low on the competency cluster (mean = 3.93)."

Moreover, women with "high competency" who had worked seven years or less had a mean of 3.12 children versus a mean of 3.13 when they worked eight years or more, virtually identical. In contrast, among "low-competency" women who worked seven or fewer years, the mean was 4.43 versus 3.30 for those working eight years or more. First, therefore, it would appear that women who possess an "instrumental" or "male" or "competency-oriented" perception of themselves, have fewer children than women with the more traditional female self-conception. Moreover, in view of the fact that almost every major fertility study shows an inverse relationship between duration of wife work experience and family size, it seems quite significant that among wives with more modern self-conceptions, this relationship is obliterated. Only among the more traditional females does work duration have the expected consequences. While interpretation of the data is not without ambiguity, they do at least provide some empirical support for the hypothesis that the more traditional is a woman's view of her own role, the more children she is likely to have. They further suggest that the variable of sex role definitions may have as strong (or stronger) correlation with completed family size as (than) wife employment per se.

Rainwater, in a partial test of the Hoffman-Wyatt model, examined a subsample of middle-class wives in terms of self-descriptions," and of desired family size (1965:191–92).

There is a strong association between family size desires and how exclusively the wife sees herself as oriented to husband and outside interests as opposed to children. . . . 90 percent of those who want a small family mention outside or husband orientations, compared to . . . only 45 percent of the large-family mothers. In contrast, over 80 percent of both medium and large-family mothers mention orientation to children compared to only 30 percent of small-family mothers.

In another study, Stolka and Barnett (1969) used a series of three items to measure the "role of woman" both in the family and in connection with her career efforts. They report that less traditional female role orientations were the single most important attitudinal factor in terms of depressing "motivations toward childbearing." Thus their work too provides some confirmation of the "feminist-fertility" linkage.

Finally, Rossi, (1970), in a carefully designed longitudinal study of 15,000 women college graduates, found that those "with high career commitments tend to want fewer children . . . [and] to be willing to let others take . . . care of [their] children . . . [than] women who have no career goal for the future, but expect to be exclusively homemakers. . . ."

Besides the foregoing reports which specifically link varied measures of sex role to fertility, the Census Bureau (January, 1971) has recently published some data which are exceedingly suggestive. In 1967, for the first time, the Bureau obtained from a national sample of wives (age 14 to 39, husband-present) the variable of family size *expectations*. They found that (younger) wives ages 14 to 24 expect a mean of 2.8 children, compared to the 3.3 expected by wives ages 30 to 39. The same pattern held when comparing younger and older white wives (2.9 versus 3.2), younger and older black wives (2.8 versus 4.2), younger and older wives living in metropolitan areas (2.9 versus 3.2), and also in nonmetropolitan areas (2.8 versus 3.5), younger and older wives who are high school graduates (2.8 versus 3.0), and also who are not graduates (2.9 versus 3.8).

The trend toward younger wives expecting fewer children than older wives was discovered by Whelpton *et al.* in their 1960 national sample. They assessed this as "one of our most important findings . . . [which] may forecast a reversal of the postwar trend toward larger families, and . . . will have an important influence on the birth rate during most of the 1960's" (1966:57–58). We now know, in fact, that younger cohorts of women are actually bearing significantly fewer children than did older cohorts when they previously were at the same life-cycle stage (Current Population Reports: July, 1970). Ryder and Westoff (1969) contend that the current decline in the American fertility rate began prior to the effects of "pill technology," and that the continuance of the decline cannot be explained totally by the pill.

Moreover it would appear from several sources that the best predictor of completed family size is fertility desires. Therefore, one could suggest that younger women in America are having and will have fewer children in part, at least, because they *want* fewer children.[2] To the degree this assumption is valid, the critical question becomes, why might younger women want fewer children? It is possible to speculate and to hypothesize that these lessened desires are a manifestation of gradual alterations in traditional sex role definitions. Could it be perhaps that younger women perceive certain kinds of rewards (occupational pursuits in particular) as viable alternatives to exclusive pursuit of traditional "feminine activities"?

This process may be largely nonconscious, and not necessarily the outgrowth of an overt, ideological commitment to feminism per se. Instead, simply because women, as well as men, operate within the context of an achievement-oriented society, the pursuit of achievement-type rewards may, in very pragmatic fashion, come to limit the desire for certain types of "ascriptive-type" rewards (traditional motherhood). To the extent these speculations are valid, the recent Census data may indicate that while the female sex role has been changing slowly for almost two centuries, the current decades may signal a juncture at which the pace of change may accelerate and the consequences become more profound than ever before.

IMPLICATIONS FOR CHANGES IN MALE SEX ROLE AND CONJUGAL FAMILY STRUCTURE

It is beyond the scope of this paper to consider in detail the consequences for the male sex role of these kinds of female role alterations, especially since they have been considered elsewhere. The currently predominant form of conjugal family structure is based on role *specialization*—the husband being chiefly instrumental and achievement-oriented, playing the provider role, while the wife is basically expressive and home-oriented. To the degree that wives become achievement-oriented, and it perhaps becomes legitimate for them to occupy the position of provider *in the same sense as husbands,* to that degree specialization will be replaced by role interchangeability. Interchangeability implies that provision of material and status rewards for the conjugal unit could be equally the responsibility and right of either or both husband and/or wife at any point in the life cycle. The wife would share this position not because the family is poor, or in debt, or simply to enhance family life style, but because of the same desires for achievement and success that currently motivate husbands. Presumably many women would eventually come to "shake off" the "fear of success" which Horner claims to be debilitating to current female achievements (1970). Hence, just as a strong female achievement-orientation might alter family function (reproduction), it might also alter the male sex role and conjugal family structure as well.

SOCIAL DIFFERENTIATION, SEX ROLE, AND FERTILITY

We alluded earlier to the classic inverse relation between socioeconomic variables (education, occupation, income) and fertility. Though the relationship persists (Kiser, 1968), it has been growing steadily weaker. Nevertheless Blau and Duncan (1967:427) argue that "on theoretical grounds . . . some differential fertility is an ingrained characteristic of industrialized society and will persist." Their argument is based on the general notion of reward-alternatives stressed throughout this paper. They contend that the less successful (male) achiever (lower-status, blue-collar), in order to compensate for his lower material and status position, seeks alternative rewards in the form of a larger family: "the unsuccessful find a substitute in the authority they exercise in their role as fathers over a number of children." Their argument concludes on the contention that since, in an industrial society, some men will inevitably continue to fill less desirable occupations they will therefore probably continue to have more children.

In terms of alternative rewards and *female* achievement, it would appear that it is the more educated women who are currently pressing for greater opportunities, and it is they who will be in the vanguard of any movement toward genuine sex-role redefinitions that might occur in the future. Better-educated women generally marry better-educated men who, according to Blau and Duncan, "need" fewer children than less-educated men. If, in addition, such wives "need" and seek fewer children than less-educated women because of alternative rewards via occupational achievement, then this may be a second factor which may influence the classic inverse status-fertility linkage. Higher status families may come to consist of husbands and wives both of whom, as a result of achievement rewards, perceive less "need" for traditional kinds of rewards in the form of children.

CONCLUSION

This paper has presented an argument which on theoretical and empirical grounds suggests that the sex-role orientations of women, in particular their orientations toward occupational achievement, may be critical in influencing fertility behavior. This possibility presents social scientists with a set of potentially significant variables in a period when many conventional demographic factors are gradually declining in their ability to differentiate segments of the population. Concomitantly, the argument suggests that changes allegedly occurring in the female role, if they continue in their presumed direction, may have implications for future family structure as well as population trends. As with any formal scheme of this sort, an empirical test is requisite to determine its degree of validity, if any. Such a test is currently being planned under the auspices of the Center For Population Research, National Institutes of Child Health and Human Development. Once these data are collected and analyzed, we should have a much more accurate picture of what the actual impact is of sex-role definitions on family fertility.

NOTES

1. This in no way denies the reality of discrimination against women both in terms of hiring and of wages. Very likely, discrimination accounts partly for the low median incomes.

2. Care must be taken to observe Ryder's caveat (1968) that to explain changes in fertility patterns by asserting changes in preferences is insufficient. Other variables must be introduced into any such model—in this case the variable of sex-role redefinitions.

REFERENCES

Blake, J. 1965. "Demographic science and the redirection of population policy." Journal of Chronic Diseases 18:1181–1200.

Blau, P. M. and O. D. Duncan. 1967. The American Occupational Structure. New York: Wiley.

Clarkson, F. E., S. R. Vogel, I. K. Broverman, and D. M. Broverman. 1970. "Family size and sex role stereotypes." Science (January, 1970):390–92.

Collver, A. and E. Langlois. 1962. "The female labor force in metropolitan areas: an international comparison." Economic Development and Cultural Change 10 (4):367–85.

Davis, K. 1967. "Population policy: will current programs succeed?" Science 158 (November, 10):730–39.

Delger, C. N. 1965. "Revolution with ideology: the changing place of women in America." Pp. 193–210 in R. J. Lifton (ed.), The Woman in America. Boston: Beacon Press.

Freedman, R., P. K. Whelpton, and A. A. Campbell. 1959. Family Planning, Sterility, and Population Growth. New York: McGraw-Hill.

Freedman, R. and L. Coombs. 1966. "Economic considerations in family growth decision." Population Studies 20 (November):197–222.

Goldberg, D. 1960. "Some recent developments in American fertility research." Pp. 137–51 in Demographic and Economic Change in Developed Countries. Princeton, N.J.: Princeton University Press.

Goode, W. J. 1963. World Revolution and Family Patterns. New York: Free Press.

Harbeson, G. E. 1967. Choice and Challenge for the American Woman. Cambridge, Mass.: Schenkman.

Hoffman, L. W. and F. Wyatt. 1960. "Social change and motivations for having larger families: some theoretical considerations." Merrill-Palmer Quarterly 6:235–44.

Horner, M. S. 1970. "Femininity and successful achievement: a basic inconsistency." Pp. 45–66 in J. M. Bardwick *et al.*, Feminine Personality and Conflict. Belmont, California: Wadsworth.

Kiser, C. V., W. H. Grabill, and A. A. Campbell. 1968. Trends and Variations in Fertility in the United States. Cambridge, Mass.: Harvard University Press.

Oppenheimer, V. K. 1970. "Demographic influences on female employment and the status of women." Unpublished Paper, Department of Sociology, University of California, Los Angeles.

Rainwater, Lee. 1965. Family Design: Marital Sexuality, Family Size, and Contraception. Chicago: Aldine.

Rossi, Alice. 1970. "Deviance and conformity in the life goals of women." Unpublished Paper, Goucher College, Baltimore, Md.

Ryder, N. B. 1968. "The time series of fertility in the United States." Unpublished Paper, Department of Sociology, University of Wisconsin, Madison.

Ryder, N. B. and C. F. Westoff. 1969. "Fertility planning status: United States, 1965." Demography 6 (November):435–44.

Stolka, S. M. and L. D. Barnett. 1969. "Education and religion as factors in women's attitudes motivating childbearing." Journal of Marriage and the Family 31 (November):740–50.

Taeuber, Karl E. and Alma F. Taeuber. 1966. "The Negro population in the United States." Pp. 96–160 in John P. Davis (ed.), The American Negro Reference Book. Englewood Cliffs, N.J.: Prentice Hall.

Tomasson, R. F. 1966. "Why has American fertility been so high?" Pp. 327–38 in B. Farber (ed.), Kinship And Family Organization. New York: Wiley.

Westoff, C. F. and R. H. Potvin. 1967. College Women and Fertility Values. Princeton, N.J.: Princeton University Press.

Westoff, C. F. and N. B. Ryder. 1969. "Recent trends in attitudes toward fertility control and in the practice of contraception in the United States." Pp. 388–412 in S. J. Behrman *et al.* (eds.), Fertility and Family Planning. Ann Arbor: University of Michigan Press.

Whelpton, P. K., A. A. Campbell, and J. E. Patterson. 1966. Fertility and Family Planning in the United States. Princeton, N.J.: Princeton University Press.

U.S. Bureau of the Census. 1969. Current Population Reports. Series P-60, No. 64 (October 6).

———. 1970. Current Population Reports. Series P-20, No. 205 (July 22).

———. 1971. Current Population Reports. Series P-20, No. 21 (January 26).

26

Coercive Pronatalism and American Population Policy*

Judith Blake

The achievement of zero population growth implies that American child-bearing be limited to an average of approximately two children per woman. Since women who are currently approaching the end of the reproductive age span have borne an average of three children, advocates of population stablization are concerned about the mechanisms for achieving a two-child average.[1] The search for measures to insure us a reproductive level that is both low and nonfluctuating is intensified by a growing recognition of the lead-time required to achieve zero population growth. For example, the two-child average will afford us zero growth only *after* the age structure of the population has become less favorable to reproduction than is currently the case. Until the baby-boom babies, who have grown up to be mothers and potential mothers, move out of the reproductive ages, the achievement of zero growth implies fewer than two children per woman.[2] It is clear, therefore, that long-run population stability will require either that Americans, in general, restrict themselves to micro-families, or that a substantial share of the population remain childless (and/or have only one child) while others have the moderate-sized families to which we are now accustomed.

It is perhaps not surprising that such a major change in our reproductive behavior would seem to call for the introduction of state-imposed coercions on individuals—an abrogation of the "voluntary" character of child-bearing decisions.[3] This popular view of what must be done in order

Reprinted from the report of the Commission on Population Growth and the American Future, pp. 1–22, by permission of the author.

* The author gratefully acknowledges support by the Ford Foundation of the research presented in this article.

to achieve population stability is, of course, both shocking and frightening to government officials. In the face of suggestions regarding state "control" over reproduction, programs that promise population stability through the elimination of "unwanted" fertility alone seem reassuringly inoffensive. Understandably, they are embraced with relief regardless of how unlikely it is that they will be effective.[4] Their selling point is "the right to choose" one's family size and this "right" is celebrated as an ultimate end. In the words of Frank Notestein:

> Family planning represents a new and important freedom in the world. It will surely be a happy day when parents can have and can avoid having children, as they see fit. . . . It is a matter of major importance that this kind of new freedom to choose, now existing for the bulk of the population, be extended to its most disadvantaged parts. If it were extended, reproduction would be brought fairly close to the replacement level. However, I would advocate the right to choose even if I thought the demographic consequences would be highly adverse, because it will always be possible to manipulate the environment in which the choice is made.[5]

However, both the coercion approach and the laissez-faire approach ("the right to choose") suffer from a serious empirical flaw. They each assume that free choice and voluntarism now exist and that they are marred only by incomplete distribution of contraceptives. One approach says that voluntarism must be curtailed, the other claims that it must be preserved at all cost. Neither recognizes that it does not exist right now. Neither takes into account that at present, reproductive behavior is under stringent institutional control and that this control constitutes, in many respects, a coercive pronatalist policy. Hence, an effective antinatalist policy will not necessarily involve an increase in coercion or a reduction in the "voluntary" element in reproduction, because individuals are under pronatalist constraints right now. People make their "voluntary" reproductive choices in an institutional context that severely constrains them not to choose nonmarriage, not to choose childlessness, not to choose only one child, and even not to limit themselves solely to two children. If we can gain insight into the coercions and restraints under which we currently operate, it may become more obvious that an antinatalist policy can be one that is *more* voluntary—allows a wider spectrum of individual choice—than is presently the case. Let us first examine why individuals may be said to be under constraint and suffer coercion, in any society, regarding reproduction. We may then turn to the main body of our paper—the actual nature of some important existing reproductive coercions in American society.

THE SOCIOLOGY OF THE FAMILY AND
THE REPRODUCTIVE FUNCTION

In order to understand the long-run determinants of birth rates, in so far as these relate to motivational and not conditional factors, one must translate birth rates into the operational context of reproduction.[6] People do not have birth rates, they have children. Their willingness to bear and rear children—to expend their human and material resources in this manner—cannot be taken for granted. Rather, childbearing and childrearing take place in an organizational context which influences people strongly to do one set of things—reproduce, and not to do other sets of things—activities that would conflict or compete with reproduction. The bearing and rearing of children thus represents one kind of allocation and organization of human and material resources. In all viable societies social control has operated to organize human beings into childbearing and childrearing groups—families—that, by definition, have proven to be highly efficient reproductive machines. Reproductively inefficient societies have not survived for historical man to study.

As with other forms of social control, that responsible for the support of the family as an institution rests on informal and formal (legal) rules of behavior. These will range from behavior that must be performed—prescribed, to behavior that is forbidden—proscribed. Large areas of behavior are simply permitted or preferred. What leads us to abide by these rules? Clearly, the same mechanisms of social control that lead us to abide by any rules. First of all, we are socialized from the beginning both to learn the rules and to believe they are right. Second, the everyday process of interaction with others puts us in constant contact with the norm-enforcement process, since other people have a stake in how we behave. They can reward us with approval, or punish us with rejection. If these informal sanctions are not effective, then formal ones may be invoked such as, for example, the law. Finally, the master control of all is what might be called the "sociological predicament." This is that any existing social organization represents a selection of possible roles and statuses, goals and activities, etc., available to individuals. Not only are persons with certain characteristics allocated to particular roles and statuses and proscribed from others, but all individuals in a given society typically have available to them, as the outer perimeter of their expectations, what the society has to offer from a role and status point of view. Such limitation of role alternatives obviates the need for many more direct coercions. Individuals are usually not afforded role options that might be deviant. This fact is abundantly documented by the social sciences. An illustration of particular relevance to this paper is Burgess and Wallin's criticism of Waller's well-known theory of the function of romantic love. Waller presupposed that the idealization and euphoria of being "in love" are necessary to propel people into marriage. He reasoned that a powerful force is needed to overcome the attractions of alternative ways of life. Burgess and Wallin's point is simple —such attractive alternatives do not exist.

> The woman who does not marry is likely to be judged a failure, the implication generally being that she was not chosen, she was not desired. Apart from the injury to her self-esteem, nonmarriage imposes difficulties and frustrations. Adult social life tends to be organized around married couples. Sexual satisfaction is not easily obtained without risk by the unmarried female who desires it, and the experience of motherhood is denied her....
>
> [As for men,] . . . to marry is to be normal, and from childhood on we are exposed to the idea of marriage as something to be desired, the risk of divorce notwithstanding. Although some men can secure their sexual satisfaction outside of the matrimonial relationship, most of them are strongly attracted by the promise of sexual gratification with the regularity, convenience and comfort which marriage affords.[7]

In sum, reproduction and replacement, like other societal functions, require an organized allocation of human and material resources. Societies have resolved this problem of resource allocation by means of diffused control mechanisms (rather than a government planning board, for example), but the mechanisms are nonetheless quite palpably there. And they involve the individual in an articulated and coercive set of constraints. He has some choice among fixed alternatives, but, as we shall see, even his "choices" are deeply influenced by his past social experience and the kind of person he has been influenced to become. His behavior is "voluntary" only in a restricted sense—not in the sense of being unpatterned, uncontrolled, or unrestrained. In effect, regardless of whether a typical birth cohort of individuals contains a large proportion of persons who might be unsuited to family life, human societies are so organized as to attempt to make individuals as suited as possible, to motivate them to want to be suited, and to provide them with little or no alternative to being suited as they mature. By fiction and by fiat, parenthood is the "natural" human condition, and to live one's life as a family member is the desideratum. In this context, individuals make their reproductive "choices."

The present paper will concentrate on two such diffused and implicit pronatalist coercions in modern American society—the prescribed primacy of parenthood in the definition of adult sex roles and the prescribed congruence of personality traits with the demands of the sex roles as defined. I believe it can be shown that there is, in American society, not only an absence of legitimate alternatives to sex roles having parenthood as a primacy focus, but that change is particularly difficult to effect because those individuals who might aspire to such alternatives are suppressed and neutralized. My thesis is that unless we realize that we have been locking pronatalism into both the structure of society and the structure of personality, the problem of fertility control will appear to be the reverse of what it actually is. We will continue to believe that our principal policy problem is one of *instituting* antinatalist coercions instead of *lifting* pronatalist ones. We will see fertility reduction as involving *more* regimentation than presently exists, when, in fact, it should involve *less*, since individuals will no longer be universally constrained to forsake other possible interests and goals in order to devote themselves to the reproductive function.

ROLE DIFFERENTIATION BY SEX AND THE PRIMACY OF PARENTHOOD

Role differentiation by sex in American society makes actual or anticipated parenthood a precondition for all other aspects of men's and women's roles. The content of sex roles—men's and women's "spheres"—uses as a bench mark the sexually differentiated relation to childbearing and rearing. The feminine role is normatively maternal and, hence, intra-familial, "integrative," emotionally supportive, and "expressive." The masculine role is normatively paternal and, as a result, primarily the complement of the maternal role—extra-familial, protective, economically supportive, and "instrumental" (or "task-oriented").[8] By according primacy to the kinship statuses of "mother" and "father" these role expectations thus assume that parenthood is implicit in the very definition of masculinity and femininity. Moreover, not only does the identification of masculinity and femininity with parenthood mean that reproduction is implicitly prescribed for everyone but, as might be expected, it means that alternative role definitions for the sexes are, at best, tolerated, and, at worst, proscribed.

Since we have been speaking of the United States, it is worth asking whether the identification of gender with parenthood is unusual in human socities. Are Americans odd? The answer is, of course, negative. We share this linkage of sex roles and parenthood functions with a large number of primitive and technologically backward peoples, as well as with some more modern ones.[9] Indeed, it is probably true that, insofar as men and women engage in reproduction in families, this division of labor will be subject to only minor modifications. What is open to question, however, is the demographic appropriateness for a low-mortality society of rigidly identifying, for *everyone,* the sexual with the parental role. Since sex is an aspect of a person's identity that begins its influence from birth, we appear to be locking ourselves into reproduction through sex-role expectations that ceased to be demographically necessary for our entire population before most of us were born.

What is the evidence for the identification of sex roles with traditional parental functions in American society? Is such an identification really normative? One significant way of answering this question is to see what happens when the norm is challenged, or when there is some large-scale defection from the sex-role expectations as defined. If the norm is operative, we would expect to discover that a variety of sanctions are invoked to bring behavior back into line. Additionally, we might expect to see an effort to label the deviation as not merely contranormative but pathological as well.

In the remainder of this section on sex roles, we shall examine a number of challenges to the traditional expectations for the sexes in American society. These challenges are: the labor force participation of women, higher education for women, feminism, and male homosexuality. We shall find, in all cases, widespread opposition to the recognized threat to sex-role expectations. Furthermore, in the case of the first three, we shall see that adjustment to this opposition has taken place so effectively as to substantially neutralize these sources of change in sex-role expectations. In the case of the last example, the deviancy is regarded as an aberration (a pathology) for which diverse causes and cures are sought. There is systematic refusal to recognize that *intra*-sex variability in temperament, personality traits, and physical and mental capability may, in actuality, be fully as important as *inter*-sex variation, if one but excludes the difference in reproductive capacity.

THE WORKING WOMAN AND THE PRIMACY OF PARENTHOOD FOR BOTH SEXES

Nothing better illustrates the absence of genuine options to parental roles in our society than the nature of the opposition to having women work outside the home. The most salient and enduring objections to a genuine career role for women—a commitment to outside work—have been two: First, that no women—even unmarried women—should be allowed to challenge men's prior claim on jobs since men must support families; and second, that outside work is unsuited to women physically and mentally since their natural fulfillment lies in another sphere entirely—motherhood. In effect, the opposition to work-commitment by women has reaffirmed *both* the male's role as father and family supporter and the female's role as mother and housewife. Smuts documents legal and public concern along these lines since the 1870's.[10] Although, as he shows, the emphasis on the physical inappropriateness of outside work for women has disappeared, the "psychological" and temperamental uniqueness of women is still emphasized strongly. Hence, jobs are sex-typed, women are "protected" by legislation, and both hiring and firing take advantage of the typical women's marginal commitment to full-time, long-term employment. Through an analysis of articles on women's labor force participation in major American popular magazines since 1900, Betty Stirling has shown that the dual considerations of concern for protecting the man's family-supporting job and concern for protecting the woman's motherhood role has characterized opposition to female employment outside the home from the beginning.[11] Public opinion polls have demonstrated the same anxieties.[12] Religious opposition to women working has been particularly vocal in the Catholic press and marriage manuals—specifically on the bases of threats to the supporting role of men and the motherhood role of women.[13]

In effect, although economic opportunities might have led us to expect the emergence of a career role for a numerically important group of unmarried, and married but childless, women, in actual fact the immense increase in labor force participation by women took a different tack entirely. Women's labor in the market has been utilized and tolerated only on condition that it supported and enhanced the traditional parental roles for both sexes. In the words of the National Manpower Council:

> Americans view the man in the family as the primary breadwinner and, when jobs are scarce, are inclined to believe that women workers should not compete with men who have families to support. Americans also believe that mothers should personally care for their children during their early formative years. Consequently, even though there are today over 2.5 million mothers in the labor force whose children are under six, there is still little sympathy with the idea of mothers holding full-time jobs when their children are of preschool age, unless they are compelled to do so by economic necessity. . . .[14]

The difficulties women experienced who wished to challenge the identity of sexual and parental roles have not been simply "male dominance" or "male power," but rather the intense societal supports for the *family roles* of mother and father. The opposition to women working thus stemmed fully as much from the obligatory nature of family formation (and the sex differentiation of parents), as from a fear of the diminution of male authority generally. We shall see, moreover, in a later section, that, after World War II, when women's educational and economic opportunities could, objectively, have provided some challenge to the primacy of the parental role, the unmarried and married but childless, women came under attack from "scientific" sources. In the face of declining religious influence, a breakdown of Victorian "traditions," and expanding career opportunities for women, "science" stepped in, in the guise of psychoanalysis, to provide an authoritative prescription of parenthood, and severe condemnation of the career women. Not surprisingly, few unmarried or childless females were available to redefine the role of the working woman along career lines. Women's labor force participation evolved as an adjunct, not an alternative, to motherhood.[15] The peculiar character of this participation—low wages, dead-end jobs, and sex-typing—tends moreover, to be self-perpetuating. Each generation of girls views the market and finds few realistic career options therein. The primacy of men's and women's family roles has successfully absorbed what might have been a genuine alternative to reproduction for a number of women. As Smuts says: "the woman who urgently wants to develop and utilize her abilities in work still has barriers to overcome. Employers tend to judge all working women on the basis of their experience with the majority who are content with modest rewards for modest efforts...."[16]

Higher Education for Women: The Mother's Helper

Theoretically, the provision of higher education to women constituted a major challenge to the primacy of motherhood as *the* sex role for American females. Far more than the franchise, higher education seemed to imply that women *should* be given career avenues equal in all respects to the channels afforded to men. In this sense, it cast into doubt the norm that motherhood is the primary role for all but the unhappy few.

The initial efforts in the United States to provide higher education for women were met with much explicit verbalization concerning the possible undermining of the wife-mother role—the only proper feminine role. This history is well known and need not concern us here.[17] More important is the mounting evidence that genuine educational opportunities for women have been subtly infused by an implicit (occasionally even explicit) premise—the unchallenged assumption that the wife-mother role is a precondition for all other roles women might wish to play. As Mabel Newcomer has said:

> The fact that homemaking is woman's most important role has never been seriously questioned either by those arguing in favor of college education for women or by those opposing it. Those opposing higher education for women have usually expressed the fear that it will encourage them to pursue independent careers, foregoing marriage; or if they marry, that it will make them dissatisfied with the homemaker's lot. Those promoting higher education have, on the contrary, insisted that college women make better wives and mothers than their less educated sisters. Even those who have been concerned with the rights and interests of unmarried women have never argued that higher education might encourage women to remain single, except as it occa-

sionally offered a reasonably satisfactory alternative when the only available young men were not entirely acceptable.[18]

Indeed, the women's colleges—in the vanguard of higher education for women—early learned to stress that their effect on diverting their charges from the path of wifehood and motherhood would be nonexistent. Defensively, they assured their trustees, their backers, the prospective parents of their tuition-paying student bodies that higher education for women would leave unchallenged woman's *role* and women's *expectations*.[19]

The stated "aims" of the colleges, as reviewed by Newcomer in the late 1950's, were sufficiently vague concerning the purposes for which young girls were attending as to leave unthreatened either the classical feminine role definition, or the intellectual fantasies of the students.[20] Clearly, the educators of young women had learned the hard way that the uncomfortable resolution between the promise of "equality"—even for some—and the reality of motherhood for all was best left to each individual girl to resolve as best she could. The college was not to be the champion of the "odd-ball" girl.

The most obvious deviant among the college presidents and promoters of women's education was Lynn White, Jr. (then President of Mills College), who attempted to clarify and make explicit the hidden agenda behind women's education in America. Almost all women do marry, few women pursue systematic careers, and even these careers are typically "feminine" rather than masculine. Why not face it? Why not educate our daughters in the light of definitively sex-linked capabilities and the appropriate social roles that express these capabilities?[21] So eager was White to clinch his point, that he fell into the familiar position adopted by some of the feminists—the moral *superiority* of the traditional female virtues over the crasser male qualities. Thus, if women were constitutionally debarred from the more highly regarded cultural pursuits, they should not feel badly. These pursuits have been overrated anyway.[22] White thus invoked the position that helped legitimate the downfall of feminism—women's battles were to be on higher ground as befits their universally more civilized, sensitive, and gentle natures. Of similar sentiments expressed by the feminists, O'Neill has written, "Definitions like this left men with few virtues anyone was bound to admire, and inspired women to think of themselves as a kind of super race condemned by historical accident and otiose convention to serve their natural inferiors."[23] In keeping with his effort to legitimate separate and unequal education for women, White celebrated motherhood as women's noblest pursuit.[24] He even deplored the antifamily bias that, he alleged, was being transmitted to men by the "celibate tradition" in higher education. For men as well as women, the family should come first, "unless men as well as women can be given the conviction that personal cultivation and career are secondary to making a success of the family, and indeed that both are bleak satisfactions apart from a warm hearth, we shall not have found wisdom."[25] In a significant chapter that constitutes a paean to motherhood, he claimed that the American population was not replacing itself, that "the best" people were particularly remiss in their reproductive obligation, and that it was the duty of high-minded American women to devote themselves to maternity.[26] Repeatedly he emphasized the hopelessness of combining a genuine career with a family of sufficient size, and enjoined college women not to be inhibited by a college education from "flinging themselves with complete enthusiasm and abandon" into family life.[27]

Is the aim-inhibition that has suffused higher education for women, its absorption into the anticipated motherhood role, merely an intellectual preoccupation of the educators, or have young college women themselves received the message that their college experience must be adapted to their future role as mothers? Two studies of American college girls, one done by Komarovsky in the 1940's, and another done by Goldsen and others in the 1950's, show clearly that the pressures on women to remain undiverted from motherhood followed them into college.

Komarovsky, writing in 1953, expressed the concern of the educator over holding out to women impossible and contradictory goals.

> The very education which is to make the college housewife a cultural leaven of her family and her community may develop in her interests which are frustrated by other phases of housewifery. We are urged to train women for positions of leadership in civic affairs when, at the same time, we define capacity for decisive action, executive ability, hardihood in the face of opposition as "unfeminine" traits. We want our daughters to be able, if the need arises, to earn a living at some worthwhile occupation. In doing so, we run the risk of awakening interests and abilities which, again, run counter to the present definition of femininity.[28]

Her case studies of women students seemed to indicate to her that these young women were presented with "equally compelling" but "contradictory" pressures. Actually, the data seem to trace a temporal change in parental and peer pressure concerning academic and occupational achievement and the traditional female role. Parents and peers were encouraging achievement until it seemed to stand in the way of marriage and motherhood. Then, for the girl who had not already received "the message" by means of less obvious cues, sanctions came into play. She was effectively told that she should not allow academic or professional achievement "to get in her way." For example:

All through grammar school and high school my parents led me to feel that to do well in school was my chief responsibility. A good report card, an election to student office, these were the news Mother bragged about in telephone conversations with her friends. *But recently they suddenly got worried about me: I don't pay enough attention to social life, a woman needs some education but not that much.* They are disturbed by my determination to go to the School of Social Work. Why my ambitions should surprise them after they have exposed me for four years to some of the most inspired and stimulating social scientists in the country, I can't imagine. They have some mighty strong arguments on their side. What is the use, they say, of investing years in training for a profession, only to drop it in a few years? Chances of meeting men are slim in this profession. Besides, I may become so pre-occupied with it as to sacrifice social life. The next few years are, after all, the proper time to find a mate. But the urge to apply what I have learned, and the challenge of this profession is so strong that I shall go on despite the family opposition.

I . . . work for a big metropolitan daily as a correspondent in the city room. I am well liked there and may possibly stay as a reporter after graduation in February. I have had several spreads (stories running to more than eight or ten inches of space), and this is considered pretty good for a college correspondent. Naturally, I was elated and pleased at such breaks, and as far as the city room is concerned I'm off to a very good start on a career that is hard for a man to achieve and ever harder for a woman. General reporting is still a man's work in the opinion of most people. *I have a lot of acclaim but also criticism, and I find it difficult to be praised for being clever and working hard and then, when my efforts promise to be successful, to be condemned and criticized for being unfeminine and ambitious.*[29]

The 1952 study of both male and female Cornell students by Goldsen, Rosenberg, Williams, and Suchman shows that the coeds had almost universally accepted motherhood as a precondition for any other activity.

A traditional middle-class idea that a woman's only career should be her family is rejected by almost all the students. Instead, they are neither unequivocally for nor unequivocally against the idea of women having careers. The attitude seems to be, "It's okay providing. . . ." Providing she is not married, or providing she has no children, or providing her children are "old enough"—a notion about which there is a wide range of opinion. Let the women have careers, indeed encourage them, but be sure it does not interfere with her main job of bearing and rearing children.[30]

Interestingly, the young women in the Cornell study had adjusted their ideas of the proper jobs for women to the demands of their motherhood role. Unlike the new feminists of the 1960's and 1970's, these women assumed that their labor market activity would not be equal in demands or prestige with that of men. "Our data indicate that just about every college girl wants to marry and have children, and that she fully expects to do so. . . . Most of them see no essential conflict between family life and a career—the sort of career, that is, that they consider 'suitable' for a woman. . . . The occupations women choose to go into are quite different from those chosen by men. They overwhelmingly select the traditional 'women's occupations.' "[31]

Why did they want to work at all? One reason was to keep occupied before marriage. Another was insurance—against the remote possibility of remaining single, and against adversity in their marriage. More significant, however, was ambivalence about the suitability of homemaking and motherhood to their interests and temperaments. A striking feature of these data is that these young women did not appear to be overwhelmingly *attracted* to maternity, they simply did not see any alternative role as realistic.

> There is no question that college girls count on building up equity in family life, not in professional work. A dedicated career-girl is a deviant: in a real sense she is unwilling to conform to her sex-role as American society defines it. For professional work among women in this country (and the college-trained women agree) is viewed as an interlude, at best a part-time excursion away from full-time family life which the coeds yearn for, impatiently look forward to . . . and define as largely monotony, tedium, and routine.[32]

The intention to work, the vision of personal realization through the use of the talents and capabilities they had come, through their college training, to know they possessed, represented the psychological life-preserver they promised themselves to keep at hand.[33]

By what mechanism was the "career girl" role rendered so deviant? One mechanism was clearly the girls' perception of what men wanted in a woman. The Cornell study found, for example, that other than the condition that an ideal mate love her spouse, two-thirds of all college men in the sample cited "interested in having a family" as highly important in a mate.[34] To the young college woman, a way of life as deviant as a genuine and demanding career represented a journey toward an unknown, inappropriate, and potentially tragic destination. She might never meet *any* man who was interested in such a freak. Half of the Cornell men were quite clear in stating that they either did not approve of women having careers, or approved only if the woman was unmarried or, if married, had no children. Only 22 percent of the men approved of a woman having a career regardless of the age of her children, and most of the remainder approved only if the children were of high school age or older.[35] Finally, the young women's sense of constraint concerning premarital sexual relations made an indefinite postponement of marriage appear lonely and sexless. Even among girls who were interested in careers, sexual relationships were defined only in romantic, emotional terms, and close to 40 percent felt that premarital sex relations were "never justified" for women. Among young women who ranked low on careerism, half felt that premarital relations were "never justified."[36]

Has it all changed by 1971? Obviously, there have been many external changes. The development of contraception—especially the pill—has greatly altered the conditions under which young college men and women may consider nonmarital relationships. Public policy is increasingly concerned with equal educational and occupational opportunity for women, and the country has been literally deluged by antinatalist and neofeminist propaganda. How have college women reacted? And what reactions must they cope with in college men? Is there yet a perceived alternative to marriage and a family, or simply a scaling down of family size desires? In an attempt to clarify this and other issues, I inserted a set of questions on family size preferences, preferred age at marriage, nonmarriage, attitudes toward the pill and abortion in a special youth study conducted by the Gallup Poll in June 1971. The study included two samples of young people aged 18–24 —one a college sample and one a representative national sample of persons in this age group. Table 1 presents some relevant data for the college sample.

The results indicate clearly that few men or women in this college sample would like to be childless, or have only one child. More than half of the men, and approximately half of the women would like to have a two-child family. A third of the men and almost 40 percent of the women want three or more children. Although these results show that family-size preferences are smaller than those expressed in the 1950's and 1960's, the desire for at least two children is clear and apparently firm.[37] A question on the family size considered "too small" demonstrates that an acceptable family size begins with two children. On the other hand, there seems to be no clear proscription against even a relatively large family. A question concerning the size family the respondent would consider "too large" shows that three children are tolerated by all but a minority of respondents—20 percent. Even at the level of five children, 27 percent of the men and 40 percent of the women have not yet designated the family as "too large."

Turning to age at marriage we see that, according to both men and women, women should definitely be married by age 25. Men believe that women should marry earlier than do women themselves, but there is consensus that age 25 is the upper limit. Although the best age at marriage for men is clearly older than for women, there is remarkable consensus between

TABLE 1. Family-Size Preferences and Attitudes Toward Age at Marriage and Nonmarriage Among a National Sample of White American College Students, June 1971. Percentages.*

	College Men	College Women
How many children would you like to have?		
None	7	9
1	3	49
2	56	49
3 or more	33	38
Total	100	100
(N)	(548)	(348)
According to your personal tastes and preferences, what size family do you think is too small— a husband, wife, and how many children?		
No children	36	31
One child	53	58
Two children	7	6
Three or more	4	5
Total	100	100
(N)	(529)	(331)
And what size family do you think is too large—a husband, wife, and how many children?		
One child	1	0
Two children	1	1
Three children	19	16
Four children	25	21
Five children	25	23
Six children	11	15
Seven or more children	17	25
Total	100	100
(N)	(548)	(350)
What do you think is the best age for a girl to marry?		
Under 18	1	0
18–19	5	2
20	14	12
21	21	16
22	23	20
23–25	31	44
Over 25	5	6
Total	100	100
(N)	(529)	(343)

TABLE 1. (cont.)

	College Men	College Women
What do you think is the best age for a man to marry?		
Under 21	5	3
21–22	22	20
23–24	26	26
25	24	27
26–30	21	24
Over 30	2	1
Total	100	100
(N)	(533)	(344)
Do you think a woman can have a happy life even if she never marries?		
Yes	81	82
No	16	15
DK	3	3
Total	100	100
(N)	(562)	(355)
What about a man—do you think he can have a happy life if he never marries?		
Yes	87	84
No	12	13
DK	1	3
Total	100	100
(N)	(562)	(355)
Total Respondents	(562)	(355)

* The difference between N's shown under the various questions and the total number of respondents (562 males and 355 females) constitute the NA/DK category in each case.

men and women concerning what this age should be. Not before age 21, not after age 30. Preferably between ages 21 and 25. However, although marrying and having a family are clearly the norm, the college men and women in this sample do not deny that either a man or a woman can have a happy life in the unmarried state. There is a clear recognition that at least *some* people can do this. Unfortunately, we do not know, from this single question, whether respondents believe the "average" or "normal" person can be happy unmarried, or whether they believe only an unusual person can so exist.

These results may seem surprising in today's context. Has neo-feminism had no effect? Why is there no clear break with the family role altogether among a substantial number of the college elite?[38] In order to understand their position, one must realize that no call has come to make such a break, no models have been presented, no champion of a genuinely alternative role has appeared. "Women's liberation," like higher education for women and women's labor force activity, has absorbed, in its turn, the norm that the American woman's adult role *includes* motherhood. To have done otherwise would have been to sacrifice its principal constituency, as we shall see. It, like higher education for women and jobs for women, has *accommodated* itself to maternity and even become its militant champion. Motherhood is, after all, one of "women's rights."

Feminism and the "Do Both" Syndrome

It is often assumed that the present-day "woman's liberation" movement is essentially antinatalist in ideology and that its effects will be antinatalist as well. Actually, however, the main thrust of the movement's stand is supportive of motherhood for all; what is decried is the relative disadvantage that women experience because of childbearing and rearing. In effect, women's liberation is concerned with lowering the exclusionary barriers for women in the labor force, opening up educational channels, elevating women's awareness of subtle forms of discrimination against them in the outside world *and* supporting women's right to have families as well. Rather than concerning itself with the atypical spinster, or childless woman, the movement has gained popularity through its recognition of the problems of women who already have made a choice to be mothers and who then are dissatisfied with their impaired occupational chances, or who find motherhood less than they expected it to be and wish to switch gears. Betty Friedan's book, *The Feminine Mystique,* was addressed primarily to this group of women—those suffering from "the problem that has no name." However, although the movement has pitched its appeal to women who have already made their reproductive choices and urged them to seek out an alternative identity as well, its general philosophy for *all* women is one of *combining* marriage and motherhood, on the one hand, with a nonfamilial role, on the other. Indeed, it is this militant statement that women should not *have* to make a choice that gives the movement wide appeal. For example, Friedan says, "when enough women make life plans geared to their real abilities, and speak out for maternity leaves or even maternity sabbaticals, professionally run nurseries, and other changes in the rules that may be necessary, they will not have to sacrifice the right to honorable competition and contribution *any more than they will have to sacrifice marriage and motherhood.*"[39]

The movement sees the major injustice toward women as inhering in the expenditure of time and effort on childbearing, together with the loss of seniority and skills in the labor market due to interrupted career patterns. This philosophy is embodied in the Statement of Purpose of the National Organization for Women.

The modern liberationist position, which requires that women generally be enabled to forego choice in their dominant career roles and shift childrearing onto outside agencies, has been elaborated by a number of sociologists.

Writing in 1964, Alice Rossi claims that:

There is no sex equality until women participate on an equal basis with men in politics, occupations, and the family. . . . In politics and the occupational world, to be able to participate depends primarily on whether home responsibilities can be managed simultaneously with work or political commitments. Since women have had, and probably will continue to have, primary responsibility for child-rearing, their participation in politics, professions or the arts cannot be equal to that of men unless ways are devised to ease the combination of home and work responsibilities.[40]

Rossi goes on to outline the need for mother-substitutes, child-care centers, less sexual demarcation in personal traits, and a less demanding definition of the mother's role in socialization. However, she accepts the parental roles for both sexes. Rather than recognizing that men and women may be variably suited to parenthood, she assumes that all are suited and all could be androgynous. Thus they could reconcile the demands of child care and the desire of the woman to excel outside the home by having both parents play the "inside" and "outside" roles.[41]

Epstein sees the primacy of motherhood obligations for women as the principal barrier to occupational commitment and success. Yet, like Rossi, she does not question the basic premise of the universal desirability of motherhood. As she notes, being single or childless is being a "nonconformist." Thus, the basic inequality lies in the fact that although women are normatively held to child care and the home, men can ignore their families with impunity. She says,

The man who spends too much time with his family is considered something of a loafer. . . . In extreme cases of neglect, wives may be permitted to complain, but clearly the absorption of the man in his work is not considered intolerable. Professors who prefer their work to their wives or children are usually "understood" and forgiven. A similar absorption in work was reported by Stanley Talbot in Time magazine; he found that the business tycoon (not surprisingly) clearly preferred his work to his family. There is no comparable "lady tycoon" with a husband and children to neglect; and the lady professional who gives an indication of being more absorbed in work than in her husband and family is neither understood nor forgiven. The woman, unlike the man, cannot spend "too much time" with her family; her role demands as mother and wife are such that they intrude on all other activities.

She remains on call during any time spent away from the family and, if she works, many of her family tasks must be fitted into what usually would be working time.[42]

We thus see that, far from questioning the basic premise that all women *should* be mothers, or for that matter that all men should be fathers, the woman's liberation movement accepts the goal of reproduction for all as a basic "good." Childlessness is regarded as an inherent deprivation for some (perhaps even many). Women who cannot share equally with men in ignoring and neglecting their children are "disadvantaged." Unquestioned is the notion of why persons of *either* sex who have such a marginal commitment to child-rearing should be pressed into having children. If a man wishes to spend virtually his entire time on occupational achievement, travel, and golf, why should the parental status be socially supported as obligatory, or his way of life condemned as self-centered and hedonistic? At present, he has to buy his way out of censure by having a family as "window-dressing" even though he may not change his way of life as a result.[43] Similarly, if a woman wishes to enjoy an externally oriented way of life, it is intensely pronatalist to specify that nominal parenthood—shored up by maids, nurseries, and child-care centers—be required as a badge of respectability, normality, or conformity.

The woman's liberation movement thus parts company with antinatalism by failing to recognize that it is not in society's interest to encourage the emergence of families in which *neither* parent is committed to parenthood. Rather, a genuine antinatalist policy would be aimed at the *indiscriminate* nature of the family-building vortex that now exists. At present, marriage and parenthood are almost ascribed statuses. They are not really chosen, they happen to people, as the Burgess and Wallin quotation cited earlier states admirably. Moreover, the state takes an essentially frivolous attitude toward the *contracting* of the marital obligation, far more carefree than the attitude it takes toward business contracts. This point is well made by Robert Kingsley in an article on the grounds for granting annulments in the United States.

> A few courts have said that the issue was whether or not the party was mentally capable of entering into an ordinary commercial contract; but the later cases have held that there is no necessary connection between the capacity to make commercial contracts and the capacity to become married. The test today is usually put as requiring the mental ability to "understand the nature of the marriage-relation and the duties and obligations involved therein." So put, it is clear that the capacity to enter into business relations has no bearing on the capacity to marry. . . . For the numerically considerable group of mentally weak persons,

whose estates are controlled by guardians but who are permitted to go at large in the community, a legal prohibition on marriage would simply result in fornication, temporary liaisons, and similar socially undesirable practices. Consequently, the law wisely has permitted such persons to marry if it appeared that, concerning that particular kind of relationship, they had a reasonably intelligent attitude.[44]

Clearly, the state has, as a matter of public policy, viewed marriage not as the licensing of parental responsibility, but as a sop to Mrs. Grundy. Yet, the modern interest of the state concerning a marriage lies in the quality of the children produced, not in the prevention of premarital fornication. Nonetheless, the law of marriage is still geared to a time when it was important to use sex as a means of enticing people into marriage and childbearing. In this regard we may suggest that a significant control over reproductive motivation in the future could be the further development of the legal personality of the child, and a diminution of his being treated, at law, as the property of his parents. The "rights" of parents to "choose" parenthood, and the number of offspring they will have could be tempered by the rights of children to certain legal guarantees from their parents.[45] If fathers have already been "liberated" from many parental obligations, and mothers are on the way to "liberation," then obviously the rights and welfare of children must come under far more detailed legal and social scrutiny.

It is of some interest that the origins of the acceptance of (even insistence on) universal motherhood were clearly visible in the suffragist movement. As O'Neill points out:

> Having already taken the economic context of American life as essentially given, feminists went on to do the same thing for the marital and domestic system, accepting, for the most part, Victorian marriage as a desirable necessity. In so doing they assured the success of woman suffrage while guaranteeing that when women did get the vote and enter the labor market in large numbers, the results would be bitterly disappointing. . . .
>
> While feminism was born out of a revolt against stifling domesticity, . . . by the end of the century most feminists had succumbed to what Charlotte Perkins Gilman called the "domestic mythology." . . . the original feminists had demanded freedom in the name of humanity; the second generation asked for it in the name of maternity. What bound women into selfless sisterhood, it was now maintained, was their reproductive capacity. . . .
>
> So the effort to escape domesticity was accompanied by an innovation of the domestic ideal—woman's freedom road circled back to the

home from which feminism was supposed to liberate her. In this manner feminism was made respectable by accommodating it to the Victorian ethos which had originally forced it into being.[46]

Charlotte Perkins Gilman, however, recognized the logical problems inherent in the motherhood emphasis and presaged the feminist movement of the 1960's and 1970's by a formula that is now familiar to us: Women, generically, should both have families *and* take an equal place with men, in the non-familial world. In order to enable them to do this, the society must provide mechanisms to relieve them of their homemaking burdens.[47]

The assumption was made then, as it is now, that men—most or all men—find self-expression and fulfillment in the labor market, and that parenthood (and the economic obligations it involves) essentially leaves men's, but not women's, life chances untouched. Since the movement is a special pleading device, it could not be expected to recognize that those differential social and economic advantages that men experience as patriarchs have constituted an incentive for them to undertake the economic obligations of domesticity and parenthood. In many cases, men's chances for social and personal mobility, for education, for promotion, etc., may be impaired by parenthood, although these personal losses may be concealed or dulled by the satisfactions of conforming and the lesser social approval attached to bachelors and the childless. As with women, so with men, the society has many mechanisms for obscuring the costs of parenthood. The fact that men's story of frustration and despair has found expression in a context different from women's—that of liberation from external economic exploitation—should not obscure the relevance of this story for our concern with pronatalist coercions. The dominant, powerful male of the feminist, woman's liberation script, the male in whose interest and for whose pleasure the society appears to exist, is clearly not the same character who appears in the Marxist-New Leftist script. In the latter, modern man is enslaved by a "system," forced to labor at meaningless tasks from which he is totally alienated, an "un-person," a "nothing." As Marcuse has said:

> Men do not live their own lives, but perform preestablished functions. While they work, they do not fulfill their own needs and faculties but work in *alienation*. Work has now become *general*, and so have the restrictions placed upon the libido: labor time, which is the largest part of the individual's life time, is painful time, for alienated labor is absence of gratification, negation of the pleasure principle. Libido is diverted for socially useful performances in which the individual works for himself only in so far as he works for the apparatus, engaged in activities that mostly do not coincide with his own faculties and desires.[48]

Although neither the feminist nor the New Left movements can be taken as unbiased observers of the social scene, the quotation from Marcuse cautions us not to forget that men undergo both direct and opportunity costs in meeting their economic obligations to their families. It is possible, indeed probable, that many men would choose a different way of life were it both honored and accessible. . . .

CONCLUSION

The formulation of explicit antinatalist policies requires an awareness of existing pronatalist ones. Lacking such awareness, action is side-tracked by a spurious controversy as to whether coercion should be instituted or voluntarism maintained. Actually, as this paper has tried to show, our society is already pervaded by time-honored pronatalist constraints. Thus, I have argued, we cannot preserve a choice that does not genuinely exist, and, by the same token, it makes no sense to institute antinatalist coercions while continuing to support pronatalist ones. Insofar as we wish to move in the direction of stabilized zero population growth, the first job for policy would seem to be to eliminate coercive pronatalist influences in a manner that is minimally disruptive of social order.

The scope of this task reminds us that a demographic revolution has more profound implications than might appear from a mere consideration of birth, death, and growth rates. These are only indicators of a society's ability to cope with the survival problem in a particular way. Behind them lie the social organization and control mechanisms that channel resources into the production and rearing of offspring on the one hand, and the effort to avert death, on the other. Population policy, therefore, inevitably goes to the heart of our way of life. To move from one policy (albeit implicit) to another (perhaps explicit) raises issues that threaten many of our established norms and habits. We are bound to experience anxiety in even thinking about the changes that may lie ahead. On the other hand, to allow a diversion of resources from reproduction may help to resolve social problems that are currently engendered by pronatalist constraints. Certainly our increased reproductive efficiency does not, of itself, imply the need for greater regimentation but rather the opposite. It makes possible a fuller expression of human individuality and diversity. After all, each generation provides us with the raw materials for evolutionary adaptation. The problem of adapting to low mortality is, therefore, not one of browbeating biologically specialized individuals out of behavior that is "natural" for all. Rather, it is one of directing cultural and social institutions into the use of human variability for meeting the new functional demands of a modern, low mortality society. In this endeavor, freedom for the development of individual potential may be greatly enhanced. I seriously doubt that it will be curtailed.

NOTES

1. *Vital Statistics of the United States,* Vol. I-Natality, 1968, pp. 1–15. By January 1, 1969, women aged 35–39 had borne 3,124 children per 1,000 women. If it were possible to relate this cumulative cohort fertility to *ever-married* women only, we would find that births per ever-married women (what we think of as "family size") were considerably higher.

2. Tomas Frejka, "Reflections on the Demographic Conditions Needed to Establish a U.S. Stationary Population Growth," *Population Studies,* 22 (November 1968), pp. 379–97.

3. See, for example, Garrett Hardin, "The Tragedy of the Commons," *Science,* 162 (December 13, 1968), pp. 1243–48; Paul R. Ehrlich and Anne H. Ehrlich, *Population, Resources, Environment* (San Francisco: W. H. Freeman & Co., 1970), pp. 254–56 and 272–74; and Kenneth Boulding, *The Meaning of the 20th Century* (New York: Harper and Row, 1964).

4. Bumpass and Westoff have calculated a "medium" estimate of the number of "unwanted" births in the United States for the period 1960–1965 as 19.1 percent of all births. Larry Bumpass and Charles F. Westoff, "The 'Perfect Contraceptive' Population," *Science,* 169 (September 18, 1970), pp. 1177–82. For a demonstration that the current level of "unwanted" births in the United States is much lower than the Bumpass and Westoff estimate, see Judith Blake, "Reproductive Motivation and Population Policy," *BioScience,* 21 (March 1, 1971), pp. 215–20. This paper also shows that the inoffensiveness of the family planning approach is overrated. "Unwanted" births occur most frequently among politically sensitive sub-groups in our population.

5. Frank W. Notestein, "Zero Population Growth," *Population Index,* 36 (October-December 1970), p. 448.

6. Conditional factors affecting birth rates are, for example, involuntary infecundity or the inability to find a mate because of an imbalance in the sex ratio due to migration. Conditional factors are those over which the individual has no control—his efforts cannot affect them, hence, his motives are not relevant to the outcome.

7. Ernest W. Burgess and Paul Wallin, "Idealization, Love, and Self-Esteem," reprinted in *Family Roles and Interaction,* ed. Jerold Heiss (Chicago: Rand McNally, 1969), pp. 121–22.

8. Although the primary focus of the typical masculine role might seem to be occupational in modern societies, the structural basis for the man's claim on an occupational role relates very clearly to his family obligations. Indeed, as will be seen later in this paper, a man's prior claim, over a woman, to a job has rested on his role of provider for a family. A married man who is a father has a similar prior claim to a job (or to a promotion) over a bachelor. From the man's subjective point of view, except in a few independently attractive occupations, the economic role is merely instrumental to the private (usually familial) existence.

9. For a cross-cultural analysis (based on almost 50 primitive and modern societies) of sex-role differentiation, see Morris Zelditch, Jr., "Role Differentiation in the Nuclear Family: A Comparative study," in *Family, Socialization and Interaction Process,* ed. Talcott Parsons and Robert F. Bales (Glencoe, Illinois: The Free Press, 1955), pp. 309–51. Although of great value, Zelditch's analysis was not designed to bring out some of the variability among societies in the availability of alternative sex roles. For example, one contrast between many European countries and the United States is the existence, in the former but not in the latter, of an established religion having a celibate clergy. Additionally, European countries have suffered from numerous unintended antinatalist constraints—devastating wars on their own territories, acute housing shortages, and, as compared with overseas European countries, fewer op-

portunities for upward social mobility and more parental control over the means to marry. It is of some interest that, in the mid-1960's, only 10 percent of American women remained single in the age group 20–29. Among European countries, in the same period for the same age group, percentages single among women were, on the average, approximately double that of the United States. For a discussion of contrasts between Europe and the United States, see Judith Blake, "Demographic Science and the Redirection of Population Policy," in Mindel C. Sheps and Jeanne Clare Ridley, *Public Health and Population Change* (Pittsburgh: University of Pittsburgh Press, 1965), pp. 41–69; and "Parental Control, Delayed Marriage, and Population Policy."

10. Robert W. Smuts, *Women and Work in America* (New York: Columbia University, 1959), pp. 110–55.

11. Betty R. Stirling, "The Interrelation of Changing Attitudes and Changing Conditions with Reference to the Labor Force Participation of Wives," unpublished Ph.D. dissertation, University of California, Berkeley, 1963, pp. 6–72.

12. *Ibid.*, pp. 73–81.

13. *Ibid.*, pp. 180–83.

14. National Manpower Council, *Womanpower* (New York: Columbia University Press, 1957), pp. 15–16.

15. Oppenheimer's statistical analysis of the interaction of supply and demand in women's increased labor force participation between 1940 and 1960 illustrates this point. The supply of what had, historically, been the "typical" female worker, a young, unmarried woman, remained stationary or declined. Hence, the only mechanism whereby the observed increase in the female labor force could have taken place was through the participation of another category of women. This category was principally the older, married woman whose childbearing obligations were either ended or greatly lessened. Valerie K. Oppenheimer, "The Interaction of Demand and Supply and its Effect on the Female Labor Force in the United States," *Population Studies,* 21 (November, 1967), pp. 239–59.

16. Smuts, *op. cit.*, p. 109.

17. See, for example, Dorothy Gies McGuigan, *A Dangerous Experiment. 100 Years of Women at the University of Michigan* (Ann Arbor: Center for Continuing Education of Women, 1970).

18. Mabel Newcomer, *A Century of Higher Education for American Women* (New York: Harper & Brothers, 1959), p. 210.

19. *Ibid.*, pp. 146–47.

20. *Ibid.*, p. 60.

21. Lynn White, Jr., *Educating our Daughters* (New York: Harper & Bros., 1950), pp. 46–48.

22. *Ibid.*, pp. 46–47.

23. O'Neill, *op. cit.*, p. 37.

24. White, *op. cit.*, pp. 71–76.

25. *Ibid.*, p. 76.

26. *Ibid.*, pp. 93–96.

27. *Ibid.*, p. 101.

28. Mirra Komarovsky, *Women in the Modern World* (Boston: Little, Brown & Company, 1953), pp. 66–67.

29. *Ibid.*, pp. 68–69, 69–71, 72. Italics mine.

30. Rose K. Goldsen, Morris Rosenberg, Robin M. Williams, Jr., and Edward A. Suchman, *What College Students Think* (Princeton, New Jersey: Princeton University Press, 1960), pp. 46–47.

31. *Ibid.*, pp. 47–49.

32. *Ibid.*, p. 58.

33. *Ibid.*, pp. 58–59.

34. *Ibid.*, p. 90.

35. *Ibid.*, p. 48.

36. *Ibid.*, p. 53.

37. Although no exactly comparable data on a college-*attending* population are available for the earlier period, it is worth noting that among college-*educated* men and women under age 30 in the late 1950's mean *ideal* family size was 3.3–3.4, in contrast to 2.4–2.5 as the mean *desired* family size in this current sample of college students. Data for 1971 on *ideal* family size among college-educated respondents in the reproductive ages show means varying between 2.6 and 2.8. These recent data will be published shortly by the author.

38. It should be noted that, as might be expected, the noncollege sample of 18–24 year olds is more pronatalist in its attitudes than the college group.

39. Betty Friedan, *The Feminine Mystique* (New York: Dell Publishing, 1963), pp. 381–82. Italics mine.

40. Alice S. Rossi, "Equality Between the Sexes: An Immodest Proposal," *Daedelus* (Spring, 1964), p. 610.

41. *Ibid.*, pp. 639–46.

42. Cynthia Fuchs Epstein, *Woman's Place* (Berkeley and Los Angeles: University of California Press, 1970), pp. 99–100.

43. According to Whyte, the good executive's wife is one who accedes to and abets the husband's total commitment to the organization. The company views the man's family as instrumental to its ends and tolerates it only in so far as this proves to be the case. For this reason, the executive's wives are screened in order to see whether they are willing to play the required role. In this manner, many large corporations endeavor to hire men who are, effectively, domesticated bachelors. See William H. Whyte, "The Wife Problem," *Life* (January 7, 1952), reprinted in Robert F. Winch, Robert McGinnis, and Herbert R. Baringer (eds.), *Selected Studies in Marriage and the Family* (New York: Holt, Rinehart, Winston, 1962), pp. 111–26.

44. Robert Kingsley, "What are the Proper Grounds for Granting Annulments?" *Law and Contemporary Problems* 18 (1953), pp. 40–41.

45. For a discussion of American family law and the shift "from a patriarchal family structure to one in which the spouses are more nearly equal as between themselves but dominant in their legal relations with their children," see Herma H. Kay, "The Outside Substitute for the Family," reprinted in *The Family and Change*, ed. John N. Edwards (New York: Knopf, 1969), pp. 261–69. Kay also documents indications that "the future path of legal development will be directed toward the emergence of the child as a person in his own right." p. 266.

46. William O'Neill, *Everyone Was Brave: The Rise and Fall of Feminism in America* (New York: Quadrangle Books, 1968), pp. 30–36.

47. Carl N. Degler, "Revolution Without Ideology: The Changing Place of Women in America," *Daedalus* (Spring, 1964), p. 668.

48. Herbert Marcuse, *Eros and Civilization* (New York: Vintage Books, 1962), p. 41.

27

A Small Failure in Birth Control

Mahmood Mamdani

> But they were so nice, you know. And they came from distant lands
> to be with us. Couldn't we even do this much for them? Just take
> a few tablets? Ah! even the gods would have been angry with us. They
> wanted no money for the tablets. All they wanted was that we accept
> the tablets. I lost nothing and probably received their prayers. And
> they, they surely must have gotten some promotion.

So the hakim, the traditional doctor, explained why many villagers had
taken the contraceptive tablets, although they had not used them. He
smiled and took another deep puff from his hand-rolled bidi, or cigarette.
It was six in the morning, and several farmers squatted at the village gate
listening to Hakimji tell of how the times had changed.

"Aho, aho, well said. No one will ever go back from this village saying
we are not hospitable," several chimed in unison, as heads nodded in agreement.

A hundred miles and six hours away from this village of Manupur
was the new and shiny capital of Indian Punjab. Sitting in a new government office, one of the two assistant field directors of the Khanna Study,
Dr. Sohan Singh, reflected upon the project's unsuccessful attempt to introduce birth control in rural Punjab: "The villagers are ignorant, you know.
What they need first of all is some education.

The Khanna Study—named after the market town where its field
headquarters were located—was the first major field study in birth control
in India. It was conducted in seven "test" villages with a total population of
8,000 people. Its field operations lasted a total of six years, from 1954 to
1960, and the study cost approximately $1 million. It was a failure.

In July 1953, the Harvard School of Public Health had prepared a report on the "population problem," the thesis of which was that although recent advances in the field of public health had resulted in spectacular and welcome declines in the death rate in "underdeveloped countries," these very declines had generated another major problem: populations were rising at an unprecedented rate. The Harvard sponsors went on to propose a long-term population field study aimed at devising methods that could later be employed to solve the "population problem."

The proposal found several sympathetic ears and a number of sponsors—the Rockefeller Foundation and the Indian government, in particular—which financed the six-year field study and the follow-up study in the summer of 1969.

The follow-up study showed that the birth control program had been a failure. Although the crude birth rate of the study population was 40 per 1,000 in 1957, and 35 per 1,000 in 1968, this reduction could not be traced to the birth control program since it occurred among both the test and the control populations.

From the outset, the Khanna Study was quite aware that it would be operating in another cultural milieu. What it feared most was the possibility of misunderstandings and misperceptions stemming from a "cultural prejudice," and precautions were taken to minimize this possibility.

In fact, the study was plagued very little by the sort of "cultural" misunderstanding that it had feared in the earlier stages. What *did* plague it was the directors' basic perception of the problem. To them, overpopulation was a disease. "Excessive population pressure" was a "social malady" and the "birth control program" a "remedy." The perception of overpopulation as a disease became an analytical tool for misunderstanding.

As the villagers remained unreceptive to the birth control program, concern grew in the higher echelons of the staff. As a result, the staff was asked to improve the content and form of its communications to the villagers: they had not been given sufficient information on their own population problem to be convinced of the urgent necessity of practicing contraception; nor had this information been transmitted through the most effective channels of communication.

What is most interesting about this analysis is the way it betrays the elitism of the social engineer. The underlying assumption is that the behavior of the population, given the environment and its constraints, is not rational: it is thus susceptible to "education." And if education fails, it is merely a question of not having used the right "techniques." In fact, the directors were saying that the fundamental problem lay not with the study but with the perception the villagers had of their own environment.

The fact is that an overwhelming majority of the people in the Khanna

Study area have a large number of children because they want *larger* families. More important, they want them because they *need* them.

The study had misplaced its fears of acting out a cultural bias. All efforts had been expended to ensure that the field workers were all Punjabis and that the American supervisors had considerable familiarity with India. But the staff, though Punjabis like the villagers, were all members of the urban, educated middle class. What they shared with the directors was a bourgeois culture. What plagued the study was not a *national* (Western vs. Indian) bias but a *class* bias. This bias pervaded its staff as well as its directors, without distinction of race, religion or "culture."

The struggle for survival and continued existence occupies the better part of an individual's time in Manupur. There exists an urgency and immediacy about material interests that cannot escape even the casual visitor. In Manupur, life *is* work.

The family structure in Manupur is rigidly patriarchal and authoritarian. An older man—and in Manupur that means one past his forties—who has a number of children in the house is assured a certain ease in life. When he returns from work, whatever the work may be, his youngest will massage his head and feet, or his body, if it aches. Children perform a variety of small tasks that adults regard as tedious, time-consuming and timesome. Whether you are rich or poor, you are ensured these small luxuries if you have enough children.

There is no adolescence in Manupur. There is only childhood and adulthood. The young in Manupur seldom display the carefree, spontaneous attitude that industrial society proverbially associates with youth. Children learn that if they are to be part of the family, they must contribute to it. Thus, children grow, not into youths, but into young adults.

The fact that the family is the basic unit of work has important social implications. The discipline of work is reflected in the discipline of the family. For an overwhelming majority in Manupur, the family enterprise is the source of economic security. When a couple grows too old to work, their only shelter is among their children, and parents have a socially approved claim on the resources of their children. When no children have survived or none were born—most unusual, in either case—the parents continue to live in the family home and survive on the charity handed out by relations or other caste members.

Children—especially sons—are vital to the people of Manupur. And so it is to be expected that religion, myth, tradition and ritual will reinforce the belief in this necessity. A variety of media—song, story, proverb or even the mere explanation of phenomena—are used for this purpose. The message transmitted is always the same: it is one's dharma, one's religious and social obligation, to have children. To desire as many children as possible is not only in the natural order of things but also an indication of virtue. Severe penalties are imposed on the "barren" wife, and this includes not merely women who have no sons. Childlessness is the main reason for divorce and the only socially acceptable justification for polygamy.

The majority in Manupur found it difficult to believe that the Khanna Study had actually come to introduce contraceptive practices. Even though the Khanna Study was a reality obvious to all, even though its staff lived in the village for a number of years, and even though the whole enterprise "must have cost an incredible amount of money," the majority of the villagers never understood why so much money and effort was being spent on family planning when "surely everybody knows that children are a necessity in life."

To the directors of the Khanna Study, all this was evidence of a communications problem: that the "right" leaders had not been contacted, that the "right" kind of information had not been given out. Yet it is clear that there were no leaders, that the whole enterprise seemed fantastic to almost everybody. Furthermore, it was precisely the "right" kind of information—stating that birth control and family planning were the "real" purposes of the Khanna Study—that the people found most incredible. A Jat farmer, gently stroking his young son's hair, told me: "These Americans are enemies of the smile on this child's face. All they are interested in is war or family planning."

To be sure, there are people in Manupur who will echo the arguments of the "outsider." These people maintain that the farmer should be afraid of land fragmentation and should thus limit his family, that he should realize that "population pressure" exists and should thus be motivated to use family planning. Those who think this way come either from among the few who own large and mechanized farms or from those who are outside of the agricultural economy: a teacher, a family-planning worker or a money-lender. They either forget, or do not realize, that their own material circumstances have led them to limit their families. Although they live in Manupur, they share the prejudices of the Khanna Study directors and its staff. It is here that the *class* basis of perceptions becomes evident.

One man was an exception to this class prejudice in Manupur. He was Pandit Pritamdasji, a 50-year-old Brahman who worked as a clerk at the school, an "educated" man who had left the village in preindependence days to fight with the Indian National Army against the British colonial government. In one of our many discussions, he said: "Africa has on the average 90 persons per square mile, very little population and no 'population pressure.' Yet it is poor. We are not poor because of our numbers. The reason is another...."

The reason he seemed to point to was the class system. And, because of it, the conclusion was and is that India's poverty cannot be "cured" by a pill.—Intellectual Digest Ed.

Population Politics and Policies

Introduction: A. Population Policy: National and Worldwide

The term population policy is ideally limited to political decisions that have legal status and are aimed at influencing the size, growth, nongrowth or composition of the population of some political unit. This conceptualization implies that the political action of some authority body is a conscious, deliberate, and explicit attempt to influence the population. These actions, depending upon the nature of the political authority, may be in the form of decrees, laws, regulations, or administrative orders. But when we move from the realm of the nominal definition to reality there are at least two features of population policies that complicate analysis. The first of these complications is that there are often laws, regulations, or administrative orders that affect the population, but they do not have the explicit aim of influencing population. The key word in this statement is explicit. There are many laws, regulations, and orders that are aimed at nonpopulation issues, but they have the unintended or incidental effect of influencing population. These are the latent functions that may accompany *any* structural change. Thus, for example, selective service laws or home loan policies may influence age at marriage and, by extension, the fertility of a population. These kinds of policies might be successfully identified and separated from actual population policies were it not for an additional problem that seems to be generated by the political process. That is, the tendency of governmental authorities to disguise what are, *in fact*, population policies as something else. As sociologist Robin Williams pointed out many years ago political behavior often contains "cultural fictions." One type of cultural fiction occurs when a statement is made about some action, but when almost everyone, including the person making the statement, knows that the reason being given is not the real reason. For example, when a president gives glowing praise and warm thanks to a public official who is being forced to resign or is being fired, most people recognize that the president is not expressing his true feelings. He is simply perpetuating the cultural fiction that all public servants are always good and loyal. Sometimes cultural fictions are easy to detect and even familiar, other times they are not so obvious.

The history of population policies shows them to be particularly susceptible to cultural fictions. The liberalization of abortion laws has invariably had a dramatic effect upon fertility, but changes are usually advocated under some cultural fiction. While I cannot document it, I believe that the liberalization of abortion laws in the last decade in the United States was largely due to the response of many legislators to the perceived excessive fertility of the population. But even more pointed, I believe that many legislators voted for liberalized abortion laws because they believed there was excessive fertility in some particular sector of the population: for example, unmarried welfare recipients. But what lawmaker said this? To my knowledge almost no one, except perhaps some of the *opponents* of liberalized abortion laws. Most of the abortion laws were passed under the guise of maternal health. This is not unique to the United States. Eastern European countries, Japan, and Mainland China have all used maternal health as the reason for accepting more liberalized abortion laws. At least in the latter two cases most observers believe that the *real reason* was to slow down excessive population growth that was impeding, or threatened to impede, the achievement of some other goal.

All of this leaves us in an awkward position when we attempt to understand and anticipate population policies for the United States, or any country. Objectively, it may be impossible to distinguish the latent or indirect effects of a nonpopulation policy from a population policy that is clothed in some cultural fiction. About the only explicit population policy we have ever had in the United States was the essentially racist national-quota immigration policy adopted in the 1920's. It was a fairly explicit policy that said "we don't want many more of 'those kinds' of people." Even in this case, however, I expect that a reading of the Congressional debates over the national origins quota system would reveal a few cultural fictions.

While we may bemoan this kind of political misdirection about population policies, it may be more enlightening to analyze *why* it occurs. This may tell us something about some underlying population values and allow us to make a more realistic analysis of what kind of explicit population policy we may expect in the future. Historically, I think it can be documented that population policies that lead to *population growth*, either through a decrease in mortality or the increase in fertility have usually been explicit. The case of France is illustrative. Since France was one of the first industrial countries to experience a decline in fertility that threatened to decrease her population, the French engaged in specific actions to stimulate the fertility of the populace. Family allowances were used in France, as they have been in many countries, to increase fertility rates. The explicit aim was to produce a larger French population. Both nationalism and ethnocentrism made this population policy acceptable to politicians and the people alike.

Similarly, death-control policies (usually through public health measures), which also increase population, have been explicitly and openly proclaimed. Reducing infant mortality and prolonging life, as death-control policies, were acceptable because they added to the population of the nation. This acceptance of population growth policies may be deduced directly from the premise that "Our nation is good and our ways are the right ways." Therefore, it must be good to have more national citizens. This logic does not usually extend to immigration because *too many aliens* are suspect. Even Australia, which encourages immigration, makes severe limitations on who may enter the country. In Australia, and most other countries, the immigrant who is racially or culturally different from the native population is not usually welcomed, and is often explicitly excluded.

It seems that population policies are usually a function of two underlying values. The first is the value placed on life generally. *Life is good; nonlife is bad.* (Nonlife refers both to death and nonfertility.) This value is as close to a universal societal value as we may ever find. The exceptions (such as infanticide or geriatricide), while dramatic, are demographically insignificant. The second value is also probably universal, though it has taken on different historical manifestations. It is the very familiar ethnocentric notion that the group we belong to is the best group, the superior or chosen group. In its modern manifestation this is usually the national group, but it can be some subgroup within a national population (usually either a religious or racial category).

From this set of values we may deduce that *the population policy of a nation-state will be more likely to be explicit if it is aimed at increasing the population, with the proviso that it must retain the character and integrity of the existing population.* A population policy that is aimed at decreasing the population or changing its character will be viewed with apprehension by the populace and thus approached very gingerly by political leaders (even the most autocratic).

Some demographers have called for a national population policy for the United States, or even a comprehensive world population policy. But there is one very practical problem that arises whenever serious discussion begins. If a society is large and heterogeneous, *any population policy* (whether it be a growth or nongrowth policy) will have such diverse ramifications and implications that it may be almost impossible to get a national consensus. Changes in population have social, economic, environmental, religious, political and humanitarian implications and effects. With these diverse and often countervailing perspectives, can it be any wonder that agreement is difficult to achieve? Almost any proposed policy (on, say, growth or nongrowth) will infringe upon someone's needs or desires. The more heterogeneous the society, the more difficult it is to achieve an acceptable population policy.

The papers in Part A of this section are the views of four demographers on the population policy labeled "zero population growth." Frank Notestein begins this discussion with his observations on the goal of zero population growth. Basically he advocates a "voluntaristic road" to a zero growth population, for while he recognizes that it will be slower, he feels that the goal will ultimately be achieved and at a lesser cost in personal freedom. The following article (29) brings together the responses of Philip Hauser, Judith Blake, and Paul Demeny in criticism and reaction to Notestein's statement. As a set, these papers bring out most of the important issues related to a zero population growth policy.

28

Zero Population Growth

Frank Notestein

Zero population growth, as platitude, sales slogan or urgent goal, has caught the public by storm—and included in that public are many biologists and economists, as well as a considerable number of sociologists and demographers.

From one point of view, favoring zero population growth is somewhat like favoring the laws of motion. Anyone who knows how to use a table of logarithms must be aware that in the long run the average rate of population growth will approach zero as a limit. If, for example, the world's population had grown at its present rate since the beginning of the Christian era, the water content of the human race would fill a sphere having a radius more than ten times that of the earth. Zero growth is, then, not simply a desirable goal; it is the only possibility in a finite world. One cannot object to people who favor the inevitable.

There is another group that values zero population growth because it is a powerful sales slogan. They are willing to accept, even to promote, the slogan, despite its ambiguity, because of the energy and resources it brings to the subject of population. Some of these supporters foster the popular impression that population growth could be stopped quickly by acceptable means if only the public were alerted to the dangers of the situation; and a few of them advance this line despite their private opinions to the contrary. They justify this lack of candor on the grounds that egregious overstatement is necessary to arouse public interest. They seem to feel that it takes massive advertising to sell both soap and the ecological necessity for a prompt end to population growth. With that I am inclined to agree. But it is a sad day when we see professionally expert distortions of the truth peddled to the public under the highest scientific auspices, as if

Reprinted from *Population Index*, 36, no. 4 (October-December, 1970), pp. 444–51, by permission of the author and the publisher.

truth can be fostered best by untruth. When scientists become concerned with reform, as I think duty indeed requires, they will at their peril abandon the ardent respect for truth that lies at the basis of their professions. It is hard enough to stick to the truth when one tries. Fortunately, this huckstering group is only a small part of those who see zero population growth as a slogan that arouses interest in objectives perceived to be both timely and important. To this there can be no objection. It is our obligation to stick to the truth, but we are not compelled to be dull about it.

Many of its most earnest advocates obviously see zero population growth as more than a slogan, and more than a platitude about long-run objectives. They want, or at least some of them want, zero growth, if not yesterday, at least now. They want it, moreover, if not on any terms, at least with the sense of urgency that makes them willing to accept many second- and third-order effects without careful examination. It is to these questions that we must turn our most careful attention. This means that we must ask with what urgency it is necessary to seek zero growth under varying circumstances. What are the advantages and disadvantages of attaining the goal with varying speeds, and what are the advantages and disadvantages of using various methods for its attainment? The assessment of the means is quite as important as the assessment of the goal.

There may be different answers for the technologically more developed and less developed countries, because of differences in the severity of the problem as well as differences in the availability of means for their solution. Let us consider first the problem in developed countries, and particularly the United States.

ZPG IN THE DEVELOPED REGIONS

Here the ecologists take the hardest line. Some of them seem to be saying that we now stand in mortal danger if our population continues to grow; indeed, that we already have too much population and should start reducing the size. On matters of resources, energy, and ecology I am outside of my professional field, but I have read some and listened more, and I find these ecologists' case wholly unpersuasive. There are no substantial limits in sight either in raw materials or in energy that alterations in the price structures, product substitution, anticipated gains in technology and pollution control cannot be expected to solve.[1] Subject to one condition, my statement seems to be in agreement with the overwhelming weight of professional opinion. The limitation arises from the fact that on the side of resources and technology we can look ahead only about a generation in terms of specific technology and known raw materials. Obviously our human interests run much farther into the future; but we cannot spell out the nature of a technology not yet developed. One can, however, on the assumption of an ordered world, reasonably predict immensely powerful developments based on cheap and virtually unlimited energy and, thanks partly to that, on an enormously expanded availability of conventional and new raw materials.

Much of the pessimistic argument is based on the idea that there are nonrenewable resources in our finite world. This seems to me to miss the point. Basically resources are not material; they are socially defined. Coal did not become a resource until a few centuries ago. It is barely one hundred years since petroleum had any but medical and magical uses. Nuclear energy is only beginning to become a resource, although it has almost unlimited prospects. We talk of diminishing returns from nonrenewable resources, but so far as I know almost all materials usually put in that category have declined in relative worth. Even with modern machinery it no longer pays to clear land in the United States. Indeed, land has never been so abundant. The fact is that basically we have only one nonrenewable resource, and that is space. Otherwise, mankind's basic resources are knowledge and skill, mainly of the organizational kind.

Nor do I share in that ocean of guilt now flooding the literature because our small fraction of the world's population consumes the lion's share of the world's resources. I hope our share becomes smaller as others gain, but I do not want a reduction of our per capita consumption. Thanks, indeed, to the high consumption of the developed world we have generated the knowledge and techniques that have greatly expanded both the supplies and the reserves of such raw materials in the world. There has often been outrageous waste but, on balance, our heavy use is expanding the world's resources, not diminishing them. We can get into intricate discussions about whether the more developed regions have paid enough for the raw materials they have purchased from the less developed regions,[2] but we cannot fail to see that substantial reductions of our purchases from those regions would bring them to economic chaos and greatly retard their development. Our sin is not use. Rather, it is the failure to pay the costs of use by avoiding pollution and by recycling minerals instead of further degrading them. I think it is time that social scientists look at resources in the same dynamic terms with which they have become accustomed recently to study population.

If we consider the evidence, not the inchoate fears, there is not the slightest indication that per capita income in the United States would be consequentially different if we had 50 or 100 million more people than we have, or 50 or 100 million fewer people. At present, the costs of both energy and raw materials represent such a small proportion of our total costs that they could be drastically increased with a negligible effect on per capita income.

Moreover, the current excitement about the size of population as a cause of pollution is almost completely without merit, save in the sense that there can be no pollution without polluters. That there is severe pollution is all too evident; but it is equally evident that pollution is related almost exclusively to mismanagement and to our high standard of living. It is related negligibly to our numbers. If we had half the population and the same per capita income, we would have much the same kind of urban concentration and much the same local pollution. Australia is sparsely populated but has 80 percent of its people concentrated in huge cities, and has much the same kind of smog and other pollution as do we.

Moreover, it is silly to suggest that reductions in population would drastically help in attacking pollution while we continue to raise our per capita incomes. There has been a vast increase in use of electricity in this country since World War II—a fact which has worried those concerned with heat and air pollution. But if we wished to achieve the per capita use of electricity of 1960 without increasing the total produced above the 1940 level, we would need to reduce our United States population below 25 million. Pollution control of all kinds will involve social and economic changes of considerable magnitude, but manipulation of the numbers of people in the society to solve this problem is probably not a realistically open option.

Nor, incidentally, does the exhortation that people should stop aspiring to lift their standards of living come gracefully from college professors, already sitting comfortably in the top ten percent of the income distribution of the richest nation on earth. I doubt that we members of the international jet set will be very effective in telling others that they should not aspire to live half as well as we do, lest pollution destroy our narrowly balanced ecology.

In political terms, relating pollution to population may have done harm to a serious attack on both pollution and population growth. It weakens interest in the present by concentrating on a distant goal. The effective approach to pollution is to make the polluters pay, and to start doing so as soon as possible. This will cost all of us money, for we are all polluters. We also need research on a vastly increased scale. That, too, is expensive. Particularly, we need research in ecology. It is time for some solid information to replace the bad dreams of the enthusiasts, their yearnings for traditional biological equilibria, and their reasoning by analogy. It is a distraction from an immediate attack on pollution to concentrate attention on the importance of stopping population growth in, say, 20, 30 or 50 years. Similarly, it is a distraction from legitimate concern for the nation's population policy to base the attack on ecological ghost stories instead of the actual inhumanities of our reproductive process. The present population-pollution axis, by raising false issues, deters rather than helps realistic and urgently needed efforts in both fields.

My own interest in speeding the end of population growth in the United States is based on much less urgent problems than the constraints of dwindling resources and energy or the risk of insoluble ecological problems. It is clear that growth must stop sometime, both here and in the world as a whole. It does not seem that we are likely to grow in national effectiveness by virtue of increasing numbers. At least, I have difficulties thinking of any national need for which we do not have enough population to provide the economies of large-scale production. On esthetic grounds it seems to me that we should avoid becoming a highly crowded nation. Europe is much more densely settled, but we are a more mobile people, and more space will almost certainly add to our enjoyment. I would like to come to zero population growth, but with no great haste and without making important sacrifices in the process of accomplishing it.

It is also clear that some costs will be entailed if we come to an end of growth. I shall not detail them, because they are well set out in the prewar literature on stagnation. I doubt that the costs of stopping growth will be nearly as high as then envisioned. Much has since been learned about managing the level of economic activity. But some adjustments will have to be made. Our entire economy has developed in a period of population growth with the relatively young populations that high birth rates produce. Nevertheless, this is an adjustment that must be made sometime unless we start lifting the death rates of the oldsters drastically—a proposal with which I have an understandable lack of sympathy. In short, I would like to see population growth come to a gradual end in the United States. But my lack of a sense of great urgency makes me unwilling to accept drastic means such as those often proposed by the people to whom the problems of energy, resources, and ecological protection have high saliency.

I would be happy if, for example, we could reach replacement level of reproduction in 10 or 15 years and stay there until the end of the century. After that I would have no objection to an intrinsic rate of natural decrease of a quarter of one percent for a time. If we did this, we would still come to a maximum population of something like 300 millions in some 70 to 90 years. These to me are acceptable goals as to numbers. They are not very important, however, compared to the means for their attainment.

The rates of population change and the factors determining them are very much more important than the size of the population. Family planning represents a new and important freedom in the world. It will surely be a happy day when parents can have and can avoid having children, as they see fit. We are coming close to realization of that goal—a goal that has given new dignity and new importance to the individual. We have not yet arrived at it. Larry Bumpass and Charles F. Westoff[3] have shown that the proportion of unwanted births was substantial in the first half of the 1960's.

It was very much higher in the lower educational groups, in the lower income groups, and, partly as a consequence of this, among Negroes. It is a matter of major importance that this kind of new freedom to choose, now existing for the bulk of the population, be extended to its most disadvantaged parts. If it were extended, reproduction would be brought fairly close to the replacement level. However, I would advocate the right to choose even if I thought the demographic consequences would be highly adverse, because it will always remain possible to manipulate the environment in which the choice is made.

I happen also to favor the repeal of laws against abortion in the belief that parents should control the destiny of the nonviable products of their bodies. I do not favor it on demographic grounds, and hope that when abortion becomes legal, no one will advocate it as anything but the personal tragedy which it inevitably is. One may expect, however, that easy abortion will further reduce the birth rate.

It is not at all beyond belief that, with contraceptives of ever increasing efficiency and legal abortion, fertility may fall below the replacement level. And, of course, it also may not. But, lacking a sense of urgency in matters of population size and believing in the importance of voluntary parenthood as a human freedom, I hope we do not accept drastic proposals to reward or penalize reproduction. We should wait at least until all of the population has ready access to effective contraception, and we can see under these conditions how the trend is going.

It seems to me dangerous to endeavor to penalize reproduction by various economic constraints because almost certainly the political process would result in maximum pressures on the most defenseless sectors of the population. There is too often willingness on the part of the bulk of the population to blame its troubles on the poor and ignorant minorities. But economic sanctions taken against the poor to compel a reduction of fertility seldom work. Generally, fertility does not fall in response to the lash of poverty. The most fertile sectors of the population will reduce their fertility with maximum speed if they can have easy access to competent contraception and the kind of support that brings them into the mainstream of the economy and society. At least in the present temper of the times, I would rather accept growth than step up the constraints which we have reason to expect would fall most heavily on the poor and their children.

It must also be recognized that the actual adoption of drastic programs designed to restrict fertility would, if they were successful, contain the seeds of their early reversal. If we could imagine a program that would drop the crude birth rate to the crude death rate in five years, we would have to imagine, as Tomas Frejka[4] has shown, a net reproduction rate of less than 0.6—not a two-child, but a one-child family—which if maintained for a few years would evoke the specter of rapid population decline, cries of race suicide, and a turnabout. It is to be noted that no nation, however heavily populated and poor, has adopted a policy for population decline. At best they want to bring the rates of growth down to two or even one percent, and just possibly to become stationary in the long run. It is interesting to note that Japan is already talking of the dangers of slow growth, that Rumania repealed its liberal abortion law because of plummeting birth rates, and that in Hong Kong one hears a great deal of talk about a labor shortage. Quickly successful policies of a drastic nature would certainly contain the seeds of their own reversal. I think there is every reason to believe that the quick way to a stationary population is the gentle one, both in action and in propaganda. And herein lies the weakness of the hucksters. Their line is successful until people realize that they have been misled. Then even sensible discussion suffers, for people once burned are twice cautious.

ZPG AND THE LESS DEVELOPED REGIONS

The situation of that two-thirds of the world's population living in the less developed regions contrasts sharply with that of the United States. In general, in the less developed regions the economy rests heavily on subsistence agriculture and other extractive industries; per capita income and literacy are very low, birth rates are very high, and death rates range from the world's highest to the world's lowest, as do the densities of population. Rates of growth vary from a little under two percent to well over three percent. Moreover, where the increase is relatively low, as in parts of Africa, it is clear that it will rise as soon as rudimentary health protection can be introduced.

It is evident that most of these populations are already too large to rise from poverty on the basis of a traditional subsistence agriculture. Their only hope of achieving reasonable per capita incomes, literacy, and health lies in the modernization of their economies. Such modernization entails heavy investment in productive equipment, transport, education, and health. Rapid progress in this direction is considerably deterred by the necessity of meeting the costs of rapid population growth at the same time. Indeed, I think that there is grave danger that population growth will so retard economic transformation and the improvement of living conditions that there will be a breakdown of civil order in a number of large countries. This risk gravely threatens the lives of tens, perhaps scores, of millions of people.

It seems difficult to exaggerate the importance of reducing the rate of population growth as soon as possible throughout most of the less developed regions. Indeed, even the areas now viewed as too sparsely populated might well benefit from the reduction of the rate of increase. In these circumstances, wisdom may enjoin favoring development at the expense of population growth where possible. This is not the place to discuss the issue, but it is my impression that there are extremely few places in the less developed regions that would not be aided in their struggle for modernization by a slower rate of population growth.

From my point of view, then, the need for slowing population growth is vastly greater in the less developed than in the more developed regions. A rapid decline of fertility for some decades until there is even a small negative rate of increase would be desirable. But zero growth, as a meaningful proposal in the near term, is idle talk. It could be achieved only by a rise in the death rate, which no one will accept as a goal of policy for his own people. During the next century, for theoretical purposes, zero growth is not low enough, and, for practical purposes, it is too low. Although the problems of the less developed regions are much greater, unfortunately the opportunities for relevant action are far fewer than in the rest of the world.

A rather large and growing number of countries in the less developed regions have national policies designed to foster the reduction of the birth rate and thereby a slowing of population growth. But even in these countries there would be minimal support for zero population growth. Policies in support of family planning have been widely adopted because the provision of services to the citizens who want them entails few political risks, and much of the top leadership realizes that the unprecedented speed of growth is blocking efforts at development. It is one thing to favor a reduction of the pace of population increase, and another thing to ask for a complete stop. When one begins to talk about growth rates of less than one percent, attention quickly shifts to the rate of growth of the traditional enemy or rival. Israel's victories in the Six-Day War did much to devalue large populations as a source of power; but the rivalry of numbers remains. It is possible that, among small countries, Hong Kong and Singapore would be content to stop growing fairly soon; and, among large countries, India and Pakistan might accept the idea at the level of top leadership. I can think of no other countries where this position would be accepted. Even where leadership agreed on the long-run objective, it would almost certainly wish not to advertise that fact, because more limited objectives would be expected to attract more widespread political support and serve program needs as well.

A number of scholars have been critical of people of my persuasion who advocate voluntarism through family planning as a means of slowing population growth and who have concentrated efforts on contraceptive methods, information and service. They hold that since the difficulty lies in the lack of motivation for restriction, it makes little sense to concentrate on the means while failing to strengthen the motives.

Naturally, I think that my approach represents the first and most effective step in strengthening the motivation for fertility restriction. Obviously, there are large numbers of people who are behaving in the traditional manner, governed by the values of the traditional society. But the number is larger in the minds of the leadership than it is in reality. Surveys, trials, and national experiences show that major proportions, often, indeed, a heavy majority, of the population express an interest in limiting their fertility. To be sure, they generally want more children than are needed to maintain a stationary population. To be sure, also, many aspects of their society still foster the ideal of the large family. I am aware that values influence behavior, but I am also aware that behavior influences values. It seems to me that the example of successful fertility limitation set by those now motivated is probably the most effective means of fostering both new values and innovative behavior. Moreover, I am greatly impressed by the speed with which the restrictive behavior has spread where family planning programs have been skillfully introduced.

I am happier than the critics with the progress that has been made, possibly for two reasons. On the one hand, I view the ultimate constraints to population growth as less narrowly drawn than they do. On the other hand, in the light of the situation a decade ago, I think there has been great and accelerating progress. By contrast, I am much less hopeful than are the critics of voluntarism about the feasibility of using more drastic measures to lift incentives for the restriction of fertility. The leadership would accept them in very few countries. Indeed, even in many of the countries having policies to foster family planning, the opposition in influential parts of the leadership group remains substantial—more substantial, I think, than among the people. In the near term more drastic means will be entirely unacceptable almost everywhere.

In the less developed regions, moreover, it would, simply for administrative reasons, be impossible to introduce even such measures as fiscal sanctions and rewards. Even now, weak administration is proving more of an obstacle to the spread of family planning than lack of public interest. Almost all of the governments are far too poor and weak to carry out a drastic program. Few of them can even count the number of their births and deaths, or have more than rudimentary medical services and facilities, or social security systems. It is hard to remember how poor they are. Canada, for example, with some 21 million people, has a larger national income and federal budget than the Government of India, with more than 500 million people. It is at best idle to talk of governments in this position drastically coercing their people's reproductive behavior. They are governments that can do something to educate and lead, but, save in the most primitive matters of public order, they cannot coerce.

The inability to coerce is perhaps fortunate in this field. I think we have reason to believe that voluntarism through education and service is the most direct route, as it is certainly the most civilized.

My own reaction to zero population growth, therefore, comes out about the same way for the less developed regions as for the more developed regions. The countries that could apply drastic constraints to human fertility do not need to; the countries that need drastic constraints cannot apply them; and in any case, the path of voluntarism through family planning is likely to be both more efficient and more civilized.

If zero population growth means the downgrading of voluntarism and the strident demand for a quick end to population growth, then it will do more harm than good. If, on the other hand, it is taken as an organizing focus for research and educational efforts concerning the importance of a worldwide trend to a stationary population and the means by which it is ultimately to be achieved, then it should be enthusiastically welcomed.

REFERENCES AND NOTES

1. The very extensive literature is summarized in a nutshell by R. Philip Hammond in a letter to *Science* 167 (3924):1439, March 13, 1970, reading in part as follows: "Even 20 × 10⁹ people, each producing 20 kilowatts of heat (twice the U.S. average), would add only 1/300 of the present atmospheric heat load. This would raise the average temperature of the earth by about 0.25°. . . . At an energy budget of 20 kilowatts per person, we could maintain a worldwide living standard near the present U.S. level even when we have exhausted our high-grade mineral resources. We could do this without placing an impossible heat load on the earth for a very large population, but not for an 'unlimited' one."

2. By more developed regions, I mean Europe, the Soviet Union, Japan, Northern America, temperate South America, Australia and New Zealand. The remainder of the world comprises the less developed regions.

3. Larry Bumpass and Charles F. Westoff. The "perfect contraceptive" population: extent and implications of unwanted fertility in the United States are considered. Unpublished manuscript. [Editor's note: The paper was published in *Science* 169(3951):1177–82. Sept. 18, 1970.]

4. Tomas Frejka. Reflections on the demographic conditions needed to establish a U.S. stationary population growth. *Population Studies* 22(3):379–97. Nov. 1968.

29

Discussion of Notestein's "Zero Population Growth"

Philip M. Hauser, Judith Blake, and Paul Demeny

COMMENT BY PHILIP M. HAUSER, UNIVERSITY OF CHICAGO

Not surprisingly, Frank Notestein, in his paper on zero population growth, displays wit, irony, and wisdom. Wit serves as a point of departure for telling and caustic criticism of the "hucksters" and distorters of population and environmental problems; the irony reveals Notestein's own value system and attitudes with respect to the problems involved; the wisdom reflects the many years that Notestein has served the population field as teacher, researcher, policy maker, and director of action programs. In view of the fervent interest worldwide, and especially in the United States, in excessive population growth and environmental pollution, Notestein's essay is a useful document containing sober perspectives. It is designed to prick the over-statements, the half-truths, and the erroneous information found in the emotional rather than rational reactions to various aspects of the relationship between rapid population growth and environmental pollution.

I should like to express complete agreement with Notestein's position that to believe in zero population growth is equivalent to believing in the laws of motion. Given a finite globe, it is clear that in the long run any rate of population increase would produce saturation and that mankind has no alternative to the achievement of a zero rate of growth. A zero rate of growth will inevitably come. The only questions, as Notestein indicates, are how it is to be achieved and when. It may be said that the only questions are whether the zero rate of growth will be achieved by nature or by man, and, if by man, by relatively rational and desirable or by irrational and undesirable means. If zero growth were to be achieved by nature, the means

Reprinted from *Population Index*, 36, no. 4 (October-December, 1970), pp. 451–65, by permission of the authors and the publisher.

probably would be pestilence and famine, disease and starvation, as discussed by Malthus. If it were to be achieved by man, the relatively undesirable and irrational methods would include—drawing on history—war, homosexuality, and cannibalism. Rational and desirable methods would include conception control, birth control, and population control, terms often used interchangeably in the literature, as if they referred to the same types of control. Actually they are quite different. Conception control refers to all the means, behavioral, mechanical, chemical, physiological, and surgical, whereby conception is prevented. Birth control includes conception control and abortion, the latter still the most widely used method of birth control. Population control involves the interrelations of fertility, mortality, and migration, and the broad area of social, economic, and political policy that may affect these components of population change. Conception control has been the chief method advocated by family planning movements throughout the world. Abortion, however, has been more widely used than conception control. Population control has not yet been achieved by any nation.

Although Notestein's essay must be regarded as a useful addition to the literature, it is not without its faults—faults both of commission and omission. He can be faulted for the following types of observation that seem to be taken for granted by many deeply involved in family planning movements but that, in my judgment, are open to question and require research for validation. First, Notestein is among those who believe the dissemination of "contraception methods, information and service" constitutes "the first and most effective step in strengthening the motivation for fertility restriction." It does not seem that this contention is supported by the present use of clinical family planning services available to peoples in the developing areas, including India, where perhaps the most ambitious program is underway.

Second, Notestein states that "surveys, trials, and national experiences show that major proportions, often, indeed, a heavy majority, of the population express an interest in limiting their fertility." To be sure, such an "interest" is expressed in KAP studies but, as I have indicated elsewhere,[1] this expression is erroneously interpreted as the equivalent of effective demand.

Third, Notestein states, "I am greatly impressed by the speed with which the restrictive behavior has spread where family planning programs have been skillfully introduced." If he is referring to the experiences of Taiwan, South Korea, Hong Kong, and Singapore, the statement does not take into consideration the fact that in these places motivation and incentive were generated by rising education and higher levels of living that initiated fertility decline and preceded any effective family planning programs. Such programs, no doubt, helped to accelerate the decline of the birth rate. I have yet to learn of any nation in which a family planning program has initiated a decline in fertility, that is, I have yet to learn where "restrictive behavior" has spread with "speed" in a population still mired in illiteracy and poverty and characterized by traditional behavior.

Fourth, Notestein, in dealing with the "critics," deals only with those who have been associated with proposals to use "drastic measures to lift incentives for the restriction of fertility." There are also critics, of whom I am one, who challenge the basic premise on which most of the present family planning programs are based, or who advocate alternative "voluntaristic" approaches. That is, it may be quite possible to depend on voluntarism for restriction of fertility by means other than those now being depended upon by family planning programs throughout the world.

Fifth, Notestein states, "Even now, weak administration is proving more of an obstacle to the spread of family planning than lack of public interest." This caveat, often repeated by people associated with family planning movements, is yet to be verified. It is my judgment, based on observation of family planning programs in various parts of the world, that strong administration would not necessarily accelerate the acceptance of family planning behavior. Strong administration, I am convinced, would not resolve the constraints imposed by the norms, values, and traditional behavior of premodern societies.

Notestein can be faulted also for the following acts of omission. First, as has already been indicated, he ignores critics, including myself, who have proposed alternative voluntary means for effecting fertility reduction. He apparently dismisses such alternatives, as he has in the past, as too theoretical, too impractical, and too complex. This conclusion, I insist, lacks research documentation. Second, Notestein refers only casually to the need for additional research and educational effort. In my judgment, the time has long since passed for a great increase in the resources allocated to the testing of alternative methods to achieve fertility reduction in the less developed areas. It would be desirable, in my opinion, to allocate perhaps 10 to 15 percent of the funds expended for family planning programs to experiments designed to test various ways of accelerating motivation and incentive for the acceptance of small-family norms, even at the expense of reducing the proliferation of Fifth-Avenue-style mass communication campaigns and birth control clinics.

I have only recently returned from India, where I had the opportunity to observe, among other things, the family planning program in Ghandigram. I can say that there a population of some 100,000 persons in Athoor Block, which is still mired in poverty and illiteracy, is having its birth rate reduced through a well designed program. But the program does not obtain in all of India. It is an intensive program involving inputs of funds and of human resources that are not extensible to all of India, or, for that matter, to any other developing region. It is a program that, in my judgment, is an holistic effort—including a family planning component—to change the life style of the community. The Ghandigram program, in my estimation, constitutes an empirical test of the hypothesis I have elsewhere stated[2] of the need for an integrated approach to the reduction of fertility. The program in its present form, although not extensible because of the enormous inputs required, can serve as a basis for continued experimentation to see what may be accomplished as various elements of present inputs are reduced or eliminated. Such experimentation could conceivably result in programs extensible to India and to other developing areas.

I should like to close with some general observations about zero population growth and its relation to environmental pollution. First, perhaps it should be mentioned that it is intriguing to see contemporary youth pick up the slogan of zero population growth in the belief, I am sure, that it not only would help to solve problems of environmental pollution, but also would serve as a slogan for organizing a larger revolt against the "establishment." Apparently many of the young do not understand, and perhaps I should not inform them, that success in the achievement of this objective would produce a population having an average age of 40 years. This, of course, might help to solve some of the present problems relating to youth, and perhaps this is one reason why zero population growth should be achieved as quickly as possible. From the Coale-Demeny tables, one can ascertain that zero population growth produced with an expectation of life of 77.5 years and birth and death rates of 12.9 would result in a population of which only 19 percent is under 15 years of age, contrasted with the present 29 percent in the United States, and of which 24 percent is 60 and over, contrasted with the present 14 percent. Such a population, incidentally, would average 2.1 children ever born to women of age 50 with 2.0 children surviving to age 20. Various problems associated with zero population growth have been ably set forth by our moderator, Ansley Coale.[3] Consideration of the concomitants of zero population growth may cool the ardor of those who wish to bring it about as quickly as possible with whatever means required.

Next, I should like to point out that zero population growth would not necessarily solve the problem of environmental pollution. On the contrary, in the United States, as in most economically advanced countries, environmental pollution is more likely the result of increased affluence and increased consumption levels than the result of increased population growth. For example, two-thirds of the increase between 1940 and the present time in electric power consumption, with its attendant pollution, is attributable to increased income per capita—only one-third to increased population growth. If the population of the United States should stop growing tomorrow, we could still experience greatly increased environmental pollution.

Next, I should like to point out that it is erroneous to hold that environmental pollution is a product of the free-enterprise capitalist system. Environmental pollution also afflicts the socialist countries. It is a product neither of the capitalist nor of the socialist economies but, rather, the result of deficiencies in both types of systems—namely, the absence of agencies with sufficient authority and funds to protect what may be thought of as common property resources—air, water, and land. Until such agencies are established at appropriate levels, international, national, and local, the environment will be polluted in both capitalist and socialist countries. In this connection, it is amusing to note that the Soviet Union has recently complained about the diminished production of caviar, hardly a consumption essential, because of the increased pollution of the Caspian Sea.

It is ironic that at this point in history demographers should have to take issue with "angry ecologists" overstating their case and using "the population explosion" as a major enemy in their effort to stem environmental pollution. There are two dangers inherent in this situation. One, the danger that the problems of environmental pollution and the population explosion may be used as a smoke screen to obscure other problems that should have priority, including the problems of the slums, racism, and the "urban crisis" in general. Second, the overstatements of the case that include naive predictions of mass starvation and poisoning of populations during the 1970's will, without question, prove to be untrue. Such overstatements and predictions, that the course of events will certainly prove groundless, may do great harm if boomerang effects follow.

Nothing I have said, however, should be interpreted to mean that there is not an urgent need to deal with problems of excessive population growth and with environmental pollution. There is no one-to-one relationship between the two, however; both require persistent, methodical, and continuous attention of the type not likely to result from unfounded distortions of the truth, nor from huge annual demonstrations, such as Earth Day. There is more than a little danger that the scaremongers and hucksters of the population explosion and of environmental pollution may set back rather than advance their admittedly worthwhile cause.

COMMENT BY JUDITH BLAKE, UNIVERSITY OF CALIFORNIA, BERKELEY

Favoring zero population growth is platitudinous, according to Notestein, as "it is the only possibility in a finite world." By this reasoning, the human effort to control the time and manner of all sorts of inevitabilities—the effort expended on postponing death, maintaining houses, saving money—is also pointless. The spokesmen for ZPG do not argue that a stationary world population will never come about without a ZPG policy, but rather that, without directed effort, zero growth will occur only after human numbers have greatly increased over present levels, and perhaps then by the mechanism of high mortality instead of fertility control.

Our choice lies in the timing and manner of accomplishing a stationary population. Since this choice will doubtless color our destiny as a species, widespread interest in the problem should not, in my opinion, be downgraded. As observers, demographers cannot, by definition, say what human beings, as actors, should desire for themselves or for their children. But we can certainly inform our fellow men of the probable consequences of a ZPG sooner rather than later, and of the fact that the timing is not beyond our control. Indeed, I learned a share of what I have just said as a graduate student reading Professor Notestein's articles some 18 years ago. I believe that he has now been goaded by the popularity of the Zero Population Growth movement into taking an unreasonable position against it.

Notestein characterizes ZPG as a "powerful sales slogan." He sees "professionally expert distortions of the truth peddled to the public under the highest scientific auspices." The ZPG *movement* is certainly open to this criticism, but so are movements—like family planning—that are close to Notestein's own door. Those who live by the slogan ("Five Million Women," "Children by Choice," "Trouble Parking? ? ? Support Planned Parenthood"), must be prepared to die by shinier slogans. That's the way it crumbles, hucksterwise.

With respect to timing, Notestein asks whether ZPG is as urgent a goal as its supporters claim. Dealing first with developed countries, he accuses the ecologists of stating that we are "in mortal danger," from scarcity of resources, if our population continues to grow. In refutation, he takes the traditional position that our principal limitation is not a shortage of resources but a want of imagination: we cannot envision what technological miracles lie ahead, nor what new resources will be discovered. However, in dismissing the urgency of ZPG for developed countries, I think he underestimates the intellectual sophistication of ecology. This discipline is a long way ahead of merely bemoaning the disappearance of nonrenewable resources. Rather, it deals with the *interrelation* among resources as itself an independent limitation. In effect, the limiting factor is not a resource, or a set of resources, but rather the set of conditions under which resources can be maintained as an interrelated system. Ecology is restating Malthus. Whereas Malthus saw a factor—land—as the limiting element, ecology sees the conditions supporting environmental balance and equilibrium as imposing limits to population growth. The *deus ex machina*—technology—has turned out to be far from cost-free. Ecologists may not always be able to pinpoint the costs of massive technological intervention, but they have alerted us to the principle involved. Only a crank would deny that technology can do wonderful things, but Notestein, inconsistently, would have us believe that it is a panacea for demographic folly.

Notestein says that the current argument about population as a cause of pollution is without merit. Pollution is due to "mismanagement" and our "high standard of living." When is management to be dubbed "mismanagement?" Since he relies on price structures and the market as mechanisms of control, perhaps he can explain why these mechanisms have allowed so much "mismanagement" of the pollution problem. Whence will come the machinisms that manage it? How far will mismanagement go before enlightened self-interest puts a stop to it? In effect, Notestein is saying that if developed countries achieved greater control over economic activity, they could sustain a larger population without pollution. Since he offers no reason why economic activity should be under such constraint, while population is given free rein, his argument is unclear. The same is true of his criticism of the level of living of developed countries. To be sure our living levels cause pollution, but little will be gained by lowering them simply to accommodate more people. Nor is it true that, in the future, we will necessarily confine ourselves to an index of living levels based on the production of goods. Clean air and water, open spaces, privacy, and quiet will increasingly be in demand, and will probably be regulated and distributed by the market, as are other scarce goods in developed societies. A "high standard of living" may thus increasingly become one that insures, at high cost, the qualities of life that we used to think were free.

Notestein's bias in favor of individual reproductive freedom, at the expense of any other values and freedoms that might get in the way, is unexplained but persistent. He advocates the "right to choose" one's family size, even if "the demographic consequences would be highly adverse, because it will always remain possible to manipulate the environment in which the choice is made." It is, of course, his privilege, as an individual, to entertain any bias he chooses. But if he is speaking as a demographer, he should recognize that it is not his job to advocate one freedom over another, or to make unsubstantiated claims about unlimited environmental manipulation. As demographers, our contribution to public policy is not to air our opinions in fields outside our own, but to tell people about the tradeoffs available to them concerning population issues.

Notestein points out correctly that as countries approach zero population growth (and frequently experience reproduction rates below unity), they back off from population limitation. He believes that this is an argument for a "go-slow" policy regarding zero growth. From the point of view of the observer, however, international reluctance is not, in and of itself, an argument against ZPG. Such reluctance is simply one of the obstacles with which a ZPG policy has to deal. Obviously, there are innumerable obstacles to the achievement of zero growth. Were this not the case, we would have it. The question for us, as demographers, is why nations become so skittish when the reality of population limitation is borne in upon them. What are the political and military constraints (plus all the other intra-societal constraints) that set a floor under population growth?

Equally, ZPG's aging effect on population structure cannot be regarded as axiomatically baleful. To be sure, there are doubtless intrinsically unde-sirable features in having a high proportion aged, features rooted in man's physiological decline with age. However, many of the undesirable features are socially induced and, in any event, the problem remains one of tradeoffs, not absolutes. We cannot have low mortality and low fertility without an aging population, and we cannot have low mortality and moderate fertility without fairly rapid growth. That is the reality of the situation. If, as seems to be agreed, population limitation is desirable, our scientific interest does not require reraising the issue of its desirability at every turn. Rather, we must apprise ourselves of the forces that induce individuals and nations to accept the undesirable side effects of the desired goal, and we must examine possible ways in which the side effects can be minimized.

Taking into account that, on the average, ZPG implies a mini-family, one can make an even stronger case than Notestein's for the potential unpopularity of a stationary population, other things being equal. Birth limitation to the levels required by ZPG will confine family life to a brief period and will require, therefore, a reorganization of our present interests, activities, and goals. Otherwise, ZPG will be experienced as a poignant de-privation. The problem will be increasingly to encourage the development of alternatives to life in families, because life without them will characterize more and more of our total existence as ZPG is established. A zero popu-lation growth policy will inevitably involve some redefinition of the choices available to individuals and some change in the rewards held out to them, just as present policy (albeit implicit) directs their current choices and manipulates their existing rewards. It is important to bear in mind, however, that an antinatalist policy would not necessarily be less "voluntaristic" than a pronatalist one. What would be altered is not the amount of social control, but the things for which people "volunteer." This is what we call social change, and we do not ordinarily regard it as a disaster.

Notestein's support for "voluntarism" in family planning seems to be a support for voluntarism under existing and unchanging pronatalist incen-tives and coercions. His version of voluntarism is precisely what leads biol-ogists and ecologists to take many of the coercive suggestions concerning fertility control that he regards as frightening and extreme. His theoretical model contains no clue as to how reproductive motivation can be changed. Hence, nonsocial scientists, who also have no clue, propose that we start knocking heads together. To our biological colleagues, this suggestion looks like business, *en finale*. To Notestein, it is apparently like being the protagonist in a Greek tragedy. To me, it is only a measure of my discipline's failure so far to see the problem clearly and outline the solution. The failure, I am afraid, is not that of the ecologist but that of demographers of the Notestein stamp.

As the *coup de grace*, Notestein not only phrases population policy in terms of coercion, but states categorically that it will put maximum pressure on the poor, rather than on other sectors. To brand all possible antinatalist policies—regardless of content—as having the poor as the butt is not only patently inaccurate but also subversive of the rational discussion that Notestein professes to desire. It stifles all discussion on the spot, for certainly no one in academic life, or in a rich foundation, or in government, wants anyone to be able even to hint that he harbored a thought that could conceivably be interpreted perhaps to mean that the poor could be induced to do anything—even in their own interest.

In short, in his pique with the ZPG movement, Notestein tries to put the Indian sign on important problems and to spook us into thinking that they are irrelevant, impractical, or illiberal. In fact, anything but the mindless distribution of contraception in ever wider concentric circles is a "no-no." In response, I feel constrained to tell him that our field is no longer waiting for signs from on high. We have moved into the public domain, and the problems to be discussed, together with the solutions to be offered, are not the ones he alone is to choose. The days when the charter members of the Population Association of America caucused to decide what should be discussed and researched in the field are over. Demographers and others are discussing and doing research. They are as individuals acting under their own steam and with support from diverse constituencies. And they have mass exposure. Such times separate the tyros from the pro— not by fiat, nor by the laying on of well manicured hands—but by intellectual challenge. To meet this challenge one has to deliver some goods. Simply telling the world what one approves and disapproves of will no longer succeed. It will take far more than Notestein's polite but empty derogation to exorcise Paul Ehrlich.

COMMENT BY PAUL DEMENY, EAST-WEST POPULATION INSTITUTE

The beginning of a new millennium is approaching. Figurative speech aside, it is barely 30 years away. In apparent preparation for the event, the twentieth century has been treating us to wondrous happenings of all sorts: most recently it has brought us ZPG. Unless the world is to come to an end, we are told, zero population growth soon is inevitable, and, to be on the safe side, it had better come tomorrow. This is depressing news, since mankind's inclination to comply with this ukase is somewhat doubtful. The goal set forth by ZPG may appear attractive on many grounds, but, as with the goal of getting rid of sin, its prospects of being actually achieved in the near term are less than promising.

Picture for a moment the familiar graph that adorns Chapter One of so many books of the demographer's trade, depicting the growth of the world population (or the growth of population in the United States) in the past few hundred years. It is an unbroken line curving upward ominously, with unsurprising smoothness. Picture now a sudden kink in this curve, flattening it out completely by, say, 1980, or at least a sharp bend bringing it to a zero growth rate by the year 2000. If supplied with the figures charting such a broken curve, a skilled draftsman, with or without mental biases imparted by some exposure to differential calculus, would feel a vague sense of unease even if he knew nothing about the subject matter of his graph. He would suspect that something must have gone wrong with the figures. *Natura non facit saltus,* as Leibnitz has suggested. If asked to place a bet on the size of the world population—say, 100 years from now—closer to five or closer to 10 billion? I think most of us would bet without much hesitation on the latter figure, even those who, like myself, would prefer to see less people and more giraffes in mankind's future.

These somewhat skeptical comments are not to be taken as disputing the possibility of concerted human action to influence the future course of population growth. Also, in fairness to ZPG, one must of course concede its right to focus on the question of what *should be* in preference to prosaic predictions of what *will be.* After all, ZPG defines itself as a political action organization whose purpose is to bring about population stability in the United States, then in the rest of the world. Given the prevailing passion for setting distant national goals, adopting long-range planning, and listening to futurologists, ZPG's predilection for holding up an ultimate objective as a guide for today's many examples of foolish acts committed in the name of noble goals, and because of my distrust of man's ability even to pick the right distant goals, I would consider a more marginalist approach in setting the right population policy superior to ZPG's grand design. But these comments may be mere quibbles. When I look at concrete policy proposals thus far advanced by zero population growth advocates, I invariably find myself in nearly full agreement with their substance. Why not join the ZPG bandwagon then? In partial answer to the question I will review briefly four main areas where I take exception to the posture represented by ZPG. Naturally I realize that there exists no unified body of ideology possessed by that organization. My comments here will refer to a kind of statistically derived ZPG doctrine as I read it, and are not to be interpreted as a dispute with its membership as a whole or with particular persons among its adherents.

First, there is a dilemma of choice between scientific objectivity and political expediency. To bring up this antinomy in the present context may appear irrelevant, since ZPG forthrightly presents itself as a political action organization. The fact remains that a commitment to seek knowledge and the kind of political commitment that seems to be required by ZPG mix badly. One cannot dispute, of course, the scientist's right to participate in political action as his preferences dictate. Neither can one dispute the possibility that scientists often may be able to support certain political causes *qua* scientists. Zero population growth may eventually prove to be such a cause. It is not now—certainly not in the instance of the United States. The proposition appears to be amply proven by the inadequacy of the scientific props thus far presented to support the overall policy objective of ZPG, by the biases and selectivity in the pertinent arguments of its academic supporters, and by the contradictions in the scientific machinery put to work by the organization depending on the coloration of the particular audience whose support it seeks.

Given these circumstances, I take it for granted that when members of the academic community lend their pens and names to what, from a scientific viewpoint, one can only describe as shady practices, they do so under the compulsion of what they consider their social responsibility. There is a notion that the capital of credibility of science is justifiably spent when the survival of mankind is at stake. Perhaps my view on those stakes is more relaxed because it is less informed than that of others. Whatever is the case, I take a different view of the social responsibility of scientists and of science in general. It seems to me that the prestige of academic institutions and academics that has accumulated as a result of the work of generations of scientists searching for objective truth will evaporate rapidly if the public discovers that it has been fed scientific pablum in the service of an ideology, no matter how well intended. Such a discovery, I am convinced, will be made only too quickly, even when that feeding comes from the platform of highly respected academic institutions. If it comes, it will hurt all scientists, not only those culpable. If it comes, it will be a sad day not only for science but for our prospects of tackling population problems as well.

My second objection concerns, more properly, the fundamental political approach represented by ZPG. If my understanding is correct, that approach is derived from an ecological view of the interaction of human aggregates with their physical environment that leads to a proposition about the optimal size and growth rate of human populations. Once that proposition has been accepted, notably once the necessity of a zero growth rate is promulgated, it is in turn translated into rules of behavior to be observed by individual members of those populations. I am unwilling to proceed along that route. I prefer to consider society as an aggregate of individuals, and to see the welfare of a society as a sum total of individual welfares. Subject to some qualifications that would justify a paternalistic conception of the state, qualifications that I do not accept as valid in developed countries, this view leads to the general rule that individuals should be left free to work out their own destiny as they see it best, that the proper role of the state is to enhance that freedom, and that that freedom should not be curtailed by the state unless it is adequately demonstrated (1) that individual actions would infringe upon the freedom of others in well specified ways and (2) that it is agreed through a democratic political process that the costs of correcting for such untoward effects of individual behavior are both as low as feasible and smaller than the costs that would be incurred in the initial injury. In short, I do not accept that demonstrations of presumed macroeconomic or other aggregate gains that might be consequent upon an induced macrodemographic change have any direct relevance to legitimate propositions of population policy that, by necessity, must operate through individual actors. I readily concede that situations often will occur in which the practical policy consequences derived both from the ecological and the individualistic approaches would be the same. Such agreements may even be the rule rather than the exception. The coincidence, however, does not remove the fundamental importance of the differences in the philosophical grounds on which similar or identical policies are justified.

The third area of disagreement has to do with the objective of zero population growth itself. I appreciate the attraction of the simplicity of the slogan and the intuitive justness of self-replacement as a rule of behavior. Like most people, I tend to picture the future as an improved but not too different version of the present, and I am inclined to think that qualitative improvements in the human condition would be far more likely to come about if quantitative growth in the numbers of mankind could be somehow brought to an early halt. Yet I am unable to share the single-minded and aggressive self-assurance of ZPG in asserting the supreme desirability of a zero rate of growth as soon as possible. This is partly because of my already indicated preference for a marginalist and individualistic approach as a more defensible way to chart a path for population policy. But even if I were to accept the ZPG approach of trying to find out the "final objective" for mankind or for any given country defined in some monolithic sense (and I am prepared to do that only for the sake of the present argument), some of my reservations about the zero growth objective would still remain.

As Frank Notestein points out, the proposition that a zero rate of growth must come sooner or later is, of course, platitudinous. Our finite world imposes ultimate limits on the size of the human anthill. But it is equally true that the long-term average of zero growth need not imply zero growth in any finite historical period. Indeed, with what little we know about our past it is safe to say that human history thus far is better described as a succession of civilizations whose long period of slow demographic expansion are followed by the *tabula rasa* of a sudden collapse or by rapid decay within the span of a few generations. I have commented above on the sheer lack of plausibility inherent in the self-confident assumption that our society will be, or indeed can be, the only exception; that somehow our society will be permanently saved from the fate of an ultimate doom and, instead, at some point may settle down to the pleasures of the stationary state.

But, quite apart from the likelihood of failure in achieving zero population growth in the foreseeable future, can we really be so certain that a policy aimed at the fastest possible demographic slowdown to zero growth is offering such an unqualified desideratum for individual advanced societies, or even for an integrated, advanced world society? On precisely what historical, moral, philosophical, or ecological grounds do we declare unacceptable a future in which demographic expansion continues, say, at the rate characteristic of today's Western Europe for the next few hundred years? Such a course would be merely in keeping with the seemingly inexorable course our industrial civilization has thus far exhibited. To be sure, it is a course that sooner or later would end not with a whimper but with a bang. Could we put the blame for such an end on population growth? Perhaps yes, but population growth is only one of the potential causes of such a calamity.

We know, for instance, that at least two contemporary societies now have the capacity to engineer self-destruction on a world scale and that such an event may occur tomorrow, if only as a result of plain, bad luck. By no stretch of the imagination could such a near future catastrophic event be ascribed to excessive population growth or size, except in the trivial sense that blames Adam and Eve for all our earthly troubles. It would be certainly just as easy to argue that we avoided a nuclear catastrophe in the past decade or two—and have a good chance of avoiding it in the foreseeable future—because poverty and overpopulation made the third world an unappetizing field of competition between the two great powers that emerged on the world scene with such a sudden force at the end of World War II.

But if population growth were to continue and the eventual collapse were to come at a level of a world population of, say, 50 billion people, it would seem only fair to argue that society finally had paid the price for its failure to put an end to population growth in time. It should be noted that the state of human society just before the end need not, or, as Fred Hoyle[4] argued, cannot, be envisaged in dismal Malthusian terms. The collapse may come suddenly under the burden of organizational complexities, perhaps at the very fulfillment of all the outstanding and unique potentialities that mark our technical civilization. If that is at all plausible, by what line of argument can we reach the automatic conclusion that it would have been better to stop the growth and avoid the eventual collapse? What if zero population growth achieved in the twentieth century merely helped to reinforce another possible developmental line, that toward a smug, fat, and self-satisfied society—a society of shuffleboard, color television, and dope? Isn't it just possible, on the other hand, that a society that had had the challenge and stimulus of continued demographic expansion would be amply compensated for its ultimate demise at the end of the road by the fun of getting there?

Variations on similar speculations could be multiplied at will. For instance, is the choice of growth versus no growth really open to us? Suppose that a radical slowing down of the world population growth, if successfully achieved, would be indeed desirable. But what if the desire for such a slowdown merely reflects the will of those of us who got tired of travel and who want to get off the train to get a good rest? Those who "cop out" to St. Petersburg may be simply bypassed by history, as the civilization of Cape Kennedy merrily marches on. Mankind may have a covenant with the devil that forces them to explore to their ultimate limits their Faustian powers, a covenant not subject to unilateral cancellation by efforts of ZPG lobbyists in Washington, D.C.

I should emphasize again that I do not consider such speculations worthwhile, because I believe that they do not lead us to ask answerable questions. We cannot answer even infinitely simpler questions involving comparisons between actual historical states or between projections to the present from the basis of some well specified past situation. Surely the qualities of American society today and, say, at the time of Thomas Jefferson have some relationship to the difference between the respective population sizes and demographic makeup. Which society and which demographic configuration is better? Well, we cannot tell. Or, to ask an even simpler question, would America be better off today if its population growth had come to a halt around 1900? The question is legitimate. After all, virtually without exception, ZPG arguments for a cessation of growth could have been made just as strongly 70 years ago as they are made today. Again, we do not know the right answer. The half of us who would be alive under this hypothesis could be living in a twentieth-century version of classical Athens, close to the fulfillment of the philosophers' dream. Or again, that hypothetical America could be a vassal state of some overseas power, ruled by an Adolph Hitler or a Joseph Stalin.

I hope that the relevance of these rather silly speculations to the issue under examination is reasonably clear. Much of the appeal of ZPG comes from its brazen assertion that it has an unequivocal and scientifically backed recommendation to make concerning at least one key policy issue bearing on the future of human society. But it has no such thing. Its aggressiveness in supplying a set of easily identified villains for many or all of our troubles, its lack of self-doubt and distaste for qualification, its capacity to see black and white where there are only shades of grey serve it well with a public that abhors complexity and yearns for simple answers and tangible scapegoats. However, these assets are bound to turn out to be short-term advantages only. Reliance on cheap futurology backfires as soon as its admirers realize that they have been taken for an easy ride. Scenario writing, like the population bomb, can be anybody's baby.

If these are intemperate criticisms, I should perhaps add that in the meantime the movement may do some good. For one thing, it provides some temporary outlet for the energies of those promising and exuberant cohorts resulting from the Great American Baby Boom. It also fills with a feeling of pride and self-satisfaction some of those who, for reasons of their own, have or plan to have one, two, or no children, and who now can choose to interpret their behavior as an act of self-sacrifice for mankind. It may even persuade some couples to stay in this patriotic group even if otherwise they would have preferred to produce a third or fourth baby, although it must be observed that the historical record does not induce one to make too sanguine an estimate as to the likely number of such couples. Finally, and most positively, ZPG's propaganda may contribute or may have contributed already to the adoption of useful policy measures, even though the justification for such measures by no means requires the ideological underpinnings of the ZPG movement.

This last observation brings me to the fourth area of my quarrel with ZPG. It seems to me that there is a vast discrepancy between ZPG rhetoric and ZPG policy proposals. Elsewhere I have discussed at some length the question of what constitutes an acceptable theoretical base for governmental intervention in reproductive processes in a free society. I can make only some general points here. I do not think we should set norms for which societies should strive with respect to their growth rate or numbers. We should make certain that individual decisions as to procreation are made in an optimal framework and then accept what comes out as the aggregate of individual decisions. In order to determine what constitutes an optimal framework we may envisage two possible situations: one in which the consequences of decisions with respect to family size are borne and enjoyed entirely by the family that has taken the action, and another where such actions involve certain externalities—that is, impose burdens or confer benefits on other families as well. Even the pure no-externalities model, surely an unrealistic construct, would upon closer examination reveal imperfections in the decision-making process with respect to fertility that unambiguously justify policy measures—diffusion of information about birth control, provision of contraceptive services, development of better methods of contraception, and so forth—to be adopted by governments to insure that all babies born are wanted babies. Removal of subsidies attached to childbearing, that disturb the unbiased play of parental preferences, is also a straightforward requirement that flows from the logic of the model. When we take into account externalities as well, the range of policy measures justifiable on simple laissez-faire principles is further and greatly extended.

What is added to this arsenal of policy measures by advocates of ZPG? Personally, I am unable to discern how substantive ZPG policy proposals differ from those implied by the liberal-individualistic framework sketched above, which has served this country well in the past. A careful examination of lists of measures supported by ZPG leads to the anticlimactic conclusion that a vast majority of these measures are simply declarative, exhortatory, or propagandistic in character. They promise speeches, talks, and demonstrations, urge population stability, reject growth mania, support commissions, encourage discussions and the like. Items that come to grips with what might be properly called action proposals are far less numerous. These call for provision of birth control services, increased research to improve contraceptive technology, and the repeal of archaic abortion laws. Finally they urge elimination of pronatalist measures built into tax laws as well as into medical and other insurance laws. With the possible exception of a hint that tax laws should actually be modified to discourage large families rather than be merely neutral—a provision greatly weakened by the stipulation that we should not penalize children already born—there is not a single element in these advocated policies that would not be consistent with a mild liberal program incorporating Adam Smithian ideas and very little else. To suggest that the advocacy of such measures depends on one's embracing ZPG's rhetoric is nonsensical, and to imply that such measures, if adopted, will somehow result in zero population growth is irresponsible. They, of course, may; but just as likely they may not. ZPG's apparent lack of realization of the gap between what it promises and what it is likely to deliver shows massive naïveté, but this is beside the point. Shorn of their rhetoric and stridency, I consider the action programs proposed by ZPG for the present U.S. situation entirely sound.

But I also believe in the rule of parsimony. That would suggest that if we have a simple and sound basis for a policy, it is unwise to advocate it on contrived and controversial grounds. Murder may be opposed on the strength of the argument that the country has a labor shortage and needs more people, but there ought to be simpler reasons to justify its banning. ZPG invokes tenuous and unproven propositions about the dire consequences of continued growth in order to support measures that neither guarantee the achievement of the avowed objective of zero growth nor depend for support on ZPG tenets. ZPG needs Occam's razor badly.

NOTES

1. Philip M. Hauser. "Family planning and population programs": a book review article. *Demography* 4(1):397–414. 1967.

2. *Idem.* Non-family planning methods of population control. Pp. 58–66 in: Nafis Sadik et al., Editors. *Population control: implications, trends, and prospects.* Lahore, West Pakistan: Sweden Pakistan Family Welfare Project, 1969.

3. Ansley J. Coale. Should the United States start a campaign for fewer births? *Population Index* 34(4):467–74. Oct.-Dec. 1968.

4. F. Hoyle. *A contradiction in the argument of Malthus.* Hull, England: University of Hull Publications, 1963. 22 pp.

Introduction: B. President's Commission on Population Growth and the American Future

As noted above, the United States has never had an explicit and total population policy. However, beginning in the 1960's, more national and political leaders became interested in and concerned about the problems related to population growth. Both Presidents Kennedy and Johnson recognized that attention had to be given to "the population problem." However, it was not until 1969 that then President Nixon recommended to the Congress that a presidential commission be established that would study all aspects of population and make policy recommendations. In March 1970, Congress established The Commission on Population Growth and the American Future. The Commission was headed by John D. Rockefeller III who had for many years been concerned about excessive population growth, especially in the underdeveloped countries. The Commission was composed of twenty-four prominent political, economic, scientific, medical and academic people. The Commission in turn asked for research papers from leading experts on a variety of population related topics. The paper by Judith Blake in Section V, "Coercive Pronatalism," was excerpted from her research report to the Commission. Richard Lincoln (article 30) summarizes the major findings and recommendations of the Commission. This brief paper gives only a taste of the final report itself, but it does show what the Commission learned and why it made the recommendations it did. Of course, the final report is a reflection of the many excellent research papers that were prepared by scientists and scholars for the Commission. As a set of documents these research reports represent some of the best current knowledge and thinking about population-related issues. Since these reports are all government documents, students who wish to examine some of these issues more closely will generally find them in the U.S. Government documents section of most major libraries.

The political response to the Commission's final report has been most interesting. President Nixon, who originally called for the establishment of the Commission, received the report, but for all practical purposes ignored it. He spoke out publicly against two specific recommendations of the report. He expressed his opposition to the Commission's recommendation that contraception be made available to teenage youngsters more freely. The Commission made this recommendation because there was substantial evidence that a high percentage (80 percent) of sexually active unmarried teenage girls were not using any contraception. The Commission's recommendation was based on its expressed concern for the resultant unwanted pregnancies and births. President Nixon also made known his personal disapproval of the Commission's recommendation that abortion be available upon request. Aside from these two negative reactions there has never been any other presidential response to the Commission's report. We seem to be as far as ever from a national population policy.

30

Population and the American Future: The Commission's Final Report

Richard Lincoln

A conscious government policy to help "improve the quality of life" by gradually slowing and eventually halting U.S. population growth was recommended by the Commission on Population Growth and the American Future. The Commission's final report was delivered to the President and the Congress in March after two years of deliberation. The 24-member panel pointed out that "at a minimum, we will probably add 50 million more Americans by the end of the century" as an echo-effect of the post-World War II 'baby boom.' Beyond that, the Commission held, continued growth would confer no possible benefit to the nation or its people, while it would aggravate some of our most pressing social and economic problems. Slower growth, the Commission stated, will not eliminate these problems, "but it will reduce the urgency, the 'crash program' character of much that we do. It will buy time for the development of sensible solutions."

The Commission members emphasized that while slower growth "provides opportunities, it does not guarantee that they will be well used. It simply opens up a range of choices we would not have otherwise. . . . Successfully addressing population requires that we also address our problems of poverty, of minority and sex discrimination, of careless exploitation of resources, of environmental deterioration, and of spreading suburbs, decaying cities, and wasted countrysides."

The Commission pointed out that the country could "cope with rapid population growth for the next 30 to 50 years. But doing so will become an increasingly unpleasant and risky business . . . adopting solutions we don't like . . . before we understand them."

Reprinted from *Family Planning Perspectives*, 4, no. 2 (April, 1972), pp. 10–22, by permission of the publisher.

The Commission, therefore, called upon the nation to "welcome and plan for a stabilized population," emphasizing that "achievement of population stabilization would be primarily the result of measures aimed at creating conditions in which individuals, regardless of sex, age, or minority status, can exercise genuine free choice. This means that we must strive to eliminate those social barriers, laws, and cultural pressures that interfere with the exercise of free choice and that governmental programs in the future must be sensitized to demographic effects."

While advocating an eventual *average* two-child family, the panel stated that this average could—and ought only—be obtained by voluntary means with "respect for human freedom, human dignity, and individual fulfillment; and concern for social justice and social welfare. To 'solve' population problems at the cost of such values would be a Pyrrhic victory. . . ."

DIVERSITY ENCOURAGED

The Commission indicated that an average two-child family may be achieved "by varying combinations of nonmarriage or childlessness" combined with "substantial percentages of couples who have more than two children." The Commission found it "desirable" that stabilization be attained "in a way which encourages variety and choice rather than uniformity."

In the long run, *average* zero population growth, the panel pointed out, "can only be achieved . . . with fluctuations in both directions." If, through individual informed free choice, the population grows at less than the replacement level for a period of time "we should prepare ourselves not to react with alarm, as some other countries have done recently [e.g., Japan and Rumania] when the distant possibility of population decline appears." Indeed, the Commissioners found, "there might be no reason to fear a decline in population once we are past the period of growth that is in store," and, "in any event it is naive to expect that we can fine-tune such trends." Certainly, we should not withhold the means to prevent or terminate unwanted pregnancies since "a nation's growth should not depend on the ignorance or misfortune of its citizenry."

Of the many possible paths to achievement of population stabilization, the Commission stated its preference for a gradual course "which minimizes fluctuations in the number of births; minimizes further growth of population; minimizes the change required in reproductive habits and provides adequate time for such changes to be adopted; and maximizes variety and choice in life styles, while minimizing pressures for conformity." Population stabilization could not be reached quickly, the panel pointed out, without social and economic disruption caused by an "accordion-like continuous expansion and contraction" of average family size over the next several decades.

One such "optimal path," which could achieve replacement fertility in 20 years and population stabilization at 278 million in 50 years (excluding the effect of immigration), would involve:

1. a decline in the proportion of women becoming mothers from 88 to 80 percent,
2. a decline in the proportion of parents with three or more children from 50 to 41 percent,
3. an increase in the proportion of parents with one or two children from 50 to 59 percent,
4. an increase of two years in the average age at which a mother bears her first child,
5. an increase of less than six months in the average interval between births.

ACT NOW TO BUILD ON CURRENT TRENDS

The Commission found cause for belief that "something close to an optimal path can be realized" providing that deliberate action which can encourage desirable trends is taken quickly. Favorable developments cited by the panel include: a historic long-term decline in average family size (temporarily interrupted by the post-World War II baby boom); continued birthrate declines over the last decade despite the coming to reproductive age of the baby-boom babies; improvements in the employment and social status of women; mounting public concern over the negative effects of population growth; a decline in the number of youthful marriages; preferences by younger couples for smaller families than their elders desired; improved effectiveness of contraceptives; increased access to legal abortions; the experience of at least 10 other countries which have, in the last half-century, experienced periods of replacement fertility.

The panel warned, however, that if its recommendations were not adopted quickly, instead of encouraging a desirable trend "we may find ourselves in a position of trying to reverse an undesirable trend."

The Commission cited several "unfavorable elements which threaten the achievement of stabilization," including the potential for a repeat baby boom; our "ideological addiction to growth"; "pronatalist" laws and social institutions, including mass media projections of stereotypical women's roles; restrictions on availability of contraception, sex education and abortion; reawakened fear of 'race suicide,' such as occurred during the Depression.

Action now is also important, the report stated, because the 1970s are probably a "critical . . . decade in the demographic transition . . . involving changes in family life and the role of women, dynamics of the metropolitan process, the depopulation of rural areas, the movement and the needs of disadvantaged minorities, the era of the young adults produced by the baby boom, and the attendant question of what their own fertility will be—baby boom or baby bust."

POLICY RECOMMENDATIONS

The Commission indicated that it sought to make policy recommendations which were technically, politically and economically feasible; recommendations which, while speaking to population issues, embodied goals "either intrinsically desirable or worthwhile for reasons other than demographic objectives."

To move the nation toward realization of these goals, the Commission assessed a broad range of current policies and programs and recommended a comprehensive set of changes in existing policies or adoption of new policies. The Commission's principal recommendations called for:

1. elimination of involuntary childbearing by substantially improving the access of all Americans (regardless of marital or socioeconomic status) to effective means of fertility control;
2. the improvement of the status of women;
3. more education about population, parenthood, sex, nutrition, environment and heredity;
4. maintenance of foreign immigration levels, and more rational guidance of internal migration to metropolitan areas;
5. increased biomedical research in human reproduction and contraceptive development;
6. more and better demographic research, including social and behavioral research, and census reporting, and statistical reporting and evaluation of family planning services; and
7. organizational changes in government necessary to attain the recommended objectives.

INVOLUNTARY CHILDBEARING

Some dozen of the Commission's major recommendations were designed to enable "all Americans, regardless of age, marital status, or income . . . to avoid unwanted births." The panel pointed out that while most couples plan to have between two and three children, because of "youthful marriage, far-from-perfect means of fertility control, and varying motivation, many of these couples will have children before they want them and a significant fraction will ultimately exceed the number they want." Citing the 1970 National Fertility Study, the panel pointed out that of all births to currently married women between 1966 and 1970, "15 percent were reported by the parents as having never been wanted." An additional 29 percent were reported as having been born before the parents wanted them. Thus, a total of 44 percent of all births to married couples in those five years were unplanned (see Table 1). The Commission made a "conservative" estimate from these findings that "2.65 million births occurring in that five-year period would never have occurred had the complete availability of perfect fertility control permitted couples to realize their preferences." The panel pointed out that the incidence of unwanted fertility, with its "enormous" financial, social, health and psychological costs, remained highest for the poor and poorly educated. "Mainly because of differences in education and income—and a general exclusion from the socioeconomic mainstream— unwanted fertility weighs most heavily on certain minority groups," such as blacks and, "probably," Puerto Ricans, Mexican Americans and Indians, as well. (Thus, the panel reported, "if blacks could have the number of children they want and no more, their fertility and that of the majority white population would be very similar.")

TABLE 1. Unwanted Fertility in the United States, 1970*

Race and Education	Most Likely Number of Births per Woman	Percent of Births 1966–1970 Unwanted	Percent of Births 1966–1970 Unplanned (including unwanted)	Theoretical Births per Woman without Unwanted Births
All Women	3.0	15	44	2.7
College 4+	2.5	7	32	2.4
College 1–3	2.8	11	39	2.6
High School 4	2.8	14	44	2.6
High School 1–3	3.4	20	48	2.9
Less	3.9	31	56	3.0
White Women	2.9	13	42	2.6
College 4+	2.5	7	32	2.4
College 1–3	2.8	10	39	2.6
High School 4	2.8	13	42	2.6
High School 1–3	3.2	18	44	2.8
Less	3.5	25	53	2.9
Black Women	3.7	27	61	2.9
College 4+	2.3	3	21	2.2
College 1–3	2.6	21	46	2.3
High School 4	3.3	19	62	2.8
High School 1–3	4.2	31	66	3.2
Less	5.2	55	68	3.1

* Based on data from the 1970 National Fertility Study for currently married women under 45 years of age.
Source: *Population and the American Future*, p. 164.

While only one percent of the first births were reported by their parents as having never been wanted, nearly two-thirds of sixth and higher order births were so reported; these births were concentrated in the later years of childbearing, the Commission found, where mother and child are at greatest risk of death or damage. Eliminating unwanted births in the older ages would also sharply reduce the incidence of such hereditary diseases as mongolism. Similarly, the Commission pointed out, 17 percent of all births occur to teenagers at a time when the likelihood of adverse health and social consequences for mother and infant is much greater than if the birth were postponed to the years between 20 and 35. The postponement of these early mistimed births to later ages could result in a "distinct improvement in the survival, health, and ability" of the children born.

So "that only wanted children are brought into the world," the Commission adopted a series of recommendations to:

1. provide full financing of all health services related to fertility,
2. enact affirmative state statutes providing for abortion on request,
3. extend the family planning project grant programs,
4. eliminate legal restrictions on access to contraceptive information and services,
5. increase investment in reproductive research and contraceptive development,
6. eliminate administrative restrictions on voluntary contraceptive sterilization,
7. develop programs to train required medical and paramedical personnel to deliver fertility-related health services,
8. develop programs of family planning education.

LEGAL RESTRICTIONS

Twenty-two states have laws restricting or regulating the sale, distribution, advertising or display of contraceptives, and six more have restrictions on selling or advertising prophylactics. These laws range from prohibition of contraceptive sales to the unmarried in Massachusetts and Wisconsin (recently declared unconstitutional by the U.S. Supreme Court) to laws prohibiting sale of contraceptives or prophylactics through vending machines, advertising them on outdoor billboards or even displaying them in drugstores. The Commission held that such laws "inhibit family planning education as well as family planning programs, and/or impinge on the ready availability of methods of contraception to the public. By prohibiting commercial sales, advertising displays, and the use of vending machines for nonprescription contraceptives, they sacrifice accessibility, education, and individual rights. . . ."

The Commission recommended that states not only "eliminate existing legal inhibitions and restrictions on access to contraceptive information, procedures, and supplies," but "develop statutes affirming the desirability that all persons have ready and practicable access" to them.

The Commission pointed out that some three million couples in the childbearing years had, by 1970, elected contraceptive sterilization; this comprised nearly one in five couples able to bear children who did not want to have any more. Despite the great—and increasing—popularity of this method of family limitation, the Commission pointed out that many physicians would not perform such operations because of fear that they might be sued or prosecuted, and many hospitals imposed requirements limiting the operation to persons of specified age or previous parity. The Commission recommended that all such requirements be eliminated so that the decision for contraceptive sterilization "be made solely by the physician and patient."

The Commission found that "the various prohibitions against abortion throughout the United States stand as obstacles to the exercise of individual freedom: the freedom of women to make difficult moral choices based on their personal values, the freedom of women to control their own fertility, and finally, freedom from the burdens of unwanted childbearing." The Commission also held that such prohibitions "violate social justice," forcing women to bear unwanted children, or to undergo dangerous and illegal abortions to avert unwanted births, with less burden on the rich woman— who has had access to medically safe, and expensive, abortions—than the poor woman, "forced to risk her life and health with folk remedies and disreputable practitioners."

The Commission stated that "abortion on request" in New York, California and eastern European countries brought the procedure "from the backrooms to the hospitals and clinics" with consequent reductions in illegal abortions and resultant maternal mortality. (Thus, in New York City, maternal mortality rates "dropped by two-thirds the year after abortion became available on request . . . [and] there is reason to suspect that the maternal death ratio will continue to decline.") The Commission also pointed to evidence that New York's abortion law had sharply reversed illegitimacy rates, which had been rising since first recorded in 1954. (There were nearly 10 percent fewer out-of-wedlock births for the first nine months of 1971 in New York City as compared to the same months in 1970.)

Legalizing abortion would also "exert a downward influence on the United States birthrate," the Commission predicted, based on the evidence in New York City. (New York showed a 12 percent decline in births in 1971 over 1970—three times the national decline.) The panel warned that "abortion should not be considered a substitute for birth control, but rather as one element in a comprehensive system of maternal and infant health care." It affirmed that "contraception is the method of choice for preventing an unwanted birth," and predicted that "with the increasing availability of contraceptives and improvements in contraceptive technology, the need for abortion will diminish." At the present time, however, the more than half-million legal abortions and "an unknown number of illegal abortions" performed in the year ending June 30, 1971 indicate that there is still a widespread "social and personal failure in the provision and use of birth control," and many Americans still "must resort to abortion to prevent an unwanted birth."

For these reasons, the majority of the Commissioners affirmed that "women should be free to determine their own fertility, that the matter of abortion should be left to the conscience of the individual concerned, in consultation with her physician and that states should be encouraged to enact affirmative statutes creating a clear and positive framework for the practice of abortion on request."

The Commission recommended that "with the admonition that abortion not be considered a primary means of fertility control . . . present state laws restricting abortion be liberalized along the lines of the New York State Statute, such abortions to be performed on request by duly licensed physicians under conditions of medical safety."

The Commission also recommended that "federal, state, and local governments make funds available to support abortion services in states with liberalized statutes [and] that abortion be specifically included in comprehensive health insurance benefits, both public and private."

Dissents from the majority recommendation on abortion—on various grounds[1]—were registered by five of the 24-member panel: Alan Cranston, John N. Erlenborn, Paul B. Cornely, Grace Olivarez and Marilyn Brant Chandler.

REPRODUCTIVE, CONTRACEPTIVE RESEARCH

Unwanted pregnancies will continue to occur, the Commission declared, until methods of fertility control are made universally available which are "safe and free of any adverse reactions; effective, acceptable, coitus-independent, and accessible commercially rather than medically; and inexpensive, easy to use, and reversible. This goal will be reached only if research efforts equal the magnitude of the task." The report stated that while the pill and the IUD "represented significant breakthroughs in a field which has been largely neglected by science for most of human history," in terms of the potential technology which should be feasible, these methods remain "fairly primitive." This, the Commission said, is because "our knowledge of basic reproductive biology is inadequate." We do not yet know "the role and functioning of the ovary and the testes, of the egg and the sperm, of the process of fertilization itself, and the normal course of gestation." In addition to such basic investigation, far more effort than is currently being expended must be devoted to development of new contraceptive methods and evaluation of the safety and effectiveness of existing ones. The Commission found the $75 million for 1973 research expenditures projected by DHEW's Five-Year Plan "modest" in terms of the need, but "far above the total amounts requested" for this purpose by DHEW—only $44.8 million for FY 1973. "This amount is far too small," the panel declared, "for a task which is crucial both in dealing with the population problem and in improving the outcome of pregnancy for women and children." The Commission projected that at least $250 million annually would be needed for population-related research: $100 million (in federal funds) for basic biomedical research in human reproduction, $100 million (mostly in federal funds) for developmental work on methods of fertility control, and at least $50 million (in federal funds) for behavioral and operational research.

The Commission recommended that "this nation give the highest priority to research in reproductive biology and to the search for improved methods by which individuals can control their own fertility." The panel called for the appropriation and allocation in FY 1973 of "the full $93 million authorized for this purpose," rising to "a minimum of $150 million by 1975; and that private organizations continue and expand their work in this field."

UNWANTED BIRTHS AND THE POOR

The 1965 and 1970 National Fertility Studies showed that while all socio-economic groups experience unwanted pregnancies, "they occur most often and have the most serious consequences among low-income couples." Since 1967, the Commission report pointed out, the federal government has sought to increase the availability of family planning to low-income couples, largely through project grant programs carried out by DHEW's National Center or Family Planning Services and by the Office of Economic Opportunity. "With a relatively modest federal investment, organized family planning programs have succeeded in introducing modern family planning services to nearly 40 percent of low-income persons in need." To reach the majority of those in need who remain unserved, the Commission reported, "will clearly require additional federal authorizations and appropriations as well as increased support for these programs from state and local governments, and from private philanthropy." The Commission estimated that

perhaps $50 million annually might be forthcoming for family plan-
ning services from state and local governments and private sources
and urged more financial support from these sources; the bulk of the
funds, however, will have to come from the DHEW and OEO
project grant programs. Specifically, the Commission recommended
new legislation to extend the current family planning project grant program under Title X of the Public Health Service Act from FY 1973 to FY
1978, and provide "additional authorizations to reach a federal funding
level of $225 million in fiscal year 1973, $275 million in fiscal year 1974, $325
million in fiscal year 1975, and $400 million thereafter. . . ." It also recom-
mended maintenance of the project grant authority under Title V of the
Social Security Act beyond 1972 at the current level of funding (about
$30 million annually), and continuation of OEO family planning programs
"at current levels of authorization" (about $21.5 million annually).

The Commission urged that "no means test be applied in the administration of these programs. Their purpose must be to enlarge personal freedom for all, not to restrict its benefits only to the poorest of the poor."
The Commission pointed out that "there are many nonpoor individuals who
need but do not receive adequate fertility control services" who may become poor through unwanted childbearing if they are denied services.

The panel considered and rejected proposals to revise tax policies, or
provide financial incentives—or disincentives—to encourage couples to
have small families, or to discourage them from having large families.
"Clearly, no proposal to penalize childbearing or reward nonchildbearing
can be acceptable in a situation in which fertility control is not completely
reliable and large numbers of unwanted births occur." The Commission
pointed out that, in practice, proposed bonus payments for not bearing
children, and withdrawal of public benefits from those who bear too
many, have been directed toward the poor, and "almost without exception . . . toward one group—welfare recipients."

What is more, all proposals to penalize childbearing—even those not
specifically directed at the poor—"have the effect of penalizing the child
and his siblings."

In addition to dismissing such proposals on the grounds of social
equity, the Commission dismissed the frequently asserted claim that "because assistance payments are based upon the number of children in the
family, welfare mothers have more children in order to increase their
monthly payment." The panel added that there is no "evidence that present
tax policies and public expenditures promote the birth of additional children in any social class." Rather, the Commission found, "the reverse might
be true." As an example, the panel cited the fact that births to welfare
mothers in New York City declined from 18.9 percent in 1959, when pay-

ments were low, to 11.3 percent in 1970 when the payments were much higher; and for the nation as a whole the average family size of welfare recipients declined between 1967 and 1969, a period when welfare payments were increasing.

The Commission also reviewed—and rejected—various proposals to require parents to assume all or a greater proportion of the costs of their children by withdrawing subsidies for education, health and social services; levying a fee for childbearing or providing a bonus for not having children; or relieving nonparents of some or all of the tax costs of education, health and other services for children. "The only reason to alter present policies which are supportive of children," the panel said, "would be if an even higher good were to be served. We cannot foresee any goal with a higher priority than insuring the welfare of future generations."

FERTILITY-RELATED HEALTH SERVICES

In order that "future generations of Americans . . . be born wanted by their parents, brought into the world with the best skills that modern medicine can offer, and provided with the love and care necessary for a healthy and productive life," the Commission recommended "a national policy and voluntary program to reduce unwanted fertility, to improve the outcome of pregnancy, and to improve the health of children." To implement this program, the Commission urged that public and private health financing mechanisms pay the full cost of all fertility-related health services, including prenatal, delivery and postpartum services, pediatric care for the first year of life, contraception, voluntary sterilization, safe termination of unwanted pregnancy and medical treatment of infertility.

The Commission estimated the total cost for such a program to range from $6.7 to $8.1 billion annually in the next five years, but pointed out that all but about $1 billion of this total cost is already being financed (although these critical services are distributed unevenly, with many persons receiving only some of them or receiving services of poor quality).

The Commission added that the "costs . . . would, in all probability, be more than offset by the benefits to individuals and society of the delivery of healthy children and the prevention of unwanted pregnancies." The panel held that the financing of these services "could easily be integrated into current publicly administered health financing systems, and made part of a new comprehensive national health insurance system. Congress should include this coverage in any health insurance system it adopts."

Covering the costs of such a program would not guarantee the delivery of these services to those in need of them, the Commission pointed out, declaring that "systematic attention" must also be given "to the organization and delivery" of the services. To accomplish this, the Commission recommended that programs be created to train doctors, nurses and paraprofessionals in the provision of all fertility-related health services, develop new patterns for the use of such personnel, evaluate improved methods of organizing service delivery, and establish the capacity to provide services in areas which have few health resources.

TEENAGE SERVICES AND EDUCATION

A number of the recommendations in the Commission report were addressed to meeting the health and social problems leading to and resulting from adolescent pregnancy.

The Commission cited a recent national study by Drs. John Kantner and Melvin Zelnick of Johns Hopkins University, which showed that 27 percent of unwed girls 15–19 years of age had already experienced some sexual intercourse. This rose from 14 percent of 15-year-old girls to 44 percent of 19-year-olds. Only 20 percent of sexually active teenage girls used contraceptives regularly, with the majority using them not at all or seldom (although almost all of them had heard about the pill). "Such a low incidence of contraceptive use," the report stated, "is particularly significant when less than half of these girls knew when during the monthly cycle a girl can become pregnant." Significant rates of sexual activity and little use of contraception among teenagers has led to rising rates of adolescent pregnancy, venereal disease, illegitimacy, forced (and unstable) marriage and recourse to abortion, the report stated.

The Commission pointed to the fact that out-of-wedlock adolescent birthrates had increased as much as threefold between 1940 and 1968 and venereal disease had become "epidemic." In 1968 more than 600,000 infants —17 percent of all births—were born to teenagers; and one-fourth of girls who recently reached their twentieth birthday had already borne a child. At best, the Commission pointed out, adolescent pregnancy—especially in the early teens—involves serious health and social consequences—far more severe than for women over 20. The infants of these young mothers "are subject to higher risks of prematurity, mortality, and serious physical and intellectual impairments than are children of mothers 20 to 35." Those girls who bear a first child at an early age—inside or outside of marriage— tend to bear subsequent children at a rapid rate. ("Sixty percent of girls who had a child before the age of 16 had another baby while still of school age.") Education and employment opportunities of these girls are likely to be seriously impaired. ("Pregnancy is the number one cause for school drop-out among females in the United States.") The psychological effects, the report states, "are indicated by a recent study that estimated that teenage mothers have a suicide rate 10 times that of the general population."

The Commission attributed much of the recent rise in adolescent pregnancy—with all its attendant social and health problems—to the denial of accurate information about sexuality, parenthood and birth control and the inaccessibility of effective birth control services.

The Commission was highly critical of those "well-organized and vocal" opponents of sex education who, to the panel members' "regret," had "successfully forestalled sex education in 13 states." Keeping youngsters in ignorance, the Commission members stated, "does not serve to prevent sexual activity, but rather promotes the undesirable consequences of sexual behavior—unwanted pregnancy, unwanted maternity, and venereal disease."

The Commission urged that "funds be made available to the National Institute of Mental Health to support the development of a variety of model programs in human sexuality" based both in schools and the community. The panel recommended that "sex education be made available to all, and that it be presented in a responsible manner through community organizations, the media and especially the schools." Because of the "serious social and health consequences involved in teenage pregnancy and the high rates of teenage out-of-wedlock pregnancy and venereal disease," the Commission also urged "the elimination of legal restrictions on access to contraceptive and prophylactic information and services by young people." It recommended that "states adopt affirmative legislation" permitting minors to receive such information and services "in appropriate settings sensitive to their needs and concerns." It asked that organizations such as the American Law Institute, the American Bar Association and the Council on State Governments "formulate appropriate model statutes."

The Commission urged that not only should "birth control services and information be made available to teenagers . . . regardless of age, marital status, or number of children," but that there be implemented "an adequately financed program to develop appropriate family planning materials, to conduct training courses for teachers and school administrators, and to assist states and local communities in integrating information about family planning into school courses such as hygiene and sex education."

While stressing "the necessity of minimizing adolescent pregnancy by making contraceptive information and services available" to sexually active youth, the Commission urged that adolescents who do become pregnant "not be stigmatized and removed from society." It urged that "school systems . . . make certain that pregnant adolescents have the opportunity to continue their education, and that they are aided in gaining access to adequate health, nutritional, and counseling services." It also held that the "word 'illegitimate' and the stigma attached to it have no place in our society." The panel recommended that "all children, regardless of the circumstances of their birth, be accorded fair and equal status, socially, morally, and legally." It called for "revision of those laws and practices which result in discrimination against out-of-wed-lock children."

EDUCATION IN POPULATION, FAMILY LIFE AND HUMAN REPRODUCTION

In addition to sex and birth control education, the Commission made numerous other recommendations in the educational field to help young people "make rational, informed decisions about their own and their descendants' future...."

The Commission called for a program of population education to provide young people with "knowledge about population processes, population characteristics, the causes of population change, and the consequences of such change for the individual and for the society." The Commission could find "no evidence that anything approaching an adequate population program now exists in our schools. Very few teachers are trained in the subject and textual materials are scant and inadequate." Citing evidence that "federal funds amounting to $25 million over the next three years are needed in this field," the panel pointed out that no appropriations have been made under authorization which has existed for the past two years, and that DHEW has requested only $170,000 for population education in FY 1973.

The Commission recommended the enactment of a Population Education Act "to assist school systems in establishing well-planned population education programs so that present and future generations will be better prepared to meet the challenges arising from population change." It asked that federal funds be appropriated for teacher training, curriculum development, materials preparation, research and evaluation, support of "model programs," and for assisting state departments of education "to develop competence and leadership in population education."

At the college level, the Commission urged that population study be included in all introductory social science courses.

The panel advocated education for parenthood, encompassing "a diversity of styles of family life in America today," including acceptance "without stigma" of those individuals who choose to remain childless. It urged that young people be made aware of the real costs of raising children, both emotional and financial (the latter estimated to average $60,000 from birth through college for a first child): "With some idea of the financial demands of children, parents can plan ahead and be better prepared to provide the kind of life they want for their children."

The Commission chided the mass media for depicting family life in a way that "bears little resemblance to that experienced by most of the population," and urged the media ("a potent educational force . . . American children and adults spend an estimated average of 27 hours a week watching television") to "assume more responsibility in presenting information and education for family living to the public." The Commission also called on community agencies, "especially the school," to assume a more active and more sensitive role in education for parenthood, and that financial support be provided for such programs by DHEW.

The panel, citing estimates that one in 15 children may be born with "some form of genetic defect," also called for increased support of research to identify genetically related disorders; development of better screening techniques, and better ways to provide genetic counseling services; improved care of those suffering from genetic disorders; and "exploration of the ethical and moral implications of genetic technology." To this end, increased private and public funding was urged to "develop facilities and train personnel to implement programs in genetic screening and counseling."

The Commission stated its belief that "genetic education is an important component in any program of education for parenthood." The panel also urged that such material be included in school curricula, and that professional education of medical and health workers be expanded so that they learn to "recognize genetically related problems and . . . refer them to available genetic counseling services."

THE STATUS OF WOMEN

The report pointed out that women today "marry earlier, have smaller families earlier, and live longer than they did 50 years ago." With less and less of their lives spent in maternal functions, women more and more are beginning to work, seek higher education and "choose roles supplementary to or in place of motherhood." While this trend is likely to continue, and even intensify, with more women foregoing motherhood entirely, the Commission found that our society has "not yet fully accommodated these changes in our social, legal, and economic structures." The panel remarked that "it would seem good social policy to recognize and facilitate the trend toward smaller families by making it possible for women to choose attractive roles in place of or supplementary to motherhood." This change, the report stated, should not be sought on demographic grounds alone, but as a means of offering "a greater range of choice" so that men and women can "be free to develop as individuals rather than being molded to fit some sexual stereotype." The Commission stated that it would be "particularly helpful if marriage, childbearing, and childrearing could come to be viewed as more deliberate and serious commitments rather than as traditional, almost compulsory behavior."

The panel expressed doubt that jobs usually open to women, of low pay and status, have much effect in reducing fertility. It indicated, however, its belief that "attractive work may effectively compete with childbearing and have the effect of lowering fertility. . . ." The Commission also found "abundant evidence" that higher education is associated with smaller families, and urged that "institutional discrimination against women in education should be abolished."

Despite improvements in the legal status of women over the past century, the Commission stated that "equal rights and responsibilities are still denied women in our legal system." It urged that the proposed Equal Rights Amendment to the U.S. Constitution (approved in March by the Congress) be ratified by the states, and the "federal, state, and local governments undertake positive programs to ensure freedom from discrimination based on sex."

CHILD CARE

The Commission found that the child-care arrangements made by working mothers—especially those with limited incomes—"are frequently inadequate." The Commission pointed to the "critical significance of the first three years of life for the emotional, and intellectual, as well as the physical, development of children." Adequate full-time developmental child-care programs, the Commission held, could tap the enormous learning potential of preschool children, and might also work to reduce fertility by offering women who want to work the opportunity to enter or reenter the labor force much sooner than they would be able to otherwise. While such programs are expensive (the Commission cited one estimate of $20 billion per year for the "best kind" of program for the 18 million children from families with incomes under $7,000), the panel indicated that those who could afford to pay should do so, and union and industry programs should be expanded to help defray the costs. The Commission stated, however, that public funds would still be necessary to "stimulate innovative programs and research, and to subsidize services for lower-income families."

The Commission recommended that "public and private forces join together to assure that adequate child-care programs, including health, nutritional, and educational components, be available to families who wish to make use of them." It also urged continuing research and evaluation of the benefits and costs to children, parents and the public of various child-care arrangements.

ADOPTION

The Commission found that "the demographic impact of adoption on the birthrate in the United States is minimal." Nevertheless, "the symbolic value of adoption as a mode of responsible parenthood ["adopt after two"] may come to outweigh its direct demographic impact." The Commission urged "changes in attitudes and practices to encourage adoption thereby benefiting children, prospective parents, and society"; such changes might include more subsidizing of poorer families qualified to adopt, and a review by appropriate bodies of "current laws, practices, procedures, and regulations which govern the adoptive process." Such a review, the Commission urged, should examine legal eligibility requirements, such as age, race, marital status, religion, socioeconomic status and labor-force status of prospective mothers.

IMMIGRATION

The Commission pointed out that immigrants are now entering the United States at the rate of almost 400,000 a year, and that net immigration accounted for about 16 percent of total population growth between 1960 and 1970. If immigration were to continue at the present rate, and each immigrant family were to have an average of two children, then immigrants arriving between 1970 and the year 2000 and their descendants would account for almost a quarter of the population increase during that period. To achieve population stabilization and continue immigration at the present rate would require an average of 2.0 children per woman, rather than the 2.1 children needed for stabilization if there were no immigration. Such stabilization would occur at a later date and imply an eventual population about eight percent larger than if there were no international migration.

Immigrants not only contribute to the growth of the population, but affect its distribution. Immigrants tend to prefer metropolitan areas and are concentrated in a few of the largest cities; two-thirds of recent immigrants indicated their attention to settle in six states. The Commission urged that the flow of immigrants "be closely regulated until this country can provide adequate social and economic opportunities for all its present members, particularly those traditionally discriminated against because of race, ethnicity, or sex." Despite the problems associated with immigration, the Commission majority felt that the present level of immigration should be maintained because of "the compassionate nature of our immigration policy" and in recognition of "the contribution which immigrants have made and continue to make to our society." The Commission recommended, however, that "immigration levels not be increased and that immigration policy be reviewed periodically to reflect demographic conditions and considerations."

While urging a freeze on the level of *legal* immigration, the Commission called for a crackdown on *illegal* entry—which, it said, "exacerbated" many of our economic problems. The panel called for Congressional legislation imposing "civil and criminal sanctions on employers of illegal border-crossers or aliens in an immigration status in which employment is not authorized."

MIGRATION AND METROPOLITAN GROWTH

With ever-increasing rapidity, the United States has been transformed in this century from a rural to a metropolitan society. At the beginning of the century, the Commission pointed out, six in 10 Americans lived on farms or in villages. Today, nearly seven in 10 live in cities of 50,000 or more, or in their suburbs; this proportion is likely, the Commission predicted, to grow to 85 percent before the century's end. Such metropolitan growth is the inevitable consequence, the report stated, of "the social and economic transformation of the United States . . . from an agrarian, to an industrial, and now to a service-oriented economy." Migration has been from low-income rural areas and from abroad to metropolitan areas, from one metropolitan area to another, and from central cities to suburbs. This pattern of growth has left in its wake such well-publicized problems as congestion in central cities, air and noise pollution, aesthetically unattractive suburban growth, and emergence of the "two societies"—poor blacks in the central cities, affluent whites in the suburbs.

"Population growth *is* metropolitan growth," the report declared. The Commission pointed out, however, that while past migration to big-city areas lies at the root of present concentrations, natural increase is now "the dominant source of metropolitan growth" (three-fourths of such growth over the past decade). The trend toward bigness of metropolitan areas cannot be checked substantially unless national population growth is slowed or stopped. Thus, the Commission reported, "the most effective long-term strategy for stabilizing local [metropolitan] growth is through national stabilization, not redistribution."

Nevertheless, the Commission held, there is a need to do something now about the problems brought about by population maldistribution; and there will still be problems of "congestion, pollution, and severe racial separation" in large metropolitan areas, even after stabilization is attained. The Commission called for "attenuating and simultaneously better accommodating" present trends in population distribution through a "dual strategy":

1. "encouraging the growth of selected urban centers in economically depressed regions," and
2. seeking "to enhance choices of living environments for all members of society. . . ."

The Commission recommended that the federal government "develop goals, objectives, and criteria for shaping national population distribution guidelines" as a basis for regional, state and local plans and development. Other federal action urged by the Commission included:

3. anticipation, monitoring and evaluation of the demographic effects of such governmental activities as defense procurement, housing and transportation programs, zoning and tax laws,
4. development of a national policy to establish criteria for the use of land "consistent with national population distribution objectives and guidelines,"
5. provision of technical and financial assistance to regional, state, metropolitan and local governmental planning and development agencies,
6. coordination and implementation of a "growth center strategy."

The Commission advocated such a "growth center strategy" (encouraging migration to cities in the 25,000–350,000 population range with "a demonstrated potential for future growth" to 50,000–500,000 people) "as an alternative to the traditional paths to big cities," since in some chronically depressed areas "the most prudent course is to make the process of decline more orderly and less costly. . . ."

Such a strategy, the Commission stated, should emphasize "human resource development"—namely, quality education, training and other vital services needed to "improve the quality and mobility potential of individuals. . . ." It should also be coupled with worker relocation counseling and assistance to enable individuals "to relocate with a minimum of risk and disruption."

On the state or regional level, the Commission called for the development corporations which would have the responsibility and the necessary power to implement more comprehensive development plans—either themselves acting as the developers, or as "catalysts" for private development.

RACIAL POLARIZATION

The Commission deplored the increase in racial polarization which has occurred in the wake of metropolitan growth; it urged that "action be taken to increase freedom in choice of residential location through the elimination of current patterns of racial and economic segregation and their attendant injustices." This, the panel said, will require "vigorous and concerted steps" to promote bias-free housing within metropolitan areas and, specifically, assurance by federal and state governments that more suburban housing for low- and moderate-income families is built.

The Commission also called for more programs "to equip black and other deprived minorities for fuller participation in economic life," including coordinated programs of education, health, vocational development and job counseling.

While calling for a "long-run national policy of eliminating the ghetto," the Commission pointed to the "short-run need to make the ghetto a more satisfactory place to live." The panel urged that "actions be taken to reduce the dependence of local jurisdictions on locally collected property taxes" as one way of promoting a "more racially and economically integrated society." The Commission found that "given the heavy reliance of local jurisdictions on locally collected property taxes, the very structure of local government in metropolitan areas . . . provides incentives for people and activities to segregate themselves, which produces disparities between local resources, requirements, and levels of service, which in turn invite further segregation." The Commission called for a more "progressive" tax program, through which revenues are "raised on the basis of fiscal capacity and distributed on the basis of expenditure needs."

The Commission also advocated "restructuring of local governments" to reduce "overlapping jurisdictions with limited functions and the fragmentation of multipurpose jurisdictions. . . ." The Commission suggested that metropolitan-wide government might be appropriate for some areas, and a "two-tier system" like Toronto's for others.

VITAL STATISTICS, SOCIAL RESEARCH

The Commission emphasized that increased research into population-related social and economic problems was needed as much as more biomedical research. The panel pointed out that in FY 1972 only $6.7 million of the $39.3 million spent on population research was devoted to behavioral aspects. It indicated that federal support for social and behavioral research in population needed to be increased over the next several years to a total of $50 million annually.

The panel made a number of other specific recommendations, among them:

1. more rapid development by the National Center for Health Statistics of comprehensive statistics on family planning services, including all patients to whom family planning services are provided, with uniform statistical definitions and standards, in a coordinated federal-state-local system,

2. adequate financial support for the biennial national Family Growth Survey to be commenced by the National Center for Health Statistics late this year, as a continuation (with a substantially enlarged household sample) of the Growth of American Families and National Fertility Studies previously undertaken by private organizations,

3. exemption from the general freeze on training funds to support programs to train scientists specializing in social and behavioral research in population.

A NEW RESEARCH INSTITUTE

The Commission found that the Center for Population Research (CPR), created within the National Institute of Child Health and Human Development (NICHD) in 1968 has become "inadequate" to carry on the needed biomedical, social and behavioral population research. The panel pointed out that if all of the population research funds recommended by it for FY 1973 were approved, the CPR component of NICHD research would be greater than all other components combined.

The Commission called for moving the population research program from NICHD to a new National Institute of Population Sciences "to provide an adequate institutional framework for implementing a greatly expanded program of population research." The panel held that creation of a separate institute would provide a "stronger base" from which to carry on expanded biomedical, social and behavioral population research; could attract better scientists; would facilitate acquisition of laboratory and clinical space needed for a diversified research program as well as . . . help in commanding the level of funding that . . . is necessary but which has not been forthcoming."

The Commission also called for:

1. substantial enlargement of the capacity of DHEW in the population field by "strengthening the Office of Population Affairs and expanding its staff,"

2. creation of an Office of Population Growth and Distribution within the Executive Office of the President to "establish objectives and criteria for shaping national growth and distribution policies; monitor, anticipate and appraise the effects on population of all governmental activities. . . . and the effect that population growth and distribution will have on the implementation of all governmental programs. . . ."

THE ECONOMY AND THE ENVIRONMENT

Before making its recommendations, the Commission carefully investigated —and finally rejected—the opposing claims that, on the one hand, slowing population growth could hurt business or threaten workers' jobs, or, on the other hand, that we must take drastic measures to reach zero population growth quickly, lest we ravage all of our resources and irreversibly pollute the ecosphere.

On the economic side, the Commission stated that it had "looked for and . . . not found, any convincing economic argument for continued national population growth," in terms of the economy as a whole, of business or of "the welfare of the average person." Indeed, the Commission found, "the average person will be markedly better off" economically if we move toward replacement fertility than if families are larger.

As to ecological damage, the Commission found that population growth exacerbates but is not the "sole culprit" causing such problems. "To believe that it is," the report states, "is to confuse how things are done with how many people are doing them."

In the long run, the Commission said, the solutions to our ecological problems will require "conservation of water resources, restrictions on pollution emissions, limitations on fertilizers and pesticides, preservation of wilderness areas, and protection of animal life threatened by man." It will require "development of clean sources of energy production" such as nuclear fusion, and adequate "pricing of public facilities and common property resources . . . such as rivers and air." (The report remarked that "at present, most monetary incentives work the wrong way, inducing waste and pollution rather than the opposite.")

Gradually slowing population growth, the Commission pointed out, will not solve any of these ecological problems, but it will help us "buy time" to find sensible solutions. However, the Commission found no merit to "the emergency crisis response." Zero population growth could not be attained rapidly "without considerable disruption to society," including serious dislocations in employment, education and business as families' average childbearing was forced to shrink and expand, contract and enlarge again over several decades. In addition, the authoritarian means which would be necessary to attain these undesirable ends would probably be unenforceable, and certainly would be repugnant in a democratic society.

NOTE

1. Mrs. Chandler advocated reform of abortion laws which restrict abortion to conditions which threaten the pregnant woman's life; she favored abortion requested by a woman and approved by her physician and a hospital committee, performed in a hospital or clinic, when the gestation period does not exceed 18 weeks. Congressman Erlenborn, Dr. Cornely and Miss Olivarez opposed abortion as "destruction of human life." Senator Cranston decried the "inconsistencies and inequities" in existing state abortion laws, but said he could not join in the Commission's recommendation because of the "social and ethical implications of such action now."

Introduction: C. Birth Control and Black Americans

Population policies are always going to exist in a political and social context. It is not possible to think of any policy as existing in a vacuum and not having an impact upon other social institutions and social groups. A policy of abortion upon demand has an obvious effect upon the Catholic Church as well as other religious groups that consider abortion a sin. An immigration policy that excludes Latin Americans or Asians is going to offend the people of these nationalities both in this country and in their native lands. As I said earlier, any population policy is going to have ramifications and implications for some important segments in the society and may therefore encounter unexpected opposition.

For several years there has been an undercurrent of opposition to the family-planning movement among black Americans. As sociologist Charles Willie put it when he appeared before the Population Commission:

> "... I must state categorically that many people in the black community are deeply suspicious of any family planning program initiated by whites. You probably have heard, but not taken seriously the call by some male-dominated black militant groups for females to eschew the use of contraceptives because they are pushed in the black community as a method of exterminating black people. While black females often take a different view about contraceptives than their male militant companions, they too are concerned about the possibility of black genocide in America.

"The genocidal charge is neither 'absurd' nor 'hollow' as some whites have contended. Neither is it limited to the ghetto, whether they be low-income black militant or middle-aged black moderates. Indeed my studies of black students at white colleges indicate that young educated blacks fear black genocide."[1]

The three papers in this section document this issue fully. The first paper (Darity, et al.)shows how accurate Willie's assertion is. A very high percentage of blacks, especially the younger men, agree that the family-planning movement is for the purpose of reducing or eliminating black Americans. The second paper, by Robert Weisbord, examines the entire issue from a historical perspective, which at the very least lends credence to the genocide notion. The final paper, by Kammeyer, Yetman and McClendon, reports on an empirical test of the hypothesis that family-planning services in the United States have been initiated more frequently if there are blacks in the population. There is a strong inferential case coming from these data that the fears and concerns of black Americans about the family-planning movement are not groundless.

Population policies are inevitably a part of political and social contexts and the case of black Americans is only one example of how influential such contexts may be. Furthermore, the responses of religious groups, racial groups, nationality groups, and political groups to population policies will always complicate and impede efforts toward population policy and population control.

---

[1] Charles V. Willie, "Perspectives From the Black Community: A Position Paper," Population Reference Bureau, PRB #37, June 1971, pp. 1–2.

31

Race Consciousness and Fears of Black Genocide as Barriers to Family Planning*

William A. Darity, Castellano B. Turner,
and H. Jean Thiebaux

THE RESEARCH APPROACH

The preliminary report here is based on pilot work done as part of a larger project. One major purpose of this study (as well as the larger research project) was to determine the relationship between family planning practices and belief in a race genocide conspiracy against black Americans. A second major purpose was to determine the relationship between family planning practices and race consciousness. In addition to these general purposes, we also simply wished to determine the extent to which fears of genocide were present in the black community, the extent of rejection by blacks of sterilization and abortion, and the extent to which blacks feel that black community control of family planning programs would make a difference in the degree of receptiveness to them. This report will be limited to a comparison based on sex and on the age differential of the 30 and under age group and the over 30 age group.

Sample

A medium-sized New England city was chosen for this pilot project. Several black communities within this urban area were identified with the help of local black citizens. By means of census data and street lists it was possible to classify several black neighborhoods in terms of income level.

Reprinted from *PRB Selection No. 37* (June, 1971), pp. 5–12, by permission of the authors and the publisher, Population Reference Bureau, Inc., Washington, D.C.

* A paper presented at the *Ninth Annual Meeting of the American Association of Planned Parenthood Physicians*, Kansas City, Missouri, April 5–6, 1971.

The classification system was very simple: low income neighborhoods and middle-to-upper income neighborhoods. In those neighborhoods which had been classified as middle-to-upper income a 40 percent sample of households was initially designated; in those neighborhoods classified as lower income a 60 percent sample of households was initially designated. From this total designated group of households a 2.5 percent random sample was drawn. This procedure provided an approximately stratified sample of the black community in that city. The total sample was 159 households.

Procedure

After sampling procedures were complete, the interviewing began. When the interviewers found households empty or potential interviewees were inaccessible, a new household was randomly selected. Ten interviewers were employed to interview the head of the household or a female member of the household in the reproductive age range. Every attempt was made to balance the group in terms of age.

An interview schedule was used which contained items seeking information concerning general demographic characteristics, attitudes toward family planning methods, attitudes toward family planning agencies, racial consciousness, racial genocide and general attitude items.

Results and Limitations

Some general characteristics of the population sample should be noted. Females made up 66 percent of the sample. The median educational attainment was high school graduation.

We are aware of a possible major bias in the fact that for this paper we have not differentiated between the never married under 30, which form 72 percent of the males and 67 percent of the females, and those in that age group who were or had been married. This analysis will form a part of a subsequent review.

SPECIFIC FINDINGS OF THE STUDY

The group was asked to give their racial designation preference, that is, whether they would prefer to be ethnically known as colored, Negro, Afro-American or black. The purpose was to set a stage for analysis of data on the basis of level of black consciousness. A survey of contemporary thought and popular literature suggests to us that the degree of race consciousness increases as one moves from "colored" to "black." Due to the small number in the sample, the choices were collapsed: Those having no particular preference, Negro and colored were combined in one category and those selecting black or Afro-American in another. For males 30 and under, 83 percent selected Afro-American or black, and for males over 30, 56 percent selected Afro-American or black. For females 30 and under, 85 percent selected Afro-American or black, and over 30, 62 percent selected Afro-American or black. For the total group, 74 percent selected Afro-American or black. These results are shown in Table 1.

TABLE 1. Racial Preference Designation of Subjects
(Percent)

Question	Males		Females		Group		Grand Total (Percent)
	30 & Under	Over 30	30 & Under	Over 30	30 & Under	Over 30	
No Preference, Negro or colored	17	44	15	38	16	39	26
Afro-American or black	83	56	85	62	84	61	74
N (Male) = 53							
N (Female) = 96 TOTAL	100	100	100	100	100	100	100

These data indicate a high percentage of black Americans in the fertility age group may be highly race (black) conscious.

The findings also showed that 39 percent of the group was married, living with spouse, 41 percent never married and 20 percent were separated, widowed or divorced. A percentage breakdown is shown in Table 2.

TABLE 2. Marital Status
(Percent)

Question	Males		Females		Group		Grand Total (Percent)
	30 & Under	Over 30	30 & Under	Over 30	30 & Under	Over 30	
Married, living with spouse	22	83	25	49	24	59	39
Not living with spouse (separated, widowed, divorced)	6	17	8	44	7	37	20
Never married	72	—	67	7	69	4	41
N (Male) = 54							
N (Female) = 93 TOTAL	100	100	100	100	100	100	100

Birth Control Attitudes and Acceptable Methods

The determination of purposes and objectives of birth control services is a very important item in any program dealing with acceptability or rejection.

A series of statements dealing with birth control clinics, their purposes and objectives were posed to the respondents. In response to the statement, "Birth control projects are aimed at the low-income population," 68 percent agreed. There was a 73 percent agreement among males 30 and under and males over 30, while 59 percent of the females 30 and under agreed with the statement and 71 percent over 30 years of age agreed.

In response to the statement, "All forms of birth control are designed to eliminate blacks," 14 percent agreed with the statement while 86 percent disagreed. It is significant to point out here, however, that 29 percent of the males 30 and under agreed with the statement while 100 percent of the males over 30 disagreed with the statement.

In response to the statement, "Encouraging blacks to use birth control is comparable to trying to eliminate this group from society," 28 percent agreed with the statement and 72 percent disagreed. However, among the male subjects 30 and under, 47 percent agreed with the statement while 27 percent of the over 30 age group agreed with the statement. The distribution among the females was basically equal: 20 percent of the 30 and under agreed with the statement and 23 percent of the over 30 age group agreed.

In response to the statement, "Sterilization is a white plot to eliminate blacks," 17 percent agreed with the statement and 83 percent disagreed with the statement. However, among the males 30 years of age and under 38 percent agreed with the statement.

Although the overall findings do not indicate a high level of suspicion about the purposes and objectives of family planning, birth control, abortion and sterilization, it is evident that among black males of 30 and under higher suspicion prevails than among the other categories. See Table 3 for these findings.

In order to determine both usable and probable methods of birth control, a series of statements dealing with acceptability of birth control and family planning methods were read to respondents. These dealt with controlling family size, use of methods to control family size and the acceptability of abortion and sterilization.

The respondents agreed almost totally that the size of the family could be controlled if one wanted to do so. In response to the question, "Can the size of the family be controlled if one wants to do so?", 92 percent answered "yes." In response to the question, "Have you or your spouse ever used any method in an attempt to control your family size?", 80 percent responded "yes." However, among male respondents, 47 percent of the 30 and under age group responded "no" to the question of contraceptive use, and 30 percent of the over 30 age group. For the females 30 and under age group, 91 percent responded "yes," and 93 percent of the over 30 age group responded "yes."

TABLE 3. Analysis of Responses to Purposes and Objectives of Birth Control Methods (Percent)

Question		Males		Females		Group		Grand Total (Percent)
		30 & Under	Over 30	30 & Under	Over 30	30 & Under	Over 30	
Birth control projects are aimed at the low-income population	AGREE	73	73	59	71	64	71	68
N (Male) = 37	DISAGREE	27	27	41	29	36	29	32
N (Female) = 80	TOTAL	100	100	100	100	100	100	100
All forms of birth control are designed to eliminate black Americans	AGREE	29	—	5	18	15	13	14
N (Male) = 43	DISAGREE	71	100	95	82	85	87	86
N (Female) = 76	TOTAL	100	100	100	100	100	100	100
Encouraging blacks to use birth control is comparable to trying to eliminate this group from society	AGREE	47	27	20	23	31	24	28
N (Male) = 45	DISAGREE	53	73	80	77	69	76	72
N (Female) = 79	TOTAL	100	100	100	100	100	100	100
Abortions are part of a white plot to eliminate blacks	AGREE	34	19	15	21	24	20	22
N (Male) = 45	DISAGREE	66	81	85	79	76	80	78
N (Female) = 78	TOTAL	100	100	100	100	100	100	100
Sterilization is a white plot to eliminate blacks	AGREE	28	6	8	21	17	16	17
N (Male)	DISAGREE	72	94	92	79	83	84	83
N (Female) = 76	TOTAL	100	100	100	100	100	100	100

In response to the question, "Have you ever been to a clinic or a doctor to obtain information about not becoming pregnant?", 35 percent of the subjects responded "yes" and 65 percent "no." Among the males 30 and under, 15 percent responded "yes," and of the males over 30 years of age, 17 percent responded "yes." Among the females the response was 44 percent and 36 percent "yes," respectively. See Table 4 for these results.

Subjects were asked to respond to two specific questions related to abortions and sterilizations to determine acceptability as a part of birth control services. In response to the first statement, "If you had all the children you wanted you would allow yourself to be sterilized," 84 percent of the respondents disagreed with the statement, while 16 percent agreed. Among all males 94 percent disagreed. Among females 30 and under, 20 percent agreed and 80 percent disagreed. The rate for the over 30 age females was 25 percent and 75 percent respectively.

In response to the statement, "You would get an abortion (or encourage your wife to get an abortion) if you (she) became pregnant and you did not want the baby," 22 percent of all respondents agreed, and 78 percent disagreed. Among males, 30 years of age and under, 12 percent agreed, while 47 percent of the males over 30 agreed. Among the female subjects, 28 percent of the 30 and under age group agreed while 17 percent of the over 30 age group agreed. See Table 5 for these findings.

Community Control

The idea of community control of services has become an important factor in the delivery of health services over the last few years. In order to ascertain the feeling about community control in the delivery of family planning services, a series of statements were presented to the respondents. In response to the first statement, "Black-operated birth control clinics will be more acceptable to blacks than white-operated clinics," 71 percent agreed, and 29 percent disagreed. There was little difference in distribution of responses by sex and age.

In response to the statement, "Birth control clinics in black neighborhoods should be operated by blacks," 78 percent of the males 30 years of age and under agreed with the statement and 44 percent of the males over 30 agreed with the statement. Among females 30 years of age and under and the over 30 age group, the results of agreement were 56 percent and 62 percent respectively.

As evidence of the strength of the idea of black control, there was a 75 percent agreement among males 30 years old and under and a 44 percent agreement among males in the over 30 year age group that "All businesses in black communities should be owned by blacks." Among females, 67 per-

TABLE 4. Birth Control Usage
(Percent)

Question	Males		Females		Group		Grand Total (Percent)
	30 & Under	Over 30	30 & Under	Over 30	30 & Under	Over 30	
Have you ever been to a clinic or doctor to obtain information about not becoming pregnant? N (Male) = 25 N (Female) = 87							
YES	15	17	44	36	38	32	35
NO	85	83	56	64	62	68	65
TOTAL	100	100	100	100	100	100	100
Have you or your spouse ever used any method in an attempt to control your family size? N (Male) = 31 N (Female) = 91							
YES	47	38	91	93	80	79	80
NO	53	62	9	7	20	21	20
TOTAL	100	100	100	100	100	100	100
Can the size of the family be controlled if one wants to do so? N (Male) = 41 N (Female) = 91							
YES	85	100	91	93	89	95	92
NO	15	—	9	7	11	5	8
TOTAL	100	100	100	100	100	100	100

TABLE 5. Birth Control Usage—Sterilization and Abortion (Percent)

Question	Males		Females		Group		Grand Total (Percent)
	30 & Under	Over 30	30 & Under	Over 30	30 & Under	Over 30	
If you had all the children you wanted, you would allow yourself to be sterilized N (Male) = 50 N (Female) = 84							
AGREE	12	47	38	17	21	25	22
DISAGREE	88	53	72	83	79	75	78
TOTAL	100	100	100	100	100	100	100
You would get an abortion if you (your wife) became pregnant and you did not want a baby N (Male) = 48 N (Female) = 81							
AGREE	6	6	20	25	14	20	16
DISAGREE	94	94	80	75	86	80	84
TOTAL	100	100	100	100	100	100	100

cent of the 30 years old and under agreed with the statement. Fifty-one percent of the over 30 years old group agreed with the same statement.

It is important to point out the relative differences in points of view as demonstrated when age differences are considered in comparing the young black males with the other age group. See Table 6 for these findings.

Strength in Numbers

There is the ever-abiding concept of "strength in numbers" when discussions on family size, political mobility, economic mobility and survival are considered. In order to approach this topic, two statements were presented to the subjects. In response to the first statement, "The survival of black people depends on an ever-increasing number of black births," 41 percent of the respondents agreed with the statement; 50 percent disagreed. The data revealed a peculiar trend, where 73 percent of males over 30 agreed, 43 percent of the males 30 and under agreed. However, the second statement, "Black American families should not limit their sizes," showed that 50 percent of the males 30 and under agreed with the statement while 50 percent disagreed. However, for the males over 30 there were 18 percent who agreed and 82 percent disagreed. Among both categories of females, few agreed with the statement.

The response to the first question indicated that the over 30 age group of males appears to reverse itself where the situation is based on a more personal context. See Table 7 for these results.

Separatist Concepts

There can be expected a high level of separatist feelings when race consciousness is very high. In order to observe this phenomenon a series of statements dealing with this item was posed to the respondents. The first statement, "Black Americans should have a country of their own," received a 23 percent agreement and 77 percent disagreement. However, among the 30 and under males, there was a 35 percent agreement. In response to the statement, "Black Americans should not try any more to integrate American society," 28 percent agreed with the statement and 72 percent disagreed. Among males 30 and under 48 percent agreed and among females 30 and under 32 percent agreed, while among the males 30 and over and females 30 and over, the percent agreeing was 14 and 15 respectively. The third question posed was "It is wrong for blacks and whites to intermarry." There was a 26 percent agreement with the statement and 74 percent disagreement. However, among the males 30 and under there was a 29 percent agreement and among females in this age category a 33 percent

TABLE 6. Community Control of Birth Control Clinics, Business, etc.
(Percent)

Question		Males		Females		Group		Grand Total (Percent)
		30 & Under	Over 30	30 & Under	Over 30	30 & Under	Over 30	
Black-operated clinics will be more acceptable to blacks than white-operated clinics	AGREE	78	69	72	64	75	65	71
	DISAGREE	22	31	28	36	25	35	29
N (Male) = 48	TOTAL	100	100	100	100	100	100	100
N (Female) = 82								
Birth control clinics in black neighborhoods should be operated by blacks	AGREE	78	44	56	62	66	56	62
	DISAGREE	22	56	44	38	34	44	38
N (Male) = 48	TOTAL	100	100	100	100	100	100	100
N (Female) = 78								
All the businesses in the black community should be owned by blacks	AGREE	75	44	67	51	70	49	60
	DISAGREE	25	56	33	49	30	51	40
N (Male) = 40	TOTAL	100	100	100	100	100	100	100
N (Female) = 80								

TABLE 7. Analysis of Statements Suggesting Support for Strength in Numbers (Percent)

Question		Males		Females		Group		Grand Total (Percent)
		30 & Under	Over 30	30 & Under	Over 30	30 & Under	Over 30	
The survival of black people depends on ever-increasing numbers of black births	AGREE	43	73	38	30	40	42	41
	DISAGREE	57	27	62	70	60	58	59
N (Male) = 43	TOTAL	100	100	100	100	100	100	100
N (Female) = 80								
Black American families should not limit their size	AGREE	50	18	25	18	36	18	28
	DISAGREE	50	82	75	82	64	82	72
N (Male) = 47	TOTAL	100	100	100	100	100	100	100
N (Female) = 78								

TABLE 8.   Questions Dealing with Separatist Attitudes (Percent)

Question		Males 30 & Under	Males Over 30	Females 30 & Under	Females Over 30	Group 30 & Under	Group Over 30	Grand Total (Percent)
Black Americans should have a country of their own	AGREE	35	19	23	17	27	17	23
	DISAGREE	65	81	77	83	73	83	77
N (Male) = 42	TOTAL	100	100	100	100	100	100	100
N (Female) = 82								
Black Americans should not try any more to integrate into American society	AGREE	48	14	32	15	39	15	28
	DISAGREE	52	86	68	85	61	85	72
N (Male) = 45	TOTAL	100	100	100	100	100	100	100
N (Female) = 82								
It is wrong for blacks and whites to inter-marry	AGREE	29	8	33	24	31	20	26
	DISAGREE	71	92	67	76	69	80	74
N (Male) = 38	TOTAL	100	100	100	100	100	100	100
N (Female) = 72								

agreement, while among males in the over 30 age group, there was an 8 percent agreement and among females in the same category a 24 percent agreement. See Table 8 for these results.

DISCUSSION AND CONCLUSION

The findings presented in this paper, which have relevance for family planning program development, will be discussed briefly. First, for public relations, it would seem that the need for change in terminology in describing or referring to black clients has been demonstrated. The 30 and under age group overwhelmingly prefers either black or Afro-American to colored or Negro. This is also true of a clear majority of the over 30 age group. Because the younger males and females are either users or potential users of family planning services, it would seem desirable for administrators to encourage staff use of terminology which is more acceptable to this age group.

The finding that 68 percent of the subjects feel that birth control clinics are aimed at low-income groups could serve as a deterrent to use of these services by black participants, since such a high percentage fall into the low-income category. It would seem advisable that in family planning program development, emphasis be placed on "open services" for *all* segments of the population with public clinics and services available to *all* segments of the population.

Special attention must be given to the black male in the 30 and under age group. The highest degree of concern and negative attitudes were observed in this age group with regard to purpose and objectives of birth control services. The same negative attitudes were observed in the case of abortions and sterilization among this age group, as compared with the over 30 male and all age categories among females.

In order to reduce the suspicion evidenced in this sector, consideration should be given to their preference for community control of birth control clinics. The idea of control is supported by 78 percent of black males in the 30 and under age group. Their involvement in planning and direction, so that they will know and understand the operations of such clinics, seems important. Administrators and developers of such services should make an all out effort to include young black males.

The findings also showed that the strongest feeling for separation is among young black males. It would seem that based on the thrust for power and the separatist movement, the inclusion of young black males in policy making and executive functions in family planning services is essential. Another significant aspect of the study demonstrated that the support for "strength in numbers" is potentially strong among young black males. Fifty percent of the respondents in the age group 30 and under supported the statement that "black families should not limit their family sizes." This also indicates a need for purposeful and deliberate inclusion of this group in family planning program development.

Additionally, it may be noted that abortion and sterilization are not highly acceptable methods of birth control in any segment of the black community. Eighty-four percent of the respondents rejected sterilization as an acceptable method of birth control. Ninety-four percent of the males rejected this method. Abortion was rejected by 88 percent of the males in the 30 and under age group.

READINGS IN POPULATION

Blake, Judith and Jerry J. Donovan. *Western European Censuses, 1960: An English Language Guide.* Berkeley: Institute of International Studies, University of California, 1971. 420 pp. $3.25.

For the census scholar, a detailed reference index for all volumes of the censuses of 22 countries giving precise bibliographical citations, pagination and titles for all statistical tables, including glossaries, technical definitions, detailed appendices on major concepts and classifications and U.S. library accessibility.

Boserup, Ester. *Woman's Role in Economic Development.* New York: St. Martin's Press, 1970. 283 pp. $7.50.

A unique investigation of the role of women in the social and economic advancement of developing countries and, in turn, the effects of their new role on marriage, the family and society. Appendix contains tabulations on female occupations and labor force participation for 34 countries.

Chasteen, Edgar R. *The Case for Compulsory Birth Control.* Englewood Cliffs, New Jersey: Prentice-Hall, Inc., 1971. 230 pp. $5.95.

An alarmist discussion of the environmental and social consequences of overpopulation which points to the limited successes of current fertility control programs, reviews existing methods and new developments in contraceptive research, and calls for immediate mandatory family limitation through legal means.

Gray, Peter H. and Shanti S. Tangri, Eds. *Economic Development and Population: A Conflict?.* Lexington, Mass.: D. C. Heath and Company, 1970. 162 pp. $2.25.

Seventeen essays by internationally prominent economists on the relationship between poverty and population growth in the Third World.

Johnson, Stanley. *Life Without Birth.* Boston: Little, Brown and Company, 1970. 364 pp. $7.95.

A personal report of the mass deprivation, threats to political stability, frustrated economic development caused by accelerated population growth in Asia, Africa and Latin America, and further aggravated by the affluent consumption of highly developed nations. Ongoing country programs and the challenge of action to the UN system of agencies are discussed.

Peck, Ellen. *The Baby Trap.* New York: Bernard Geis Associates, 1971. 245 pp. $5.95.

An attempt to offer alternative, emancipated life styles for the young marrieds by an attack on the image of glorified motherhood fostered by pronatalist social, cultural and economic pressures.

Tachi, Minoru and Minoru Muramatsu. *Population Problems in the Pacific.* Tokyo: Ministry of Health and Welfare, 1971. 510 pp. Price not available.

Proceedings of Symposium No. 1 of the Eleventh Pacific Science Congress containing 74 papers by noted sociologists/demographers on population dynamics, food/resources and development, population control, family planning and demographic research and training for an area of diverse ethnic cultures and economic progress.

Tamplin, Arthur R. and John W. Gofman. *'Population Control' Through Nuclear Pollution.* Chicago: Nelson-Hall Company, 1970. 242 pp. $6.95.

A much-documented study of the health hazards and serious genetic implications of currently sanctioned levels of radiation dosage in AEC-sponsored programs. Scientists are urged to exercise their social and moral obligations in the protection of man against the nuclear powerplant, as the deadliest of polluters.

32

Birth Control and the Black American: A Matter of Genocide?

Robert G. Weisbord

During the 1960's and continuing into the 1970's, the charge that birth control and abortion are integral elements of a white genocidal conspiracy directed against Afro-Americans has been heard with increasing frequency and stridency in black communities. The genocide theory finds greatest acceptance among spokesmen for black nationalist and black revolutionary groups, but suspicion of family planning programs is not limited to them. An analysis of black leadership opinion on birth control is provided in this paper. The black debate over the desirability of population limitation is traced back approximately fifty years. It began with a dispute between those blacks who believed that in sheer numbers there was strength and those blacks, such as W. E. B. DuBois, who argued that among human races, as among vegetables, quality and not quantity counted. An appreciation of the sexual exploitation of the chattel slave in the ante-bellum period, which did not end with emancipation, is also essential to an understanding of the roots and rationale of the genocide notion which are the foci of this paper.

INTRODUCTION

In recent years amid the growing debate about population problems, much publicity has been given to the controversial idea that birth control programs constitute a thinly disguised white plot to commit genocide against people of African extraction in the United States and elsewhere. This idea is frequently voiced by black community spokesmen. Most, but certainly not all, of these spokesmen are identified with black nationalist or revolu-

Reprinted from *Demography*, 10, no. 4 (November, 1973), pp. 571–90, by permission of the author and the publisher.

tionary organizations. Discussion of the subject is usually passionate. On at least one occasion black fulminations against birth control have been translated into violence: a family planning clinic in Cleveland, Ohio, was burned by arsonists impelled by the conviction that planned parenthood meant genocide (*New York Times*, 1968).

In the past there have been surveys of black attitudes toward family planning in general and "racial genocide" in particular. Unfortunately relatively little attention has been paid to the genocide rhetoric, its roots and its rationale. These are the major foci of this article.

At the outset terminology must be clarified. For purposes of this study the term "birth control," initially coined by Margaret Sanger, "family planning," and "planned parenthood" will be used synonymously. All may be defined as "voluntary planning and action by individuals to have the number of children they want, when and if they want them." On the other hand, "population control" is used to connote the belief that, for the good of society in light of overpopulation, individuals and groups should reduce the number of children they produce. Semantic confusion necessitates a very careful examination of black pronouncements to determine the intended meaning. Perhaps the confusion is inevitable in view of the sensitive nature of the subject.

HISTORICAL BACKDROP

Anger is often generated among Afro-Americans when the black family is talked about: witness the heated and protracted argument over the "Moynihan Report" (U.S. Dept. of Labor, 1965). No wonder. In slave days the Negro family was a precarious institution which existed at the sufferance of the master. "Husbands" and "wives" and parents and children could be separated forever by the whim of a callous owner. Financial considerations preceded humanitarian ones.

Not infrequently slaves were mated as if they were livestock. Historian Frederick Bancroft (1931, p. 81) wrote that "Next to the great and quick profit from bringing virgin soil under cultivation, slave-rearing was the surest, most remunerative and most approved means of increasing agricultural capital. Thomas Dew, President of William and Mary College and a staunch defender of the slave system, took pride in the fact that Virginia was a Negro-raising state.

Male slaves were sometimes set up as stallions, and certain slave women with proven or anticipated fecundity were deemed especially valuable as "breeding wenches." "Breeding slaves," "childbearing women," "too old to breed" were everyday phrases in the vocabulary of the slaveocracy.

The progeny of slave unions were the property of the slaveowners as were the offspring of lower animals. "Suppose a brood mare is hired for five years, the foals belong to him who has part of the use of the dam," a nineteenth-century judge observed. He held that the "slave in Maryland in this respect, is placed on no higher or different grounds" (Goodell, 1969, p. 30).

Rewards were given to unusually procreative slave women. Some in Virginia were promised freedom after they bore a specified number of children. Apparently there were many cases of extraordinarily fruitful slaves (Curtin, 1969, pp. 28–29, 73, 92).

Despite special privileges bestowed during pregnancy and just after childbirth, there were slave women who refused to breed children into bondage to add to the slavemaster's wealth (Blake, 1897, p. 13). A male slave such as Henry Bibb (1850) understood all too well that slave fathers did not fulfill the traditional paternal roles of provider and protector. He deeply regretted that he had fathered one slave child. "She was the first and shall be the last slave that ever I will father for chains and slavery on this earth" (p. 44). Others too were tormented by the realization that they had sired children who would be compelled to endure the degradation and woe of chattel slavery (Anonymous and Jones, 1871, p. 8). It is impossible to know the degree to which contraceptive techniques were employed by bondsmen in the antebellum period, but it is known that birth prevention was practiced in tribal Africa (Himes, 1936, pp. 5–12). In addition, contraceptives and abortifacients form a fascinating part of black American folklore (Puckett, 1968, pp. 331–32).

Black sexual autonomy was tampered with in other ways. In the colonial period castration was not an uncommon form of punishment for recalcitrant blacks. Such barbarism was ordinarily the work of enraged sadistic mobs as a concomitant of lynching in the post-Civil War era, but in the eighteenth century the practice was sanctioned by specific statutes. South Carolina law (1722) mandated castration for slaves who had run away for the fourth time. Emasculation was also used to punish a broad range of sexual offenses, whites at that time being preoccupied with fears of sexual aggression by blacks. It is very significant that in all the colonies save Pennsylvania, castration as a lawful punishment was reserved for Negroes and Indians (Jordan, 1968, pp. 154–59). Tenuous as the links between slave breeding and birth control may be, and farfetched as the comparison between eighteenth-century punitive castration and family planning may be in white eyes, the sexual exploitation of Americans of African descent may appear to black "militants" to be a seamless web, an unbroken tradition.

There are other elements in the tradition which should not be ignored. Just after the turn of the twentieth century there were cases of black and white convicts who were sterilized. This occurred in state prisons in Indiana, West Virginia and elsewhere and was motivated by belief that surgical sterilization would suppress the sex drive and would transform unruly, disorderly prisoners into docile ones. By the post-World War I era the practice had been largely discontinued, but not entirely, and the ideological raison d'etre was periodically reaffirmed.

In 1929 Dr. Thurman B. Rice, who taught at the Indiana University School of Medicine, published a book euphemistically titled *Racial Hygiene,* in which he advocated castration as the suitable punishment and preventive technique for sex criminals—rapists, sodomists, etc. For other categories of unfit persons, for the feeble-minded, for epileptics, for the insane and deformed he recommended vasectomies. These remedies were not prescribed only for blacks, but the author did not hesitate to express his trepidation as he contemplated racial mongrelization, the curse of South America. "The colored races are pressing the white race most urgently," Rice wrote, "and this pressure may be expected to increase" (Rice, 1929, pp. 318–20, 368).

Sterilizations involving both sexes were performed during the 1930's and 1940's at the State Hospital for Negroes located in Goldsboro, North Carolina (Woodside, 1950, pp. 31–33). The percentage of black males sterilized there was higher than the percentage in comparable white institutions in North Carolina. Blacks who were rapists or troublesome to hospital authorities were castrated to tranquilize them and make them more manageable. Consent to be sterilized was not sought from the patients in advance of the operations, supposedly because of their low intelligence, but it is alleged that they raised no objections. Relatives were asked for permission, but procedural safeguards appear to have been inadequate.

Precisely how many hapless beings in the United States were the victims of coercive sterilization in those years may never be known. Recent disclosures of a forty-year-old United States Public Health Service research project involving syphilitic black males are a stark reminder of the subhuman status to which Afro-Americans have been consigned. Without their consent or knowledge four hundred of these black subjects in the so-called Tuskegee Study were deliberately denied treatment for their venereal disease for experimental purposes. In retrospect the hideous project has been described as "almost like genocide" (*New York Times,* 1972).

QUALITY OR QUANTITY—THE EARLY DEBATE

Black Americans began to debate the merits of birth control just a few years after Margaret Sanger founded her first clinic in Brownsville. W. E. B. DuBois, the titanic black scholar and civil rights activist, was one of the earliest to put his seal of approval upon family planning. More than half a century ago DuBois (1922, pp. 248–50), writing in the *Crisis* magazine which he edited for the National Association for the Advancement of Colored People (N.A.A.C.P.), gave a ringing endorsement to birth control, calling it "science and sense applied to the bringing of children into the world." Of all who required it, Dr. DuBois added, "we Negroes are first." Having endless children resulted in a criminally high infant-mortality rate, and it was inimical to the health of women. A second alternative, postponing marriage until middle age lest unwanted children be brought into the world, DuBois also rejected. Family planning was clearly preferable and would redound to the well-being of both parents and offspring.

Ten years later DuBois (1932, pp. 166–67) lamented the fact that grassroots black opinion was totally ignorant of birth control. Other blacks, intelligent ones included, regarded it as inherently immoral. Among blacks who took a jaundiced view of birth control, religious and moral considerations probably counted for more than demographic factors. In 1934 the seventh annual convention of Marcus Garvey's Universal Negro Improvement Association met in Kingston, Jamaica. The Garveyites, black nationalists par excellence, unanimously passed a resolution condemning birth control. Curiously, the resolution read much like a papal encyclical. Moved by an American black and seconded by a West Indian delegate, the resolution averred that "any attempt to interfere with the natural function of life is a rebellion against the conceived purpose of divinity in making man a part of His spiritual self." The convention counselled persons of African descent throughout the world not to "accept or practise the theory of birth control such as is being advocated by irresponsible speculators who are attempting to interfere with the course of nature and with the purpose of the God in whom we believe" (*The Black Man*, 1934).

During the Great Depression, which caused incalculable suffering among black Americans, educated blacks who wrote on family planning favored it as a necessary and desirable part of good health care. The June, 1932, issue of the *Birth Control Review* focused on the great need for planned parenthood on the part of underprivileged blacks, on the deficiency of family planning services and on Negro receptivity to birth control.

Elmer Carter, editor of *Opportunity*, pointed out that, since the economic collapse, myriad lower-class black women had sought out unqualified quack abortionists to terminate unwanted pregnancies. The real question then was whether birth control would be achieved by safe contraceptive means or by "the clumsy almost murderous methods of the medical racketeer." At that juncture the leading black communities on Chicago's South Side and in Harlem were served by only two birth control clinics. Carter (1932, pp. 169–70) wrote that it would be most unfortunate if the birth control movement remained "unmindful or indifferent to the plight of the Negro." Dr. Charles H. Garvin (1932, pp. 269–70), a prominent black surgeon practicing in Cleveland, also indicated that the movement had been dilatory in its work among blacks.

Contraception had made significant inroads in the educated black classes. And when birth control clinics were established in Baltimore, Detroit and Cincinnati, the blacks attended out of proportion to their share of the population of those cities. By the mid-1930's blacks in Harlem already had rather low birth rates. Several explanations were possible, but, in the judgment of one demographer (Kiser, 1935, p. 284), it seemed likely that the fertility situation reflected a "deliberate limitation of families among married couples who can ill afford more children in the city." Pregnancy-spacing facilities were also made available to blacks in Berkley County, a rural county in South Carolina with a tenant-farmer population. No less than eighty percent of the contacted black persons with low incomes and little schooling utilized the child-spacing methods put at their disposal (Seibels, 1942, p. 44).

To meet the family planning needs of black Americans the Birth Control Federation formed a Division of Negro Service. Its national advisory council on Negro problems included Mary McLeod Bethune, head of the National Council of Negro Women; Walter White, executive director of the N.A.A.C.P.; the Reverend Adam Clayton Powell, Jr., pastor of the Abyssinian Baptist Church; and other prominent blacks.

Despite the foregoing, family planning remained a delicate topic. Even some middle-class black institutions were chary about giving their unqualified support to the movement. In March, 1947, the *Pittsburgh Courier*, one of the most influential Negro weeklies, published an article entitled "Planned Parenthood Has the Answers to Questions Concerning Health and Happiness of the Family." A few weeks later a letter to the editor from a Roman Catholic priest who had worked among black people criticized the *Courier* for advocating a practice that was not only a violation of God's law but one which would decimate the black race (*Pittsburgh Courier*, April 19, 1947). The newspaper retorted defensively that the article in question was actually a news release from a planned parenthood agency. The *Courier* did not necessarily endorse the philosophy of family planning.

The argument that birth control was a vehicle by which blacks would be decimated or by which they would decimate themselves was not novel in the 1940's. Marcus Garvey, who is regarded by many black separatists today as the progenitor of the black-power phenomenon, seems to have said little about birth control *per se*, but he was concerned about the tragedy of racial extinction. He wanted his U.N.I.A. to strengthen the black race so as to eliminate the possibility that blacks could be exterminated as he contended the American Indian had been. In his *Philosophy and Opinions*

(Garvey, 1967), first published in 1923, the Jamaican-born black nationalist cautioned blacks against supinely sitting by and permitting "the great white race to lift itself in numbers and power." In another five centuries that would mean that this "full grown race of white men will in turn exterminate the weaker race of black men for the purpose of finding enough room on this limited mundane sphere to accommodate that race which will have numerically multiplied itself into many billions" (pp. 46–48). Global black solidarity was imperative, Garvey declared, but he did not tell blacks to multiply pell mell or to forsake contraception.

The desirability of continued growth of the Afro-American population was not wholly confined to black nationalists of the Garvey stripe. Negro anthropologist W. Montague Cobb (1939) expected life in the United States to become increasingly competitive because the American population would be growing within fixed territorial limits. He speculated about the chances of the white majority liquidating the competing black minority. His prescription for the Afro-American was as follows: "He should maintain his high birthrate observing the conditions of life necessary to this end. This alone has made him able to increase in spite of decimating mortality and hardships. If the tide should turn against him later, strength will be better than weakness in numbers" (pp. 345–46).

DuBois (1932) had written almost impatiently about those who are "led away by the fallacy of numbers. They want the black race to survive. They are cheered by a census return of increasing numbers and a high rate of increase." To DuBois the numbers game was deplorable. He believed that fellow blacks had to learn that "among human races and groups, as among vegetables, quality and not mere quantity really counts" (pp. 166–67).

Higher fertility among blacks in the depths of the depression would not mean a population gain because of poverty, malnutrition and disease which raised the death rate. Why enrich the undertakers and pack the prisons with unwanted children, asked columnist George Schuyler (1932). "It were far better to have less children and improve the social and physical well-being of those they have" (pp. 165–66).

The relationship between the fecundity of the black race and its salvation reemerged as a debatable matter at the end of World War II. Arguments on both sides changed little, if at all. Taking issue with those whom he labelled the "self-appointed guardians of the Negro race," E. Franklin Frazier (1945, pp. 41–45), the distinguished black sociologist, maintained that "more and more babies born indiscriminately, without thought of the parent's health or ability to rear them, is not the answer." Black survival and progress were not contingent upon the number of babies born but on the number who lived to become strong, healthy adults. Frazier, though a vociferous champion of planned parenthood for many years, did not view it as a cure-all for the assorted ills of the American Negro. However, he insisted that "to live decently and efficiently, whether his relative numbers are greater or smaller will depend upon knowledge and the intelligent ordering of his life rather than upon ignorance and uncontrolled impulse" (pp. 41–45).

In 1945 one of the "self-appointed guardians" of the race was Dr. Julian Lewis, a pathologist and former professor at the prestigious University of Chicago. Whereas the growth of the white race was guaranteed by a low death rate, he wrote in the *Negro Digest* (Lewis, 1945, pp. 19–22), the survival of the black race in the United States was dependent upon a high birth rate. Lewis wanted to resolve the multiple problems of illiteracy, deficient medical facilities and congested living conditions which curtailed black longevity instead of reducing the black population. He categorically denied that lowering the number of blacks would improve conditions in schools or hospitals, for example.

Almost a decade later Lewis was still apprehensive about blacks becoming an "inconspicuous group," rather than the country's largest minority. This could happen, he declared, if the black and white birth rates were equalized and the prevailing death rate for blacks was unchanged. He faulted the Planned Parenthood Federation for trying to "improve the quality of the human race at the cost of numbers" (Lewis, 1954, pp. 52–55). If blacks practiced birth control on a general scale, it would mean "race suicide," Lewis said.

"Race suicide" was the fashionable phrase at that juncture in history. Before too long it was supplanted by "genocide," a term usually applied to the implementation of Hitler's "final solution" to the Jewish problem. Blacks too utilized the term particularly after the publication in 1951 of William Patterson's book *We Charge Genocide—The Historic Petition to the United Nations For Relief From a Crime of the United States Government Against the Negro People*. The book, it should be noted, did not treat the subject of birth control.

Regardless of phraseology the "strength in numbers" philosophy has not been peculiar to blacks. Various national, ethnic, racial and religious groups have voiced their anxiety about the possible long-range effects of birth control. Thus a French law in 1920 forbade the spread of "contraceptive propaganda" in the hope of boosting the Gallic population. Procreating for the state was deemed virtuous in Mussolini's Italy, and the Nazis padlocked Germany's birth control clinics. Professor John T. Noonan (1967, pp. 488–89, 610) has shown that a few decades ago contraception was regarded as a potential danger by some clerics because it "could deprive society of a fair share of Catholics." Those prelates wishfully thought that the Church might expand if Catholics limited their reproductive activities less than other people.

There were also those who were convinced that general use of contraception would eventuate in the extinction of the entire species. The irrelevance of this "race suicide" argument to specific acts of contraception and its absurdity in the face of demographic changes have led to its virtual obsolescence, at least insofar as undifferentiated homo sapiens are concerned.

But particular groups which have suffered oppression continue to associate safety and security with additional numbers. From time to time Jews are exhorted to be fruitful, to multiply and to turn a deaf ear to all talk of a global population explosion. They are told that the Jewish demographic situation is unique. Jews have an extraordinarily low birth rate. Moreover, the Nazi holocaust meant a staggering population loss for European Jewry, which Jews have the right, nay the obligation, to regain. David Ben-Gurion (1971, p. 839), Israel's first prime minister, now an octogenarian, has written that any fertile Jewish woman who does not bear at least four healthy children is derelict in her duty to the Jewish nation. Her dereliction was equated with that of the male who evades military service. Notwithstanding Ben-Gurion's "the more the better" demographic doctrine, American Jews are, by and large, very enthusiastic practitioners of contraception. There is no talk of Gentiles liquidating Jews by foisting birth control upon them although it is noteworthy that during World War I Margaret Sanger was accused by opponents of establishing her clinic "to do away with the Jews" (Sanger, 1938, p. 226).

Nowadays Spanish-speaking Americans, minorities belonging to the country's underclass, sometimes engage in rhetoric about population control as a genocidal plan. For example, the Young Lords, the Puerto Rican counterpart of the Black Panthers, have expressed concern about the dilution of Puerto Rican strength on the mainland through government-sponsored population programs. Some nationalistic Puerto Ricans on the Caribbean island have taken the position that greater numbers will expedite the achievement of independence from the United States. Mexican-Americans have been known to comment that their bargaining position vis-a-vis the Anglo majority would be improved by the sheer weight of numbers. A government plot to attenuate the power of *la raza* has been perceived by some Chicanos who recall that past experimental contraceptive research has utilized Puerto Rican and Mexican-American subjects (Warwick and Williamson, 1971).

NUMBERS AS AN ANSWER TO GENOCIDE

For many black opponents of fertility limitation, the remarkably durable "strength in numbers" argument is the most persuasive. "Our safety, our survival literally, depend on our ever increasing numbers and the heavy concentration of our people in the financial heart of America—namely in the large urban centers" (Watts, 1969, p. 3). So editorialized black nationalist Daniel H. Watts, an architect by training, who publishes the monthly journal, the *Liberator*. Rejecting the idea that there is any paucity of space or shortage of food in the United States, a country with allegedly forty million white racists, Watts has written that one of the best warrantees of black survival is "a more vigorous effort on our part to reproduce our own" (p. 3). Speaking in support of birth control for black Americans is tantamount to speaking in support of genocide.

A black physician in Pittsburgh put it this way: "Our birth rate is the only thing we have. If we keep on producing, they're going to have to either kill us or grant us full citizenship." One of the stated goals of the pro-natalist E.R.O.S. (Endeavour to Raise Our Size), a California-based group, has been to increase the voting power of Afro-Americans (Cowles, 1966). A spokesman for the Five Percenters, a little-known black splinter organization in New York City, envisioned the uses of an inflated black population a little differently. As told in an *Ebony* article (Smith, 1968, p. 29), he pointed to a pregnant black girl and remarked, "She's having another baby for me. I need an army and this is how we're going to get it." In sum, the line of argument is that whether future blacks function within the political system or act to undermine it, greater numbers will be a help, not a hindrance.

Demographic changes have probably given the old numbers game new vitality. The percentage of Negroes in the United States population declined steadily from 19.0 in 1810 to 9.7 in 1930. In absolute numbers the black population had increased from 757,208 in 1790 to 11,891,143 in 1930, but, owing to the legislative termination of the Atlantic slave trade (which sharply reduced the importation of slaves even if it did not actually end it) and to the European immigration to the United States, the proportion of persons of African extraction decreased. Since 1930 when the effects of restrictive immigration laws were reflected in the decennial census, the percentage of blacks has risen markedly. As of 1971, the official black population was twenty-three million, eleven percent of the general population, up .2 percent from 1965. Blacks frequently scoff at these figures, contending that blacks are undercounted. Every chance he gets Dick Gregory states publicly that he disbelieves the census statistics published by the government. James Forman, among others, claims that the black population is actually thirty million.

Perhaps more meaningful than the total Afro-American population is its distribution. According to the Census Bureau, blacks now constitute a clear majority in six cities, including Newark, New Jersey; Washington,

D.C., the nation's capital; and Atlanta, Georgia. Eight additional cities have a population that is forty percent black. These phenomena are attributable in large measure to a white exodus from the decaying inner cities. In any case fifty percent of America's blacks are to be found in fifty cities, and one-third of the total black population is concentrated in just fifteen cities.

Do these figures warrant Daniel Watts' conclusion that the "city has become the Black man's land"? By virtue of their size black communities have managed to elect mayors in Gary (Indiana), Cleveland, Newark, and elsewhere. But whether the quality of life for black residents of those urban centers has improved even slightly is debatable. The crucial economic relationship between whites and blacks has not really been altered.

Census data in 1970 disclosed that there are one hundred and two counties, all in the South, that are at least half black. Taken in conjunction with the voting rights which blacks increasingly exercise, these statistics point to a tremendous new political potential. Afro-Americans are already electing public officials of their race at a rate unparalleled since Reconstruction. If the one man vote concept is fully realized, blacks are bound to further augment their political strength. But there are Afro-Americans who feel that the price may be exorbitant. Dr. Martin Luther King (n.d., p. 5) once stated that Negroes "do not wish for domination purchased at a cost of human misery. Negroes were once bred by slave owners to be sold as merchandise. They do not welcome any solution which involves population breeding as a weapon."

The "strength in numbers" school of thought has been ridiculed on tactical as well as moral grounds and not only by so-called "moderates." Julius Lester (1969, pp. 140–43) believes that black revolutionaries should urge their women to postpone having children so that they may fully participate in the battle. "There is power in numbers," he has conceded, "but that power is greatly diminished if a lot of those numbers have to sit at home and change diapers instead of being on the front lines, where most of them would rather be."

"My Answer to Genocide," an *Ebony* cover story by the social critic-humorist Dick Gregory (1971, pp. 66ff) is probably the best-known single article on the subject of birth control and blacks. Quite simply, Gregory's answer was "eight black kids—and another baby on the way." Gregory, a vegetarian, explained that birth control was contrary to nature. Therefore he could never use it. But the principal point that emerges from the essay is that Gregory is mistrustful of any white-devised policy for blacks.

> For years they told us where to sit, where to eat, and where to live. Now they want to dictate our bedroom habits. First the white man tells me to sit in the back of the bus. Now it looks like he wants me to sleep under the bed. Back in the days of slavery, black folks couldn't

grow kids fast enough for white folks to harvest. Now that we've got a little taste of power, white folks want us to call a moratorium on having children (p. 66).

Gregory blurred the distinction between the concept of family planning and the ideal of the small family. Furthermore, he grossly distorted the latter by suggesting that it meant no childbearing at all. Perhaps most important of all Gregory seems to have said that nothing of value to blacks could come from the white power structure. He is not alone in this respect.

H. Rap Brown (1969, p. 138), successor to Stokely Carmichael as head of the Student Non-Violent Coordinating Committee (S.N.C.C.), has also subscribed to the theory that governmental birth control programs designed for indigent masses are an attempt at genocide. In his *Die Nigger Die* Brown (1969, p. 55) gave a straightforward testament of the philosophy of doing and believing the opposite of whites: "If the white folks say it's more cultured to whisper, you talk loud. If white folks say gray suits are fashionable, you go buy a pink one." Brown has written that even as a teenager he "knew white folks couldn't do wrong right, so whatever they thought was good, I knew wasn't." Whatever the enemy opposed deserved support. Whatever he supported merited opposition. Given the melancholy history of white subjugation of blacks in American history, this attitude, while self-defeating, is understandable. It overlooks the fact that, even if a minority of whites foster black family planning for base motives, it may still be in the best possible interests of blacks to accept family planning.

In a sense the success of the birth control movement may militate against its acceptance by blacks whose alienation from the United States is almost total. Martin Luther King (n.d., pp. 2–3) once spoke of the striking kinship between the civil rights movement and the early birth control movement, both aiming at the alleviation of horrible slum conditions. Margaret Sanger, like Dr. King, had nonviolently resisted unjust laws and had been jailed. The birth control movement has come a long way from that era when public and clerical officials prevented meetings on birth control from being held, when physicians were loath to discuss contraception, and welfare workers were forbidden to do so. Birth control is now generally respectable. Since the early 1960's, American presidents have openly professed a concern about population problems. On a limited scale federal funds finance family planning services and population research. Laws curbing the circulation of family planning information are still on the statute books of twelve states but, according to a mid-1971 public opinion poll, ninety percent of all Americans believe that such information should be made available to men and women who want it (Lipson and Wolman, 1972, p. 39).

It may be said then that, although there is still some opposition, birth control has been accepted, perhaps grudgingly, by the Establishment and consequently anti-Establishment forces will be skeptical about it. The greater that acceptance is and the more available the contraceptive service, the deeper the skepticism will be, especially when other needs of the black poor are ignored. Thus, an anonymous black nationalist at Indiana University noted that abortions were free but aspirin costs money (Yette, 1971, p. 244). When Congress is remiss in its responsibility to rid the ghetto of rats, when it fails to deal with the grave problem of lead poisoning among black slum dwellers, positive congressional action on family planning is bound to raise many black eyebrows.

Family planning is rarely seen in isolation from the black American dilemma, past and present. The Black Panther Party newspaper (1969; 1970; 1971) has bracketed planned parenthood, black participation in the Vietnam War, venereal disease and prostitution. All are part of the same picture. Coercive sterilization bills and restrictive welfare legislation are in the picture. So are inhuman living conditions, "police murders," rat bites, frequent fires and accidents brought about by dilapidated houses. Together these constitute a malicious plan of genocide of black people concocted by the United States Government. Additional evidence of the plan cited by the Panthers has been the reluctance of the government to institute a meaningful program of diagnosis, prevention and treatment of sickle cell anemia. The United States was capable of sending men to the moon, and it was scientifically able to cure other diseases, the Panther newspaper observed bitterly, but it "has refused to research or *disclose* [emphasis mine] the cure for a disease, practically all of whose victims are Black People" (*The Black Panther*, 1969; 1971).

The Panthers have also invoked the "strength in numbers" argument. In 1970 when New York State liberalized its abortion law, the move was lambasted in the Black Panther organ: "Black people know that part of our revolutionary strength lies in the fact that we outnumber the pigs—And the pigs realize this too. This is why they are trying to eliminate as many people as possible before they reach their inevitable doom" (*The Black Panther*, 1970).

Brenda Hyson, one of the female Panthers sharply critical of birth control, saw passage of the new law as a victory of an "oppressive ruling class who will use this law to kill off Blacks and other oppressed people before they are born." It was just a matter of time, she wrote, before voluntary abortion led to involuntary abortion and compulsory sterilization. She predicted that black women would shun "legalized murder" as they had "rejected the attempt to force family planning in the guise of pills and coils" (*The Black Panther*, 1970).

The Panthers are actually Marxist black revolutionaries, not nationalists. Not every nationalist subscribes to the genocide philosophy, but most of the caustic criticism of family planning emanates from nationalist camps. A rejection of birth control programs as genocidal was embodied in a resolution passed at the first national conference on black power held in Newark in 1967. Epitomizing the black nationalist point of view was a strongly worded article by Brother Kahlil (1971, pp. 20–21) in *Black News,* a youth oriented bi-weekly published in Brooklyn. It excoriated the white man and charged him with perpetrating "deceptive genocide" by means of birth control. The "beast with an evil intellect" wanted to create a "blond-haired, blue-eyed world." To that end black women were duped into having unnecessary hysterectomies and surgical sterilization. The use of birth control pills and other contraceptives was vigorously disapproved by *Black News.* Of the condom it was said, ". . . the hidden meaning of the Trojan was to emasculate the black man by convincing him that he should throw away his living sperm in the white man's rubber contraption rather than to put it into his woman's fertile womb" (pp. 20–21).

THE BLACK MUSLIMS

No black separatist organization has been more vitriolic in its condemnation of population control and family planning than the Nation of Islam, or the Black Muslims as they are popularly known. The fear that birth control is a "death plan" is starkly expressed by Elijah Muhammad, leader of the Chicago-based movement. In his book *Message to the Blackman in America,* Muhammad admonished fellow blacks to be aware of the "tricks the devils [whites] are using to instill the idea of a false birth control in their clinics and hospitals" (pp. 64–65). Blacks are further warned "of being trapped into the kind of disgraceful birth control laws now aimed exclusively at poor, helpless black peoples who have no one to rely on." Muhammad argued that the teachings of both the Bible and Holy Koran are against contraception. The white man's motive in supporting planned parenthood is seen not as that of promoting the well-being of Negro families, but of exterminating those families in the future. Muhammad (1965) actually saw a parallel between birth control and Pharoah attempting to destroy ancient Israel by murdering male Hebrew infants. Although such an analogy seems unbelievably simplistic, even paranoid, he cites as supporting evidence the example of a clinic in Fauquier County, Virginia, where impoverished black women were "pressured into accepting sterilization" (pp. 64–65).

Birth control, it should be remembered, plays a crucial role in the central myth underlying the Black Muslim racial ideology. The original race was black, the Muslims say. The Caucasian race came about when a renegade black scientist Yacub made use of a rigid birth control law to kill off all the black babies on the mythical island of Pelan. After six hundred years,

Goodman (1971, p. 56) once asserted, "all they had left was a pale-skinned, blue-eyed, blond-haired thing that you call a man. But actually the Bible calls him the devil."

Malcolm X's views on planned parenthood were more complex than those ordinarily communicated by the Muslims. In a 1962 interview Malcolm expressed a preference for the term "family planning." The phrase "birth control" was distasteful to him, and he opined that "people, particularly Negroes would be more willing to plan than to be controlled" (Cowles, 1962). Malcolm informed Wylda B. Cowles, a black field consultant for the Planned Parenthood Federation, that Black Muslim dogma did not proscribe family planning. He implied that techniques requiring discipline, e.g., the rhythm method or coitus interruptus, were used. It was apparent to the interviewer that Malcolm favored the use of planned parenthood services for health and economic reasons. Mention of over-population elicited questions from him about why major efforts to control population growth were directed toward colored nations. Malcolm did arrange contact between Black Muslim women leaders and Planned Parenthood. Two women attended sessions at the Planned Parenthood clinics for some time.

In the following years the Muslims took an inflexibly hostile position. *Muhammad Speaks,* the widely read Black Muslim weekly, has published numerous articles decrying the "deadly nature and diabolic intention behind birth control schemes" (*Muhammad Speaks,* January 24, 1969). Family planning is seen as an integral element in a pattern of white oppression of blacks. A 1969 article in *Muhammad Speaks* alerted its readers to the "fact that, in this country, they are birth control targets far out of proportion to their percentage of the population—just like the Black soldiers in Vietnam are drafted, wounded and killed far out of their proportion in the population" (August 29, 1969). Another article (May 23, 1969) contended that the "alarm and feverish attention now given to the 'population explosion' has long been one of the key 'alternatives' agreed upon by white world powers for preserving white supremacy." A 1970 piece entitled the "Many Faces of Genocide" recalled that overt genocide against Africans began with the trans-Atlantic slave trade four hundred years ago. Population control, a white neo-Malthusian plot, was nothing more or less than genocide in a more sophisticated and subtle form (November 20, 1970).

Muhammad Speaks cartoons have graphically conveyed the Muslim antipathy to birth control. For instance, one drawing which was juxtaposed with a criticism of the Ford Foundation for its backing of fertility research portrayed a cemetery with open graves each containing the body of a black infant. Inscribed on the grave markers were "scientist," "doctor," "lawyer," "teacher," "engineer," and "inventor," suggesting the future professional attainments of the dead babies. A black woman standing at the graveside holding a box of birth control pills (the box marked with a skull and crossbones) is thinking "Death For My Babies . . . And Race." A white grave-digger's comment is "Birth Control (Death) . . . Now There Will Be No More Negroes and Indians" (January 24, 1969).

In the same vein was a cartoon showing a white physician handing pills to a black woman. The woman is staring into a roaring furnace on which there is a sign reading "Birth Control—Death Of A Nation." The caption reads "Kill the Black Babies and Save the White—Orders By the Father (Yakub) To the White Race—Kill-Kill-Kill" (October 11, 1968).

Abortion reform has also drawn the wrath of *Muhammad Speaks*. In January 1971 it reported on a pro-abortion women's march in Washington, D.C. during which one black feminist averred that, "Black women are uniting to control their own bodies. We will not be prone for you men any longer. We want the right to have abortions" (January 3, 1971). Other black females echoed her sentiments, but *Muhammad Speaks* emphasized the infinitesimal black showing at the march. "Black women reject abortion as cure-all" was the title of the *Muhammad Speaks* story.

Minister Louis Farrakhan (1972, p. 3), probably the Muslim's most dynamic spokesman since the defection of Malcolm X, has written that, "When the Black woman kills her unborn child, she is murdering the advancement of her nation." He has stated confidently that there is sufficient food on earth to feed mankind.

Women occupy a subordinate position in the Nation of Islam. On those rare occasions when they do make public statements they do not challenge well-established dogma. Shirley Hazziez (*Muhammad Speaks*, 1971) has written that Pharaoh's bid to exterminate the Israelites was child's play compared with the devil's efforts to destroy black babies with birth control pills and drugs. Miss Hazziez assured her readers that Allah was able to feed and care for black infants. She appealed to the black women to decline the pill, "a deadly poison," and to rebuff the white enemy that advised blacks to decrease their numbers.

BLACK FEMALES AND THE GENOCIDE NOTION

Except for women in the Nation of Islam and the Black Panther Party, women, including self-styled revolutionaries and nationalists, have often defiantly claimed the right to exercise freedom of choice in the matter of their own fertility. Dara Abubakari (Virginia E. Y. Collins) (1970, pp. 360–61), a vice president of the separatist Republic of New Africa, has been quoted as follows: "Women must be free to choose what they want. They should be free to decide if and when they want children. Maybe in this phase of the game we feel that we don't need any children because we have to fight the liberation struggle. So we won't have any children. We have the right to say so. Men shouldn't tell us."

Written along the same lines was a manifesto by a black women's liberation group in Mount Vernon, New York, signed by two welfare recipients, two housewives, a domestic and others. The statement indicted black men for making black women the "real niggers in this society-oppressed by whites, male and female, and the black man too." The essence of their case was that

> Black women are being asked by militant black brothers, not to practice birth control because it's a form of Whitey's committing genocide on black people. Well, true enough, but it takes two to practice genocide and black women are able to decide for themselves, like poor people all over the world whether they will submit to genocide. For us birth control is the freedom to fight genocide of black women and children. . . . Having too many babies stops us from supporting our children, teaching them the truth . . . and from fighting black men who still want to use and exploit us (Black Women's Liberation Group, 1970, pp. 360–61).

Black women are beginning to look out for their own best interests, Carolyn Jones (1970) has written. Black men who preached against abortion were nowhere to be found when child support was necessary. Miss Jones has found that "young black women who watched their own mothers and grandmothers struggle to raise a family alone, are no longer willing to listen to the black man's cry of genocide" (p. 49).

Maxine Williams and Pamela Newman (1971, p. 9), two black women members of the Young Socialist Alliance, are cognizant of the pilot experimental birth control projects which used Puerto Rican women as subjects. Therefore, they have said that they understand why "Third World" women sometimes view birth control and abortion as genocide. However, they believe that the central issue is the right of women to control their own bodies. Women and not male supremacists ought to determine for themselves whether to have children or not.

Some black spokeswomen have unequivocally disavowed the genocide interpretation. Shirley Chisholm, the indomitable Congresswoman from Brooklyn, has been among the most passionate apostles of planned parenthood. She was honored in the summer of 1969 by United Planned Parenthood for her stalwart support of the movement. In December of that year Mrs. Chisholm gave spirited testimony on behalf of a bill to expand, improve, and better coordinate the family planning services and population activities of the federal government (Lincoln, 1970, p. 12). She testified that in her own "Bedford-Stuyvesant community, black women are glad to get direction in the area of family planning. I know that thousands of black women have been maimed by botched abortions because they couldn't get the family planning help that white women get."

Mrs. Chisholm has called the portrayal of legal abortion programs and family planning as genocide "male rhetoric for male ears. It falls flat to female listeners, and to thoughtful male ones." In her book, *Unbought and Unbossed* (1970, pp. 124–36), she has argued that two or three wanted youngsters who will be loved and educated can contribute more to racial progress than any number of children who are ill-fed, ill-clothed, ill-housed and neglected. To Mrs. Chisholm racial pride and simple humanity buttress this attitude which, in effect, restates DuBois' dictum about quality and quantity.

On occasion black women have asserted themselves and have clashed head-on with black men purveying the genocide philosophy. In December, 1967, the *New York Times* reported that local family planning clinics had been accused of taking action to keep the birth rate among blacks as low as possible. The clinics were accused of operating "without moral responsibility to the black race." It was said that they had become an instrument of genocide. Dr. Charles Greenlee, a Pittsburgh physician who made these charges, also complained about "pill-pushing" by inquisitive, untrained white workers in black neighborhoods (*New York Times*, 1967). Dr. Greenlee, who was identified with the N.A.A.C.P. in Pittsburgh, subsequently protested that those workers approached only black women in poverty areas (*Pittsburgh Press*, 1968). The physician told the press that he was not opposed to planned parenthood as such. Rather he objected to programs sponsored by the Office of Economic Opportunity (O.E.O.), which allegedly concentrated family planning clinics in black neighborhoods. The motive, Dr. Greenlee declared, was "to make less niggers so they won't have to build houses for them" (*New York Post*, 1968).

Greenlee's highly vocal ally was one William Bouie Haden, a former grocery store proprietor, who led a black organization called the United Movement for Progress. The pill, Haden cautioned his followers, could "lead to a bigger massacre of black people than the German's killing of the Jews (*Pittsburgh Courier*, 1968). Haden was incensed because the white political establishment was unwilling to appropriate money for rat control in the ghettos, but will "spend thousands to make sure you can't have any babies" (*Pittsburgh Press*, August 21, 1968).

After the mobile planned parenthood clinic in the black Homewood-Brushton area of Pittsburgh was closed due to the combined efforts of Greenlee and Haden, the latter had warned that firebombings and rioting would result "if anyone tries to operate a birth control project in the area" (*Pittsburgh Press*, August 15 1968). Protests by seventy black women who wanted the clinic reopened were to no avail. In February, 1969, five other poverty neighborhoods were denied funds for planned parenthood facilities owing mainly to Haden's activities.

Black women spearheaded the counterattack. The local branch of the Welfare Rights Organization, whose members were recipients of public assistance, was upset by the decision to eliminate clinics in their neighborhoods. The Welfare mothers clarified their support for planned parenthood in a press release on 24 February, 1969. They did not want to be told how many children to have. "We think a mother can better care for her family if she can control the number of children she bears, and we think that a mother deserves the opportunity to decide when her health and well-being is better served by preventing conception." Free choice was the crux of the dispute. The Welfare Rights Organization also observed that "most of the anti-birth control pressure is coming from *men!*—Men who do not have to bear the children. We're speaking for the women and we want the Planned Parenthood Centers to stay in our neighborhoods." As a consequence of agitation by a few hundred poor black women, the federal funds originally earmarked for birth control were restored in March. Haden had been snubbed by the very people he had claimed to represent. Little has been heard from Haden or Greenlee since.

INTEGRATIONISTS AND THE GENOCIDE ISSUE

Greenlee's position was hardly typical of the N.A.A.C.P., which is the oldest and largest of the civil rights organizations. Considerations of family well-being prompted the N.A.A.C.P. in 1966 at its fifty-seventh convention to adopt a policy statement which said in part: ". . . mindful of problems of family health and economic stability, we support the dissemination of information and materials concerning family health and family planning to all who desire it" (*Crisis*, 1970, p. 78). Four years later an editorial in the *Crisis* (1970) talked of the population explosion, a phenomenon which required that greater attention be paid to family planning. "The future of the entire human race is at stake." It took note of the division within the black community over the issue of birth control and criticized those blacks who seemed to espouse the "Hitler doctrine of babies and more babies, regardless of the circumstances into which they were born or of the prospect of their attaining the good life" (pp. 78–79). On the other hand, it pointed out that more babies were needed and poor black people should not reject parenthood out of despair. The need for more babies was not elaborated upon. To be sure, among rank and file members of the N.A.A.C.P. and among local branch activists, there are those who have reservations about birth control for blacks, but, as recently as April 1972, John Morsell (1972), the assistant executive director wrote: "It is a fact that the national leadership of the N.A.A.C.P. believes in family planning as a social value and rejects the notion . . . that this is a form of genocide."

The National Urban League, which is also bi-racial, middle-class and pro-integration, has endorsed family planning for more than thirty years. Concerned with strengthening family life and with reducing individual and family dependency, the League's Board of Trustees in 1962 care out four square for "positive and realistic programs of family planning." All persons were entitled to know about the various methods of birth control and to choose among them consistent with their own value sysems and religious convictions. At that time many welfare departments still refused to involve themselves in family planning even as referral agencies. The Urban League charged that this practice undercut the effectiveness of programs to make welfare recipients self-supporting, and stated that, "To prohibit case workers in public welfare agencies from discussing family planning resources with their clients is a discrimination which denies to welfare recipients one of the principal means of family health and progress utilized by more affluent couples" (National Urban League Board of Trustees, 1962). Whitney Young, the late executive director of the Urban League, once wrote that the responsibility of tax-supported welfare and medical agencies to impart information about birth control was as basic as their obligation to share information about the availability of polio innoculations or X-rays.

In the 1960's and 1970's eminent black individuals who are usually categorized as moderate and anti-separatist have normally taken pro-birth control stances. In 1966, two years before his assassination, Martin Luther King was the recipient of the Margaret Sanger Award in Human Rights. Dr. King (n.d., pp. 3-4) in accepting the award remarked that:

> Negroes have no mere academic nor ordinary interest in family planning. They have a special and urgent concern. . . . The Negro constitutes half the poor of the nation. Like all poor, Negro and white, they have many unwanted children. This is a cruel evil they urgently need to control. There is scarcely anything more tragic in human life than a child who is not wanted.

Other prominent black proponents of family planning are Bayard Rustin, chief organizer of the 1963 march on Washington; A. Philip Randolph; and James Farmer, national director of the Congress of Racial Equality (C.O.R.E.) when that organization was still integrationist in orientation and make-up. Dr. Jerome H. Holland, a distinguished Negro sociologist and educator and a former American Ambassador to Sweden, served for a time as chairman of Planned Parenthood—World Population. The members of the Congressional Black Caucus have co-sponsored family planning legislation in the House of Representatives.

But three and a half centuries of persecution have left a legacy of mistrust which affects the thinking of some of the most reasonable, responsible, "moderate" blacks. That mistrust is often apparent in their statements on population questions. The multi-talented Langston Hughes (1965) wrote a column on the "Population Explosion" in which his famous character Simple said, "White folks are not thinking about being sterilized, neither in war nor peace. It is India, China, Africa and Harlem they is considering— 300 million dollars worth of birth control for us! You know I really do believe white folks has always got something up their sleeve for colored folks. Yes, they has."

Julian Bond, the dynamic Georgia legislator addressing a Syracuse University commencement audience, suggested that the intense interest in the population explosion could lead to genocide of Afro-Americans and other poor people. "Without the proper perspective the *Population Bomb* becomes a theoretical hammer in the hands of the angry, frightened and powerful racists, as well as over the heads of black people, as the ultimate justification for genocide" (*Providence Journal,* 1970; *Springfield Sunday Republican,* 1970). He implied that Afro-Americans had good cause to be alarmed.

The *Population Bomb* to which Julian Bond alluded was the title of a controversial book by a population biologist at Stanford University, Dr. Paul R. Ehrlich. A frightening exposition of the population problem and its attendant dangers to mankind, the book was also an eloquent plea for stabilizing the world's population, for lowering the growth rate to zero, even "making it go negative." Erhlich himself is honorary president and past president of Zero Population Growth (Z.P.G.), a national organization originally founded in California to educate the public in general and legislators in particular about the issue of overpopulation; to press for enactment of far-reaching birth control programs; and to promote research into population problems and more effective contraception. Most advocates of Z.P.G. talk about arresting population growth by means of tax incentives not to reproduce beyond a certain limit, by legalizing abortion and by making population education an integral part of school curricula. A minority profess a belief in the necessity of compulsory birth regulations, e.g., adding sterilants to water supplies. Not surprisingly, it is the extreme coercive techniques which receive the greatest publicity and give the movement to curb population growth an unfavorable image with certain blacks. Dr. William Darity, chairman of the Public Health Department at the University of Massachusetts, has bluntly called Z.P.G. "genocide for our black people." At a Yale University debate in January, 1972, he said that Z.P.G.'s emphasis on planned parenthood is designed to reduce and control the black population (*Yale News,* 1972).

By and large black spokesmen were dubious about the ecological "craze" of the late 1960's of which growing apprehension of a population explosion was one facet. Blacks were worried that national attention and, more importantly, public money desperately needed in the ghettos could be diverted to environmental causes. At the First National Congress on Optimum Population and Environment (1970) the discontented black caucus submitted that "the elimination of dangerous species such as rats, roaches and other vermin is of more immediate concern to Black people than the preservation of brook trout, buffalo and bald eagles." Although the caucus did not reject birth control *per se*, they pointed out that it was no remedy for the health problems of the living. The caucus also wanted an assurance that *"no coercive* family planning or population stabilization measures are allowed to become part of a national or local legislative policy."

COERCION—A CRUCIAL ISSUE

Coercion was not an academic matter. Across the country public officials, reflecting the wave of popular indignation over escalating welfare costs, have put forward punitive proposals. These measures have often been seriously debated in state legislatures. Typically they provide for imprisonment or compulsory use of birth control (if such is possible) or mandatory sterilization after a woman on welfare has given birth to a certain number of illegitimate children. Continued eligibility for welfare payments would depend on compliance.

Punitive sterilization bills have been proposed in the Mississippi legislature since 1958 ostensibly to solve the problem of illegitimacy. A 1964 measure in Mississippi was denounced by Dr. Alan F. Guttmacher, President of the Planned Parenthood Federation, and by the Association for Voluntary Sterilization. (The Planned Parenthood Federation has steadfastly defended voluntarism in family planning. It has filed *amici curiae* briefs to fight anything that smacks of compulsory birth control. It has argued that compelling women to practice birth control is an infringement of the Fourteenth Amendment to the U.S. Constitution and violates the right of privacy.) Quick to recognize the racist overtones of the bill, S.N.C.C. issued a pamphlet entitled *Genocide in Mississippi*. S.N.C.C. quoted one advocate of sterilization who prophesied during the legislative debate that, "When the cutting starts, they'll [Negroes] head for Chicago" (quoted in Paul, 1968, p. 90).

In 1971 there was a spate of similarly coercive bills proposed in state legislatures. As might be expected, blacks strenuously opposed this legislation. A black doctor from Chicago commented about an Illinois measure that the "connection . . . to Nazism is so close it scares me (*New York Times,* 1971). Sterilization of Jews in the Nazi era has been well documented. The precedent is there and blacks know it. Notwithstanding his pro-birth control stand, Julius Lester (1969, p. 140) considers forced sterilization of welfare mothers to be a genocidal weapon against the Afro-American community. Jesse Jackson (1971, p. 25) considers it "an inhuman social proposition based upon race rather than population."

Although punitive birth control legislation has not been enacted to date, rumors are often circulated about black women who have been sterilized without any medical necessity for the procedure. They are widely believed by blacks. While most allegations of this nature are never substantiated, an indeterminate number have certainly been performed either for financial or racist reasons or for both. Dr. Herbert Avery (*Los Angeles Times*, 1968) of the Watts Extended Health and Family Planning Group claims to have examined numerous black Southern women who had been sterilized without their consent "because they were having too many children."

What appears to be a most outrageous example of unwarranted sterilization recently occurred in Alabama. Two black sisters, one twelve years of age, the other fourteen, were sterilized at a Montgomery family planning clinic funded by the Office of Economic Opportunity. The clinic steadfastly maintains that Mrs. Lonnie Relf, the mother of the two girls, though illiterate, understood the nature of the surgical procedures to be performed on her daughters. Mrs. Relf denies this and claims that she thought she was simply giving permission for vaccinations. A one million dollar damage suit has been filed on behalf of the girls. In the black community the case has triggered charges of racism, Nazism and genocide. Should allegations that approximately ten other black minors had previously been involuntarily and unnecessarily sterilized be substantiated, the matter could become a cause celêbre.

This study has dealt primarily with the public utterances and writings of black American opinion makers. Between their pronouncements on birth control and the practice of contraception by millions of Afro-Americans there may be a sizeable gap. There is substantial evidence suggesting that the black masses are no more responsive to the genocide notion than American Catholics are to papal encyclicals on artificial contraception. In a study published in 1970 Donald Bogue found that eighty percent of his Chicago sample of black women ghetto dwellers approved of birth control and seventy-five percent were actually practicing it. Bogue thought it "possible that the controversy over birth control for Negroes has eroded approval of family planning somewhat although it is still overwhelmingly positive" (p. 33). A recent opinion study (Lipson and Wolman, 1972) revealed that a significant majority of blacks wish the government to provide contraceptive information and supplies, want the government to make abortion available to all women and desire the legalization of sterilization operations.

Unwanted fertility has declined steeply for blacks in the last five years according to data drawn from National Fertility Studies (Westoff, 1972). This is largely reflective of the more effective use of contraceptives by blacks. Impoverished blacks have made excellent use of birth control clinics. The inescapable conclusion is that contraception is not anathema despite the genocide rhetoric.

But there may be a dark cloud or two on the horizon. Data from a New England study (Darity, Turner, and Thiebaux, 1971) indicated that black males under thirty were much more likely to concur with the genocide-conspiracy theory and were much more hesitant about condoning limitation of black family size than were older black males.

Whether such feelings are matched by behavior remains to be seen. It may be surmised that black women who will have to bear and raise black children are not likely to be animated by abstract political and philosophical questions. Data from the New England study confirm this. Nevertheless, the genocide rhetoric will surely continue to be heard, for black "paranoia" is anchored in historical reality. Black anxiety about birth control may be partially dissipated by inviting black community involvement in birth control projects, by integrating family planning into comprehensive health care programs, and by utilizing black personnel wherever possible. But until America comes to grips with the manifold problems of the seething cauldrons which are our black ghettos, until such time as blacks cease to be an exploited underclass, until such time as black Americans believe they possess the power to shape their own destinies, it is unlikely that the genocide rhetoric will be muted.

ACKNOWLEDGMENTS

Research for this paper was made possible by a grant from the Ford and Rockefeller Foundations Program In Support of Social Science and Legal Research On Population Policy. The author wishes to express appreciation to Professor Leon Bouvier of the University of Rhode Island for his advice and encouragement. The help of graduate assistants Richard Kazarian and Edith Beckers is also gratefully acknowledged.

REFERENCES

Abubakari, Dara (Virginia E. Y. Collins). 1972. The Black Woman Is Liberated In Her Own Mind. Pp. 585–87 in Gerda Lerner (ed.), Black Women in White America—A Documentary History. New York: Pantheon Books.

Anonymous, and Thomas H. Jones. 1871. The Experience of Thomas H. Jones Who Was A Slave for Forty-Three Years. New Bedford: E. Anthony and Sons.

Attah, Ernest B. 1972. Racial Aspects of Zero Population Growth: Some Perspectives With Demographic Models. A paper presented at the Annual Meeting of the Population Association of America, Toronto, April, 1972.

Bancroft, Frederick. 1931. Slave-Trading in the Old South. Baltimore: J. H. Furst Co.

Ben-Gurion, David. 1971. Israel—A Personal History. New York: Funk and Wagnalls, Inc.

Bibb, Henry. 1850. Narrative of the Life and Times of Henry Bibb, An American Slave. New York: Published by the Author.

Black Man, The. November 1934.

Black Panther, The. 4 January 1969; 4 July 1970; 10 April 1971; 8 May 1971.

Black Women's Liberation Group, Mt. Vernon, New York. 1970. Statement on Birth Control. Pp. 360–61 in Robin Morgan (ed.), Sisterhood is Powerful. New York: Vintage Books.

Blake, Margaret Jane. 1897. Memoirs of Margaret Jane Blake of Baltimore, Maryland. Philadelphia: Press of Innes and Son.

Bogue, Donald J. 1970. Family Planning in the Negro Ghettos of Chicago. Milbank Memorial Fund Quarterly, Part II 48:283–99.

Brown, H. Rap. 1969. Die Nigger Die. New York: The Dial Press.

Carter, Elmer A. 1932. Eugenics for the Negro. Birth Control Review 16:169–70

Chisholm, Shirley. 1971. Unbought and Unbossed. New York: Avon Books.

Cobb, W. Montague. 1939. The Negro as a Biological Element in the American Population. Journal of Negro Education 8:336–48.

Cowles, Wylda B. 1962. Memo to Dr. Alan F. Guttmacher concerning the Interview with Malcolm X, May 29, 1962.

———. 1966. Memo to Dr. Alan F. Guttmacher concerning meeting with E.R.O.S. in Berkeley, California on February 23, 1966.

Crisis. 1970. Planned Parenthood. Crisis 77:78–79.

Curtin, Philip D. 1969. The Atlantic Slave Trade—A Census. Madison: University of Wisconsin Press.

Darity, William A., Castellano B. Turner, and Jean H. Thiebaux. 1971. An Exploratory Study on Barriers to Family Planning: Race Consciousness and Fears of Black Genocide as a Basis. A paper presented at the Ninth Annual Meeting of the American Association of Planned Parenthood Physicians, Kansas City, Missouri, April, 1971.

Dubois, W. E. B. 1922. Birth. Crisis 24:248–50.

———. 1932. Black Folk and Birth Control. Birth Control Review 16:166–67.

Ehrlich, Paul R. 1971. The Population Bomb. New York: Ballantine Books

Essence. 1971. Conversation: Jesse Jackson and Marcia Gillespie. Essence (July 25).

Farrakhan, Minister Louis. 1972. The Black Woman. Essence (January).

Frazier, E. Franklin. 1945. Birth Control for More Negro Babies. Negro Digest 3:41–44.

Garvey, Marcus. 1967. Philosophy and Opinions of Marcus Garvey. London: Frank Cass and Company.

Goodell, William. 1969. The American Slave Code in Theory and Practice. New York: The New American Library.

Goodman, Benjamin (ed.). 1971. Malcolm X, the End of White World Supremacy—Four Speeches, New York: Merlin House, Inc.

Gregory, Dick. 1971. My Answer to Genocide. Ebony 26 (12):66–72.

Himes, Norman E. 1936. Medical History of Contraceptives. Baltimore: The Williams and Wilkins Co.

Hughes, Langston. 1965. Population Explosion. New York Post, December 10, 1965.

Jones, Carolyn. 1970. Abortion and Black Women. Black America 1:48–49.

Jordan, Winthrop D. 1968. White Over Black—American Attitudes toward the Negro 1550–1812. Chapel Hill: University of North Carolina Press.

Kahlil, Brother. 1971. Eugenics, Birth Control and the Black Man. Black News (January 14):20–21.

King, Martin Luther, Jr. n.d. Family Planning—A Special Urgent Concern. New York: Planned Parenthood-World Population.

Kiser, Clyde V. 1935. Fertility of Harlem Negroes. Milbank Memorial Fund Quarterly 13:273–85.

Lester, Julius. 1969. Birth Control and Blacks. Pp. 140–43 in Revolutionary Notes. New York: Richard W. Baron.

Lewis, Julian. 1945. Can the Negro Afford Birth Control. Negro Digest 3:19–22.

———. 1954. Is Birth Control A Menace To Negroes? Jet (August 19):52–55.

Lincoln, Richard. 1970. July 1970 Senate Bill 2108: Capitol Hill Debates the Future of Population and Family Planning. 2 (1:6–12).

Lipson, Gerald, and Dianne Wolman. 1972. Polling Americans on Birth Control and Population. Family Planning Perspectives 4:39–42.

Moore, Emily C. n.d. Native American Indian Values: Their Relation to Suggested Population Policy Proposals. Unpublished report to the Commission on Population Growth and the American Future. U.S. Commission on Population Growth and the American Future.

Morsell, John. 1972. Private communication with the Author, April 24, 1972.

Muhammad, Elijah. 1965. Message to the Blackman in America. Chicago: Muhammad Mosque of Islam No. 2.

Muhammad Speaks. 11 October 1968; 29 August 1969; 31 May 1969; 23 May 1969; 24 January 1969; 20 November 1970 and 3 January 1971.

New York Post. 7 October 1968.

New York Times. 23 May 1971; 26, 27, 28 July 1972; 8, 9 August 1972.

Noonan, John T., Jr. 1967. Contraception—A History of Its Treatment by the Catholic Theologians and Canonists. New York: Mentor-Omega.

Patterson, William L. (ed.). 1970. We Charge Genocide—The Historic Petition To The United Nations for Relief From a Crime of the United States Government Against the Negro People. New York: International Publishers.

Paul, Julius. 1968. The Return of Punitive Sterilization Programs—Current Attacks on Illegitimacy and the AFDC Program. Law and Society Review 111 (1):90.

Pearl, Raymond. 1936. Fertility and Contraception in Urban Whites and Negroes. Science 83:503–06.

Pittsburgh Courier. 14 April 1947; 29 March 1947; 24 August 1968.

Pittsburgh Press. 21 August 1968; 15 August 1968.

Puckett, Niles N. 1968. Folk Beliefs of the Southern Negro. New York: Negro Universities Press.

Rice, Thurman B. 1929. Racial Hygiene—A Practical Discussion of Eugenics and Race Culture. New York: Macmillan Company.

Sanders, Thomas G. 1970. Opposition to Family Planning in Latin America: The Non-Marxist Left. American Universities Field Staff Reports. West Coast South America Series XVII, No. 5.

Sanger, Margaret. 1938. Margaret Sanger: An Autobiography. New York: W. W. Norton and Company Publishers.

Schuyler, George S. 1932. Quantity or Quality. Birth Control Review 16:165–66.

Siebels, Robert E. 1941. A Rural Project in Negro Maternal Health. Human Fertility 6: 42–44.

Smith, Mary. 1968. Birth Control and the Negro Woman. Ebony 23 (5):29–37.

Tannenbaum, Frank. 1946. Slave and Citizen: The Negro in the Americas. New York: Vintage Press.

Warwick, Donald P., and Nancy Williamson. 1971. Population Policy and Spanish Speaking Americans. Unpublished report to the Commission on Population Growth and the American Future. U.S. Commission on Population Growth and the American Future.

Watts, Daniel H. 1969. Birth Control. Liberator (May, 1969).

Westoff, Charles F. 1972. The Modernization of U.S. Contraceptive Practice. Family Planning Perspectives 4:9–12.

Williams, Maxine, and Pamela Newman. 1971. Black Women's Liberation, Second Ed. New York: Pathfinder Press, Inc.

Woodside, Moya. 1950. Sterilization in North Carolina: A Sociological and Psychological Study. Chapel Hill: University of North Carolina Press.

Yette, Samuel F. 1971. The Choice: The Issue of Black Survival in America. New York: G. P Putnam's Sons.

33

Family Planning Services and the Distribution of Black Americans

Kenneth C. W. Kammeyer, Norman R. Yetman, and McKee J. McClendon

Although the family planning movement has been in existence for many decades, most observers have noted that the 1960's brought great changes in American policies and practices regarding the control of fertility (Jaffe, 1967:145). After decades of silence, or even opposition, American political leaders at all levels, from the president to local city and county officials, have become increasingly supportive of the idea of family planning. Public family planning services were initially provided primarily through affiliates of nongovernmental organizations such as Planned Parenthood. However, during the latter half of the 1960's such services were often made available through county health departments and county hospitals. After the initiation of the "war on poverty," some funds 'or famil'/ nlanning services were provided by the Office of Economic Opportunity as well.

This paper attempts to shed some light on factors that may have contributed to, or influenced, the decision of local units in the United States to provide public family planning services. In particular, we are able to demonstrate that family planning services in the United States were provided more frequently whenever there were black Americans in the population. In other words, there is a strong inferential case to be made that reactions to the racial composition of the population have influenced decisions to provide family planning services.

THE RATIONALE OF THE FAMILY-PLANNING MOVEMENT

Organizations that have fought and worked for family planning in the United States, from Margaret Sanger's American Birth Control League to

Reprinted from *Majority and Minority*, ed. Norman R. Yetman and C. Hoy Steele (2nd ed., 1975), by permission of the authors and the publisher, Allyn and Bacon, Inc., Boston.

the present-day Planned Parenthood and Office of Economic Opportunity programs, have been quite consistent about their aims. The stated objective has always been to enable the poor to have the same ability to control family size as the more affluent.

As the position has recently been expressed: "The 55 percent difference in fertility rates between poor and non-poor seems to stem largely from [the] considerable difference in the means of fertility control to which the poor have had access. The objective of national policy is to remedy this inequity by providing low-income couples with effective access to the same modern methods of fertility control which higher income Americans enjoy" (Planned Parenthood/Office of Economic Opportunity, 1969:4).

If family planning services are made available in accordance with this rationale, it might be supposed that those communities with the largest number of people who are poor would be the most likely to have such services. Such a supposition can be stated in the form of a hypothesis and labeled the *poverty* hypothesis: the availability of family planning services will be positively related to the prevalence of poverty in the population.

The family planning movement may also be viewed as activity aimed at reducing perceived high or excessive fertility. By providing contraceptive information and materials to couples who have large families, high fertility levels could be greatly reduced. Following this objective, family planning services would be initiated wherever fertility is high. If transformed into a hypothesis to explain the availability of family planning services, this may be called the *high fertility* hypothesis: the availability of family planning services will be positively related to the fertility levels found in the population.

Yet another explanation of the distribution of family planning services, but one that does not emanate from the ideology of the family planning movement, is what demographers have labeled the *diffusion* hypothesis. This hypothesis holds that birth-control methods, techniques and knowledge will be found first in urban centers and will then diffuse through more rural segments of the society. While Carlsson (1966) has made a notable attack on the diffusion hypothesis, it must be considered in this study because it may account for the distribution of family planning services in the United States.

On the basis of the *poverty* and *high fertility* hypotheses, one should find the availability of family planning services in the United States to be closely related to the amount of poverty in the population and the fertility rate. The *diffusion* hypothesis would lead us to expect family planning services to be more frequently found in urban areas. However, there is another factor that might explain the distribution of the family planning services, one having nothing to do with the rational objectives of the family planning movement or the diffusion of ideas from urban to rural areas. That is, the racial and ethnic composition of the population. Of course, the idea that family planning services would be provided more frequently when there are racial or ethnic minorities in the population is repugnant to the leadership of the family planning movement. But the objectives of the leaders of the family planning movement and the implementation of these objectives in local communities throughout the nation are quite different matters. It may be that communities, through their leaders, see the need for helping to control fertility among their poor, but they perceive this need more clearly if those poor are also racial or ethnic minorities. In simple terms, the racial or ethnic characteristics of the population may create higher *visibility* for the *need* to provide fertility control services.

The proposition that family planning services will be more likely to be made available if there are racial or ethnic minorities in the population may be labeled the *racial* hypothesis. Stated in the form of a hypothesis we may say: the availability of family planning services in the United States will be positively related to the presence of racial or ethnic minorities in the population.

The idea that birth control or family planning services are directed toward racial or ethnic minorities did not emerge from a vacuum. Even in the early days of Margaret Sanger's work, critics of the family planning movement charged that it was directed at particular groups. Since Sanger's efforts at that time were often concentrated among the impoverished immigrant Jews, she was charged with operating a clinic that "was intended to do away with the Jews" (Jaffe, 1968:234-35). Today a frequent charge against the family planning movement is that it is directed toward black Americans. Charles Willie (1971:1) has asserted that "many people in the black community are deeply suspicious of any family planning program initiated by whites." There is considerable empirical evidence to support Willie's description of black perceptions of the family planning movement. Darity, Turner, and Thiebaux (1971) questioned a sample of blacks from a medium-sized New England city and found that 29 percent of the males, and 5 percent of the females aged 30 or younger agreed with the statement that "all forms of birth control are designed to eliminate black Americans." In this same study, a less strong statement said, "Encouraging blacks to use birth control is comparable to trying to eliminate this group from society." Forty-seven percent of males aged 30 and under agreed with this statement, while 20 percent of females in this age group agreed. Among those over 30, 24 percent agreed (27 percent of the males, 23 percent of the females; Darity, et al., 1971:6-7).

But what do these figures prove? Only that among a substantial portion of black Americans, particularly males, there is some acceptance of the idea that the family planning movement is directed toward them and has the objective of reducing their numbers in the population. Perhaps black Americans have developed an ultrasensitivity to racism in general, and thus see it at every turn; perhaps it is a simple misinterpretation of the facts. The editors of the Population Reference Bureau (1971), who published Professor Willie's remarks, adopted the latter explanation. They noted:

> Government activity in the field of population thus far has been confined largely to bringing to the poor that same ability to control individual family size, in terms of contraceptives and information, that is available to the rest of society. Inevitably, this has meant that *official birth control centers have concentrated in poor communities, a disproportionate share of which are black* (emphasis added). This concentration has led some militant blacks to proclaim that family planning programs are aimed at black 'genocide.'

This position on the issue argues that if black Americans are more often the targets of family planning programs it is because they are more often poor, and the aim of the family planning movement is only to give the poor the same opportunity as the nonpoor to choose the number of children they want. This interpretation is, of course, a restatement of the poverty hypothesis presented earlier. The argument is that the distribution of family planning services is determined by the distribution of poverty. If family planning services are also found where there are disproportionate numbers of black Americans, it is due to the positive correlation between race and poverty.

The research that follows will test the racial hypothesis as an explanation of the distribution of family planning services. The poverty, high fertility and diffusion hypotheses will be considered as alternative explanations.

THE STUDY

In 1969 Planned Parenthood and the Office of Economic Opportunity issued a report on the availability of family planning services in the United States. The research for this report was conducted by the Center for Family Planning Program Development of Planned Parenthood. The purpose of the study was to provide the Office of Economic Opportunity, as well as other interested agencies and individuals, with some baseline information on the availability of family planning services in the United States. Using several data-gathering methods, information was collected on the 3072 counties of the United States. The report provided a county-by-county breakdown on the availability of family planning services, along with a variety of other measures reflecting demographic, social welfare, and medical conditions in each county. We have used the data presented in this report as the best available information on the distribution of family planning services in the United States in 1968. The report revealed that, in 1968, exactly 1200 of the 3072 counties had *some* family planning services available to the public. Specifically this meant that at least one of the following four services was available: 1. The county health department was providing family planning services; 2. The county hospital was providing family planning services; 3. A Planned Parenthood affiliate was providing family planning services; or 4. The Office of Economic Opportunity was providing funds for some agency to provide family planning services.

Our overall strategy in this study has been to treat the racial hypothesis as the primary hypothesis to be tested. If the expected relationship is found beween the minority group, or racial, composition of the counties and the availability of family planning services, then the variables reflecting the alternative hypotheses (poverty, high fertility, and urbanism) will be introduced as control variables. More specifically, using product-moment correlation, the zero order correlation between all independent variables and the dependent variables will be examined first. Then a partial correlation analysis will be undertaken. Finally, the same data will be analyzed with a cross-classification procedure, using gamma as measure of association.

The Dependent Variable—Availability of Family Planning Services

The Planned Parenthood/O.E.O. study identified all United States counties that were providing some family planning services "either by public or voluntary hospitals, health department, Planned Parenthood affiliates or other agencies" (Planned Parenthood/Office of Economic Opportunity, 1969:5). While the Planned Parenthood study sought to establish a measure that would indicate the percent of need for family planning services being met by each county, this study does not have the same objectives. Our aim was to identify those counties where public or quasi-public family planning services had been made available. This study will try to determine what differentiates those counties that had taken some action from those that had apparently taken none. The dependent variable in this analysis is therefore a dichotomous classification that distinguishes those counties where some family planning services had been provided by 1968 from those counties where none had been provided.

This measure of family planning services does not mean that a county is providing for all its family planning needs, but only that some kind of action had been taken in the county by some people—very likely those who have some degree of responsibility and power in the county. Even if, as is sometimes argued, potential users of family planning services should have initiated the request for those services, someone in a position of authority had to decide to provide it. The question that this research attempts to answer is: to what factors did the county officials respond? Was it poverty, high fertility, or race?

The Independent Variable—Racial and Minority Group Composition of Counties

Using data from the *County and City Data Book* of 1967 (U.S. Bureau of the Census, 1967), United States Census reports (U.S. Bureau of the Census, 1961), and the Planned Parenthood report (1969) referred to above, we obtained demographic data so that each county could be described in terms of the:

1. Percentage of the county population black
2. Percentage of the county population black and Indian
3. Percentage of the county population Spanish-speaking and Indian
4. Percentage of the county black and Spanish-speaking
5. Percentage of the county population black, Indian and migrant farm laborer
6. Percentage of the county population black, Indian, migrant farm laborer, and Spanish-speaking
7. Percentage of the county population black, Indian, migrant farm laborer, Spanish-speaking and foreign born.

An earlier analysis revealed that the first of these indicators, percentage of the county population black, was the strongest independent variable (Kammeyer, Yetman, and McClendon, 1972). For the United States as a whole, and in four of the five regions of the country, "percentage black" always correlated more highly with the availability of family planning services than any combination of minority groups. Since other combinations of minority groups only diminished the relationships, it is our judgment that the introduction of other groups only confounds the issue. In individual states certain unique combinations of minority groups in the population might prove to be stronger. However, in the remainder of this paper we will focus only on the percentage of the population black as the independent variable.

The Control Variables—Poverty, High Fertility, and Urbanism

The primary hypothesis to be tested is that the percentage of the county population that is black will be positively related to the availability of family planning services. However, the alternative (poverty, high fertility, and diffusion) hypotheses call for measures of these factors that can be controlled while we examine the racial hypotheses. Also for reasons that will be discussed below, we will examine the relationships separately for different regions of the country.

Providing family planning services is, as noted above, often justified on the basis of the economic need of the population. When the population is poor there is a presumed need for public or quasi-public family planning services. Therefore, if the influence of minority groups in the population is to be shown, the poverty level of the population must be held constant. In this analysis the poverty level of counties was measured in two ways: first, by using the "percentage of the families in the county with an income under $3,000 per year," and second by the percentage of women aged 15–44 in the county population who were medically indigent and in need of family planning services (Planned Parenthood/Office of Economic Opportunity, 1969).

The first of these two poverty measures uses the generally accepted 1960's poverty level of $3,000 yearly income per family. One might expect that it would be a satisfactory index of the poverty level of women in the childbearing years. However, the second measure is more appropriate since it focuses on medically indigent women in need of subsidized family planning. This measure was developed by Planned Parenthood researchers, who used it to estimate the number of women in need in 1966, for all United States counties. The measure of "medically indigent women in need" was described as "all fertile women who are exposed to the risk of unwanted pregnancy and who cannot afford medical care. It consists of all women who are: a) medically indigent; b) fertile; c) exposed to pregnancy; d) and not currently pregnant or seeking a desired pregnancy" (Planned Parenthood/Office of Economic Opportunity, 1969:238). The similarity of these two measures of poverty is revealed by the fact that they were highly correlated ($r = .934$; see Table 1). If the poverty hypothesis is to account for the distribution of family planning services in the United States, this measure should be highly correlated with the availability of family planning services. Or as a partialing variable, it should reduce correlations of other correlated measures. The latter method is the principal way in which we will employ this variable.

The high fertility hypothesis calls for some indication of fertility in the county. We used both the county fertility rate for 1966 (the number of births per 100 women aged 15–44 in 1966) and the county crude birth rate (the number of births per 1000 population). These variables, as control variables, will be discussed more fully below.

The diffusion hypothesis calls for a measure of the level of urbanism in each county. Since blacks are now concentrated in urban places (Price, 1969:11), it is important to control for the effects of urbanism. When we

TABLE 1.   Correlation Matrices Showing the Zero-Order Correlations Between the Independent, Dependent and Control Variables; For The United States and Five Regional Areas

	(1)	(2)	(3)	(4)	(5)	(6)	(7)
Correlation Matrix A—United States							
(1) Available Family Planning Services	1.000						
(2) Percent Black	.428	1.000					
(3) Percent Families with Income Under $3,000	.174	.479	1.000				
(4) Percent of Women in Need of Subsidized Family Planning	.235	.508	.934	1.000			
(5) Fertility Rate	.076	.144	−.029	−.017	1.000		
(6) Crude Birth Rate	.151	.125	.051	−.102	.655	1.000	
(7) Urbanism	.209	−.050	−.540	−.429	.080	.140	1.000
Correlation Matrix B—Region 1, West*							
(1) Available Family Planning Services	1.000						
(2) Percent Black	.466	1.000					
(3) Percent Families with Income Under $3,000	−.007	−.187	1.000				
(4) Percent of Women in Need of Subsidized Family Planning	.039	−.126	.714	1.000			
(5) Fertility Rate	.075	.077	.106	.068	1.000		
(6) Crude Birth Rate	.131	.165	.101	−.219	.378	1.000	
(7) Urbanism	.418	.439	−.390	−.177	.022	.110	1.000
Correlation Matrix C—Region 2, North Central†							
(1) Available Family Planning Services	1.000						
(2) Percent Black	.324	1.000					
(3) Percent Families with Income Under $3,000	−.268	−.141	1.000				
(4) Percent of Women in Need of Subsidized Family Planning	−.215	−.080	.980	1.000			
(5) Fertility Rate	.162	.029	−.200	−.220	1.000		
(6) Crude Birth Rate	.250	.093	−.368	−.383	.927	1.000	
(7) Urbanism	.372	.338	−.670	−.609	.124	.284	1.000

Correlation Matrix D—Region 3, Northeast‡

	(1)	(2)	(3)	(4)	(5)	(6)	(7)
(1) Available Family Planning Services	1.000						
(2) Percent Black	.409	1.000					
(3) Percent Families with Income Under $3,000	−.447	−.279	1.000				
(4) Percent of Women in Need of Subsidized Family Planning	−.367	−.197	.960	1.000			
(5) Fertility Rate	−.030	−.055	.166	.163	1.000		
(6) Crude Birth Rate	.053	.006	−.002	−.029	.880	1.000	
(7) Urbanism	.596	.499	−.693	−.572	−.069	.016	1.000

Correlation Matrix E—Region 4, West-South-Central§

	(1)	(2)	(3)	(4)	(5)	(6)	(7)
(1) Available Family Planning Services	1.000						
(2) Percent Black	.009	1.000					
(3) Percent Families with Income Under $3,000	−.043	.344	1.000				
(4) Percent of Women in Need of Subsidized Family Planning	.019	.408	.955	1.000			
(5) Fertility Rate	−.015	.103	−.047	.003	1.000		
(6) Crude Birth Rate	.022	.110	−.110	−.049	.977	1.000	
(7) Urbanism	.306	−.029	−.497	−.368	.183	.246	1.000

Correlation Matrix F—Region 5, South‖

	(1)	(2)	(3)	(4)	(5)	(6)	(7)
(1) Available Family Planning Services	1.000						
(2) Percent Black	.277	1.000					
(3) Percent Families with Income Under $3,000	.006	.301	1.000				
(4) Percent of Women in Need of Subsidized Family Planning	.038	.291	.850	1.000			
(5) Fertility Rate	.138	.426	.133	.140	1.000		
(6) Crude Birth Rate	.177	.339	.005	−.064	.866	1.000	
(7) Urbanism	.219	−.009	−.614	−.467	.009	.085	1.000

* Washington, Oregon, California, Idaho, Nevada, Montana, Wyoming, Utah, Colorado, Arizona, and New Mexico.
‡ North Dakota, South Dakota, Nebraska, Kansas, Minnesota, Iowa, Missouri, Wisconsin, Illinois, Michigan, Indiana, Ohio.
‡ New York, Pennsylvania, Vermont, New Hampshire, Massachusetts, Connecticut, Rhode Island, New Jersey, Maine.
§ Oklahoma, Texas, Arkansas, Louisiana.
‖ Kentucky, Tennessee, Mississippi, Alabama, West Virginia, Virginia, North Carolina, Georgia, South Carolina, Florida, Maryland, and Delaware.

examine the racial hypothesis, the measure of urbanism used in this analysis is the percent of the population living in places of 2500 or more This measure of urbanism follows the Census Bureau classification, and, while it may seem somewhat simplistic as a measure of urbanism, it does correlate very highly with much more elaborate urbanism measures (See Queen and Carpenter, 1953:38–43).

Finally, since blacks are unevenly distributed throughout the United States, and their rural-urban distribution varies from one geographical region to another, it is also necessary to control for region. It is especially important to ensure that the concentration of blacks in Southern states and the preponderance of family planning services in the South do not produce a spurious relationship for the nation as a whole, between "percent black" and family planning services. Moreover, examining the regions individually permits us to examine whatever regional variations there may be in the relationships being examined.

The Findings

A correlation matrix showing the zero order correlations among the major independent, the dependent, and control variables is presented in Table 1. Matrix A is for the entire United States, while matrices B, C, D, E, and F are for the five regional areas separately.

For the United States as a whole, matrix A shows the correlation between "percent black" and the availability of family planning services. The correlation coefficient is .428. Neither the percentage of families below the poverty level in the county, nor the percentage of women in need of subsidized family planning is as highly correlated with the availability of family planning. The respective correlation coefficients are .174 and .233. The two measures of fertility are even less highly correlated with the availability of family planning. The fertility rate is correlated .076, and the crude birth rate .151. Urbanism is correlated .209.

It appears that for the United States as a whole, neither the poverty hypothesis, the excessive fertility hypothesis, nor the diffusion hypothesis accounts for the distribution of family planning services as well as the racial hypothesis. However, this conclusion needs to be assessed further.

Regional Differences. In different regions of the country there are differences in the way "percent black" is related to the availability of family planning services. There is some correlation between "percent black" and family planning services in all regions of the country except the West-South-Central region, which therefore requires some special attention. The West-South-Central region is made up of Oklahoma, Arkansas, Texas and Louisiana. In 1968 Louisiana and Texas had very few counties providing family planning services (9.4 percent of the Louisiana counties, 12.2 percent of the Texas counties). Since Louisiana, in particular, has a substantial black population (32 percent of the total) it is understandable that no high correlation between "percent blacks" and family planning services was observed. Louisiana, in 1968, stood out as a clear exception to the other deep South states, since the overwhelming majority of the counties in the remaining Southern states were providing some family planning services. Probably the Catholic heritage of Louisiana accounts for this dissimilarity. However, it is of interest to note that by the time of a 1969 resurvey by Planned Parenthood, Louisiana resembled the rest of the Southern states in providing family planning services. By 1969, Louisiana had gone from the six counties, of a year earlier, to fifty-five counties providing family planning services. The latter figure represents 86 percent of the Louisiana counties, a proportion comparable to most other Southern states and far greater than the percentage in non-Southern states. Texas increased its percentage of counties providing family planning services in 1969 to about 21 percent, so while the West-South-Central region did not support the racial hypothesis in 1968, it might well have in 1969 after Louisiana had made such substantial changes.

Among the remaining regions of the country, the West showed the highest correlation between the "percent black" and family planning services. The correlation in the West was .466. It was followed by the North with .409, the North-Central with .324, and the South with 2.77.

By contrast, there was no region of the country in which poverty was correlated highly enough with the availability of family planning services that it could account for the distribution of such services. In the West, the West-South-Central, and the South the correlations between the two measures of poverty and the availability of family planning services tended to hover around zero. In the North-Central and Northeast the correlations between poverty and availability of family planning services were not even positive; they were negative. In these two regions the greater the level of poverty in a county the *less* likely it was to have family planning services. In the Northeast the high negative correlations (−.477 and −.367) might be accounted for by the fact that available family planning was highly correlated with urbanism (r. = .596). Since urbanism was negatively correlated with poverty (−.572, in the Northeast and −.693 in the North Central), it would follow that poverty would not be positively correlated with family planning. Whatever the explanation, it is clear from both the low correlations in the West, West-South-Central and the South, and the negative correlations in the North-Central and Northeast that the existence of poverty does not explain the availability of family planning services.

Measures of fertility (the fertility rate and the crude birth rate) fared equally badly as correlates of the availability of family planning services.

In the Northeast and West-South-Central regions the correlations were around zero; in the West the correlations were .075 and .131, in the South they were .138 and .177, while in the North-Central they were .162 and .250. Only in the North-Central regions did high fertility seem to have the expected positive correlations with the availability of family planning services, but, it might be noted, the correlation was still lower than the correlation beween "percent black" and family planning services.

While neither the poverty nor high fertility hypotheses explained much of the variance in the availability of family planning, either in the United States or the separate regions, urbanism was always positively related. The correlations ranged from .219 in the South to .596 in the Northeast. This suggests that urbanism could be a factor accounting for a substantial proportion of the relationship between the distribution of blacks and available family planning services. However, this is only likely to be true for certain regions of the country, namely those where urbanism is in fact related to percent black. As Table 1 shows, the positive correlation between urbanism and percent black in the West, North-Central and Northeast is not found in the South or in the West-South-Central. There is also not a positive relationship for the total United States, apparently owing to the preponderant influence of the southern regions. We used a partial correlation analysis for the United States, and for the several regions, to examine the correlation between the percentage of blacks in the county and availability of family planning services while controlling for poverty, fertility, and urbanism.

For the poverty variable we will use "women in need of subsidized family planning" since this variable correlated most highly with available family planning services. It is also a measure of poverty that has a logical affinity to the idea that it is the poor in their reproductive years who are the natural targets of family planning programs.

As an index of fertility we will use the crude birth rate of the county rather than the fertility rate. This may seem unusual since the fertility rate, which is based on the number of women in the childbearing ages rather than upon the total population, is usually assumed to be a more refined measure of fertility. There are three reasons for our decision. First, crude birth rate correlated more highly with the available family planning services than did the fertility rate. In that sense it is more likely to be able to diminish or "wash out" the correlation between "percent black" and family planning services.

The second reason for using crude birth rate rather than the fertility rate is somewhat more complex. One critical comment on an earlier version of this paper suggested that perhaps the poverty level of a county does not reduce the correlation between "percent black" and available family planning services because the age structure of the "white-poor" counties is different from the age structure of the "black-poor" counties. Specifically, it was suggested that the "white-poor" counties were more likely to be made up of many more *old* poor people than the "black-poor" counties (Williams, 1972). If age structures of "white-poor" and "black-poor" counties differed in this way, it would mean that the "white-poor" counties would have much less need for family planning services. In effect this is another perspective on the high fertility hypothesis since it is being argued that the "black-poor" counties would have more people in the childbearing ages than the "white-poor" counties. Since the crude birth rate *is* affected by the structure of the population, it turns out to be a better control variable for fertility in the present case.

The third reason for using crude birth rate over fertility rate is that the percentage of babies in the total population would be more closely related to the services that the county must provide for children. A high crude birth rate would put a heavy demand on public services while a high fertility rate would not necessarily do so if there were only a small number of fecund women in the population. Also, a high crude birth rate is more likely to be visible to public officials than a high fertility rate.

Two additional points are necessary before presenting the partial correlation analysis. First, while we will report here only the partials for "women in need" (poverty control) and crude birth rate (high fertility control), the results are the same, indeed usually more supportive of our conclusion, when the alternative control variables for poverty (percent of families with less than $3,000 income) and high fertility (fertility rate) are used. Limiting the number of control variables in this part of the analysis is done only in the interest of brevity and clarity. Second, while we argued above that crude birth rate can be used as a surrogate control for the age structure of the population, we did control for the age structure directly (women in the county population aged 15–44) with the same result. Readers interested in the full set of partial correlations or any specific partials may contact the authors directly.

The Partial Correlation Findings. Table 2 shows the partial correlations between "percent black" in the county population and the availability of family planning services. The variance accounted for by the effects of several crucial control variables has been removed, both singularly and in combination. Again the correlations are shown for both the United States as a whole and for the five regions separately. The West-South-Central region, of course, still shows no correlation between family planning services and the distribution of blacks, so the discussion will focus on the United States as a whole and on the remaining four regions.

In general, neither the poverty variable (women in need) nor the

TABLE 2. Partial Correlation Coefficients between Percentage of the Population Black and the Availability of Family Planning Services, Controlled for "Women in Need of Subsidized Family Planning," Crude Birth Rate, and Urbanism, for the Total United States and Five Regions.

			Region			
	United States	West	North-Central	North-east	West-South-Central-	South
Zero Order Correlation Between Percent Black and Available Family Planning Services	.428	.466	.324	.409	.009	.277
Control Variables			Partial Correlation Coefficient			
Women in Need	.370	.475	.315	.369	.002	.278
Crude Birth Rate	.417	.454	.312	.409	.007	.234
Urbanism	.449	.346	.227	.161	.019	.286
Women in Need and Crude Birth Rate	.345	.464	.309	.370	−.001	.231
Women in Need, Crude Birth Rate, and Urbanism	.301	.347	.223	.168	−.042	.204

fertility measure (crude birth rate), taken separately, substantially reduced the zero-order correlations. Even when the two measures were controlled simultaneously, not much of the correlation between percent blacks and available family planning services was washed out. For the United States as a whole this second-order partial dropped the correlation from .428 to .345. For the regions, the reduction produced by the combined effect of these variables was generally even less. With "women in need" and crude birth rate controlled, the correlation in the West changed hardly at all, going from .466 to .464. In the North-Central region it went from .324 to .309, in the Northeast from .409 to .370, and in the South from .277 to .231. In essence, controlling for effects of poverty and high fertility (as well as indirectly for age structure) resulted in only a modest diminution of the correlations between "percent black" and available family planning.

By contrast the third control variable, urbanism, had considerably more effect. It had a substantial effect when it was the only control variable, especially in the Northeast, and also in the third order partials when it was combined with the poverty and high fertility variables.

For the total United States, having partialled out the effects of urbanism, poverty, high fertility (and age structure with the crude birth rate) there was still a correlation of .301 between the percentage of blacks in the county population and whether or not the county had some family planning services available.

In four of five regions in the country as a whole the third-order partials, which controlled for the effects of poverty, high fertility, and urbanism simultaneously, produced correlations that were about 30 percent less than the original zero-order correlations. In the Northeast the reduction was even greater. In this region the correlation between "percent black" and available family planning services decreased by about 60 percent (from .409 to .168). This was, of course, due to the high correlation between urbanism and family planning services in the Northeast.

In the four regions of the country, still excluding the West-South-Central, the third-order partial correlations were .349 (West), .233 (North Central), .168 (Northeast) and .204 (South). In terms of the variance explained, these are not dramatically large correlations, though it can be noted again that compared to the poverty and high fertility variables, "percent black" was much more strongly correlated with the availability of family planning services. Only by putting it in the position of the primary causal variable, and subjecting it to the test of spuriousness, do we diminish its explanatory power. If we had conversely treated the poverty and high fertility variables as the primary causes of the distribution of family planning services, *as they are generally assumed to be,* and subjected them to the same tests of spuriousness, of course we would have reduced their power also. Indeed we would have virtually eliminated their correlation with the dependent variable.

By contrast, urbanism, reflecting the diffusion hypothesis, does often show an equally high, or higher, correlation with family planning services when the data are examined regionally. That was not the case for the country as a whole, where the correlation for percent black was .428, and the correlation for urbanism was .209.

Cross-Classification Analysis. While the correlation analysis indicates in a single coefficient the degree of the relationship between the racial composition of counties and the availability of family planning, the same relationship may be examined in a cross-classification analysis and displayed by means of bar graphs. We did this by dividing the several continuous distributions into categories, and cross-classifying them with the already dichotomous dependent variable. The independent variable "percent black" was divided into five categories, ranging from those counties with no blacks to those counties with more than 50 percent blacks.

Figures 1 through 7 are some selected bar graphs that show clearly

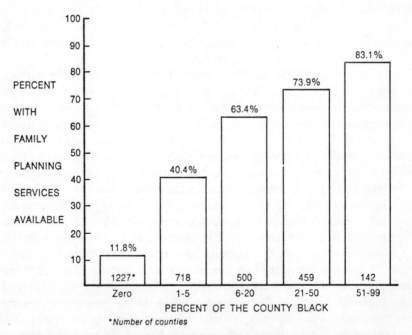

FIGURE 1.   The Relationship Between the Percent of the County Population Black and the Availability of Family Planning Services. All counties in the continental United States.

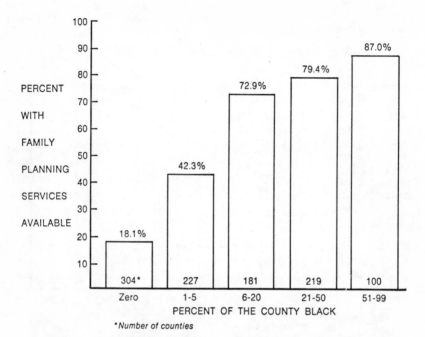

FIGURE 2.   The Relationship Between the Percent of the County Population Black and the Availability of Family Planning Services. All counties with a crude birth rate of 19 or greater.

the consistent and strong relationship between the percentage of county population black and the availability of family planning services.

For example, in Figure 1 for the total United States it may be seen that among those counties that had no blacks only 11.8 percent had family planning services. There were 1227 such counties. At the other extreme there were 142 United States counties that had more than 50 percent of the population black, and among these counties 83.1 percent had some family planning services. The counties with intermediate percentages of blacks had proportionately large percentages providing family planning services.

The remaining Figures 2–7 consistently show the same pattern. Whenever the percentage of blacks increases, the proportion of the counties providing family planning services increases. The categories shown graphically in these figures were not selected because they were the most impressive data available, but rather they were thought to be the most interesting. For example, Figure 2 shows the one-third of the U.S. counties with the highest crude birth rates, Figure 3 shows the counties with the highest percentage of "women in need," and Figure 4 shows the most

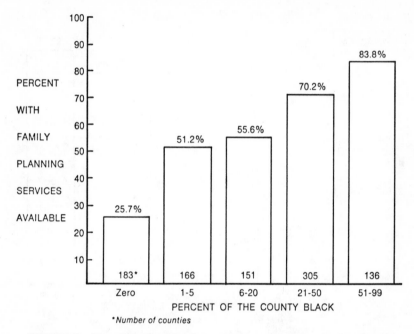

FIGURE 3. The Relationship Between the Percent of the County Population Black and the Availability of Family Planning Services. All counties with women in need higher than 24%.

heavily urban counties. In all cases the relationship between "percent black" and available family planning services is clearly evident.

In Figure 4, as in Figures 6 and 7, there were some categories of "percent black" that had fewer than ten cases. Whenever this occurred we combined that category with an adjacent one. These combinations are shown with double-width columns.

Figure 5 shows the relationship for those counties that had both a high crude birth rate and a high proportion of "women in need." While there is a slight disruption of the pattern in the first columns, there is still a clearly evident relationship between "percent black" and available family planning services.

Figures 6 and 7 show the same two categories of counties, but now divided into the least urban and most urban also. In other words, Figures 6 and 7 show the relationship while holding three variables constant simultaneously. Again the relationship is shown, even though the number of cases in Figure 7 is very small.

Since there is still the possibility that we might have been selective in

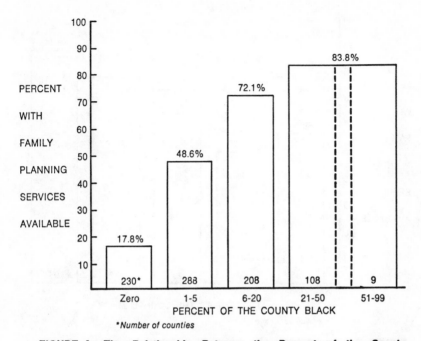

FIGURE 4. The Relationship Between the Percent of the County Population Black and the Availability of Family Planning Services. All United States counties with 50% or more of the population urban.

the choice of data for Figures 1–7, some additional summary information may be supplied. Each bar graph is drawn from a 2x5 table (family planning services available: yes or no; percent blacks in the county divided into five categories ranging from zero percent to more than fifty percent). For purposes of comparison the coefficient of association gamma was calculated for each 2x5 table. While gamma is designed for ordinal data, it may be used even for the dichotomous or nominal attributes if the order is kept the same throughout. Here we use it primarily to indicate the strength and consistency of relationships. In the cross tabulation tables that produced Figures 1–7 the gamma values were, respectively, .71, .70, .53, .67, .45, .45, .60. These values of gamma are only average or below average compared to the sets from which they come.

If we use gamma as an indication of the consistency of the relationship between percent blacks and available family planning services, we can show very clearly that the relationship holds under almost all conditions of poverty, fertility, and urbanism. To illustrate, when we divided each of the three control variables into three categories (low, medium, and high), the

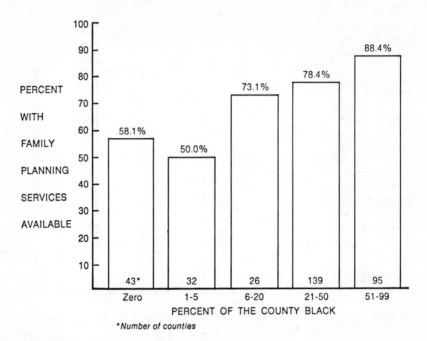

FIGURE 5. The Relationship Between the Percent of the County Population Black and the Availability of Family Planning Services. All counties with a crude birth rate of 19 or higher and women in need greater than 24%.

result was twenty-seven (3x3x3) combinations that represented particular combinations of the characteristics of poverty, fertility, and urbanism. When we examined the relationship between "percent black" and available family planning services for every combination, there was only one table out of the twenty-seven that had a gamma with a negative sign. It happened to be for a set of thirty-eight counties (low-urban, low-poverty and medium-crude birth rate) where only one county had family planning services, and it was in a county with no blacks. However since thirty-three of these thirty-eight counties had no blacks there was little chance for the relationship to be revealed in any case. The remaining twenty-six gammas were in the positive direction, with the average gamma value of .58.

A similar kind of cross-classification analysis was carried out for the five separate regions of the United States. Controlling for three categories of poverty and three categories of fertility for all five regions, we had a total of forty-five (3x3x5) cross-classifications between the percentage of blacks in the county and available family planning services. Fourteen of these tables had fewer than twenty cases, so we arbitrarily eliminated them

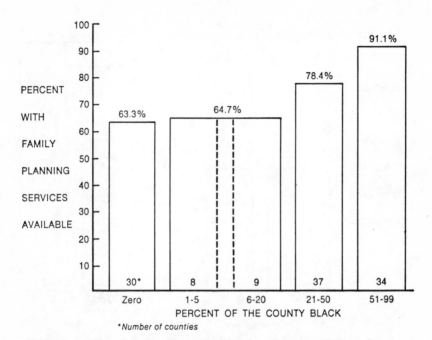

FIGURE 6. The Relationship Between the Percent of the County Population Black and the Availability of Family Planning Services. All counties with a crude birth rate of 19 or higher, women in need greater than 24% and no percent of the population urban.

from consideration. Of the remaining thirty-one tables, twenty-eight had a positive relation between "percent black" and available family planning services. Three had negative relationships. Two of these three were in the West-South-Central region, which, as we have noted, did not show the relationship in the correlation analysis. The remaining deviant case was in the North-Central region where the "women in need" variable was high but crude birth rate was low. Again this was a set of counties where sixty-eight of the eighty-one counties had no blacks, and only two of the eighty-one counties had family planning services. As before, this gave little opportunity for the relationship between "percent black" and family planning services to be seen.

In general, the cross-classification analysis revealed, just as the correlational analysis had shown, that there is a fairly strong and persistent relationship between family planning services in United States counties and the presence of blacks in the population. The percentage of blacks in the county was the single strongest independent variable for explaining variation in the availability of family planning services. Support for the

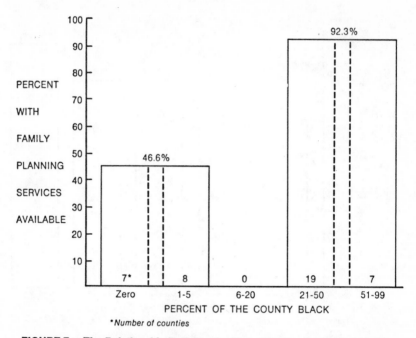

FIGURE 7.   The Relationship Between the Percent of the County Population Black and the Availability of Family Planning Services. All counties with a crude birth rate of 19 or higher, women in need greater than 24% and more than 50% of the population urban.

racial hypothesis was clearly greater than for either the poverty or fertility hypotheses. Further, even when controlled for urbanism, poverty, fertility, and indirectly age structure, the relationship between "percent black" and available family planning services did not disappear.

CONCLUSION

There are several perspectives from which the findings of this research may be viewed. First, it must be emphasized that the unit of analysis in this study is the county. The act is one of making family planning services available to the population of that county. This research has demonstrated that counties that have made family planning services available are more likely to have a higher percentage of blacks in the population than the counties that have not. We do not know which people in these counties took what precise action, and we certainly do not know from these data what motivated them to do what they did. We only know that in most regions of the country, in poor counties and rich counties, in rural and urban counties, the same pattern appears: family planning is more likely to be available if there are black Americans in the population.

Why have family planning services been established first in areas with high concentrations of black Americans? Our findings are subject to alternative interpretations. On the one hand, our data make it clear that the claim of many black Americans that family planning has been selectively directed toward them is not a totally unfounded and irrational perception. Whether such programs represent deliberate, conscious, systematic efforts by members of the majority group to curtail black fertility, or whether they reflect a genuine concern for the health and well-being of black Americans, the *effect* of the many individual decisions has been the same: populations with a higher proportion of blacks are more frequently the target of such programs. This fact gives apparent substance to charges that such programs are designed not simply to assist the poor, but to control the growth of the black population.

Given the prevalence of racism in this country, such an interpretation of these data is not implausible, nor should it be summarily dismissed as purely ideological. Racism in America has been extremely pervasive and has often been uncovered in many subtle and unsuspected forms in the most benign institutions. Black Americans have understandably come to regard new activities with suspicion and cynicism, and often search for latent rather than manifest functions of any programs that purport "to do something for" them. This suspicion derives from the perception that governmental agencies are alien and that programs of governmental assistance for minority groups do not reflect the interests of black people. On the contrary, they often reflect the concern of the majority group to maintain and perpetuate its own power and privilege.

To view the matter from a contrary view, the data of this study could been seen as revealing a pattern of preference for assistance to black Americans. This pattern could be interpreted as discriminatory against whites, who have been systematically excluded from the benefits of family planning services. Certainly if we had found an opposite pattern—one in which there was an inverse, rather than a direct, correlation between family planning centers and percentage of blacks in the population—an alternative but equally plausible case of racism might have been made. For had this been found, it could have been said that blacks had been systematically excluded from services available to other Americans.

It may be that public officials have been more responsive to pressures by black poor, who in the past decade have been more strident and insistent in their demands for equal justice. Thus higher "visibility" of black poor may have been a function not of higher fertility or of the salience of race, *per se*, as by the fact that blacks had made their demands for equal justice and for programs of governmental assistance more keenly felt in the minds of officials responsible for making decisions. Thus the patterns we discerned could be attributed to a responsiveness on the part of those in power to the needs of poor black Americans.

A problem with this "responsive" interpretation is that, given the relative dearth of black political power in most local communities in the United States, the "success" of obtaining family planning services would appear to be an anomaly. Even if there were black pressures for the establishment of such programs (and how frequently this occurred is problematic), in order for such programs to be implemented some person or persons in power in each county had to make those decisions. That would raise the question of why there was acquiescence of agreement on the part of local officials on *this* particular issue. Why were officials likely to attempt to institute this particular program "to do something for" blacks?

Since the family planning movement continues to grow, it would appear that most places in the country will have some family planning services within a few years. The Planned Parenthood/Office of Economic Opportunity follow-up study of 1969 (eighteen months after the original survey) revealed that there had been a 20 percent increase in the number of counties providing services, even in that short period of time (Planned Parenthood/Office of Economic Opportunity, 1972). This could be interpreted to mean that our findings have only transitory historical significance. However, we feel that this research is important not only for the substantive issue investigated, but also for what it reveals about public policy formation. This study indicates that race may be a crucial latent determinant of policies and programs in which it is generally assumed that such considerations are absent.

REFERENCES

Carlsson, Gosta. 1966. "The Decline of Fertility: Innovation or Adjustment process." Population Studies 20:149–74.

Darity, William A., Castellano B. Turner, and H. Jean Thiebaux. 1971. "Race Consciousness and Fears of Black Genocide." Population Reference Bureau Selection No. 37 (June):5–12.

Jaffe, Frederick S. 1967. "Family Planning, Public Policy and Intervention Strategy," Journal of Social Issues 23 (July):145–63.

————. 1968. "Family Planning and Public Policy: Is the 'Culture of Poverty' the New Cop-Out?" Journal of Marriage and the Family 30 (May):228–35.

Kammeyer, Kenneth C. W., Norman R. Yetman, and McKee J. McClendon. 1972. "Family Planning Services and the Distribution of Black Americans." Paper presented at the annual meeting of the Population Association of America in Toronto, Ontario, Canada.

Kelly, Francis J., Donald L. Beggs, and Keith A. McNeil with Tony Eichelberger and Judy Lyon. 1969. Multiple Regression Approach. Carbondale and Edwardsville: Southern Illinois University Press.

Nunally, Jim C. 1967. Psychometric Theory. New York: McGraw-Hill.

Planned Parenthood/Office of Economic Opportunity. 1969. Need for Subsidized Family Planning Services: United States, Each State and County, 1968. Washington, D.C.: U.S. Government Printing Office.

Planned Parenthood/Office of Economic Opportunity. 1972. Need for Subsidized Family Planning Services: United States, Each State and County, 1969. Washington, D.C.: U.S. Government Printing Office.

Population Reference Bureau. 1971. Selection No. 37. Washington, D.C.: Population Reference Bureau.

Price, Daniel O. 1969. Changing Characteristics of the Negro Population. A 1960 Census Monograph. Washington, D.C.: U.S. Government Printing Office.

Queen, Stuart A., and David A. Carpenter. 1953. The American City. New York: McGraw-Hill.

U.S. Bureau of the Census. 1961. U.S. Census of Population: 1960. General Population Characteristics, Final Report PC (1)-B. Table 28. Washington, D.C.: U.S. Government Printing Office.

U.S. Bureau of the Census. 1967. County and City Data Book, 1967. Washington, D.C.: U.S. Government Printing Office.

Weisbord, Robert G., "Birth Control and the Black American: A Matter of Genocide." Demography 10 (1973):571–91.

Williams, Roberta. 1972. Population Reference Bureau, Personal Communication.

Willie, Charles V. 1971. "A Position Paper" Presented to the President's Commission on Population Growth and the American Future. Washington, D.C.: Population Reference Bureau Selection No. 37 (June):1–4.

Index

Abortion, 83, 84, 325, 358, 385, 391, 408, 410, 411, 415–16, 419, 420, 431, 438, 445, 448, 452, 460. 463. 464, 465; laws, 376, 405, 430 n. 1; and maternal health, 376; rejection of, 433; and welfare recipients, 376

Abubakari, Dara (Virginia E. Y. Collins), 463

Accidental death, 261; data on, 263

Adams, John Quincy, 292

Adams, Samuel, 292

Adoption, symbolic value of, 329, 425

Advisory Committee on Problems of Census Enumeration, 106

Age composition, 38; crime statistics for, 60; and child dependency, 37; of Florida, 17; impact of, on crime rates, 62; and mortality, 35

Age distribution, 33; and fertility, 34

Age at marriage, 14, 358

Age-specific analysis of data, 63

Age-standardized rates, 277–78 n. 7

Agricultural methods, improvement in, 27

Aid to Families with Dependent Children (AFDC), 222–23, 235 n. 1

Alienation, 16, 49–58; from work, 365

American Birth Control League. See Sanger, Margaret

Americans, as consumers, 382

Antonovsky, Aaron, 275

Arithmetical growth, 131

Association for Voluntary Sterilization (AVS), 469

Aubrey, John, 75

Baby boom, 148, 346, 411, 412

Bacon, Lloyd, 233

Back, Kurt W., 4, 5, 10, 212, 215, 219

Bancroft, Frederick, 449

Barnett, L. D., 341

Beale, Calvin L., 224, 234

Bell, Alexander Graham, 292

Ben-Gurion, David, 456

Bennett, M. K., 27

Berkson, Joseph, 260

Bernard, Jessie, 243

Bertillon, A., 141

Beshers, James, 170, 171, 214, 219

Bethune, Mary McLeod, 453

Bibb, Henry, 450

Bickel, Wilhelm, 153, 154

Bills of Mortality, 74, 79–81, 137, 139

Birth control, 116, 152, 391, 499; and the black American dilemma, 460; and blacks, 431–32, 452; as approved by black women, 470; and black feminists, 463; and Black Muslim ideology, 461, 462; black nationalist criticism of, 460–61; black support of, 466–67; and young black males, 436, 446; and Catholic Church, 313, 321; and Catholics, 297, 298; and Catholic women, 314–21; and coercion, 469–71; and class, 296, 299, 373–74; and education, 370; after marriage, 140; within marriage, 132; and

Birth control—*cont.*
race consciousness, 433; and religion, 298; respectability of, 459; use of, 416; in India, 299, 370–74
Birth control clinics, 435–38, 445, 452, 465; black operated, 438–41, 445; in Nazi Germany, 455
Birth Control Federation, 453
Birth control movement, 452–53; black support of, 451–53
Birthplace: and criminal behavior, 231–32; and imprisonment, 231; and welfare, 231–33
Birth rate: decline of, 140; factors affecting, 367 n. 6; low, effect of, 40; in Malthus's time, 121; and modernization, 156
Births, unwanted, 367 n. 4. *See also* Abortion
Blacks: and alienation, 459; and race consciousness, 434–35; distribution of, 457–58; and fertility, 413; and welfare, 225, 226, 230, 231. *See also* Race and Poverty; Race suicide; Genocide, of blacks
Blackner, C. P., 156
Blackout babies, myth of, 44
Black Panther Party, 460, 463
Black slavery, history of, 449–51
Blake, Judith, 47, 296, 299, 334, 336, 340, 346, 379, 394, 407
Blau, P. M., 343
Bogue, Donald J., 190, 470
Bonar, James, 118, 123
Bond, Julian, 468
Bourne, Stephen, 188
Bradburn, Norman, 258, 278 n. 9
Braidwood, Robert J., 23
British census, 120
Bronze Age, 24
Brown, H. Rap, 459
Brown, R. G., 159
Bumpass, Larry, 297, 298, 313, 384
Burgess, Ernest W., 348, 349, 363

Caesar, time of, 39
Cancer, 13
Caplan, Nathan S., 232
Caplovitz, David, 258
Carlsson, Gosta, 476
Carmichael, Stokely, 459
Carr-Saunders, Alexander M., 156
Carter, Elmer, 452
Carter, Hugh, 260, 273, 275, 276, 278 n. 8
Casual setting interviews, 109 n. 10. *See also* Underenumeration

Census: age-reporting errors in, 104, 107; black undercount in, 99, 107; critics of, 72, 73; first reliable, 139; frictional undercounting in, 105; special efforts to improve, 109–10 n. 15; underenumeration in, 73, 98
Center for Population Research, 429
Charles II, 76–77, 99
Child-care programs, 424
Child dependency, 37
Child Health and Human Development, National Institute of, 429
Childlessness, 298–99, 323–32, 363, 410, 422; and divorce, in India, 373; by intention, 325–26; by postponement, 326–27
Childless wives, 328–29
Children: pressure for having, 298; rewards for having, 299; rights of, 364; value of, in India, 372
Children, as protection, 264, 271; for women, 273, 277 n. 4
Chilton, Roland, 17
Chisholm, Shirley, 464–65
Circle of eligibles, 14
Cirrhosis of the liver, 265
Cities, problems of adjustment to, 232
Coale, Ansley, 2, 33
Cobb, W. Montague, 454
Coefficients of preservation, 259, 267, 270, 271, 273
Cloward, Richard A., 224
Coleman, James S., 234
Coleridge, Samuel Taylor, 131
Collver, A., 335
Commission on Population Growth and the American Future. *See* Population Commission
Common culture, 291
Conception control, defined, 391
CORE (Congress of Racial Equality), 467
Contraception, 57, 116, 142, 297–98, 318, 332 n. 7, 358, 411, 416, 419; and Catholics, 313–21, 455; laws restricting, 414–15, 459; and teenagers, 420–22; and need for development of, 412
Coombs, L., 337
Corn Laws, 122
Cowgill, D. O., 156, 157
Cowles, Wylda B., 462
Crain, Robert L., 231, 233, 234
Crime: index, limitations of, 67; rates, variations in, 66; statistics, 60
Cultural fictions, 376
Current Population Survey data, 103, 104

Darity, William, 432, 433, 468, 471, 477
Darwin, Charles, 117
Davis, Jefferson, 292
Davis, Kingsley, 47, 153, 156, 157, 295, 296, 334, 335, 340
Death control policies, 377–78
Death dip, 243, 281, 282, 284, 285, 286, 292–93; and fame, 291–92; size of, 288–91
Death rate: and acceleration in population growth, 20, 28; effect on birth rate, 40, 120–21; in Malthus's time, 121; and modernization, 156
Death rise, 285–86; size of, 288–90
Degler, C. N., 338
Demeny, Paul, 379, 398–406
Demographic analysis, 1, 2, 6, 7; formal, 135–36
Demographic: fate, 12; methods, limitations of, 98; phenomena and time, 96; research, need for, 412; transition: theory of, 29, 156–67; and cyclical theories, 157; and Malthusian theory, 156; in the 1970s, 411–12
Demography, 1, 2, 69; formal, 15, 135, 137, 147–49; classical, criticism of, 94; historical, 15; history of, 94–97; as an observational science, 69, 70; and social psychology, 4, 5, 11–14; tasks of, 135, 147–49; topics of, 10
Derner, Gordon, 267
Desmond, Annabelle, 15, 16, 18
Dew, Thomas, 449
Diabetes, 267, 268
Divorce rate, 17
"Do Both" syndrome, 361–66. See also Women, working
Dodd, Stuart, 214
Doubleday, Thomas, 138
Drake, Michael, 161
Dublin, L., 147
DuBois, W. E. B., 448, 451–52, 454, 465; and birth control, 452
Dumont, E., 21
Duncan, Beverly, 216
Duncan, Otis Dudley, 70, 216, 343
Duncan, Otis Durant, 190
Duncan, G. C., 268
Durand, John, 26
Durkheim, Émile, 259, 260, 264, 271, 272, 274, 277 n. 4 and 5, 278 n. 9

Edison, Thomas, 292
Education, European attitudes toward, 205

Ehrlich, Paul R., 468
EROS (Endeavour to Raise Our Size), 457
Epidemic, course of, 90
Epstein, Cynthia Fuchs, 362–63
Equal Rights Amendment, 424
Equilibrium analysis, 189
Erhardt, Carl, 43

Family law, 369 n. 45
Family life: and the aged, 38; alternatives to, 397; and obligations of men, 367; in urban environments, 38
Family planning, 57, 384, 421, 449; and low-income couples, 417–19; movement, 395, 475; obstacles to, 388; programs, 391, 392–93, 432; to slow population growth, 387; voluntarism in, 397–98
Family planning services, 432; and economic need, 481, 484, 486, 487, 489; and high fertility, 481, 485–86, 487; hypotheses on institution of, 476; of population percentage black, 484–86, 487, 489; direct correlation between blacks and, 491–98; and urbanism, 481, 484, 489
Family structure, in India, 372
Famine, power of, 126
Farmer, James, 467
Farrakhan, Louis, 463
Fate, 10; demography as the science of, 11
Fatalism vs. instrumentalism, 16
Feld, Sheila, 257, 258, 259, 272
Feminism, 330–31, 361–66
Fertility: control, access to, 412; decisions on, 13, 16, 47; declines in, 156–57; desire to control, 29; institutional control of, 347; longitudinal analysis of, 149; and poverty, 385; and religion, 150–51; and social class, 150–51
Fillmore, Millard, 292
Fire of London, 1666, 76
Food: arithmetical increase in, 124; effect of on population, 124–26
Forman, James, 457
Four hundred, the, 291–92
Franklin, Benjamin, 292
Frazier, E. Franklin, 454–55
Freedman, R., 335, 337
Frejka, Tomas, 385
Friedan, Betty, 361
Fumifugium (first treatise on atmospheric pollution), 85

Garfinkel, Lawrence, 267
Garvey, Marcus, 452, 453, 454
Garvin, Charles H., 453
Genocide: of blacks, 431, 448–71; black
    females and, 431–32, 463–66; of Jews,
    455, 456; of Spanish-speaking Ameri-
    cans, 456
Geometrical growth, 131
Geriatricide, 378
Gibbon, Edward, 123
Gilman, Charlotte Perkins, 364–65
Gini, Corrado, 145
Glass, Davis V., 156, 161
Glick, Paul, 260, 273, 275, 276, 278 n. 8
Godwin, William, 121, 122, 123, 131
Goldberg, D., 335
Goldsen, Rose K., 355, 356
Goldstein, Sidney, 198
Goode, W. J., 336
Goodman, Benjamin, 462
Gove, Walter, 242
Graunt, John, 70, 74–92, 137; meticulous-
    ness of, 78–79; methods of, 81
Gravitational model theorists. See Stewart,
    John W.; Dodd, Stuart D.
Great Blackout of 1965, 16
Great Depression, 452
Great Snow of 1967, 44
Green, Edward, 232
Greenlee, Charles, 465–66
Greenwood, M., 89, 91, 92
Gregory, Dick, 457, 458
Griffith, G. Talbot, 159
Groat, Theodore, 16
Growth ideology, 411
Guilford, J. P., 205
Gurin, Gerald, 257, 258–59, 272
Guttmacher, Alan F., 469

Habakkuk, Hrothgar J., 159
Haden, William Bouie, 465–66
Haenszel, W., 267
Hagood, Margaret Marman, 190
Hales, John, 75
Halley, E., 90
Hammond, E. Cuyler, 267
Hancock, John, 292
Hauser, Philip M., 1–3, 6–9, 70, 241,
    379, 390–94
Hayes, Rutherford B., 292
Hazlitt, William, 130, 131
Hazziez, Shirley, 463
Health Statistics, National Center for, 428
Henry, Louis, 15, 72
Hertzler, Joyce O., 157

Hoffman, L. W., 334, 340
Holland, Jerome H., 467
Hollingshead, August, 275
Homicide, data on, 261, 262
Homo sapiens, 22
Households, unenumerated, 98
Hoyle, Fred, 403
Hughes, Langston, 468
Hume, David, 117, 123
Humphreys, N. A., 188
Hydraulic civilizations, 24, 27
Hyson, Brenda, 460

Ideal family, 300–301, 309–310, 323
Illegitimacy rates, 57
Increasing prosperity, theory of, 140
Index of dissimilarity, 216
Indianapolis Study, 143
Indik, Bernard P., 224
Industrial Revolution, 28
Infanticide, 378
Infant mortality, 377, 452
Intercourse, and fertility, 296
Irish potato famine, 133

Jackson, Jesse, 470
Jaffe, Frederick S., 475, 477
Jefferson, Thomas, 292, 293
Johnson, Lyndon B., 407
Jones, Carolyn, 464
Juvenile court data (Florida): limitations
    of, 62; advantages of, 62; statewide, 64–
    66
Juvenile delinquency, 60; and birthplace,
    231; and crime rates, 17

Kahlil, Brother, 461
Kammeyer, Kenneth C. W., 156, 171, 212,
    214, 432, 478, 480
Kennedy, John F., 407
Kennedy, Joseph, 203–204
Kennedy, Robert, 242, 244–56
Kerner Commission, 232
Keynes, John Maynard, 115, 117, 119, 130
Khanna Study, 370–74
King, Martin Luther, 459, 467
Kingsley, Robert, 363–64
Kinman, Judith, 231
Kirk, Dudley, 190
Kiser, Clyde V., 232, 333, 343, 453
Kitagawa, Evelyn M., 241
Knowles, H. C., 268
Kohn, Melvin, 275

Komarovsky, Mirra, 355–56
Konig, Rene, 35
Kraus, Arthur, 260, 270, 274
Krause, J. T., 161

Langlois, E., 335
Leaky, L. S. B., 21
Lee, Everett, 170, 171, 173, 188, 203, 214–19, 231
Leroy-Beaulieu, 141
Leukemia and aleukemia, 269–70
Lester, Julius, 458, 470
Levasseur, Bertillon, 141
Lewis, Julian, 455
Liebow, Elliot, 232
Life chances, 240, 257; of the sexes, 277 n. 3; of men, 365. See also Mortality
Life cycle, 47
Life table, 137, 147; first, 88–90, 91
Lilienfeld, Abraham, 260, 270, 274
Lincoln, Richard, 407, 464
Lipson, Gerald, 459, 470
Logistic curve, 144–45
Longitudinal analysis, 95
Long, Larry, 212, 221–35
Lorimer, Frank, 18, 30
Lotka, A., 147
Lowry, Ira S., 224
Lung cancer, and marital status, 265, 266–67

McClendon, McKee, 171, 212, 214, 432, 478
McKeown, Thomas, 159
McMurry, Martha, 299, 333
MacKenroth, Gerhard, 153, 154
Malcolm X, 462
Malthus, Thomas Robert, 111, 114–34, 140, 391, 395, 403; economic theory of, 119; and sex, 116–17
Malthusian controversy, 138, 145
Mamdani, Mahmood, 299, 370
Mangalam, J. J., 170, 171, 173, 214
Marcuse, Herbert, 365
Marriage: contract, state's attitude toward, 363; late, 133; law of, 364; and motherhood, 361
Marital selection, choice enlarged, 14
Marital status: and mental illness, 258, 259; and mortality, 257–78
Marx, Karl, 112, 138, 140, 153
Masters, Stanley H., 233
Mayer, Kurt, 112, 135
Meaninglessness, and family planning, 50, 53, 49; and social isolation, 55

Mencken, H. L., 292
Mental Health, National Institute of, 421
Migrants, 200–201; identity of, 181–82; levels of education, 234; as members of a collectivity, 170, 175–76
Migration, 13–14, 170, 191, 203–204; consequences of, 183; currents of, 198–99; and decision making, 176, 191–93; and destination, 182–83, 189; and economics, 189, 208; and education, 203–11, 213; and the interactional system, 177–78, 189; Ravenstein's laws of, 188–89; reasons for, 182; sociodemographic variables in, 181–82; sociological study of, 175; stages of, 189; technology and, 189; theories of, 169–72, 173, 180–81, 190, 215, 218–19; volume of, 191, 194–98, 204; and welfare, 213; women and, 189, 212
Miller, Andreas, 35
Miller, H., 267
Mishler, Elliot G., 35
Mobile society, 210
Modern medicine, development of, 39
Moral restraint, 126–28, 130, 133. See also Malthus, Thomas Robert
Morita, Y., 164–66
Morris, Judy K., 111, 114
Mortality: and age, 240; and census, 94; changing causes of, 12–13; decline in, 156; and educational level, 240; and marital sex role, 242–43, 273–75; and modernization, 159; and race, 240, 241; and sex role, 240, 241, 242–43, 244, 257–78; in Ireland, 244–56; and social ties, 239, 261; and status, 239–43, 245–47, 248, 252–54; and vital statistics, 94; and effect on age distribution, 35; of widowed, 276 n. 2
Mortality rates, limitations of data on, 244
Moynihan, Daniel, 222, 449
Muhammad, Elijah, 461
Myrdal, Alva, 461

Nation of Islam, 463
NAACP (National Association for the Advancement of Colored People), 453, 465, 466
Natural law, 129
Neal, Arthur, 16
Neanderthal, 22
Negro Women, National Council of, 453
Newcomer, Mabel, 353–54
New Left movement, 365–66
Newman, Pamela, 464
New Stone Age population, 22–24

New York City, power failure in, 42–45
Nixon, Richard M., 407–408
Nonmarriage, 410
Nonparenthood, National Organization for (NON), 331
Nonrenewable resources, 382, 395
Noonan, John T., 455
Normlessness and family planning, 49, 50, 53
Notestein, Frank W., 156, 347, 379, 380–89, 390

O'Casey, Sean, 245
Occupational choice, 14
Office of Population Research, 150
Old Stone Age population, 21
O'Neill, William, 354, 364
Oppenheimer, V. K., 336
Overpopulation, 112, 371; danger to civil order, 386; and pollution, 383; and rivalry of numbers, 387. See also Zero Population Growth

Paige, Jeffrey M., 232
Paine, Thomas, 129
Parenthood, as compulsory behavior, 424; education for, 423; as "natural," 349; precondition for other roles, 350; voluntary, 385
Parish, William, 277 n. 4
Patterson, William, 455
Pearl, Raymond, 144, 145
Petersen, William, 158–63, 166, 167
Petty, William, 75–77, 89, 92
Phenomenon, abstraction of, 185 n. 7
Phillips, David P., 243, 281–93
Piven, Frances Fox, 224
Planned parenthood, defined, 449
Planned Parenthood Federation, 469
Planned Parenthood—World Population, 467
Plato, 123
Poe, Edgar Allen, 292
Political arithmetic, 137, 139
Political arithmeticians, 70, 71
Poor laws, 120, 122, 128, 131, 162
Population Commision, report of, 409–30; recommendations of, 412, 414, 427, 428, 429; and ZPG, 430
Population control, 391; defined, 449; changing attitudes in communist countries, 112; socialist opposition to, 112; and moral restraint, 122; voluntary, 410
Population: data, Japanese source of, 164,

social-historical, 161, spread-out nature of, 70–71; and ecological damage, 430; need for education about, 412; equilibrium theory of, 155 n. 8; explosion, 112, 113, 135; and food, 23, 134; and growth, acceleration of, 20, 124, 144; maldistribution of, 426–27; mobility, effect on census, 103; movements, christenings and burials used to determine, 83–86; and poverty, 409; preventive and positive checks to, 115, 118, 133, 124–25, 140; related research, need for, 416–17, 428–29; sizes, estimates of, 86, 123; stabilization, 147, 410–11, 429–30; stages of, 156, 157; theory of, 111, 136
Population Education Act (proposed), 422
Population policy, 299, 375, 431–32; and anxiety, 366; consensus on, 378; and values, 378; decisions on, 46; disguise of, 376; explicit, 377; responses of groups to, 432; and science, 400; state-imposed, 346; and welfare recipients, 418
Population Sciences, National Institute of (proposed), 429
Population studies, 1–3, 6–8, 46; examination of, 135; Malthus's affect on, 111; origins of, 137–54; and sociology, 3, 4, 6
Potato famine, Irish, 133
Potter, Robert G., Jr., 35
Potvin, R. H., 335
Poverty, blacks and, 226–27
Powell, Adam Clayton, Jr., 453
Powerlessness, 49
Precensus data, 72
Prehistory, period of, 21–22
Premarital pregnancy, 57
Price, Charles, 173
Price, Daniel O., 233, 481
Principle of population, 114, 116
Pronatal pressures: 303–305; and education, 308; and family finances, 311; and religion, 306–307; on women, 300, 304, 306, 309, 311
Pronatalism, and structure of personality, 350; and structure of society, 350
Psychological state and mortality, 257
Public health, development of, 39

Race and poverty, correlation, 478
Race suicide, 411, 455, 456
Racial polarizati⌐n, 427–28
Rainwater, Lee, 51, 340
Randolph, A. Philip, 467
Ravenstein, E. G., 188, 214

Redlich, Frederick, 275
Reproduction, lack of alternatives to, 347, 349, 357, 366
Ricardo, David, 114, 115, 119
Rice, Thurman B., 451
Right to choose, 347, 396
Rights of Man, Malthus on, 129–30
Rockefeller, John D., III, 407
Rossi, Alice, 341, 362
Rousseau, Jean Jacques, 117
Royal Commission on Population, 143
Royal Economic Society, 133
Royal Society of Philosophers, 76
Royal Statistical Society, 188
Rural-urban adjustment, 186 n. 15, 189, 426
Rushing, William, 275
Russell, Josiah C., 25, 26
Rustin, Bayard, 467
Ryder, Norman R., 297, 335, 339, 341, 344 n. 2

Sadler, Michael Thomas, 138
Sagi, Philip C., 35
Sample survey, 72, 95
Sanger, Margaret, 449, 451, 456, 459, 475, 477
Sanitation, improvement in, 39
Savitz, Leonard, 231
Scanzoni, John, 299
Schuyler, George, 454
Schwartz, Moshe, 277 n. 4
Schwarzweller, Harry K., 170, 173–84
Scientific method, 27
Scientific spirit, 16
Scripps Foundation for Research in Population, 149
Seibels, Robert E., 453
Self-destruction, world scale, 402
Sex education, 411, 420–22; denial of, 421
Sex equality, 362
Sex-role: differentiation, cross-cultural analysis, 367 n. 9; expectations, 350–51; and fertility, 299; and migration, 170–71; orientation and fertility behavior, 16; primacy of parenthood in, 349
Sexual exploitation, of slaves, 448
Sexual intercourse, 420
Sexuality, 48
Shelley, Percy Bysshe, 121
Sheps, Mindel, 260, 270, 273
Shurtleff, David, 260
Siegel, Jacob, 73
Singh, Sohan, 370
Skinkin, M., 267

Smallpox vaccination, 19
Smith, Kenneth, 133, 134
Smuts, Robert W., 351, 353
Snow babies, 45
Social capillarity, 141
Social engineer, elitism of, 371
Social isolation, 49, 50, 53
Social organization, 178–81, 186 n. 19
Social psychological concepts, 16
Social sciences, background of, 10–11
Socioeconomic status: role in contraceptive practices, 143; and specialization, 210
Sociological framework, 174
Southern migrants, and welfare, 221
Specialists, rewards of, 210
Stabilization: and immigration, 425; unfavorable social elements of, 411
Spencer, Herbert, 138
Spengler, Joseph J., 123
Spielberger, Adele, 17
Statistics, vital, system or 139
Steiner, Gilbert, 224
Sterilization, 321, 419, 430 445; of blacks, 451, 470; coercive, 451 of Jews 469; rejection of, 433
Sternlieb, George S., 224
Steward, Julian, 27
Stewart, John, 214
Stewart, T. D., 21
Stillbirths, 83
Stirling, Betty, 352
Stolka, S. M., 341
Stone Age, 20
Stouffer, Samuel A., 190, 214
Strength in numbers, 441, 445–46, 448, 454, 455, 458, 460
SNCC (Student Non-Violent Coordinating Committee), 459, 469
Stycos, J. Mayone, 296
Suchman, Edward, 277 n. 6
Suessmilch, Johann Peter, 137
Suffragist movement, 364
Suicide, 259, 261; data on, 262, 272, 274, 277 n. 4. See also Race suicide; Genocide
Sutherland, Ian, 70, 73–74

Tacitus, 123
Taeuber, Alma F., 234, 333
Taeuber, Irene B., 163–65
Taeuber, Karl E., 234, 333
Terris, Milton, 265
Tesla, Nikola, 292
Thiebaux, H. Jean, 432, 433–46, 471, 477

Thomas, Dorothy Swaine, 190
Thompson, W. S., 156
Tietze, Christopher, 43
Tilly, Charles, 231
Time-series, rational attempt to study, 90
Tolchin, Martin, 42
Tomasson, Richard T., 35, 338
Transition theory, 112; explicitness of, 157; in support of, 161; and Japanese modernization, 162–66; questioned validity of, 152–53
Transversal analysis, 95
Tuberculosis, 267
Turner, Castellano B., 432, 433–46, 471, 477
Twain, Mark, 292

Udry, J. Richard, 16, 42–45
Underenumeration: difference in white and nonwhite undercount patterns, 101; and marital status, 270; of nonwhites, 241; reasons for, 100, 101, 102
Universal Negro Improvement Association, 453
Unwanted fertility, and the poor, 185, 408, 412, 413
Urban crisis, 394
Urbanization, 141; of Negro population, 109 n. 15
Urban League, National, 467
Urban vs. rural, background, and welfare, 224; 231–33
Urban sprawl, 135

Vasectomy, 325
Veevers, J. E., 298–99, 323
Venereal disease, 420; and Tuskegee Study, 451
Veroff, Joseph, 257, 258, 259, 272
Vital Revolution, 28

Wallace, Alfred Russel, 117
Wallace, Robert, 121
Wallin, Paul, 348, 349, 363
War on Poverty, 475
Washington, George, 291
Watts, Daniel H., 457, 458
Weisbord, Robert, 432, 448–71, 480
Weisman, Carol Sachs, 231, 233, 234
Welfare, absence of, in South, 234
Welfare payments, and migration, 221, 222–33

Welfare Rights Organization, National, 234, 466
Welfare rolls, of cities, 221
Wellemeyer, J. Fletcher, 18, 30
Westoff, Charles F., 35, 297, 298, 313, 335, 339, 341, 384
Whelpton, Pascal K., 337
White, Lynn, Jr., 354
Whites, poverty status among, 227
Wife, executive's, 369 n. 43
Willcox, W. F., 92
Williams, Maxine, 464
Williams, Robin, 376
Willie, Charles, 431, 477, 478
Wives, interrupted career development of, 212
Wolff, Harold, 267
Wolman, Dianne, 459, 470
Women: biological advantage of, 247–48; black family heads on welfare, 228–29; discrimination against, 344; higher education for, 353–61; liberation of black, 464; role of, 411, 412; status of, 130, 411, 412, 423–24
Women's Liberation movement. See Feminism
Women, National Organization for (NOW), 361
Women, status of Irish. See Mortality and sex roles, in Ireland
Women, working: as deviant, 357–58; social status of, 411; opposition to, 351–53; "scientific" attack on, 352; supply and demand of, 368 n. 15
World birth rate, average of, 39
World death rate, average of, 39
World population, 18, 113, 433–71; growth of, 28, 399; problem of, 46, 462–63; size of in early Christian era, 24; survey of, 22
Wrong, Dennis H., 161
Wyatt, F., 334, 340

Yetman, Norman R., 432, 480
Young Socialist Alliance, 464
Young, Whitney, 467

Zero population growth, 299, 330, 346, 379; and aging population, 397; and ecologists, 281; as an esthetic goal, 384; inevitability of, 390; public acceptance of, 380; side effects of, 397; and timing 395

ZPG (national organization), 468; action proposals of, 405; ecological approach of, 400–401; and environmental pollution, 393; goals, limitations of, 399–406; methods of, 391; oversimplifications of, 394, 404; rhetoric and policy, 404

Zinjanthropus, 21